THE WORLD'S CITIES
Contrasting Regional, National, and Global Perspectives
A.J. Jacobs

The World's Cities offers instructors and students in higher education an accessible introduction to the three major perspectives influencing city-regions worldwide: **City-Regions in a World System**; **Nested City-Regions**; and **The City-Region as the Engine of Economic Activity/Growth**.

The book provides students with helpful essays on each perspective, case studies to illustrate each major viewpoint, and discussion questions following each reading. *The World's Cities* concludes with an original essay by the editor that helps students understand how an analysis incorporating a *combination* of theoretical perspectives and factors can provide a richer appreciation of the world's city dynamics.

A.J. Jacobs is an Associate Professor and the Director of Graduate Studies in East Carolina University's Department of Sociology. He was an Assistant Professor in the University of Cincinnati's School of Planning, a Visiting Associate Professor in Hosei University's Faculty of Business (in Tokyo, Japan), and a Visiting Assistant Professor in Michigan State University's Urban Planning Program. He received his Ph.D. in Sociology–Urban Studies from Michigan State University and his Master's in Regional Planning from the University of North Carolina-Chapel Hill.

D0207209

THE METROPOLIS AND MODERN LIFE

A Routledge Series
Edited by **Anthony Orum, Loyola University and
Zachary P. Neal, Michigan State University**

This series brings original perspectives on key topics in urban research to today's students in a series of short accessible texts, guided readers, and practical handbooks. Each volume examines how long-standing urban phenomena continue to be relevant in an increasingly urban and global world, and in doing so, connects the best new scholarship with the wider concerns of students seeking to understand life in the 21st-century metropolis.

Books in the Series:

Common Ground: Reading and Reflections on Public Space edited by Anthony Orum and Zachary P. Neal

The Gentrification Debates edited by Japonica Brown-Saracino

The Power of Urban Ethnic Places: Cultural Heritage and Community Life by Jan Lin

Urban Tourism and Urban Change: Cities in a Global Economy by Costas Spirou

The Connected City by Zachary Neal

The World's Cities edited by A.J. Jacobs

Ethnography and the City edited by Richard Ocejo

Also of Interest from Routledge:

The Community Development Reader, Second Edition edited by James DeFillipis and Susan Saegert

Housing Policy in the United States, Second Edition by Alex F. Schwartz

Neobohemia: Art and Commerce in the Postindustrial City, 2nd Edition by Richard Lloyd

China and Globalization, 3rd Edition by Doug Guthrie

Foodies: Democracy and Distinction in the Gourmet Foodscape by Josée Johnston and Shyon Baumann

Branding New York: How a City in Crisis Was Sold to the World by Miriam Greenberg

City Life from Jakarta to Dakar: Movements at the Crossroads by AbdouMaliq Simone

The World's Cities

Contrasting Regional, National, and Global Perspectives

A.J. Jacobs
East Carolina University

Routledge
Taylor & Francis Group

NEW YORK AND LONDON

First published 2013
by Routledge
711 Third Avenue, New York, NY 10017

Simultaneously published in the UK
by Routledge
2 Park Square, Milton Park, Abingdon, Oxon OX14 4RN

Routledge is an imprint of the Taylor & Francis Group, an informa business

© 2013 Taylor & Francis

The right of A.J. Jacobs to be identified as the author of the editorial material, and of the authors
for their individual chapters, has been asserted in accordance with sections 77 and 78 of the Copyright,
Designs and Patents Act 1988.

All rights reserved. No part of this book may be reprinted or reproduced or utilised in any form or
by any electronic, mechanical, or other means, now known or hereafter invented, including photocopying
and recording, or in any information storage or retrieval system, without permission in writing
from the publishers.

Trademark notice: Product or corporate names may be trademarks or registered trademarks,
and are used only for identification and explanation without intent to infringe.

Library of Congress Cataloging in Publication Data
Jacobs, A.J. (Andries Johannes)
    The world's cities: contrasting regional, national, and global perspectives /
[edited by] A.J. Jacobs.—1st ed.
    p. cm.—(Metropolis and modern life)
    1. Cities and towns. 2. Cities and town—Growth. 3. Urban economics.
    I. Title.
    HT151.J223 2012
    307.76—dc23

ISBN: 9780415894852 (HB)
ISBN: 9780415894869 (PB)

Typeset in Sabon and Helvetica Neue, Trade Gothic
by Swales & Willis Ltd, Exeter, Devon

Printed and bound in the United States of America by Sheridan Books, Inc. (a Sheridan Group Company).

For my mentors and scholarly inspirations:
Richard Child Hill, Joe Darden, and June Thomas

CONTENTS

PART TWO: NESTED CITY-REGIONS

CONCLUSIONS AND LESSONS

SERIES FOREWORD

The World's Cities: Contrasting Regional, National, and Global Perspectives, by A. J. Jacobs

This series brings original perspectives on key topics in urban research to today's students in a series of short accessible texts, guided readers, and practical handbooks. Each volume examines how long-standing urban phenomena continue to be relevant in an increasingly urban and global world, and in doing so, connects the best new scholarship with the wider concerns of students to understand life in the 21st-century metropolis.

In this addition to the series, A.J. Jacobs collects more than 20 seminal readings in the vast literature on the world's major cities. It has become increasingly clear that, driven by globalization and other forces, cities and their surrounding regions are taking on new forms and functions. However, at the same time, many different and often seemingly conflicting perspectives have emerged to explain these developments. In this volume, Jacobs introduces the reader to three particularly influential approaches, and demonstrates how they may not be so far apart. In the first section, he offers works that suggest the world's cities have been brought into direct contact with one another to form a world urban system. In the second section, he presents readings claiming that cities remain nested within their more immediate regional and national contexts. Then, in the third section, he provides a sampling of the arguments that cities and their surrounding regions are the engines of growth for tomorrow. Throughout the book, Jacobs summarizes and synthesizes these differing perspectives in a series of original essays, concluding with a multipart conceptual toolkit to guide students and scholars through their own explorations of the world's cities. Both comprehensive and insightful, this volume marks a path through the complex issues of cities and globalization that makes it clear where to go from here.

Anthony Orum
Zachary Neal
Series Editors

PREFACE

While World/Global City Theorists[1] may have received greater acclaim, there has been no shortage of excellent studies written by scholars seeking to either disprove their assertions or demonstrate that non-global factors have been the most decisive determinants driving urban growth trajectories. These arguments are important, as they have influenced the public policy decisions made by officials seeking to address the complex issues and problems confronting the world's city-regions.

Despite the importance of these debates, only a small number of books, useful for courses in higher education and intended for a non-specialist audience, have been published chronicling the abundant research on the world's city-regions. Among those already in print, most either engage the topic without a theoretical perspective or do so from only one specific vantage point. An illustration of the former is Stanley Brunn et al.'s (2012) *Cities of the World: World Regional Urban Development*, now in its fifth edition. Examples of the latter would include: Neil Brenner and Roger Keil's (2006) *The Global Cities Reader*; and the three collections edited by Peter Taylor and his compatriots connected with the 'Globalization and World Cities Research Network Group': *Commodity Chains and World Cities; Cities in Globalization*; and *Global Urban Analysis* (Taylor et al., 2006, 2010; Derudder and Witlox, 2010; GaWC, 2011). Whereas Brenner and Keil's excellent volume contains 50 shortened articles, 47 of which essentially adhere to the *World/Global City Theory*, the three other books are effectively outgrowths or spinoffs from Taylor's (2004) seminal book, *World City Network*.

Similarly, while Michael Peter Smith's (2001) *Transnational Urbanism* and Mark Abrahamson's (2004) *Global Cities* are certainly well-written, their authors naturally approach the topic strictly from their own perspective. The same is true of Saskia Sassen's now famous *Global City,* her multiple edition, *Cities in the World Economy,* and her edited volume, *Global Networks, Linked Cities* (Sassen, 1991, 2002, 2006). On the other hand, the few books that have addressed the world's cities from more than one perspective, such as Peter Marcuse and Ronald Van Kempen's (2000) *Globalizing Cities,* and Allen J. Scott's (2001) *Global City-Regions,* are now more than ten years old.

As a result of the limited choices available, students newly exposed to this dynamic and important subject are never supplied with a full picture of the many internal and external influences affecting metropolitan regions. Nor are they afforded the opportunity to compare and contrast multiple viewpoints on cities in such a way as to encourage the development of their own viewpoints. The net effect has been to inhibit the size of the audience studying the world's cities.

In contrast, this volume seeks both to open and facilitate a broader and more practical understanding of the globe's city-regions. Unlike any other collection of readings available, it provides students with a series of essays organized and presented around the multiple perspectives utilized by researchers in their examination of the world's urban areas.

It contains 24 readings drawn from a variety of theoretical perspectives and grouped into three categories: City-Regions in a World System; Nested City-Regions; and The City-Region as the Engine of Economic Activity/Growth. Each part of the book contains a brief overview essay introducing that perspective and offering a brief summary of the eight readings that follow. Each of the three parts begins with one or two condensed version(s) of influential writings which help to frame each viewpoint.

Each reading also includes *Questions for Discussion*, *Further Readings*, and *Helpful Web Links*. These have been included to enhance the learning process, by encouraging students to think more deeply about the important ideas presented. They also should serve as an additional resource for instructors.

The book concludes with an original essay entitled, *The Nexus City Model: Bridging the Local, Regional, National, and International Contexts*. Its purpose is to help students see how the various theoretical perspectives presented in the literature on the world's cities and in this volume can be usefully *integrated* and *combined*. The goal is to encourage students to think about their own "views" on the world's cities and develop their own perspectives.

By bringing together a variety of case studies, ideas, and insights, the editor aims to help students gain a better understanding of the world's major cities, while prodding them to *objectively* compare and contrast places and the various theoretical viewpoints in the literature explaining them. Similarly, the volume's three-part format, along with its references, study questions, and final essay, are all intended to enable instructors to tailor the readings easily to their semester assignments/test schedules.

Overall, it is my hope that this book fills an important teaching need in the urban studies literature, and supports a highly interactive learning experience which truly engages students and encourages them to develop a broader understanding of our world's cities. Such outcomes should make any educator proud.

DEDICATION AND ACKNOWLEDGEMENTS

This reader is dedicated to three people, Drs. Richard Child Hill, Joe T. Darden, and June Manning Thomas. Without their guidance and support, I never would have been asked to edit such a volume.

In the September of 1983, I was a transfer student at Michigan State University (MSU) majoring in Telecommunications. My dream was to be a sportscaster. For my major, I needed a 12-credit Social Science cognate. Having enjoyed 'Introduction to Sociology' at a prior school and since that transfer course was being counted towards graduation, I decided on Sociology. Throwing an obstacle into my plans was the fact that, as an out-of-state student, from Florida at the time, I had arrived in East Lansing just a few days prior to classes starting. This meant I was unable to pre-register for any classes, and had to go over to 'the Pit' to register. In the days before online micro-computer registration, college students had to fight their way through crowded auditoriums or pits, as they were called, to register for classes. For MSU students, 'the Pit' was in IM West Building. When in 'the Pit', students went to a department's table to pick up course enrollment cards. When I went over to the Sociology table, I was told only a few courses were still available. One on the list, 'Urban Sociology' sounded interesting and fit into my schedule. I secured the class registration card, stacked it with the others and proceeded to the registrar's table. The rest, as they say, is history.

The Urban Sociology course was taught by Dr. Hill, who would open my eyes to the problems in American cities, especially Detroit, a topic which would increasingly become more important to me than who won last night's games. Although I am still an avid sports fan and occasionally teach Sociology of Sport, it is not a stretch at all to say that Dr. Hill and his class rewrote my career path. By 1985, I had changed my major to Sociology, with an emphasis in Urban. The year after, I was pursuing a Masters' in Regional Planning from the University of North Carolina in Chapel Hill (UNC), followed by a six-year career as a professional urban planner. Dr. Hill also was a primary reason why, in 1994, I would again enroll at MSU, this time to pursue a joint Ph.D. in Sociology-Urban Studies. In the Spring of 1995, during his 'Political Economy' seminar, he would again unearth a new world for me, this time regarding East Asian development. Similar to the 1983 Urban course, this enlightening, along with Dr. Hill's own academic work, would greatly inspire my own research for many years to come, beginning with my dissertation, and later my articles on Japanese cities and the world's auto regions. For these reasons, I thank and dedicate this volume to Dr. Richard Child Hill.

My connection with Dr. Joe Darden began in January 1984, when as then Dean of MSU's Urban Affairs Program, he hired me to serve as his undergraduate work-study student. Through working for him on research projects, I learned almost everything there was to know at the time about the U.S. Census and related data collection. This knowledge would serve me well during my Masters' Program at UNC, my years as a professional planner, my Ph.D. Program, and during my research for many of the scholarly articles I have published as an academic. In addition, every since that first assignment, when he asked me to compile census tract data on Pittsburgh and Chicago, Dr. Darden has shown the utmost confidence in my analytical and scholarly abilities. Without his constant encouragement over the years, I may never have returned to MSU to pursue my doctorate. It was then that for four years I was fortunate enough to serve as his graduate research assistant. During this experience, he taught me the rigor necessary to publish quality scholarly work, and where I published my first article (with Dr. Darden and the late-Sameh Kamel). His research on Detroit, particularly, his book with Dr. Hill and June and Richard Thomas, *Detroit: Race and Uneven Development* (Darden et al., 1987), has inspired my own work for many years now. For these reasons and his continued friendship for nearly 30 years, I dedicate this book to Dr. Joe T. Darden.

I first met Dr. Thomas in January of 1995, when I was a Ph.D. student enrolled in her 'Urban Policy' course at MSU. In the course she challenged me to look beyond the obvious, to take a more holistic view of cities and urban policy decisions, and to strive for excellence. Her book, *Redevelopment and Race: Planning a Finer City in Postwar Detroit* (Thomas, 1997), remains my bible on the city. Her enthusiasm and positive feedback towards my scholarship, especially my dissertation, gave me the confidence I needed to succeed as an academic. This included giving me my first full-time academic position, as a Visiting Assistant Professor in Michigan State's Urban Planning Program, a place I most likely would still be, if she had been allowed to put me on the tenure-track stream. For these reasons and her continued guidance and friendship for more than 15 years, I dedicate this book to June Manning Thomas.

This reader would not have been possible without the support of many other people. First, I would like to give special thanks: to Rex LaMore, the Director of MSU's Center for Urban Affairs (now, the Center for Community and Economic Development), who began as my internship coordinator in November of 1985, and later became my assistantship supervisor, my colleague in MSU's Urban Planning Program, and my friend. The initial lessons he taught me about clarity of purpose, dedication, and sense of community have remained with me for more than 25 years; to the late-Ruth Hamilton, who served as my former teacher and mentor through my two iterations in MSU's Sociology Department, who simultaneously taught me the value of hard work and kindness. These lessons, which she first imparted on me nearly 30 years ago, have guided my teaching and research over the past 15 years; to Richard Thomas, my former professor in MSU's Urban Affairs Program, whose positive attitude and enthusiasm for Urban History and life have rubbed off on me every time I have been in his presence; to the late-Ki Mano, whose teachings provoked my initial interests in international market forces; to Rex Todd, my former supervisor with the Town of Garner, NC's Community Development Department, who taught me how to think like a professional city planner, and whose instruction has influenced my teaching of urban courses ever since; Hiroshi Fukuda at Hosei University for his many years of friendship and for his giving me the opportunity to teach in Tokyo for a year in 2004–05; and Takayuki Namiki, with Saitama Prefectural Government, for his many years of friendship, mentorship, and support with scheduling interviews with Japanese officials.

Related to this volume, I would like to offer my greatest appreciation to my graduate assistant, Sarah Searcy, who incredibly rendered 29 of the 41 maps in the volume, and improved others. I also would like to thank Steve Rutter at Routledge, and the series editors, Anthony Orum and Zachary Neal for their guidance and for asking me to participate in the series.

Next, and essentially working backward chronologically, I would like to thank the following people and organizations for their support of my academic and professional endeavors over the past 30 years: Leon Wilson, Marieke Van Willigen, Bob Edwards, Charles Garrison, Mamadi Corra, Richard Caston, and my other colleagues, staff, and friends in the Department of Sociology at East Carolina University; the International Council for Canadian Studies and Canadian Embassy in Washington; Tom Wagner, Charles Ellison, Roger Barry, Mahyar Arefi, David Edelman, and my other former colleagues, mentors, staff, and friends in the University of Cincinnati's School of Planning, as well as Rhys Williams formerly in Sociology; my former students Nobuaki Takahama, Yusuke Fukada, and the staffs of the Faculty of Business, the International Center, and main library at Hosei University in Tokyo; Steve Gold, Larry Busch, Maxie Jackson, Marilyn Aronoff, John Melcher, Richard Lyles, Fran Fowler, and all my former colleagues, instructors, and classmates at MSU; Bill Napolitano, the late-Roland Hebert, Jim Hadfield, Steve Smith, Ling Ling Chang, and my former colleagues at friends at SRPEDD in Taunton, MA; Brad Bass, Jenny Saldi, Lula Sanders, Judy White, and my other former colleagues with the Town of Garner, NC; Bill Rohe, David Godschalk, Edward Kaiser, and all of my former instructors and classmates in the University of North Carolina's Department of City and Regional Planning; and Steve Alperstein, Melvin Mitchell, Junior Moore, and my other former colleagues and friends with Metro Dade Transit Administration.

I also would like to thank the following people for informing and/or supporting my research in one way or another over the years: alphabetically, Victoria Basolo, Jon Coleman, Scott Cummings, David Edgington, Kuniko Fujita, Steve Glickman, Mark Gottdiener, Brad Hammond, Michael Indergaard, Tod Kilroy, Hyun-Woo Kim, Young-Hun Kim, Andrew Kirby, Myron Levine, Bob McMahon, Daniel Monti, Petr Pavlinek, Jim Phillips, Iko Kimura Suda, Jim Thomas, Michael Timberlake, Paul Waley, Graham Wilson, Brian York, Mark Zigmont, and Keichiro Zushi. In addition, I would like to thank Kathleen and Alex Romanovich for always welcoming me into their home during my research trips to the Southern Ontario.

I also must offer very special thanks to my in-laws, the late-Osamu and Michiko Kimura, for providing me food, shelter, and support, and affording me the greater opportunities to conduct research in Japan than I would otherwise been able to.

I am also largely in debt to my sister, Jennifer, who has proofread almost every academic article I have published since 1999, including my nearly 500-page dissertation. If not for her amazing skills, I am sure my publication record would be much smaller.

I remain eternally grateful to my late parents, Joyce and Marshall Jacobs, for their lifelong encouragement and their emotional support. I hope they were as proud of me, as I was of them.

Finally, I must give special thanks to my three best friends: Ruiko Mei Kimura Jacobs, Shuko Kimura Jacobs, and Steven R. Hicks. Steve and I have been best buddies for 30 years now, dating back to that same September 1983 when I first transferred to MSU. We have been through countless journeys ever since, most notably my attending of his wedding to his bride of 25 years, Kathy, in 1987, to his hosting of my wedding at their home in 2000, and many other cool adventures in between. In fact, Steve's friendship was an important motivating factor behind my return to MSU for my Ph.D. in August 1994.

It was then that I also would find Shuko. We met on the very first day of MSU's Sociology Department's orientation for new Ph.D. students, and have been together ever since. Without her brilliant work as my interview interpreter on my dissertation, I never would have been able to complete that document, and most likely would never have written the numerous articles on Japanese cities I have published over the years. Lastly, I must thank her for her never-ending patience and support during my countless and ever demanding years as an academic.

Last but not least, I want to thank my dancing daughter, Ruiko. Every day since her birth in 2002, she has taught Shuko and me the true meaning of the word love, and given all of our hard work and dedication a real purpose, this volume included. If I can inspire her half as much as she has inspired me, then I expect some day she will shine on her own stage.

A. J. Jacobs, February 2012

NOTE

1   *World/Global City Theory* generally refers to scholars guided by one or more of the following perspectives: John Friedmann's (1986) *World City Hypothesis*; Saskia Sassen's (1991) *Global City Theory*; Michael Timberlake's (1985) *World System's City System Theory*; and/or Peter Taylor's (2004) *World City Network Theory*.

CONTRIBUTORS

Editor, and author of Overviews, Conclusion, and Chapters 1-2, 11, 13, 16, 18, and 24

A. J. Jacobs, Associate Professor and Director of Graduate Studies, East Carolina University, Department of Sociology, A-405 Brewster MS567, Greenville, NC 27858 USA, E-mail: draj-jacobs@yahoo.com

Authors of other edited chapters:

1. John Friedmann, Honorary Professor, University of British Columbia, School of Community and Regional Planning, #433-6333 Memorial Road, Vancouver, BC V6T 1Z2, Canada. E-mail: rpf@interchange.ubc.ca

2. Saskia Sassen, Robert S. Lynd Professor, Columbia University, Department of Sociology, 713 Knox Hall—MC 9649, New York, NY 10027, USA. E-mail: sjs2@columbia.edu

3. Ben Derudder, Associate Director of the Globalization and World Cities Research Group and Network (GaWC), and Professor, Ghent University, Department of Geography, Krijgslaan 281/58, B-9000 Ghent, Belgium. Email: ben.derudder@ugent.be

   Peter J. Taylor, Director of GaWC and Professor, Northumbria University, Department of Geography and Environment, Ellison Building, Newcastle upon Tyne, NE1 8ST, UK. E-mail: crogfam@yahoo.com

   Frank Witlox, Associate Director of GaWC and Professor, Ghent University, Department of Geography, Krijgslaan 281/58, B-9000 Ghent, Belgium. Email: frank.witlox@ugent.be

   Gilda Catalano, Lecturer, University of Calabria, Department of Sociology and Political Science, 87306 Arcavacata di Rende, Cosenza, Italy. Email: gilda.catalano@unical.it

4. Christof Parnreiter, Professor, University of Hamburg, Department of Geography, Bundesstraße 55, D20146 Hamburg, Germany. E-Mail: parnreiter@geowiss.uni-hamburg.de

5. Rolee Aranya, Associate Professor, Norwegian University of Science and Technology, Department of Urban Design and Planning, NO-7491 Trondheim, Norway. E-mail: rolee.aranya@ntnu.no

6. Edward Denison, Independent heritage consultant, writer and architectural photographer. 2 St. Ann's House, Margery Street, London, WC1X 0HS, UK. E-mail: e.denison@ucl.ac.uk

7. Owen Crankshaw, Professor, University of Cape Town, Department of Sociology, Private Bag, Rondebosch 7700, Western Cape, 7701, South Africa. E-mail: Owen.Crankshaw@uct.ac.za

8. Yasser Elsheshtawy, Associate Professor, United Arab Emirates University, Department of Architectural Engineering, Faculty of Engineering, P.O. Box 17555, Al Ain, UAE. E-mail: sheshtawi@uaeu.ac.ae; yasser09@gmail.com

9. Richard Child Hill, Emeritus Professor, Michigan State University, Department of Sociology, 316 Berkey Hall, East Lansing, MI 48824. E-mail: hillrr@msu.edu.

   Kuniko Fujita, Michigan State University, Department of Sociology, 316 Berkey Hall, East Lansing, MI 48824. E-mail: fujitak@msu.edu.

10. Janet Abu-Lughod, Professor Emerita, The New School University, Department of Sociology, 65 Fifth Avenue New York, NY 10003. E-mail: nychla@aol.com

12. Chia-Huang Wang, Professor, Department of Social and Policy Sciences, Yuan-Ze University, 135 Yuan-Tung Road, Chung-Li, Taoyuan, Taiwan 32003, R.O.C. E-mail: wanghcia@saturn.yzu.edu.tw

14. Christopher Silver, Dean, University of Florida, College of Design, Construction and Planning, 331A ARCH, P.O. Box 115701 Gainesville, Florida 32611-5701. E-mail: silver2@dcp.ufl.edu

15. Michael Indergaard, Professor, St. John's University, Department of Sociology and Anthropology, St. John's Hall Room 444I-1, Jamaica, NY 11439. E-mail: indergam@stjohns.edu

17. Allen J. Scott, Professor, UCLA, Departments of Geography and Policy Studies, 1144 Bunche Hall, Los Angeles, CA 90095-1524, USA. E-mail: ajscott@ucla.edu

    Michael Storper, Professor, UCLA, Department of Urban Planning, 3250 Public Policy Building, Los Angeles, CA 90095-1656, USA. E-mail: storper@ucla.edu

19. Susan Fainstein, Professor, Harvard University, John F. Kennedy School of Government, Mailbox NR, 79 JFK Street, Cambridge, MA 01238, USA. E-mail: susan_fainstein@harvard.edu

20. Bob Jessop, Distinguished Professor and Founding Director, Lancaster University, Institute for Advanced Studies, C23b Lancaster, LA1 4YL, UK. Email: b.jessop@lancaster.ac.uk.

    Ngai-Ling Sum. Senior Lecturer. Lancaster University, Department of Politics, Philosophy and Religion, County South, B73, Lancaster, LA1 4YL, UK. E-mail: n.sum@lancaster.ac.uk

21. James Simmie, Professor, Oxford Brookes University, Department of Planning, Headington Campus, Gipsy Lane, Oxford OX3 0BP, UK. E-mail: jsimmie@brookes.ac.uk

    James Sennett, Research Associate, Oxford Brookes University, Department of Planning, Headington Campus, Gipsy Lane, Oxford OX3 0BP, UK. E-mail: jsennett@brookes.ac.uk

Peter Wood, Emeritus Professor, University College London, Department of Geography, Pearson Building, Gower Street London. WC1E 6BT, UK. Email: p.wood@geog.ucl.ac.uk

Doug Hart, University of Reading, School of Real Estate and Planning, Reading RG6 6UD, UK. Email: d.a.hart@reading.ac.uk

22. John Rennie Short, Professor, University of Maryland Baltimore County, Department of Public Policy, 1000 Hilltop Circle, Baltimore, MD 21250. Email: jrs@umbc.edu

Carrie Breitbach, Assistant Professor, Chicago State University, Geography Program, 9501 S. King Drive, Chicago, Illinois 60629. Email: cbreitba@csu.edu

Steven Buckman is in Real Estate Services, United Brokers Group, 428 S Gilbert Rd, Suite 112, Gilbert, AZ 85296. Email: stephenb@ubgrealestate.com

Jamey Essex, Associate Professor, Associate Professor, University of Windsor, Department of Political Science, Chrysler Hall North 1139, Windsor, Ontario N9B 3P4. Email: jessex@uwindsor.ca

23. Paul Waley, Senior Lecturer, University of Leeds, School of Geography, University Road, Leeds, LS2 9JT, UK. E-mail: p.t.waley@leeds.ac.uk.

Introduction

Cities and Regions Evolving in an Ever-Changing World

A.J. Jacobs

> At the beginning of the 21st Century, more than three billion persons—about half of the world's population—lived in urban areas. By 2030, this number is expected to increase ... to more than five billion. Most of this increase will occur in ... megacities of the developing world.
>
> (Gottdiener & Hutchison, 2011, p. 1)

Cities are the nexus of social, political, and economic activities. They serve as both the cores of, and the means for connecting, events taking place on the local, regional, national, and international levels. In addition, since all spatial tiers are constantly interacting with one another, cities evolve within an ever-changing development context.

English-language studies examining the human settlements we have come to know as cities began in earnest in the late 1800s. Among the earlier notable books were: Frederick Maitland's (1898) *Township and Borough;* Josiah Strong's (1898), *The Twentieth Century City;* W.E.B Dubois' (1899) *The Philadelphia Negro;* and Adna Ferrin Weber's (1899) *The Growth of Cities in the Nineteenth Century.*[1] According to Louis Wirth (1938, p. 9), the first systematic theories of urbanism were Max Weber's "penetrating essay, 'Die Stadt' (The City), and a memorable paper by Robert E. Park, 'The City: Suggestions for the Investigation of Human Behavior in an Urban Environment'" (see Park, 1915; Weber, 1958, 1978). During that same year as Park's article, 1915, Patrick Geddes also published his classic book: *Cities in Evolution* (see Chapter 2).

Greatly influenced by his mentor, Georg Simmel, Park teamed with his University of Chicago colleague Ernest Burgess to establish what would become the Chicago School of Human Ecology/Urban Sociology.[2] Park's article was reprinted ten years later in his book with Burgess and Roderick McKenzie (1925), *The City.* This volume would serve as the springboard for decades of research published by some of the most renowned urban scholars of the 20th century, most of whom were Park's colleagues and/or students.[3]

The influence of the Human Ecology School remained strong throughout the 1970s, in the USA at least, guided by works of McKenzie's most prized student at the University of Michigan, Amos Hawley.[4] This began to change in the 1970s and 1980s, beginning with the publication of Ray Pahl's (1970) *Whose City?,* David Harvey's (1973) *Social Justice and the City*, and the English translation of Manuel Castells' (1977) *The Urban Question.* This was followed most prominently by the 1979 release of the second edition of Peter Hall's (1966/1979) now classic book *The World Cities.* Thereafter, scholars began focusing more and more of their attention on globalization and its impacts on cities and regions.[5] Among the notable contributions of this period were the works of what would become known as the L.A. School of Urban Studies (Dear, 2001). Michael J. Dear, Allen J. Scott, Edward W. Soja, Michael Storper, and Mike Davis are the most well-known scholars from the L.A. School.[6]

In regards to the examination of the world's major cities, however, the major turning point in urban growth theory was a series of early to mid-1980s studies in which authors delineated what they called 'the new international division of labor' (NIDL) and the ensuing development of a world urban hierarchy led by a few command cities.[7] Ever since, detailing the impacts of globalization on metropolitan regions has become "a major preoccupation of urban scholars" in a variety of social science disciplines (Brenner & Keil, 2006, p. 5).

While the leading *world/global city theorists*[8] have been the most recognized, scholars seeking to demonstrate that national and/or local factors have remained the most decisive determinants driving urban development outcomes have been just as prolific. These theorists have examined the world's city-regions from a variety of different perspectives, each offering the urban scholarship unique insight into urban growth processes. For the sake of space and simplicity, these works might be categorized into two camps: (1) Nested City; and (2) The City-Region as the Economic Engine of Growth. Recognizing the importance of all three schools of thought, the readings in *The World's Cities: Contrasting Regional, National, and Global Perspectives* are grouped and presented in three parts.

In Part One: City-Regions in a World System, the eight selected readings fit within the paradigm known as *world/global city theory*. This school of thought generally has referred to published research guided by one or more of the following: John Friedmann's (1986) 'World City Hypothesis'; Saskia Sassen's (1991) *Global City*; Michael Timberlake's (1985, 1987) 'World System's City Theory'; and/or Peter Taylor's (2004b) *World City Network*. Led by these scholars, advocates of this model have claimed that contemporary capitalism has severely weakened the influence of national and local actors (disembedded cities), and thereby, enabled transnational corporations (TNCs) to re-organize human settlement space in their best interests. This restructuring has facilitated the creation of an international urban hierarchy, led by a few core 'world' cities: New York, London, and Tokyo. These megacities have then served as TNC global command centers for finance, production, and trade. The net result has been growing socio-economic inequality worldwide and within metropolitan areas, especially global cities. It also has induced all cities to converge (i.e., to lose their uniqueness and become more similar, over time).

Part Two: Nested City-Regions includes eight readings in which the authors subscribe to what has been called the *nested city thesis*. Led by Richard Child Hill and Kuniko Fujita (2003) and Janet L. Abu-Lughod (1999), authors guided by this perspective have maintained that each local area has its own distinct national, historical, geographical, institutional, and cultural context, and these multiple factors have remained the primary determinants of urban development paths. Moreover, for these theorists, variations in these embedded factors, such as the region of the world in which a city was located within, its national government policy, intergovernmental systems, and racial-ethnic relations, have clearly demonstrated the continued diversity of urban areas and growth outcomes.

Part Three: The City-Region as the Engine of Economic Activity/Growth presents eight chapters from well-known urbanists, including Allen J. Scott, Michael Storper, Bob Jessop, Susan Fainstein, James Simmie, and John Renie Short. Although coming at the issue from a variety of perspectives, collectively these readings assert that city-regions and/or local actors have remained the primary catalysts of urban development. Although falling under a variety

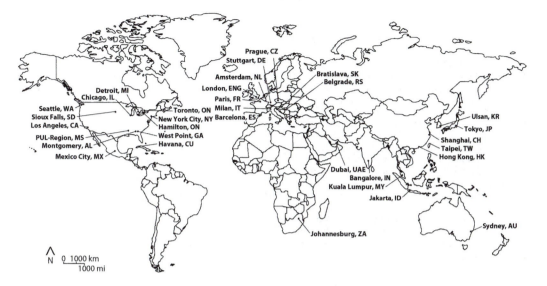

Figure I.1 Nexus Cities in the World Context

of theoretical banners, scholars in this grouping essentially have claimed that it has been those cities which have contained agglomerations of complementary industries, clusters of innovative firms, and/or reflexive, entrepreneurial local development officials that have proven to be the most successful.

In total, the book contains 24 chapter readings providing theories and lessons from more than 30 cities/regions evolving within an ever-changing world (see Figure I.1 for a geographic spread of these urban areas). Each portion of the book also contains a brief 'Overview' chapter by the editor, which introduces that particular perspective and offers a brief summary of the eight selections included within that segment. To further introduce the reader to each theory-grouping, the first chapter reading in each part presents a condensed version of an influential writing in that perspective. These works are followed by a cross-section of case studies that effectively approach their case studied from this viewpoint.

The compilation concludes with an original essay by the editor entitled, 'The Nexus City Model: Bridging the Local, Regional, National, and International Contexts'. The objective of this original essay is to summarize and integrate many of the ideas presented in the volume's readings into a 12-factor conceptual toolkit or model that can be utilized by students and scholars in their own examinations and comparisons of the world's city-regions.

Finally, to enhance the student, instructor, and scholarly experience, each chapter contains four 'Questions for Discussion', six 'Further Readings', and ten 'Helpful Web Links'. In addition, an extensive list of references cited in the readings is included at the end of the volume. These tools are intended for use in class discussion and/or course written assignments. They also are intended to aid and encourage readers to think more deeply about cities and the important ideas presented. This is critical, as in the wake of the worst world economic crisis in a generation, both greater awareness and innovative thinking are necessary if we are truly to achieve the intended goals of all urban scholars regardless of their academic discipline: (1) to help make human settlements, both big and small, better places to live; and (2) to enhance the quality of life of citizens residing in such places.

NOTES

1 For more early writings on cities, see Martindale (1958), Timberlake (1985), and Gottdiener & Budd (2005).
2 A major influence on Park was Simmel's (1950) essay, 'Metropolis and Mental Life,' which was originally completed in German in 1902–03.
3 e.g., Burgess (1925, 1926), McKenzie (1927, 1933), Wirth (1928, 1938), and Hoyt (1933)
4 See particularly, Hawley (1950, 1968, 1971, 1986).
5 See for example, Hall (1966/1979), Harvey (1982), Hill (1982), Sassen-Koob (1982), Smith (1984), Gottdiener (1985), Henderson & Castells (1987), Rodriguez & Feagin (1987), and Gottdiener & Feagin (1988).
6 See for example, Dear & Scott (1981), Soja, et al. (1983), Scott & Storper (1986), Soja (1989), Storper & Walker (1989), Scott (1990a), and Davis (1990). Although he was a founding member of UCLA's Urban Planning Program and its Director at the time, John Friedmann's work is not considered within the Neo-Marxist, L.A. School paradigm. As the discussion throughout this book reveals, Friedmann has led his own school of thought, the World City Theory (see especially the Overview for Part One: City-Regions in a World System and Chapter 1).
7 See particularly, Cohen (1981), Friedmann & Wolfe (1982), Timberlake (1985), Friedmann (1986), and Smith & Feagin (1987).
8 World/Global City Theory generally refers to scholars guided by one or more of the following perspectives: John Friedmann's (1986) World City Hypothesis, Saskia Sassen's (1991) Global City Theory; Michael Timberlake's (1985) World System's City System Theory; and/or Peter Taylor's (2004b) World City Network Theory.

PART 1

City-Regions in a World System

City-Regions in a World System: An Overview

A.J. Jacobs

Part One: City-Regions in a World System presents readings which fit within the urban theoretical perspective known as *world/global city theory*. Scholars subscribing to this paradigm maintain that the forces driving world capitalism have become the primary shapers of urban/metropolitan growth patterns. John Friedmann, Saskia Sassen, Peter Hall, and Peter Taylor are the most frequently cited contemporary scholars advocating this position.[1] Nevertheless, *world/global city theory* has a rich historical tradition dating back at least to Patrick Geddes' (1915) *Cities in Evolution*, which is generally recognized as first to use the term 'world city'.

Although not always credited, many of the guiding principles in this perspective were outlined in Roderick McKenzie's (1927) seminal *American Journal of Sociology* article 'The Concept of Dominance and World Organization.' Influenced by Charles Child's (1924) *Physiological Foundations of Behavior,* McKenzie used an ecological metaphor, essentially a spider web of interconnectedness, to describe spatial development patterns typical in American, Western European, and Asian city-regions in the early 20th century. He suggested that, similar to biological organisms, urban settlements tended to evolve towards an axial "form of spatial pattern with a dominant center and subordinated integrated parts" (p. 30). Meanwhile, advances in transportation and communications, he maintained, had brought mobility for people and production, and thereby allowed for the separation of administration/management, industry and commerce. Within city-regions, the decentralization of production sent factories to the urban fringe, making territorial boundaries less important. All of which ultimately served to reinforce existing core and periphery relationships within and between the world's city-regions.[2]

Similar to the much later arguments put forward by Andre Gunder Frank (1966, 1967) in his *dependency theory*, and Immanuel Wallerstein (1974a, 1974b) in his *world systems theory,* and Friedmann (1986) in his *world city hypothesis,* McKenzie claimed that within this world urban system, 'world' centers like London and New York had come to dominate less-developed areas or 'margins' by expanding their power/markets in three ways, depending upon the attributes of the periphery area. In the first relationship of dominance, the 'trade frontier,' mercantile-based economies, such as the British Empire, imported primary goods from the margins in order to produce manufactured goods. In 'plantation frontiers,' the governments of periphery areas supplied companies from core countries with an abundance of natural and agricultural resources for sale and consumption in other parts of the world. Lastly, a more recent expression of Western center dominance was found in the 'industrial frontier.' In these circumstances, Western firms located entire factories in lesser developed countries and then produced in the margin, exploiting low-wage labor and natural resources in their effort to create cheap finished products for export to the home country and world-wide (McKenzie, 1927, pp. 36–37).

According to McKenzie, however, the locations of these domination-subordination processes were constantly changing as, "centers of dominance arise and produce new combinations of regional interdependence" (p. 42); this idea also can be found in Wallerstein's core, semi-periphery, and periphery, related to his discussions of the historical rise and fall of nations in the world system. Presciently, McKenzie also predicted the rise of Tokyo (and Japan) as a world center of economic control over 50 years before it actually happened. In addition, it is apparent that McKenzie would not have been surprised at how modern advances in information technology have impacted the world urban hierarchy. In fact, he predicted that telecommunications would supplant transportation as the most powerful tool of global interconnectedness and core dominance.

As bigger issues, such as World War II, the Cold War, Vietnam, 'Third World' Nationalism, and internal social movements captured the spotlight, McKenzie's writings, and others from the Chicago School of Human Ecology, fell out of favor. His work was reborn, however, in Michael Timberlake's (1985) edited volume, *Urbanization in the World Economy*. Here, Timberlake reminded urban scholars of McKenzie's decades-old conclusions regarding the existence of a world city system governed by core–periphery relations. Subscribing to what might be called *world system's city theory*, Timberlake (1985, 1987), along with Rodriguez and Feagin (1987), Anthony King (1989, 1990), and Walton (1976) before them, also encouraged scholars to integrate Wallerstein's ideas into their research on the globe's urban system.

Although never citing him specifically, McKenzie's depictions of the relationships between the world urban system and the global distribution of resources were mirrored in R. B. Cohen's (1981) greatly underappreciated chapter, 'The New International Division of Labor, Multinational Corporations and Urban Hierarchy' (or NIDL), in Michael Dear and Allen J. Scott's edited book, *Urbanization and Urban Planning in Capitalist Society*. Inspired by Stephen Hymer's (1972, 1979) similarly titled, 'Multinational Corporations and the International Division of Labor', Cohen claimed that the NIDL represented "a system for production on a world scale in which even greater numbers of people are integrated into activities carried on by large international producers of goods and by international firms which service these produces" (Cohen, 1981, p. 288). He stressed:

> But in perhaps its most profound impact, the NIDL has integrated qualitatively different types of laborers, with very different levels of work experience, highly varied types of social backgrounds, and vastly divergent histories of labor organization, into . . . a complex hierarchical world system . . . under the aegis of large, highly integrated international companies. (Cohen, 1981, pp. 288–289)

He concluded that "the new changes which area as part of the NIDL have reshaped the spatial hierarchy of economic activities . . . [and led] to the emergence of a series of global cities," such as New York, London, and Frankfurt, which formerly merely served as nodes of international business and/or finance (pp. 293, 300). In the process, these places have been transformed into the command and control centers of "business decision-making and corporate strategy formulation" in the new world order (p. 300).

Cohen's work was emblematic of a dramatic sea change that was taking place in urban studies at the time. This transformation was spurred by the 1979 re-issuance of Peter Hall's 1966 book, *World Cities*. Although Friedmann was critical of Hall's overly physical, quasi-ecological approach, he so liked Hall's book title that he even adopted it for his own theory (see Friedmann & Wolff, 1982, p. 332). Borrowing from Hall, Wallerstein, Cohen, and others, Friedmann's ensuing article, 'The World City Hypothesis,' rather than Hall's book, would then profoundly shape the urban scholarship for the next 25 years. Almost as influential has been Sassen's (1991) book *Global City: New York, London, Tokyo*.

Guided by Friedmann and Sassen, *world/global city* theorists have generally claimed that contemporary neo-liberal capitalism has severely weakened the authority of nation-states and thereby disembedded or de-territorialized cities from their national boundaries (i.e., released cities from both the control and the protection of their national governments). Freed from state constraints, TNCs have re-organized urban space for their own intrinsic purposes. The ensuing economic restructuring has led to the creation of a stratified world system (i.e., the NIDL) with an urban hierarchy led by a few core megacities, New York, London, and Tokyo; more recently this list has included a few more cities, such as Paris and Hong Kong (see Taylor, 2004a, 2004b). While there certainly has been diversity in the argument, *world/global city* theorists essentially have agreed that the city-regions at the top of the global urban network, with their "extraordinary concentrations of top decision-makers," have become the frontal lobes of global finance, production, and trade (Feagin & Smith, 1987, p. 3). Or, to use contemporary computer jargon, they have become the multiple core processors powering the 'clouds' operated by the world's corporate elite.

Friedmann and Sassen's writings have inspired the scholarship of countless other urban theorists.[3] Nevertheless, despite their provocative and informative pronouncements, the *world/global city* perspective has come under fire from many directions since the 1990s. The main criticisms have focused upon the perceived lack of original and historically based comparative data in many such works, and the theory's over-estimation of the diminution in power of national (and local) governments over urban development processes.[4] More recently, in the midst of the post-2008 world economic crisis, some even have signaled the end of the paradigm's usefulness (Therborn, 2011).

One of the few earlier exceptions to the ahistorical generalization was the writings of Christopher Chase-Dunn's (1984, 1985). Addressing the issue in true Wallersteinian fashion, Chase-Dunn (1985, p. 273) wrote that despite the claims of some Global City advocates, "the system of world cities . . . did not appear in the 1950s, with cities having been 'national' before that time. Rather, cities have long been both national and international." As for the perceived lack of original data, this critique led to the creation of several global cities research collaboratives, most notably, Peter Taylor's 'Globalization and World Cities Research Network' or GaWC (2011).

Acknowledging Friedmann, Sassen, Hall, Manuel Castells and Nigel Thrift as 'honorary founders,' Taylor and his GaWC contributors, particularly Jon Beaverstock, Ben Derudder, and Frank Witlox, have spent the past 15 plus years inundating the academic literature with articles empirically delineating the world urban hierarchy.[5] Meanwhile, totally independently from and unaware of Taylor's GaWC endeavors, Smith and Timberlake (1995a, 1995b) became the first to empirically 'map' the global system of cities. A third, equally independent effort, and drawing inspiration from Stephen Hymer (1972), was Alderson and Beckfield (2004).[6] Nonetheless, although there have been theoretical and empirical differences among these authors, scholars guided by *world city network/world system's city theory* have generally concluded that the primary factors driving a city-region's growth outcomes were: (1) the number of interconnections worldwide it had with others cities; (2) which city-regions it was affiliated with; and (3) which sectors of the economy these city network linkages were. City-regions which have contained the greatest concentrations of financial and professional elites, and which have had the most interconnections with similar cities, even just air travel connections, have occupied the highest positions in the NIDL.

Cataloguing all the articles utilizing or citing Friedmann, Sassen, or Taylor's framework suggests that *world/global city theory* has been the most dominant paradigm in the urban scholarship over past 20 years. In fact, according to Therbon (2011), it may have achieved hegemonic status in urban studies. The list of publications is so vast that it is nearly impossible to select only a handful of them for presentation in any one volume. Nevertheless, the following eight chapters in Part One: City-Regions in a World System are intended to provide the reader with a basic understanding of this perspective through a cross-section of case studies from different parts of the world.

The selections begin with Chapter 1, which offers a condensed version of Friedmann's (1995) "Where We Stand: A Decade of World City Research," from pp. 21–47 of Paul Knox and Peter Taylor (eds.) *World Cities in a World System*. Here, Friedmann reviews and assesses the framework's theoretical major premises, its objectives and significance 13 years after his original article with Goetz Wolff (1982) was published. After chronicling some of the research guiding the paradigm at the time, he acknowledges the challenges of applying abstract theory to real life cases. He modestly concludes that the while the *world city hypothesis* has proven its usefulness as a theoretical framework, "we must remember that the dynamism of the political economy of capital is so great that no single paradigm is likely to remain intact for more than a couple of decades at most" (p. 35).

Most appropriately, Friedmann's reading is followed in Chapter 2 by an excerpt from pp. 32–33 and 130–148 of the 2006 third edition of Sassen's (2006) book, *Cities in a World Economy*. In this selection, she argues that the massive growth in world financial activity, beginning in the 1980s, prompted the concurrent rise of *global cities* serving as the gateways for international capital and as nexuses between national wealth and the global market. She then reviews evidence suggesting that the Digital Age has provoked a greater concentration of top-level corporate functions, rather than their expected dispersal.

She offers three reasons explaining this trend: (1) social connectivity—major financial firms and their top employees require a certain type of work and social environment to thrive, and are attracted to cities with such climates and concentrations of others like them; (2) the need for enormous resources—only very large mega-regions can handle the scale of operations required by these global command and control network; and (3) the denationalization of the corporate elite—as national attachments and identities have become irrelevant "for these global players and their customers" (p. 143). Sassen concludes that the growing use of electronic telecommunications will continue to reinforce the dominant position of these *trans-territorial centers* of contemporary capitalism.

Chapter 3, 'A Global Network Analysis of 234 Cities,' provides a condensed version of Ben Derudder, Peter Taylor, Frank Witlox, and Gilda Catalano's *Regional Studies* article: 'Hierarchical Tendencies and Regional Patterns in the World City Network: A Global Urban Analysis of 234 Cities.' Emblematic of the more than 100 articles published by GaWC contributors over the last ten years, here the authors seek to achieve two objectives: (1) to expand the analysis of the world's city network beyond the upper tier of elite cities; and (2) to provide an empirically and quantitatively based assessment of the world's urban spatial hierarchy.

Utilizing a database of 100 financial and business firms, and focusing on 22 network clusters ranging across 234 cities, Derudder et al. offer a multi-layered city classification system of the world's urban regions. Their taxonomy introduces five bands of cities outside the core regions of London and New York. Among these bands they categorize the inner ring as 'leading world cities' and the most outer ring as 'major cities on the edge.' Each band also has its own sub-categories: city type and arenas. The former contains four city types: cluster nuclei, single members, hybrid members, and isolates. The latter represents regional clusters of cities. They state that hybrid members are those "members of the cluster who share membership with another cluster . . . [while] with their 'core' and 'hybrid' memberships, the arenas are constituted by interweaving hierarchical and regional processes" (pp. 875, 880). This interesting and quite complex article would serve as one of the foundation pieces for years of research, including at least three books written and/or edited by GaWC leadership: Peter Taylor's (2004b) classic *World City Network: A Global Urban Analysis*; Taylor et al.'s (2010) *Global Urban Analysis: A Survey of Cities in Globalization*; and Derudder and Witlox's (2010) *Commodity Chains and World Cities*.

Chapter 4 supplies a shortened edition of Christof Parnreiter's (2002) 'Mexico City: The Making of a Global City?' which originally appeared in Sassen's edited book *Global Networks, Linked Cities*. Inspired by Friedmann, Sassen, Taylor, and others, Parneiter argues "that globalization processes give rise to a new form of centrality, in which a certain number of cities emerge as key places" (p. 146). He then chronicles how global flows and the authorization of the North American Free Trade Agreement in 1994 forced the Mexican government to dramatically reposition its development strategies towards foreign trade and foreign direct investment (FDI), particularly manufacturing-related FDI. He says that this new neo-liberal strategy most profoundly impacted the Federal District (i.e., the Mexico City metropolitan region), provoking violent swings in its economy, and making it increasingly more dependent upon foreign capital. In the process, Mexico City was transformed from a national metropolis into a region of advanced capitalist services, and became the "pivot between the Mexican and global economies" (p. 163).

Chapter 5, 'Location Theory in Reverse? Location for Global Production in the IT Industry of Bangalore,' is an edited selection from Rolee Aranya's (2008) paper, 'Location Theory in Reverse?' which first appeared in *Environment and Planning A*. Here, Aranya, a GaWC collaborator, studies the locational history of eight software and information technology (IT) firms from the southern Indian city of Bangalore. He argues that similar to that of advanced producer services, IT firms have strategically restructured Bangalore's urban fabric and have transformed the Indian metropolis into an important global city for IT services. In contrast to *World City Theory*, however, he claims that his findings suggest that IT firms in Bangalore have created their own unique spatial pattern, a reverse location logic which has seen "the peripheralization of control functions and a retention of routine production functions in the core urban areas" (p. 446). He maintains that the IT sector's limited need for face-to-face interactions and focus on offshore activities have driven this apparent reversal of location dynamics.

Chapter 6 provides a condensed version of Edward Denison's (2008) 'Building Shanghai: Historical Lessons from China's Gateway,' previously published in *City*. In the reading, Denison presents a historical review of the evolution of architectural styles in one of "the world's largest and fastest growing cities," and one of China's major gateways to the global economy (p. 207). In the process, he shows how contemporary capitalist forces have reshaped Shanghai's "urban landscape from an aging, dense and relatively low-rise city, into a multifaceted and ubiquitously high-rise conglomeration" (p. 207). While never denying its status as a world city, he nevertheless claims that modern Shanghai architecture, despite its transparent linkages to globalization, still retains clear echoes from its past. This, he contends, has "helped to fuel discussions about crucial issues concerning the city's future: architectural preservation, sustainable urban development and property rights" (p. 214). He concludes by reminding other municipalities to delve into their pasts when seeking solutions to their contemporary and future urban problems. It is in this way, he implies, that striving to become a capital gateway does not require eschewing a city's history.

Chapter 7 offers a condensed version of Owen Crankshaw's (2008) 'Race, Space and the Post-Fordist Spatial Order of Johannesburg,' which was first published in *Urban Studies*. Here, Crankshaw utilizes data from the *2001 South African Population Census* to measure the extent of residential racial desegregation in South Africa's capital city's expanding middle-class suburbs. His findings suggest that in the post-apartheid era, the northern suburbs have developed a much more mixed-race pattern than in more established neighborhoods in the city. Perhaps overly optimistically, he maintains that this desegregation phenomenon has the potential to erode the city's historical legacy of apartheid. If so, he argues, this will make Johannesburg an exception among world cities.

The final reading in Part One, 'Global Dubai or Dubaization' (Chapter 8), presents an edited selection from pp. 249–279 of Yasser Elsheshtawy's (2009) recent book *Dubai: Behind an Urban Spectacle*. In the particular chapter selected, Elsheshtawy focuses on the 'Dubai Model,' and the implications for other Middle Eastern cities wishing to emulate its strategies. He then tries to assess Dubai's influence on other Arab cities through case studies of Morocco, Amman, and Cairo. He maintains that Dubai's development represents a unique phenomenon, which he calls the willing accommodation of global capitalist forces by an Arabic city. Therefore, drawing upon Michael Smith's (2001) perspective in *Transnational Urbanism*, he argues that any efforts to replicate the Dubai Model in other Middle Eastern areas have been and will remain mixed, as long as Western capital ignores each city's unique politico-social histories, networks, practices, and power relations. He then instructs other cities of the world, in the Middle East and in other developing nations to be weary of the potential pitfalls of adopting Dubaization. Mirroring Friedmann, Sassen, and other *World/Global City* scholars, he cautions that while there are benefits, Dubaization may lead to the intensification of social divisions and a greater sense of injustice in those areas among citizens who are closed out of the spoils of globalization.

Overall, the diverse selections in Part One provide the reader with a beginning foundation for understanding the main arguments in *World/Global City Theory*. As stated in the Introduction, to aid in this process, the end of each chapter contains: four 'Questions for Discussion,' six 'Further Readings,' and ten 'Helpful Web Links.' These additions are intended for use in class discussion and/or course written assignments. Finally, all of the references cited in Part One's readings, as well as in this 'Overview' chapter, are compiled in a separate section entitled 'References Cited in the Readings' and supply students and scholars with an added resource for their own research or final term paper assignments. Similar to the tools, this format is repeated in Parts Two and Three of the volume.

NOTES

1   For example, see Friedmann & Wolff (1982), Friedmann (1986), Sassen (1991, 2006), Hall (1966, 1996), and Taylor (1997, 2004b).

2   In an earlier article, 'The Ecological Approach to the Study of the Human Community', McKenzie (1924, pp. 290–291) lays the foundation for his ecological classification of communities.

3   These include among others: Knox & Taylor (1995), Brenner (1997, 1999a), Keil (1998), Lo & Yeung (1998), Yeung (2000), Abrahamson (2004), and Brenner & Keil (2006).

4   On the first aspect see for example, King (1990), Abu-Lughod (1995, 1999), Short et al. (1996), Smith (2001),

and Olds & Yeung (2004). On the second, see Hill & Kim (2000), Hill & Fujita (2003), and the readings in Part II of this volume, Nested City-Regions.

5 For more a sampling of studies see Knox & Taylor (1995), Taylor (1997, 2004a), Taylor & Aranya (2008), Taylor et al. (2002a, 2002b, 2006, 2010), Taylor, Walker et al. (2002), Beaverstock et al. (1999, 2000), Derudder et al. (2010), and Derudder & Witlox (2010). Numerous other published and non-published articles are available on the GaWC's website: http://www.lboro.ac.uk/gawc/.

6 Also see Smith & Timberlake (2001), Shin & Timberlake (2000), and Alderson et al. (2010).

CHAPTER 1

Where We Stand: A Decade of World City Research (1995)

John Friedmann

As an interlocking system of production markets, the global economy is a discovery of the 1970s (Barnet and Müller 1974). At the time there was a good deal of controversy over the so-called 'new international division of labour' and a centuries-old 'world system' (Wallerstein 1974a).

The significance of these theoretical developments for the study of urbanization was not recognized until the early 1980s (Cohen 1981; Friedmann and Wolff 1982). Ten years have passed since then, and this chapter is an attempt to survey what we have learned and to assess where we stand in the study of world cities. I begin with a discussion of some conceptual issues: what is the 'theoretical object' of world cities research? How shall we define the elusive notion of world city? I then launch into an extended review of the literature, including theoretical developments in the 1980s and empirical studies in the early 1990s. The third section takes a closer look at the notion of a structured hierarchy of world cities and argues the need to remain ever alert to economic and political changes that may lead to the rise and fall of world cities that are linked to each other in 'antagonistic co-operation'. Next, I turn to consider that remnant – a majority of the world's population – that for all practical purposes is excluded from the capitalist 'space of accumulation' and consequently also from world city analysis. I argue that our understanding of the urban dynamic remains incomplete unless we

consider both the internal and external proletariats of world cities. A brief coda concludes my discussion.

CONCEPTUAL ISSUES

A certain ambiguity attaches to the world city hypothesis as originally formulated (Friedmann 1986). Is it a way of asking questions about cities in general, or a statement about a class of particular cities – world cities – set apart from other urban agglomerations by specifiable characteristics? Judging from a review of the relevant literature – the answer apparently is that it is both.

How are we to define this class? Please note that we are talking here about cities as spatially organized socio-economic systems; we are talking about *places* and *sites* rather than *actors*. With this proviso, I shall now proceed in a series of discrete steps to define, rigorously I hope, the class of cities that is the object of our study. And I will do so by positing a series of 'agreements' about what I take to be our theoretical object.

First, we have to agree that cities articulate larger regional, national, and international economies. That is to say, cities serve as *centres* through which flow money, workers, information, commodities, and other economically relevant variables. As centres they extend their influence into a surrounding 'field' or region whose economic relations they 'articulate' into the global economy or *space of global accumulation.* Amin and Thrift (1992) have stated recently why, in their view, urban centres are still required for a decentred economy. Spatial concentration, they argue, solves certain problems of corporate management, including *representation* (how to think and talk about the global system), *social interaction* (gathering information, tapping into particular capitalist structures, making agreements, forming coalitions, cementing relations of trust), and *innovation* (incubating product innovations, marketing new products, experimenting with financial innovations, and gaining access to representation and interactive networks).

Second, we have to agree that there is such a thing as a *space of global accumulation,* that is, a set of national and regional economies that serves the purposes of capital accumulation on a 'world-wide' scale. This space includes areas of primary production (e.g. rainforests and minerals in the Amazon Basin), specific production sites (localizations of production), and, of course, spatial concentrations of consumers.

In one sense this global space is co-terminous with planet Earth: from the Arctic to the Antarctic, from the Atlantic to the Pacific, there is no place that is not actually or potentially of use in the process of capital accumulation. But in another and more relevant sense the space of global accumulation is much more restricted. Large parts of the world's population are not incorporated into this space or, if they are, make only a marginal contribution as either direct producers or consumers. I shall come to speak of this in a moment. For now it will be sufficient to say that the space of global accumulation, defined by a set of interdependent regional and national economies, encompasses only a fraction of the earth's surface and an even smaller fraction of its population. It is this more restricted set of space economies precisely that is the space being articulated, or organized, through the network of world cities.

Third, we have to agree that world cities are large, urbanized regions that are defined by dense patterns of interaction rather than by political–administrative boundaries. Typically they have populations of between one and twenty million or more.

Fourth, we have to agree that these regional cities – the commanding nodes of the global system – can be arranged into a *hierarchy of spatial articulations,* roughly in accord with the economic power they command. At the top we find the command and control centres of the global economy, New York, London, and Tokyo (Sassen 1991). After that, the going becomes more contentious because we lack unambiguous criteria for assigning particular cities to a specific place in the global system. There are cities that articulate large national economies into the system, such as Paris, Madrid, and São Paulo; others have a commanding multinational role, such as Singapore and Miami; and still others, such as Chicago and Hong Kong, articulate important subnational (regional) economies.

But establishing such a hierarchy once and for all may, in any event, be a futile undertaking. The world economy is too volatile to allow us to fix a stable hierarchy for any but relatively short stretches of time. Assigning hierarchical rank may therefore be a less compelling exercise than recognizing the existence of differences in rank without further specification and, based on this rough notion, investigating the articulations of particular world cities with each other.

Hierarchical relations are essentially relations of power, and competition for place is always severe among cities. Not only are world cities constantly engaged in an equilibrating act to adjust their economies to the processes of 'creative destruction' that are endemic to industrial capitalism, they are themselves driven by relentless competition, struggling to capture ever more command and control functions that comprise their very essence. Competitive *angst* is built into world city politics.

Fifth, and last, we have to agree that the

dominant culture of world cities is cosmo
politan, as defined by its controlling social
strata whom Sklair (1991) calls the transnational capitalist class. The capitalist class
leads its members to be clairvoyant in some
regards, but also to be self-deceptive and even
blind in others. Typically, they confuse their
own class interest – which is the smooth,
uninterrupted functioning of the global system of accumulation – with national or local
territorial interest, as in the notorious words
of Charles Wilson: 'What is good for General
Motors is good for the United States.'

A growing social schizophrenia has resulted
between, on the one hand, regional societies
and local institutions and, on the other hand,
the rules and operations of the economic system at the international level. The more the
economy becomes interdependent on the global scale, the less can regional and local governments, as they exist today, act upon the
basic mechanisms that condition the daily
existence of their citizens. The traditional
structures of social and political control over
development, work, and distribution have
been subverted by the placeless logic of an
internationalized economy enacted by means
of information flows among powerful actors
beyond the sphere of state regulations.

Let me now sum up the five agreements
that, together, constitute a definition of our
'theoretical object'.

1   World cities articulate regional, national,
    and international economies into a glo-
    bal economy. They serve as the organiz-
    ing nodes of a global economic system.
2   A space of global capital accumulation
    exists, but it is smaller than the world
    as a whole. Major world regions and
    their populations are, at present, virtu-
    ally excluded from this space, living in a
    permanent subsistence economy.
3   World cities are large urbanized spaces of
    intense economic and social interaction.
4   World cities can be arranged hierarchi-
    cally, roughly in accord with the eco-

nomic power they command. They are
cities through which regional, national,
and international economies are articulated with the global capitalist system of
accumulation. A city's ability to attract
global investments ultimately determines
its rank in the order of world cities. However, its fortunes in this regard, as well as
its ability to absorb external shocks from
technological innovations and political
change, are variable. Cities may rise into
the rank of world cities, they may drop
from the order, and they may rise or fall
in rank.
5   The controlling world city strata consti-
    tute a social class that has been called the
    transnational capitalist class. Its interests
    are the smooth functioning of the global
    system of accumulation; its culture is cos-
    mopolitan; and its ideology is consumer-
    ist. Its presence gives rise to often severe
    conflict between itself and subaltern
    classes who have more locally defined
    territorial interests and whose rise into
    the transnational class is blocked.

RECENT RESEARCH

I want to turn now to some recent studies
that have used the emerging world city paradigm for their subject matter. I will do so in
three steps. First, I would like to tell the back-
story to the emerging paradigm: what are the
theoretical debates that underlie world city
research? Second, I will review two large-
scale, comparative studies of world cities at
the very apex of the global hierarchy. And
third, I will take a brief look at some specific
city studies.

Backstory

At the outset, I would like to insist that
what we are studying here is a historically unprecedented phenomenon and not
merely a continuation of what, in one form
or another, has been around for a very long

time (Chase-Dunn 1985). I shall therefore follow Amin and Thrift (1992) when they write that between the 1970s and 1980s there occurred an important shift, 'a move from an international to a global economy'. They describe this new economy in terms of four characteristics: the functioning of industries on a world scale through the medium of global corporate networks; an increase in oligopolistic, progressively centralized power; an ongoing process of corporate decentralization through new forms of subcontracting, joint ventures, and other forms of networked organization and strategic alliances; and finally, a new, more volatile balance of power between nation-states and corporations, resulting in the increasing prominence of cross-national issue coalitions uniting fragments of the state, industries, and firms in a worldwide network. One can debate the particulars of this formulation and still conclude that the capitalist economy today is organized in ways that are dramatically different to those that existed right up to the 1960s.

An ongoing controversy about the precise nature of this new world economic order is found in the literature on Fordism, a term originally coined by Antonio Gramsci but given currency by Lipietz and his followers in the French 'regulationist' school (Lipietz 1989). In Lipietz's formulation the Fordist regime of accumulation was based, in the final instance, on the idea of mass production, mass consumption, and a Keynesian system of state regulation. A controversy has sprung up on precisely the question of whether we are now moving into a new regime of post-Fordist, flexible accumulation or are merely in an unnamed 'restructuring phase' of capitalism. But all participants in the debate seem to agree that we are facing a new economic landscape along with a new alignment of class forces within the continuing evolution of the capitalist mode of production.

Building on the path-breaking work of Piore and Sabel (1984) among others, Storper and Walker (1989) forge new ground in the geography of flexible accumulation. Theirs is a Schumpeterian vision of capitalism, where periods of rising waves of technological and product innovation are followed by declines of older and rapidly obsolescing industries in a never-ending and competitively driven process of 'creative destruction'. In its specificity, their work goes beyond Iipietz, however, with their emphasis on new technologies and forms of capitalist organization (i.e. 'flexibility'). Mass consumption plays a secondary role in their account, to the primacy of gains in productivity and the extraction of surplus value. Consequently they focus on production ensembles (above all, in manufacturing) and on a geography of production sites that is in many ways reminiscent of Isard's (1956) production complexes of some forty years ago.

Manuel Castells' book, *The Informational City*, was published in the same year as Storper and Walker's (1989) and draws on some of the same literature. In this essentially synthetic work Castells tries – to define an 'informational mode of development'. The book is important in a number of ways. Like so many contemporary economic sociologists and geographers, Castells is transfixed by the ensemble of advanced, information-based technologies for which the microchip may stand as symbol. These technologies, argues Castells, have created a deterritorialized 'space of flows' which overcomes terrestrial barriers by creating instantaneous access to a network of strategic stations located around the world. Access to this space, and control over its principal nodes, have become critical for the players in the game of capital accumulation. By the same token, those who lack access to this networked space are disempowered and, to varying degrees, dependent on whatever crumbs of information power holders may be willing to share. Inherent in this formulation is a dualism of incorporation/exclusion which foreshadows some of the facets of world city research on which I will comment below.

The final background to which I would like to draw attention is Sklair's *Sociology of the Global System*. He writes 'the primary agent in the political sphere is a still-evolving *transnational capitalist class*. The institutions of the *culture-ideology of consumerism,* as expressed through the transnational mass media, are the primary agents in the cultural-ideological sphere' (Skiair 1991: 53). Sklair thus draws our attention to the social and political actors who have created the new global economic order and who will have to maintain ('reproduce') it. He also reminds us of the importance of ideology in undergirding the hegemony of global capitalism and its 'space of flows'. I shall return to this point later.

Major Comparative Studies

Now I want to comment on two exceptional, very different, recently published books on world cities: Sassen's (1991) *Global City,* an and Sudjic's (1992) essay in *The 100 Mile City* and bypasses academic debates to present us with a close-up view of how the 'global city' has come about. Its object is the built environment.

Since Manuel Castells' (1983) influential work on the politics of cities which, he claimed, revolves around issues of collective consumption, scholars have treated urban phenomena primarily from the perspective of social reproduction. For their part, neo-classical economists, to the extent that they treated them at all, subsumed much of what we know about cities under vaguely defined (and rarely specified) agglomeration economies. Labour economists focused additionally on the functioning of urban labour markets. Explicitly rejecting these approaches, Sassen favours a paradigm that emphasizes the *production of financial and producer services,* not as a residual category subsumed under an estimated employment multiplier with manufacturing at the base, but as a productive activity in its own right. What these services produce, she argues, is

'control capability' over a geographically dispersed set of global production sites and service outlets. Geographical decentralization requires centralization of command structures and, for the global economy as a whole, control capability has come to be centred, among others, in the three metropolitan areas of New York, London, and Tokyo. Sassen approaches global cities as sites for the production of producer services and as financial market-places for the buying and selling of securities.

This proves to be an exceedingly useful point of departure. Sassen draws out of her research a series of fascinating hypotheses, speculations, intuitions, and questions that will do much to inform our work in the years ahead.

By far the most fascinating, because least familiar, global city discussed by Sassen is Tokyo. Only seven years ago, Rimmer expressed surprise at his discovery that 'the parallels between Tokyo and Los Angeles [as putative world cities] were greater than imagined' (Rimmer 1986: 152). Now Japanese scholars have begun their own investigations into urban restructuring. A recent article by Takashi Machimura carries the telling subtitle 'Transforming Tokyo into a world city' (Machimura 1992). Machimura pauses on the horns of a dilemma: is Tokyo to be merely 'a giant growth machine solely for the processing of global capital and information?' Implied in this question is the fate of Tokyo as the capital of Japan, an island nation which, like the United Kingdom, has a strong sense of its own identity.

Like other writers, Sassen poses a similar question when she defines her set of global cities as a 'new type of city', though she is careful to moderate this abstract conception by insisting that each city is also a specific place, with its own history and way of life. What I should like to add to this is that it may be helpful to distinguish global cities that are national capitals (Paris, Madrid, London, and Tokyo *inter alia*) and those, such as Frankfurt, New York, Toronto, Los Angeles, São Paulo, and Osaka, that are not. Of necessity, capital cities are less likely than other cities to become 'giant growth machines' to the exclusion of national/local considerations. Where capital cities are concerned national governments may impose their own will on the city.

A second point to remember in the comparative study of global cities (or world cities: I will, henceforth, use the two designations interchangeably) is that countries have very different policies with regard to foreign immigration, and this has major consequences for world city formation. Tokyo's case is notorious, and although Sassen discovers an 'underclass' of foreign workers there, their numbers are (still?) relatively insignificant. More than 95 per cent of Tokyo's resident population remains Japanese. This is obviously not the case with New York or London nor, increasingly, with cities on the European continent.

My third and final comment on Sassen's excellent book relates to her chosen focus on producer and financial services. I would agree with her that these services are essential to the management of the global production complex. But I would also argue that we must consider, as a separate category, the cultural services that are crucial for ensuring the hegemony of transnational capitalism through what Sklair calls its culture-ideology of *consumerism* major news services, television, the motion picture industry, major newspapers, publishing, communications consultants, and advertising agencies. It is their understanding of the world that we feed off, that shape our ideas and our responses to political situations. Professionals in these industries are every bit as important as bankers, accountants, realtors, and insurance agents. They are increasingly networked internationally, employ tens of thousands of workers across the entire spectrum of jobs, from newspaper delivery boys and movie 'gophers' to the moguls of recording and TV studios, and they are concentrated in global cities. Their task is to create and reproduce a popular consensus around transnational interests. As instruments of hegemony they do not always play by the rules, but their role in creating a positive image of global capitalist accumulation is critical.

I now pause briefly to consider Sudjic's book.

What is new is Sudjic's complete immersion in the city-building processes of the global city. Unsentimentally, he embraces change as inevitable. Sudjic's is an eye-opening new reading of the physical form of the five cities he has studied: Paris, London, New York, Los Angeles, and Tokyo. His sharpest criticism fall on those who would be blind to the values of the cosmopolitan culture of world cities, especially the idolaters of territorially based communities. Overall, Sudjic succeeds in describing the new regional city in ways that will be instantly familiar to Sassen and the rest of our 'invisible college'.

Specific City Studies

Of the single city studies, the volume recently edited by Mollenkopf and Castells is by far the most impressive (Mollenkopf and Castells 1991). *Dual City: Restructuring New York* explores some of New York's characteristics as a global city, including its information economy, the public sector, the new dominant social strata, social (dis)organization, political inequality, the informal economy, and even a bow in the direction of comparative studies with Los Angeles and London. The editors' conclusion takes up the theme of socio-economic polarization, already raised by Friedmann and Wolff in 1982 and taken up in Sassen: New York society, they say, is dominated by two opposing forces:

(a) The upper professionals of the corporate sector form an organizational nucleus for those whose interests are directly linked to the development of New York's corporate economy.

(b) The remaining social strata occupying increasingly diverse positions and have plural interests and values.

They then go on to deconstruct the formulation of a polarized society by stressing the diversity among the second, subaltern group, arguing that within each category there are further social 'cleavages'. In this way polarization is made almost to disappear into a celebration of postmodern 'difference'.

To stress social disorganization as a *source* of subalternity is misleading. Theoretically more consequential would be the relative access of subaltern groups to the information flows of the global economy. In his earlier study (1989) Castells had stressed this lack of access as a structural source of disempowerment. It is surprising not to see his argument restated, perhaps in more elaborate form, in *Dual City*.

London has produced two books that avail themselves of the world city paradigm. One, by Leyshon and Thrift (1997) was not available at the time of writing. The other is King's *Global Cities: Post-Imperialism and the Internationalization of London* (1990). King is particularly interested in the physical city, a concern he shares with Sudjic. But unlike the latter, he is deeply concerned with history. He sees London's present-day status as global clearing-house as a continuation of her imperial role in earlier centuries. In the first part of this chapter I was at pains to argue that the global economy we live in has a new and unprecedented structure, that we are *in transition* from one type of economy to another. King acknowledges this change, understood by him as a change in the spatial division of labour. But he emphasizes continuities [in history].

It is a point worth pondering, both methodologically and in terms of world city theorizing. Theory soars into abstract regions where fine differences scaled to an earthly terrain tend to become invisible. If we neglect the other face of world cities – their rooted-ness in a politically organized 'life space', with its own history, institutions, culture, and politics (the difference between Paris and London, for example) – much of what we observe will remain unintelligible.

King sums up his own impressions of London in the era of Margaret Thatcher, and of world cities more generally, by observing that the city has become increasingly 'unhooked from the state where it exists, its future decided by fortunes over which it has little control' (King 1990: 145–6). The Docklands scheme – Europe's largest real-estate venture during the 1980s – is placed in evidence of this claim. Meanwhile, with the demise of Olympia and York, its largest developers, the Docklands have fallen on very hard times. During the Thatcher era it was called the 'flagship' of the government's urban policy. King might have pointed out that during the Thatcher era national interest was perceived to be largely coincident with the interests of the transnational capitalist class, and no inherent conflict between the two was claimed to exist.

Finally, I want to draw attention to a volume of *Comparative Urban and Community Research* edited by Michael Smith (1992) which contains several world city essays, most notably by Roger Keil and Peter Liescr on Frankfurt (1992) and a comparative piece on Amsterdam and Los Angeles by Edward Soja (1992). Soja's piece is an excellent demonstration of how differences in scale can influence comparisons. Central Amsterdam would seem to have little in common with Los Angeles, but as soon as our eyes are raised to the level of the regional city, some startling similarities emerge. Soja remains agnostic on the question of a new post-Fordist regime of accumulation; he is more comfortable with the vaguer, more pragmatic notion of 'restructuring'. Applying this notion to both Dutch and southern Californian regions, centred in Amsterdam and Los Angeles respectively, he finds both world cities undergoing very similar processes of economic, social, and spatial change.

Keil and Lieser, on the other hand, focusing on the municipality of Frankfurt as the core of their world city region, report on a new policy of urban regulation, which has helped to shape the globalization processes of that city. They make use of Lipietz's Fordist and post-Fordist terminology, and state that:

> the integration of the local, national, and global levels of analysis is a precondition for an understanding of current processes of world-city formation here.

Both modest and radical reform might be able to modify the 'inevitability' of growth, economic development, racism and selective exclusion, local powerlessness, and the fetishism of the urban image. Their success will depend partly on the social and political mobilization of their clientele in the civil society of the city and any given system or local regulation, is indeed only a temporary arrangement suffering from a chronic instability. Its spatial borders, its class structure, and its economic base are constantly being redefined. Smith (1992, pp. 59–60).

In conclusion, when we look back at this review of the literature, it becomes clear that we stand on a threshold in our research. The works under review have opened up a vast research terrain. Many more partial studies than those reviewed here become intelligible only within the world city paradigm (see, for example, Heskin, 1991; Zukin, 1992). At the same time, we must remember that the dynamism of the political economy of capital is so great that no single paradigm is likely to remain intact for more than a couple of decades at most. The world city hypothesis has proved useful as a theoretical framework, but the real city is swiftly changing into something else, and eternal vigilance over

ongoing change processes is the price of our knowledge.

CONCLUDING COMMENTS

Having reviewed where we stand in our research I conclude that the world city paradigm has not only been productive of interesting research hypotheses but is sufficiently robust to guide our efforts in the years ahead.

I use the term 'paradigm' advisedly. What I still called 'hypothesis' in 1986 has been fleshed out into a solid research paradigm which allows us to explore in a number of different directions. As an explicitly spatial framework it requires bifocal vision: one eye directed at the dynamic capitalist system at the core – the space of global accumulation and its articulations – and the other at the fragmented periphery of the excluded. The two must be brought together into a stereoscopic view. Or, to use another metaphor, they must be read as parts of the same story; their separate narratives hang together.

The beauty of the world city paradigm is its ability to synthesize what would otherwise be disparate and diverging researches – into labour markets, information technology, international migration, cultural studies, city building processes, industrial location, social class formation, massive disempowerment, and urban politics – into a single meta-narrative. It is said that meta-narratives are no longer fashionable. But surely that is only because the meta-narrative of capital remains largely invisible. *Without a counter-narrative to place into high relief, it is as if it did not exist.* The world city paradigm not only allows us to make portions of the meta-narrative of capital visible but also provides us with a basis for a critical perspective.

QUESTIONS FOR DISCUSSION

1. In two or three paragraphs, discuss the main themes of Friedmann's chapter.
2. In 1–2 pages, use specific examples from the chapter to illustrate Friedmann's main themes.
3. From the 'Further Readings' list below, summarize some of Friedmann's conclusions in greater detail. What thoughts were provoked in your mind from reading Friedmann's chapter? Was it surprising to find that in an ever-globalizing economy, only a few cities seem to dominant economic decision making? In two or three paragraphs, discuss your thoughts concerning Friedmann's findings.
4. The 'Helpful Web Links' below provide the English websites for some of the second-tier urban areas that Friedmann and others have labeled as existing or emerging 'World' cities. Utilizing these websites, the 'Further Readings,' and other sources, conduct some research on three of these city-regions. Then, in 2–3 pages, describe some of the most interesting facts, similarities, and differences among these cities and present your findings to the class.

FURTHER READINGS

Cohen, R. 1981. The New International Division of Labor: Multinational Corporations and Urban Hierarchy. In M. Dear and A. Scott, eds., *Urbanization and Urban Planning in Capitalist Society,* London: Methuen, pp. 287–315.

Friedmann, J. 1986. The World City. *Development and Change,* 17 (1): 69–83.

Friedmann, J. 2001. World Cities Revisited: A Comment. *Urban Studies,* 38 (13): 2535–2536.

Friedmann, J. 2002. *The Prospect of Cities.* Minneapolis: University of Minnesota Press.

Friedmann, J. 2011. *Insurgencies: Essays in Planning Theory.* New York: Routledge.

Friedmann, J. and G. Wolff. 1982. World City Formation: An Agenda for Research and Action. *International Journal of Urban and Regional Research* 6 (3): 309–344.

HELPFUL WEB LINKS

Brussels Capital Region, Ministry of 2012. Welcome to the Brussels Capital Region Portal: Home Page of the Brussels Capital Region of Belgium, Online. Available at: http://www.brassels.irisnet.be/, last accessed, January 15, 2012.

Dusseldorf, City of. 2012. Landeshauptstadt Dusseldorf: Official Website of Dusseldorf, Germany, the State Capital of North-Rhine Westphalia. Online. Available at: http://www.duesseldorf.de/en/index.shtml, last accessed, January 15, 2012.

Houston, City of. 2012. City of Houston eGovernment Center: Official Site of Houston, TX. Online. Available at: http://www.houstontx.gov/, last accessed, January 9, 2012.

Madrid Visitors and Convention Bureau. 2012. esMadrid.com: Business in Madrid, Spain. Online. Available at: http://www.esmadridxom/en/business-madrid, last accessed, January 15, 2012.

Melbourne, City of. 2012. Home Page for the City of Melbourne, Australia. Online. Available at: http://www.melbourne.vic.gov.au/Pages/default.aspx, last accessed, January 15, 2012.

Munich, City of. 2012. The Official Website of the City of Munich, Germany. Online. Available at: http://www.muenchen,de/int/en/, last accessed, January 15, 2012.

Rotterdam, City of. 2012. English Home Page for the City of Rotterdam, The Netherlands. Online. Available at: http://www.rotterdam.nl/home_english, last accessed, January 15, 2012.

Sao Paulo, Government of. 2012. Porto do Governo do Estada de São Paulo: Portal of the State Government of São Paulo, Brazil, English Home Page. Online. Available at: http://www.saopaulo.sp.gov.br/en/conhecasp/, last accessed, January 13, 2012.

Vancouver, City of. 2012. Home Page for the City of Vancouver, British Columbia. Online. Available at: http://vancouver.ca/, last accessed, January 2, 2012.

Vienna City Administration. 2012. Wien.at: City of Vienna Home Page. Online. Available at: http://www.wien.gv.at/english/, last accessed, January 2, 2012.

CHAPTER 2

Cities in a World Economy (2006)

Saskia Sassen

Global cities are strategic sites for the management of the global economy and the production of the most advanced services and financial operations that have become key inputs for that work of managing global economic operations. The growth of international investment and trade and the need to finance and service such activities have fed the growth of these functions in major cities. The erosion of the role of the government in the world economy, which was much larger when trade was the dominant form of international transaction, has shifted some of the organizing and servicing work from governments to specialized service firms and global markets in services and finance. A second, much less noted, shift of functions to this specialized service sector concentrated in cities comes from the headquarters of global firms. The added complexity and uncertainties involved in running global operations and the need for highly specialized knowledge about the law, accounting, business cultures, and so on, of large numbers of countries has meant that a growing component of headquarter functions is now being out sourced to specialized corporate services firms. Therefore, today there are two sites for the production of headquarter functions of global firms: One is the headquarters proper, and the other is the specialized service sector disproportionately concentrated in major cities. Thus, when firms globalize their operations, they are not necessarily only exporting jobs, as is usually argued. They export certain jobs, for example, labor-intensive manufacturing and clerical work, but they actually may be adding jobs to their top headquarter functions. One way of putting it is to say that when Detroit lost many of its manufacturing jobs, New York City actually gained specialized service jobs, as the work of major auto manufacturing headquarters became increasingly complicated and required state-of-the-art legal, accounting, finance, and insurance advice, not to mention consulting of various kinds and new types of public relations efforts. Headquarters of firm that operate mostly globally tend to be located in global cities. But given the option to outsource the most complex and variable headquarter functions, headquarters can actually locate anywhere, a trend evident in the United States but less so in countries where there is only one major internationally connected city.

The[se] trends point to the emergence of a new kind of urban system, one operating at the global and transnational regional level (Taylor 2004b). This is a system in which cities are crucial nodes for the international coordination and servicing of firms, markets, and even whole economies that are increasingly transnational.

GLOBALIZATION AND CONCENTRATION: THE CASE OF LEADING FINANCIAL CENTERS

Perhaps with the exception of the United States, all the major economies in the developed world display a similar pattern of sharp concentration of financial activity and related producer services in one center: Paris in France, Milan in Italy, Zurich in Switzerland, Frankfurt in Germany, Toronto in Canada, Tokyo in Japan, Amsterdam in the Netherlands, and Sydney in Australia. The evidence also shows that the concentration of financial activity in such leading centers has actually increased over the last decade.

Is this tendency toward concentration within each country a new development for financial centers? A broader historical view points to some interesting patterns. Since their earliest beginnings, financial functions were characterized by high levels of concentration. They often operated in the context of empires, such as the British or Dutch empires, or quasi-empires, such as the disproportionate economic and military power of the United States in the world during the last 50 years. Although some of the first financial centers in Europe were medieval Italian cities such as Florence, a city whose currency, the florin, was one of the most stable in the continent, by the seventeenth century a single financial center became dominant. It was Amsterdam, which introduced central banking and the stock market, probably reflecting its vast international merchant and trading operations, and the city's role as an unrivaled international center for trading and exchange. One hundred years later, London had emerged as the major international financial center and the major market for European government debt. London remained the financial capital of the world, clearly as a function of the British Empire, until well into the twentieth century.

By 1914, New York, which had won its competition with Philadelphia and Boston for the banking business in the United States, emerged as a challenger to London. London, however, was also the strategic cog in the international financial system, a role that New York was not quite ready to assume. But after World War II, the immense economic might of the United States and the destruction of Britain and other European countries left New York as the world's financial center. But the context had been changing, especially since World War I. Against the earlier pattern of empires, the formation of nation-states made possible a multiplicity of financial centers, typically the national capital in each country. Furthermore, the ascendance of mass manufacturing contributed to vast, typically regionally based fortunes and the formation of secondary financial centers in those regions. By the 1960s, these various trends had contributed to a proliferation of financial centers inside countries (e.g., Italy had 11 financial centers, and Germany had 7), highly regulated banking systems, and strict national protections. The dominance of mass manufacturing over the preceding half century meant that finance and banking were to a large extent shaped by the needs of manufacturing economies and mass consumption. Although New York may have been the leading international financial center since the early twentieth century, it was so as part of a national U.S. government strategy seeking global dominance along patterns that differed from the contemporary phase.

The developments that took off in the 1980s represented a sharp departure from this pattern of fairly closed and protected national financial systems centered on mass production and mass consumption. The opening of national economies to foreign investors and the explosion in financial innovations that raised the speculative character of finance and began to replace highly regulated national commercial banking as a source of capital strengthened the tendencies toward concentration in a limited number of financial centers. Although this is reminiscent of older imperial patterns, the actual conditions and processes involved are different.

In the 1980s, there was massive growth in the absolute levels of financial activity worldwide. But this growth became more sharply concentrated in a limited number of countries and cities. By the late 1990s five cities—New York, London, Tokyo, Paris, and Frankfurt—accounted for a disproportionate share of all financial activity. Strong patterns of concentration were also evident in stock market capitalization and *in* foreign-exchange market.

This (see Table 2.1) level of concentration happened in the context of enormous absolute increases, deregulation, and globalization of the industry worldwide, which means that a growing number of countries have become integrated into the world markets. Furthermore, this concentration happened at a time when financial services are more mobile than ever before—in the context of massive advances in telecommunications and electronic networks. One result has been growing competition among centers for hypermobile financial activity. There is also a functional division of labor among various major financial centers. In this sense, at work here is also a single global system with a division of function across multiple countries.

The hypermobility of financial capital puts added emphasis on the importance of technology. It is now possible to move money from one part of the world to another and make deals without ever leaving the computer terminal Thanks to electronics, there are disembodied marketplaces—what we can think of as the cyberspace of international finance (Sassen, 1998).

Finally, the globalization of the industry has raised the level of complexity of transactions, and deregulation has promoted the invention of many new and increasingly speculative instruments. This change has contributed to the power of the leading centers, insofar as they are the only ones with the capability to produce authoritative innovations and to handle the levels of complexity in today's financial system.

In the next section, I examine these issues in greater detail with a particular focus on the networks that connect these centers and the impact of digitization on place.

WHY DO WE NEED FINANCIAL CENTERS IN THE GLOBAL DIGITAL ERA?

The global financial system has reached levels of complexity that require the existence of a cross-border network of financial centers to

Table 2.1 Foreign Exchange Turnover by Country, Percentage Share, Selected Years 1992–2004 (US$ billions)

	1992	1995	1998	2001	2004
United Kingdom	27.0	29.5	32.4	31.2	31.3
United States	15.5	15.5	17.8	15.7	19.2
Japan	11.2	10.2	6.9	9.1	8.3
Singapore	6.9	6.7	7.1	6.3	5.2
Germany	5.1	4.8	4.8	5.4	4.9
Hong Kong	5.6	5.7	4.0	4.1	4.2
Australia	2.7	2.5	2.4	3.2	3.4
France	3.1	3.7	3.7	3.0	2.6
Canada	2.0	1.9	1.9	2.6	2.2
Netherlands	1.9	1.7	2.1	1.9	2.0
Denmark	2.5	2.0	1.4	1.4	1.7
Sweden	2.0	1.3	0.8	1.5	1.3

Source: Bank for International Settlements (2005) (Sassen, 2006, p. 134)

Note: Turnover of spot, outright forwards, and foreign exchange swaps (adjusted of local interdealer double service the operations of global capital. This network of financial centers differs sharply from earlier versions of the international financial system. In a world of largely closed national financial systems, each country duplicated most of the necessary functions for its economy; collaborations among different national financial markets were often no more than the execution of a given set of operations in each of the countries involved, as in clearing and settlement. With few exceptions, such as the offshore markets and some, of the large banks, the international system consisted of a string of closed domestic systems and the limited, mostly routinized interactions among them.

The global integration of markets that took off in the 1980s led to the something approaching one system embedded in all countries linked to the global financial system raising the importance of leading financial centers; these centers have all the resources to execute the tasks, in part because they created many of the standards and rules that had to be adopted by all participating countries. Rather than each country with its own center for global operations, a leaner system is emerging, with fewer strategic centers and more hierarchy. In this context, London and New York, with their enormous concentrations of resources and talent, continue to be the powerhouses in the global network for the most strategic and complex operations for the system as a whole. They are the leading exporters of financial services and typically are part of any major international public offering, whether it is the privatization of British Telecom or France Telecom. This dominance, on the one hand, does not preclude the fact that one of the ways in which the global financial system grows is by incorporating more and more *national* economies, a process that happens through the development of a state-of-the-art financial center in each country—which often evolves into a second- or third-tier global city. On the other hand, in the case of the European Union, the formation of a single-currency Eurozone is spelling the end of an era in which each country had its full-fledged financial center. A steep hierarchy is very likely with Frankfurt and Paris at the top in the Eurozone and a crisscross of alliances centered in either of these major centers or among centers not included in those alliances.

The major financial centers of a growing number of countries worldwide are increasingly fulfilling gateway functions for the in-and-out circulation of national and foreign capital. Each of these centers is the nexus between that country's wealth and the global market and between foreign investors and that country's investment opportunities. The result is that the numbers of sources of, and destinations for, investment are growing. Gateway functions are their main mechanism, for integration into the global financial market rather than, say, the production of innovations to package the capital flowing in and out; the production of innovations tends to remain concentrated in the leading centers, as these have not only the specialized talents but also the clout to persuade investors to buy innovative instruments. Further, the complex operations in most second- and third-tier financial centers tend to be executed by leading global investment, accounting, and legal services firms through affiliates, branches, or direct imports of those services.

These gateways for the global market are also gateways for the dynamics of financial crises: Capital can flow out as easily and quickly as it flows in. And what was once thought of as *national* capital can now as easily join the exodus.

Finally, although electronic networks are growing in number and in scope, they are unlikely to eliminate the need for financial centers (Sassen 2006, chap. 7). Rather, they are intensifying the networks connecting such centers in strategic or functional alliances among exchanges in different cities. These alliances may well evolve into the equivalent of the cross-border mergers and acquisitions of firms. Electronic trading is also contributing to a radically new pattern whereby one market—for example, Frankfurt's Deutsche Eurex—can operate on screens in many other markets around the world, or one brokerage firm, notably Cantor Fitzgerald, could have its prices of Treasury futures listed on screens used by traders all around the United States.

Electronic trading will not eliminate the need for financial centers because these combine multiple resources and talents necessary for executing complex operations and servicing global firms and markets. Frankfurt's electronic futures network is actually embedded in a network of financial centers. Broker Cantor Fitzgerald has an alliance with the Board of Trade of New York to handle its computerized sale of Treasury futures. Financial centers cannot be reduced to their exchanges. They are part of a far more complex architecture in the financial system, and they constitute far more complex structures within that architecture than the exchanges.

IN THE DIGITAL ERA: MORE CONCENTRATION THAN DISPERSAL

What really stands out in the evidence for the global financial industry is the extent to which there is a sharp concentration of the shares of many financial markets in a few financial centers. This trend toward consolidation in a few centers is also evident within countries. In the United States, for example, New York concentrates all the leading investment banks with only one other major international financial center, Chicago, in this enormous country. So have São Paulo and Mumbai, which gained share and functions from, respectively, Rio de Janeiro in Brazil and New Delhi and Calcutta in India. These are all enormous countries, and one might

have thought that they could sustain multiple major financial centers. In France, Paris today concentrates larger shares of most financial sectors than it did in the 1970s, and once-important stock markets such as Lyon have become "provincial," even though Lyon is today the hub of a thriving economic region. Milan privatized its exchange in September 1997 and electronically merged Italy's ten regional markets. Frankfurt now concentrates a larger share of the financial market in Germany than it did in the early 1980s, as does Zurich in Switzerland. Further, these processes of growing concentration moved fast. For example, by 1997, Frankfurt's market capitalization was five times greater than all other regional markets in Germany combined, whereas in 1992, it was only twice as large. This story can be repeated for many countries. What stands out is that this pattern toward the consolidation of one leading financial center is a function of rapid growth in the sector, not necessarily of decay in the losing cities.

Note that there are both consolidation in fewer major centers across and within countries *and* a sharp growth in the numbers of centers that become part of the global network as countries deregulate their economies. São Paulo and Mumbai, for example, joined the global financial network after Brazil and India deregulated, at least partially, their financial systems in the early 1990s.

All of these trends bring up, once again, the question as to why this rapid growth in the network of financial centers, overall volumes, and electronic networks has resulted in, or failed to reduce, the high concentration of market shares in the leading financial centers of the world. Both globalization and electronic trading are about expansion and dispersal beyond what had been the confined realm of national economies and floor trading. Indeed, given globalization and electronic trading, one might well ask why financial centers matter at all.

AGGLOMERATION IN THE DIGITAL ERA

The continuing weight of major centers is, in a way, countersensical, as is the existence of an expanding network of financial centers. The rapid development of electronic exchanges and the growing digitization of much financial activity suggest that location should not matter. In fact, geographic dispersal would seem to be a good option given the high cost of operating in major financial centers, and digitization would seem to eliminate most reasons for having a geographic base. Further, the geographic mobility of financial experts and financial services firms has continued to increase and has resulted in a variety of new industries catering to the needs of the transnational professional and managerial classes, thereby enabling even more mobility.

There has been geographic decentralization of certain types of financial activities, aimed at securing business in the growing number of countries becoming integrated into the global economy. Many of the leading investment banks now have operations in more countries than they did in the early 1980s. The same can be said for the leading accounting and legal services and other specialized corporate services, as well as some markets. For example, in the 1980s, all basic wholesale foreign-exchange operations were in London. Today, these are distributed among London and several other centers (even though the number of these centers is far smaller than the number of countries whose currency is being traded).

There are at least three reasons that explain the trend toward consolidation in a few centers rather than massive dispersal.

1. *Social Connectivity.* First, although the new telecommunications technologies do indeed facilitate geographic dispersal of financial activities without losing system integration, they have also had the effect of strengthening the importance of central coordination and control functions for financial firms and, even, markets. This is particularly so, given the trend toward making financial exchanges into private corporations and hence developing central management functions of sorts. While operating a widely dispersed network of branches and affiliates and operating in multiple markets has made central functions far more complicated for any firm, this is especially so in finance given the speed of transactions possible in electronic markets. The exchanges are also increasingly subject to these trends. The execution of these central functions requires access to top talent and to innovative milieux—in technology, accounting, legal services, economic forecasting, and all sorts of other, many new, specialized corporate services. Financial centers have massive concentrations of state-of-the-art resources that allow them to maximize the benefits of telecommunications and, in the case of leading centers, to organize and govern the new conditions for operating globally. Even electronic markets such as NASDAQ and E*Trade rely on traders and banks located somewhere, with at least some in a major financial center.

One fact that has become increasingly evident is that to maximize the benefits of the new information technologies, you need not only the infrastructure but also a complex mix of other resources. And this means the material and human resources—state-of-the-art office buildings, top talent, and the social networking that maximize the benefits of connectivity. Any town can have fiber-optic cables. But do they have the rest?

A second fact emerging with greater clarity concerns the meaning of *information*. There are, one could say, two types of information. One is the datum: At what level did Wall Street close? Did Argentina complete the public sector sale of its water utility? Has Japan declared such-and-such bank insolvent? But there is a far more difficult type of information, akin to a mix of interpretation, evaluation, and judgment. It entails negotiating a series of data and a series of interpretations of other data in the hope of producing a higher-order datum. Access to the first kind of information is now global and immediate, thanks to the digital revolution. You can be a broker in the Colorado mountains and have access to this type of information. But the second type of information requires a complicated mixture of elements—the social infrastructure for global connectivity—and it is this that gives major financial centers a leading edge.

You can, in principle, reproduce the technical infrastructure anywhere. Singapore, for example, has technical connectivity matching Hong Kong's. But does it have Hong Kong's social connectivity? When the more complex forms of information needed to execute major international deals cannot be gotten from existing databases, no matter what a firm can pay, then that firm needs the social information loop with the associated interpretations and inferences that come with bouncing off information among talented, informed people. The importance of this input has given a whole new weight to credit-rating agencies, for example. Part of the rating has to do with interpreting and inferring the quality of a firm's or government's resources. Credit-rating firms are in the business of producing *authoritative* interpretation and presenting them as information available to all. Firms, especially global firms in finance, often need more than what credit-ratings firms sell. They need to build this advanced type of interpretation into their daily work process, and this takes not only talent but also information-rich milieux. Financial centers generally, and leading ones especially, are such milieux.

Risk management, for example, which has become increasingly important with globalization as a result of the growing complexity and uncertainty that comes with operating in multiple countries and markets, requires enormous fine-tuning of central operations. We now know that many, if not most, major

trading losses during the decade of the 1990s have involved human error or fraud. The quality of risk management depends more heavily on the top people in a firm than simply on technical conditions, such as electronic surveillance. Consolidating risk-management operations in one site, usually a central one for the firm, is now seen generally as more effective. This is the case of several major banks: Chase and Morgan Stanley Dean Witter in the United States, Deutsche Bank and Credit Suisse in Europe.

In brief, financial centers provide the social connectivity that allows a firm or market to maximize the benefits of its technological connectivity and to handle the added pressures that speed brings to financial firms.

2. *Need for Enormous Resources.* Global players in the financial industry need enormous resources, a trend that is leading, first, to rapid mergers and acquisitions of firms and, second, to strategic alliances between markets in different countries. Both of these are happening on a scale and in combinations few had foreseen a decade ago. Examples from the late 1990s, when these trends took off, are the mergers of Citibank with Travelers Group (which few had predicted just two years earlier), Salomon Brothers with Smith Barney, Bankers Trust with Alex Brown, and so on. Analysts fore-see a system dominated by a few global investment banks, about 25 large fund managers, and an increasingly consolidated set of specialized service firms. A similar trend is expected in the global telecommunications industry, which will have to consolidate to offer a state-of-the-art, globe-spanning service to its global clients, among which are the financial firms; indeed, the early 2000s saw the demise of several large telecommunications firms and their partial absorption by some of the remaining firms.

Another kind of merger is the consolidation of electronic networks that connect a very select number of markets. Europe's more than 30 stock exchanges have been seeking to shape various alliances. Euronext is Europe's largest stock exchange merger, an alliance among the Paris, Amsterdam, and Brussels bourses. Also, small exchanges are merging.

These developments are likely to strengthen intercity, links in the worldwide network of about 40 cities through which the global financial industry operates and may well ensure the consolidation of a stratum of select financial centers at the top of the worldwide network.

Does the fact of fewer global players affect the spread of such operations? Not necessarily, but it will strengthen the hierarchy in the global network. For example, institutional money managers around the world controlled approximately $15 trillion by early 1999. The worldwide distribution of equities under institutional management shows considerable spread among a large number of cities that have become integrated in the global equity market with deregulation of their economies and the whole notion of emerging markets as an attractive investment destination over the last few years. However, this global market is characterized by a disproportionate concentration in the top six or seven cities. London, New York, and Tokyo together accounted for a third of the world's total equities under institutional management at the end of 1998.

These developments make clear a second important trend that in many ways specifies the current global era. These various centers don't just compete with each other: There is collaboration and division of labor. In the international system of the postwar decades, each country's financial center, in principle, covered the universe of necessary functions to service its national companies and markets. The world of finance was, of course, much simpler than it is today. In the initial stages of deregulation in the 1980s, there was a strong tendency to see the relations between the major centers as one of straight competition, especially among the leading centers—New York, London, and Tokyo. But in my research at the time, I had already found a division of labor among these three centers, along with competition in certain areas. What we are seeing now is yet a third pattern: strategic alliances not only between firms across borders but also between markets. There is competition, strategic collaboration, and hierarchy.

In brief, the need for enormous resources to handle increasingly global operations and the growth of complex central functions discussed earlier produce tendencies toward concentration among the top centers and hierarchy in the expanding global network of financial centers.

3. *Denationalization of the Corporate Elite.* Finally, national attachments and identities are becoming weaker for these global players and their customers. Thus, the major U.S. and European investment banks have set up specialized offices in London to handle various aspects of their global business. Deregulation and privatization have further weakened the need for *national* financial centers. The nationality question simply plays differently in these sectors than it did as recently ago as the early 1980s. Global financial products are accessible in national markets, and national investors can operate in global markets. It is interesting to see that investment banks used to split up their analysts team by country to cover a national market; now they are more likely to do it by industrial sector.

The sophistication of the global economy lies in the fact that its organizational side (as opposed to the consumer side) needs to involve only strategic institutional areas—most national systems can be left basically unaltered. China is a good example. It adopted international accounting rules in 1993, an advantage for a country with an accounting system that differed sharply from the prevalent Anglo-American standards generally being used in international transactions. But China did not have to go through a fundamental reorganization to do this: It only used those standards when transacting with foreign firms. Japanese firms operating overseas adopted such standards long before Japan's government considered requiring them. In this regard, the organizational side of globalization is quite different from the global mass-consumer markets, in which success necessitates altering national tastes at a mass level.

This process of denationalization in the realm of the economy has an instrumental and practical connotation, unlike what might be the case in processes of identity formation or in the rising anti-immigrant politics evident in many of the European countries today, subjects examined in Chapter 6. For example, I argue that denationalization of key economic sectors in South Korea and Thailand was facilitated by the 1997–98 Asian financial crisis because it enabled foreign firms to buy up large numbers of firms and property in these countries where once their national elites had been in full control. In some ways, the Asian financial crisis has functioned as a mechanism to denationalize, at least partially, control over key sectors of economies that, while allowing the massive entry of foreign investment, never relinquished that control.

Major international business centers produce what can be thought of as a new subculture. In a witty insight, *The Economist,* in its coverage of the January 1997 World Economic Forum meeting held in Davos, titled one of its stories "From Chatham House Man to Davos Man," alluding to, respectively, the "national" and the "global" version of international relations. The resistance to mergers and acquisitions, especially hostile takeovers, in Europe in the 1980s and 1990s or to foreign ownership and control in East Asia points to national business cultures that are somewhat incompatible with the new global economic culture. I find that global cities and financial centers contribute to denationalizing the corporate elite. Whether this is good or bad is a separate issue; but it is, I believe, one of the conditions for setting in place the systems and subcultures necessary for a global economic system.

CONCLUSION: CONCENTRATION AND THE REDEFINITION OF THE CENTER

The central concern in this chapter was to explain the counterintuitive tendency for the top-level functions of leading global and often digitized sectors to evince significant agglomeration economies. This concentration has occurred in the face of the globalization of economic activity and revolutionary changes in technology that have the power to neutralize distance.

I examined the case of the leading financial centers in the world today to see whether the concentration of financial activity and value has declined given globalization of markets and immense increases in the global volume of transactions. The levels of concentration remain unchanged in the face of massive transformations in the financial industry and in the technological infrastructure this industry depends on.

But what exactly is the space of the center in the contemporary economy, one characterized by growing use of electronic and telecommunication capabilities. In the past, and up until quite recently, in fact, the center was synonymous with the downtown or the CBD. Today, the spatial correlate of the center can assume several geographic forms. It can be the CBD, which remains as the most strategic center in most global cities, or it can extend into metropolitan areas in the form of a grid of nodes of intense business activity, as in Frankfurt and Zurich, for example.

Elsewhere (Sassen, 1991), I argued that we are also seeing the formation of a transterritorial *center* constituted via intercity electronic networks and various types of economic transactions; I argued that the cross-border network of global cities can be seen as constituting such a transterritorial terrain of centrality *with regard to a specific complex, of industries and activities.* At the limit, there exist terrains of centrality that are disembodied and lack any territorial correlate: These are electronic spaces of centrality.

QUESTIONS FOR DISCUSSION

1. In two or three paragraphs, discuss the main themes of Sassen's chapter. Then, in 1–2 pages, using specific examples from the chapter, explain Sassen's main themes and discuss what you think were the strongest and weakest elements in her arguments.

2. Was it surprising that high-end financial services have continued to cluster within the core of the world's largest cities despite the decentralization potential of the digital age? What happened to the predicted future of the home office and working anywhere? In 1–2 pages, discuss why you think the digital age has not resulted in the decentralization in high-end financial services.

3. With new and constant advances in cell phones, tablets, and wireless technologies, do you expect this clustering pattern to change in the future? In 2–3 pages discuss what you think the fixture spatial distribution of financial services will be. In your answer, discuss how they will look worldwide, and within large metropolitan areas that you know about, such as New York, Los Angdes, Chicago, or your home region.

4. Utilizing the 'Further Readings', 'Helpful Web Links' and other sources, conduct some further research on three of Global Financial Centers. Then, in 2–3 pages, describe some of the most interesting facts, similarities, and differences among these cities and New York, Los Angeles, and Chicago and present your findings to the class.

FURTHER READINGS

Sassen, S. 1991/2001. *The Global City*. Princeton, NJ: Princeton University Press.

Sassen, S. 1999. Global Financial Tenters. *Foreign Affairs,* 78(1), 75–87.

Sassen, S. 2001. Global Cities and Developmentalist States: How to Derail What Could Be an Interesting Debate. A Response to Hill and Kim. *Urban Studies,* 38(13), 2357–2540.

Sassen, S. 2002. *Global Networks, Linked Cities*. New York: Routledge.

Sassen, S. 2003. Global Cities and Global City-Regions. In A. Scott, ed., *Global City-Regions*. New York: Oxford University Press, pp. 78–95.

Sassen-Koob, S. 1984. The New Labor Demand in Global Cities. In M. Smith, ed., *Cities in Transformation*. Beverly Hills, CA: Sage, pp. 139–171.

HELPFUL WEB LINKS

Chicago, City of. 2012. Welcome to the Official City of Chicago Website. Online. Available at: http://www.cityofchicago.org/city/en.html, last accessed, January 9, 2012.

Frankfurt, City of. 2012. Frankfurt am Main: Welcome to Frankfurt, Germany. Online. Available at: http://www.firankfurt.de, last accessed, January 15, 2012.

London, City of. 2012. Home Page of the City of London, United Kingdom. Online. Available at: http://www.cityoflondon.gov.uk/Corporation/homepage.html, last accessed, January 14, 2012.

New York, City of. 2012. NYC.gov: Official Website of the City of New York. Online. Available at: http://www.nyc.gov/portal/site/nycgov/?front_door=trae, last accessed, January 9, 2012.

Paris, City of. 2011. Welcome to the Portal of the City of Paris! Online. Available at: http://www.paris.fr/english, last accessed, December 31, 2011.

San Francisco, City and County of. 2012. Welcome to SF GOV: City and County of San Francisco Official Site. Online. Available at: http://www.sfgov.org/, last accessed January 15, 2012.

Singapore, Government of. 2011. Singapore Government Home Page. Online. Available at: http://www.gov.sg/government/web/content/govsg/classic/home, last accessed, December 31, 2011.

Seoul, Special City of. 2012. Hi Seoul, Soul of Asia. Online. Available at: http://english.seoul.go.kr/, last accessed January 7, 2012.

TMG. 2012. Tokyo Metropolitan Government. Online. Available at: http://www.metro.tokyo.jp/ENGLISH/, last accessed January 7, 2012.

Zurich, City of. 2012. Home Page of the City of Zurich, Switzerland. Online. Available at: http://www.stadt-zxierich.ch/content/portal/en/index.html, last accessed January 15, 2012.

CHAPTER 3

Hierarchical Tendencies and Regional Patterns in the World City Network . . . (2003)

Ben Derudder, Peter J. Taylor, Frank Witlox, and Gilda Catalano

One of the most salient propositions in John Friedmann's seminal World City Hypothesis (Friedmann, 1986, p. 71) refers to the fact that: "key cities throughout the word are used by capital as 'basing points' in the spatial organization and articulation of production and markets. The resulting linkages make it possible to arrange world cities into a complex spatial hierarchy." However, the lack of theoretical agreement on the defining characteristics of world cities has resulted in ad hoc taxonomies (e.g., Friedmann, 1986; Knox, 1995) often limited to the highest ranks of the hierarchy (e.g., Sassen, 1991; Abu-Lughod, 1995). Apart from the lack of an undisputed definition of world cities in and by itself, the main reason for these somewhat eclectic approaches has been a lack of data (Smith & Timberlake, 1995a; Short et al., 1996), a problem that is, of course, related to the absence of undisputed defining characteristics of world cities. One of the major consequences of the problems pertaining to a description of Friedmann's 'complex spatial hierarchy' is that the lower rungs of this transnational urban hierarchy have remained un-assessed. The prime purpose of this paper is to rectify this limitation: we investigate a very large number of cities, many of which have never figured at all in previous discussions of world cities . . .

EMPIRICAL RATIONALE

Drawing on Sassen's (1991, 1995, 2006) work on the role of advanced producer services in world city formation, a theoretically grounded endeavor of data acquisition has been undertaken by Globalization and World Cities Research Group and Network GaWC (GaWC, 2011). Treating world cities as global service centers, GaWC has developed a methodology for studying world city network formation. Rather than assuming world cities form an urban hierarchy, this approach specifies a network in which 'hierarchical tendencies' may be revealed. The empirical research has been based upon: first, a rectification of the data deficiency problem; and second, incorporation into the analysis of many more cities than heretofore in world cities research.

In initial work, 125 cities were assessed for 'world city-ness' in devising a 'roster' of 55 world cities (Beaverstock et al., 1999). These 55 cities were subsequently used for creating some experimental data on 46 service firms for a first global multivariate analysis of world cities (Taylor & Walker, 2001). The success of the latter stimulated a new data collection exercise covering 316 cities and 100 global service firms (Taylor et al., 2002a), and new analyzes of the 123 most connected cities (Taylor et al., 2002b). These cities were selected for having network connectivities at least one-fifth of the highest city connectivity. Analysis was limited to 123 because as the size of the data matrix increases (i.e. inclusion of more cities) it becomes relatively 'sparse' (lots of zero entries) which make analysis less reliable. Nevertheless, this is the largest published analysis of cities across the world that we are aware of but it still leaves several regions relatively unrepresented. For example, in inter-tropical Africa there are only two cities (Lagos and Nairobi) that qualify in the top 123 connected cities.

In this paper we go beyond these previous studies in two ways. First, using the same data based upon 316 cities we analyze 234 of them; we include all cities in which at least 20 of the 100 service firms have a presence. Second, for the 234 cities set we employ fuzzy set analysis in order to cope with the resulting sparser data matrix better; this is a technique that deals with this problem reasonably well. Thus we are able to include more than 100 additional cities. The result is that we have a fuller representation of regions across the world. For example, there are now 12 African cities included outside South Africa and the Arab north.

The end-product is an analysis of the world city network at a level of geographical detail never before attempted. We create a global ordering of cities into 22 urban arenas. These exhibit both hierarchical tendencies—the arenas are arranged into a center surrounded by five bands of different levels of connectivity— and regional patterns with arenas showing specific geographical concentrations of cities.

Conceptual Problems

The contemporary study of world cities started with Friedmann and Wolff's (1982), identification of 'command centers' to control and articulate the 'new international division of labor' being created by multinational corporations. This model reflected the later recognition by Amin and Thrift (1992) of a shift from an international to a global economy, characterized by increasingly integrated global networks of production and services. World cities are then the basing points in these networks, and their specification therefore relates to the identification of 'cities in global matrices', as Smith and Timberlake (1995a) reminded us.

Related discourses focus on a "global network of cities" (King, 1990, p. 12), a "transnational urban system" (Sassen, 2006, p. 45), "functional world city system" (Lo & Yeung, 1998, p. 10), or a "global urban network" (Short & Kim, 1999, p. 38). The implications of these various different conceptualizations have never been fully discussed in the world city literature.

Formal specifications of the cities acting as 'command centers' are fraught with difficulties. While it is obvious that cities like London and New York are world cities, there has hardly been a consensus as to the status of less significant cities in this context (Beaverstock et al., 1999). In other words, the highest ranks of the world city network may very well stand out, but the absence of more detailed taxonomies of cities below the leading cities in the world economy is a problem. As a consequence, somewhat vague discourses on patterns of global competence in the outer reaches of the world city network have dominated the debates. For instance, some authors have reified the lower ranks of the hierarchy as 'sub-global cities' (e.g., O'Connor & Stimson, 1995), while this is particularly problematic given the pervasive nature of globalization . . . 'medium cities' have just as much need to respond to globalization trends as their larger neighbors. In other words, it would be wrong to designate the outer reaches of the world city network as 'sub-global'. Rather, their capacity to operate in a global economy is merely less when compared to the upper ranks of world cities. All cities operate at a myriad of scales, and although the importance of their respective functions may vary, it would be wrong to pin down a clear-cut border between world cities, thoroughly influenced by and influencing globalization, and other cities deemed 'sub-global'. The outlined problems pertaining to the formal identification of world cities can hence be traced back to a lack of characteristics that have been agreed upon to qualify for world city status. As a result, in the original outset of the *World City Hypothesis*, Friedmann

(1986) restricted the associated taxonomy to 30 world cities (with some hierarchical notes on these cities), in addition to an accompanying suggestion on regional patterns in the world city network (i.e., three subsystems: North America, Europe, Pacific Asia). World cities outside these three subsystems primarily served as an outlet of other economies into these subsystems, providing a basic spatial structure for the world-system, as outlined by Wallerstein (1979). Friedmann (1986, p. 71), asserted, however, that the lower rungs were highly uncertain, for the importance of some semi-peripheral world cities was derived from the articulation of significant economies, whereas secondary structures in Europe were difficult to specify "because of their relatively small size and often specialized function." As a result, "the list of secondary cities . . . is meant only to be suggestive."

The GaWC approach to overcoming these discourse and classification problems has been to build upon aspects of Sassen's work on place and production in a global economy, which pertains to the wider debate over the extraordinary changes that have occurred in global economic systems in the last few decades. One of the most fundamental changes, according to Daniels (1995), has been the . . . transformation of the economic bases of cities from manufacturing to services, a conversion that can be traced back to the observation that a growing number of manufacturing and service industries, unable to cope with the accelerated pace of structural change and the increasing pressure for product innovation on their own, are becoming more and more dependent on specialized business services. For Sassen, the salient point is that these business services are in and by themselves an indispensable production factor that has a growth potential of its own, as opposed to other domains of service sector growth that is the strict result of derived demand of other sectors. The reason for this is that such corporate service firms have benefited immensely from the technological advances in computing and communica-tions that have allowed them to broaden the geographical distribution of their service provision. For instance, law firms have been traditionally associated with a particular city and its local client base—a 'New York law firm', a 'Boston law firm' and so on—but under conditions of contemporary globalization, a few firms have chosen to pursue a strategy of providing legal services across the world (Taylor et al., 2002a).

Based on these observations, Sassen (1995, p. 63) has ascertained that: "a focus on the production process in service industries allows us . . . to examine the proposition that there is a producer services complex which, while catering to corporations, has distinct locational and production characteristics. It is this producer services complex more so than headquarters of firms generally that benefits and often needs a city location." Following this lead, GaWC conceives world cities as the production sites for the leading service industries of our time, i.e., places where knowledge-based (expert/profession/ creative) services to other corporations are concentrated. It has indeed been argued elsewhere that new technologies, heavily used by advanced producer services firms, may neutralize distance as an impediment in locational decision making (e.g., O'Brien, 1992), but the reality of the locational strategies of these service industries seems to imply a new form of concentration in the face of economic globalization (Swyngedouw, 1997). The fact that these new forms explicitly offer their global networks to possible clients, underpins that locational decisions are of the utmost importance to students of world cities. In other words, the concentration of these services in specific places should be at the basis of research on the world city network.

WORLD CITIES AS GLOBAL SERVICE CENTERS

In GaWC research, world cities are treated as global service centers—locales where advanced producer services are concentrated for servicing their global corporate clients. From this starting point, the world city network is formally specified as an inter-locking network. Full details of the specification are given in Taylor (2001); here we summarize the argument to provide the rationale for data collection and measurement of connectivity.

An inter-locking network has three levels: a network level, in this case cities connected in a world economy; a nodal level, the cities; and a sub-nodal level, the firms providing the advanced producer services. It is at the latter level that world city network formation takes place. Through their attempts to provide a seamless service to their clients across the world, financial and business service firms have created global networks of offices in cities around the world. Each office network represents a firm's global strategy for dispensing its services; it is an outcome of location decision making at the scale of the world-economy. The world city network is therefore defined as the aggregate of the many service firms pursuing a global location strategy. In this way it is global service firms that 'inter-lock' world cities into a network of global service centers: they are the prime producers of the contemporary world city network.

This model can be formally represented by a matrix [of] . . . the 'service value' of city i to firm j. Service value is the importance of a city to a firm's office network which depends upon the size and functions of an office or offices in a city. Thus every column denotes a firm's global strategy and every row describes each city's mix of services . . .

. . . The advantage of a precise specification of the world city network is that techniques of network analysis can be used. Using elementary network analysis, the most basic measure of a city is its connectivity in relation to all other cities in the matrix. . . . These links can be aggregated to produce an inter-city interlock link. . . . Each city has such an interlock link with every other city.

Aggregating all the inter-lock links of a city produces the global network connectivity . . . of the city . . .

The limiting case is a city that shares no firms with any other city so that all of its elemental links are 0 and it has zero connectivity. In practice, with large data sets the global network connectivities can be quite large numbers. To make them manageable in our use below, we express city connectivities as proportions of the largest computed connectivity in the data thus creating a scale from 0 to 1. These scores will be used below to indicate hierarchical tendencies within our analysis.

METHODOLOGY

Data Collection

Global service firms were defined as firms with offices in 15 or more different cities, including at least one in each of the prime globalization regions: northern America, Western Europe and Pacific Asia.

Firms meeting this criterion were selected from rankings of leading firms in different service sectors. The other key criterion was purely practical—whether adequate information could be found on the firm's website. A supplementary criterion was to only consider sectors in which at least 10 firms could be included to facilitate inter-sector comparisons. In the event 100 firms were identified in six sectors: 18 in accountancy; 15 in advertising; 23 in banking/finance; 11 in insurance; 16 in law; and 17 in management consultancy.

Selecting cities was much more arbitrary and was based upon previous GaWC experience in researching global office networks. Capital cities of all but the smallest states were included plus many other important cities in larger states. A total of 316 cities were selected.

Data collection focused on two features of a firm's office(s) in a city: first, the size of office (e.g. number of practitioners); and second, their extra-locational functions (e.g. regional headquarters). The main problem with this type of data collection exercise is that the exact nature of the information collected for each firm differed to that for every other firm. The solution was to standardize the information. Information for every firm was simplified into 'service values' ranging from 0 to 5 as follows. The city housing a firm's headquarters was scored 5, a city with no office of that firm was scored 0. An 'ordinary' or 'typical' office of the firm, resulted in a city scoring 2. With something missing (e.g. no partners in a law office), the score was reduced to 1. Particularly large offices were scored 3 and those with important extra-territorial functions (e.g., regional offices) scored 4. The end-result was a 316 by 100 matrix . . . [with] ranges from 0 to 5.

Fuzzy Classification

One of the most popular data analysis techniques for studying large data matrices is cluster analysis. Applied to the matrix produced here, a traditional clustering algorithm would compute mutually exclusive clusters of cities, based on the various service values for the world cities. However, this classical approach towards cluster analysis is fraught with various sources of problems (Derudder & Witlox, 2002) . . . In order to represent the data structures more comprehensively, therefore, we propose to replace the crisp separation of clusters . . . by a fuzzy notion . . . where 'n' is the number of cities that need to be classified; 'C' is the number of clusters; and the membership value of [a] city in cluster is 'c' (ranging from 0 to 1). A fuzzy classification scheme computes grades of membership in different clusters rather than providing information on mere membership (Sato et al., 1997; Hoppner et al., 1999). This approach can reflect the expected complexity of multiple and intertwined profiles in any classification, since it is reflected by hybrid membership in different clusters. . . . This

yields a roster of 234 cities for analysis. . . . Here, we will focus on the results for C = 22. This is a pragmatic choice after assessing several solutions of different classes. With 22 clusters we find a broad diversity in hierarchical and regional patterns in the world city network that provides for a particularly insightful interpretation. For the clarity of the argument, the results below are reported in a simplified form that identifies 'core' and 'hybrid' members of clusters.

URBAN ARENAS: HIERARCHICAL AND REGIONAL TENDENCIES

The 22 clusters in the fuzzy classification of 234 cities are grouped together in three different ways. First, there is a strong hierarchical dimension to the clusters: cities with similar levels of global network connectivity tend to be classified together. Second, there is a strong regional dimension to the clusters: cities from the same part of the world tend to be classified together. Third, there is a tendency for interaction between these two dimensions: clusters with low average connectivity tend to be more regionally restricted in membership. These geographical features mean that our results show more than clusters in an abstract 'service space', they represent urban arenas in a geographical space that is the world city network.

This is an important interpretation because it indicates that cities are not creating and reacting to a simple process of globalization leading to an overarching world city hierarchy. There is a multifaceted geography of arenas through which cities operate as service centers for global capital. Hence, as well as the commonplace notion that individual world cities represent critical local–global nexuses, there are also urban arenas that represent regional–global nexuses within contemporary globalization.

This new complex global urban geography is shown in Table 3.1 and Figure 3.1. The table highlights the hierarchical tendency in the results with arenas listed in terms of average global network connectivity for cluster members. These cluster connectivities are in turn used to denote five bands of arenas to represent the hierarchical tendency around cluster A, which is by far the most important arena in terms of connectivity. The latter is called the 'center' of the bands for reasons that will become clear when we look at Figure 3.1. The largest gap in connectivity is between cluster A and Band I but all the bands are identified using gaps in the levels of connectivity. To get a feel for the structure and geography of the fuzzy classification, Table 3.1 shows also the size of each cluster, including overlapping cities, and also the most typical city in each cluster.

The regional tendency in the results is added to the hierarchical tendency in Figure 3.1: arenas are depicted in their respective bands around the center and in addition they are located in roughly their geographical

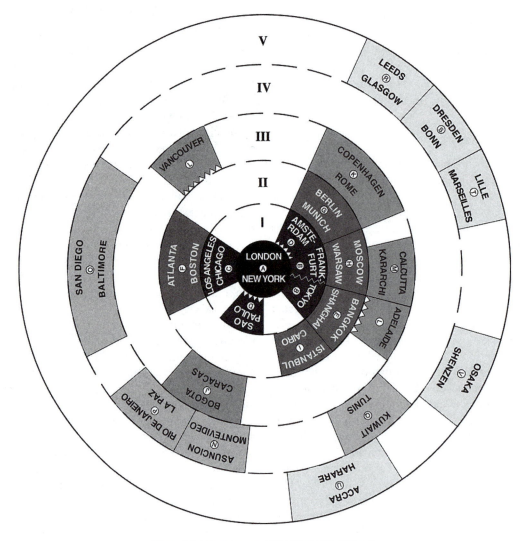

Figure 3.1 Urban arenas of the World City Network

Table 3.1 Bands of Arenas in the World City Network

Cluster/arena	Average connectivity	Band	No. of members[1]	Typical city[2]
A	.988	Center	2(0)	London
B	.613	I	7(2)	Frankfurt
C	.574	I	3(0)	Chicago
D	.539	I	11(2)	Amsterdam
E	.438	II	8(0)	Bangkok
F	.401	II	5(1)	Atlanta
G	.384	II	4(0)	Berlin
H	.379	II	6(0)	Warsaw
I	.371	II	9(3)	Istanbul
J	.297	III	7(4)	Caracas
K	.297	III	12(8)	Copenhagen
L	.231	III	23(6)	Adelaide
M	.225	III	12(2)	Calcutta
N	.201	IV	9(4)	Montevideo
O	.193	IV	23(0)	Baltimore
P	.180	IV	16(10)	La Paz
Q	.179	IV	19(12)	Kuwait
R	.158	V	14(5)	Leeds
S	.157	V	8(0)	Dresden
T	.148	V	13(3)	Lille
U	.141	V	22(8)	Accra
V	.121	V	13(3)	Osaka

Source: Derudder et. al (2003, p. 880).

Notes:
1 Membership is defined as affiliation of 0.3 and above; figures in brackets refer to hybrid cities with membership of other clusters.
2 Member with the highest affiliation.

position. The latter are articulated about a trans-Atlantic center of London and New York. Two member cities are shown for all arenas to aid in initial reading of the carto-gram. In addition to the center arena, there are only three other arenas that have strong trans-regional membership, two in Band I, and one, perhaps surprisingly, in Band IV. This means that 18 of the arenas have relatively clear-cut regional identities thus showing the strength of the regional tendency in these results.

Further interrogation of the results requires a detailed look at the content of the arenas. For each cluster/arena we have searched for four sets of cities:

1. The cluster nucleus is made up of those cities with affiliations above .7;

2. Other singular members are cities with affiliations between .3 and .7 and with no important membership of another cluster;

3. Hybrid members are the other members of the cluster who share membership with another cluster (clusters without hybrid members we refer to as distinc-tive); and

4. Near isolates are cities that are members of no clusters (they have no affiliation as high as .3), but have their highest affilia-tion to a given cluster.

As above, we begin by ordering the argument through bands before focusing on the regional patterns.

The Center and Band I: Leading World Cities

Table 3.2 shows the four sets of cities for the Center arena and Band I arenas. The former is simple to the extreme. It consists of a two-city nucleus and nothing else. The *Center arena* is 'main street, world-economy'; by far the most important link in the world city network in terms of connectivities (again, see Table 3.1), it is also a wholly distinctive dyad. This is the justification for terming the arena the center and so locating it as the pivot of our cartogram (again, see Figure 3.1).

The Band I arenas are also relatively small and simple. This is especially the case with *Arena C* which includes just the three U.S. cities that rank below New York. It is a distinctive arena with no hybrids. The other two Band I arenas are cross-regional and link western European cities with cities in other parts of the world. *Arena B* links Paris and Frankfurt with the leading Pacific Asian cities. Although Sassen has suggested that Tokyo should be ranked next to New York and London, our analysis does not show this. This is because there is a wide range of business services in our data and Tokyo's global prowess is largely restricted to banking/ finance firms. *Arena D* links other leading European cities with leading world cities outside the other two main globalization arenas (U.S. and Pacific Asia) in European-settler regions, notably Latin America. These two arenas share Brussels and Barcelona as members. The distinction between the two arenas is the particular dominance of banking/finance services in the arena including Pacific Asia.

The Center and Band I arenas define the 21 most important cities within this analysis of the world city network. They also suggest specific relations amongst these leading world cities. Beyond the Center, it is the European cities that appear pivotal in linking to other cluster that includes all the important Pacific Asian regions; the leading U.S. cities arena appears as relatively cities not in Band I arenas; *Arena G* is a distinctive isolated in global service provision.

Bands II and III: Major Regional World Cities

The Band II and III arenas (Tables 3.3 and 3.4) are regional clusters of important world cities. There are three classic examples in Band II: *Arena E* is a distinctive cluster that includes all the important Pacific Asian cities not in Band I arenas. *Arena G* is a distinctive cluster

Table 3.2 Center and Band I Arenas

City Type	A	B	C	D
Cluster Nucleus	London New York	Frankfurt Hong Kong Paris Singapore Tokyo	Chicago Los Angeles	Amsterdam Zurich Madrid Milan Sao Paulo Mexico City
Singular Members			San Francisco	Sydney Buenos Aires Toronto
Hybrid Members		Brussels > D Barcelona > D		Brussels > B Barcelona > B
Near Isolates				

Source: Derudder et al. (2003, p. 881)

Table 3.3 Band II Arenas

City Type	E	F	G	H	I
Cluster Nucleus	Bangkok Jakarta Kuala Lumpur Manila Seoul Shanghai	Atlanta Boston Dallas	Berlin Dusseldorf Munich	Warsaw Moscow Prague St. Petersburg	Istanbul Dubai
Singular Members	Beijing Taipei	Washington	Hamburg	Budapest Vienna	Mumbai Cairo
Hybrid Members		Miami > J			Dublin > K Lisbon > K Athens > K Amman > Q Beirut > Q
Near Isolates				Kiev	Geneva

Source: Derudder et al. (2003, p. 882)

Table 3.4 Band III Arenas

City Type	J	K	L	M
Cluster Nucleus	Caracas Bogota	Copenhagen	Adelaide Brisbane Perth Vancouver Montreal	Calcutta Karachi Bangalore
Singular Members	Medellin	Rome Stockholm Helsinki	Auckland Hamilton, Bermuda Cape Town Winnipeg Calgary Ottawa Christchurch Edmonton Johannesburg Melbourne Hobart	Islamabad Chennai Dhaka Riyadh Jeddah Lahore New Delhi
Hybrid Members	Lima > P Santiago > P San Jose > N Miami > F	Dublin > I Lisbon > I Athens > I Riga > Q Vilnius > Q Tallinn > Q Sofia > Q Bratislava > Q	Canberra > P Monterrey > P Guadalajara > P Birmingham > R Manchester > R Southampton > R	Nairobi > Q Colombo > U
Near Isolates	Curitiba	Oslo	Durban Wellington Ruwi Manama	Ho Chi Minh Bucharest

Source: Derudder et al. (2003, p. 882)

that includes all important German cities not in *Band I* arenas; and *Arena H* is a distinctive cluster that includes all the important eastern European world cities. The latter has a near isolate, relatively unimportant city but appropriately located geographically for arena—Kiev. Not quite distinctive but otherwise similar to the above arenas, *Arena F* includes important U.S. cities not in the Center or Band I. In this case there is one hybrid member, Miami, which is linked into *Arena J* in Band IV. The latter is the arena of leading Latin American cities that are not in Band I. Clearly this analysis is picking up the regional articulation role of Miami between the U.S. and Latin America (See Brown et al., 2002).

Arena J also links down the bands to less important Latin American arenas. This nondistinctive structure, sharing cities with other clusters, is typical of the other arenas in Bands II and III. *Arena I* brings together important Asian cities outside the Pacific Rim but also has links to a lower band arena of Asian cities and to

Arena K which is a cluster of important 'outer' European cities. This odd combination combining northern, southeastern and southwestern European cities replicates previous findings based on just European cities (see Taylor & Hoyler, 2000). *Arena M* is more distinctive than the others and is clearly a south Asian arena with just two hybrids. Finally, *Arena L* is a cross-regional cluster that covers the old British Commonwealth.

This 'cultural' historical throwback arena again replicates previous findings (see Taylor et al., 2002b). Membership covers Australian, Canadian, New Zealand and South African cities not found in Band I arenas. Note the dearth of British cities, only three appear as hybrids. They link to a particular British arena in Band V.

With the exception of the latter unusual cluster, these arenas show that below the top echelons of the world city network, important cities tend to be very regional in the focus of their global service provision.

Bands IV and V: Major Cities on the Edge

In Bands IV and V we come to cities that are rarely if ever mentioned as world cities (see Tables 3.5 and 3.6). This does not mean, of course, that they are not involved in the same globalization processes as the cities we have dealt with above, but they are less intensively connected to the world city network. Given our conclusion concerning Band II and III arenas, we would expect the arenas in these two lower bands to be even more regional in their memberships . . . This is indeed the case: there are three European arenas, two each from Asia and Latin America, and one from Africa and the U.S. The latter, *Arena O*, is distinctive and large and incorporates all remaining continental U.S. cities if the near isolates are included. The cluster of less important German cities, *Arena S*, is similarly distinctive but much smaller. It also includes some neighboring European cities as singular members and near isolates. Both the UK (*Arena R*) and France (*Arena T*) have their own urban arenas of less important cities albeit less distinctive in nature than *Arena S*. The UK arena includes the

Commonwealth arena hybrids; France includes other neighboring European singular members, hybrids and near isolates.

The Latin American and Asian clusters are much less clear-cut as geographical arenas. In particular, *Arena N* and *Arena P* both include less important Latin American cities from across the region with no obvious geographical division of the region. For instance, Central American and Caribbean cities are found in both clusters. In contrast, the Asian clusters, *Arena Q* and *Arena V*, have geographical concentrations in west and East Asia respectively. The former thus includes Middle Eastern cities not previously appearing in a cluster and the latter includes almost all the Pacific Asian cities not included in earlier clusters. Perhaps appropriately they share central Asian cities as hybrid members.

Table 3.5 Band IV Arenas

City Type	N	O	P	Q
Cluster Nucleus	Montevideo Asuncion	Baltimore Columbus Kansas City Richmond Charlotte Cincinnati New Orleans St. Louis San Diego Indianapolis Portland	La Paz Quito	Kuwait Tel Aviv Tunis Dalian
Singular Members	Port Louis Guayaquil Guatemala City	Honolulu Sacramento Pittsburgh Tampa Phoenix Philadelphia Cleveland Minneapolis Buffalo Denver Hartford San Jose, CA Detroit	Porto Alegre Belo Horizonte Rio de Janeiro	Zagreb Casablanca Nicosia
Hybrid Members	San Jose > J Panama > P Santo Domingo > U San Salvador > U		Kingston > U Managua > U Port of Spain > U Tegucigalpa > U Canberra > L Monterrey > L Guadalajara > L Lima Santiago Panama City	Bratislava > K Riga > K Vilnius > K Tallinn > K Sofia > K Nairobi > M Beirut > I Amman > I Tashkent > V Almaty > V Ankara > V Ljubljana > T
Near Isolates		Seattle Houston Rochester Las Vegas	Palo Alto Limassol Nassau	Abu Dhabi

Source: Derudder et al. (2003, p. 884)

Arena Q also shares less important outer European cities with *Arena K*. Finally, there is an African cluster: *Arena U*. All inter-tropical African cities belong to this arena except for Nairobi. Furthermore all these African cities are part of the nucleus or are singular members; the hybrids of this arena are non-African. This reflects the lowly and relatively isolated position of inter-tropical African cities in the world city network.

Arena 'Gaps': Regional and National Geographies

The findings are from a global urban analysis and this is how we have interpreted them

Table 3.6 Band V Arenas

City Type	R	S	T	U	V
Cluster Nucleus	Leeds Aberdeen Glasgow Belfast Liverpool Newcastle	Dresden Bonn Hanover Nuremburg	Lille Lyons Marseilles Strasburg Bordeaux	Accra Dar Es Salaam Gaberone Kampala Lusaka Lagos Harare	Osaka Tehran Shenzhen Yangon Yokohama
Singular Members	Bristol Edinburgh Nottingham	Leipzig Stuttgart Cologne Utrecht	Basel Lausanne Seville Bologna Bern	Doula Brazilia Abijan Dakar Doha Windhoek Maputo	Tianjin Guangzhou Baku Labuan Nagoya
Hybrid Members	Birmingham > L Manchester > L Southampton > L Bilbao > T Valencia > T	Valencia > R	Ljubljana > Q Bilbao > R Port of Spain > P	Kingston > P Managua > P Tegucigalpa > P Colombo > M Santo Domingo > N San Salvador > N	Tashkent > Q Almaty > Q Ankara > Q
Near Isolates		Essen Rotterdam Gothenburg The Hague Luxembourg	Antwerp Turin Malmo		Hanoi

Source: Derudder et al. (2003, p. 885)

above. However, the identification of urban arenas does point to some interesting 'sub-global' conclusions. Specifically we can comment upon how contemporary globalization seems to be impinging on long-established national and regional 'urban systems', the traditional concern of urban geographers studying relations between cities. Figure 3.1 is particularly informative in this respect.

First we can contrast the location of the arenas featuring cities in Europe's leading three economies.

Whereas German cities are featured in three bands (I, II, and V), British and French cities are concentrated in two bands (Center and V for the UK; I and V for France). This clearly shows the different national patterns of cities with Germany's distinctive 'horizontal' city relations compared with the UK and France's 'vertical' city relations. Although this is by

no means a surprising result, it is relevant to the workings of contemporary globalization, whereas London and Paris cast an inhibiting 'shadow' over their compatriot cities, Frankfurt has no such effect on other German cities. Clearly this is of vital importance to how each of these national economies relates to globalization processes.

U.S. urban arenas have a similar pattern to German arenas in being represented in four bands (Center, I, II, and IV). This is perhaps to be expected given the large number of U.S. cities within the data. However this fact makes the lack of a U.S. arena in Band III interesting. There appears to be a gap created in the globalization of U.S. cities between the likes of relatively important cities such as Boston and less important cities such as

Baltimore. This certainly implies policy incentives for cities in *Arena O* to try and 'move up' and create a new U.S. arena in a higher band. More generally, the U.S. arenas are typified by their high levels of distinctiveness. New York, as half of the Center, and Miami as an important hybrid city linking to Latin America, are the only continental U.S. cities to share arenas outside their own country. This relates to the sheer scale of the U.S. economy and its long-developed, massive market in financial and business services that provides less of an incentive for firms 'to go global' to the same degree as global service forms from other world regions. This highlighting of the ambiguous role of U.S. cities in contemporary globalization is an important result of this research.

Finally the most important result of this research is the light it shines on erstwhile 'third world' cities in the world city network. The main point is that both Asian and Latin American urban arenas are quite well represented across all bands beyond the center. In the case of Africa, its Arab cities and South African cities feature in relatively important Asian and Commonwealth arenas, but the inter-tropical cities all cluster in one Band V arena. The exception is Nairobi which is a hybrid in two Asian clusters in Bands II and IV. Here we have the only signs of an authentic African world city emerging.

CONCLUSION

Conceptualizing world cities as global service centers, GaWC has developed a methodology for studying world city network formation. In this paper, we have complemented previous exploratory analyses of the world city network with as main objectives: (1) the unraveling of the fuzzy spatial dimensions behind world city formation; and (2) the description of the network at a level of geographical detail never before attempted.

Although we specify world cities as an interlocking network to which we apply a global level analysis, our results clearly reveal both hierarchical and regional tendencies within the data. First, the hierarchical tendencies contra Sassen's (1991) famous global trilogy, a dual city arrangement heading the network: London and New York form a distinct arena and Tokyo appears in an arena at the next level of connectivity. Overall, hierarchical tendencies interact with regionality: clusters with low average connectivity tend to be more regionally restricted in membership. These geographical features suggest that our results show more than clusters in an abstract 'service space'; they represent *urban arenas* in a geographical space that is the world city network.

Second, the regional tendencies show the three world-economy core regions—northern America, Western Europe and Pacific Asia—to be quite different in their allocations to arenas. In northern America, U.S. cities seem to be typified by: (1) high levels of distinctiveness (except for Miami); and (2) with a connectivity gap created in their globalization. In contrast, European cities are both linked into other continents and cover all levels of arena. Pacific Asia shows a globalization gap larger than that of the U.S. Arguably, the most important result is the light our analysis shines on non-core ('third world') cities in the world city network. While both Asian and Latin American urban arenas are quite well represented across all bands beyond the center, and Arab cities and South African cities feature in relative important Asian and Commonwealth arenas, inter-tropical African cities (except for Nairobi) all cluster in a single arena with a marginal position in the network,

In conclusion, we have tried to enhance insight into globalization through the depiction of a new and detailed geography of the world city network. We have not limited 'globalization forces' to just 'global cities' but have incorporated a very large number of cities into a single global urban analysis. Contemporary globalization is not an end-product in itself but an ongoing bundle of processes. This means that the gaps in the pattern that we have identified may be filled in the coming years as connectivity within the world city network intensifies. On the other hand the gaps may widen as global services become more concentrated in fewer cities. We cannot know which of these future scenarios will come to pass, but we do know that we will not be able to assess such changes unless we have a good empirical understanding of the contemporary-world city network.

QUESTIONS FOR DISCUSSION

1. In two or three paragraphs, discuss the main themes of Derudder et al.'s chapter.
2. In 1–2 pages, using specific examples from the chapter, explain Derudder et al.'s main themes in more detail and try to discuss what you think were the strongest and weakest elements in their arguments.
3. What cities were was surprising about the distribution of cities Derudder et al.'s Bands of Arenas (I–V)? In 2–3 pages, list five or six cities you were surprised by their position in the world city hierarchy and explain why (try to write at least a paragraph about each).
4. Below are 'Helpful Web Links' to the English websites for some other major city-regions of the world. Utilizing these websites and other sources, conduct some further research on three cities within Derudder et al.'s World City Network (pick no more than one from each Arena Band in Figure 3.1). Then, in 2–3 pages, describe some of the most interesting facts, similarities, and differences among these cities and present your findings to the class.

FURTHER READINGS

Derudder, B. et al. 2010. Pathways of Change: Shifting Connectivities in the World City Network, 2000–08. *Urban Studies,* 47 (9): 1861–1877.

Derudder, B. and F. Witlox, eds. 2010. *Commodity Chains and World Cities*. New York: Wiley.

Taylor, P. 2004. *World City Network: A Global Urban Analysis*. New York: Routledge.

Taylor, P., B. Derudder, P. Saey, and F. Witlox, eds. 2006. *Cities in Globalization: Practices, Policies and Theories*. London: Routledge.

Taylor, P., P. Ni, B. Derudder, M. Hoyler, J. Huang, and F. Witlox, eds. 2010. *Global Urban Analysis: A Survey of Cities in Globalization*. London: Earthscan.

Timberlake, M. ed. 1985. *Urbanization in the World-Economy*. Orlando: Academic Press.

HELPFUL WEB LINKS

Baltimore, City of. 2012. City of Baltimore, MD Official Website. Online. Available at: http://www. baltimorecity.gov/, last accessed January 16, 2012.

Copenhagen City of. 2012. Welcome to Copenhagen, Denmark. Online. Available at: http://www. kk.dk/sitecore/content/Subsites/CityOfCopenhagen/SubsiteFrontpage.aspx, last accessed January 16, 2012.

Leeds City Council. 2012. Home Page of Leeds, United Kingdom. Online. Available at: http://www. leeds.gov.uk/, last accessed January 16, 2012.

Lille, City of. 2012. Home Page of Lille, France. Online. Available at: http://www.leeds.gov.uk/, last accessed January 16, 2012.

Oslo, City of. 2012. Oslo Kommune: Official Website of the City of Oslo, Norway. Online. Available at: http://www.oslo.kommune.no/english/, last accessed January 15, 2012.

Moscow, City of. 2012. Welcome! International Portal of Moscow, Russia. Online. Available at: http://moscow.ru/en/, last accessed January 15, 2012.

Riga, Municipality of. 2012. Riga Municipality Portal: Home Page of Riga, Latvia. Online. Available at: http://www.riga.lv/EN/Channels/About_Riga/default.htm, last accessed, January 16, 2012.

Stockholm, City of. 2011. City of Stockholm: Stockholms Stad. Online. Available at: http://international.stockholm.se/, last accessed, December 30, 2011.

Tallinn, City of. 2012. Home Page of Tallinn, Estonia. Online. Available at: http://www.tallinn.ee/eng, last accessed, January 16, 2012.

Warsaw, City of. 2012. Warsaw: The Official Website of the Capital of Poland. Online. Available at: http://www.um.warszawa.pl/en, last accessed, January 16, 2012.

CHAPTER 4

Mexico City: The Making of a Global City? (2002)

Christof Parnreiter

With a population of 17.9 million people in the year 2000, Mexico City[1] is the third-largest urban agglomeration in the world, behind Tokyo and Bombay. This leads into thinking of it merely as a Third World megacity, which is a simplified picture, because beyond the large size, new dynamics of urbanization—related to economic globalization—may be at work. Though these new dynamics are far more easily seen in First World metropolises—they are also present in Third World cities.

To overcome this deficit I focus on the global integration of Mexico City. My main

Figure 4.1 Mexico City in Mexico

argument is that it is not quantity—in terms of population size—which shaped Mexico City's destiny in the last two decades, but the changing quality of relations with the national economy on the one hand, and with the world economy on the other hand. I maintain that the city's development was strongly biased by the radical shift in the country's economic strategy toward foreign markets, because this shift implied a revalorization and reordering of economic activities, of space, and of capital–labor relations.

My approach is based on global or world cities research (see for example, Friedmann, 1986; Sassen, 1991; Knox and Taylor, 1995). In short, the argument is that globalization processes give rise to a new form of centrality, in which a certain number of cities emerge as key places. These global cities link larger regional, national, and international economies with the global economy, and by doing so serve as nodal points where the flows of capital, information, commodities, and migrants intersect and from which they are directed. Concentrating command and control functions, global cities are both production sites and trade places for specific goods, namely financial and other advanced producer services, which are essential for global integration (Sassen 1991). Finally, global cities are linked to each other by flows of capital, information, commodities, and migrants, thus creating a cross-border network of cities. The emergence of a global urban system alters the geography of the world system (perceived traditionally as a collection or hierarchy of nation-states), because it operates both through nation-states and by bypassing their boundaries.

In the following section I will analyze major development in Mexico City in light of global embeddedness. Thus, because of globalization, and as part of it, Mexico City turns from a national metropolis into a pivot between the Mexican and the global economy. By doing so, Mexico City contributes to the "production" of globalization.

MEXICO IN THE GLOBAL ECONOMY

The integration of Mexico into the world system is by no means a recent phenomenon. From the Spanish conquest to the externally stimulated and pushed modernization during the rule of Porfirio Díaz (1876–1911), to massive indebtedness at the end of import substitution, Mexican destiny has been shaped to a great extent by factors beyond its territory. However, in the two decades following the debt crisis in 1982, Mexico's integration into the international division of labor has become ever deeper and has changed its form. By joining the General Agreement on Tariffs and Trade (today the World Trade Organization) in 1986 and the North American Free Trade Agreement (NAFTA) in 1994, the country's government institutionalized its course toward globalizing Mexico.

The collapse of import substitution, marked by the debt crisis, forced Mexico to a radical change of its economic strategy. In order to guarantee the payment of interest (and, to a smaller extent, the repayment of debt), to restore public finance and to create opportunities for highly profitable investment for both foreign capital owners and national business elites, governments implemented neoliberal policies. A good part of the country's economy and labor market was deregulated, the financial sector liberalized, land reform halted, tariff protections dismantled and import restrictions eliminated, state-owned enterprises privatized, manufacturing and agriculture reorientated toward foreign markets, and wages and social transfers reduced. All these changes show that globalization thus did not simply "happen" to Mexico. Rather, the state—or the elite controlling it—was a crucial agent. Globalization resulted from a deliberate reshaping of relations of capital, state, labor, and space, carried out to assert the interests of a specific set of private firms, namely those operating on a global scale.

As a result, the character of the Mexican economy has changed profoundly in the last two decades. Inward development was replaced by outward development, as demonstrated by the drastic growth of foreign trade and foreign investment. Annual exports grew more than sixfold between 1983 and 2000, up to $166 billion. Imports grew fifteenfold, amounting to $174 billion in 2000. The share of foreign trade in the national gross domestic product increased from less than 20 percent of GDP in the late 1970s to 59 percent in 2000. Another result of the greater opening of Mexico to the world market is that foreign capital flew into the country at unprecedented levels. Annual foreign direct investment (FDI) increased eightfold between 1980 and 2000, amounting to $13.1 billion in 2000. Between 1980 and 2000, $124.1 billion was invested in Mexico as FDI, and an additional $91.5 billion came into the country as portfolio investment. As a consequence of this increase, FDI reached 13.9 percent of all investment and 2.5 percent of the GDP in 1998, compared to 3.3 percent of all investment and 0.8 percent of GDP in 1980.

Data unmistakably indicate a shift from inward development, as was pursued in the era of import substitution, to an economy that is strongly oriented and tied to the world market. This shift implies a profound transformation of the Mexican economy, increasing the importance of export production (in particular the maquiladora industry) and of the financial sector. Thus, in the last two decades both the mode of Mexico's insertion into the world economy and the nature of the Mexican economy itself have changed radically.

ECONOMIC, SOCIAL, AND DEMOGRAPHIC TRANSFORMATIONS IN MEXICO CITY

For the purpose of this chapter it is crucial to ask what this transformation meant for Mexico City (the Zona Metropolitana de la Ciudad de México, or ZMCM). At first glance, transformation reduced the economic weight of Mexico City. The combined share of the Federal District and the state of Mexico in the national GDP went down by nearly 10 percent, reducing the share of Mexico City to 33.1 percent (see Table 4.1). This decline was mainly due to the breakdown of the manufacturing sector in Mexico City in the early 1980s. Industrial output shrank in absolute terms (down 5.8 percent annually between 1980 and 1985), and its share in Mexican manufacturing fell from 48.6 to 32.1

Table 4.1 Shares of Regions in the National GDP, 1980–1999 (Percent)

	1980	1985	1994	1999
Mexico City	36.2	32.1	34.2	33.1
Central region	43.5	40.0	42.4	41.6
Extended North/Central region: all those above plus Guanajato, Jalisco, Xacatecas, Aguascalienties, San Luis Potosi.	56.6	53.2	56.5	55.6
Northern border region	19.3	19.4	21.9	23.3
Gulf region	10.3	11.9	7.1	6.6
South	4.1	4.1	3.4	3.2
Southeast	1.1	1.6	2.6	3.0

Source: Authors calculations based on INEGI (various years). Central region: Federal District, State of Mexico, Hidalgo, Morelos, Puebia, Querétaro, Tlaxcala. Northern border region: Baja California, Chihuahua, Coahuila, Nuevo Leon, Sonora, Tamaulipas. Gulf region: Campeche, Tabasco, Veracruz. South: Chiapas, Oaxaca. Southeast: Yucatan, Quintana Roo.

percent. Additionally, the Federal District lost importance as a national center of economic decision making. Though 287 of the Mexican "Top 500" companies were there in 1982, this number had declined to 145 by 1989.

Due to the losses of the ZMCM, the share of the country's central region in the national GDP also declined. At the same time some states in the country's center or north of it (Aguascalientes, Querétaro, Guanajuato) increased their share. States in the northern border region (particularly Baja California, Chihuahua, Coahuila and Nuevo León), where most of the maquiladora industry is located, increased their share of the national GDP considerably. Finally, the Southeastern state of Quintana Roo (the destination of a good part of international tourism) also augmented its share of national GDP.

As regards the labor market, it is even more obvious that transformation weakened economic concentration in Mexico City. Though in 1980 nearly 41 percent of the workforce employed in the formal sector was in the ZMCM, this share had dropped to less than 30 percent in 1994. The reduction was strongest in Mexico City's manufacturing sector, where even the absolute number of workers declined. For the second half of the 1990s, available data suggest that the downward trend continued.

With the beginning of neoliberal restructuring in the second half of the 1980s Mexico City's share in the national GDP rose again, although without reaching 1980 levels (see Table 4.1). The recovery was driven mainly by an upswing of the Federal District where growth rates of GDP amounted to 3.5 percent annually (1988–1996), which was markedly higher than the national average (2.5 percent). The extent to which the city's economy recovered is shown also by the fact that the Federal District is one of the few regions in Mexico where GDP per capita was higher in 1995 than in 1980. Though it stagnated nationwide and grew only slightly (0.2 per-

cent annually) in the dynamic northeastern border region, it increased by 1.4 percent in the capital. Consequently, GDP per capita in the Federal District was 3.3 times the national average in 1995, while in 1980 it was only 2.6 times higher. This increase points to the concentration of highly productive economic activities.

Economic recovery in Mexico City stems mainly from two trends. First, manufacturing in the Federal District overcame the crisis, regaining annual growth rates of nearly 4 percent from 1993 to 1999. Consequently, the share of the Federal District s industrial GDP in the total Mexican manufacturing GDP remained constant in the 1990s, at a level slightly over 20 percent. Although this is, of course, much lower than in the 1970s, it is important to note that the downward trend in terms of production was stopped. Thus, speaking of a "deindustralization" of Mexico City would be misleading for various reasons. First, due to its historical weight and the stabilization of the manufacturing sector, the ZMCM still is by far the most important single city for manufacturing in Mexico, although states like Tamaulipas, Aguascalientes, Chihuahua, or Baja California have far higher growth rates in manufacturing. Second, employment that was formerly counted as manufacturing might appear as part of the service sector because of the internal reorganization of firms, even though the employment may still be attached to manufacturing. Third, part of the city's manufacturing might have become informalized, which would mean a reduction in statistical employment but not in output.

For the economic recovery of Mexico City the growth of the service sector was even more important than manufacturing. Services became the city's most important sector both in terms of the GDP and employment. Yet, the growth of the service sector does not simply reflect a shift toward services in general, since the subsectors "trade, restaurants, and hotels" and "municipal, social, and personal services" barely grew. Rather, growth was concentrated on "transportation and communication" and "finance, insurance, and real estate." Both sub-sectors had annual growth rates of about 5 and 4 percent, respectively (1993–1999). Consequently, the weight of "finance, insurance, and real estate" within the Federal District's GDP nearly doubled over the last 15 years (from 10.7 percent in 1985 to 19.0 percent in 1999). Within advanced producer services, financial services in particular expanded rapidly. With an annual growth rate of more than 8 percent, banking outperformed any other subsector of the urban economy.

A strong expansion of employment in producer services also indicates that the economic upswing of Mexico City in the 1990s was very much linked to advanced services. Employment in real estate, financial, and professional services grew by 75 percent between 1987 and 1997. In addition, advanced services accounted for nearly a third of all new employment in the Federal District in the second half of the 1990s. Amounting to 8.6 percent of the city's total formal employment in 1997, advanced services employed about half as many people as did manufacturing. Finally, headquarters returned to the capital in the 1990s. In 1998, 213 of the Mexican Top 500 were located in the Federal District (up from 145 in 1989), while the state of Nuevo Leon, where Monterrey is situated, had 59 (up from 51 in 1989), and Jalisco, housing Guadalajara, had 40 (the same as it had in 1989)

During the process of recovery, the city underwent two major socioeconomic transformations. First, its economic profile was changed. Until the 1970s trade and manufacturing were the most important sectors. By 1999 municipal, social, and personal services dominated (30.4 percent of the capitals GDP) followed by trade, restaurants, and hotels (21.4 percent), manufacturing (19.6 percent), and finance, insurance, and real estate (19.0 percent). Already in 1993 the Federal District

had become, according to the Coefficient of Local Specialization, highly specialized in services related to finance and insurance, and, to a lesser degree, in professional services. Second economic recovery was reached at the expense of employment and social standards. Though employment grew throughout the 1990s, it grew slower than the Mexican average, resulting in a further decrease of Mexico City's share in national employment. In particular, manufacturing which provided more than 50 percent of formal employment in the ZMCM in 1980, employed only 20 percent of all (formally) occupied people in 1999.

Economic recovery was also obtained at the expense of income. In general, real wages in Mexico have declined severely in the last two decades, losing 43 percent of their purchasing power from 1980 to 1998. Real minimum wages shrank even more by 60.5 percent. Yet, the decrease was even more pronounced in the Federal District. Though in 1980 real minimum wages paid in the capital were about 20 percent higher than the national average, this difference had almost disappeared by the second half of the 1990s. Futhermore even greater numbers of people worked in the unregulated informal economy, where work tends to be poorly paid. Although by the very nature of the informal economy it is difficult to assess exactly how many people work there, some studies (of the International Labour Organization [ILO], for example) estimate that the number might reach up to 50 or 60 percent of the economically active population—a sharp increase since the 1980s. Even the National Institute for Statistics, Geography, and Computer Sciences (INEGI) points out that the number *and* the share of people who work under precarious conditions increased notably in the 1990s. For example, 50 percent of the workers in the ZMCM have no welfare benefits. It is interesting to note that various indicators suggest that informality is higher in Mexico City than the national average.

As to social polarization, data on the income structure of the employed population in the ZMCM (INEGI, various years) have to be analyzed carefully because the INEGI does not reflect on the loss of the real value of wages. Yet this loss is a decisive factor, since a person earning five times the minimum wage in 1999 in reality obtained only slightly more real purchasing power than did a person earning twice the minimum wage in 1987. If this sharp contraction of real wages is taken into account, the notable decrease of people earning less than double the minimum wage between 1987 and 1999 (from 83.6 to 56.1 percent) does not mean that the actual share of people earning incomes below the poverty line really declined. On the contrary: taking five times the minimum wage as the income necessary to purchase the basic basket of goods at the end of the 1990s, compared to twice the minimum wage in the mid 1980s, the share of the employed population that obtained incomes below or up to the poverty line increased slightly (from 83.6 in 1987 to 85 percent in 1999). On the other extreme of the income scale the group with the highest earnings grew, although it remained very small (amounting to 2.8 percent in 1993). Thus, in terms of earnings, a trend toward polarization can be identified, though this trend is not very strong. However, data on the income distribution among households of Mexico City point to a somewhat declining inequality during the first half of the 1990s. The richest tenth obtained 34.6 percent of all income in 1996, compared to 39.5 percent in 1989. Conversely, the poorest 30 percent of the urban population expanded their share from 8.9 to 10.1 percent (INEGI, various years). However, this result has to be taken carefully since some distortion might result from the fact that city-related data for the 1980s are missing. This decade was, at least on the national level, one of pronounced growth of inequality. Thus, it is likely that despite a decrease in inequality in the first half of the 1990s, the level was still higher than in 1980.

The labor market, too, shows rising inequalities with a growing polarization between jobs at the top and at the bottom of the hierarchy for the period between 1970 and 1990. This tendency seems to have continued through the 1990s, although in an altered and less pronounced way. Between 1992 and 1998, petty traders and street vendors, a group that certainly corresponds to the bottom of the labor market hierarchy, expanded their share of total urban employment by 5 percent. By doing so, this segment of the labor market grew faster than any other sector.

A final transformation happening in Mexico City that is worth mentioning is the turnaround regarding migration patterns. Mexico City, which has been the most important destination of migrants for decades, turned—in only one decade—into the country's main sending area. The migration balance of the ZMCM became negative in the second half of the 1980s, amounting to a net loss of 223,700 people. In other words, Mexico City grew not because of immigration, but despite emigration. Population growth was driven only by birthrates being higher than mortality.

As a consequence, between 1980 and 2000, the combined share of the state of Mexico and the Federal District (that is, in essence, the share of Mexico City) of all internal migrants shrank from 47 percent to 40.2 percent. Federal states attracting a growing number of migrants are Baja California and Chihuahua in the North, Morelos and Puebla in the country's center, and Quintana Roo in the Southeast. The emergence of new patterns of migration becomes even more evident if one excludes intraurban mobility from data and focuses on migration balances instead of gross immigration, in which case the most important destination for internal migrants between 1985 and 1990 was Baja California, followed by Chihuahua and Quintana Roo. The state of Mexico came in fourth, and the Federal District had, as already mentioned, a negative migration balance.

DEBT CRISIS AND THE END OF IMPORT SUBSTITUTION

The loss of Mexico City's share of national GDP and employment and the emergence of new migration patterns may, to a certain extent, be seen as decentralization of the country's economy and population. In fact, since the 1970s, Mexican governments had elaborated various plans to promote more balanced development. However, in the opinion of many researchers the defacto decentralization that happened in the 1980s cannot primarily be attributed to these plans. Some maintain that diseconomies of scale (e.g., high land prices, traffic jams, or pollution) affected industries with high consumption of land, water, and infrastructure, which might have forced them to relocate in nearby states in central Mexico or in the northern border region.

The most important changes contributing to the decrease of Mexico City's share of the national GDP in the early 1980s are the definite end of import substitution and the crisis that accompanied the transformation to an outward-oriented development. Data previously mentioned suggest that the first half of the 1980s was particularly critical to the ZMCM. In addition, evidence shows that Mexico City was harder hit by the crisis than other cities. This may be surprising, given that Mexico City was the unchallenged "epicenter" of the Mexican economy, with a rather developed and diversified economic base, above national average levels of productivity, and considerable foreign investment.

The immediate cause of the crisis was that indebtedness had grown so high by 1982 that Mexico could no longer pay interest. However, this bankruptcy did not arise from simple insolvency. Rather, 1982 marked the definitive end of import substitution and thus can be seen as a watershed in Mexican history. Problems with import substitution had become apparent by the 1970s. Thanks to the oil boom in the second half of that decade and the fact that foreign credit was easily available and rather cheap at that time, the Mexican government disregarded the first signs of serious economic problems. When terms of trade for oil worsened to the disadvantage of Mexico and when interest rates in the United States increased drastically in the early 1980s, Mexico could not meet its obligations.

Though import substitution was relatively successful through the decades, it never developed a base for intensive growth. Rather, it had to rely on extensive growth, meaning a steady increase of inputs. In the 1970s, agriculture slid into a profound crisis, making it unable to generate enough export revenue to pay for manufacturing imports. Industry itself lost its capacity to achieve productivity gains; plants and technology became obsolete. Consequently, the Mexican economy could not generate the amount of exports and therefore foreign currency necessary to finance imports. Thus, inflation increased, problems in the balance of payments became notorious, and indebtedness rose drastically.

The reorientation of the economy toward foreign markets further deteriorated Mexico City's position. With production gearing to exports, domestic markets lost importance, devaluing the large urban agglomerations first as markets and then as production sites. In the neoliberal model, the masses aren't needed as consumers as much as they were during the era of import substitution. As workers, the population came under pressure because economic success depends on rationalization of economic activity and gains in productivity. Moreover, wage reductions that were crucial for becoming competitive in the world market reduced domestic purchasing power, additionally contributing to the devaluation of domestic markets. By far the biggest market, Mexico City was hardest hit by these developments.

Location Patterns of Headquarters

A first step to study the relationship between the new dynamic of Mexico City's economy and global functions is a closer analysis of the location patterns of the most important firms registered in Mexico. The results can be summarized as follows: the greater a firm's sales volume and the stronger its links to the global economy in terms of exports, imports and foreign capitalization, the higher the probability that its headquarters are in the Federal District. Regarding sales, 70 percent of the top ten Mexican companies had headquarters in the Federal District in 1998, compared to 42.6 percent of the top 500. Mexico City's dominance emerges even more clearly by including the communities of the state of México that belong to the ZMCM, in which case half of the biggest 500 companies have their main offices in Mexico City. The only other Mexican state with a significant number of main offices is Nuevo León, with its capital, Monterrey (11.8 percent).

Since the primary concern of this article is Mexico City's global links, export orientation and foreign capital participation are among the most meaningful facts about the location of company headquarters. Companies dominated by international capital are much more likely to locate in Mexico City than are Mexican-owned private firms. Breaking the top 500 Mexican firms down according to whether they are Mexican-owned private companies or have mostly foreign capital, different location strategies emerge. Whereas 39.4 percent of companies with primarily private Mexican capital have their main offices in the Federal District, 58.3 of the foreign-controlled corporations have their headquarters there. This trend increases with the size of the firm and if one considers the whole metropolitan area (ZMCM). For example, 78.9 percent of internationally controlled companies among the top 100 firms are based in Mexico City. Regarding foreign trade (except for the maquiladora industry),

the results show the same tendency: Mexico City is strongly preferred for headquarters, and the preference increases the more a company exports or imports. Nine of the ten biggest export firms are located in the Federal District, and 73.4 percent of the exports of the 100 biggest export companies (again excepting the maquiladora industry) originate in the Federal District, a huge lead over Nuevo León (11.8 percent).

To sum up, the Federal District is where the biggest Mexican companies prefer to set up their headquarters. This preference increases with: (1) sales volume; (2) foreign capital participation; and (3) export production. The location of main offices in the Federal District points to a close link between the city's economy and the global economy. The data suggest that transnational companies situated in Mexico and Mexican companies capable of adapting to the world market and becoming global players prefer to locate their headquarters in the Federal District. Consequently, the Federal District has global city functions insofar as it is where the Mexican economy (or at least parts of it) become globalized. In that sense, Mexico City's loss of manufacturing employment suggests that deindustralization fits into a new division of labor, in which the ZMCM specializes in functions commonly attributed to global cities, while other cities in central Mexico and the U.S. border region expand manufacturing.

In this context it is important to note that the high concentration of headquarters in the Federal District does not translate into concentrated production is striking that *together* the six northern border states, which contain 86 percent of all maquiladora production, attracted only 29.2 percent of FDI—less than half the share of FDI invested in the Federal District. Mexico City's dominance is even greater if one considers that most of the FDI in the State of Mexico may have been directed to firms located in the ZMCM. In that regard, Mexico City's share was nearly two-thirds of all FDI. Portfolio investment data on regional distribution are lacking, but it is likely that here the concentration in the Federal District is even higher than for FDI since the stock and employment. Instead, the big firms have spread their production across various cities in the country, maintaining only specific segments in Mexico City. This points to the city's role as a central node in the international and regional division of labor.

The Mexican branches of General Motors, Daimler-Chrysler, Volkswagen, Ford and Nissan are, for example, leading enterprises in terms of sales, exports, and foreign investment. All but Volkswagen have their headquarters in the Federal District, yet production plants are spread all over the country. Although Mexico City is not totally negligible as a manufacturing site, most automobile production takes place either in central states (state of Mexico, Guanajuato, Aguascalientes, and Morelos), or in northern border states (Coahuila and Chihuahua). The same applies to the computer industry, a fast-growing sector with massive exportations to the United States. IBM, which came to Mexico City in 1957, shifted its plants to the state of Jalisco in 1975, leaving only its main office in the Federal District. Future research should analyze the links between production sites, the regional headquarters in Mexico City, and foreign cities, where the capital, specific services or semi-finished products might come from. That would indicate the world economic network or commodity chain into which headquarters articulate Mexican production.

Regional Distribution of Foreign Investment

As previously stated, both FDI and portfolio investment grew significantly as a consequence of the opening of Mexico's economy. In fact, global capital flows represent one of the most important links between the Mexican and the world economy. In 1998–99 Mexico was, behind China, Hong Kong, Brazil, and Argentina, the fifth-largest recipient of FDI among Third World countries. Both FDI and portfolio investment are highly concentrated in the Federal District. Between 1994 and 1999, $29.4 billion or 60.3 percent of all FDI went to the Federal District market and. the headquarters of all major banks—and hence their accounting departments—are located in the capital.

However, not all capital that enters the Federal District is necessarily invested there. For example, a transnational corporation that makes a greenfield investment may set up a new plant anywhere in Mexico, whereas that company's regional headquarters, which controls and services local production, is located in Mexico City. This applies to the biggest single investments of 1998–99. Daimler-Chrysler and Ford invested $1.5 billion each, but Daimler-Chrysler's resources went toward expanding an existing plant in Coahuila, whereas Ford spent its on building a new one in Chihuahua. The same principle applies to mergers and acquisitions. The U.S. brewing company Anheuser-Busch invested $556 million to buy 13 percent of Mexico's Grupo Modelo, which brews Corona. Grupo Modelo has its main office in the Federal District and has breweries in 77. In these cases foreign investment is entered in the Federal District (because accountancy is carried out there) and then redistributed to production sites throughout Mexico. As in the case of the headquarters, however, it is necessary to trace capital flows from the global investor to the local use. This would reveal an urban network in which different cities occupy different positions, tasks, and degrees of power. Key issues for future research include: (1) identifying the command-and-control linkages between headquarters in the Federal District and production faculties elsewhere in the country; (2) the spatial and sectoral distributions of investment; and (3) the role played in that division of labor by banks, financial institutions, and other services located in Mexico City.

Between 1980 and 2000 the proportion of finance, insurance, and real estate in the Mexican GDP increased from 11 to 15 percent, and national employment in real estate, financial, and professional services grew by 45 percent between 1992 and 1997 (INEGI, various years). This growth was strongly concentrated in Mexico City. In 1999, 27.1 percent of the national GDP in the category of "financial services, insurance, and real estate" came from the Federal District, compared to 22.5 percent of the total GDP and 20.6 percent of GDP in manufacturing. The combined share of the Federal District and the state of Mexico (that is, in essence, Mexico City) amounted to 36.8 percent. It is remarkable that Mexico City's share in the national GDP in advanced producer services increased through the 1990s, while the share of the northern border region, which takes on increasingly more manufacturing, declined slightly (see Table 4.2).

Similarly, employment in advanced producer services is concentrated to a high degree in Mexico City. In 1997 the ZMCM had 47.8 percent of all national employment in real estate, financial, and professional services. Additionally, with 8.6 percent of formal employment, advanced services make up a higher share of urban employment in the ZMCM than in any other major Mexican city (Guadalajara: 6.8 percent; Monterrey: 7.8 percent); thus they have a greater impact on the city's economic and social development. Also, Mexico City is the only Mexican city where productivity in advanced services is above the national average in all subbranches, while rival cities such as Monterrey and Guadalajara exceed the national average in no more than half the categories.

To sum up, the evidence clearly suggests that a new form of centrality is emerging. Mexico City concentrates most activities related to economic globalization even though its share of the national GDP and employment has decreased since the 1970s. The location patterns of headquarters, regional distribution of foreign direct investment, and distribution of advanced producer services indicate that the opening of the Mexican economy and the growing orientation toward global markets has intensified the concentration of activities essential to the globalization of the Mexican economy in the Federal District. Thus, as part of the production of globalization, Mexico City has changed from a national metropolis into a pivot between the Mexican and the global economies. In other words: Mexico City increasingly takes on global city functions. The articulation of export production (aside from the maquiladora industry) with the world economy, for example, is mainly organized and controlled from Mexico City. In a similar vein, capital flows to Mexico are channeled through the Federal District and in particular its service sector.

WHICH PLACE IN THE GLOBAL URBAN NETWORK?

Given the evidence that clearly shows that Mexico City is indeed assuming world city

Table 4.2 Regional Shares of National GDP in "Financial Services, Insurance, and Real Estate," 1993–1999 (percent)

	1993	1994	1995	1996	1997	1998	1999
Federal District	26.6	27.4	26.9	26.6	27.4	27.0	27.1
State of Mexico	9.0	8.9	9.1	9.4	9.4	9.7	9.8
Mexico City	35.6	36.3	36.0	36.0	36.8	36.7	36.9
Central region	43.4	44.0	43.7	43.7	44.4	44.3	44.5
Northern border region	20.3	20.1	20.3	20.0	19.5	20.0	20.2

Source: Author's calculations based on INEGI (various years).

functions and that the city is well integrated into the cross-border urban network, two questions arise. First, do the functions that Mexico City carries out in and for the world economy exceed the national territory and economy? Differently put, is Mexico City a regional center for Central America? Second, to which other world cities is Mexico City linked, and what is, in terms of power relations, the nature of these connections?

In Latin America, there are five cities identified by the GaWC as world cities: Mexico City, São Paulo, Buenos Aires, Caracas, and Santiago. Since a majority of Latin American countries do not possess world cities, their access to the specialized knowledge of advanced producer services has to be cross-border. Could it be, that in the case of Central American and Spanish-speaking Caribbean countries, that Mexico City is the place where these services are bought? Evidence available suggests that that may not be the case. According to Taylor (2000), where the region is the Americas, New York is the centre but where Latin America is a designated region then Miami is the centre. This argument is based on the fact that six out of eleven London-based major producer service firms have their regional office in Miami, which makes that city the clear regional center even though it is not a particularly important world city in its own right. Nijman (1996) reaches the same conclusion. Although Miami does not play an important role either on the national scene in the United States or in trade relations with most of the world's regions, it is the dominant city for U.S.–Latin American connections. In the early 1990s, the city handled more than a third of all U.S. trade with Latin America, and the tendency was growing. For Central America and the Caribbean the share was even higher (47 and 43 percent, respectively). Yet, it is crucial to note that these data *exclude* Mexico. Regarding U.S.–Mexican trade, Miami virtually plays no role—it handles less than 1 percent. Thus, one can assume

that the reach of Mexico City as a global city does not exceed the national economy and territory, given that Miami seems to be the central node for the rest of Latin America. On the other hand, regarding the articulation of Mexico into the world economy, Miami is not involved. Consequently, in that case the main node is Mexico City.

Though evidence clearly suggests that Mexico City is becoming a world city, it is not the whole urban agglomeration that is inserted into cross-border flows. What one observes is the making of a global city *in some parts of the city*—which does not enclose the historical center that is dominated by public services and informal street vendors. Thus, the transformation of Mexico City into a global city implies not only the emergence of new forms of centrality, but also the creation of new spaces of centrality within the city—the five *delegaciones* of the Federal District that were noted earlier in this chapter for their communications infrastructure. It is in these districts that nearly two-thirds of the capitals GDP and three-fourths of its GDP in services are produced, where the vast majority of companies with headquarters in the Federal District can be found, where the conversion of the use of urban space toward services is most pronounced, where infrastructure for global telecommunication is centralized, where most private investment is directed to, where many of the urban megaprojects (like shopping malls or modern office complexes) are (going to be) realized, and where prices for land and real estate are the highest.

However, the "new center" needs the urban peripheries (in economic, social, and spatial terms) because they are functionally linked to the core. An indigenous woman living in a poor neighborhood like Valle de Chalco and working as a *muchacha* (domestic servant) in a banker's household in Las Lomas is attached to the global, as is a street vendor who sells branded articles. Both contribute in a specific niche to the reproduction of global capitalism. Though rich studies on the links between the informal and the formal economy exist, we need more research to establish whether the transformations that Mexico City is undergoing create a section of society which is functionally irrelevant to the system—as Castells (1991: 213) contended was true for whole states.

NOTES

1. Mexico City refers to the whole Metropolitan Area (Zone Metropolitana da la Ciudad de México [ZMCM]). The ZMCM is formed by the Federal District, which is the country's capital and forty-one communities (*municipios*) of the surrounding state of Mexico, which have grown together with the Federal District. Nearly half of the city's overall population of 17.9 million live in the Federal District.

QUESTIONS FOR DISCUSSION

1. In two or three paragraphs, discuss the main themes of Parnreiter's chapter.
2. In 1–2 pages, use specific examples from the Parnreiter's chapter to illustrate his main points.
3. From what you have just read and other articles/knowledge, list what you think were the major forces driving Mexico City growth in the late-20th Century and into the present Then, in 2–3 pages, discuss how these factors influenced Mexico City's growth. Where possible, use Friedmann, Sassen or Taylor's discussions to add depth to your discussion.
4. Utilizing the 'Further Readings', 'Helpful Web Links', and other sources, conduct some further research on Mexico City and on three other large cities in Latin America. Then, in 2–3 pages, write up some of the most interesting facts you discovered about these cities and present your findings to your class.

FURTHER READINGS

Aguilar, A. 1999. Mexico City Growth and Regional Dispersal: The Expansion of Large Cities, and New Spatial Forms. *Habitat International*, 23 (3): 391–412.

Brown E., G. Catalano and P. Taylor. 2002. Beyond World Cities: Central America in a Global. Space of Flows. *Area*, 34 (2): 139–448.

Garza, G. 1999. Global Economy, Metropolitan Dynamics, and Urban Policies in Mexico. *Cities*, 16 (3): 149–470.

Newson, L. and J. King, eds. 2009. *Mexico City through History and Culture*. New York: Oxford University Press.

Parnreiter, C. 2010. Global Cities in Global Commodity Chains: Exploring the Role of Mexico City in the Geography of Global Economic Governance. *Global Networks*, 10 (1): 35–53.

Scott, A. 2001. Industrial Revitalization in the ABC Municipalities, Sao Paolo: Diagnostic Analysis and, Strategic Recommendations for a New Economy and a New Regionalism. *Regional Development Studies*, 7(1): 1–32.

HELPFUL WEB LINKS

Aguascalientes, State Government of 2012. Welcome to Aguascalientes, Mexico. Online. Available at: http://www.aguascalientes.gob-mx/idiomas/ingles/, last accessed, January 13, 2012.

Buenos Aires, City of. 2012. Official Tourist Site of Buenos Aires, Argentina City Government. Online. Available at: http://www.bue.gov.ar/?ncMenu=785&&lang=:en, last accessed, January 13, 2012.

CHAPTER 5

Location Theory in Reverse? Location for Global Production in the IT Industry of Bangalore (2008)

Rolee Aranya

Global outsourcing of production in the information technology (IT) industry . . . to countries like India and China has received more than its fair share of media attention. It is in fact a very real example of globally integrated production and service provision made possible by the rapid developments in communication technology. 'IT', as understood in this paper, is the production of software applications, embedded software, software customization, and IT enabled services (ITES) provision. The 'IT firms' referred to are of two types—software and ITES. Software firms include all firms that undertake production of programming applications for end users or carry out production of applications or parts of applications on contract to other firms. ITES firms are those firms that provide services enabled by communication technology for labor-intensive back office operations. These operations may involve direct contact, as in the case of call centers and customer services, or may relate to back office functions for airline bookings, medical transcription, and so forth.

In the case of India multinational IT firms took advantage of the skilled labor available from various public sector industries, universities, and research organizations, and established offshore production centers in the late 1980s. From an initial interest shown by large multinational corporations (MNCs), such as Texas Instruments and Hewlett Packard, there emerged a growth and agglomeration dynamic, which has now led to most major

software firms in the world locating in India, accompanied by rapid growth and the internationalization of domestic firms. . . .

According to a recent estimate, India now has the highest number of IT export-related jobs and revenues in the world. . . . Most of the export-related IT firms in India are located in and around the major cities. Of these, Bangalore, Hyderabad, Chennai, Mumbai, suburban Delhi, and Pune lead in attractiveness for location. While the first multinational IT firms were located in Bangalore, making it the city most identified with industry in India, realization of the market potential for attracting offshore investment in the sector has more or less driven national urban policy over the last decade (see Figure 5.1).

Cities have become valuable resources for state governments to compete for footloose global investment. Bangalore has become a success story that other cities are vying to emulate. Unfortunately, while urban policy is strongly oriented towards creating an edge in a dynamic economic environment, very little study has focused on the spatial implications and patterns of location of these firms in an urban setting. . . .

The purpose of this paper is to present detailed studies on selected firms involved in offshore production of IT in Bangalore and to highlight their unique patterns of location. The example of patterns and spatial restructuring observed in Bangalore is used as an illustration of the inadequacy of

Figure 5.1 Bangalore in India and South Asia

location studies of producer services (i.e., services provided by specialized firms to other firms, as opposed to individuals), for analysis of export-oriented IT firms, especially in the context of developing countries, where they are most often located.

THE GLOBAL IT INDUSTRY IN BANGALORE

The city of Bangalore, located in the southern state of Karnataka, has acquired international acclaim and is often known by names such as the 'Silicon City of India', the 'IT Capital of India', and the 'Technology Hub'. Its transformation from the 'Garden City' and the 'Pensioners Paradise' to the 'Silicon City' has been a steep curve of change effected in the last decade. Bangalore had 1,154 registered IT firms in 2003 . . . [up] from a paltry 13 firms in 1992. These firms exported software and services worth US$2.67 billion in 2002–03, or almost half of India's entire IT export.

The first MNC (Texas Instruments) to locate in Bangalore (in 1984), acted as a precursor to other such firms, creating confidence in investors to locate in the city. Thereafter, agglomeration economies were set in place for future investments. The nature of the industry changed gradually to include the whole gamut of research and development, routine software customization, and, more recently, back office services. As a result of this diversification there is wide variety of firms located in the city. A significant development in the IT industry in Bangalore has been the growth of domestic firms such as Wipro, Infosys, and Satyam Computers into large MNCs, as a result of the boom in offshore business coming to India. It is these firms that have moved up the value chain and have taken up end user application products and services.

STUDYING INTRA-METROPOLITAN LOCATION IN BANGALORE

This paper is based on an empirical study conducted to understand intra-metropolitan location of IT firms in Bangalore, both at an overall city level and also through a detailed analysis of location histories of selected firms. Location histories of firms and the logic of location decisions were reconstructed through 43 interviews (conducted between 2001 and 2003) with key decision makers in the selected firms. The information derived from these interviews was supplemented with discussions with property developers (four interviews), real estate consultants (eight interviews), business promoters (three interviews), and local planning agencies (seven interviews). In addition to the interviews, spatial patterns at the city level were analyzed through an address database of all registered firms in the city in 2002 (STPI, 2004) and data on property value trends maintained by the real estate consultants that were interviewed.

In order to get a wide mix of firms for the study of intra-metropolitan location in Bangalore . . . the eight case studies [Wipro, I flex,

IBM, V Moksha, Mind Tree, Info Quark, First Ring, and Acusis] vary according to their level of revenues, ownership, and types of products. They are all export-oriented firms with the majority of the production being for an external market. In that sense they may all be considered 'global firms'. All the firms have a considerable presence in Bangalore with their headquarters or Indian headquarters located in the city. The oldest firm is Wipro Ltd, which began operation in the software sector in 1983, and the newest firms Acusis, which began operation in late 2001.

Semi-structured interviews of about 45–60 minutes were conducted with key people in the firms. These people were typically chief operating officers (COOs) and managers of administration and facilities, human resources, and real estate portfolios. On average five or six people in different managerial positions were interviewed in each firm. The questions that were asked were divided into four substantive groups: details on nature of work, size, and history of the firms; location history of the firms; factors that influenced location, internal, and external linkages of the firm; and lastly the extent to which the firms utilize local resources.

Although a checklist of indicators on which information to be collected was prepared before undertaking the interviews, the attitudes and communicativeness of the firms differed. The larger the size of the firm, the more hesitant the executives were in sharing information. Spatial decisions, in the case of multinational firms, are sometimes made by people who are located elsewhere; therefore the local management had limited awareness of the rationale behind spatial decisions. The domestic firms, on the other hand, were concerned about the image that they portrayed locally and were reticent in discussing aspects such as local resource utilization and company policies on location, housing, and transport—issues which would jeopardize their position with the local public authorities. Due to these roadblocks in free communication with the interviewees, the strict schedule of questions had to be abandoned in most cases. Wherever a problem of a limited interview was faced, key information on opinions and decisions was obtained from the interviews and supplemented with information from other sources. . . .

LOCATION PATTERN AT THE CITY LEVEL

The concentration of firms in the Bangalore Metropolitan Area . . . as well as the development of infrastructure for the IT industry, has led to two distinct urban phenomena—multi-nucleation and peripheralization of offices and retail space. As firms seek out areas for expansion and dispersal, the city has changed from a single-core Central Business District (CBD) to multiple commercial and retail cores.

Several industrial location and urban policies have contributed to the peripheralization of office-space. The first was the location of the satellite earth station in an industrial area (Electronics City) to the south of the city in 1995 (see Figure 5.2). The communication technology available at that time required a clear sight link with the wireless transmitters. This prompted firms to choose locations within the range of the wireless network. Additionally, state government policy to encourage the sector has translated into the development of two major technology parks in the periphery that are aimed at providing high-quality telecommunication infrastructure and commercial space to firms. Plans are underway to extend the technology parks to a much larger technology corridor, which would offer further incentive to firms to shift their offices to suburban and peripheral locations. Urban policy made by the Bangalore Development Authority is also oriented towards offering firms a 'hassle-free' location. The IT policy of the state has facilitated location of offices to anywhere in the juris-

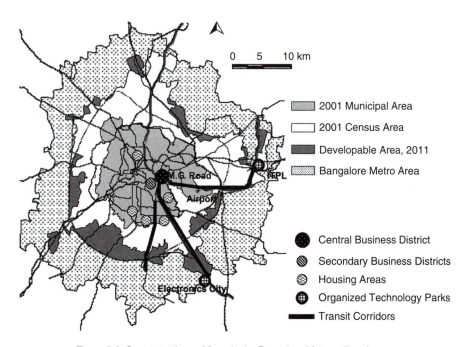

Figure 5.2 Concentrations of firms in the Bangalore Metropolitan Area

diction of the development authority, often overriding zoning regulations of the master plan . . . Similarly, office development by private builders is permitted with exemptions from the master plan if the development is being custom built for IT firms (Millennium IT Policy, 2001). As a result of these incentives offered by the state, the [IT] real estate market in Bangalore was flooded with small-time entrepreneurs who wanted to capitalize on the demand for space from firms. [The ensuing] oversupply of space eventually led to a crash in values when the global industry went through a slowdown in 1997. . . . In effect, IT firms in Bangalore have had access to a buyer's market for office space in the city. Supportive industrial policies of the state have facilitated firms having access to favored locations that are often linked to tax incentives. [Moreover], supply for space has not been a limiting factor for location. . .

Analysis of the location history and the future location plans of the firms studied suggests a sequential process of location and relocation. A common strategy of the firms is to make a distinction between administrative and production functions after reaching a certain size. While administrative functions are related to the running of the firm, production functions are those that are directly associated with the realization of the project/technical work of the firm. Production is often undertaken in what are called 'development centers' or 'offshore development centers' ('ODCs'). [An] ODC is a model of functioning in which the offshore office becomes an extension of the office of the client, and all systems are set up as replicas of the client. Therefore, the ODC is segregated from the other project offices, either physically or through electronic security systems. Separation of the ODCs from each other and from the administrative functions is as much a function of growth of the firms as it is the need to protect client information, and has implications for location decisions of firms. . . . This is illustrated in the following detailed studies of the location history of

five of the eight firms studied. . . . These firms have been selected because they show a clearer history of location in the city compared with some of the newer firms.

WIPRO TECHNOLOGIES

This firm belongs to a large business group that diversified into IT in 1983. . . . The city of Bangalore had been the headquarters of the business group for thirty years before the IT firm was set up. Hence, Bangalore was also its natural choice for headquarters for the new firm. Initially, the administrative office of Wipro Technologies was located in the CBD, and the software development centers were located in three other offices around the CBD. The period of 1985–95 was a testing phase for the firm, and no major investment in property was considered until certainty of growth in this sector was established. Until 1995, the firm had grown from 30 employees to almost 2,000 employees, who were divided equally in each of the four offices in the CBD. The period of 1995–96 brought about a shift from purely onsite to offshore software production by Wipro. Onsite production was undertaken by sending project teams abroad to the clients, whereas offshore production meant that projects could be worked on remotely. Once the credibility of the firm had been established clients were willing to increase the offshore element in the projects. Since expansion in the CBD was restrained by the phenomenally high rental and lack of large floor space, the firm rented space for new development centers in the residential areas while maintaining the corporate office in the CBD. Subsequently, as large projects were acquired by the firm, new space was leased in the proximity of the earlier development centers and an ODC established. Therefore, Wipro developed a network of development centers in the city and chose not to consolidate them in a single physical location later. As the IT industry boomed in 1996 and the firm had established its brand name, Wipro started a phase of investing in property in the city. They undertook two major projects, one to own and develop their largest development center in the periphery in special economic zones, and the second for consolidation of the corporate headquarters of all the businesses in a single location. In late 2001, both projects were completed and the corporate headquarters of all Wipro companies were moved to a peripheral location about 12 km from the municipal area boundary.

The stages of location of the Wipro can be divided into the following three phases (see Figure 5.3):

- phase 1: (1983) initial location of headquarters and development centers in the CBD and SBDs in commercial complexes; 30 employees and 9,300 m² of office space.
- phase 2: (1995–96) expansion of development centers into independent buildings and commercial space in residential areas; 2,000 employees and 20,630 m² of office space.
- phase 3: (2000–01) decentralized development centers in various locations (suburban and municipal areas) and centralization of corporate headquarters in suburban locations; 5000 employees and 122,630 m² of office space.

IBM INDIA

IBM, which has been located in Bangalore for the last ten years, has a number of large offices all over India, but still decided to locate its headquarters for its India operations there. In 1993, when it started operation in the city, the firm arrived as a joint venture between the Tata Group (large Indian business conglomerate) and IBM international. The firm then occupied an office space owned by the partner firm in a prime commercial complex near the airport. This office still remains today the registered office of IBM India. In 1997 the stake of ownership by the Tata Group in IBM was reduced to 20% and IBM Global Services was extended to India. This was the time that software development had taken off in India, and the firm leased two office spaces for development centers, one in each of the CBD and the SBD. In 1998 the ownership was transferred completely to IBM International and the firm became a fully owned subsidiary. At the same time, in order to expand the IBM R&D located in Bangalore, the firm made a decision to consolidate its space in the city. A long-term lease agreement was made with a builder and landowner for a space about 10 km from the CBD along the corridors leading to the special economic zones. The agreement

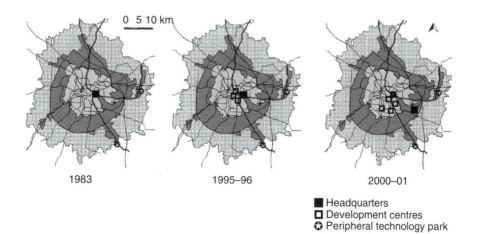

1983   1995–96   2000–01

■ Headquarters
□ Development centres
✪ Peripheral technology park

Figure 5.3 Stages in the location of Wipro

involved renovation of an existing building to suit the needs of the firm and a special agreement for future expansion in the land abutting the building. Though the firm had two options for sites for a consolidated campus, one being along an alternative corridor at a distance of about 15 km from the CBD, the current site was selected due to easier terms of the lease agreement and the employees' choice to stay closer to the city. After the crash of the IT global business, expansion plans for the construction of a large campus on the site were put on the back burner, but the development centers were mostly moved out to this single consolidated space. Though the office near the airport and the other two city offices are maintained as a backup space, the development centers and the headquarters are concentrated in the suburban location.

The shifting of location of the IBM India can be divided into three phases (see Figure 5.4):

- phase 1 (1993): initial location near the airport in leased offices in a commercial complex; 25 employees and 500 m² of office space.
- phase 2 (1998): expansion into prime commercial complexes in the CBD and SBD locations; 800 employees and 1,800 m² of office space.

- phase 3: (2001) relocation to a place along the highway into a single-user occupied building while the original office is maintained; 1,500 employees and 3,700 m² of office space.

I FLEX

I flex is an independent firm and was set up in Bangalore in 1993 and was once a part of Citigroup. . . . The year 1998 marked the emergence of I flex Ltd as an independent firm selling Citigroup's banking-related software. The original location of I flex was a leased office space in a prime commercial complex in the CBD. This office was already available to the firm as a part of Citicorp. However, with the expansion needs and the rapid growth of the firm by 1998, additional space for the second development center was leased in a commercial complex in the SBD. In 1998 the headquarters of the firm was also moved to Mumbai to achieve proximity to financial institutions. In the next planned move of the firm a site has been purchased in a suburban locality that lies to the east of the city, near the special economic zone. Construction of a 12 500 m² building and campus has already been initiated and the scattered development centers and the headquarters was scheduled to have moved to the new campus by the end of 2003.

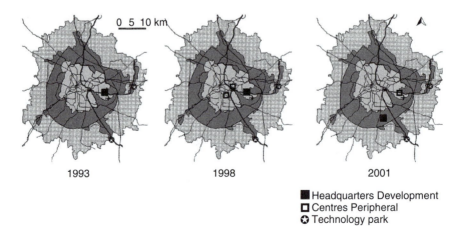

Figure 5.4 Shifts in location of IBM India

As with the previous two cases the location cycle of I flex leads to ultimate suburbanization and a consolidation of activities in a single campus. The phases can be distinguished as follows (see Figure 5.5):

- phase 1 (1993): initial location in a commercial complex in the CBD; 150 employees and 1,060 m² of office space.
- phase 2: (1998) expansion into an additional office space in the SBD; 25 employees and 2,500 m² of office space.
- phase 3: (2003) consolidation of space in a campus in a suburban location; 25 employees and 15,000 m² of office space.

FIRST RING AND ACUSIS—ITES FIRMS

There is a dissimilarity of location requirements for the production of software-enabled and internet-enabled services. The location of ITES firms takes place as a result of a trade-off between rent, transport and employee costs, and additional costs of communication networks with sufficient speed and reliability.

Among the case studies First Ring and Acusis are both service firms which provide IT-enabled Services that are very much dependent on high-speed internet connectivity. The basic infrastructure for these kinds of firms is now available throughout the city because of a newly laid fibre-optic network, and yet they opt for completely opposite locations for their facilities. First Ring is located in the technology park, almost 15 km from the airport, and Acusis is located near the CBD. When the locations of Acusis and First Ring are compared, the influence of business models on location choice is illustrated. Acusis, a medical transcription firm, relies on high-speed communication to get voice data from its clients (large hospitals) in the US that has to be transcribed and sent back before the doctors return to work the next day. The speed of communication and of the transcribers is key to sustaining the business. Similarly, First Ring is also a service firm which offers back office operations such as airline bookings, customer support, and call centers, which have short turnaround times. Both of the firms have parent firms that are located in the US through which work is channeled to the main service centers located in India.

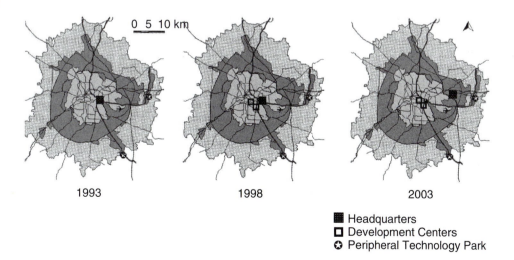

Figure 5.5 Stages in the location of I flex

However, First Ring, prioritizing the quality of infrastructure, chose to locate itself in the technology park (20 km from the city center) and transports its employees, working in 12-hour shifts, from all over the city to this peripheral location.

On the other hand Acusis has chosen to locate itself near the CBD. The firm is based on a model of 'home based transcription' (HBT) which enables the employees to get work at home through a high-speed communication network and to be able to transmit the output to the head office via the same network. The firm aimed to employ approximately the same number of employees as First Ring by the end of 2003, but the employees would not have been required to travel daily to the office, thereby saving huge costs which have been channeled into having a smaller but centrally located office. The finance manager of the firm stated that the central location was selected to ensure that in case the employees involved in the HBT needed to contact the office, they could do so without having to travel large distances thereby saving time and money.

Contradiction in the above location choices lies in the fact that one firm prioritizing high quality communication networks opted for a high-rent and high-transport-cost location, whereas a similar firm opted to locate in a smaller and cheaper office in the city and employed technological solutions to minimize transport costs.

FINDING PATTERNS IN INTRA-METROPOLITAN LOCATION

Though there are differences among the firms, and not all of them are at the same level of business development, a three-phase process of location and relocation can be identified (see Table 5.1).

In each phase of location and relocation, different factors influence decisions in firms. Table 5.2 divides these factors at each phase of location into four categories—communi-

Table 5.1 Three-phase firm location-relocation process within metropolitan locations

Phase 1 Initial location at start-up
Phase 2 Expansion of development centers
Phase 3 Consolidation of control functions in suburban locations and pattern of dispersed development centers maintained

Source: Aranya (2008, p. 460)

cation factors, organizational factors, policy factors, and value preferences.

Communication factors relate to the considerations regarding physical transport and the substitutability of contacts with advanced technology. Organizational factors relate to changes to the way a firm operates. Policy factors are those incentives and spatial policies such as zoning regulations and tax incentives that the firms avail of and are subject to in the urban context. Value preferences are socio-cultural aspects of location such as the aspiration to a certain image associated with office space and preferences for a better urban environment.

In the first phase, firms select an initial location in the city. The initial location of firms is mainly dependent on organizational factors such as ownership, size of firm, local partnerships that the firm has made, and size of the capital investment. Among the case studies, large firms such as Wipro, IBM, and I flex, who had business partners in the city or were backed by large capital (in case of Wipro), prime CBD locations were preferred. Smaller start-up firms like Mind Tree and InfoQuark opted for more obscure offices with lower rents. As discussed earlier, for ITES firms, location is based on a trade-off between quality of infrastructure and cost of transport.

In the second phase, as firms establish their credibility in the market, multiple development centers are needed. While administrative

Table 5.2 Theoretical classification of determinants at each phase of location

	Communication factors	Organizational factors	Policy factors	Value preferences
Phase I	Trade-off between quality of infrastructure and transport cost for ITES firms	Ownership of the firm and its existing size		
		Size of initial capital investment		
		Local partnerships and initial contacts	Maximum taxation benefits	
Phase II	Separation of projects from competing clients	Shifts from onsite to offsite production		
		Increase in employee strength		
		Organizational change		
Phase III	Relative proximity to other development centers	Upgraded infrastructure	Maximum taxation benefits	Image
		Consolidation of control functions		Prevention of disruption due to disasters
		Size of firm		Better urban environment

Source: Aranya (2008, p. 460)

functions are not moved from initial locations, development centers are either expanded or multiplied. This phase is often accompanied with a shift to offsite production (remote working) rather than sending project teams to client offices. As firms start to get increasing offshore business, development centers need to be created and hence employee strength is enhanced.

Since firms create a specialized niche in the market they sometimes handle projects of competing clients. For example, I Flex, which specializes in banking-related software, or Wipro, which is a specialist in enterprise resource planning (ERP) and e-commerce, often have projects from firms which are competitors in their own consumer markets. To maintain the levels of project security required to attain client confidence a physical separation of work is required. Separation of

projects from competing clients thus becomes a factor for maintaining physically dispersed development centers. This fosters the creation of a network of offices of single firms within the city. The dispersal is maintained either in physical terms or electronically if the development centers are consolidated at a later date. Expansion of markets for firms also leads to organizational reorganization. For example, as Wipro expanded its business it split its project teams by regional markets, and located them in separate offices. In addition to these organizational and communication factors, local incentives offered to IT firms begin to dictate location. Under the software technology parks (STP) scheme of the central government, individual premises are declared as 100% export oriented units, making them eligible for sales tax concessions. If a multiple office network is maintained projects can be moved around within the intra-city network depending on the level of export segment in the output. Not all premises of firms are registered as STPs and so are not obligated to achieve the stated goals for export. Firms use this incentive scheme to their advantage through maintaining multiple development centers in the city. The scheme does not impose restrictions on the physical location of the firms, as long as they are within the jurisdiction of the Bangalore Development Authority. The human resource manager of Wipro conveyed this during an interview:

> Projects are allocated to specific offices depending on how easily a team can be put together. Projects are also moved around between offices to get tax benefits from the STP Scheme.

The logic of multiple offices in the city was also explained by a need to prevent disruption due to disasters. Backups of key information and multiple links in networks are facilitated by the multiplicity of offices . . . This was a significant factor in the case of IBM, which has adopted this policy in its global offices.

In the third phase, firms consolidate control functions and some key development centers in user-specific campuses while a dispersed pattern of development centers is maintained. Because only suburbs and peripheral locations offer the possibility of large campuses, these are located outside the city with a high quality of firm-owned infrastructure. A campus model which was initiated by Infosys (the second largest IT firm in India), has become a matter of prestige. Facilities such as large conference halls, video conferencing, employee entertainment facilities, firm-owned satellite linkups, complete captive power backups, incubators, and so forth have become symbolic of a firm's success. The importance of image as a factor for relocation was stressed by the real estate manager for Wipro:

> As a start-up firm we [Wipro Technologies] needed maximum visibility. An office in the CBD was required. As the firm has grown, we now have to consider the image we portray to our overseas clients when they visit. A campus has become a necessity.

The motivation behind the suburban and peripheral location for campuses is that large consolidated space is available at an affordable price. The suburbs offer a good environment and an option to escape from the overcrowded city center. The selection of location for the campus is based on a relative proximity to other development centers. In order to maintain the network of offices in the city, firms set up local area networks and centralized servers where project information is saved and accessed. Despite this, proximity adds to the convenience of movement between offices for face-to-face interactions.

As reported by the manager of Administration Facilities at Wipro Technologies, the functions within IT firms are divided into three groups: technology, communication, and enterprise. Technology areas are the development centers, where actual production takes place; communications is the functions which are required to manage interaction between dispersed offices; enterprise is related to management and administrative functions. The consolidation and dispersal of these three categories of functions differ from firm to firm but a relative consolidation takes place in enterprise and key communication and technology functions in a campus. However, size of the firm is an important factor in deciding whether firms will consolidate all functions in a single peripheral location or whether they will maintain a dispersed pattern. This is apparent from the fact that IBM opted for a single location with a backup office, as compared with the fact that Wipro has multiple offices.

The three-phase process of location change observed among the case-study firms can be described as a dual process, where firms have varying tendencies both to disperse from city cores and also to centralize in other locations.

DIVERGENCE FROM STUDIES
OF OFFICE LOCATION

The observed spatial pattern of location of IT firms in Bangalore seems to correspond with location/relocation of offices and urban restructuring in most cities of advanced economies. Multi-nucleation, as put forward by Daniels (1985), and succession of location, suggested by Schiller (2001) in his Seed Pod model, are apparent in the spatial canvas of Bangalore city, influenced to a large extent by location decisions made by IT firms. Case studies of firms discussed in this paper confirm the dual process of peripheralization and centralization of offices in suburban and core areas. However, unlike the cities that these location models are based on, Bangalore's suburbanization has not followed the same sequences of residential, retail centers, and office location. The demand for office space has fast-tracked suburban growth from agricultural land to offices. Residential and retail development is following as a result of office location.

Studies of office location conducted in the 1970s and 1980s were based on deciphering contact patterns of producer service firms. . . . The main argument being that face-to-face contacts could be replaced by technology-driven telecommunication and this had enabled firms to split their functions at an intra-metropolitan level. However, these studies were based on services that developed as a result of unbundling of 'office functions' from traditional manufacturing in postwar developed economies. These services agglomerated in the major cities and created a demand for office space in CBDs. This prompted an investigation into the contact patterns of firms and the possibility of splitting functions in firms to reduce pressure for space in CBD locations.

Though IT firms are very much an 'office-based industry', the export-oriented nature of their production is a critical factor that distinguishes them from producer services and is decisive in determining location at an intra-metropolitan level. The key aspects of the work done in IT firms that creates this unique pattern are:

1. IT firms in Bangalore are involved mostly in export-related production of software and services.
2. Owing to their export-oriented nature, clients of these firms are located mostly overseas.

This limits their need for face-to-face contacts in local physical proximity.

Alternatively, producer service firms in advanced economies service clients in the market in which they are located. They offer their services to other businesses that may have global operations, but which usually have strategic offices in the cities where producer service firms agglomerate. Interdependence of co-location of offices of producer services and their clients that are major global businesses is an assumption that underlies the studies of office location. Major 'global cities' such as London, New York, and Tokyo are understood to create a demand for advanced producer services, which becomes an indicator of the level of integration of these cities in the global economy.

Unlike producer service firms, as IT firms involved in export-related service provision expand and split functions, they do not face issues of loss of strategic contacts if they move the location of their offices. Strategic contacts for maintaining competitiveness of IT firms are not related to the city in which they are located. In some cases strategic contacts with clients are maintained by establishing liaison offices in the markets from where business is outsourced. For example, Wipro, I Flex, and Info Quark, from among the case firms, have subsidiary offices in the US and UK which are involved in business development and promotion. At an intra-metropolitan level, the stress is on 'intra-firm' internal contacts rather than 'inter-firm' external contacts. . . . Interviews conducted during this study revealed how intra-firm contacts determined location in the city.

According to the real estate manager of Wipro on the future location pattern of the firm:

> The site [Sarjapur Road Campus] for the Corporate Headquarters was selected because of its proximity to the previous businesses and the growth of the firm has been this side. It has proximity to our other offices and we are sort of planning to consolidate all offices in this area. It helps our people to move between offices for meetings.

If the factors that determine location at each phase in the sequence (Table 5.2) are analyzed, it is apparent that all communication factors influencing software firms are related to intra-firm contacts. These may be related to opting for physically separated development centers to discourage interaction among employees working on projects of competing clients or maintaining relative proximity to other development centers for frequent meetings. ITES firms, on the other hand, opt for location based on the model of operation on which they work. This is still an intra-firm consideration that is dependent on the quality of communication infrastructure available to them. Recent security concern over data leakage from these firms would definitely have a bearing on the home-based working model employed by one of the case firms. It would be interesting to see how location decisions would be altered by this added factor.

Predominance of 'intra-firm' or internal contacts in everyday operation of the firm makes them relatively footloose for location. They are not bound to CBDs for location, divergence from location theory of offices occurs when firms are able to shift strategic and administrative functions to peripheral locations while retaining routine functions in the core city. But this is a logical pattern for IT firms because the technical employees of the firm, who are directly involved in the production process, travel shorter distances to the development centers if they are located in the main urban fabric. High-level managers and administrators, having higher affordability and being fewer in number than technical employees, can travel larger distances to peripheral locations.

One example of such reasoning was observed in the location decisions of IBM. As explained by their administration manager:

> We wanted to create a new image for IBM Global Services as a R&D center and thought of doing it through a new campus. There were two choices for location—one was on Banerghatta Road [10 km from the CBD] and the other was in Whitefields [20 km from the CBD]. We had a vote among our employees. The management did not mind travelling longer but the other employees opted for the closer location.

Although IBM ultimately opted not to split its management and development centers, the location closest to the CBD was selected for a consolidated office.

In the absence of external contacts being a limiting factor of location, alternative dimensions guide the location of firms in Bangalore. Significant among these are organizational and policy factors. Value preferences come into play at later phases of a firm's growth. Organizational restructuring . . . is more relevant at a regional or, in fact, a 'global' scale. Offshoring of business to firms in Bangalore from advanced economies is, in itself, a manifestation of the split of functions in multinational firms. But the same is observed in Bangalore at an intra-metropolitan level. Organizational expansion, which may have occurred as a result of change in business model (e.g. a shift from on-site to offshore production), an increase in business volume leading to employee growth, or splitting of functions for project security, are all factors that have had an impact on location.

Policy and value preference factors that influence location at later phases of a firm's growth are significant in their contextual relevance. The policy factor that has influenced location in the case-study firms relates to the taxation incentive available to firms involved in export. Forming a part of industrial policy of the national government, it contributes towards firms maintaining multiple offices in the city. By declaring selected offices as export-oriented units they are able to move around projects among their multiple locations, thereby not having to conform to export targets. When aggregated over a city level the choice of firms to maintain dispersed development centers contributes to the development of a multinucleated urban pattern and conversion of residential properties for office use.

Value preferences come into play when a firm has reached a certain size, and image considerations become important with respect to its competitors. A single-firm campus-like office has become a symbol of achievement among firms in the city. All firms aspire to set up a campus with a high level of infrastructure and a large amount of land in the periphery. The decision to consolidate key development centers and managerial functions in peripheral locations is as much an image boosting decision as a genuine need for functioning of the firm.

To summarize the discussion on determinants of location, the difference in nature of work and services produced by IT firms and other producer service firms leads to different outcomes in terms of location of offices. Unlike the findings from existing theories of office location the stress is not on factors of communication and face-to-face versus indirect contact, but on aspects relating to intra-firm communication and organizational factors. Since firms located in Bangalore have very little local market orientation, their inter-firm contacts are focused more on their parent or subsidiary firms located elsewhere. The firms have more backward linkages with the city than forward linkages. Their primary interaction with the city is in terms of availability of skilled labor. In such a situation organizational factors and other factors, such as policy and value preferences, determine their location at an intra-metropolitan level. Very simply put, firms locate in the city, expand and multiply offices, expand further, and then consolidate key administrative functions in peripheral locations. . . .

QUESTIONS FOR DISCUSSION

1. In two or three paragraphs, discuss the main themes of Aranya's chapter.
2. In 1–2 pages, use examples from the chapter to illustrate these main themes and then discuss what you think were the strongest points supporting Aranya's arguments.
3. From what you have just read and other articles/knowledge, why do you think IT jobs have been transferring to Bangalore and India, in general? In 2–3 pages, discuss some of the reasons for this shift is occurring, and why the jobs are transferring to Bangalore over, say, China or Mexico. Conclude your discussion with a couple of paragraphs about which city-region(s) or nation you think will be the center(s) of the IT industry in 20 years, and why. In your answer, try to discuss/think about where different work functions in the IT industry will be located in the future (i.e., where will management positions be located in the world, research & development jobs; factory production work; and other office related services; will they be in large central cities, suburbs, rural areas, home offices, etc.).
4. Utilizing the 'Further Readings', the 'Helpful Web Links', and other sources, conduct some further research on Bangalore and three other large cities in India. Then, in 2–3 pages, write up some of the most interesting facts you discovered about these cities and present your findings to your class.

FURTHER READINGS

Benjamin, S. 2000. Governance, Economic Settings, and Poverty in Bangalore. *Environment and Urbanization*, 12 (1): 35–56.

Chaminade, C. and J. Vang, J. 2008. Globalisation of Knowledge Production and Regional Innovation Policy: Supporting Specialized Hubs in the Bangalore Software Industry. *Research Policy,* 37 (10): 1684–1696.

Nair, A., D. Ahlstrom, and L. Filer. 2007. Localized Advantage in a Global Economy: The Case of Bangalore. *Thunderbird International Business Review*, 49 (5): 591–618.

Parthasarathy, B. 2004. India's Silicon Valley or Silicon Valley's India? Socially Embedding the Computer Software Industry in Bangalore. *International Journal of Urban and Regional Research*, 28 (3): 664–685.

Parthasarathy, B. and Y. Aoyama. 2006. From Software Services to R&D Services: Local Entrepreneurship in the Software Industry in Bangalore, India. *Environment and Planning A,* 38 (7): 1269–1285.

Taylor, P. and R. Aranya. 2008. A Global 'Urban Roller Coaster'? Connectivity Changes in the World City Network, 2000–04. *Regional Studies*, 42 (1): 1–16.

HELPFUL WEB LINKS

Ahmedabad, Municipal Corporation of. 2012. E-governance Site, Ahmedabad (AMC), India. Online. Available at: http://www.egovamc.com/, last accessed, January 13, 2012.

Delhi, National Capital Territory of. 2012. Welcome to the Delhi Government's Home: Online. Available at: http://delhigovt.nic.in/index.asp, last accessed, January 13, 2012.

Greater Mumbai (Bombay), Municipality of. 2012. Welcome to the Municipal Corporation of Greater Mumbai, India. Online. Available at: http://www.mcgm.gov.in/, last accessed, January 13, 2012.

Hyderabad, Municipality of. 2012. Welcome to the Greater Hyderabad Municipal Corporation. Online. Available at: http://www.ghmc.gov.in/, last accessed, January 13, 2012.

Jaipur. District Administration of. 2012. Official Website of the Collectorate of Jaipur, India. Online. Available at: http://www.jaipur.nic.in/, last accessed, January 13, 2012.

Karnataka, State Government of. 2012. Government of Karnataka, India, Department of IT, BT, and S&T. Online. Available at: http://www.bangaloreitbt.in/index.html, last accessed, January 13, 2012 (contains the City of Bangalore).

Kolkata (Calcutta), Municipality of. 2012. Official Website of the Kolkata Municipal Corporation. Online. Available at: https://www.kmcgov.in/KMCPortal/HomeAction.do/, last accessed, January 13, 2012.

Lucknow, District Administration of. 2012. Official Website of Lucknow District, India. Online. Available at: http://lucknow.nic.in/, last accessed, January 13, 2012.

Surat, Municipality of. 2012. Home Page of Surat Municipal Corporation, India. Online. Available at: http://www.suratmunicipal.gov.in/Default.asp, last accessed, January 13, 2012.

Tamil Nadu, State Government of. 2012. The Government of Tamil Nadu Welcomes You: Tamil Nadu Districts (Includes the District of Chennai). Online. Available at: http://www.tn.gov.in/districts.html, last accessed, January 13, 2012.

CHAPTER 6

Building Shanghai: Historical Lessons from China's Gateway (2008)

Edward Denison

Located at one of the key gateways to the world's most populous country, Shanghai has long enjoyed a [modern] image (see Figure 6.1). Today, as one of the world's largest and fastest growing cities, this image is dutifully sustained as Shanghai offers unprecedented opportunities for domestic and international architects who have enjoyed

Figure 6.1 Shanghai in China and Asian context

considerable commercial success while help-ing to transform the urban landscape from an aging, dense and relatively low-rise setting into a modern, multifaceted and ubiquitously high-rise conglomeration in little under two decades.

However, the scale of change and such narrow timeframes belie a broader narrative that deconstructs the pervasive and argu-ably superficial image of the city. By adopt-ing a wider historical view, the city's radical modernity appears more as an evolutionary rather than revolutionary process in which key issues such as rapid development, urban continuity and the dominance of foreign architects all have played an important role in shaping the city since the mid-19th cen-tury. This paper explores these issues from the perspective of Shanghai's urban fabric and the socio-economic influences that have helped to shape it, revealing, in the process, potentially instructive parallels between the past and present that in turn might better inform urban practices in the future.

SHANGHAI'S ARCHITECTURAL TRANSFORMATION FROM THE 19TH CENTURY TO THE 1950S

Architecturally, few things come close to matching the magnitude of China's jaw-dropping developments since the early 1990s, but a prominent contender would be the piles of literature that eulogize the prod-ucts of this phenomenal period of growth. The foundation on which much of the often repetitive commentary stands is the unprec-edented nature of China's experience. The excited chatter about foreign architects and their iconic creations on the blank canvas that is China's urban realm invariably clads the structure of this commentary, but as the dust finally starts to settle after more than a decade of remarkable construction, some are beginning to question this work and its broader impact. It might be no surprise to hear one observer voice of the preponderance

of foreign architectural influence in China: "... every variety of Western hideousness can be studied in detail, from the simple biscuit box type to the economically pretentious" (King, 1919, p. 563).

What might be surprising, however, is that this was said in the early years of the 20th century. Nearly 100 years later, in an age transfixed by the future, the past in China appears all too often overlooked. History not only offers some notable parallels that serve to inform contemporary practitioners, but while running the risk of stating the obvi-ous, the past is also where cities, in all their complex magnificence, came from. To over-look this by concentrating only on idealized futures, as history so often proves, can be a terrible mistake. By seeing beyond the erro-neous yet often-quoted view of China as an architectural tabula rasa it is easy to see that although China's current architectural expe-riences are quantitatively unique, they do have a historical precedent. Furthermore, it was during the epoch in which this precedent was set, before the Second World War, that the foundations of many of China's leading cities were laid. Perhaps the most outstand-ing example that demonstrates these issues in a distinct urban ensemble is Shanghai.

Shanghai provides an interesting and somewhat paradoxical study because the city has always prided itself on being modern, on shunning the past, yet it is this modish char-acter that has, over time, become an essential facet of its heritage. Following its inaugura-tion as a Treaty Port in 1842, after which it was said to be [very backwards] from an architectural point of view, it has consist-ently maintained its position as the primary gateway through which modern ideas and technology permeated China. It was the first city in China to plan (1863) and operate a railway (1876), the first to commercially generate electricity (1882), the first to have electrical street lighting, the first to process gas (1866) and the first to install a mod-ern waterworks. These developments were fundamental to the establishment of modern industries that by the end of the 19th century made Shanghai China's largest port and industrial powerhouse, transforming it from a city [with] little architectural beauty in the 19th century into . . . [a] model settlement by the Second World War.

Then, as now, the city relished its [modern] identity reinforced by media headlines domestically and internationally extolling the highrise lust for wealth that epitomized Shanghai's architecture. But the "New Billion-Dollar Skyline" (*Far Eastern Review*, 1927, p. 254) of the late 1920s that bestowed to Shanghai its epithet Manhattan of the Far East had then only recently evolved through relatively rapid phases of architectural development following the establishment of foreign settlements adjacent to the former walled city.

On this land were built most of Shanghai's first foreign buildings, typically designed . . . in a 'compradoric' style [blending the of Classic Colonial-style architecture from Britain with a native Chinese-flavor], said to be imported from Guangzhou by a Cantonese contractor called Chop Dollar (who "developed a style of compradoric architecture peculiar to the place" (Kingsmill, 1911, pp. 76–77). Compradoric buildings were invariably symmetrical, two storeys high and skirted by a veranda, and were seen as anything from 'simple in the extreme' (Dyce, 1906, p. 34) to creating a 'grand and imposing appearance' (Wright, 1908, p. 85).

By the end of the century, as Shanghai's compradoric architectural character was giving way to larger, towering enduring structures of three or four storeys . . . [in a style evoking immense praise from] the city's oldest resident Reverend William Muirhead:

> These splendid hongs and houses, banks and offices imparting an air of beauty and order . . . We might well point to the English homes we have formed here . . . How different is this from what we know to be the characteristic of Chinese homes. (Shanghai Mercury Office, 1893, pp. 60–61)

Such loaded sentiments had a long pedigree in China and reflected a discernable lack of interest in or respect of China's architecture among popular foreign opinion since Sir William Chambers' views (which had done so much to precipitate Europe's love affair with Chinese design in the 18th century) had fallen out of favor. To survey the terrain of Western architectural literature composed by foreign visitors to or residents in China since the 18th century is to witness a landscape strewn with derision and contempt. Even the most celebrated architecture, Beijing's Forbidden City, widely considered to be the very embodiment of Chinese architectural design and planning, failed to escape scorn [from Western travelers].

Such sentiments demonstrate the prevailing foreign mindset at a time in which foreignness equated to civilization and in the case of Shanghai and many other Treaty Ports provided the undisputed distinction between their magnificent world of the foreign settlements and the repugnant Chinese city. Architecturally, this world underwent a complete revolution at the turn of the century with the three years from 1914–16 aptly reflecting the nature of this 'revolution' . . . Rampant construction caused the demolition of old buildings and the erection . . . of ostentatious well-lit 'tiny' palace-like residences all over the Foreign Settlements, including the city's formerly rural perimeter . . . Change [was] so rapid, that residents lamented that . . . many of the [city's] ancient landmarks would soon be gone (Gamewell, 1916).

The process of renewal was not simply quantitative or purely stylistic. New materials and construction techniques facilitated qualitative changes in the construction industry that allowed for entirely new building types. One such example was Shanghai's Public Market off Nanjing Road, designed by the British engineer, Frederick Gratton (1859–1918). Opened on January 1, 1899, the 575 ton steel-framed structure with a glass roof was among the first of its kind in

China. In the same year, a German architect, H. Becker, established an office in Shanghai and together with R. Steel from Yokohama designed the Russo-Chinese Bank, completed in 1902, which was the first non-industrial building in China to use steel and concrete in its construction. By 1908, Shanghai's first entirely reinforced concrete office building, the six-storey Shanghai Mutual Telephone Company building designed by the British firm Davies & Thomas, was completed. Seven years later, the Union Assurance Company, China's first steel-framed office building, designed by the Hong Kong-based firm Palmer & Turner was built.

Ironically, although modern, the steel frame or concrete structure that paved the way for various modernizing influences was "purely Chinese in idea; very much similar to the Chinese system of posts and beams" that had characterized Chinese architecture for millennia (Lu, 1929, p. 98). Indeed, the essence of the wooden frame was noted by some at the time to be "actually the precursor of modern building where the pillars are replaced by concrete or steel, and where the walls are screens and not supports" (King, 1919, p. 562). Yet the architectural implications of this were only fully explored through the lens of Japanese architecture before the Second World War, while China struggled to move beyond mere stylistic appendage. Nevertheless, steel and reinforced concrete ushered in a new phase of largely foreign architecture in China, characterized by larger, taller structures. Nowhere in China embraced these new manifestations of modernity more than Shanghai. Although the city's infamously boggy soil, consisting of hundreds of meters of aqueous mud, gave [countless] architects and engineers sleepless nights, by the 1920s technological innovations and new materials helped to change professional opinion, which had previously considered six storeys to be Shanghai's safe height limit (Wilson, 1930).

Modern standards of living, new construction methods, materials and engineering techniques, allowed for different configurations of rooms, thinner walls, a greater efficiency in the use of space internally and externally and, importantly, taller structures. These improvements combined with the wider prevailing political and economic conditions in China at the end of the 1920s and in the early 1930s, heralded Shanghai's architectural heyday. Coinciding with the Great Depression, trade stalled and a currency crisis decimated the value of silver on which the Chinese currency was based. Speculators consequently ploughed money into [the city] . . . fueling a land and property boom [unparalleled] in the settlement's history.

This prolific phase witnessed also a shifting attitude in architectural discourse. From his belittled position the Chinese architect was growing in confidence and collectively China's growing architectural community was becoming increasingly critical of the dominance of foreign influence in China. One of the first of China's professionally trained architects to question the quality of foreign architects' work in China was Lu Yan Zhi, a graduate of Cornell University and one of the first of the first-generation of Chinese architects to have returned home after studying overseas. In 1919, Lu began work in the Shanghai office of the American architectural firm, Murphy & Dana. In 1922, he left his job to establish one of the first ever Chinese architectural practices. In his resignation letter he declared his career intent "to combat the ever present 'compradoric' architecture . . . which is disfiguring our bigger cities and countryside" (Cody, 2001, pp. 148 and 167n). (Lu went on to win first prize for the design of the Sun Yet Sen Mausoleum in Nanjing in 1925 and the following year he won the competition for the design of the Sun Yet Sen Memorial Auditorium and Monument in Guangzhou.) Another critic, Du Yan Geng (1935, p. 26), proclaimed some years later:

There are some architects and engineers that have two common diseases. One is to pursue the Western style, and the other is to pursue the popular style. One of these two is enough, but to have both is unbearable! Such people, how can they be mentors? How can they lead society?

Architectural arguments aside, Shanghai's architectural peak witnessed astonishing growth: from 1927 to 1930 the construction of foreign stores increased by over 1000 per cent, foreign residences by 800 per cent, apartment buildings by 400 per cent and Chinese houses by 250 per cent. From 1925 to 1930, 11,838 Chinese and 972 foreign buildings were demolished and the expansive gardens of former luxury mansions were subdivided to make way for new developments as land prices soared by 1000 per cent from 1924 to 1934.

With increasing land values, a rising population and large numbers of foreign residents seeking modern, comfortable alternatives to the insecurity of living outside the foreign settlements, the apartment building prospered. Shanghai's first purpose-built high-rise apartment building was completed in 1924. From 1926 to 1934, 55 apartment buildings were built, some being the biggest buildings in Asia. This period also witnessed the construction of what was China's tallest building until the 1980s: the Joint Savings Society Building. Designed by the Shanghai-based Hungarian architect Laszlo Hudec and completed in 1934, this represents arguably Shanghai's architectural zenith.

While this affluent epoch was apt for the construction of larger structures, the most profitable and certainly the most numerous building type was the lane house. One acre of land could accommodate 120 units, giving Shanghai a population density of 600 people per acre, one of the most densely populated metropolitan areas in the world at the time. The lane house, or Shikumen, a curious fusion of the British terrace house and the Chinese courtyard dwelling, first emerged in the mid-19th century to house Chinese refugees in the foreign settlements. These successive waves of migrants caused Shanghai's property market to go "perfectly mad" (Laurie, 1866, p. 4), covering former rural areas in "a maze of new streets and alleyways with thousands of new tenements" (Montalto de Jesus, 1909, p. 206) whose memory can still be recalled in the grain of Shanghai's downtown street pattern over 150 years later. No other building type surpassed the Shikumen in forging Shanghai's urban character.

The physical memories of Shanghai's developments before the Second World War remain markedly palpable due to the events that subsequently overwhelmed the city. These events, which stifled construction and eventually cocooned the city, began in 1932 when architectural activity in Shanghai was subdued by Japan's bombing of the Chinese suburbs. When Japan finally invaded China and the Chinese administered areas of Shanghai in 1937, construction virtually halted. By the time war had engulfed the rest of the world, Shanghai's physical character was set. From 1945 to 1949 Shanghai witnessed minimal development and thereafter became a Communist city.

At the time, Shanghai's housing stock comprised 72.5 per cent old and new style Li Long, 13.7 per cent temporary huts (in the outlying suburbs), 9.5 per cent garden houses and 4.3 per cent apartments. Communist land and property reform saw over 15,000 foreign properties surrendered and caused all public buildings and all housing to be nationalized in 1952 and 1954, respectively. In a similar time-frame, (1949–57), while Shanghai's population grew by 44 per cent from approximately 5 million to 7.2 million, housing standards "declined sharply . . . reaching intolerable levels" for many (Howe, 1981, p. 171).

CONTEMPORARY SHANGHAI: TOWARDS A GLOBAL CITY ARCHITECTURE

The lack of investment in and maintenance of Shanghai's physical fabric had the result of effectively suspending the city in space and time, a situation that changed rapidly following Deng Xiao Ping's visit in 1990. This provided a clear signal to the Municipal Government that it was time for Shanghai to rekindle its commercial spirit and proceed swiftly along with a select few cities that received favorable economic policies from the Central Government. Vital to this scheme was the re-development of the industrial district of Pudong, Shanghai's former backyard on the eastern bank of the Huangpu (see Figure 6.2).

However, while the plans for China's new financial hub in Pudong were being drafted, the policy towards the rest of the city resembled a gargantuan land auction whereby the right to build was granted to any developer willing to pay the right price. This policy met with little opposition early on, since the often appalling living conditions of those residing in Shanghai's lane houses, not only under-maintained for nearly half a century but also subdivided and occupied by multiple families, provided the ideal pretext for the subsequent demolition that has taken place. However, as the right to build on prime city-centre sites increased, so too did the opposition to this policy of seemingly unconstrained development. Residents started questioning and openly resisting the fragmentation of established communities that threatened to undermine the unique high-density, low-rise, multi-functional character of Shanghai. The developer's view, in contrast, was founded on the opinion that these residents are legitimate scapegoats, squatters even, since none technically owned the homes they occupied.

To put these scenarios into figures better illustrates the scale of change in just one and a half decades. In four years from 1993, the leases for 1,334 land parcels covering 78.4 million sq. meters were sold to developers. This coincided with, and was dependent on, large-scale relocations affecting 900,000 households, who were moved from the city's most desirable areas to the city's rapidly expanding margins. This process saw 4.3 million sq. meters of shabby and dilapidated houses razed. In return, the construction

Figure 6.2 The Pudong Financial District in the mid-2000s (Denison, 2008, p. 213)

of 16.2 million sq. meters of accommodation in the outlying districts, more than 'the total housing construction area in the first 30 years of the 'New China', nearly trebled the average individual space from under five sq. meters per person to 13.8 square meters by 2003.

While these transformations have fashioned a city that appears patently modern, futuristic even to many foreign observers, beneath the estimated 4,000 high-rises built in the last two decades and behind the abundant rhetoric that supports this giddy growth there are clear echoes from the past that, contrary to a prevailing trend, have helped to fuel discussions about crucial issues concerning the city's future: architectural preservation, sustainable urban development and property rights. As Shanghai stands at this potentially significant juncture, there is a strong sense of déjà vu as the city witnesses once again outdated buildings being demolished, old landmarks disappearing, new construction techniques and materials permitting taller structures, and a preponderance of foreign architectural influence.

Now, as in the past, questions are being increasingly asked about all of these issues, but while new construction is necessarily dependent on the demolition of old structures and while new technologies, materials and practices permit often very much larger structures, the range and extent of foreign influence in Shanghai, and more broadly throughout China, is a cause of growing deliberation. Unique cultural, economic and political pressures weigh heavily on China's architectural and urban development and cannot be easily resolved by anything less than an acute sensitivity to these problems; the antithesis to the foreign notion of China being a tabula rasa.

Since foreign attitudes to Chinese architecture have not yet returned to the elevated ground from which they fell swiftly and ignominiously after the 18th century, it is easy to see why 'from India and the West, China has received much architecturally but given little' (Jun, 1938, p. 410). Giving also requires receiving. As Dong Da You (1936, p. 358), an eminent Chinese architect before the Second World War and Government advisor to the major Shanghai Civic Centre project in the 1930s suggested: "Chinese architecture has never been considered important in the history of architecture, because it has developed independently and has exercised little, if any, influence on the main stream of architectural development outside China."

So it is in the 21st century, that architecture and urban planning policies in China remain largely foreign in nature and do little to resolve the escalating problems China faces as its cities grow and transform on a scale never before witnessed by humankind. With a few exceptions, rigorously marketed computer generated utopias that blanket whole areas of China's burgeoning cities necessarily erase history from their versions of reality because to include history with all its thorny complexity, these creations would appear instead as part of an evolutionary continuum that would make them far less laudable than the headlines suggest. Extolled in the black and white text of newspaper's pages, celebrated in the high gloss of architectural portfolios and in the kaleidoscopic color of weekend supplements and self-promoting trade journals, this new world of China that belongs exclusively to the third millennia more than echoes the eulogizing that took place in Shanghai's previous heyday when the Manhattan of the Far East's New Billion Dollar Skyline was proudly boasted to the world.

However, now, as then, the alleged architectural marvels appear viable, attractive even, only when shown out of context and viewed in pristine isolation. Just as [when] in the city's former prime [a haphazard] mob of smaller buildings [grew] behind Shanghai's celebrated river frontage, so too behind today's headlines can be found a different perhaps less savory story. In the real world, where cities appear as staggeringly complex entities whose fabric has been woven from countless human interventions, the image of China as an empty [landscape] or canvas for . . . innovation, exposes a very different picture; a picture all too often, perhaps expediently, overlooked yet one that reveals history in all its glorious, grubby and gritty detail, and one that is far the richer for it. It will be in this realm that the real solutions to China's myriad urban problems are tackled and solved and not in the virtual world of inaccessible mega-structures that come with the prerequisite architectural name tag municipalities demand.

As these massive problems become more acute, one can only hope that more municipalities heed another historical precedent and, in seeking solutions to these problems, look beyond the iconic building or showcase development and demonstrate the same confidence in their own architects that their forebears did when they extended exceptional opportunities to the likes of Lu Dong and may other young aspiring Chinese architects from the 1920s onwards.

QUESTIONS FOR DISCUSSION

1. In two or three paragraphs, discuss the main themes of Dennison's chapter.
2. In 1–2 pages, discuss what you think were the most relevant/interesting points Denison made about the connections between Shanghai's past and the modern-day city skyline.
3. Utilizing the 'Further Readings' and 'Helpful Web Links', list what you think were the three or four major forces driving Shanghai's growth from the late 20th century to the present. Then, in 2–3 pages, discuss how these factors influenced Shanghai's growth and changing urban architecture. Where possible, draw upon Friedmann, Sassen, and Derudder et al.'s discussion of World/Global Cities.
4. Utilizing the 'Further Readings', the 'Helpful Web Links', and other sources, conduct some further research on Shanghai and three other large cities in China. Then, in 2–3 pages, write up some of the most interesting facts you discovered about these cities and present your findings to your class.

FURTHER READINGS

Han, S. 2000. Shanghai between State and Market in Urban Transformation. *Urban Studies*, 37 (11): 2091–2112.

Wang, J., and S. Lau. 2009. Gentrification and Shanghai's New Middle-Class: Another Reflection on the Cultural Consumption Thesis. *Cities*, 26 (2): 57–66.

Wu, F. 2000. The Global and Local Dimensions of Place-Making: Remaking Shanghai as a World City. *Urban Studies*, 37 (8): 1359–1378.

Wu, W. 1999. City Profile: Shanghai. *Cities,* 16 (3): 207–216.

Yang, Y. and C. Chang. 2007. An Urban Regeneration Regime in China: A Case Study of Urban Redevelopment in Shanghai's Taipingqiao Area. *Urban Studies*, 44 (9): 1809–1826.

Zhang, L. 2003. Economic Development in Shanghai and the Role of the State. *Urban Studies*, 40 (8): 1549–1572.

HELPFUL WEB LINKS

Beijing, Government of. 2012. Beijing Official City Website International: eBeijing, the Official Website of the Beijing Government. Online. Available at: http://www.ebeijing.gov.cn/, last accessed, January 13, 2012.

China Internet Information Center. 2011. An Introduction to China's Provinces, Municipalities, and Autonomous Regions. Online. Available at: http://www.china.org.cn/english/features/ ProvinceView/164868.htm, last accessed, December 31, 2011.

Chongqing, Municipal Government of. 2012. Welcome to Chongqing, China. Online. Available at: http://english.cq.gov.cn/, last accessed, January 13, 2012.

Harbin, Government of. 2012. Official Website of Harbin, China. Online. Available at: http://www.harbin.gov.cn/english/, last accessed, January 13, 2012.

Nanjing, Government of. 2012. Official Website of Nanjing, China. Online. Available at: http://english.nanjing.gov.cn/, last accessed, January 13, 2012.

Shanghai, Municipal Government of. 2012a. Official Website of Shanghai, China. Online. Available at: http://www.shanghai.gov.cn/shanghai/node23919/node24025/index.html, last accessed, January 13, 2012.

Shanghai Baoshan District. 2012. Welcome to Baoshan. Online. Available at: http://english.baoshan.sh.cn/About_Baoshan/201005/t20100505_118477.html, last accessed, January 7, 2012.

Shantou, Government of. 2012. Official Website of Shantou, China. Online. Available at: http://english.shantou.gov.cn/, last accessed, January 13, 2012.

Tianjin, Municipal Government of. 2012. The People's Government of Tianjin City, China. Online. Available at: http://www.tj.gov.cn/english/, last accessed, January 13, 2012.

Wuhan, Municipal Government of. 2012. Official Website of Wuhan, China. Online. Available at: http://english.wh.gov.cn/, last accessed, January 13, 2012.

CHAPTER 7

Race, Space and the Post-Fordist Spatial Order of Johannesburg (2008)

Owen Crankshaw

INTRODUCTION

Johannesburg . . . is roughly divided into the northern neighborhoods, which are mostly White and middle-class, and the southern neighborhoods, which are mostly Black and working-class. The middle-class northern neighborhoods . . . have all the characteristics of an 'edge city' and the Black southern neighborhoods . . . are typical 'excluded ghettos'. In the 1970s, the northern neighborhoods could accurately have been described as suburbs, since they served an almost purely residential function. Today, however, they comprise large clusters of offices, shopping malls, manufacturing parks and recreation facilities in the form of cinemas, restaurants and sports centers. These areas have become

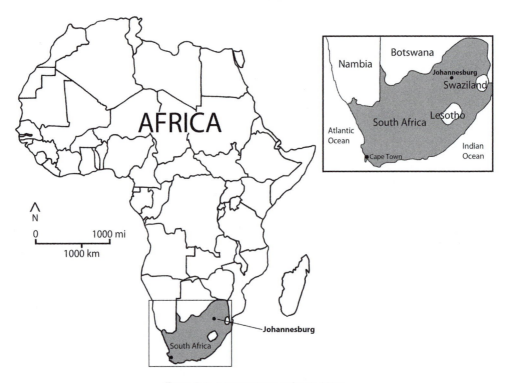

Figure 7.1 Johannesburg in South Africa

'totalized suburbs' in the sense that they now function independently of the central business district of the central city.

Indeed, one could say that the old city center has been eclipsed by the size of these edge city developments. Not only did the northern neighborhoods attract the lion's share of growing service-sector business, they were also the destination of choice for all kinds of businesses that abandoned the old city centre. In the south, the Black neighborhoods were created from the 1950s onward as racially segregated areas by the apartheid government. They were typical ghettos for working-class Blacks. However, the decline in manufacturing employment has transformed many of these Black neighborhoods into 'ghettos of exclusion' with extremely high unemployment levels.

During the apartheid period, edge city development in the northern neighborhoods reinforced racial and class segregation in Johannesburg. The difference with cities in the US, obviously, is that racial segregation was secured by government legislation rather than through discriminatory housing subsidies and title deed restrictions. The occupation of houses and apartments in the northern neighborhoods was restricted by the Group Areas Act for Whites only. The exception was the African neighborhood of Alexandra, which is located in the heart of the northern neighborhoods. . . . However, since the abolition of the Group Areas Act in 1991, Blacks have been free to live in the northern neighborhoods, if they can afford to do so. The extent to which Blacks have moved out of the ghettos to live in the northern neighborhoods will therefore be an indication, not only of the repeal of the Group Areas Act, but also of the extent of upward class mobility and increased wealth among Blacks. The question therefore is whether edge city development in Johannesburg will continue to exclude Blacks or not. Put differently, what are the post-Fordist spatial dynamics of race and class in a city such as Johannesburg, where Whites are the minority race?

Some authors argue that Johannesburg's post-apartheid spatial order is just as racially unequal as it was during apartheid. This study tests this argument by using the results of the 2001 population census to examine the extent to which edge city development in Johannesburg is characterized by racial residential desegregation. Its results show that the northern suburbs are undergoing fairly substantial desegregation. To the extent that this trend continues, the geography of apartheid racial divisions will be eroded and Johannesburg's racially mixed edge city will become an exception among world cities.

RACIAL POST-FORDISM: THE CHANGING SPATIAL ORDER OF JOHANNESBURG

The foundations for the division between the middle-class northern neighborhoods and the working-class southern neighborhoods were established during the decades immediately after the Second World War. During this period, the city experienced dramatic economic growth that was driven by both the manufacturing and service sectors. By this time, Johannesburg's gold mines were largely exhausted and employment here was in decline. Manufacturing and mining establishments were located on the south side of the central business district, in a strip running along an east-west axis (see Figure 7.2). This strip of industrial development followed the rail and road networks that linked them to the gold mines and industrial areas in the towns to the east and west. By contrast, most service-sector establishments had their offices and shops in the centre and northern flank of the central business district. These service-sector establishments included shops, entertainment venues, offices and government departments. By the end of the 1960s, these offices and shops had expanded northwards and taken over large areas of the erstwhile residential neighborhood of Braamfontein (Beavon, 2004).

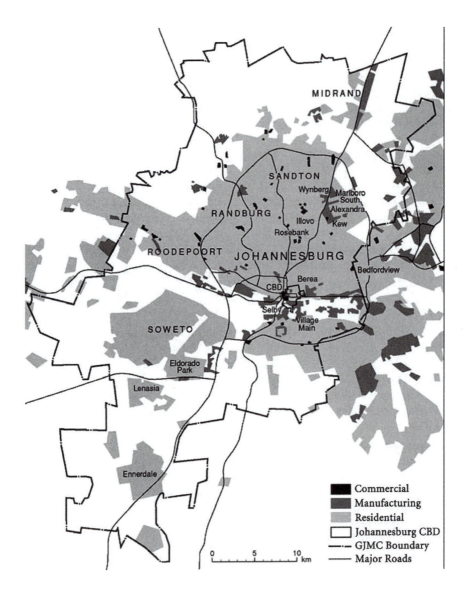

Figure 7.2 The post-Fordist geography of Johannesburg

Source: Crankshaw (2008, p. 1693)

Residential settlement patterns corresponded roughly with this north-south division between the manufacturing and service sectors. The population of the northern neighborhoods tended to be more middle-class, with higher percentages of residents who were managers and professionals (Hart, 1976a).

The residents of the southern neighborhoods tended to be working-class, with higher percentages of residents employed as artisans, semi-skilled machine operatives and in other manual occupations. How did this occupational class divide correspond to the racial divisions in Johannesburg? The middle class in the northern neighborhoods was exclusively White. The working class in the southern neighborhoods, by contrast, comprised both Blacks (Africans, Coloreds and Indians) and Whites. At this time, the races were residentially segregated by law. Whereas the White population lived in the neighborhoods to the east, the Black population lived in the neighborhoods to the west. The concentration of working-class Blacks in the southern neighborhoods was a direct result of apartheid policies that forcibly relocated Blacks from the inner city and suburbs in the north and west of Johannesburg to the new southern suburbs of Soweto, Eldorado Park and Lenasia (Crankshaw, 2005).

This phase of the apartheid period has aptly been described as "racial Fordism" (Gelb, 1991, p. 2). The apartheid government's policies at this time still aimed to prevent the growth of a Black middle class in Johannesburg. Policies and regulations that governed the employment, education and housing of Blacks, and Africans in particular, were therefore designed to ensure that Blacks were restricted to their role as cheap working-class labor in a system of mass production. Mass consumption was, in effect, reserved for the White middle class and skilled (artisanal and supervisory) working class.

The end of racial Fordism in Johannesburg can be said to have started with the decline of the manufacturing sector from about the mid-1970s. According to the population censuses, employment in the manufacturing sector fell from about 200,000 in 1980 to 110,000 in 2001 (Central Statistical Service, various years). By contrast, employment over the same period in the community, personal and social services sector grew from about 255,000 to about 267,000. Similarly, employment in the commercial sector grew from about 169,000 to 178,000 over the same period. Finally, employment in the financial intermediation, insurance, real estate and business services sector (FIRE) more than doubled from about 79,000 to 181,000 (GJMC, 1948–2001) . . .[1] By 2001, Johannesburg had a distinctly post-Fordist character, with the manufacturing sector contributing only 13 per cent to all employment. By contrast, tertiary-sector employment (commerce, FIRE, community, personal and social services) amounted to 73 per cent of all employment.

The 1970s also marked the start of Black upward mobility into jobs that were previously the preserve of Whites. The gradual desegregation of the national labor market was accompanied by reforms to racist legislation that governed both education and employment. By the end of the apartheid period, a sizeable Black middle class had therefore been established (Crankshaw, 1996, 1997). The rate of growth of this class has obviously accelerated during the post-apartheid period. In Johannesburg, the Black share of middle-class employment grew from 15 per cent in 1960 to 50 per cent in 2001 (see Table 7.1).

Unlike the other large metropolitan areas of Cape Town and Ethekwini (Durban), the Black middle class is mostly African, rather than Indian or Colored. In 2001, Africans

Table 7.1 The Changing Racial Composition of the Middle Class in Johannesburg, 1960–2001

	1960	1970	1980	1991	1996	2001
African	12	11	16	16	33	34
Colored	2	2	2	3	6	6
Indian	1	2	2	4	7	9
White	85	85	79	77	54	50
All races	100	100	100	100	100	100
All Blacks	15	15	21	23	46	50

Sources: Bureau of Statistics (1968); Central Statistical Service (various years); Department of Statistics (1976).

accounted for 69 per cent of Black middle-class employment in Johannesburg, as compared with only 46 per cent in Ethekwini and 20 per cent in Cape Town. These results suggest that Blacks have benefited from the growth of professional and managerial jobs that was driven by the expanding service sector. But has the growth of this Black middle class been associated with a racially segregated post-Fordist spatial order?

The deindustrialization of Johannesburg took a particular spatial form. In summary, the northern neighborhoods have become the effective new city centre with the lion's share of the growth of new office and retail developments while the old city centre has borne the brunt of the decline of the manufacturing sector. More specifically, this new post-Fordist spatial order was driven by two dynamics. The first dynamic was that both tertiary- and secondary-sector businesses favored locations in the 'edge cities' of the northern neighborhoods such as Rosebank, Randburg, Sandton and Midrand (again, see Figure 7.2). This meant that new companies have opened establishments in the northern neighborhoods and many established ones have relocated from the old city centre to the northern neighborhoods. The second is that, since most manufacturing establishments were once located near Johannesburg's central business district, the absolute decline in the number of manufacturing establishments was concentrated in the old city centre. From 1989 to 1999, almost half of all the factories in central Johannesburg closed down. By contrast, manufacturing employment in the northern neighborhoods actually doubled as a result of the establishment of 200 new factories, many of which had relocated from the CBD (Rogerson & Rogerson, 1997). As far as office developments were concerned, by the year 2000 there was twice as much office space in the northern neighborhoods as in the central business district (Beavon, 2004). Similarly, by 1999, the amount of shopping space in the large malls of the northern neighborhoods was almost double that of central Johannesburg.

Contemporary Johannesburg therefore has some of the characteristics of a post-Fordist spatial order. The northern neighborhoods meet the criteria of an edge city by: their independence from the old Johannesburg CBD through the 'totalizing' character of their combined residential, recreational, commercial and industrial activities; and, the middle-class and family character of their residents. However, the northern neighborhoods do not conform to Marcuse and van Kempen's (2000) model by being the preferred residential location of the business and political elite. These authors argue that the elite are to be found in the enclosed and protected high-rise 'citadels' in downtown, such as Battery Park in New York City. In contrast, Johannesburg's elite still prefer the neighborhoods near to the new edge city of Sandton. Instead of living in enclosed citadels, members of the elite tend to live in the new luxury walled communities (Harrison & Mabin, 2006; Jurgens & Gnad, 2002) that conform to Marcuse and Van Kempen's (2000, p. 254) concept of the 'exclusionary enclave'.

. . . The residents of the 'excluded ghettos' are working-class Blacks, comprising those who have been both discriminated against in the long term by apartheid legislation and who are also newly excluded from employment by the skill and spatial mismatch brought about by the decline of employment in the manufacturing sector and the generally slow employment growth across all sectors of the economy.

This post-Fordist spatial order has been described by some authors as possibly even more polarized than the racial Fordist order that characterized Johannesburg during high apartheid. There is some disagreement, however, on whether or not this post-Fordist spatial order is more racially equal than it was during high apartheid. Beall *et al.* (2002) have argued that, although the city is now more spatially unequal than before, racial segregation is probably in decline. Their reasoning is that during the late- and post-apartheid period, many middle-class Blacks, who were previously forced to live in the segregated Black southern neighborhoods, moved to live in the inner city and the northern neighborhoods. However, their evidence, based upon Crankshaw and White (1995), is restricted to studies of the inner-city neighborhoods and not the northern neighborhoods themselves. By contrast, contemporary Johannesburg has been described by Beavon (2004) as a 'neo-apartheid' city. His reasoning is that the White population of Johannesburg is still concentrated in the northern neighborhoods, precisely those neighborhoods that are characterized by the highest personal incomes, the best shopping facilities and the lion's share of office-based businesses and jobs. He further argues that, although there has been some residential desegregation of the formerly Whites-only neighborhoods, the percentage of African homeowners has remained extremely low.

Beavon's evidence comes from two sources. The first source is the 2001 population census, which shows that the northern neighborhoods are still dominated by Whites and that the overwhelming majority of Blacks still live in the erstwhile Black neighborhoods that are marginalized from the modern developments in Johannesburg. The second source is a study of property transactions between 1993 and 2000, which showed that only 3.3 per cent of all properties in the northern neighborhoods were purchased by Africans (Prinsloo & Cloete, 2002). This argument, that the post-apartheid period is characterized by persistent racial residential segregation, is also made by Christopher (2001, 2005). He has analyzed the population census data using a dissimilarity index to show that levels of desegregation in urban areas across the country have not declined.

This dispute therefore revolves around the extent to which the northern neighborhoods are becoming racially desegregated. However, both contributions to the debate have not provided adequate evidence on the social and racial character of residential desegregation in the northern neighborhoods of Johannesburg . . .

The debate between Beavon (2004) and Beall *et al.* (2002), over whether racial residential desegregation is eroding racial inequality in Johannesburg, also rests upon different ways of interpreting the evidence. There seem to be two elements to Beavon's interpretation of racial inequality. The first is that the concentration of the White population in the northern neighborhoods is itself a measure of inequality. In other words, in order for racial equality to be achieved, the White population would need to be proportionately distributed throughout the erstwhile Black neighborhoods of the northern and southern neighborhoods of Johannesburg. The second element of Beavon's argument is that the desegregation of the residential population is not an adequate indicator of racial equality. Instead, he argues that it is necessary to establish the number of Black property owners in the northern neighborhoods. . . . He concludes that there are "no real signs of a significant intermingling of races in the former older, whites-only, middle- and upper-class suburbs north of the Witwatersrand ridge" (Beavon, 2004, p. 267).

MEASURING RACIAL INEQUALITY IN JOHANNESBURG

To advance this debate, I have analyzed the 2001 population census data of all formerly Whites-only Johannesburg neighborhoods. The first aim of this analysis is to establish whether or not the northern neighborhoods continue to be the home of middle-class residents. The second aim of this analysis is to accurately measure the extent of residential desegregation in the formerly Whites-only neighborhoods and to measure the extent to which Blacks who have moved to these formerly Whites-only neighborhoods are equal to the Whites with respect to their housing tenure.

Measuring the social characteristics of residents in South African cities is complicated by the presence of live-in domestic workers. One of the contradictions of apartheid was that African domestic workers (housekeepers and gardeners) lived with their White employers in Whites-only neighborhoods. So, although Africans were forbidden by apartheid laws from occupying homes within Whites-only neighborhoods, African domestic workers were permitted to live in separate servants' rooms in Whites-only residential areas and still do so today. This phenomenon is a marked feature of Johannesburg, where most properties in middle-class neighborhoods have servants' rooms in their backyards (Hart, 1976b). Since the population census recorded all individuals at their place of residence, regardless of whether they were domestic workers or ratepayers, the census results therefore inflate both the number of working-class residents and the number of African residents in the formerly Whites-only neighborhoods.

The methodological problem, therefore, is how to exclude these African domestic workers from the data . . . I therefore had to rely upon the race and occupation variables to exclude live-in African domestic workers from the formerly Whites-only neighborhoods. One consequence of this method is that it measures residential desegregation in terms of the employed population. The unemployed and economically inactive residents are excluded.

Another advantage of this method is that it measures desegregation among a homogeneous group (the employed), which means that the estimate of desegregation is not shaped by racial differences in dependency ratios (reflected in the economically inactive population). Since Blacks living in the northern neighborhoods do have a higher unemployment rate than Whites, this method therefore underestimates the extent of residential desegregation.[2]

The following statistical analysis was restricted to the 379 formerly Whites-only residential neighborhoods of Johannesburg. Of these, 18 were designated as part of the inner-city belt, 301 were designated as the northern neighborhoods and 60 were designated as the southern neighborhoods. I have defined the northern neighborhoods as all the formerly Whites-only neighborhoods that lie to the north of Empire Road and Louis Botha Avenue. This list of formerly Whites-only neighborhoods has been carefully developed in order to exclude Black residents who are not living in homes that were built for White occupation. This was achieved through fieldwork and the analysis of dwelling types using the population census data. Neighborhoods that were excluded from the analysis included industrial areas with hostels for African workers, shack settlements occupied by Coloreds and Africans, and post-apartheid low-income housing developments occupied mostly by working-class Coloreds and Africans. The only exception was the suburb of Country View, which was a non-racial neighborhood established in 1990. This was one of the first non-racial areas to be established under the auspices of the Free Settlement Areas Act of 1989, only a few years before the abolition of the Group Areas Act. I have not excluded it from this study because of its middle-class and racially mixed character. Overall, my aim has been to avoid inflating the numbers of Black residents in the northern neighborhoods by including Blacks who are not living under the same conditions as the White middle class.

THE CLASS CHARACTER OF NORTHERN NEIGHBORHOOD RESIDENTS

In order to establish the extent to which the population of the northern neighborhoods is middle class, I have defined the middle class to include the occupational groups of managers and professionals. This definition therefore excludes all associate professional, technical, clerical and sales staff. The percentage that this middle class contributed to the total number of employed residents in each formerly Whites-only neighborhood was calculated and represented graphically using natural breaks in the percentage distribution. The results show a marked difference in the occupational class composition of the northern and southern neighborhoods. Whereas, all the neighborhoods with more than two-thirds of the population classified as middle-class are situated in the northern neighborhoods, none is to be found in the southern neighborhoods (Figure 7.3). Moreover, even within the northern neighborhoods, almost all these middle-class neighborhoods fall within a radial segment that centers on the Sandton CBD. These results therefore confirm the middle-class character of the edge city of the northern neighborhoods.

RACIAL RESIDENTIAL DESEGREGATION

To what extent are the houses and apartments of the northern neighborhoods still occupied by Whites? If we exclude African domestic workers from the data, the census results show that just over two-thirds (69 per cent) of the population of the northern neighborhoods was still White in 2001. One-fifth of the population was African. Coloreds and Indians made up the remaining 11 per cent in roughly equal proportions.

This estimate of the extent of residential desegregation will be higher than other estimates because it includes residents who live in all types of accommodation. This means that, in addition to the residents of houses and apartments, this estimate includes residents who live in backyard rooms, in rooms on a shared property or in communal facilities. Since a higher percentage of Africans (21 per cent) than of Whites (6 per cent) live in these kinds of accommodation, this estimate will include more Africans than other estimates.

Arguably, this first estimate does not represent true residential desegregation, since it is not a measure of the extent to which Blacks are living in the main house on the property. A second estimate, which includes only residents living in the main house on the property or in an apartment, gives a somewhat reduced level of desegregation. By this measure, 27 per cent of the population in the formerly Whites-only northern neighborhoods was Black in 2001. Africans comprise 16 per cent of this population and the percentage of Coloreds and Indians . . . 11 per cent (see Table 7.2).

These are the first precise estimates of the level of racial desegregation in the formerly Whites-only northern and southern neighborhoods of Johannesburg. Considering that Whites comprise only 16 per cent of the population of Johannesburg, these results confirm Beavon's argument that they are over-represented in the northern neighborhoods.[3] However, these results also support the argument that there has been significant change in the racial composition of residents in the northern neighborhoods. When we judge the rate of this change, we should bear in mind that the process of desegregation is dependent upon the natural turnover of residents

Table 7.2 Percent Racial Distribution of Residents of the Formerly Whites-only Townships in Johannesburg, 2001 (Only Residents Living in the Main House or Flat)

	Inner city	*Southern neighborhoods*	*Northern neighborhoods*	*Total*
Africans	88	28	16	30
Coloreds	3	11	4	5
Indians	3	9	7	7
Whites	5	52	72	58
Total	100	100	100	100

Source: Central Statistical Service (various years)

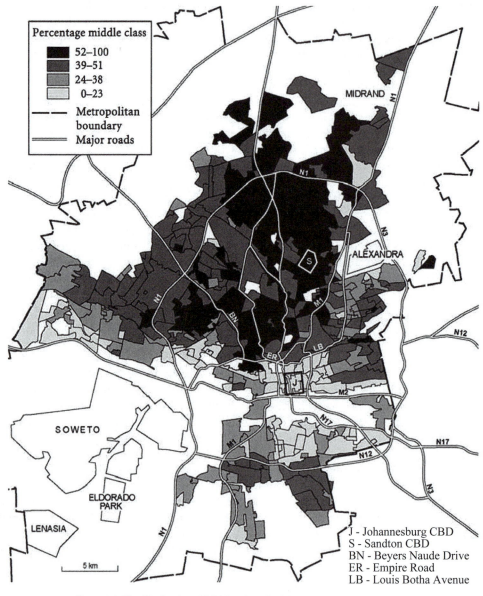

Figure 7.3 The Distribution of Middle-class Residents in Johannesburg, 2001

Source: Crankshaw (2008, p. 1702)

and that Black residence in these formerly Whites-only neighborhoods has been legal for only 10 years. On balance, I think that it is fair to say that this level of desegregation is too high to be described as 'low' or not 'significant' as suggested by Beavon.

The full significance of the level of residential desegregation in the northern neighborhoods only becomes apparent upon an analysis of its spatial character. . . . The results show that residential desegregation is not restricted to small pockets within the northern neighborhoods. It is true that high levels of desegregation (with more than 44 per cent of residents being Black) are clustered in neighborhoods that are adjacent to the inner city and the formerly Blacks-only neighborhoods of Eldorado Park, Lenasia, Soweto and Alexandra. It is also true that the southern neighborhoods are much more desegregated than the northern neighborhoods.

However, it is also true that neighborhoods with modest levels of de-segregation (with 15–44 per cent of residents being Black) are distributed throughout the northern neighborhoods. Over half (59 per cent) of all formerly Whites-only neighborhoods fall within this category. Only one-quarter (25 per cent) of neighborhoods have Black populations that comprise less than 15 per cent of all employed residents. This general pattern is much the same even if we restrict our analysis to the wealthier radial segment that lies to the east of Beyers Naude Drive. In this more middle-class area, 61 per cent of formerly Whites-only neighborhoods have modest levels of desegregation (with 15–44 per cent of employed residents being Black).

The spatial pattern of African residence in the formerly Whites-only neighborhoods is similar to the pattern for Blacks, but at lower levels of desegregation (see Figure 7.4). About two-thirds (64 per cent) of formerly Whites-only neighborhoods have low levels of desegregation (with 0–15 per cent of employed residents being African). One-third (34 per cent) are moderately desegregated (with 14–44 per cent of employed residents being African). In the remaining neighborhoods, 6 per cent of neighborhoods, more than 44 per cent of the employed residents are African. Nonetheless, the spatial pattern of desegregation is still a widespread one.

These results also reveal that there is no sign that White flight is resulting in the creation of new, mostly White, suburbs. Instead, White flight probably takes the form of emigration or migration to other cities. So, although the White response to racial residential desegregation may be the same as elsewhere, it takes a different form with different consequences for residential desegregation.

Residential desegregation does not indicate, on its own, complete equality between the races. A reasonable argument, proposed by Beavon, is that although residential desegregation is 'noticeable', evidence from the literature suggests that it is characterized by Black tenants rather than Black homeowners. Since the 2001 population census asked residents whether they rented or owned their accommodation, the census results can therefore be used to test this argument for *all* the formerly Whites-only neighborhoods in Johannesburg. Restricting the analysis to houses and apartments, the results show that over half (59 per cent) Black (African, Colored and Indian) residents in the northern neighborhoods own their accommodation (see Table 7.3)

The percentage of African homeowners in the northern neighborhoods is somewhat lower, at 42 per cent (see Table 7.4). Nonetheless, this is a substantially higher rate of African homeownership than the estimate of 3.3 per cent provided by Prinsloo and Cloete (2002). The discrepancy between these findings is due largely to Prinsloo and Cloete's sample, which is restricted to the more expensive of the northern neighborhoods and to house sales that took place from 1993 to 2000. . . . A possible explanation for this discrepancy is that African homeowners began buying homes and apartments before 1993. . . . If this is true, then the cumulative number of African homeowners would be higher than that measured over the period from 1993 to 2000. Another possible reason for these different estimates is that the population census was conducted one year later than their study—namely, in 2001.

These findings therefore demonstrate that the expansion of employment, shopping and recreational facilities in the edge city of Johannesburg's northern neighborhoods is increasingly being enjoyed by the growing

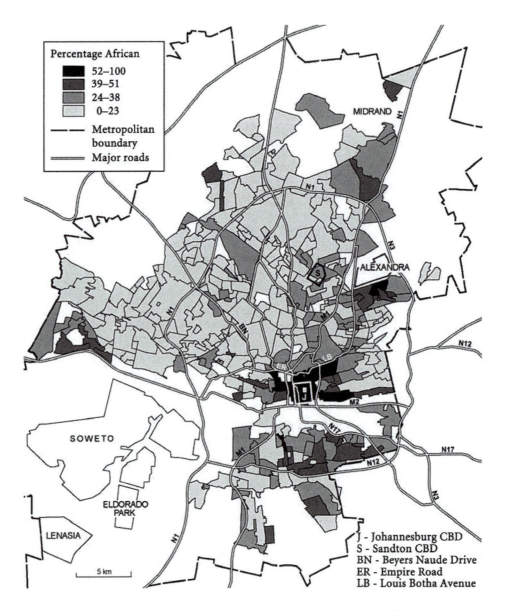

Figure 7.4 African Residential Patterns in Johannesburg's ex-Whites-only Suburbs, 2001

Source: Crankshaw (2008, p. 1705)

Black middle class. Although substantial residential desegregation is still a long way off, the process is well underway.

These results also raise the question of what social dynamics are driving residential desegregation in Johannesburg. Residential desegregation is proceeding at a faster rate in neighborhoods characterized by rental tenure rather than homeownership. This is probably due partly to the higher rate of turnover among tenants than among home-owners and partly to the fact that rental tenure is usually

Table 7.3 Tenure of Black Residents of House and Apartments in the Formerly Whites-only Townships of Johannesburg, 2001 (Only Residents Living in the Main House or Flat)

	Inner city	Southern neighborhoods	Northern neighborhoods	Total
Owned	11	65	59	42
Rented	88	32	34	54
Other	1	3	7	4
Total	100	100	100	100

Source: Central Statistical Service (various years)

Table 7.4 Tenure Status of African Residents of House and Apartments in the Formerly Whites-only Neighborhoods of Johannesburg, 2001 (Only Residents Living in the Main House or Flat)

	Inner city	Southern neighborhoods	Northern neighborhoods	Total
Owned	10	51	42	34
Rented	84	37	33	60
Other	6	12	25	6
Total	100	100	100	100

Source: Central Statistical Service (various years)

cheaper than homeownership (initially, at least) and does not require large savings.

On the basis that Black middle-class residents are, on average, younger, less qualified and earn less than their White counterparts, one would expect more of them to live in less expensive areas and where rental properties are found. This would explain the high levels of desegregation in the inner city and southern neighborhoods. There is also the question of choice. The results show that there are higher levels of desegregation in neighborhoods near to Blacks-only neighborhoods. Is this due to choice or is it a result of White flight due to the violent political turmoil of the 1990s? Finally, has there been any White resistance to residential desegregation that may have affected the pattern of desegregation? These questions present an interesting research agenda.

RACE, CLASS AND EDGE CITY DEVELOPMENT IN JOHANNESBURG

How does the racial and class character of edge city development in Johannesburg compare with cities elsewhere? In respect of its occupational class character, Johannes-

burg's edge city is quite typical with its predominantly middle-class residents. What sets Johannesburg apart from racially divided cities in the US, is the extent of residential desegregation in its edge city. In the US, the residential mobility of middle-class Blacks out of the ghettos has little impact on the overall racial composition of most edge cities. The main reason for this is that Blacks are still a small minority in most US cities. This is obviously not the case in Johannesburg, where Africans make up 74 per cent of the population and Blacks in general make up 84 per cent of the population. This majority status of Blacks means that, although they are underrepresented in the middle class in relative terms, by sheer weight of numbers they make up half of the managerial and professional middle class in Johannesburg. Since residential desegregation is being driven by the growth of the Black middle class, the extensive desegregation of formerly Whites-only neighborhoods is inevitable. This fact is often overlooked by scholars who have studied residential desegregation in racially divided cities. The post-Fordist spatial order of Johannesburg may be more unequal than its Fordist and apartheid past, but it is certainly less racially unequal.

Johannesburg differs from US cities in another important respect by having a single metropolitan government. This means that municipal policies to create a racially integrated edge city can be implemented. One of the policy goals of the South African government's Urban Development Framework is to undo the racial residential segregation of the apartheid era (Pieterse, 2003). Initiatives in Johannesburg have included new housing developments in the northern neighborhoods, such as Cosmo City and Jerusalem, that are aimed at providing homes for residents of all races with a range of incomes, from the very poor to the middle class (Dlamini, 2005, 2007; SACN, 2007). However, the size of these initiatives is unlikely to change the middle-class character of the northern neighborhoods.

CONCLUSION

The racial-Fordist spatial order of Johannesburg was characterized by both racial and class polarization. Whereas the southern neighborhoods tended to be occupied by working-class Blacks, the northern neighborhoods tended to be occupied by middle-class Whites. This research has attempted to measure the extent to which Johannesburg's post-Fordist spatial order is either entrenching this apartheid spatial order or eroding it. In class terms, it is probable that the post-Fordist period is even more spatially polarized than the racial-Fordist period. Without comparative data,

however, the extent of this change cannot be confirmed. What the results do show is that formerly Whites-only neighborhoods with a majority of managers and professionals are only found in the north and not in the south. To what extent is this class polarization still associated with race? The results show that the residents of the northern neighborhoods of Johannesburg are no longer exclusively White. There has been substantial desegregation by a Black middle class, just over half of whom are homeowners.

These results have interesting implications for the relationship between the post-Fordist spatial order and racial inequality in Johannesburg. They suggest that the racially exclusive character of middle-class neighborhoods is in widespread decline. If this trend continues, then the class division between the southern neighborhoods and the northern neighborhoods will not always be associated with a racial division. Such a racially mixed post-Fordist future would prove to be an exception in the world of global cities.

NOTES

1   The Greater Johannesburg Metropolitan Council (GJMC) is a relatively new metropolitan authority and includes the former local authorities of Johannesburg, Randburg, Roodepoort, Sandton and Soweto (again, see Figure 7.2). Since the boundaries of the GJMC are relatively new, data prior to 1996 was based on Magisterial Districts.

2   The unemployment rate in the northern suburbs was 18 per cent for Africans, 19 per cent for Coloreds, 7 per cent for Indians and 4 per cent for Whites.

3   This figure is calculated from the entire population and not just the employed workforce.

QUESTIONS FOR DISCUSSION

1. In two or three paragraphs, discuss the main themes of Crankshaw's chapter.
2. In 1–2 pages, use specific examples from the chapter to illustrate his main points.
3. From what you have just read and other articles/knowledge, list what do you think were the major forces driving Johannesburg changing post-Fordist spatial order.

> Then, in 2–3 pages, discuss how these factors, particularly race relations, influenced this change and whether or not Crankshaw's Johannesburg conforms to Friedmann's World City.
>
> 4. Utilizing the 'Further Readings', the 'Helpful Web Links', and other sources, conduct some further research on the Johannesburg and two other cities in South Africa. Then, in 2–3 pages, write up some of the most interesting facts you discovered about these cities and present your findings to your class.

FURTHER READINGS

Bremner, L. 2004. *Johannesburg: One City, Colliding Worlds*. Parktown: STE Publishers.

Crankshaw, O. 1997. *Race, Class and the Changing Division of Labour under Apartheid*. London: Routledge.

Crankshaw, O. 2005. Class, Race and Residence in Black Johannesburg, 1923–1970, *Journal of Historical Sociology*, 18 (4): 353–392.

Gaule, S. 2005. Alternating Currents of Power: From Colonial to Post-apartheid Spatial Patterns in Newtown, Johannesburg. *Urban Studies,* 42 (13): 2335–2361.

Parnell, S. and J. Robinson. 2006. Development and Urban Policy: Johannesburg's City Development Strategy. *Urban Studies,* 43 (2): 337–355.

Pirie, G. 2010. Trajectories of North—South City Inter-relations: Johannesburg and Cape Town, 1994–2007. *Urban Studies,* 47 (9): 1985–2002.

HELPFUL WEB LINKS

Buffalo City, Municipality of. 2012. Buffalo City Metro: The Official Website of Buffalo City Municipality, South Africa (includes the City of East London). Online. Available at: http://www.buffalocity.gov.za/, last accessed, January 13, 2012.

Cape Town, City of. 2012. City of Cape Town, South Africa Official Website. Online. Available at: http://www.capetown.gov.za/en/Pages/default.aspx, last accessed, January 13, 2012.

Ekurhuleni, City of. 2012. Ekurhuleni Metropolitan Municipality, South Africa. Online. Available at: http://www.ekurhuleni.gov.za/, last accessed, January 13, 2012.

eThekwini, Municipality of (Durban). 2012. Durban: The Official Website of the eThekwini Municipality, South Africa. Online. Available at: http://www.durban.gov.za/Pages/default.aspx, last accessed, January 13, 2012.

Johannesburg, City of. 2012. Official Website of the City of Johannesburg, South Africa. Online. Available at: http://www.joburg.org.za., last accessed, January 13, 2012.

Mangaung Metro Municipality. 2012. Home Page for Mangaung Metropolitan Municipality, South Africa (includes the City of Bloemfontein). Online. Available at: http://www.bloemfontein.co.za/last accessed, January 13, 2012.

Nelson Mandela Bay, Municipality of. 2012. Official Website of Nelson Mandela Bay Municipality, South Africa (includes the City of Port Elizabeth). Online. Available at: http://www.nelsonmandelabay.gov.za/, last accessed, January 13, 2012.

Nkangala District Municipality. 2012. Welcome to the Nkangala District Municipality, South Africa. Online. Available at: http://www.nkangaladm.org.za/, last accessed, January 13, 2012.

South African Cities Network. 2012. *South African Cities Network Newsletter*, Online. Available at: http://sacities.net/, last accessed, January 13, 2012.

Tshwane, City of. 2012. Welcome to the City of Tshwane, South Africa (includes the City of Pretoria). Online. Available at: http://www.tshwane.gov.za/Pages/default.aspx, last accessed, January 13, 2012.

CHAPTER 8

Global Dubai or *Dubaization* (2010)

Yasser Elsheshtawy

It is appropriate to look at Dubai's place in the world or, more tellingly, how Dubai sees itself globally (see Figure 8.1).

The Dubai phenomenon is part of an upheaval in the Arab region whereby the center of power has shifted to the Gulf states (GCC). Leading this 'revolution' is the city of Dubai. A variety of terms are beginning to describe this phenomenon: the Dubai model; Dubaization; Dubaification. The idea here is

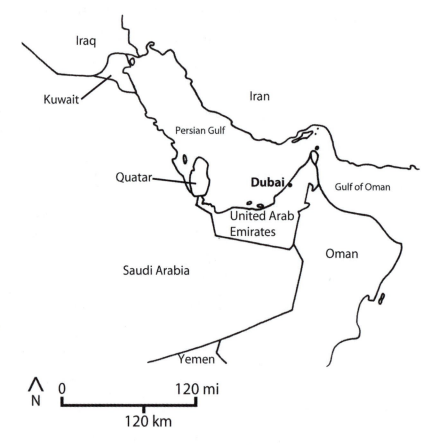

Figure 8.1 Dubai in the Gulf Region

to show that the mode of development taking place in the city is so unique and different from what has been taking place throughout thousands of years of urbanization that a new term needs to be invented. But, is there such a thing as a 'Dubai model'? And if it exists, is it desirable to export elsewhere—in other words, to what degree can this 'model' be replicated in other parts of the region? And how has the financial turmoil, which began as early as summer 2007 according to some reports, affected the perceived attractiveness of this model?

Sheikh Mohamed bin Rashid al Maktoum, Dubai's ruler, in a 2008 *Wall Street Journal* article, observed that Dubai is 'A big city like no other'. And while acknowledging that Dubai's 'ethos' is commerce, he was keen to highlight its multicultural, and tolerant nature: 'the ethos of Dubai was, and is, all about building bridges to the outside world; it was, and is, about creating connections with different cultures'. He points out that Dubai has no political ambitions. More recently and within the context of the global financial crisis, he rightly notes the degree to which it has become integrated into the global financial system—that any blow to Dubai would have serious repercussions in the region, because we live in a 'global village'.

But, there is a sense of difference, which is not just projected in official rhetoric but finds its way into the local media. Hardly a day passes without reports indicating the supremacy of Dubai over other Middle Eastern cities and its determination to join the ranks of leading world cities. But these do not just appear in the local media; international publications, such as *The Economist,* are filled with articles about the city, heralding the arrival of an Arabian tiger. But beyond such anecdotal evidence is there hard empirical data supporting Dubai's projected supremacy and success?

My aim in this chapter is to investigate these issues. To that effect it is divided into three parts: first I look at the 'Dubai model'

in detail, examining the rhetoric which has accompanied this term. My focus then shifts to a discussion of specific cases, to illustrate the degree to which this 'model' has been adopted both regionally in the Middle East as well as globally. A more detailed case study focusing on the city of Cairo follows this and concludes the chapter, where I question the focus on Dubai's megaprojects and suggest that potentially more useful lessons could be found by looking at the city's hidden spaces.

THE DUBAI MODEL?

I first introduced the term 'Dubaization' in 2004 during the International Association for the Study of Traditional Environments conference in Sharjah, in a paper discussing the influence of Dubai on Cairo, citing specific projects which I found to be inspired, directly or indirectly, by Dubai. I elaborated on this argument further during a workshop at the American University in Cairo and also during the International Union of Architects conference in Istanbul in 2005. These issues were further developed in two publications (Elsheshtawy, 2004, 2006). The dominance of Dubai during that time, and the proliferation of its megaprojects, made such a connection, however tenuous, very attractive. Yet since then the term itself—Dubaization— has been adapted and used in many discussions, papers and forums. An urban forum held in Panama defined Dubaization as 'the dense construction of high-rise buildings' in a discussion centring on the proliferation of these developments in Panama City. Energy experts in India decry the 'Dubaization' of its cities—equated here with the construction of what they call 'glass towers'.

While in these instances the term refers to locally initiated developments, on other occasions there is direct intervention from Dubai-based developers. In Istanbul, locals refer to the construction of luxury towers in the financial district of Levent (one is called Dubai Towers) as 'the Dubaification of

Istanbul'. In a similar vein, Asad Yawar discusses the extent to which Dubai-based entities are buying UK football stadia and sponsoring British teams. He observes that 'the economic vibrancy of Dubai has made such a strong impression globally that some are beginning to talk of a "Dubai model" that poor countries can leverage to catapult themselves into first-world levels of affluence'.

In some instances the term goes beyond the incursion of real estate companies and mega-developments to denote certain qualities—and it is here that it acquires a negative dimension. For many the word connotes fakedness and artificiality. For example, the demolition of an old playhouse building in New York is derided by preservationist groups because it only preserves the façade. One commentator argued that: 'They want the Dubaization and aggrandizement of NYU and nothing else' (Chan, 2008). An *Economist* article, titled 'Fake Parks: Dubai in America', discusses the construction of fake parks (developing activities which mimic nature in an artificial setting): 'Is America catching up with Dubai, home of desert skiing, the world's only seven-star hotel and other outlandish attractions?' (The Economist, 2006). Given these discursive representations of the Dubai phenomenon, how does Dubai see itself in all of this? How does it project its power, and are such depictions heralding the emergence of a hegemonic, empire-like status? In the following two sections, I discuss this in some detail.

Rhetoric: Debating the Dubai Moment

The notion of a Dubai model has been raised by local commentators and researcher. Chief among them is Abdul Khaleq Abdullah, a Dubai based political scientist who has written extensively about the virtue of this model—to the extent of noting that we are witnessing a 'Dubai moment'. He elaborated on this argument in a 2006 articles—written in Arabic—comparing Dubai to Tokyo, Shanghai, Singapore, Frankfurt, London and New York. He then observes.

> At this moment Dubai is the Arab city rushing forward to emphasize its global presence . . . Dubai has transformed into a model (Arabic: qudwa) city in the Arab region and has become a developmental, urban and population phenomenon, raising debate. (Abdullah, 2006a, p. 58)

And because of this, 'This is Dubai's moment in history . . . which she has waited for, for a long time' (ibid., p. 61). His argument is centered on the notion that Dubai is the most globally integrated city in the region and because of its success there will be some sort of Arab renaissance.

In aggressive and provocative language, he notes that whatever Dubai does or initiates becomes a source for emulation among its neighbors. He then applies the model theory to everything: Dubai has the model airport, model hotels, etc. Because of this 'Dubai moment' there is deep resentment among Arabs. He recognizes that the city is not a model in some aspects such as the population imbalance, loss of identity, exaggeration of its accomplishments, absence of transparency and proliferation of prostitution. In an insightful depiction, he notes the fleeting nature of this model:

> Dubai is building a new Arabian dream and no one knows for how long this will last. Especially since it is not supported by a solid foundation—through public participation, institutional development and social debates. Instead the city is administered through individuals, more as a company than a government. (ibid., p. 70)

Samir Amin, noted economist, in a robust rebuttal refutes the existence of such a model. Writing from a neo-Marxist perspective, essentially viewing the entire planet engulfed in what he has called elsewhere 'Americanization', he argues that regional powers, which would include Dubai, 'will not be allowed to have a margin of movement allowing them to become a center combining between financial and political power' (Amin, 2006, p. 159). This became evident when the Washington regime refused to allow the UAE to use its money to buy companies administering some US ports. What is acceptable, according to Amin, is for these monies to be put under US control, which in turn entails ownership rights: 'This is the limit that colonialists will not allow to be transgressed' (ibid., p. 159).

On the notion of Dubai being another Singapore, he argues that there are some similarities, for instance acting as a mediator for giant transnational firms. But Singapore contains productive activities which are conducted by these firms, whereas this is not the case in Dubai. And since this mediator—Dubai or Singapore—benefits financially from the situation, this does not give it the chance to be promoted to a 'new center', thus having the benefits of the real center, that is controlling decisions, and having complete control over capitalist ownership. And while Dubai is seeking to become a financial center, going beyond the 'oil economy' to become a 'local post-oil company', there are, according to Amin, limitations for such a system.

Amin thus argues that while there are certain aspects of global centers that exist in Dubai, political and economic limitations pertaining to 'American' hegemony more or less prevent the city from becoming a real center—which is only 'allowed' to happen in the financial capitals of the world—the triad: London, New York, and Tokyo. Yet clearly such a view could be disputed by many economists and political scientists. For instance, the emergence of BRIC economies (Brazil, Russia, Ireland, and China), as well as the recent global financial meltdown, indicate that the centers of power are shifting. This argument is also made by Abdul Khaleq Abdullah in responding to this rebuttal. He disputes Amin's notion of true centers, arguing that in the current globalizing condi-

tions there are no more absolute centers vs. those at the margin. New centers emerge all the time, and Dubai will become a center for a new region (Abdullah, 2006b). Moreover, he refutes Amin's example of the Dubai Port episode, which he suggests was a minor episode in Dubai World's global acquisitions and that in the case of the US the blockage of the deal was racially motivated.

Of course this whole debate about the supremacy or existence of a 'Dubai model' has not addressed its viability or sustainability. According to some critics the 'model' is neither sustainable nor should it be emulated as it is based on certain conditions which do not exist elsewhere. For instance, Asad Yawar (2006) discusses the limitations of the Dubai 'model'. He disputes the officially perpetrated vision/megaprojects version of the city and asks if 'Dubai [is] a realistic, or even a desirable, model for emulation'. He then enumerates a set of factors which show its unique situation: unique location as a port city; location in an oil-rich region; and proximity to the lucrative markets of Asia. The global economic condition prior to 2008 is an additional factor: 'Dubai is now awash with literally hundreds of billions of dollars in surplus funds from nearby Arabic- and Persian-speaking states that would in other times have found a home in New York or Zurich'.

Furthermore, he argues that there is a series of problems with the Dubai model that 'render it not just hard to copy, but potentially unmanageable'. There is no transfer of skills from expatriates to locals; business arrangements do not boost the indigenous skills base; the 'model' is 'contingent to an important degree on almost fantastical levels of exploitation of foreign labor at the lower levels of the economy' (he cites as an example the Burj Dubai project which he suggests is put together by labourers earning $4/day); lack of the possibility of citizenship (even for those born in the UAE) leads to lack of attachment—in times of financial hardship this could potentially lead to 'societal tumult.' Further, environmental feasibility is another problem—'the modern city has been designed as if global warming did not exist'.

Also, the city's developmental strategy based on cheap mass international transport could be thrown into disarray if there are rises in jet fuel prices.

Yet, in spite of all these criticisms directed at this particular mode of development, looking not just at the region but also globally, we can see that Dubai's developers have been active in perpetuating their urban development vision. In many instances, though, such incursions are encouraged by local governments and investors who are in the end motivated by profit.

Competitive Dubai

Going beyond the rhetoric—either for or against the model—reports and studies do in fact suggest that Dubai has surpassed its Middle Eastern neighbors. For example, the Arab World Competitiveness Report commissioned by the United Nations places the UAE (and/other Gulf cities) squarely ahead of Egypt, Algeria, and Lebanon, among others (Lopez-Claros and Schwab, 2005). Another study, developed by the consulting firm Ernst & Young, compares Dubai with Cairo and other cities, using various criteria that track favorable business environments. No surprise here, either: Dubai supersedes Cairo on all counts (e.g. infrastructure, telecommunications, regulatory environment, etc.) (MRG, 2003).

A recent Global City Index report released in 2008 by the Urban Land Institute (ULI) shows that London and New York still rank among the world's most successful cities, but face increasing competition from other global cities, according to an analysis of thirty major global indices and other data. Both cities—according to the report—face formidable challenges from global cities such as

Tokyo, Hong Kong, Paris, Shanghai, Dubai, and Mumbai (ULI, 2008). And there are, of course, many other indicators which seem to show that Dubai's distinctive status, particularly in the Middle East, finds some affirmation. For instance, the 2008 Global Cities Index developed by Foreign Policy, with A.T. Kearney and the Chicago Council on Global Affairs, using a broad range of indicators, has shown that Dubai ranks 27th among 60 cities included in the survey—the only other Middle Eastern city to come close is Cairo at 38 (Foreign Policy, 2008)

DUBAIZATION IN THE MIDDLE EAST

The phenomenon of spectacular developments based on the construction of megaprojects has engulfed the entire Middle East; it is not just relegated to Dubai anymore. In Saudi Arabia for example, Prince Fahd bin Sultan has begun construction of what is intended as a showcase for a new Saudi Arabia: a $300 billion multicultural metropolis designed to lure 700,000 inhabitants from around the globe. The construction of this and five other megacities scheduled for completion by 2020 will be funded by oil revenue.

Damascus is another example of a city reconfigured to cater for global capital and various investment interests. For instance, reports indicate that there are plans to bulldoze two ancient districts just outside the city's northern gates to build an eight-lane motorway flanked by high-rise blocks skirting the city. This has prompted some to argue that 'While Baghdad is being destroyed by war . . . are we to see Damascus destroyed by vested interests?' (The Economist, 2007, p. 35). Another report examines the recent boom in consumption in Syria due to the policies of Bashar Al-Assad's government, which has 'pushed economic development and private enterprise in an effort to make up for the loss of oil export'. This rush to consume is extending to almost all types of goods and services. New clothing shops, shopping centers, cafés and restaurants are opening daily. New hotels are being planned, especially in Damascus, which has only about five four- and five-star hotels compared with dozens in Beirut. Various Gulf conglomerates and development companies have allocated hundreds of millions of dollars to build shopping malls, hotels and residential complexes (Oweis, 2007).

In Khartoum, investors are coming from the Gulf, China, India, and Malaysia. To cater for this growing business, the government of Sudan approved a project to provide 'state-of-the-art' facilities for business executives. Called the Al Mogran Development Project, it is next to the Hilton Hotel and the Ministry of Investment, at the confluence of the 'White and Blue Niles, and is developed by Al Sunut Development Company Sudan's leading real estate firm. At an estimated cost of over $4 billion, it is spread over several thousand acres' (Marques, 2007, p. 9). Described by some as an effort 'to build a new Dubai' it consists of a vast complex of gleaming offices, duplexes and golf courses.

Opposite Al Mogran, on the Omdurman side, Saudi and Kuwaiti investors have bought a large plot of land on which they intend to build a huge financial center. Interestingly, Al Mogran is not the only huge construction site in Khartoum. About 15 km (9 miles) across the city the largest American embassy in Africa is going up, which will supposedly house the biggest CIA listening post outside America (El-Fasher, 2006).

In Istanbul, Sama Dubai, the real-estate arm of the state-owned Dubai Holding, is to develop a site in the city's business district, previously used as a bus stop, to build the previously mentioned Dubai Towers complex (WAM, 2007). And in Iraq, the President of the American Chamber of Commerce said that Dubai's economic model could be applied for every region in the country. This would include the building of an international airport and a $200 billion

investment arm in the Kurdish region (Aris, 2007)

Dubai's Emaar is developing the Zowara-Abou Kemash area on the Mediterranean coast near Tripoli, Libya. It is considered to be one of the largest projects in Emaar's portfolio (380 million square metres) (Gulf News, 2007).

In Algiers, reports indicated a multibillion dollar project to modernize part of its antiquated waterfront—but there are no concrete proposals yet. In Morocco, rules are streamlined and projects fast-tracked for the benefit of Gulf developers. These projects are not just restricted to Dubai-based investors. There is, for instance, the $350 million Mazagan Resort under construction south of Casablanca developed by Dubai World and an assortment of local and international investors and Qatar investors have launched a $600 million coastal complex of hotels, holiday homes and a golf course near Tangier in the north. In Tunisia, Emaar is developing Marina Al Qussor, a US$1.88 billion, 4.5 million-square-meter development of the country's eastern coastline. The deal was endorsed in 2007 by Tunisian legislators with particular emphasis placed on the jobs that would be created by the development, an interesting observation given the high unemployment rate in the country. Another project in Tunisia, called 'Century City', and described as a 'luxury real estate development', is proposed by Sama Dubai, at a value estimated around US$14 billion.

Inspired by Dubai: The Case of Amman

In Amman, the real estate industry is expanding significantly due to an influx of Iraqis as well as developments across a range of industries. Leading this growth is Mawared, a state-owned development and investment company. One of their key projects is Abdali carried out in partnership with the Hariri family and the Kuwaiti investment group Kipco.

Abdali will eventually become a fully functioning city center for Amman. The project is viewed as an anchor that will attract global business to Jordan. The case of this development in Amman is interesting here because it is modelled after the Solidere development in Beirut.

Rami Daher, an architectural scholar and practitioner in Amman, observes that the Abdali project is part of wider phenomenon in Amman, which includes a proliferation of mails and gated communities in addition to luxurious towers which represent a form of 'living above the city' (Daher, 2008). He notes that these transformations are part of what he calls neoliberal urban restructuring—a privatization of public space.

It is interesting to place this project in a wider context involving the city of Amman which is increasingly being demarcated along economic lines—a rich eastern area, site of the Abdali project and various upscale malls, and a poorer western part containing slums and refugee camps. Development efforts are increasingly geared towards the former. Daher makes an interesting point related to urban governance, namely the notion of resistance.

Resisting the Model: Beyond the Middle East

In the previous two sections I looked at the extent to which Dubai is either directly influencing or inspiring developments throughout the Middle East. But elsewhere in the world one can see a similar 'Dubaization' process. For instance in the UK, Dubai Ports World acquired a deal to develop a new port east of London which will help 'the UK compete with Rotterdam as a vital European distribution hub'. In India, Sama Dubai is planning to construct 'Smart City', envisioned as the largest business park in India and based on the Internet and Media City model in Dubai. There was strong local opposition to the project and as a result terms of the deal

were revised: Smart City is leasing the land for 99 years, as opposed to outright ownership. Such forms of resistance are rare and may offer a lesson for the Middle East. Similar objections have also accompanied the planning of a luxury resort in South Africa, on the grounds that it will displace local farmers.

The South African case is particularly interesting as it highlights the degree to which some of these proposals are clashing with local interests and raising issues that are not applicable in Dubai's *tabula-rasa*-like landscape. The project in question is called Amazulu World and is developed by Dubai based Ruwaad—a private developer, initially specializing in signage and branding. The project is described as being the largest leisure and shopping center in Africa and will include, among other things, a 106-metre high statue of a Zulu warrior king. The project was unveiled in 2008, but faced fierce opposition from local residents and farmers because of their planned relocation. Having occupied this land for generations, the area has cultural and religious qualities which would not exist elsewhere. Some critics liken the way in which the project has been portrayed to policies of forced settlements under the apartheid government. These objection are, however, not raised by a 'few people'—they number according to some reports, more than 10,000 families. Such insensitivities to local condition occur elsewhere. For example, at the level of retail, Emaar is planning to build India's largest mall basing its development on the Dubai Mall. There is no consideration at all for the appropriateness of constructing such provocative projects. But one cannot blame Emaar in this case: India has what is perhaps the only shopping mall in the world, in New Delhi, which charges its customers for entry to preserve its elite status!

These endeavors can thus be criticized on social grounds (intensifying existing social divisions; social inequity; displacement), but they also seem to commodity cultural symbols and as such are also a threat to the local culture. This is not the fault of Dubai of course, because local players are more than happy to appropriate their cultural heritage to maximize profit. Some of the projects which I have reviewed use regional elements (the gates of Damascus), apply them to unexpected contexts (entry to a gated community), and add other stylistic elements (arches, decorations, etc.), thus reworking the symbolism or imagery of the original and creating a new image. This new image, in turn, becomes in itself a point of reference, a Debordian spectacle.

While Dubai claims that it is nonpolitical in its outlook, the mere fact that all these interventions are taking place and the degree to which they create economic and cultural situations that many would construe as problematic seems to undermine the political neutrality claim.

The mere act of intervention and development is political.

THE IT CAPITAL OF THE MIDDLE EAST

In 1999 Sheikh Muhammad bin Rashid announced the creation of an IT center called Dubai Internet City (DIC). A year later, with landscaping and high rises as its finishing touches, the project was complete, and has since then become an unqualified success. Occupied by big names in the IT industry, it has made Dubai the IT hub of the region. Comprised of a series of office buildings overlooking an artificial lake and lush gardens, the center is located adjacent to Sheikh Zayed Road. One is led through a gate designed to reflect a traditional wind tower, on to a series of screens with 'Islamic' motifs, and then to a sequence of glass buildings such as one might find in any high-tech park in Malaysia or Silicon Valley. Although entry is free to anyone (provided they have a car), a protective fence surrounds the devel-

opment. Located nearby is Media City, a project similar to Internet City, although in this case the occupants are from the media industry. This 'city' also comprises office blocks set in an artificial landscape. It houses studios and newsrooms and has become a regional center for media companies such as Reuters, CNN, MBC, and others. The anonymity of the office blocks in both these 'cities', which are distinguished only by the logo of their respective inhabitants, seems to highlight the fact that they operate primarily on a regional and global level, in some way disconnected from the surrounding reality.

CONCLUSION: THE TRUE DUBAI MODEL

The flight from Cairo or Beirut to the Gulf states takes only a couple of hours, and in that time the traveler is transported to what might as well be a different planet. He leaves behind a world of decay and dulled tones and steps into one of glitter and dazzle. (Lamb, 2002, p. 34)

The above is reflective of a popular viewpoint propagated by journalists and casual observers. Thomas Friedman, for example, proclaims in all seriousness that 'Dubai is precisely the sort of decent, modernizing model we should be trying to nurture in the Arab-Muslim world' (Friedman, 2006). Lee Smith, another journalist, compares Dubai to Baghdad during its Abbasid heyday, since the city has reincarnated the ideals of this ancient capital—openness, tolerance and curiosity. Furthermore, he declares that the 'Dubai model suggests how the Arab world might revive its historical role as a trade and communications center'. In that way 'the Arab world itself becomes a free zone, embracing not only liberal economic policies and new media technologies but eventually political and social reforms'. Finally 'what's good for Dubai may in turn be good for the Arab world' (Smith,

2006). The city, according to these view-points, should thus be groomed to become the center for a new Middle East, molded in the image of neoliberal agenda makers.

Along similar lines Ashfin Molavi (2007) argues that key 'caravan posts' on the new Silk Road are regional economic 'winners' or rising stars: Dubai, Beijing, Mumbai, Chennai, Tokyo, Doha, Kuala Lumpur, Singapore, Hong Kong, Riyadh, Shanghai, Abu Dhabi. The old Silk Road civilization centers such as Persia (Iran), the Levant (Lebanon, Syria, Jordan) and Mesopotamia (Iraq) lag behind. Thus ' *Dubai, it might be argued, is the unofficial Middle East capital of the new Silk Road*—a gathering place of capital, ideas and traders fueling the growth—and Iran, once a central force, is the sick man, albeit with enormous potential' (my emphasis).

Dubai is seemingly becoming a center of, and model for, urbanism in the Arab world. Furthermore, a number of events suggest that Dubai is becoming the center of a 'new' Middle East. Other cities are influenced as well. Some observers have noted that Beirut has been overshadowed by Dubai, which has in effect assumed the Lebanese capital's previous mantle as a 'gateway to the East' (Champion, 2004). The recent wars in Lebanon, particularly the Israeli offensive of 2006, only strengthen Dubai's position. The influence is not, however, restricted to traditional Middle Eastern centers, as I have argued in this chapter, but extends to Gulf cities as well. Qatar is at the present constructing an island named 'the Pearl,' which is modelled on the Palm Islands in Dubai. Similar developments are occurring in Kuwait (City of Silk) and in Muscat (The Blue City).

Dubai has thus become, for better or worse, a model for cities throughout the Arab world. But, and this is a critical question, is there any harm in this? It could be argued that such intensification of social divisions, caused by adapting Gulf-based modes of

urbanism may lead to a sense of injustice and hence may drive some residents towards acts of resistance.

I am not suggesting that there is a direct correlation between terrorism and Emaar constructing megaprojects in Cairo and other cities. But places like Dubai lend themselves to this kind of *tabula-rasa* development—and thus are quite successful for (almost) everyone. 'Everyone' here would refer primarily to the city's high-income population, investors, an assortment of tourists and world, millionaires. The global financial crisis has, however, questioned even this degree of success. Of more concern is the juxtaposition of slums with luxury developments which is not yet as characteristic of Dubai as it is of Amman and, especially, of Cairo. Megaprojects and enclaves of the 'new Dubai'-type are, nevertheless, inherently rife with *explosive* socio-political issues.

But does Dubai's 'mode of development' offer anything positive, any potential lessons? It may be more useful to argue that Dubai is a model for the Arab world not through its megaprojects, but because it accommodates multiple nationalities, a fact that may contribute to its unique response to globalizing condition. The discourse on Dubai typically ignores these spaces by focusing instead on the megaproject. However, as I noted, a form of informal unbanity is emerging which caters for a largely migrant and transient community. These new citizens of the global economy—one might call them 'the foot soldiers of globalization'—appropriate such public setting by connecting to the local while at the same time maintaining ties to their homelands. In that way vibrant settings are created in which one finds an intermingling of different nationalities supported by the structure of the built environment. This is—in my view—the true 'Dubai model' where the rest of the 'dysfunctional' and 'crumbling' Middle East may find some useful lessons.

QUESTIONS FOR DISCUSSION

1. In two or three paragraphs, discuss the main themes of Elsheshtawy's chapter.
2. In 1–2 pages, use specific examples from the chapter to illustrate Elsheshtawy's main points.
3. From what you have just read and other articles/knowledge, list what you think were the major forces driving Dubai's growth in the late 20th century and into the present. Then, in about one page, discuss how each of these factor influenced Dubai's growth.
4. Utilizing the 'Further Reading', the 'Helpful Web Links', and other sources, conduct some further research on Dubai and some other cities in the Islamic World. Then, in 2–3 pages, explain what Elsheshtawy means by 'Dubaization' by offering some examples of this phenomenon in other cities.

FURTHER READINGS

Elsheshtawy, Y., ed. 2004. *Planning Middle Cities: An Urban Kaleidoscope.* New York: Routledge.

Elsheshtawy, Y., ed. 2008a. *The Evolving Arab City: Tradition, Modernity and Urban Development.* New York: Routledge.

Elsheshtawy, Y., ed. 2009b. *The Superlative City Dubai and the Urban Condition in the Early Twenty-First Century.* Cambridge, MA: Harvard University Press.

Elsheshtawy, Y. 2010. *Dubai: Behind an Urban Spectacle.* New York: Routledge.

Marchal, R. 2005. Dubai: Global City and Transnational Hub. In M. Al-Rasheed, ed., *Transnational Connections and the Arab Gulf.* London: Routledge.

Smith, M. P. 2001. *Transnational Urbanism: Locating Globalization.* Malden, MA: Blackwell.

HELPFUL WEB LINKS

Abu Dhabi City, Municipality of. 2012. Welcome to the Municipality of Abu Dhabi City. Online. Available, at: http://www.adm.ae/en/home/index.aspx, last accessed, January 12, 2012.

Casablanca. City of: 2012. Grand Casablanca's Official Website. Portal for Region of Casablanca, Morocco. Online. Available at: http://www.casablanca.ma/index/portal/media-type/html/user/anon/page/entrepreneurEn.psml?noteid=3023, last accessed, January 11, 2012.

Doha, City of. 2012. Welcome to Doha City, Qatar. Online. Available at: http://dohacityqatar.com/home.php, last accessed, January 12, 2012.

Dubai, Government of. 2012. Dubai Municipality Portal, United Arab Emirates (UAE), Available at: http://www.dm.gov.ae/wps/portal/MyHomeEn, last accessed, January 12, 2012.

Greater Amman Municipality. 2012. Home Page of Amman, Jordan. Online. Available at: http://www.ammancity.gov.jo/en/gam/index.asp, last accessed, January 12, 2012.

Istanbul Metropolitan Municipality. 2012. Home Page of the Istanbul Metropolitan Municipality, Turkey. Online. Available at: http://www.ibb.gov.tr/en-US/Pages/Home.aspx, last accessed, January 12, 2012.

Karachi, City of, 2012. City District Government of Karachi, Pakistan. Online. Available at: http://www.karachicity.gov.pk/, last accessed, January 12, 2012.

Persian Gulf.org. 2012. Welcome to the Persian Gulf: Cities of the Persian Gulf. Online. Available at: http://www.thepersiangulf.org/cities/, last accessed, January 12, 2012.

Riyadh, City of. 2012. Website of Riyadh City, Saudi Arabia. Online. Available at: http://www.arriyadh.com/eng/, last accessed, January 11, 2012.

Tunis. City of. 2012. Portal of Tunis City, Tunisia. Online. Available at: http://www.commune-tunis.gov.tn/publish/content/default.asp?lang=:=en#, last accessed, January 11, 2012.

PART 2

Nested City-Regions

Nested City-Regions: An Overview

A.J. Jacobs

Part Two: Nested City-Regions presents readings which fit within the urban theoretical paradigm known as *nested city theory*. Although perhaps currently best known for their critiques of the *world/global city hypothesis*, led by Richard Child Hill and Kuniko Fujita, 'city' scholars subscribing to this perspective maintain that city-regions have remained tightly embedded or nested within their particular national and local development contexts (see, for example, Hill & Fujita, 2003; Fujita, 2011). In other words, they contend that national and local factors have remained the foremost determinants of urban/metropolitan growth patterns.

Although a number of 19th century scholars, such as List (1966 [1885]), supplied similar theories regarding national development, Max Weber is generally regarded as the father of embeddedness scholarship, even in regards to the study of cities (Martindale, 1958; Jacobs, 2006). In his 'Concepts and Categories of the City,' Weber (1958, 1978) examined the forces driving growth in cities of the world and devised a four-category model which grouped cities based upon a series of contextual factors (e.g., their geographical location, infrastructure, politico-economic elite, mixture of firms, and labor-force skills).

In Weber's *Producer Cities,* population and economic capacity expanded in these areas as a result of them being the site of large factories, small manufacturers, or home–work industries. Income was then generated through the sale of these manufacturers to local entrepreneurs, workers, craftsman, and merchants, and/or through exports to outside territories. Weber offered the German cities of Essen and Bochum as examples of *Producer Cities*. Other past and contemporary examples might include the cities of Manchester, Detroit, Ulsan, and Toyota.

In *Merchant Cities*, Weber stated that economic growth was driven by commercial trade. He said such cities frequently were home to large multinational trading houses and/or joint stock corporations, and flourished due to their locations at major trans-loading points, where principal modes of transportation intersected. According to Weber, the major European seaports of London, Paris, Berlin, and Dusseldorf, where shipping and railyards were conjoined, represented prototypical examples of *Merchant Cities*. Today's New York and Frankfurt would fit this category.

For Weber, *Consumer* or *Rentier Cities* were those dependent upon the investment activities of the national government and/or *rentiers* (e.g., large private, aristocratic, and/or feudal landowners). As such, the economic opportunities and incomes of residents in these cities were derived from their providing of services, either directly or indirectly, to the national bureaucracy and/or *rentiers* and others attached to them. Although any national capital might conform to this grouping, for Weber (1978, p. 1215), "an example of a city of [national] officials might be Peking [Beijing], with an example of a city of land-rent consumers, Moscow, before the abolition of serfdom." Tokyo, Paris, and London are past and present examples of *Rentier Cities*.

Weber did not give any examples for his *Agrarian Cities*. He did state, however, that these cities were urban settlements with market centers based upon the production of food/agriculture for local consumption and export. If cities whose economies were driven by extraction of resources and the energy sector were included, most of the cities in the Canadian and American prairies, such as Edmonton, Calgary, Saskatoon, Omaha, Tulsa, and Houston, among others, might be contemporary representations of this category.

A second important influence on the development of *nested city theory* was Jane Jacobs. In her books *The Economy of Cities* (1969) and *Cities and the Wealth of Nations* (1984), she described the many embedded factors provoking economic growth in certain areas and decline or stagnation in others. She argued that geographical location, such as the existence of a deep harbor, local industrial mix (diverse or over-concentrated) and labor-force skills, were some of the factors predicting urban growth trajectories. She loosely grouped the world's city-regions into five categories. She stated that *growth cities* were those which expanded as a result of multiplier effects induced by their firms' exports to other places. Conversely, *supply regions* were those shaped by the market activities of other distant cities. Third, *transplant regions* were areas without their own native industries, but which attracted factories from other cities. Next, she said, there were *backward cities*, or areas in lesser developed nations whose economies were dependent upon imports from core growth cities. Finally, there were *bypassed places*, or those declining settlements which had been forgotten or abandoned by modern capitalism.

While Jane Jacobs discussed the impacts of embedded factors, the central place theorist Richard Preston (1978), in his 'The Structure of Central Place Systems,' was one of the first to use the term *nested hierarchies* in reference to city development. For Preston, nestedness described the functional interdependency among municipalities within nations. Peter Dicken, (2011) in the six editions of his book *Global Shift*, has regularly utilized the term 'embedded' to describe the varying local and national contexts for industrial development. Claiming that the state was not 'dead,' he concluded that national government policies still greatly influenced the geographic location of manufacturing production. Similarly, and drawing directly upon Weber, Ted Gurr and Desmond King (1987) in their book *State and the City* also maintained that the nation and local states have remained primary actors in the promotion and economic decline of urban areas.

Another important contribution to *nested city theory* has come from Ash Amin and Nigel Thrift (1994, 1995) in their writings on what they called *institutional thickness*. For these authors, whereas institutional embeddedness referred to the complex institutional interrelationships situated within national and sub-national contexts, institutional thickness represented "a plethora of institutions of different kinds, all or some of which can provide a basis for the growth of particular local practices and collective representations" (Amin & Thrift, 1994, p. 14). They claimed that city economic success was highly dependent upon the ability of local and supra-local officials to cultivate institutional thickness and utilize it to positively support local firms and markets. They concluded that capital cities and core metropolitan areas were "clearly types of localities which can derive competitive advantage from the presence of many institutions of governance in economic, political, and cultural life" (Amin & Thrift, 1995, p. 105).

As mentioned, however, over the past 20 years *nested city theory*, proposed by Hill and Fujita, and supported by their former students from Michigan State University (MSU), has served as the primary counter and sometimes foil to the *world city hypothesis* (see Hill & Kim, 2001; Friedmann, 2001; Sassen, 2001). While Hill and Kim's (2000) article 'Global Cities and Developmental States: New York, Tokyo, and Seoul' has been the most frequently cited, the framework for the 'MSU School of Urbanism' began to take shape in Hill's (1987, 1989, 1990a, 1990b) comparative studies of automotive production regions in the USA and Japan.[1] Thereafter, Hill and Fujita gradually incorporated theories of national developmentalism and embeddedness into their work. Their ideas were complemented by a growing number of non-MSU scholarly works advocating similar positions, such as those by Chris Pickvance and Edmond Preteceille (1991), Takashi Machimura (1992, 1998), Ann Markusen (Markusen & Park, 1993; Markusen & Gwiasda, 1994) and Abu-Lughod (1995, 1999).[2] This culminated in the official naming of the theory by Hill and Fujita in their introductory article to their 2003 special issue of *Urban Studies*, which they entitled 'The Nested City: Introduction.'[3]

Recognizing the significance of their work, Chapter 9, the first of the eight readings in Part Two: Nested City-Regions, presents Hill and Fujita's seminal 'The Nested City' article, which outlines the basic suppositions in their theory. In the reading, the authors reject the claims of *world city* scholars that: (1) global forces have de-territorialized cities from their national contexts; and (2) contemporary global capitalism has provoked the convergence of the world's major cities (i.e., the loss of their uniqueness, related to their levels of social diversity, economic inequality, and other social problems). Rather, they argue that while it is true that global forces are expanding their influence relative to other scales, they "are not the decisive determinants of urban form and functioning" (p. 207).

Next, they claim that city growth trajectories and identities continue to be "stamped both from the inside and outside," with public and private sector actors from all spatial tiers (the global, supranational-regional, national, state/provincial, metropolitan, municipal, neighborhood, household, family, and the individual) exerting influence over it (p. 208). In addition, they maintain that globalization and embeddedness are not mutually exclusive: "Globalization does not entail convergence. [On the contrary,] growing interdependence in the global whole is perfectly consistent with differentiation within" and among all spatial tiers of the world system (p. 212). Finally, they critique *world city theory* in general by stating that: "Because cities are nested in diverse national and regional configurations, the implications of globalization for urban life cannot be deduced from any structural or market deterministic logic; they must be ascertained through comparative study of cities in their nested configurations" (p. 213). They conclude by asserting that such analyses clearly show that nation-states have retained their centrality, and that metropolitan areas continue to follow their own unique development models, evolving within their own particular, nested national and sub-national, historical, geographical, institutional, and cultural contexts.

Following Hill and Fujita, Part Two offers seven case study readings from a relevant cross-section of city-regions in the North America and East and Southeast Asia. The selections are heavy on Asia, as urban scholars studying cities in that part of the world have been the most frequent adherents to *nested city theory*.

Chapter 10 provides an edited selection from pp. 1–4 and 399–426 of Janet L. Abu-Lughod's (1999) aforementioned book, *New York, Chicago, Los Angeles: America's Global Cities*. Here, Abu-Lughod's presents her main concepts and conclusions from her in-depth study of America's three largest city-regions. Similar to Hill and Fujita, she emphasizes the importance of comparative urban research, and how such studies allow us to more clearly discern how historical variations in geography, politics, and inter-group relations, among other factors, have fostered differentiation in local development contexts and outcomes. In the process, she rejects the *world city* convergence argument, stating that despite being in the same nation, New York, Chicago, and Los Angeles are very different places. She says their unique geographic settings, transport technology, inter-city links, politics, and inter-group relations, among others factors, have produced three divergent physical and social terrains.

More specifically, she claims that Chicago's location in the American Midwest, its manufacturing base, its proportionately lower and less diverse levels of immigration, and its historical political machine, have made its ideological, economic, and inter-racial context very different from that in the gateway cities of New York and Los Angeles. Similarly, New York's eastern seaboard location has created a different development environment than in Los Angeles, situated on the West Coast and in relative close in proximity to Mexico. These terrains then have interacted with, and have been influenced by, international forces in distinctly different ways.

Chapter 11, 'Race, Fragmentation, and Divergent Outcomes in Detroit and Toronto,' represents a condensed and edited version of my own previously published *Journal of Urban Affairs* article, 'Embedded Contrasts in Race, Municipal Fragmentation, and Planning: Divergent Outcomes in the Detroit and Greater Toronto-Hamilton Regions 1990–2000' (Jacobs, 2009b). In this reading, I compare post-1990 growth trends in the Detroit and Greater Toronto Area-Hamilton Regions (GTAH), two areas within the same natural geographic region and closely linked by industrial production flows, yet politically situated within separate federalist states. Drawing upon census data and field interviews, I reveal how variations in: (1) inter-racial-ethnic relations, including immigration; (2) municipal fragmentation; and (3) multi-jurisdictional planning, especially at the state/provincial level, have foster divergent spatial patterns in the two regions. I conclude that whereas the Detroit Region's development context has provoked a now five-decade population and economic decline in the City of Detroit, the GTAH's embeddedness has helped to prevent the depopulation of, and wide-scale disinvestment in, its central city, Toronto (and to a relative degree in its second core, the City of Hamilton).

Chapter 12, 'Planning Taipei,' presents an edited selection from Chia-Huang Wang's (2006) *Town Planning Review* article, 'Planning Taipei: Nodal Status, Strategic Planning and Mode of Governance.' Wang, also a former student of Richard Child Hill, presents a case study of Taipei, which he calls "a secondary world city within the semi-periphery" (p. 283). Utilizing what he calls a "bottom-up approach, in contrast to the top-down one prevalent in research on the world-city system," he explores how Taipei's primacy in Taiwan's urban hierarchy and national politics has influenced local strategic planning and governance. He claims that Taipei's national-local mode of governance has set the context that has enabled, constrained, and conditioned the city's strategic planning actions and responses to global forces. He concludes that Taiwan provides a prime example of how world cities have remained embedded in nested politico-economic structures, and how these local structures "represent the interactions between a world city's actions and responses, contextual settings and globalizing forces" (p. 283). He closes suggesting that his bottom up framework can be applied not only to the study of Taipei, but also in conducting comparative analyses of other world city-regions.

Chapter 13, 'Expanding Income Stratification in the Tokyo Region,' builds upon the ideas and techniques discussed in a handful of my previously published articles on Japanese cities and/or Tokyo.[4] I begin the chapter by investigating whether or not income stratification by municipal place has expanded in the Tokyo Metropolitan Region (TMR) over the past 30 years. I then reveal evidence suggesting that while income inequality has increased noticeably within the TMR, its levels remain much less severe than that in America's three largest metropolitan areas, New York, Los Angeles, and Chicago. Next, I review some of the factors explaining the TMR's rise in stratification, namely, the area's declining industrial employment, expanding income inequality nation-wide, falling land prices in central Tokyo, and the waterfront redevelopment policies of the Tokyo Metropolitan Government. Lastly, I discuss how Tokyo's unique racial-ethnic context and the municipal merger policies of Japanese Government were two of the many factors helping to keep the TMR's level of income inequality far below that in America's largest urban regions.

Chapter 14, 'Experiencing Jakarta,' supplies an edited selection from Chapters 2, 3, 5, and 7 of Chris Silver's (2008) book *Planning the Megacity: Jakarta in the Twentieth Century*. The reading begins by briefly examining Jakarta's history as a colonial capital in the Dutch Empire. Silver then discusses the historical influence of overseas Chinese in the city, which began in the in 19th century. Next, he reviews the city's explosive population growth between 1931 and 1971, especially since 1948, as the capital city of the independent nation, Indonesia. Thereafter, he chronicles how the policies of the national government, under President Suharto, sought to further expand, revitalize, and restructure the central city and its surrounding urban fringe, in an effort to transform Jakarta into a global city. The result, he shows, has been a steady outflow of people from the inner city to new suburbs. The reading concludes with Silver's planning vision for the Jakarta's future in the 21st century, and his description of some of the challenges it faces.

Chapter 15, 'Actor Networks and Hybrid Developmental States: Malaysia's Multimedia Super-corridor and New York City's Silicon Alley,' offers an edited selection from Michael Indergaard's (2003), *Urban Studies* article 'The Webs They Weave: Malaysia's Multimedia Super-corridor and New York City's Silicon Alley.' Guided by *actor-network theory*, Indergaard compares the embedded forces driving the creation of, and inter-workings within, the digital districts in the two areas. He argues that whereas venture capitalists brought together a myriad of entrepreneurs in New York, the Malaysian national state took the lead role in the development of the multimedia super-corridor (MSC). He then demonstrates how the Malaysian state devised a comprehensive plan and utilized various devices, including recruiting venture capitalists, in their efforts to make their massive project a reality. He concludes by suggesting that Malaysia's development approach represents a hybrid model, weaving in elements of both developmentalism and neo-liberalism. In the interim, he introduces to the scholarship an expanded version of his mentor Hill's *nested city theory,* one that contains a new third category, which he calls *developmental hybrid states*. He states that this grouping represents a middle position between the typical binary neo-liberal and state-led dichotomy. The research conducted for this article would form the foundation for a book, *Silicon Alley: The Rise and Fall of a New Media District* (2004), and influence Indergaard's research on New York for a decade thereafter.[5]

In the final reading in Part Two, Chapter 16, 'Ulsan: South Korea's *Great Industrial City*,' I chronicle some of the forces driving the transformation of the port city of Ulsan from a fishing village into the home of the world's largest auto production complex, most expansive shipyard, and second biggest petrochemicals combine.[6] Through the case of Ulsan, I introduce the concept of the *great industrial city*, which I define as large urban conurbations with manufacturing sector(s) that have become highly influential, even dominant, internationally. In the process, I seek to: (1) remind scholars and practitioners about the continued importance of industrial cities for national economies and in global capitalism; (2) enhance the English language knowledge of South Korean urban areas; and (3) demonstrate how the world's city-regions have been decisively shaped by both international and embedded/nested forces, with no one level having primacy. I close by encouraging scholars to more seriously consider industrial regions when delineating the global urban hierarchy, and thereby, to expand the *world/global-nested city* debate beyond merely analyzing large financial centers.

NOTES

1   A sampling of articles advancing or critiquing *nested city theory* published by Dr. Hill's former MSU Sociology-Urban Studies students include Hill & Kim (2000, 2001); Indergaard (2003); Wang (2003, 2006, 2007), and Jacobs (2002, 2003b, 2009b, 2009c, 2011a, 2011b), not to mention those by Dr. Fujita, who also originally was a Ph.D. student of Hill's at MSU.

2   Some other more recent important critiques of *global city theory* have included Machimura (2003), Ho (2003), Olds & Yeung (2004), and Therborn (2011). Markusen also received her Ph.D. from MSU during Hill's tenure in that university's Sociology Department and Urban Affairs Program, but in Economics.

3   Prime examples of this include: Fujita (1991, 2000); Hill (1996, 2004); Fujita & Hill, (1993, 1997, 1998); and Hill & Fujita (1995, 2000, 2003). Hill & Fujita and their protégées frequently have drawn upon the developmental state and embeddedness theories of Polanyi (1957 [1944]), Johnson (1982), Gurr & King (1987), Huber (1994), Evans (1995), and Hollingsworth & Boyer (1997).

4   See for example, Jacobs (2003a, 2004, 2005, 2006, 2008, 2012).

5   See for example, Indergaard (2002, 2004, 2009, 2011) and Tillman & Indergaard (2008).

6   Earlier version of this chapter was published in *The Open Studies Journal* (Jacobs, 2011b). The Chapter 16 version was greatly condensed, edited, and contains updated data in the text and in Tables 16.1 and 16.5, and a entirely new table, Table 16.2.

CHAPTER 9

The Nested City (2003)

Richard Child Hill and Kuniko Fujita

The papers in this Special Issue of *Urban Studies* were originally prepared for presentation at an international conference on "City, State and Region in a Global Order" held in Hiroshima, Japan, in December 1998. Conference organisers were sceptical about claims that globalisation was forcing convergence in social patterns among the world's major cities: for example, the thesis that New York, London and Tokyo are converging on a global city model that transcends national and regional location (Sassen, 1991; Taylor 1995), or the claim that Los Angeles' 'postmodern' institutional and spatial mix models the future world metropolis (Soja, 1989; Miller, 2000), The re-appearance of convergence theories seemed particularly egregious when viewed from the vantage-point of great cities in highly urbanised, non-Western regions of the world, like Pacific Asia.

The world's major cities are, indeed, key participants in the globalisation process: providing infrastructure and expertise that enable corporations to co-ordinate and control their far-flung activities, serving as prime sites for incoming and outgoing foreign investment, and operating as central nodes for the international transmission of all kinds of information. But is it valid to draw inferences about a city's economic base, spatial organisation and social structure from these 'global' facts alone?

Cities are embedded in multilevel spatial and institutional configuration. Those con-figurations are changing and the global level is taking on added weight relative to other scales of organisation. But global variables are not the 'decisive' determinants of urban form and functioning. The whole multilevel configuration in which the city is nested, including, most especially, the nation-state and region of the world, must be taken into account. The studies presented in these pages leave no doubt as to the continued importance of nation and region in east Asian urban development and they point the way towards a richer and more nuanced programme of Comparative, multilevel, urban research. In this respect, this Special Issue of *Urban Studies* joins the recent turn towards variation, contradiction and complexity in globalisation studies (Hay and Marsh, 2000).

COMPLEXITY'S ARCHITECTURE

We are accustomed to thinking of hierarchy as top down control, the relationship of vertical command. But hierarchy has a second meaning in the social sciences: the nesting of parts within larger wholes, the relationship of levels. In us superior—subordinate meaning, hierarchy is one among many possible forms of human relationship. In its nested meaning, hierarchy is a natural aspect of all forms of complex organisation.

In a nested hierarchy, parts and wholes are not subordinated one to the other. Rather, the relationship is one of energetic tension, and is constantly changing to meet new situations. Nestedness is a duality: everything is both part and whole, both cause and effect, both separate from and dependent upon other entities. Neither part nor whole can fully account for human interaction. Instead, the self-contradiction must be juggled. Human societies are intrinsically multilevel systems but the number of levels, and the relative autonomy and power of entities at each level change through history. Cities occupy an intermediate scale in human societies today. Cities are bounded by entities with wider sweep: subnational regions, nation-states, transnational regions, the world. And cities bound entities of lesser scope: neighbourhoods, households, families, the individual. A city's identity is stamped both from the inside and from the outside; it is *a part of and apart from* other levels of human organisation.

Levels of society are bound together through various means. Economic integration occurs through markets, corporate hierarchies, states, networks and associations political integration through intergovernmental relations, negotiated rules and norms, political parties and the courts; cultural integration through shared memories, ideologies, values, the popular arts and habitual ways of doing things. But since entities at each societal level are also relatively autonomous and path-dependent, there is considerable variation, from one area of the world to another, in the content and mix of institutions that co-ordinate human behaviour. A capitalist system of production, for example, combines "industrial relations, worker and managerial training, corporate structures, interfirm relations, finance, beliefs about distributive justice, state policies, laws and morality". But real-life capitalist political economies "vary in the ways firms approach profits, measure efficiency, consider social peace and egalitarian distribution, emphasise quantity versus quality of production, and innovated" (Hollingsworth and Boyer, 1997, p. 2).

Established hierarchies can break down when societies experience prolonged bursts of uncertainty. During most of the 20th century, the world centred upon relatively independent nation-states embedded in multilevel systems with substantial differences in economic, political and cultural institutions. But in recent decades, the centrality of the nation-state has been challenged by deregulation, the expansion of market ideology and computer mediated communication networks.

Hollingsworth and Boyer (1997) envision a 'double movement', global and subnational, eroding the power of the nation-state today. A nation's power is constrained from above by increased global competition, the expansion of supranational rules of the game and greater integration with other nations in trade, finance, production and services National power is constrained from below by regional and community networks better able to nurture trust and 'tacit knowledge' than national-scale organisations. The challenge from above is exemplified by alliances among multinational corporations operating in different countries. The challenge from below is indicated by the proliferation of local networks of small firms sustained by neo-corporatist social contracts and local-government-sponsored Infrastructure, research and development, training and education policies. Institutions operating primarily at the national level during the post-war era are now dispersing to multiple spatial levels, Hollingsworth and Boyer, conclude. Today's actors perforce find themselves nested in institutional arrangements "linked at all levels of reality" (Hollingsworth and Boyer, 1997, p. 472).

NATION-STATES

The weakening of the nation-state should not be exaggerated, however. Paradoxically, the global forces challenging the nation-state are themselves contingent upon the nation-state.

As Ignatieff (1993) has so powerfully demonstrated national belonging continues to override other methods of unity. Belonging is first and foremost protection from violence and, without the protection, of a nation-state, no other form of belonging is secure. In fact, Ignatieff argues, the cosmopolitanism of the world's great cities depends upon the rule-enforcing capacities of their national governments. Belonging also means being recognised and understood, and national identity based upon language, land and history, still far outweighs global cosmopolitanism in the collective psyche.

The nation-state remains the ultimate locus of legitimate authority and global markets depend upon the legitimacy of national political regimes (Pauly, 1997). Markets cannot regulate themselves. The norms and rates required for mutually beneficial exchange necessitate intricate political negotiations among nation-states. International markets are intrinsically intertwined with domestic polities in these negotiations because states cannot open their markets unless they can also manage the domestic consequences of doing so. When international collaboration fails to deliver national prosperity, citizens question why they must acquiesce in decisions reached beyond their borders and they look to their national political authorities for the answers. Economic globalisation is thus conditioned upon political accommodations within and among nation-states.

Powerful nations attempt to create international regimes that favour their own firms and industries. Each would-be-hegemon would have competitor countries cast their productive systems in its image. International financial integration, for example, is not the automatic outcome of an unhindered market; it has been advanced by the US during the post-World-War-II era, and reflects a US-led "balancing of many nations' interests" (Pauly, 1997, pp. 131–132). And, as Louis Pauly farther remonstrates

All the work of central bankers, bank supervisors, and accounting standards come to naught if the central organs of government responsible for macro economic policy in powerful states move in different directions. Such a movement would crack the foundations of 'global' finance and no superior force exists to fix it. (Pauly, 1997, pp. 131–132)

The cross-border activities of multinational corporations (MNCs) continue to depend upon national institutions. Doremus *et al.* (1998) remind us that MNCs must be chartered by nation-states, and nation-states continue to shape corporate operating environments and retain the political authority to steer corporate activities. The authors' comparative study of MNCs based in the US, Japan and Germany demonstrates that national politics and culture continue to shape how these business goliaths govern themselves, approach long-term financing, programme research and development, invest abroad and trade with other firms. We are still a long way from a "world where gigantic corporations are truly global and where the state is in retreat", their study concludes. Rather,

The overarching story is one of increasing economic openness in national economies and deepening integration across dynamic markets—all conditioned and ultimately constrained by the extent to which still divergent national governing structures can accommodate themselves to one another. (Doremus *et al.*, p. 141)

WORLD REGIONS

The emerging global order is not a single system superimposed on a collection of withering nation-states. Global trade, production and financial networks are tied into different regional and national variants of capitalism (Stallings, 1995; Dore *et al.*, 1999). The contrast between the American influence in the Western hemisphere and Japanese influence in east Asia is particularly sharp. The American model advocates a drastic scaling back of state participation in the economy, decreased trade protections and openness to all types of foreign capital. The Japanese model, while promoting some privatisation and liberalisation, is based upon collaboration between government and private sector and a tradition of 'developmental slate' activism (Johnson, 1982; Hatch and Yamamura, 1996).

The neo-classical explanation of the 'east Asian miracle' (World Bank, 1993) is based upon the market-driven global convergence view: East Asian newly industrialising countries (EA-NICs) grew so rapidly because they conformed to the Washington model and adopted rational, market-oriented policies, But in fact, Japan and the EA-NICs took a quite different, state activist route to development. East Asian states strategically influenced the flow of investment to create dynamic comparative advantage (Amsden, 1989; Berger and Dore 1996)

East Asia's 'four tigers'—South Korea, Taiwan, Hong Kong and Singapore—have all profited by association with Japan's rise to economic prominence and by privileged access to Japanese finance. All four nations have mounted successful export-oriented development strategies. All four have managed to upgrade incrementally their products. And all four have become big foreign investors themselves. South-east Asian nations are following the east Asia tigers in a 'flying geese' formation. They were the primary beneficiaries of Japanese direct foreign investment (DFI) after the 1985 Plaza Accord and then DFI from Korea, Taiwan, Hong Kong and Singapore, and are now firmly bound into east Asian production and trade networks (Kojima, 2000).

As we would expect from the nested hierarchy principle, south-east Asian nations are connected to but also apart from their north-east Asian neighbours. There is much greater ethnic, cultural and religious diversity in south-east than in north-east Asia. Straddling sea trading routes between China and India,

south-east Asian countries have traditionally had a more outward economic orientation than nations in the north-east. South-east Asian Chinese family-based companies have developed their own horizontally integrated conglomerates alongside the vertically integrated, regional division of labour and are extending their agribusiness, tourism, banking and property development activities into neighbouring countries Singapore's government-linked corporations (GLCs) are building airports and seaports in Vietnam, Cambodia and Laos and providing management expertise in civil aviation, ports administration, telecommunications, public housing, health care and urban planning.

Japan and the EA-NICs ran into difficulties in the 1990s, partly due to their own past successes. Growth in production stimulated the diffusion of domestic manufacturing abroad and created competitive opportunities for less developed countries in the region Success in international trade triggered US protectionism to reduce the American trade deficit. Capital mobility punctured the wall the EA-NICs had erected between their domestic capital markets and foreign investors to enable national economic management and planning.

The EA-NICs responded with a strategy of 'managed openness' (Cowley and Aronson, 1993). They moved towards economic liberalism but they did so within the developmental state tradition. EA-NIC states facilitated the globalisation strategies of national firms by helping to finance their foreign acquisitions, mergers and factories. They targeted overseas assistance to infrastructure projects designed to complement their national firms' overseas investment and trade. They only slowly opened up to foreign investment, placed limits on foreign stock ownership in domestic companies and continued to stress long-term gain over short-term profit. They orchestrated national industrial upgrading by opening to foreign investors in the technically most advanced sectors, by channelling outside investment into strategic sectors to enhance the capability of local firms, by using government procurement to induce strategic alliances between TNCs and local firms, by funding research on the use of critical technologies and by setting up semi-public firms to commercialise prototype manufacturing technologies developed in state research labs. In short, the rationale for state intervention has changed, but the state continues to guide economic restructuring.

Restructuring triggered a wave of DFI from the EA-NICs to south-east Asia and China. Bilateral trade and production networks among the EA-NICs and between the EA-NICS and China have grown dramatically. The percentage of EA-NIC exports going to the Asia-Pacific region has ballooned with a corresponding contraction in exports to the US. Trade within industries is outpacing trade between industries, drawing the east Asian region closer to the European Union model Pacific Asia is now a collection of dynamic growth zones in which complex production and distribution networks link local firms co sub-regional metropoles and, through them, to regional and world markets.

WORLD CITIES

Globalists believe that national political authorities

> are increasingly relegated to the role of adapting themselves, as well as the societies over which they have receding control, to the convergent logic of market rationality, a worldwide division of labor and integrated technology base, all unified by corporations that owe allegiance to no state. (Doremus *et al.*, 1998, p. 138)

The globalist viewpoint permeates the literature on world cities. Saskia Sassen (1999, p. 86) for example, claims that globalisation produces a world city system that transcends national institutions, politics and culture. Becoming a global finance centre, she

argues, means abandoning national ties and embracing supranational alliances. Structural changes occurring within the city, John Friedmann (1986, p. 318) hypothesizes, are now decisively determined by "the form and extent of a city's integration with the world economy and the functions assigned to the city in the new spatial division of labor". In short, globalisation produces a convergence in the economic base, spatial organisation and social structure of cities, corresponding to the functional role a city plays in the globalisation process and the level a city occupies in the international division of labour (Friedmann, 1986, p. 318; Sassen, 1991, p. 4).

The nested hierarchy principle suggests an alternative hypothesis. Because cities are lodged within an interdependent world order divided among differently organised regional formations and national systems, the economic base, spatial organisation and social structure of the world's major cities are determined by the entire multi-level configuration—global niche, regional formation, national development model local historical context—in which each city participates. Globalisation does not entail convergence. Growing interdependence in the global whole is perfectly consistent with differentiation *within and between* regional, national and city levels of the system. As constituent elements of the global order, cities both facilitate the globalisation process and follow their own, relatively autonomous, trajectories.

World capitalism does not conform to one overarching model. Regionally differentiated and nationally anchored capitalisms co-exist and compete. Evidence from the US, Germany and Japan does not suggest that differences in core national patterns of corporate structure and strategy are eroding substantially as a single global system of industrial enterprise and technological innovation emerges (Doremus *et al.*, 1998, p. 142). Countries are attempting to open their markets to foreign competition *and* pursue national and regional industrial policies simultaneously. The institutional scope of the nation-state may be contracting, but national passions still take precedence over global cosmopolitanism in the collective psyche and economic globalisation continues to depend upon political accommodations within and among nation-states.

An evolutionary rather than a convergent vision of urban change is compelling. Rather than becoming more alike in economic base, spatial organisation and social structure under circumstances of global competition and transnational organisation, the world's major cities are evolving in various ways depending upon social and political context and historical timing. Different systems of production can be equally competitive in world markets. Path-dependence among complementary institutions makes convergence among cities lodged in different world regions and nation-states unlikely. Economic globalisation generates a political backlash when market dynamics encroach too corrosively on national identities and safety-nets.

NESTED CITIES

National institutional arrangements are more dependent on international and sub-national forces today than at any time in the postwar era. The centrality of the nation-state remains, however, even as the coordinating institutions at various spatial levels recombine into new configurations (Brenner 1999a). While interdependence among nations has grown continuously in the past two decades, the world political economy does not operate according to a single unifying mechanism, be it market co-ordination or anything else. While there is arguably a single global system, there are many globalisations. Social systems co-exist like limbs and branches on a tree, in multi-level configurations.

New York and Tokyo, for example, participate in the same global order but their nested configurations in the world system are markedly different. The implications of globalisation for a city derive from the entire multilevel configuration in which the city participates. The state plays a more directly activist role in Tokyo's configuration than in New York's, for example. Tokyo's institutional mechanisms for global co-ordination and control centre in slate bureaus as contrasted with private producer service networks in New York. Globalisation triggered massive deindustrialisation and class polarisation in New York but not in Tokyo (Hill and Kim, 2000). Tokyo's neighbouring cities in the Asia-Pacific region, like Taipei and Singapore are closer to Tokyo's trajectory than to New York's. London. New York's cousin in the West Atlantic region, looks more like New York than like Tokyo, Taipei or Singapore, But at the same times New York, London, Tokyo, Taipei and Singapore are each following there own distinctive paths.

Because cities are nested in diverse national and regional configurations, the implication of globalisation for urban life cannot be deduced from any structural or market deterministic logic: they must be ascertained through the comparative study of cities in *their nested configurations*. Tokyo for example, is nested in relationships with the Tokyo metropolitan government, the Kanto region, Japan's unitary and developmental state, an east Asian region characterised by a distinctive 'flying geese' division of labour and a Confucian heritage. New York City has nested ties of an entirely different political and cultural sort—to the state of New York, the north-eastern US, the American federalist and regulatory state and the West Atlantic region.

Each scale contributes to the form and definition of urban life. But nested configurations are not complete hierarchies, like a set of Chinese boxes: they are partial hierarchies, organised like a tree, McDonald's 'Golden Arch' is a global brand image shared by the company's franchises worldwide; but McDonald's in Norway serves salmon burgers, a national variation absent in other countries; and McDonald's in Beijing is a hangout for the elderly, a striking contrast to McDonald's clientele in wealthier, less space-starved societies.

Nation-states and cities do not simply 'filter' or 'mediate' global functions. Causality runs back and forth among levels of society. Interaction creates new configurations. The interplay among regional national and local institutions can lead cities to globalise differently. There is no single authority at any level with the power to monitor and regulate the whole system. We live in a world of unprecedented complexity (Hollingsworth and Boyer, 1997)

THE STATE AND URBAN DEVELOPMENT IN EAST ASIA

The papers in this *Urban Studies* Special Issue on "Nested Cities: The State and Urban Development in East Asia" confirm the value of analysing cities in relation to the multilevel systems in which they are nested.

Peter Marcotullio ("Globalisation, Urban Form and Environmental Conditions in Asia-Pacific Cities") highlights the distinctiveness of urbanisation in Pacific Asia. The region's major cities are interlinked through state-sponsored transport and communication infrastructure into an urban coastal corridor stretching from Tokyo to Jakarta. In Marcotullio's telling, the great cities of Pacific Asia are both converging and diverging in urban form. They are converging as a consequence of globalisation-induced economic integration. They are diverging according to the varied roles they play in the regional division of labour and according to their specific environmental conditions, national institutions and public policies (Marcotullio, 2003).

Kuniko Fujita ("Neo-industrial Tokyo") explains how differences in national regulatory systems in Japan and the US result in quite different world city trajectories in Tokyo and New York. She especially emphasises how Japan's developmental state has shaped Tokyo's urban pattern. The strength of local industrial districts in Japan, for example, does not come at the expense of national power; on the contrary, Tokyo's small business networks are firmly embedded in a national innovation infrastructure. But while causality runs from Japan's central state down to Tokyo's metropolitan government (TMG), if runs up levels, as well. The TMG has initiated 'strategic globalisation' policies, for example, and Fujita also shows how Tokyo's world city development is connected to Pacific Asia's 'flying geese' regional division of labour (Fujita, 2003).

Asato Saito ("Global City Formation in Capitalist Developmental State: Tokyo and the Waterfront Sub-centre Project") presents a closer look at the involvement of the Japanese state in Tokyo's world city trajectory. By capitalist developmental state, Saito means political-economic co-ordination through a non-partisan bureaucracy, administrative guidance and society consensus on the authority, indeed, the duty, of national officials to intervene in the economy, The Tokyo Waterfront Sub-centre development is a 'flagship project' for global city creation, a means to promote the concentration of command-and-control functions in Tokyo (Saito, 2003).

In Saito's telling, the global city is a project of the nation-state in Japan and Tokyo is first and foremost a national champion. The national government defined the project's basic policy direction through the Fourth National Development Plan. The TMG manages the project as landlord and developer. The substantive content of the project was decided through political give and take between the central government and the TMG. The private sector came on board only after the state had sorted out the development agenda.

A developmental state also plays the leading role in Taipei's world city efforts, according to Chia-Huang Wang ("Taipei as a Global City"). But Taipei differs from Tokyo in its level of economic development and its position in the Asia-Pacific regional division of labour. Parallelling Saito's analysis of Tokyo, Wang shows how Taipei's trajectory as a world city hinges on the political and administrative relationships between the Taiwanese central state and the Taipei municipal government. The central-local relationship is moulded by ethnic party) politics in Taiwan—specifically, the struggle for power between the Mainlanders (KMT) and the Taiwanese (DPP). Wang's study suggests that a cohesive national identity may he a pre-condition for global city development, echoing Michael Ignatieff's (1993) conclusions about the relationship between civic nationalism and global cosmopolitanism (Wang, 2003)

A. J. Jacobs ("Embedded Autonomy and Uneven Metropolitan Development") compares the impact of intergovernmental system, national approach to development and institutional support for metropolitan planning on patterns of urban development in Detroit (US) and Nagoya (Japan). Even though the Detroit and Nagoya economies are both based upon the automobile industry, and even though auto production is a global industry, and even though the two cities are headquarters sites for the world's most powerful transnational automobile companies, the development pattern in the two metropolitan areas differs fundamentally. Nagoya has not experienced the deindustrialisation and severe uneven development afflicting Detroit (Jacobs, 2003b).

Hideo Aoki's ("Homelessness in Osaka: Globalisation, *Yaseba* and Disemployment") depiction of homelessness in Osaka, Japan, parallels Jacobs' findings in certain respects. Homelessness is increasing in Japanese cities, as in the US, and is connected to economic globalisation in both societies. But the urban pattern is very different in the two nations. There are many more homeless in the USA

than in Japan relative to population size— New York City alone has twice as many homeless as the whole of Japan. In Japan, the homeless are almost all male, single or divorced, middle-aged and older, and current or former day labourers mostly in the construction industry. The homeless in the US include men, women, children, whole families and a much wider range of occupational groups (Aoki, 2003).

Homelessness in Japan stems primarily from the collapse of the day labour system. Structural unemployment among unskilled casual workers is a growing problem and has been exacerbated by fiscal-crisis-induced state cutbacks in construction outlays. Homelessness in the US is primarily due to poverty, of which unemployment is just one component. Lack of institutional care for the mentally ill and drug abuse also play an important role in the US, Japan has social policies for the homeless but has depended most on company welfare systems and family kinship networks to address the problem, but these institutions are weakening under the impact of globalisation, Aoki concludes.

Michael Indergaard ("The Webs They Weave") compares New York City's Silicon Alley and Kuala Lumpur's Multimedia Supercorridor (MSC) and shows how "images, relationships and space" in the two high-technology multimedia districts are differently shaped by the national development model and regional context in which they are situated. US federal policies had an indirect effect on Silicon Alley through telecommunications deregulation and a political climate favouring private financiers, venture capitalists and stockholders. There was little direct public-sector involvement in Silicon Alley; private entrepreneurs, especially venture capitalists and real estate agents, took the lead. Kuala Lumpur's MSC, by contrast, is championed by Malaysia's version of the developmental state. As in Tokyo and Taipei, Malaysian public agencies perform many of the financial and real estate development functions carried out by private entrepreneurs in New York City. While Silicon Alley was "a temporary base for circulating capital", Malaysia's MSC may be a more enduring foundation for digital industry, Indergaard concludes (Indergaard, 2003).

John Clammer ("Globalisation, Class, Consumption and Civil Society in South-east Asian Cities") explores the contradictory impact of internationalised ways of consuming on urbanism, class and culture in south-east Asian cities. Mass consumption has widened the political horizons of the new middle classes and has opened new possibilities for civil society, while at the same time increasing the gulf between the newly affluent and the poor. But, as Clammer richly reveals, new middle-class practices vary markedly among cities in the region depending upon the character of the national state and local ethnic and religious traditions—from soft authoritarianism in Singapore to a more thorough-going statism in Jakarta, and from social movements based upon religious fundamentalism to grass-roots efforts devoted to the environment and human rights (Clammer, 2003)

K. C. Ho ("Attracting and Retaining Investments in Uncertain Times: Singapore in South-east Asia") pinpoints the commanding role of the state in Singapore's successful structural adjustment to the 1997–98 Asian financial crisis, In Ho's telling, the state's capacity is based upon its "embedded autonomy", in relation to Singaporean society, and with neighbouring Malaysia and Indonesia. Embedded autonomy is a central aspect of the developmental state (Evans, 1995), whereby the government is able to neutralise lobbying efforts and claims on state resources, while maintaining incentives for performance and restructuring efforts.

In Singapore's successful response to the region's financial crisis, the state was able to circumvent efforts by property developers to sustain high land prices and efforts by retailers to buttress consumption, while at the same time implementing a substantial society-wide wage reduction with the help of the National Trades Union Congress. At the regional level, Singapore has managed to protect its core position as a financial hub and coordinating centre for industrial branch plants in Indonesia and Malaysia, even though the city-state is hugely overshadowed in population size by Indonesia and depends totally on Malaysia for its water supply. The state has managed this balancing act largely through the strategic use of foreign assistance and the cultivation of countervailing relationships with nations outside south-east Asia (Ho, 2003)

QUESTIONS FOR DISCUSSION

1. In two or three paragraphs, discuss the main themes Hill and Fujita's chapter,
2. In 1–2 pages, use specific examples from the chapter to explain what the authors mean by the concept of Nested City.
3. Now that you have read both Friedmann and Sassen's Global City thesis and Hill and Fujita's 'Nested City', in 1–2 pages discuss the major differences between the two theories.
4. Utilizing the 'Further Readings', 'Helpful Web Links', and other sources, conduct some research on three 'Nested Cities' in Japan and South Korea. Then, in 2–3 pages, describe some of the most interesting embedded factors you discovered and present your findings to your class.

FURTHER READINGS

Fujita, K. 2000. Asian Crisis, Financial Systems and Urban Development. *Urban Studies*, 37 (12): 2197–2216.

Fujita, K. 2011. Financial Crises, Japan's State Regime Shift, and Tokyo's Urban Policy. *Environment and Planning A*, 43 (2): 307–327.

Hill, R. 1989. Comparing Transnational Production Systems: The Automobile Industry in the USA and Japan. *International Journal of Urban and Regional Research*, 13 (3): 462–480.

Hill, R. and K. Fujita. 1995. Osaka's Tokyo problem. *International Journal of Urban and Regional Research*, 19 (2): 181–193.

Hill, R. and K. Fujita. 2000. State Restructuring and Local Power in Japan. *Urban Studies*, 37 (4): 673–690.

Hill, R. and J. Kim. 2000. Global Cities and Developmental States: New York, Tokyo, and Seoul. *Urban Studies*, 37 (12): 2167–2195.

HELPFUL WEB LINKS

Daejeon Metropolitan City. 2012. It's Daejeon. Welcome to Daejeon Metropolitan City, South Korean. Online. Available at: http://www.daejeon.go.kr/language/english/index.html/, last accessed January 7, 2012.

Fukuoka, City of. 2012. City of Fukuoka English Home Page. Online. Available at: http://www.city.fukuoka.lg jp/english/index.html/, last accessed January 7, 2012.

Hiroshima, City of. 2012. Hiroshima City Overview. Online. Available at http://www.city.hiroshima.lg.jp/www/genre/0000000000000/1001000000023/index.html, last accessed January 7, 2012.

Incheon Metropolitan City. 2012. Fly Incheon: Home Page of Incheon Metropolitan City. Online. Available at: http://english.incheon.go.kr/, last accessed, January 4, 2012.

Nagoya, City of. 2012. City of Nagoya: English Home Page. Online. Available at: http://www.city.nagoya.jp/en/, last accessed January 7, 2012.

Osaka, City of. 2012. City of Osaka: A Metropolis to Make Home. Online. Available at: http://www.city.osaka.lg.jp/contents/wdu020/english/, last accessed January 7, 2012.

Sakai, City of. 2012. Sakai City: Foreign Residents and Visitors. Online. Available at: http://www.city.sakai.lg.jp/index_en.html/, last accessed January 7, 2012.

Sendai, City of. 2012. Sendai City Official English Website. Online. Available at: http://www.city.sendai.jp/language/english.html, last accessed January 7, 2012.

Seoul, Special City of. 2012. Hi Seoul, Soul of Asia. Online. Available at: http://english.seoul.go.kr/, last accessed January 7, 2012.

TMG. 2012. Tokyo Metropolitan Government. Online. Available at: http://www.metro.tokyo.jp/ENGLISH/, last accessed January 7, 2012.

CHAPTER 10

New York, Chicago, Los Angeles: America's Global Cities (1999)

Janet L. Abu-Lughod

This chapter focuses on three gigantic urbanized places that currently occupy hegemonic positions in the spatial structure, aesthetics, economy, changing demography, contentious politics, and evolving cultural meanings of American history: New York, Los Angeles, and Chicago. By the 1990s, each had become a gigantic regional constellation or galaxy of man-imposed constructions, strewn apparently like confetti over vast landscapes of terrain and encompassing the lives of seventeen, fourteen, and eight million persons, respectively (see Figure 10.1).

These settlements are perhaps the most impressive objects our culture has produced, and their scatterings are not random. We shall be searching for those shapes and their causes, and we shall trying to capture the processes whereby the three original urban settlements evolved into ever more complex forms—each contribution to which may have been "intended," but whose composite whole was never planned nor could have been fully anticipated.

These three urbanized regions offer a particularly fertile arena for investigating the

Figure 10.1 New York, Chicago, and Los Angeles in the USA

nature of global cities and for tracing not only the role they play in the international community today, but also the ways in which their changing embeddedness in an evolving world system and their unique responses to those challenges over time have created significant variations within the general category of global cities.

THE CONCEPT OF GLOBAL CITIES

The theme of "global cities" has recently captured the imagination of urbanists, but as I shall argue, much of this exciting literature has been, remarkably ahistorical, as if contemporary trends represent a sharp break from the past, if not an entirely new phenomenon. Furthermore, both the general descriptions of "world cities" and the accompanying causal analyses that attribute their commonalities to general forces residing at the highest level of the international economy neglect variations in global cities' responses to these new forces.

Contemporary scholars, trying to define the "global city," imply that it is a relatively *new* phenomenon that has been generated in the present period by the development of an all-encompassing world system—variously termed late capitalism, post-industrialism, the informational age, and so on. Among the hallmarks of this new global city are presumed to be an expansion of the market via the internationalization of commerce, a revolution in the technologies of transport and communications, the extensive transnational movement of capital and labor, a paradoxical decentralization of production accompanied by a centralization of control over economic activities, and the increased importance of business services, particularly evident in the growth of the so-called FIRE economic sector—finance, insurance, and real estate. Accompanying these changes, and often thought to result from them, is a presumed new bifurcation of the class structure within the global city and increased segregation of the poor from the rich.

The value of such insights cannot be denied, but it is questionable whether the phenomenon is as recent as is claimed. As I shall argue, *all of these characteristics*, at least in embryo form, had already made their appearance in New York City before the last quarter of the nineteenth century, when that city was clearly recognizable as a "modern" global city. And even though the pace and scale of today's globalized economy—and thus of the global cities that serve as its "command posts"—are faster and vaster, and the mechanisms of integration more thoroughgoing and quickly executed, I contend that the seeds from which the present "global city" grew were firmly planted in Manhattan during the middle decades of the nineteenth century. Chicago and Los Angeles would eventually (and sequentially) follow that model with time lags of thirty and sixty years, respectively, although they would naturally do so in a changed world context and under revised regimes of production, circulation, and consumption, as well as politics.

Examining the earlier histories of these three cities, then, should help to identify in each the origins of its global functions and embeddedness, albeit acknowledging that these have become more pronounced and widespread in our day. But this book is not merely a comparative urban history that singles out economic and institutional variables solely for the purpose of predicting global functions. Although it treats economic and political structures, it also takes space seriously, in the manner that urban geographers do, and for very sociological reasons. In the current literature on global cities, space has almost disappeared as a focus. And yet one of the major differences obvious to anyone who has ever visited the three cities is their unique spatial arrangements and, related to those characteristics, the ways of life and social relations within them. Spatial patterns are deeply associated with variations in social life and the relationships among residents, and it is these social relations that yield differences in the patterns of urban living that give to each city its quintessential character.

THE LOGIC OF GLOBAL CITY COMPARISONS

Generalizations about the nature and functions of global cities in the contemporary era tend to underplay variations that arise from the unique national institutions that serve as the context for their development. Because so many disparate cases are included in the comparative study of global cities, it is difficult to untangle the mechanisms that operate within them and to trace how these mechanisms yield quite different spatial configurations on the ground. Because the built environment is itself the accumulated product of past forces, it is impossible to differentiate present effects from past residual influences, much less to distinguish between those that have been shaped by local social and physical conditions and those generated at the international level.

The challenge of comparing global cities has furthermore been compounded by the varying depths of their historical heritages. Most megalopolitan agglomerations that today serve as "world" or "global" *cities*—for example, London, Paris, Amsterdam, Tokyo—have developed over many centuries. They thus contain accretions of successive types of settlements that have layered, one upon the other, vastly different patterns of development and reconstruction, until the composite whole becomes difficult to grasp. Not only are their landscapes difficult to "read," but they are not easily compared with one another, because the national and cultural contexts in which they developed are so different.

These difficulties are somewhat eased in a more controlled comparison of the three largest global cities of the United States, each of which was essentially built on a tabula rasa of terrain and imposed upon a preurban tradition that was for all practical purposes irrelevant to the uses to which European newcomers would put their sites. Furthermore, the physical development of each is only a century or two old, having been formed almost exclusively within the so-called modern period of mercantile/industrial capitalism and within a world system that for some five centuries was dominated by the hegemonic powers of western Europe and then their Atlantic offspring. Although there were dramatic changes over time in both the systems of economic production and the levels of technology the sources of these transformations came essentially from within the same general framework of cultural and economic evolution. And although the political context shifted, as the United States changed from a primarily rural/agrarian society to an urban/industrial one, all three cities developed within that common, albeit changing, legal framework.

Nevertheless, the three urbanized regions, although similar in their overarching economic, technological, social, and political contexts, offer enough significant variations to make comparisons among them a fertile source for new insights into the processes of urban change in the contemporary era. If all are, in one way or another, to be placed in the category of global cities, the variations among them should offer a better chance to differentiate between global and local causes.

The three differ in fundamental ways with respect to, inter alia,

1. their natural geographic settings, as defined by climate, resources, and terrain, which set significantly different parameters for their growth and functions;

2. their spatially specific links to an external world whose contours have shifted dramatically over the more than two centuries of their existence;

3. their original economic functions, political sponsorships, and first settlers, which to some extent helped to define cultural patterns that left lasting marks;

4. the moments of their most dramatic physical expansion (what I shall call *cohort* or *generation*), during which the basic template for the future form of the particular city was established;

5. the timing of their growth spurts and the changing sources of their in-migrant populations, which framed their subsequent racial and ethnic compositions and their persisting political structures and practices;

6. the technologies of transport during initial phases that generated armatures of passage in the three urbanized regions in radically different ways;

7. the social and technological organization of production and communication over time that shaped the imperatives of land, location, and scale in unique ways; and

8. the interclass and political relations that gave, to each region its own modus vivendi: characteristic patterns of power relations, conflict, and modes of conflict resolution—what I shall refer to as its distinctive *civic culture*.

By tracing *how* these differences have resulted in the unique variations on the "global city" phenomenon that we find today in the metropolitan regions of New York, Chicago, and Los Angeles, I intend to shed fight on the mechanisms that yield both the common and special qualities of global cities.

THE GEOHISTORICAL CONFIGURATION OF THE WORLD

I have argued that the topics of globalization and global cities require a much closer attention to history than they have thus far received. Such a historical approach needs to take into consideration the changing shape of the world system that constitutes the largest context for developments within today's major cities; the history of the expansion of the United States over the course of the nineteenth and twentieth centuries, within which

the national urban hierarchy developed; and more specifically for New York, Chicago, and Los Angeles, the more detailed histories of these individual, urbanized regions that, over time, have generated the physical and social "terrain" onto which the newer global forces are now being inscribed and with which they interact.

It may be appropriate here to review these changing contexts briefly but more systematically.

The Historical Context of Globalization and Global Cities

Cities as nodes in networks are not a new phenomenon. Indeed, the fact that cities lie at the center of complex networks constitutes their *essential* feature. Throughout-world history, certain cities—some of them imperial capitals remarkably large-for their times, but a few relatively tiny "city-states"—have served as key nodes through which wider circuits of production, exchange, and culture have been coordinated, at least minimally. But in these earlier manifestations of integration, the territorial reach of even the most extensive "transnational/transimperial" systems was limited to only small fractions of the globe. Entire continents were excluded or were in touch at their peripheries only with the outer fringes of core regions. Nevertheless, urbanization per se was, in fact, both a symptom and a consequence of the construction of such regional systems, whose cores exerted dominance over their agricultural hinterlands and/or, via rivers or even the edges of the sea, increased the surplus available to the cities through conquest and/or tribute or through favorable terms of trade with distant points.

The Geohistorical Context for American Development

For much of the first centuries of its existence, then, New York remained a key American link into a world system that focused increasingly on the Atlantic. Throughout the nineteenth century and into the early years of the twentieth, American history reads as the integration and eventual consolidation of a transcontinental subsystem, spreading from east to west. Even when the midcontinent was settled up to the Mississippi, and St. Louis (soon to be overtaken by Chicago) became the hinge for the drive to Manifest Destiny, New York retained and indeed strengthened its dominance as a core in its own right. As I have argued, it was, almost from its start, a "global city." Chicago could never have achieved the eminence it did without its prime outlet to the sea, New York.

It is important to recall that the integration of Chicago with the nascent U.S. system to its east and south was initially by water, the historically preferred transportation pathway. In the first quarter of the nineteenth century, decades before the railroad terminals consolidated Chicago's lead as midcontinental nexus, the outlets to the Atlantic coast via the Erie Canal-Great Lakes system and to the Caribbean Sea via the internal thoroughfare of the Mississippi River were already in place. What the rails did that waterways could not do, however, was link the zones west of the Mississippi to Chicago and from there on to New York. Without these linkages, Los Angeles's later growth (at least in the form it took) would have been inconceivable.

It was not until the tiny Mexican settlement of Los Angeles, conquered a bare quarter of a century before, was finally connected to the U.S. network via railroads—at first indirectly through San Francisco in 1875 and then via a direct route a decade later—that its modern growth spurt began. And it was not until the twentieth century, after the formation of America's first "overseas empire" (thanks to territories ceded in the 1898 Spanish–American War), that the Pacific became a true, albeit still a secondary, focus of American geopolitics. Heightened by these strategic interests, the sea circuit from the Pacific to the Caribbean was significantly shortened a

dozen or so years later by the construction of the Panama Canal. Thus New York was the point of departure for Manifest Destiny, Chicago was its midwestern switching yard, and Los Angeles ultimately became its terminus.

Institutional and Technological Factors

It would be an error, however, to think in such geographically determined ways. Although an advantageously located site is a sine qua non for urban development, the agency of "men" (and they *were* mostly men in those days), acting politically and economically, has always intervened to favor certain of several otherwise equiprobable locations and to mobilize private and public financing to exaggerate the potential of such favored sites. And changes in technological capacity often have served to reduce or increase the viability of any natural setting.

Thus New York's port, so favorably endowed by nature, did not expand dramatically until the commercial invention of direct port auctions gave the city's brokers a monopoly over foreign trade, and until the engineering achievement of a through waterway to the Great Lakes made New York the dominant break-in-bulk point in internationally linked trade. And it was the capital accumulation facilitated by sophisticated institutions of insurance, banking, and credit that consolidated New York's lucrative role as broker for the slave-produced cotton crop, in preference to any southern port.

Similarly, both drainage of Chicago's waterlogged site and the clever machinations of land-speculating politicians in attracting rail termini and "hub" functions were essential in consolidating that city's lead over potential competitors, just as the later engineered reversal of the flow of Chicago's river reduced the need for portage to the Mississippi. "Nature's metropolis" may have drawn upon a rich agrarian and mineral hinterland, but it was, in the last analysis, the city's skill at centralizing the processing of these raw riches by means of machines and accounting inventions that made it "the metropolis of midcontinent."

The case of Los Angeles is even clearer, because initially the region had neither a water supply sufficient to support a major city nor a natural harbor able to compete with the better-endowed ports at San Francisco to the north or San Diego to the south. Only the political clout of local businessmen, exploiting access to both local and national public funds, enticed a continental rail terminus to the area, secured distant water for the municipality's monopoly and gained the enormous federal subsidies necessary to construct an expensive, artificially enhanced massive port complex.

Differential Urban Growth as Affected by Military Conflicts

Unhappily, wars also play their part in creating locational advantages out of potentials. Just as Los Angeles's modern history was born in the 1847 conquest, expanded in the 1898 Spanish–American war, and further consolidated with the construction of the Panama Canal just before World War I, so the city was not decisively catapulted into the first ranks of the American urban system until World War II, when the Pacific arena drew the United States into an irreversible involvement with the "East" (to its west). World War II also boosted the economies of New York and Chicago: the former primarily through its ports, from which lend-lease shipments were funneled to Europe, and its expanding shipbuilding and airplane manufacture directed to the European theater; the latter through the burgeoning demand for war materiel produced by its heavy Fordist industries.

By then, the world system was moving into the culminating phase of late-modern globalization. The evidence is obvious. One has only to contrast the First World War with the Second. The first had really encompassed only a portion of the European-Adantic "world." The second signaled that the world system had incorporated the countries of Asia and the Pacific Rim as well. To this day, the postwar period has seen the "reach" of this system extend to virtually all parts of the globe, including most of Central and South America. Only a few mountainous redoubts, some interior deserts in Africa, Asia, and Australia, and a handful of off-course islands lie temporarily beyond global reach, and their days are numbered.

Weapons of war, produced first in the United States for its own defense, have fueled the remarkable economic prosperity of the Southwest, including Los Angeles; have partially infused the economies of the Northeast and Mid-Atlantic states, including New York's extended region; and have, by their absence, further undermined the economies of the Midwest, including Chicago's. But weapons produced for export have also enhanced the hegemonic position of the United States in the world economy and, through sales to Third World countries and the deployment of forces in subregional conflicts, have reconfigured the shape of the entire world system.

CONTEMPORARY INTERACTIONS BETWEEN CONTEXT AND THE THREE CITIES

History, however, does not end with globalization. The present fates of the urbanized regions of New York, Chicago, and Los Angeles are linked to a changing geography of power, and thus, ultimately, to the shape of the larger system. Reflecting the Janus-like position of the contemporary United States as both an Atlantic and a Pacific power, and the increased integration of North America with the Caribbean and the Latin American continent, the three seacoasts of the United States have become even more important magnets for people, both through internal migration and external immigration. In recent decades the population of the United

States has continued to decant toward those coasts, not only in the conventional directions of east and west but southward as well. The rapid rise of gateway Miami almost to world-class status is certainly linked to the growing importance of the Caribbean and "our neighbors to the south," as that zone of influence is increasingly integrated with the American core, if only, it sometimes seems, by illegal traffic in drugs. Chicago's tragedy is that it is not in these growth zones.

The Global and the Local within New Technological Parameters

Technological advances have continued the age-old process of disengaging decisions from actions on the ground, with the ironic effect of facilitating the dispersal of production and people while increasingly centralizing what many analysts now refer to as "command functions." We saw this at earlier moments: the substitution of the commerce in "chits" in New York for the "real" midwestern wheat that remained in place in Chicago's silos; the removal of factories to the outskirts of cities at the same time company headquarters expanded in city centers, where telephones and later computers could monitor production farther afield and even abroad; the diffusion of stock ownership at the same time professional managers concentrated their hold over important decision making.

To some extent, these processes continue, but the scales at which they now operate often disengage or camouflage any clear lines between causes and effects, between those who command and those who labor, as capital and labor move with increasing freedom beyond not only the metropolitan boundaries but national borders as well. This disengagement means that healthy growth in command functions is not incompatible with dire destitution in those parts of the system (whether highly localized, at the national level, or at the global level) that are "out of the loop." Such marginalized zones can now

be found in Manchester and Sheffield, England, in downtown Detroit, in the South and West Side ghettos of Chicago, in South-Central Los Angeles, in Bangladesh, and in many parts of the African continent.

SPACE STILL MATTERS IN THE DIRECT ECONOMICS OF GLOBALIZATION

Common to all three cities have been general forces generated at the global level, even though their consequences have not been uniform because they have fallen upon different preexisting terrains. As we have seen, in Chicago the major effects have come from the global restructuring of production methods and the redistribution of places of production, with less coming from the concentration of foreign investments or foreign immigrants. In contrast, although both New York and Los Angeles have been the recipients of major "restructurings" in their economic bases, some of these shifts have made them more unlike (Los Angeles continues Fordist industrial production, whereas New York's minor Fordist base has virtually disappeared), whereas other changes, such as their enhanced attractiveness to foreign investments and company (sub)headquarters, indicate their common greater reliance on the international system. New York and Los Angeles are also capitalizing on their touristic appeal, especially to international visitors (more Asians to Los Angeles, more Europeans to New York), and the media centers of both cities are having disproportionate effects on the transmission of American popular culture to the rest of the world.

Such changes are directly attributable to the increased internationalization of trade, investments, cultural production and consumption, and the communications revolution itself. As before, however, social and technological innovations in space-based transportation and more fungible communications systems have reshaped the roles of all three.

Foreign Trade, Shipping, and Air Freight

Although theoretically one would expect that the tonnage and value of commodities involved in international trade would be important measures of globalization, the actual figures reveal so many anomalies that this crude measure must be used cautiously. True, geographic position still determines the flow of imports and exports through specific ports. Thus Chicago's Custom House, with direct access to only one water-adjacent foreign country (Canada), cannot be expected to process as much international shipping as the major coastal seaport regions. Because of the city's location, many of the bulk commodities originating at Chicago terminals that are destined for overseas will be transshipped through other coastal ports.

Nor, more surprisingly, are the ports of the New York and Los Angeles regions hegemonic. For example, raw figures for 1988–90 indicate that with respect to foreign tonnage, the ports of both Houston and New Orleans outranked those of the New York region, and that Los Angeles ranked only tenth. Chicago's rank among American ports was even lower (fifty-eighth in 1988, forty-fourth in 1989, and fifty-ninth in 1990). Comparing only New York, Chicago, and Los Angeles on raw tonnage of imports and exports, the range is narrowed somewhat, New York ports receive far more tonnage than they ship out: in contrast, import and exports are more nearly balanced through the ports of the Los Angeles region.

As might be anticipated, however, given the increasing importance of airborne shipping, the gaps are much reduced when commodity transfers via air freight are compared. In recent years, the airports in the three urbanized regions have accounted for about one-third of all revenue tons enplaned in the United States, confirming their hegemonic position as global cities.

Real Estate and Control Exercised through Corporate Headquarters

Globalization is also apparent in the landscapes of the three cities, because one important area in which foreign investment has had a visible impact has been in prime urban real estate, especially commercial and office structures in downtown areas. Foreign investors (Dutch, Middle Eastern, and Japanese in New York; Japanese, Taiwanese, and Hong Kong Chinese in Los Angeles) have purchased or built impressive banks, spending surplus funds on "trophy" properties with famous names and have opened headquarters for their transnational firms in all three cities. They are seeking immediate access to the headquarters of major American firms and to the business and legal services that cater to them; and have naturally flocked to New York, Los Angeles, and Chicago, where these "command" functions remain concentrated. By the end of the 1980s, of the 500 largest corporations in the United States (most of them with transnational connections), the New York metropolitan region was home headquarters for 138; Chicago occupied second place with 42; and Los Angeles ranked third with only 25. The degree of centralized dominance, however, varied with the type of business. Large firms engaged in retail trade, commercial banking, insurance, utilities, and transportation were least concentrated, whereas headquarters of manufacturing, advertising, and diversified financial companies (all singled out by theory as exercising "control" functions) were most likely to be concentrated in the three world cities and their extended suburban regions.

REGIONAL POPULATION MATTERS AND IS SPATIALLY GROUNDED

Large size, high density, and demographic diversity have always been defining qualities of cities because, as impressive as the international comings and goings may be, most economic and transcultural activities are still manifested locally. Some of the differences among our three cities can be attributed to overall growth rates in their regions, not all of which are traceable to international causes. This is particularly evident with respect, to Chicago. Even though O'Hare's boast that it is the busiest air terminal in the country is not to be dismissed, it must be acknowledged that the vast midwestern and plains hinterlands of that city have not been growing as before, and indeed, the population in many parts of it has actually been in decline, relatively if not in absolute numbers. The demographic "failure to thrive" of the Midwest, Chicago's service-area cachement zone, has had serious repercussions on the city's economic health that compound, as well as in turn are caused by, the loss of its Fordist base. Thus only a portion of these consequences flow from specifically local causes, such as post-Fordism or even Chicago's contentious race relations, although the negative effects have been experienced most severely by poor people of color.

In contrast, the easternmost and westernmost "gateway cities" to the United States, while to some extent subject to the same evisceration of their old-style production bases as Chicago (New York far more so than Los Angeles), have continued to hold their own demographically because, especially in the past three decades, they have served as major magnets for the expanded numbers of immigrants now being admitted to the United States. When the unbounded conurbations around them, rather than the zones within their legal city limits, are the units of analysis, both conurbations have continued to grow.

Thus the "hollowing out" of the continent has been achieved not only through low rates of natural increase and internal migration out of the Great Plains but, increasingly, through the recently enlarged streams of immigrants from abroad whose "ports of entry" remain the coastal cities—even though the movers now travel by air (or foot) rather than ship. The recent demographic recovery of the New York urbanized region and, even more so, the growth of the Los Angeles megalopolis (despite the recent defection of "Anglos") is clearly attributable to the heightened immigration from abroad that resulted from changes in national policy. Whereas this is clearly an indirect result of the new globalization, it can also be seen as a revival of earlier patterns of recruitment, albeit from very different sources.

The Insertion of Immigrants into the Existing Class and Racial Structures of the Three Cities

Given the diversity of the new immigrants by race and national origin, and given variations in the human and economic capital they bring with them, it is to be expected that their insertion into the unique racial, class, and occupational structures already existing in their cities of destination would take quite different forms and have radically different effects on their political cultures and on their native-born minority populations. Not only do different sending countries provide immigrants with widely varying human capital characteristics, but once within the country, developments at the more local level help to determine how immigrants will be absorbed, what economic niches will be open to them, and how they will interact with native-born citizens, both white/Anglo and African American.

Structures of opportunity intersect with the skills that immigrants bring with them, but not in the same ways in all places. Number and composition of the immigrant stream have of course, been crucial in shaping responses. The fact that California received more "legal" immigrants than any other state [since the 1980s], at the very time when the local economy was contracting, explains in part, but only in part, why the backlash there has been so much more extreme than in

New York or even in Chicago. The fact that the largest percentage of California immigrants were drawn from Mexico and that these "legal" number were supplemented by another 750,000 (or 75 percent of all undocumented immigrants) suggests that responses to this form of "globalization" are deeply affected by the scale and composition of the immigrant population.

In Chicago immigration has been proportionately lower than in either Los Angeles or New York, and has been only moderately diverse. The backlash against immigrants has thus not been extreme, and the older Chicago pattern of ethnic enclaves (which tends to "separate the combatants") seem to be persisting. African American and Latino tension, however, continue. And although both groups are disproportionately disadvantaged and are largely concentrated in the inner city, they are more likely to live adjacent to one another but not to intermingle, as poor Latinos and blacks have done in South-Central Los Angeles.

CONSEQUENCES OF GLOBALIZATION

In the foregoing I have perhaps belabored the proof that the three cities whose evolution I have traced in this book are, despite their differences, quintessential global cities. That, however, does not mean that everything or even most things that take place within these urbanized regions are attributable, either directly or even indirectly, to the current processes of world system restructuring or the role of the United States as the dominant, if no longer the completely hegemonic, player. If international forces were so overwhelmingly powerful, one would anticipate that their effects in the three cities would differ only in degree. That is patently untrue, as I have tried to illustrate through the comparisons presented here.

This, then, returns us to the larger question: Given the large changes in the worlds restructuring, why are the effects on the three

cities so different—not only in economic but in social and spatial terms? My argument throughout has been that common forces originating at the level of the global economy operate always through local political structures and interact with inherited spatial forms. They are therefore always manifested in particular ways that differentiate cities from one another and that militate against the facile generalizations that have hitherto been made about a class of cities called *global*.

Clearly, then, I believe that there are no absolutely inevitable consequences of globalization, even in places that clearly warrant inclusion in that category. To conclude, I focus on three fundamental sources of differentiation that have shaped the developments in New York, Chicago, and Los Angeles: (1) the problem of political boundaries; (2) the problem of income distribution, presumed to be bifurcating; and (3) the problem of social relations as these occur within the *spatial* terrains and inherited *cultural* patterns of the three urbanized regions. Although these differences may perhaps appear obvious, some of their consequences, and especially the interrelationships among them, need to be teased out.

The Problem of Political Boundaries

Many American urbanized regions are particularly difficult to plan for and coordinate for several reasons, including the peculiar history of unmovable state boundaries; the special characteristics of the American federal system, which theoretically operates only in those zones of power not reserved to the states; and the dependent juridical character of municipalities, which never completely independent of the governmental level that created them. Some of the variable degrees of freedom that our three cities can exercise to respond to the challenges of globalization are linked to inherited boundaries, because of the impossibility of making adjustments across state borders and the increasing resistance to annexation on the part of their suburbs. The recent solution in many metropolitan areas has been to try to move urban functions up to the surrounding county unit, but this solution is not open to all.

Ironically, of the three cities covered Angeles, with its strangely fragmented city jurisdictions (albeit all within a single county in a single state), seems in the strongest position to overcome some of the problems generated by irrational boundary conditions. As we have seen, functions such as water and education have already been moved up to the county level, thus placing subareas and municipalities that contain highly differentiated ethnicity-, race-, and class-specific populations within a single governmental jurisdiction. The downside of this arrangement, of course, is the lack of an adequately representative governmental institution that could serve as a truly democratic arena for the resolution of controversies and the expression of dissent. On the positive side, the county itself is a level of government that makes coordination with surrounding counties somewhat easier. This asset is enhanced by the fact that the urbanized region falls within a single state, a second boundary issue of the greatest import.

The Chicago urbanized region also benefits from its virtual containment within a single state, although admittedly there is some overflow into western Indiana and southern Wisconsin. Furthermore, the region has a certain neat symmetry, in that the city lies nested within (and occupies most of the territory of) a single county, which, in turn, is neatly surrounded by its collar counties. Theoretically, this should facilitate common governance. However, this potential is never realized; indeed, the potential for coordination founders on the same "race question" that has plagued much of Chicago's history throughout the twentieth century. Fearful that minorities will "invade" suburban communities or that they will make claims on the tax bases of the more affluent wider region, the Maginot Line of the persisting border

wars has now been reset at the city limits, and where that line of defense fails, at the outer limits of Cook County (which on the west is identical to the city border).

It is hard to avoid the conclusion that the maintenance of racial-ethnic segregation has been the overarching goal of regional strategies. Within the sectorally segmented region, whites have essentially ceded the southern quadrant to minorities (with the exception of the University of Chicago's enclave, whose planned *cordon sanitaire is* now firmly in place, thanks to destruction around it). A certain amount of white "reconquest" of the central business district is also taking place. Although Michigan Avenue north of the river and the residential Gold Coast that fans out from it along the lakefront remain the zones of highest prestige (and the whitest), the south Loop, now anchored at the new Harold Washington Library at Congress Street and stretching into the Printers Row/Dearborn Station renewal area, has succeeded, to some extent, in continuing "Negro removal." And to the west of the Loop, redevelopment zones have deposited elegant commercial and residential high-rises on land formerly claimed by the poor. Minorities, both black and Latino, have been pushed farther west until they reached the city limits at the final defense line of Austin/Cicero. As we have seen, the largest fraction of Chicago's economic vitality is funneled into the north and northwest quadrants, both inside and beyond the city and county limits. This portion of the urbanized region is largely white and becoming more so. Decaying "in-fill" zones in the northwest quadrant that were temporarily preempted by minorities are now beginning to undergo gentrification and "bleaching." The current (white) ruling elite of Chicago has managed to manipulate borders and to gain needed regional coordination through the long preexisting system of special districts that bypass conventional governmental boundaries, and has equally controlled its fiscal problems by passing on to the state government responsibility for covering many costs that would otherwise have had to be borne by urban and suburban residents. This has been achieved despite the traditional tensions between Chicago and "downstate" in the state legislature. Thus, although borders may hinder or facilitate, they do not predetermine goals or prevent political maneuvering around them to achieve solutions.

In the New York region, however, none of these regional solutions has proven very adequate, and the relations with adjacent states, not to mention those between "city" and "upstate," remain contentious. The latter is evidenced annually in the battles over the budget that are waged long beyond the end of each fiscal year and, most recently, have been highlighted—in the almost quintessentially western drama of a standoff at the old corral—when proponents favoring retention of state rent regulations (of vital concern mostly to renters in New York City) squared off against those who preferred to let the law lapse (mostly owners throughout the state). The antagonists argued well beyond the midnight deadline for renewal of the regulations, before a compromise extension was worked out.

Underlying the perennial budget controversy vis-à-vis the state government is the issue of how much New York City's tax revenues subsidize state expenses and what proportion of locally raised taxes ought to be returned to the city to cover its fairly liberal but costly social benefits. City politicians complain that New York's wealth is siphoned off not only to the federal government, as I have shown, but to "upstate" as well. In return, the state attempts to micromanage and impose limits on the city's expenditures and its welfare programs. As Ester Fuchs has astutely noted more than once, New York, in comparison to other large cities, has the largest fiscal burden and the least control over its policy.

All of these problems are compounded by the intractable issue of state borders, especially now that the urbanized region sprawls not only over New York and New Jersey (as before), but into adjacent areas of Connecticut and, most recently, even parts of Pennsylvania. This leads to what can only be described as the New York regions unsolvable problem of governance.

One idea that recurrently surfaces in New York is the (unrealistic) suggestion that the region *could* become manageable if only its parts were "detached" from their containing states and the zone unified politically as a "city-state." This would presumably make the city solvent—by retaining the funds that now go to Albany, by freeing it from incompatible legal restraints (although more effective home rule might be a less draconian solution), and by muting the fierce zero-sum competition between New York and New Jersey with respect to industrial and commercial location, taxation, and especially investments and revenues from its ports and airports. A lesser, but no less facetious, suggestion is for the city simply to secede from the state of New York. Periodically, the suggestion is floated, as it was during the 1969 mayoral campaign, that New York should become the fifty-first state.

Regardless of how seductive these suggestions may appear, they remain a pipe dream. The New York region will have to continue to temporize, not only because of intractable boundaries but because entrenched interests are not likely to be dislodged. Nonetheless, the patchwork of jurisdictions does militate against the simple class bifurcations that some have argued are a direct effect of globalization. It is to this argument that we now turn.

Is Class Bifurcation in Global Cities Really Just a Function of Globalization?

First set forth in 1982 as a tentative hypothesis in Friedmann and Wolff's article on world cities, the proposition that changes at the international level are leading, via a clear causal line, to growing inequality in global cities has now become an article of faith in the growing literature. It is easy to slip into the obverse, namely, that because class inequalities on the local level are largely attributable to causes originating "elsewhere," they therefore lie beyond the capacities of states and cities to rectify.

I have already argued that whereas since the time period coinciding with post-1973 restructuring, the United States has indeed experienced a widening class gap between the richest and poorest segments of its population, this has largely been a *reversal* of a trend that, since the empowering of labor unions under New Deal legislation and the prosperity of the war and postwar periods, had succeeded in narrowing a gap that had formerly been easily as wide. In the preceding era, the labor shortages entailed by reduced immigration and by the booming postwar economy had raised the floor for all but dirt farmers and inner-city blacks. The creation of an admittedly modest welfare state for dependent children and the elderly also contributed to the process of leveling upward.

Toward the end of the 1960s, however, this process began to unravel. The inflationary stagnation of the 1970s and regressive government policies thereafter rapidly culminated in the present moment, undermining many of the labor empowerment programs initiated in the 1930s and 1940s and curtailing entitlements that had expanded in the decades thereafter. We seem now to have returned to a status quo ante, albeit one in which the new international options (more footloose overseas investments and more liberal immigration policies) provide the leverage by making people at the bottom seem more expendable.

It may be true that in today's global cities there is a return to the old pattern of "the citadel" and "the ghetto," as Friedmann and Goetz have suggested, but the causes run deeper than the overarching process of globalization. If bifurcation were a mechanical and inexorable consequence of globalization, one would expect to find few variations from country to country and from global city to global city. This is clearly not the case. I do not question the general finding of growing inequality, but the story of its causes and its spatial consequences is far more complex and is being played out somewhat differently region by region and in rural and urban places both large and small. The evidence from the three cities suggests important variations that call into question a single monolithic set of causes.

In the New York region, for example, economic restructuring and the wild fluctuations on Wall Street pull in opposite directions, which may be a fairly new phenomenon. [In 1996,] New York City's unemployment rate climbed even as Wall Street repeated record highs. This has led to greater disparities in income and unemployment rates. However, if in New York one can partially blame the problem of rising inequality on the new failure of Wall Street to serve as an economic multiplier (hardly a sufficient cause), in Chicago the inequities appear chiefly to be due to the end of Fordism. In Los Angeles, the in-migration of poorly educated Mexicans seems to be the most significant factor in growing inequality.

Thus, even if the global system itself does generate greater inequities by removing some of the privileges formerly enjoyed in a fortress United States with less permeable borders, the chains of causation are highly complex and the results are felt in local areas well beyond those of mere global cities, and even differently in the global cities themselves. And, as I have already noted, the whole matter is complicated by political policies adopted at the state and federal levels. In the last analysis, these variations are needed to account for the fact that other "developed" countries seem to have followed more redistributive policies and, therefore, now exhibit less inequality than the United States. Untangling such knotty problems lies far beyond the task of this book.

Bifurcations in the Spatial Patterns of Global Cities

Friedmann and Wolff's metaphor of the citadel and the ghetto, however, was intended to have meaning not only in socioeconomic space, but in physical space and in power relations as well. The metaphor tries to capture class-based spatial segregation as well as the antagonistic relationship between two "camps"—one that requires walls and fortifications to keep some in and others out. Although walls are certainly rising—around gated communities-and heavily guarded commercial and residential high-rises of the wealthy, as well as along the racial *cordons sanitaires* of white Chicago—the contrasts among the three cities are as illuminating as the common elements and are not manifested exactly the same patterns.

As I have indicated, such disparities are only indistinctly reflected on the urban-scape in New York. In Manhattan, the classes are probably more mixed spatially than they were in earlier times and, at least in public space, assorted racial and ethnic groups now mix more freely than in Chicago or Los Angeles. Whether this should be attributed solely to cultural differences, however, cannot be determined. Certainly, rent regulations in that borough have inhibited gross sittings and sortings by income and race/ethnicity—more so than in the outer boroughs, where, given higher rates of home ownership and a narrower discrepancy between regulated and open-market rents, demographic successions have been more volatile and extreme. In short, much more than global forces are at work.

The Social Consequences of Spatial Patterns

Throughout this book I have paid special attention to the evolution of spatial patterns in New York, Chicago, and Los Angeles, not only as indicators of the sites on which they were constructed and the technological, economic, and political forces that shaped their forms, but because their contrasting physical appearances constitute the most visible "signatures" of their individual characters.

If you were to ask anyone familiar with all three urban places (or even someone who has only seen photographs) whether they could ever confuse one city with the others, the answer would probably be a laugh. True, they are all "global cities" and thus manifest, admittedly in different ways, some of the attributes of this contemporary genre of cities. True, they are all gigantic primates of their regions, and thus, regardless of their problems, exercise the controls and dominance to which their size and resources entitle them. True, they are cosmopolitan in their demographic compositions, bringing diverse types of people together in concentrated space (the bedrock of any definition of *urban*), even though the exact components of their diversity vary in significant ways.

But it is also true that they are places of strong physical/symbolic representation, containing icons so internationally recognizable that one does not need to append a city name to locate the Statue of Liberty, Sears Tower, Hollywood, Times Square, the Loop, the Outer Drive. Their skylines and streets, and often their heroes and villains, are engraved on the retinal memories of most moviegoers. And stereotypes of popular culture, accents, and behavior patterns also abound. There are shared preconceptualizations about "typical New Yorkers," "broad-shouldered Chicagoans," and laid-back occupants of "LaLaLand."

In short, these cities are more than the sums of their parts, just as they are much more than the products of globalization. Throughout my analysis I have so often picked apart the pieces that I seem somehow to have lost their essences—what I have always referred to as the unique "personalities" of individual cities. I cannot end, then, before reassembling the parts to demonstrate how different are the cityscapes, the mannerisms, and indeed the social relations that people form with one another in these three "typical" American global cities.

I begin with urbanscape, because in many ways cities provide the stage settings that channel the movements of their actors and choreograph their steps. But from such obvious physical differences we are led to more abstract elements such as persisting plots and mannerisms, because these stage plays have had a long run. Actors, even new ones joining the cast, must learn their parts from those already on the scene; they must learn how to fit into the patterns already etched on the urbanscape, learn to adapt to what is expected of them. It is in this sense that stereotypes are not totally false, although there is always more variation than the superficial ones allow. Furthermore, like open-ended improvisations in hyperspace, the plots do keep being modified, as scenery is rearranged and fixtures added or removed, and as the stage is periodically crowded with large groups of strangers who arrive with their own props and pursue subplots that do not exactly match or mesh. Furthermore, stage designers (planners?), investors, and directors leave one city stage to alight in another, cross-pollinating designs for living that will influence, but not determine, the effects.

Space, in its grossest sense, is one such shaper of behavior, and impressionistic journalists are sometimes better able to capture essential differences than are more cautious social scientists. One attempt I like very much is by Joseph Giovannini, who explores his reactions to moving from Los Angeles to Manhattan and the alterations this required in his own behavior. He argues that "there is no such thing as a genetic New Yorker or Angeleno" and that "if you drop any New Yorker other than Woody Allen in Los Angeles, he will eventually become acquisitive about cars . . . if you drop any Angeleno

other than a Beach Boy in New York, he will eventually choose his neckties for their coded social meanings" (Giovanni, 1983 p. 147).

Although this may be too extreme a comment, Giovannini does capture the fact that the two cities are based on "fundamentally different spatial premises": "Space in New York collects people; in Los Angeles it separates them. New Yorkers occupy a community; Angelenos occupy their own privacy." He contrasts his privatized driving commute to work in Los Angeles with his highly sociable walk to work in Manhattan.

This makes New York quite different from Los Angeles, which is a private rather than a public city. In Los Angeles, commuting by car "extends the privacy of the single-family house . . . keeps you circulating among people you know . . . [which] limits your exposure to other age groups, social classes, even races." Furthermore, in Los Angeles, "the street is often without sidewalks . . . whereas the street in New York is often a place . . . that collects all the other people who have left their incomplete apartments." Because of this, public spaces have very different ambience in the two cities. In New York, "many public spaces are slightly small for the traffic they bear, and the sense of overflow that pervades them . . . gives New York a feeling of enormous energy . . . . New Yorkers pick up the tensions of the city. . . . But if Los Angeles has few surface tensions to make it taut, it can be appreciated for its tranquility (Giovannini, 1983, pp. 144, 147–49).

I, too, have lived in both places, as well as spent much more time in Chicago than in either, and like a chameleon I have learned to adapt to the different settings, savoring what they have to offer but also missing elements only possible in the others. As did Giovannini, I live in the collective hive of Manhattan, which spews crowds onto the streets at all times of day and night, especially when the weather is beautiful. Who can remain in a crowded apartment when the spectacle of the streets beckons?

Last evening I returned from the movies (on foot, of course, because some ten movie houses lie within walking distance of my apartment). Passing through Union Square Park, on the paved, relatively small open rectangle that several days a week hosts a movable farmers' market, I stopped with my companion to marvel at a juxtaposition one would be extremely unlikely to find at a single location in Los Angeles or Chicago. Despite the hot night, a group of medieval jousters in full coats of armor (and Reeboks) wielded heavy cudgels against each others' shields. Just adjacent to this show, but respectfully careful not to infringe on its space, young men seriously practiced their skateboard skills, oblivious of their interracial mixing and blind to the equally diverse passersby. On a raised wooden platform, recently constructed by the labor intensity that makes blue-collar workers so visible in the city, two black musicians were grooving in percussion (plastic pails and drumsticks), while at nearby tables people read by the poor streetlight or conversed quietly in small groups. We stopped to decipher a small stone marker usually obscured by the makeshift stands of the farmers' market; it commemorated the massacre of Armenians so long ago and far away. We nodded. We had experienced quintessential New York.

A few weeks earlier in Chicago, I caught a more formally planned collective event—the Blues Festival set up in Grant Park at the lakefront, in which most of the "audience" sat in rows of folding chairs set up in front of provisional stages. Beer and bratwurst were in the air. The music and almost all of the musicians were "black," and Chicago could have been in the Deep South, except that because this event was being staged at the lake, almost all of the informally dressed attenders and appreciators were white. Authentic, and perhaps even better, blues are available in the Black Belt, but this would have been considered off-limits by most listeners. I thought this was quintessentially Chicago.

And in the ten months I lived and worked in Los Angeles, I had to relearn (with great trepidation) how to drive, a skill I had lost in the ten years I had been living in New York. I trained myself to stare down adjacent drivers and to exercise extreme caution when a tight-lipped blonde girl was behind the wheel of the next car. And I experienced, the exhilaration—and freedom—of executing skillful and swift maneuvers on highways that seemed to lack true lanes and rules. As Giovaninni notes, however, "in LA you can see the sky" and the "car moves at just the right speed to appreciate the landscape; on foot it is rather boring" (p. 149). But most of the time I lived in Los Angeles I did without rented wheels. On buses I admired the courtliness of the Mexican American drivers and the cordial Spanish banter when the bus picked up (again, mostly) Mexican passengers at corners near the sweatshops at the fringe of "downtown," only to discharge them all at the single intersection along Wilshire Boulevard where the city changes abruptly from Latino to Anglo. I also did a lot of walking, despite the distances that result from low density. Except along the promenades of Santa Monica or the "ethnic" shopping streets, I was often the sole walker, although sweating joggers often veered around me; occasionally, I overtook homeless men with shopping carts, and one of my self-appointed "jobs" was to help them negotiate their carts over humps in the seldom-used sidewalks. Along the half mile of elegant houses but empty streets (except for Latino gardeners and repairmen) between my apartment and the UCLA campus, I once counted 176 small signs that threatened "armed response" from three different private protection agencies. Chicagoans are subtler in their exclusions and New Yorkers, although used to more mixing on the streets and in the subways, have an "en garde" personal alertness to potential incursions by others.

But even these poetic fancies fail to capture the cities. For every crowded street in Manhattan there are more relaxed places where kids still play stoop-ball and neighbors chat over shared driveways and rose gardens. My graduate students and I have even invented the phrase "Brooklyn is another country," to acknowledge how little Manhattan can stand for the city or region. But so also are Jackson Heights and Chinatown and Boerum Hill and Washington Heights. The same is true for Chicago and Los Angeles, for all three places are now microcosms of an American world that includes the "rest of the world."

If the three cities can be said to have special personalities, we must acknowledge that these personalities are by now split into multiple personae. In this book I have tried to trace some of the roots of these differences, both those internal to the cities and those that distinguish among them. At the end, however, I must admit to inevitable failure, because cities must be directly experienced. Writing about them is only the weakest substitute for being in them.

QUESTIONS FOR DISCUSSION

1. In two or three paragraphs, discuss the main themes Abu-Lughod's chapter. Make sure to discuss Abu-Lughod's view of Global City theory.

2. List three or four of the nested factors mentioned by Abu-Lughod's as having differentially impacting New York, Los Angeles, and Chicago's development path. Then, in 1–2 pages, use specific examples from the chapter to explain these factors and how they have created varying development contexts, class and inter-racial relations, etc. in the three cities.

3. Now that you have read Abu-Lughod, discuss some of major similarities and differences between her view of cities in the world and Friedmann and Sassen's Global City theory.

4. Utilizing the 'Further Readings','Helpful Web Links', and other sources, conduct some further research on three other American cities. Then, in 2–3 pages, describe some of the most interesting facts, similarities, and differences among these cities and New York, Los Angeles, and Chicago and present your findings to the class.

FURTHER READINGS

Abu-Lughod, J. 1990. New York and Cairo: A View from Street Level. *International Social Science Journal*, 42 (3): 307–318.

Abu-Lughod, J. 1991. *Changing Cities: Urban Sociology*. New York: HarperCollins.

Danielson, M. and J. Doig. 1982. *New York: The Politics of Urban Regional Development*. Berkeley, CA: University of California Press.

Fuchs, E. 1992. *Mayors and Money: Fiscal Policy in New York and Chicago*. Chicago: University of Chicago Press.

Mollenkopf, J. and M. Castells, eds. 1991. *Dual City: Restructuring New York*. New York: Russell Sage Foundation.

Waldinger, R. ed. 1997. *Ethnic Los Angeles*. New York: Russell Sage Foundation.

HELPFUL WEB LINKS

Atlanta, City of. 2012. City of Atlanta Online. Online. Available at: http://www.atlantaga.gov/, last accessed, January 9, 2012.

Chicago, City of. 2012. Welcome to the Official City of Chicago Website. Online. Available at: http://www.cityofchicago.org/city/en.html, last accessed, January 9, 2012.

Cleveland, City of. 2012. City of Cleveland Home Page. Online. Available at: http://www.city.cleveland.oh.us/CityofCleveland/Home, last accessed, January 9, 2012.

Houston, City of. 2012. City of Houston eGovemment Center: Official Site of Houston, TX. Online. Available at: http://www.houstontx.gov/, last accessed, January 9, 2012.

Los Angeles, City of. 2012. Official Site of the City of Los Angeles–Home. Online. Available at: http://www.lacity.org, last accessed, January 9, 2012.

New York, City of. 2012. NYC.gov: Official Website of the City of New York. Online. Available at: http://www.nyc.gov/portal/site/nycgov/?firont_door=true, last accessed, January 9, 2012.

Philadelphia, City of. 2012. PHILA.GOV. Welcome to the City of Philadelphia. Online. Available at: http://www.phila.gov/Pages/default.aspx, last accessed, January 9, 2012.

Phoenix, City of. 2012. Welcome to the City of Phoenix: Official Site of the City of Phoenix. Online. Available at: http://phoenix.gov/, last accessed, January 9, 2012.

St. Louis, City of. 2012. City of St. Louis, MO: Official Website. Online. Available at: http://www.stlouis-mo.gov/, last accessed, January 9, 2012.

Washington, DC. 2012. The District of Columbia: Home Page of Washington, DC. Online. Available at: http://dc.gov/DC/, last accessed, January 9, 2012.

CHAPTER 11

Race, Fragmentation, and Divergent Outcomes in Detroit and Toronto (2013)

A.J. Jacobs

The Detroit-Ann-Arbor-Flint Consolidated Metropolitan Area (CMSA) or the Detroit Region, and the urban agglomeration defined by the Ontario Government as the Greater Toronto Area-Hamilton (GTAH) Region, provide two fine examples of how variations in national and sub-national structures have fostered diverse outcomes in the world's

Figure 11.1 Detroit, Toronto, and Hamilton in the Great Lakes Region

city-regions. Located only 230 miles (370 kilometers) apart within North America's Great Lakes Region, the two urban agglomerations had populations that were similar in size, and economies closely linked by industrial production and bilateral trade flows (see Figure 11.1). Both also are nested within Federalist nation-states, the U.S. and Canada, respectively. However, except for its new sports stadiums, casinos, and other scattered projects, whereas Detroit's urban core has continued on a now five-decade decline, the core of the GTAH, Toronto, has remained vibrant and economically healthy city.

Drawing upon census data and field interviews in these two regions, this chapter chronicles how variations in: (1) inter-racial-ethnic relations, including immigration; (2) municipal fragmentation; and (3) multi-jurisdictional planning (i.e., embeddedness, especially at the state/provincial level), have helped provoked these divergent outcomes.

REGIONS DEFINED[1]

Extending out from the shores of Lake Erie, the Detroit Region, as defined by the *2000 U.S. Census*, encompassed Southeastern Michigan's Detroit-Ann-Arbor-Flint CMSA, a ten-county metropolitan region that was

1   Genesee
    1a Flint
2   Lapeer
3   St. Clair
4   Livingston
5   Oakland
6   Macomb
7   Washtenaw
    7a Ann Arbor
8   Wayne
    8a Detroit
9   Lenawee
10 Monroe

0   25   50   100 Miles

Figure 11.2 The Detroit CMSA in Michigan

6,565-square-mile in land, contained 5.46 million residents, and 330 city, village, charter township, and general law township governments (see Figure 11.2). Located on the shores of Lake Ontario, the GTAH Region, as defined in Ontario's *Places to Grow: Growth Plan* (MPIR, 2006), represented the inner ring of South Central Ontario's Greater Golden Horseshoe (GGH), and encompassed a 3,155-square-mile which, in 2001, contained 5.57 million inhabitants (see Figure 11.3).[2] It consisted of only 30

municipalities: 24 'lower-tier' local municipalities; two 'single-tier' municipalities, the cities of Toronto and Hamilton; and four upper-tier regional municipalities, Durham, Halton, Peel, and York.

The latter four, which along with Toronto also were within the Greater Toronto Area (GTA), contained 24 lower-tier municipalities. Toronto and Hamilton were consolidated cities, which became single-tier municipalities when the: (1) six lower-tier municipalities in the Metropolitan Munici-

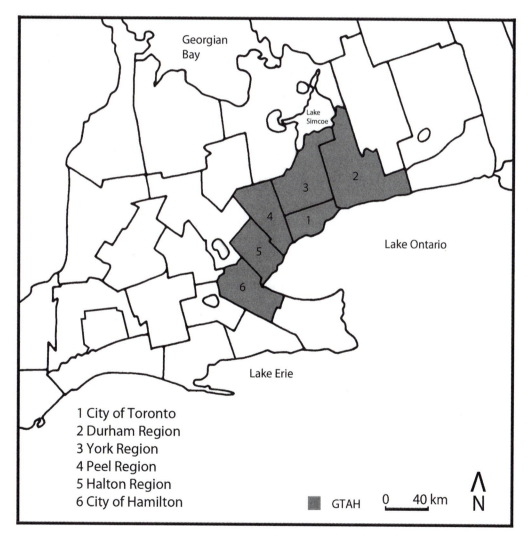

Figure 11.3 The GTAH Region in southern Ontario

pality of Toronto (or Metro) merged in 1998; and (2) the six localities governed by the Region Municipality of Hamilton-Wentworth amalgamated in 2001. According to provincial and local officials, the area's integrated transportation network/commuting patterns suggest that the GTA and Hamilton has come to function as one consolidated region (Ontario, 1998).

The Detroit and the GTAH Regions have represented North America's two largest automobile production agglomerations, with Detroit serving as its brain center. In 2004, the latter region employed 132,995 in Transport Equipment Manufacturing, with an estimated 96% of these working in Motor Vehicle Manufacturing, primarily in the area's 14 automotive plants. Automotive firms employed 51,000 in the GTAH in 2004, with about 40% of these in the region's six large Big Three assembly complexes. These plants have regularly produced roughly 1.1 million cars, trucks, and minivans per year (GTMA, 2006). Hamilton has supported these efforts as the heart of Canada's steel industry. Moreover, despite its automotive prowess, the GTAH has historically had a much more diversified economy than the Detroit Region.

Table 11.1 Population Change in the Detroit Region with White/Minority Change, 1990–2000

	2000 Population	Population Change 1990–2000	% Change 1990–2000	Change NH White Population 1990–2000	% Change NH White Population 1990–2000	Change Minority Population 1990–2000	% Change Minority Population 1990–2000
Detroit Region	5,456,428	269,257	5.19%	−29,039	−0.74%	298,296	23.79%
Detroit city	951,270	−76,704	−7.46%	−112,357	−52.93%	35,653	4.37%
Flint city	124,923	−15,818	−11.24%	−17,951	−23.92%	2,133	2.93%
Rest of Region	4,380,215	361,779	9.00%	83,532	2.29%	278,247	76.19%
Rest of Region							
Rest of Genesee County*	311,198	21,500	7.42%	10,773	8.97%	12,246	47.40%
Lapeer County	74,768	13,136	17.57%	10,773	14.92%	2,363	92.92%
Lenawee County	98,890	7,414	8.10%	4,383	5.23%	3,031	39.51%
Livingston County	156,951	41,306	35.72%	38,343	33.98%	2,963	105.15%
Macomb County	788,149	70,749	9.86%	34,402	5.00%	36,347	121.48%
Warren city	138,247	−6,617	−4.57%	−14,745	−10.56%	8,128	156.82%
Rest of Macomb	649,902	77,366	13.51%	49,147	8.97%	28,219	114.08%
Monroe County	145,945	12,345	9.24%	9,203	7.18%	3,142	58.06%
Oakland County	1,194,156	110,564	10.20%	13,452	1.40%	97,112	77.51%
St. Clair County	164,235	18,628	12.79%	13,599	9.69%	5,029	94.65%
Washtenaw County	322,895	39,958	14.12%	12,095	5.19%	27,863	55.73%
Rest of Wayne County*	1,109,892	26,179	2.42%	−44,235	−4.54%	70,414	63.77%

Sources: U.S. Census Bureau (2010a).

Notes: NH White refers to Non-Hispanic Whites
* The Rest of Genesee excludes Flint, and the Rest of Wayne County excludes the City of Detroit

RECENT POPULATION AND DEMOGRAPHIC TRENDS

As illustrated in Table 11.1, the Detroit Region's population increased by 269,257, or 5.19%, between 1990 and 2000. However, this development occurred extremely unevenly. While the cities of Detroit and Flint contracted by 76,704 (or 7.46%) and 15,818 (or 11.24%) inhabitants, respectively, the remainder of the region expanded by 361,779 residents, or 9.00%. Growth was most prominent in the northern parts of Macomb and Oakland Counties, as well as in the western edge counties of Livingston and Washtenaw. This was a continuation of a five-decade trend of population flight from the region's core.

As again presented in Table 11.1, while the region's Non-Hispanic White (NHW) population declined by 29,039 or 0.74% during this period, its Minority population increased by 298,296 or 23.79%. NHW decline was most apparent in the cities of Detroit and Flint, which lost 112,357 (or 52.93%) and 17,951 (or 23.92%) of their NHW population, respectively. In contrast, the rest of the region experienced an NHW increase of 83,532 or 2.29%. In particular, Livingston and Macomb Counties each added more than 34,000 NHW. Macomb's growth was even more impressive when the inner ring City of Warren's loss of 6,617 NHW was excluded. Spillover from Macomb's expansion occurred in neighboring Lapeer and St. Clair Counties.

As a result, by 2000, although the Detroit Region was 71.56% NHW and 21.06% Black, the cities of Detroit and Flint had become 89.50% and 59.97% Minority, and 81.55% and 53.27% Black, respectively; the City of Detroit's NHW population fell below 100,000 for the first time in over a century. Meanwhile, as shown in Table 11.2, the rest of region was 85.31% NHW and only 7.07% Black. That meant that in 2000, roughly 60% of the region's minorities were concentrated in Detroit and Flint, an area encompassing only 2.62% of its land.

As for the GTAH Region, as shown in Table 11.3, its population increased by 884,673 or 18.87% between 1991 and 2001. Growth was strong in all six sub-regions, including Toronto and Hamilton. Similar to Detroit, the suburban sub-regions out-paced these two core areas, collectively expanding by 640,347 residents or 32.67%. Nonetheless, both Toronto and Hamilton grew by roughly 9% after 1991, adding 205,723 and 38,603 residents, respectively. Although most of this growth was in the former suburban portions of the two core areas, the old pre-merger boundaries of both Toronto and Hamilton still experienced relatively healthy increases of 40,957 or 6.45% and 12,622 or 3.96%, respectively. Additionally, Whites had not, as of yet, abandoned these core cities, as had been the case in the Detroit Region.

As also depicted in Table 11.3, between 1996 and 2001, the number of Whites in the GTAH Region rose by 69,685 or 1.92%. This included a small increase within the old city borders of Toronto of 2,410 (or 0.52%) and a slight decrease of 2,065 (or 0.74%) in pre-merged Hamilton. Conversely, the entire Toronto amalgamated city sub-region suffered a net decline of 77,330 Whites (or 5.25%) after 1996. This was as the product of a combined loss of 79,740 Whites (or 7.88%) in Toronto's five former Metro suburbs, most of which occurred in the northernmost ex-municipalities of North York (or 31,775 or 9.05%) and Scarborough (31,730 or 11.98%).

On the other hand, the number of minorities (i.e., the combined total of persons defined by the *Canadian Census* as either Natives of Aboriginal Identity or Visible Minority), increased by 400,300, or 28.11%, between 1996 and 2001. As a result, as shown in Table 11.4, exactly 33% or 1.82 million of the GTAH's population were minority group members in 2001, up from 27.9% in 1996; 1.79 million of this total was Visibly Minority.

Table 11.2 Racial Distribution in the Detroit Region in 2000

White 2000	2000	% NH 2000	% Asian & % Minority 2000	% Other Pacific Black 2000	Non- Whites Islander 2000	% Hispanic
Detroit Region	71.56%	28.44%	21.06%	2.37%	3.51%	2.86%
Detroit city	10.50%	89.50%	81.55%	1.00%	5.19%	4.96%
Flint city	40.03%	59.97%	53.27%	0.45%	4.89%	2.99%
Rest of Region	85.31%	14.69%	7.07%	2.73%	3.11%	2.40%
Rest of Genesee*	87.76%	12.24%	7.16%	0.98%	2.97%	2.06%
Lapeer County	94.42%	5.58%	0.82%	0.39%	2.61%	3.11%
Lenawee County	89.18%	10.82%	2.12%	0.46%	4.91%	6.96%
Livingston County	96.32%	3.68%	0.46%	0.60%	1.81%	1.24%
Macomb County	91.59%	8.41%	2.71%	2.16%	2.48%	1.58%
Warren city	90.37%	9.63%	2.67%	3.11%	2.92%	1.35%
Rest of Macomb	91.85%	8.15%	2.71%	1.96%	2.38%	1.63%
Monroe County	94.14%	5.86%	1.90%	0.47%	2.21%	2.13%
Oakland County	81.38%	18.62%	10.11%	4.16%	2.98%	2.43%
St. Clair County	93.70%	6.30%	2.10%	0.42%	2.52%	2.19%
Washtenaw Co.	75.89%	24.11%	12.29%	6.34%	3.97%	2.74%
Rest of Wayne*	83.71%	16.29%	8.40%	2.35%	3.74%	2.71%

Sources: U.S. Census Bureau (2010a)

Notes: NH White refers to Non-Hispanic Whites; All other races include Hispanics.
% Other Non-Whites includes all other races not listed but not White Hispanics
* The Rest of Genesee excludes Flint, and the Rest of Wayne County excludes the City of Detroit

Included in this total were 492,260 South Asians, 420,450 Chinese, and 329,585 Black/Afro-Caribbean. In the process, in 2001, the GTAH's was 8.91% South Asian, 7.61% Chinese, and 5.96% Black/Afro-Caribbean, as well as 10.53% in other races. Many in these categories were among the 278,490 foreign-born residents that moved to the GTAH after 1996.

Finally, in terms of spatial distribution, data infer that, although sizeable clusters of South Asians, Chinese, and Blacks have evolved in three of its six sub-regions—Peel, York, and Toronto— residential patterns in the GTAH have been quite different from Detroit's racially bifurcated metropolis. The rigorous residential segregation index calculations of Darden (2004) and others have supported this assessment. As shown in Tables 11.5 and 11.6, the index of dissimilarity for Blacks in all three of the Census defined Metropolitan Areas (MSA) within the Detroit Region (Detroit, Flint, and Ann Arbor) in 2000 remained markedly higher than the 2001 index for any group in three defined Canadian Census Metropolitan Areas (CMA) in the GTAH (Toronto, Hamilton, and Oshawa). In fact, at .847, the index for Blacks in the Detroit MSA, the largest MSA in its region, was almost twice that for Blacks and All Visible Minorities in the Toronto CMA, the GTAH's most segregated CMA. It also was .270 higher than that for Chinese, the most segregated group in the Toronto CMA. Meanwhile, Flint's Black index was significantly higher than that for any group in the GTAH, as was Ann Arbor's index for Asians, the only MSA in Detroit with a substantial Asian population.

Overall, although its population has been decentralizing and some of its neighborhoods have become more racially uniform, the extreme levels of central city decline, White flight, and racial segregation prevalent in the Detroit Region, have not, as of yet, come to exist in the GTAH. As the next section

Table 11.3 Population Change in the GTAH, 1991–2001, with White/Minority Change 1996–2001[R]

	2001 Population	Population Change 1991–2001	% Change 1991–2001	Change in White Pop. 1996–2001	% Change White Pop. 1996–2001	Change in Minority Pop. 1996–2001[N]	% Change Minority Pop. 1996–2001[N]
GTAH Region	**5,572,094**	**884,673**	**18.87%**	**69,685**	**1.92%**	**400,300**	**28.11%**
Toronto city (A)	2,481,494	205,723	9.04%	–77,330	–5.25%	170,265	19.08%
Hamilton city (A)	490,268	38,603	8.55%	9,125	2.19%	12,705	27.46%
Rest of Region	2,600,332	640,347	32.67%	137,890	7.90%	217,330	44.76%
Sub-regions							
Durham	506,901	97,831	23.92%	28,840	7.08%	18,645	38.70%
Halton	375,229	62,093	19.83%	24,610	7.85%	10,365	43.21%
Peel	988,948	256,150	34.96%	20,965	3.60%	115,295	43.06%
Brampton city	325,428	90,983	38.81%	6,125	3.29%	51,095	63.16%
Mississauga city	612,925	149,537	32.27%	5,330	1.49%	63,035	34.01%
Hamilton (A)	490,268	38,603	8.55%	9,125	2.19%	12,705	27.46%
Hamilton city (P)	331,121	12,622	3.96%	–2,065	–0.74%	10,395	26.09%
Rest of Hamilton	159,147	25,981	19.51%	11,175	8.12%	2,320	36.25%
Toronto (P)	2,481,494	205,723	9.04%	–77,330	–5.25%	170,265	19.08%
Toronto city (P)	676,352	40,957	6.45%	2,410	0.52%	18,435	9.87%
Rest of Metro	1,805,142	164,766	10.04%	–79,740	–7.88%	151,825	21.52%
East York borough (P)	115,185	12,489	12.16%	–415	–0.57%	7,875	23.42%
Etobicoke city (P)	338,117	28,124	9.07%	–10,885	–4.78%	19,825	20.03%
North York city (P)	608,288	45,018	7.99%	–31,775	–9.05%	50,160	21.49%
Scarborough city (P)	593,297	68,699	13.10%	–31,730	–11.98%	65,885	22.74%
York city (P)	150,255	10,436	7.46%	4,930	–5.20%	8,080	15.84%
York	729,254	224,273	44.41%	63,480	14.31%	73,020	50.13%
Markham town	208,615	54,804	35.63%	–605	–0.65%	35,810	44.78%
Richmond Hill	132,030	51,888	64.75%	9,890	14.49%	20,230	60.86%
Vaughan city	182,022	70,663	63.46%	35,740	32.13%	13,550	64.26%
Rest of York	206,587	46,918	29.38%	18,455	10.78%	3,430	30.14%

Sources: Statistics Canada (2007).

Notes:
(A) Post-amalgamation and (P) Pre-amalgamation boundaries.
N   Includes both Visible Minorities and Natives of Aboriginal Identity.
R   All figures and the percentages that they were based upon were rounded at the source

Table 11.4 Percent White and Other Major Groups in GTAH Population, 2001[R]

	% White 2001	% Minority 2001[N]	% South Asians 2001	% Chinese 2001	% Black 2001	% All Others 2001
GTAH Region	**67.00%**	**33.00%**	**8.91%**	**7.61%**	**5.96%**	**10.53%**
Toronto city (A)	56.75%	43.25%	10.34%	10.57%	8.31%	13.15%
Hamilton city (A)	87.83%	12.17%	2.27%	1.54%	2.16%	4.78%
Rest of Region	72.83%	27.17%	8.79%	5.93%	4.45%	7.38%
By Sub-Region						
Durham	86.71%	13.29%	2.95%	1.15%	4.48%	3.75%
Halton	90.78%	9.22%	2.71%	1.39%	1.52%	3.05%
Peel	61.14%	38.86%	15.73%	4.22%	7.17%	11.21%
Brampton city	59.31%	40.69%	19.48%	1.68%	9.89%	8.98%
Mississauga city	59.34%	40.66%	14.92%	5.89%	6.20%	13.18%
Hamilton (A)	87.83%	12.17%	2.27%	1.54%	2.16%	4.78%
Hamilton city (P)	84.63%	15.37%	2.59%	1.85%	2.86%	6.25%
Rest of Hamilton	94.46%	5.54%	1.62%	0.90%	0.70%	1.71%
Toronto (A)	56.75%	43.25%	10.34%	10.57%	8.31%	13.15%
Toronto city (P)	69.25%	30.75%	4.69%	9.63%	5.29%	10.07%
Rest of Metro	52.09%	47.91%	12.44%	10.92%	9.43%	14.32%
East York borough (P)	63.67%	36.33%	14.95%	6.29%	3.93%	10.10%
Etobicoke city (P)	64.88%	35.12%	11.71%	2.74%	9.20%	10.75%
North York city (P)	52.97%	47.03%	8.95%	11.47%	8.65%	17.32%
Scarborough city (P)	39.60%	60.40%	17.91%	17.87%	10.17%	13.58%
York city (P)	60.32%	39.68%	4.66%	3.17%	14.42%	16.40%
York	69.86%	30.14%	6.53%	13.88%	2.23%	7.01%
Markham town	44.32%	55.68%	12.68%	29.99%	3.78%	8.91%
Richmond Hill	59.37%	40.63%	6.22%	21.85%	2.01%	10.20%
Vaughan city	80.93%	19.07%	5.87%	3.76%	1.97%	7.33%
Rest of York	92.76%	7.24%	1.05%	1.36%	1.01%	2.88%

Source: Statistics Canada (2007).

Notes: (A) Post-amalgamation boundaries; (P) Pre-amalgamation boundaries
[N] Includes both Visible Minorities and persons of Aboriginal Identity.
[R] All figures that these percentages were derived from were rounded at the source

discusses, a main reasons for these differences have been the two region's quite dissimilar inter-racial, governmental, and planning contexts for development.

DETROIT'S INTER-RACIAL CONFLICT VS. THE GTAH'S MOSAIC

Another important factor dramatically influencing spatial growth patterns in the Detroit and GTAH Regions has been their starkly different inter-racial contexts. First and foremost, although racial and ethnic discrimination persist in the GTAH, the region does not wear the scars of slavery nor has it ever experienced the "Black/White fault line and stratification that have so powerfully shaped" Detroit's development context (Boyd, 2000, p. 143).

In addition to slavery, a long history of institutional racism (both legal and non-legal

Table 11.5 Dissimilarity Index for MSA in Detroit Region, 1990 and 2000[1]

Detroit Region	Blacks 1990	Blacks 2000	Asians 1990	Asians 2000	Hispanics 1990	Hispanics 2000
Detroit MSA	.875	.847	*.429	*.459	.398	.457
Flint MSA	.813	.767	*.381	*.352	.352	.273
Ann Arbor MSA	.615	.632	.561	.587	.393	.379

Table 11.6 Dissimilarity Index for CMA in the GTAH, 1996 and 2001[1]

GTAH Region		Blacks 1996	Blacks 2001	Chinese 1996	Chinese 2001	South Asians 1996	South Asians 2001	All Visible Minorities 2001
Toronto CMA								
Darden/Walks & Bourne	(A)	.467	.487	.529	.577	.570	.535	.435
Fong/Hou	(B)	.522	.43	.525	.53	.557	.48	
Hamilton CMA								
Walks & Bourne (2006)			*.385		*.465		*.422	.319
Oshawa CMA								
Walks & Bourne (2006)			.302		*.427		*.365	.268

Source for Detroit: Darden et al. (2007, p. 148–49).

Source for GTAH: (A) = Darden (2004. p. 440) for 1996 and Walks & Bourne (2006, p. 283) for 2001

Notes

(B) = Fong (2006, p. 57) for 1996 and Hou (2006, p. 1199) for 2001. For Fong, the index is for each group compared with Canadians of British descent. His calculation for Chinese is actually for East and Southeast Asian.

(I) = Index of Dissimilarity measuring the degree each group is segregated from Whites.

* = Represented less than 2 percent of the total area population, so index may be skewed.

controls), has built a wide chasm between Whites and Blacks in the Detroit Region. According to Thomas (1992), the area's inter-racial context began to dramatically change during World War I, when labor shortages in the automotive sector stimulated massive Black migration to the region. As the number of Blacks in the city of Detroit expanded more rapidly than White controlled housing and job markets were willing to accommodate (from 5,741 in 1910 to 120,066 in 1930), inter-racial conflicts, including police brutality on Blacks resulting in deaths, grew more frequent every year.

Blacks again flocked to Detroit during World War II, seeking employment in the region's bustling but undermanned industrial plants. After the War, as Whites were enticed to the suburbs by new housing construction, low-interest mortgages, and roads, urban renewal clearance, freeway construction, and discriminatory national and local housing policies displaced tens of thousands of Blacks. Combined with the fact that many Whites refused to accept mixed neighborhoods, this combination of factors led to the hyper-concentration of Blacks in the region's most deteriorating neighborhoods.

After decades of racial injustice, intolerance and brutality, the situation boiled over on July 23, 1967, when a 3:00 am police raid of the Blind Pig tavern exploded into one of the most intense civil rebellions in America history, leaving 42 dead and 7,231 people arrested. The region has still yet to fully rebound from this event. During the 1970s and 1980s, neither the Black politically controlled central city, nor White suburban leaders, were willing to repair the divide. During the 1990s, through zoning ordinances and other land use practices, suburban officials continued to subtly restrict the entrance of Blacks into their municipalities. Moreover, since the riots, fear and ignorance among most Whites have made it extremely difficult for the region's core cities to attract Whites back into their areas. "Meanwhile, a lack of fair and open housing has kept Blacks pinned in the city" (Thomas, 1997, p. 7). Overall, Detroit's combative interracial context has been a primary embedded catalyst of central city decline, uneven development, White flight, and hyper-segregation region-wide.

Without discounting its own historical structures of exclusion and stratification, the GTAH clearly has been much less racially divided than Detroit. In contrast to Detroit's separatism, the GTAH's inter-racial context has befitted a form of cultural accommodation known as a racial-ethnic mosaic. Lipset (1990) argued that such variations were inherently nested in the clearly dissimilar ideological and related institutional foundations of American and Canadian political-economy. An important element of this was Canada's establishment as a bilingual society and its government's efforts to placate its French linguistic minority. On the other hand, Bibby (1990), Reitz and Breton (1994), and others have argued that ideological differences between the two countries have been negligible at best. Rather, they maintained that in addition to not suffering from the fallout of slavery, Canada's greater social integration has been a function of: (1) racial minorities consistently representing a much smaller proportion of Canada's population, thus reducing the risk of racial conflict in the GTAH; and (2) economic inequality among groups has been less severe in Canada and in the GTAH than it has been in America.

However, the first factor no longer applies to the GTAH. As previously presented, in 2001, at 33.00%, the GTAH's percent minority was greater than that of the Detroit Region's, 28.44% in 2000, with its three largest minority groups, South Asian, Chinese, and Black/Afro-Caribbean (22.5%), constituting a combined higher proportion of the region than Blacks in the Detroit Region. Although methodologies changes make pre-1996 data not truly comparable with 2001 Visible Minority data, according to *Canadian Census* data on Ethnic Origin, these three groups comprised 11.17% of the region in 1991. Moreover, as other data showed, unlike Detroit, as the minority population rapidly expanded in the GTAH, Whites did not immediately flee its core.

Although perhaps an exception in Canada, it appears that support for a multicultural racial-ethnic mosaic has remained strong in the GTAH, especially among younger and better educated residents. As for economic inequality, a primary reason it has remained relatively lower in the GTAH than in Detroit has been Canada's highly selective immigration policies, which have given favored entry status to immigrants with high levels of educational attainment and economic status in their home nations. In other words, national immigration policy and local immigration histories have been important nested variations in the both inter-racial/inter-group and development contexts in the Detroit and GTAH Regions.

Other national policies also suggest that the Canadian Government has taken its own unique approach regarding the connection between inter-group relations and urban configurations. Among these strategies have included: (1) a 1969 law enshrining English and French as the two national languages; (2) the promulgation of the Multicultural Act in 1971 (reaffirmed in 1988); and (3) the establishment of a Multicultural Directorate in 1972. The Multicultural Act, in particular, has institutionalized "the symbolic importance of diversity in Canadian society," and has had an indirect, but positive influence on the experiences of minority group members, helping to create an inter-racial context in which Canadian minorities were less likely to fall into the urban underclass than they were in the USA (Boyd, 2000, p. 143). The Act has been supported by other Federal policy statements and initiatives which have stressed the positive contributions that minorities and immigrants could make to Canadian society if they were allowed to maintain their cultural heritage.

While the embedded inter-racial context in the GTAH seems to have been less conducive than Detroit's at promoting White flight, racial polarization and central city decline, its own situation has become more complex as a result of the region's growing diversity. For example, while White elites might not have dismantled the region's core cities, they may have been successful at pushing minorities to the suburb. Still, despite its own growing problems, the GTAH's inter-racial context has far from approached convergence with Detroit's legacy of racism.

FRAGMENTED DETROIT, AMALGAMATIONS GTAH

The Detroit and GTAH Regions' quite dissimilar frameworks for municipal governance provide another example of how embedded institutional structures have uniquely shaped urban trajectories in each area. The U.S. was built upon a philosophy of strong institutions of local government. As such, Michigan, similar to other American States, has granted its municipalities expansive administrative, financial, and implementation autonomy. In contrast, although Canada also was established as a federated system, provincial–local relations have been hierarchical, with limited municipal home-rule. As such, the Province of Ontario has retained either direct or indirect approval over most important local functions. A perfect illustration of this has been laws governing municipal incor-

porations, which although both contain roughly 5.5 million residents, has produced a fragmented metropolis of 330 localities in Detroit, as compared with only 30 in the GTAH.

Until 1970, Michigan's intergovernmental system permitted areas of only 750 inhabitants to be established as new cities, and the chartering of home-rule villages with as little as 150. While the state raised the city threshold to 2,000 in 1970, the proverbial 'horse was already out of the barn' by that time. Next, in 1978, Michigan law enabled suburban townships in the Detroit Region with as few as 2,000 residents and with densities of only 150 persons per square mile, the right to become Charter Townships. This designation authorized them municipal corporation status, with powers fairly similar to that of cities. Most important, it has effectively granted them boundary protection from annexation by adjacent cities, and thereby, provoked a new form of municipal fragmentation in the region.

Between the 1978 Charter Township Act revision and December 2007, the number of Charter Townships in the Detroit Region jumped from four to 55. Moreover, since the revision, the only annexations that have taken place in the region have been those that were previously circumscribed by legal boundary agreements, such as between the City of Ann Arbor and Ann Arbor Township. Even in this case, however, property owners in the township successfully challenged the annexation in court.

Such a context for local government has landlocked the region's core cities, rendering them incapable of enhancing their tax base through territorial expansion; Detroit city has not completed a successful annexation since 1927. As rural and suburban representatives have come to outnumber city representatives in the Michigan State Legislature, townships have gained control over the State Congress and bureaucracy, making it impossible to reverse the tide of fragmentation.

Overall, with their limited taxing authority and lower mileage rates than cities, Charter Townships have served as another funnel draining residential and non-residential development out of the region's central cities. Between 1980 and 2002, for example, place of work employment in the City of Detroit contracted 498,000 to 304,000. By comparison, employment in the pre-amalgamated city limits of Toronto expanded 492,000 in 1983 to 557,000 in 2001.

In contrast to Michigan, the Ontario law has entitled the provincial government to closely regulate GTAH local action, and at various times, to reorganize municipal powers, functions, and territorial boundaries when it believed it was in the best interest of the province as a whole. Next, during the late 1960s, the province instituted a two-tier municipal government system. 'Metropolitan' and 'Regional Municipalities' have comprised the 'upper-tier' in this system. For many important functions, such as water and sewer service distribution, these directly elected authorities have effectively been home-rule counties, with powers over 'lower-tier' local municipalities—cities, towns, townships, and villages—within their provincial sub-regions. Moreover, it also has protected central cities through its authorization of 'single-tier' municipalities, such as Toronto and Hamilton, whose 'upper-tier' were dissolved as part of their mergers with their suburbs. Although conflicts between tiers and between central cities and suburbs have far from disappeared, according to local officials, single-tier and regional municipalities have served as a compromise between efficiency and democracy for GTAH residents, intended to put the best interest of the many over the parochial interests of the few.

Ontario's two-tier system was promulgated on January 1, 1954, when the then City of Toronto and 12 other municipalities in the southern half of York County federated to create the province's first upper-tier municipality, the aforementioned, Metro. This was followed in the 1960s and 1970s by a series of reorganizations which reduced the number of municipalities in the province from 955 in 1951, to 820 in 1975. This included the: 1967 merger of 13 Metro communities into the six municipalities which later amalgamated to create the current City of Toronto; and the authorization of 11 other regional municipalities, including Durham, Halton, Peel, York, and Hamilton-Wenworth in the GTAH.

Also during the 1970s, provincial officials began discussing the consolidation of Metro municipalities into one mega-city, and the merging of others to create cities with at least 200,000 residents. Little movement on these fronts took place until 1988, when Ontario established the provincial Office of the GTA (OGTA), in order to ease political tensions among municipalities in the region. Then in April 1995, Ontario Premier Bob Rae created the so-named Golden Task Force, to address, among other issues, the significant fiscal problems of municipal governments in the region prompted by structural changes in the global economy and Canada's worst recession since the 1930s. The work of the Golden Task Force culminated in the amalgamation of Toronto and its Metro suburbs in 1998.

Pushed forward by the administration of the next Premier, Mike Harris, Toronto became part of a wave of consolidations that reduced the Ontario's municipalities (at all tiers) from 815 in 1996 to 445 in 2004. From the perspective of the Ontario's Ministry of Municipal Affairs and Housing (MMAH), such restructuring was necessary in order to both enhance the GTAH's and the province's international competitiveness, and to improve local government efficiency, effectiveness, and accountability in the long-term. However, there has been significant ongoing debate regarding the reasons for, and the merits/demerits of, these mergers. In fact, citizens in a few cities were even considering de-amalgamations.

Democratic or not, as a result of its 1990s consolidations, in 2007, Ontario, a province of 354,500 square miles, had only 445 municipalities, including counties. In contrast, Michigan, at less than one-sixth its size (56,804 square miles), had 1,776 municipalities plus 83 counties. Similarly, while the GTAH had only 30 municipalities serving 5.57 million people in 2007, the Detroit Region, despite having a land area that was twice as large (6,565 to 3,155 square miles), had 330 municipalities (and 10 counties), or 11 times as many serving its 5.46 million residents. Additionally, although after Detroit's post-1978 municipal count effectively remained constant, 51 of its townships expanded their autonomy by becoming Charter Townships.

Legally enabled by Michigan Law to create separate islands of Whites and affluent residents, large-scale municipal fragmentation in the Detroit Region has served to exacerbate its conditions of uneven development, White flight, and racial segregation. Conversely, limited fragmentation seems to have helped to lessen these occurrences in the GTAH. On the other hand, some have believed that the GTAH's mergers may have come at a cost: a loss in local representation. Perhaps to address this issue, in 2001, Ontario's authorized a new *Municipal Act*, representing the "first comprehensive overhaul of its municipal legislation in 150 years" (MMAH, 2003, p. 2). The new Act granted municipalities broader powers, in order to allow them to more effectively and flexibly carry out their responsibilities. Further reforms were introduced on January 1, 2007, when new versions of the *Municipal Act,* the *Planning Act,* and *City of Toronto Act* went into effect (see for example, Ontario, 2006).

DETROIT'S 'COLUMBUS SYNDROME' VS. SUB/MICRO-REGIONAL PLANNING IN THE GTAH

A final factor which decisively shaping growth patterns in the Detroit and GTAH Regions has been their local contexts for inter-municipal collaboration. One of the positive aspects of Michigan's intergovernmental environment has been that it has given localities the freedom to creatively manage their own affairs. Michigan's combination of expansive local autonomy, municipal fragmentation, and a 'hands off' state has greatly inhibited cooperative planning efforts in the Detroit Region. Although inter-jurisdictional service agreements have existed, it would be more accurate to characterize the viewpoint of most local politicians as competitive, even combative, and 'not interested', in collaboration. What was noteworthy about this was the fact that a framework for intra-regional collaboration has been in place for more than 60 years.

The Southeast Michigan Council of Governments (SEMCOG), covering seven of the ten counties within the Detroit Region, has existed in some form since 1945. SEMCOG, along with the two other regional commissions serving the remaining counties in the consolidated region (Genesee, Lapeer, and Lenawee), was established to promote development planning in their region. Unfortunately, nestled within a context dominated by strong local parochialism, it was never authorized the necessary powers to carry out its intended purpose. In fact, several communities have challenged their decisions in court, claiming they violated of their constitutional right of local autonomy.

Evidence suggests that the City of Detroit also deserves a fair amount of the blame for its own problems. For example, during the 1950s, city leaders firmly believed that the city would profit more from collecting suburban water and sewer fees than it would be harmed by rapid suburban growth. As a result, the city began acquiring suburban water supply systems under agreements to extend city water (and later sewer) as quickly as possible to any suburb willing to pay for it. In doing so, they failed to envision how such a same policy would later provoke large-scale disinvestment out of the city over the next 50 years. Once water and sewer were extended to open suburban lands, all they could do was watch as the greenfields filled up with houses and factories followed by shopping malls and later office parks.

Overall, although municipal planners in the Detroit Region now clearly understand the desperate need for multi-local planning, they have come to believe that, unless substantial state or federal financial inducements were created to encourage local participation, such efforts will always remain politically infeasible, even at the *micro-regional scale* (two to three municipalities). Within such a context, municipal officials have developed what one area planner called the *Columbus Syndrome*: "Planners and politicians in the region act as if the earth is flat and they would fall off the end of the earth if they considered anything beyond their corporate boundaries. I guess they are blind to the fact that roads go through and do not stop at their borders" (Jacobs, 1997–2008). Such attitudes did little to discourage White-flight, central city decline, and uneven growth in the region during the 1990s.

In contrast, while far from free of its own inter-local in-fighting, Ontario's intergovernmental system has facilitated a greater degree of multi-jurisdictional planning in the GTAH, relative to most American regions. The provincial government began cultivating this climate in the 1920s, when it first proposed the creation of Metro. Although this was initially rebuffed, the province continued its effort to improve inter-local relations by establishing the Ontario Department of Municipal Affairs in 1935, the predecessor of the MMAH. Ever since, this ministry, in concert with the Ontario Municipal Board [OMB], has been crucial in resolving inter-municipal disputes; initially authorized in 1897, the OMB, is an "adjudicative tribunal [which] . . . hears appeals and applications on a wide range of municipal matters" (OMB, 2004, p. 2).

While it has had its critics and problems, Metro, established in 1953, ultimately would become one of North America's best known positive examples of metropolitan administration. As Rose (1972) explained, at the time, post-war growth in the region was occurring so rapidly that even the Conservatives in power at the time were convinced that planning for infrastructure, social services, and urban development was best carried out at the regional scale. It also was believed that Metro would create a framework for local planning and orderly suburbanization, while easing existing tensions between Toronto and its suburbs.

In other words, in many ways, the initial post-war development and planning context in the GTAH was not that much different than it was in Detroit. Thereafter, however, a major difference in the two was the Ontario's authorization of new forms of governance that promoted inter-local cooperation, such as Metro, and later, regional municipalities. According to GTAH officials, the purposes for these "upper-tier" regional municipalities were fourfold. First, they were responsible for planning and providing major urban services within their sub-regions, such as highways and water and sewer lines. Second, they were to serve as arbiters to reduce inter-local competition for development. Third, they were to facilitate and lead multi-local land and development planning. Finally, they were charged with ensuring capability among all goals, plans, policies, ordinances, regulations, capital improvement programs, and implementation strategies initiated by jurisdictions within their sub-region (i.e., effectively planning consistency and infrastructure concurrency). In the process, the province offered North America an example of how sub- and *micro-regional* planning ('small r') could provide a first step toward region-wide planning ('Big R').

Interestingly, after authorizing these regional municipalities, over the next ten years, the province decided to distance itself from municipal affairs and planning. Then, in the mid-1980s, amidst growing social diversity, inter-local political turmoil, and phenomenal growth in the "905 Area Code Belt" outside of Metro, which were threatening the financial stability of Toronto and the governance capacity of Metro itself, the province aggressively re-entered development planning . In 1988, as part of this initiative, it established the aforementioned OGTA. Spurred by the OGTA, first York, and then the other regional municipalities began formulating their own strategic plans.

While provincial policies created a climate for multi-jurisdictional collaboration, perhaps the most significant variation in institutional structures between the GTAH and the Detroit Region has been the *Ontario Planning Act*. First authorized in the 1940s, but having undergone several substantial revisions, the Planning Act has provided the legislative foundation for land-use planning decisions in Ontario. Acting within its framework, the Ontario Government has sought to: (1) prevent the policies implemented in one jurisdiction from unfairly affecting neighboring areas; (2) foster vertical (among tiers), horizontal (among municipalities), and internal planning consistency (within municipal plans); and (3) encourage the authorization of local policies and plans that were representative of the provincial interest (Ontario, 2005).

Prior to 1998, consistency was ensured through provincial review of municipal plans, ordinances, and related amendments, as well as by technical assistance to localities regarding provincial policy objectives. After 1998, revisions to the Planning Act officially assigned the MMAH conformity approval for upper-tier and single-tier municipal plans. Meanwhile, upper-tiers with approved master plans were granted oversight authority over lower-tier municipal plans within their respective region.

As mentioned earlier, since 1988, regional municipalities in the GTAH have aided consistency compliance through their own strategic plans. Together with their multi-local infrastructure activities, these plans have effectively served as metropolitan (Toronto and Hamilton), sub-regional, and *microregional master plans*. In the process, they have coaxed municipalities into considering the interests of other jurisdictions outside their own. While far from perfect, these actions represented a significant difference from Detroit.

Other post-1990 amendments to the Planning Act have further demonstrated the province's commitment to planning consistency. This has included: (1) mandating all municipalities to prepare official plans; (2) periodic review of these plans every five years; (3) the defining of the necessary measures to be taken to attain plan goals and objectives; and (4) requiring internal consistency between plans and municipal ordinances, such as zoning by-laws. Related to this, the Act has granted the MMAH, alone or together with any other ministry, the expressed discretion to issue policy statements on matters relating to municipal planning that were in the opinion of the MMAH of provincial interest. This has evolved into official Provincial Policy Statements (PPS), specifically defining the province's development priorities. The 1996 and 2005 PPS called for the institution and maintenance of a pro-active long-range planning process, containing well integrated master plans at all tiers of government (MMAH, 1996, 2005b).

Furthermore, the Planning Act was amended to state that where the MMAH was "of the opinion that a matter of provincial interest as set out in a PPS is likely to be affected" by a local plan, they may request the amendment of the respective municipal plan to ensure vertical consistency (Ontario, 2005, Section 23–1); the municipality may appeal such a ruling to the OMB. It should be noted that since the 2004, the Planning Act has also required that all decisions made by local, regional and provincial bodies be consistent with the PPS.

Finally, several provincial plans, such as the *Oak Rides Moraine Plan* and the *Niagara Escarpment Plan*, continued to promote planning consistency in the GTAH during the 2000s. However, the most significant documents for the region's future will be the recently authorized *Greenbelt Plan, 2005* and the *Places to Grow, Growth Plan for the Greater Golden Horseshoe, 2006* (MMAH, 2005a; MPIR, 2006). Combined, these growth management plans have called for the intensification of development and the realization of planning consistency in the entire GGH, to be achieved through a collaborative multi-municipal planning process.

Overall, the GTAH's embedded intergovernmental environment has promoted integrated regional and sub-regional planning and development to a much greater degree than Detroit. In contrast, the only mechanism for potential regional planning in the Detroit Region has been the U.S. Government's 1991 *Intermodal Surface Transportation Efficiency Act*, and its 1998 and 2005 re-authorizations. This legislation, however, has merely required regional transportation plans in areas of non-attainment of federal clear air standards. It does not mandate multi-local development plans or consistency as part of the authorization of regional transportation plans. As a result, it has done nothing to inhibit further core city disinvestment, White flight, and uneven development in the Detroit Region.

SUMMARY, CONCLUSIONS: TOWARD A NUANCED NESTED CITY THEORY

This study compared post-1990 development trends in the Detroit and GTAH Regions, two closely linked urban areas within the same natural region, with fairly similar population sizes, but situated within separate Federalist states. It chronicled how dissimilarities in three contextual factors, inter-racial relations, municipal autonomy, and multi-jurisdictional planning, have helped to foster the divergent spatial patterns that have come to exist in the two regions. Of course, these were not the only factors influencing urban configurations in these regions. Moreover, there certainly has been interplay among these factors, and among international, national, and local forces. Nevertheless, the article's discussion demonstrated how urban growth trajectories in the two areas have remained nested within their particular multi-level spatial and institutional configurations. Its findings also suggest the need for greater consideration of state/provincial factors when conducting cross-national comparisons of cities, even those within Federalist states.

In closing, recently released 2006 *Census* data showed that the City of Toronto gained another 21,787 total residents between 2001 and 2006, and the new City of Hamilton added 14,291. Both also got more racially-ethnically diverse. Looking to the future, it will be interesting to discover if this and other nested differences will continue to inhibit Detroit-like urban outcomes in the GTAH. Hopefully the province and local municipalities will react to their evolving context and address any potential issues in a highly collaborative, rather than combative, manner. Here's hope that Detroit learns from its past and the GTAH and follows suit.

NOTES

1   Unless otherwise indicated, data sources for this chapter can be found in Tables 11.1 to 11.5.

2   On June 20, 2008, the Ontario Ministry of Public Infrastructure Renewal and the Ministry of Energy were merged to create the Ministry of Energy and Infrastructure. The two were then again split into two ministries on August 18, 2010, and the *Places to Grow Growth Plan* was placed under the authority of the new Ministry of Infrastructure.

QUESTIONS FOR DISCUSSION

1. In two or three paragraphs, discuss the major themes and theories introduced in Jacobs' chapter.
2. In 1–2 pages, using specific examples from the chapter, list and briefly explain the major differences in the Detroit and Toronto local/regional development contexts.
3. Then, in 2–3 pages, utilize Hill and Fujita's Nested City Theory to briefly explain how the major differences in the Detroit and Toronto local/regional development context have provoked divergence growth outcomes in each region.
4. Utilizing the 'Further Readings', the 'Helpful Web Links', and other sources, conduct some further research on the Detroit and Greater Toronto Regions. Then, in 2–3 pages, write up some of the most interesting facts you discovered about these cities and present your findings to your class.

FURTHER READINGS

Darden, J. 2004. *The Significance of White Supremacy in the Canadian Metropolis.* Lewiston, NY: Edwin Mellen Press.

Darden, J., R. Hill, J. Thomas, and R. Thomas. 1987. *Detroit: Race and Uneven Development.* Philadelphia: Temple University Press.

Fong, E., ed. 2006. *Inside the Mosaic.* Toronto: University of Toronto Press.

Sancton, A. 2000. *The Assault on Local Government.* Montreal: McGill-Queen's University Press.

Siegel, D. 2005. Municipal Reform in Ontario. In J. Garcea and E. LeSage, eds., *Municipal Reform in Canada: Reconfiguration, Re-Empowerment, and Rebalancing.* New York: Oxford University Press, pp. 127–148.

Thomas, J. 1997. *Redevelopment and Race: Planning a Finer City in Postwar Detroit.* Baltimore, MD: The Johns Hopkins University Press.

HELPFUL WEB LINKS

Detroit, City of. 2012. The Official Website of Detroit. Online. Available at: http://www.detroitmi.gov/, last accessed, January 9, 2012.

Hamilton, City of. 2012. Official Website of the City of Hamilton. Online. Available at: http://www.hamilton.ca, last accessed, January 9, 2012.

Macomb, County of. 2012. Official Web Site of Macomb County, Michigan. Online. Available http://www.macombcountymi.gov/index.htm, last accessed January 9, 2012.

Mississauga, City of. 2012. Mississauga.ca Home: City Home Page. Online. Available at: http://www.mississauga.ca/portal/home, last accessed January 9, 2012.

MPIR. 2006. *Places to Grow, Better Choices, Brighter Future: Growth Plan for the Greater Golden Horseshoe.* Toronto: Ontario Ministry of Public Infrastructure Renewal. Online: Available at: https://www.placestogrow.ca/index.php?lang=eng or http://www.moi.gov.on.ca/en/news/index.asp, last accessed, January 9, 2012.

Oakland, County of. 2012. Oakland County, Michigan Home Page. Online. Available at: http://www.oakgov.com/index.html, last accessed, January 9, 2012.

SEMCOG. 2012. Southeast Michigan Council of Governments: SEMCOG Home Page. Online. Available at: http://www.semcog.org/, last accessed, January 9, 2012.

Toronto, City of. 2012. Toronto.ca: Official Web Site for the City of Toronto. Online. Available at: http://www.toronto.ca, last accessed, January 9, 2012.

Wayne, County of. 2012. Welcome to Wayne County, Michigan. Online. Available http://www.wayne-county.com/, last accessed January 9, 2012.

York, Regional Municipality of. 2012. Welcome to the York Region. Online. Available at: http://www.york.ca/default.htm, last accessed, January 9, 2012.

CHAPTER 12

Planning Taipei (2006)

Chia-Huang Wang

Taipei has not been a key city in studies of the world/global city, but it deserves description and analysis because of the role it plays in east-Asian regional-city networks in particular and the whole capitalist world system in general (see Figure 12.1). A few studies do exist, but most were either published in Chinese or regard Taipei as an individual case to be compared with other world cities (Hill and Kim, 2000; Smith, 2004). The studies of C. H. Wang (2003), J. H. Wang (2004), and the contributors to *Globalizing Taipei* (Kwok, 2005) are the few cases published in English that focus specifically on Taipei. The former two characterize Taipei as a secondary world city while the latter focuses on issues of economic and spatial restructuring, state and society realignment, social

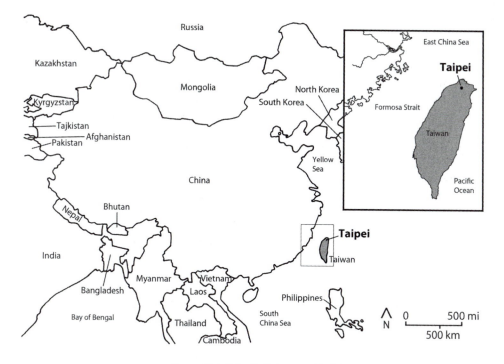

Figure 12.1 Taipei in Taiwan and in Asia

differentiation, and cultural reorientation. Nevertheless, more work is required to determine Taipei's particularities and contextual settings.

This paper is a case study on Taipei as a secondary world city within the semi-periphery. A conceptual framework is constructed to indicate that a world city's nodal status is embedded in a nested politico-economic structure and represents the interaction between a world city's actions and responses, contextual settings and globalizing forces. The nested structure consists of three levels mutually structuring one another—the city's strategic planning, its mode of governance (MOG), and the capitalist world system with its world-city hierarchy. The capitalist world system and world-city hierarchy constitute the macro structure that incorporates and positions national or local settings. A world city's MOG influences the contextual settings that enable and constrain its strategic planning. A world city's strategic planning represents the coping actions and reflexive responses of local actors in dealing with the globalizing forces.

The paper is divided into six parts . . . [Following this introduction], the second part draws upon the arguments of various scholars to describe Taipei's nodal status within the hierarchy of the world-city system. The third part discusses Taipei's major strategic planning actions. The fourth defines the MOG in Taipei as a contextual setting enabling and constraining the city's coping actions and reflexive responses. The fifth part explains Taipei's MOG, [while] the conclusion discusses the theoretical and comparative implications.

TAIPEI'S NODAL STATUS

From a macro perspective, Taipei appears to be insignificant in the world-city system in terms of its range of attributes and networking capabilities. Taipei was regarded by Friedmann (1986) as a secondary world city located in the semi-peripheral states. In contrast, Kuo (2000) considered the Taipei metropolis to be a global city-region. [Whereas,] Hill and Kim (2000) contended that it could be categorized as a state-centered and political-bureaucratic world city in their binary framework of world cities. Smith (2004) regarded Taipei as an intermediate node within global commodity chains, such as those of clothing and electronics.

The categories of Friedmann and other [world city advocates] are based on conceptual thinking and analyses of data, such as population size and socio-economic factors (e.g. financial, transportation and migration flows), but various case studies and systematic calculations demonstrate Taipei's nodal significance within the capitalist world city and the international division of labor. In terms of the power and prestige indices (data based on the interrelationships of headquarters and subsidiaries of multinational corporations) in the world-city system, Taipei ranked 37th in (prestige) significance, one of the four centrality indicators developed by Alderson and Beckfield (2004). The network analysis by Taylor (2000, 2004b) classified Taipei as a gamma world city (minor-centre status) in the world-city hierarchy, playing a minor role in international flows or activities such as specialist service cities, command centers, gateways, media connectivity, and financial connectivity.

From a micro perspective, the official data for Taipei reflect the city's status within the world-city system. Table 12.1 shows that in 2003, tertiary industry dominated Taipei's industrial structure, in terms of capital and number of registered firms (primarily in the financial and insurance sectors, but also in the wholesale and retail sectors) . . . Nevertheless, the secondary sector remains significant. This suggests that Taipei has achieved its position in the capitalist world system through [both] producer services and top-end manufacturing . . . Moreover, Taipei information technology (IT) and high-technology industries . . .

Table 12.1 Taipei's Industrial Structure in 2003

	Capital ($100 million US)	City-wide percentage	Registered firms	City-wide percentage
Construction	16,358	6.53	23,904	10.26
Wholesale and retail	15,485	6.19	90,474	38.85
Financial and insurance	94,375	37.70	5,823	2.50
Shipping, warehousing and communications	9,614	3.84	21,377	9.18
Scientific and technical service	7,637	3.05	22,437	9.63
Lodging, food and beverage	591	0.24	7,682	3.30
Cultural and recreational services	2,203	0.88	6,903	2.96
Other service industries	4,742	1.89	11,433	4.91
Other	33,565	13.41	14,460	6.21

Source: Taipei Metropolitan Government (2004)

constitute a network connecting IT engineers, investment and other resources located in Taiwan and the USA (Jou and Chen, 2001; Saxenian and Hsu, 2001). Taipei has been an interface region connecting Silicon Valley and China's south-east coastal region, thus linking globalizing flows of assets and capital (Hsu, 2005). In other words, Taipei's nodal status is supported by its IT firms and industrial zones.

These data suggest that one should not only be aware of globalizing forces, but also examine local coping actions and reflexive responses, which have either been constrained or enabled by contextual settings, that is, by the local MOG.

TAIPEI'S STRATEGIC PLANNING

Strategic planning, regional planning, and city planning constitute a spatial planning hierarchy (from top to bottom). Strategic planning sets macro visions for economic, social and spatial development. It directs, coordinates and integrates regional, as well as city, planning. These, in turn, formulate micro visions. . . . Mega projects, flagship projects, and various other entrepreneurial schemes are the final results of this systemic operation of the three levels of planning. Next, strategic planning, regional planning and urban planning

constitute a set of logical relations. Strategic planning directs, coordinates and integrates the conceptualization and implementation of regional and urban planning, based on detailed formulation. Taipei's strategic planning includes tactics, mini strategies, urban development and renewal, urban design, master plans and flagship projects to form a loose framework to guide Taipei's development. However, while its form appears to correspond to the typical ideal, Taipei's strategic planning has been a complex historical product of the city's politico-economic context, as shown below.

One of the major goals of strategic planning for Taipei is to develop the city into an international financial hub. In the late 1970s, the Xinyi Planning Area (XPA) was designated as Taipei's auxiliary urban core in which the Taipei Metropolitan Government (TMG), Taipei City Council and business office buildings would be located, and as a specialized space for international financial activities. However, as a result of speculative investment by property developers since the mid-1980s . . . and the plan of the central government under Kuomingtang (KMT) rule for the building of the Asian Pacific Regional Operational Center (APROC), the Xinyi Planning Area has become Taipei's new central business district. The Xinyi Planning

Area was planned to create the image of 'Taipei's Manhattan'. The Taiwanese Developmental State and the TMG also collaborated to develop Nanking Financial Region into Taipei's 'Wall Street'.

While developing the city as an international financial hub, the central government and the TMG did not neglect the quality of Taipei's human resources skills and the city's connections to neighboring regions. The central government and the TMG have been developing Taipei's technology corridor [with the expectation of improving the region's] hi-tech cluster effects. [It also hopes] to develop Taipei into an important hi-tech manufacturing (biotechnology, information technology and telecommunications) centre and transnational corporations' global logistics base, in order to reposition Taipei in the international division of labor and the world-city system. . . .

To attract various value-added flows, Taipei followed the central government's directions and has been developing the meetings, incentives, conventions and exhibitions (MICE) industry. Since the mid-1980s, the Taiwanese State has begun to promote the MICE sector by constructing buildings and facilities for it. Located mainly in XPA, the Taipei World Trade Centre complex consists of the World Trade Centre Exhibition Hall (Phases I and II), the Taipei International Convention Centre, the International Trade Tower and Taipei 101. To ease the spatial pressures on XPA and to balance urban industrial development, the National Bureau of International Trade's Ministry of Economic Affairs planned to establish an international exhibition center in Nangang District in 1994. It was commenced in 2000, but due to economic factors, technical details and possibly partisan politics the project was not completed until 2003. An additional facility, the Taipei Dome (Arena) was constructed by the TMG and is managed by the Eastern Arena Corporation to provide space for exhibition, recreation and convention activities.

The TMG has been promoting metropolitan/city-regional governance by hosting various policy forums, such as the Northern Taiwan Regional Development Forum (NTRF) in early 2004 and the Summit Forum of Northern Taiwan Regional Integration in 2005. Mayors and magistrates of Northern Taiwan cities and counties were invited to discuss cross-jurisdictional strategic development, coordination and cooperation for city-regional/metropolitan development. Apart from multilateral cooperation among local governments for city-regional or metropolitan governance, Taipei also planned bilateral cooperation to enhance city-regional governance. Taipei and Taoyuan County began a new round of strategic alliances in mid-2005 to deal with issues of tourism promotion, Mass Rail Transit (MRT) construction and sales of agricultural produce, as well as disaster prevention and control.

Data and the [approach] represented by the official documents and projects implemented by the TMG, suggest that central government, the TMG and business enterprises have collaborated to realize the local government's strategic planning objectives. [This structure also] appears to match the operational or model definition of strategic planning outlined earlier, but this impression needs to be carefully qualified for the following reasons. First, the central government has always played an important role in Taipei's urban development, strategic planning, and [implementation] by formulating national economic plans, establishing economic and financial laws and providing fiscal and non-fiscal assistance. [As previously mentioned], during the mid-1990s, Taipei was assigned important roles to play in the KMT government's APROC Plan. The Nangang Software Park (NGSP) was a policy product of the central government's economic bureaucracy and the TMG incorporated it into its strategic planning.

The central government's enabling roles have changed into constraining ones, however, since the Democratic Progressive Party (DPP) won the presidential election in 2000. Taipei's roles in the central government's economic plans have been downplayed and its resources cut, partly because of the political differences between the KMT and DPP (Wang, 2003; Wang, 2004). In contrast to the APROC Plan, the DPP's new economic plan Challenge 2008: National Development Plan (2002–08) only mentions that a Taipei Harbor will be built and there will be expansion of Taipei's rapid transit network. Nevertheless, the developmental state's attitudes and actions . . . [still] need to be considered when exploring Taipei's MOG, especially the dimensions of integrated planning system and intergovernmental relations.

Second, Taipei's strategic planning and urban plans are not always the direct results of the planning. Before the 1990s, there were various urban plans and urban-renewal projects based on technical and policy considerations according to mayors' reports to the city council. There was some real estate speculation during the authoritarian era, but it was not excessive, partly because of the political situation and partly because of the various styles and connections of the mayors. The concept and thinking of strategic planning did not emerge until the mid-1990s. In some cases, the mayors and bureaucracy had to adjust their plans to cope with spontaneous development and the private sector's needs or requests. . . .

These two examples suggest that while defining strategic planning is important in theoretical formulation and empirical analysis, one should also pay great attention to a (world) city's politico-economic contextual settings which could be understood by considering the city's MOG.

MODE OF GOVERNANCE: DEFINITION AND DIMENSIONS

Mode of governance (MOG) is a complex structural combination of actors, institutions, processes and relations dealing with strategic formulation and policy implementation. A city's MOG is related closely to how [it] captures the resources and opportunities brought by economic globalization, on the one hand, and deals with local interests and actors in balancing economic development, democratic participation and distributive justice on the other. The State (central and local) is an important actor within a MOG. Relationships among actors, such as the central and local governments, the private sector and the third sector, are also important. Synthesizing the insights of many scholars, the author contends that integrated planning, intergovernmental relations, political leadership, bureaucracy, public-private partnerships, as well as public participation constitute the most significant dimensions of a world city's MOG.

Integrated Planning System

An integrated planning system sets the macrostructural parameters for local governance. It mediates resource flows through supranational and sub-national spaces, shaping institutional capacities and policy making processes of various levels of governance. . . . In Taipei's case, the existence of an integrated planning system is [vitally] important, mainly because Taiwan . . . has a centralized State which controls fiscal resources and wielding power in matters of budget allocation and supervision. Whether the central government incorporates local states into its national plans of economic and spatial development deeply influences local governance and urban development.

Intergovernmental Relations

Vertical and horizontal intergovernmental relations structure the political dynamics and policy coordination of an urban or local MOG. Power structures and dynamics (e.g. centralization versus decentralization, unitary and federal states, as well as constitutional and legal frameworks), partisan politics and ideological factors shape the dynamics of intergovernmental relations. The dynamics include institutional networks, policy orientations, resource provision, cooperation and coordination, as well as competition and conflict. Regardless of the theoretical perspective chosen . . . to examine intergovernmental relations, all these [factors] are important and should be included in discussing urban modes of governance.

Many empirical researches confirm the significance of intergovernmental relations in conditioning and articulating national and urban governance. The case studies include China/Shanghai (Wu, 2000a; 2000b), Japan (Jacobs, 2003a), the USA/Hartford, CT, (Burns, 2002), Canada (Sancton, 1998), and Western European cities/regions (Newman and Verpraet, 1999). In Taipei's case, intergovernmental relations, especially the vertical ones, are extremely important, mainly because the Taiwanese state controls most resources and is the seat of power. More importantly, since the DPP won the presidential election in 2000 and controls the central government, Taipei's vertical intergovernmental relations have undergone radical changes. The new political situation has seriously constrained Taipei's governance and the effectiveness of strategic planning.

Political Leadership

In some cases, political leadership surpasses the limits set by laws and institutions, thus strengthening urban governance. A narrow definition of political leadership refers mainly to the personalities, leadership styles and politico-economic relations (with public officials and the general public). A wider definition includes more structural elements and stakeholders. Historical-institutional aspects might be taken into consideration to discuss political leadership. The wide definition is more inclusive, but it depends on which factors or actors are highlighted. Local political

dynamics could be emphasized; or the focus could be on business leadership in urban governance. In Taipei's case, the focus will be on the starkly contrasting leadership styles and local state-business relations of the two mayors in the past decade.

Bureaucracy and Public–Private Partnerships

Bureaucracy is important within a city's MOG. A strong supportive bureaucracy can complement a mayor's political leadership by fully implementing the leader's visions. A competent bureaucracy can also serve as the core of a 'good government' and be an important bridge linking the public and private sectors. However, sometimes a bureaucracy limits the exercise of political leadership or influences other stakeholders involved in urban governance. Public–private partnerships have been a core and a popular concept in urban governance, but their significance varies with regard to different issues and points of views . . . Partnerships tend to be related closely to alliances between politicians and businesses. In some cases, partnerships can lead to corruption, channeling resources between politicians and businesses, but in other cases they could lower public costs, raise working efficiency or strengthen policy efforts . . . Given Taiwan's deep-rooted bureaucratic system and tradition, the Taipei city bureaucracy's relations to, and influences on, the practices of the public–private partnerships need to be examined.

Citizen Participation

To participate in urban governance, urban planning, and in reshaping their urban space in general, is considered to be a right of citizenship . . . A variety of empirical studies on Western urban governance, however, demonstrate that the state and a few elites have always been dominant. The consideration of effectiveness tends to outweigh the ideal of local participatory democracy. In view of these findings, it is interesting to examine whether Taipei's citizens have sufficient channels to participate in city strategic planning and have access to decision making processes.

TAIPEI'S MODE OF GOVERNANCE

In the light of the dimensions outlined above, the following sections describe and discuss the features and trajectories of Taipei's MOG in order to delineate Taipei's contextual settings.

Integrated Planning System: Is There One?

Taiwan's national spatial planning system provides a legal and policy framework for strategic planning, but has not provided an integrated planning foundation for Taipei's strategic planning. This is not to say that the idea of comprehensive spatial planning has never emerged. The Urban Planning Law (1939), the Regional Planning Law (1974) and related regulations [have established a] legal framework for urban and regional planning, but not for strategic planning. A succession of various regional/metropolitan plans emerged, such as the Kaohsiung Port Metropolitan Plan (1958), the Taipei-Keelung Metropolitan Regional Plan (1963), and the Northern Taiwan Regional Construction Plan (1969), but few were able to advance Taipei's strategic planning. The Comprehensive Development Plan of Taiwan Area (CDPTA, 1979), a prototype for Taiwan's integrated planning system, was promulgated in 1979, but it did not set a comprehensive foundation for strategic planning for Taipei. The Ministry of Interior and the Council of Economic Planning and Development (CEPD), the agency responsible for the national economic development plan tried to integrate the loose spatial planning laws and policies into a comprehensive planning system by drafting the National Territorial Planning Law and by formulating the National Territorial Comprehensive Development (NTCD) Plan, but the new system has not yet been introduced.

It is, therefore, clear that Taipei's urban planning before the 1990s and strategic planning during the 1990s were more like components of Taiwan's national economic development plans and the achievements of the TMG's political leadership than they were outcomes based on a consistent, systematic, comprehensive and integrated planning system. For example, the XPA was achieved through the combined efforts of the Ministry of Economic Affairs (MOEA) and the urban planning arm of the TMG. Although the MOEA has been one of the leading agencies with substantial resources at its disposal, its main tasks do not include spatial planning, unlike the Ministry of the Interior and the CEPD. The city-regional/metropolitan policy forums promoted by the TMG in 2004 and 2005 were not based on the Urban Planning Law, the Regional Planning Law, or national spatial plans; nor were they based on a comprehensive strategic planning blueprint by the central government. The forums were based on tactical considerations: to circumvent various constraining influences of the DPP government, to support Mayor Ma's political leadership and to give certain urban scholars an opportunity to provide advice.

To date, the central government has not introduced an integrated planning system for local governance, but the Ministry of Interior, CEPD and MOEA have been shaping Taipei's urban development and local governance by means of various land use regulations and national economic plans. Nevertheless, the central state's attitudes and actions turned hostile to Taipei after the DPP won the presidential election and controlled the central government, which leads us to consider the intergovernmental relations between the central government and the TMG, and its effects on Taipei's strategic planning and MOG.

Intergovernmental Relations: From Enabling to Constraining

As a result of the Taiwanese state's emerging economic development plan and resource allocation, Taipei's intergovernmental relations were conducive to Taipei's urban governance, in general, and particularly, strategic planning, in the 1990s. The vertical intergovernmental relations helped the realization of the XPA, NGSP, and the Taipei Financial Centre (Taipei 101). However, the situation radically changed after 2000. In that year, Shui-Bian Chen, the DPP candidate, won the presidential election and the KMT were removed from central government office. For reasons of partisan politics and ideological conflicts the DPP president and his government have not been willing to give the TMG full support and sufficient resources. One of the main reasons why the DPP government has been hostile towards the TMG is that Ying-Jeou Ma, a KMT politician, defeated Chen in the Taipei mayoral election in 1998 and another DPP competitor in the 2002 election. Ma also was considered a strong candidate for future presidential elections [he was elected in 2008). The fact that Chen was re-elected as president in 2004 [further strained national-TMG relations].

The situation for the TMG is extremely serious because the Taiwanese state is a unitary state with a centralized system dominating budgetary allocation and the nomination of important personnel in local government. Without support and resources from the central government, the effectiveness of Taipei's strategic planning is bound to be limited. As an example, Wang (2004) indicates that while the Kaohsiung Municipality Government under the DPP mayor obtained additional fiscal resources from the central government, the TMG's budget was cut for political reasons . . . (e.g. to balance the development gap between Northern Taiwan and Southern Taiwan). In addition, the central government under the DPP has not supported the TMG's during their city-regional/metropolitan policy forums.

In comparison with its vertical intergovernmental relations, the TMG's horizontal intergovernmental relations appear to have been more moderate, although there were some disputes between Taipei city and Taipei County about the distribution of water supply, and [occasionally on other issues]. The policy forums held in 2004 and 2005, together by Taipei and Taoyuan County, also reflect the relatively harmonious nature of the TMG's horizontal intergovernmental relations in contrast to its central-local vertical relations.

Political Leadership: Personal Style and State–Business Relations

Between 1994 and 2006 Taipei had only two mayors, Shui-Bian Chen (1994–98) and Ying-Jeou Ma (1998–2006). While both have tried to promote Taipei's status within the world-city system . . ., Chen's and Ma's modes of leadership contrast strongly in terms of personal styles, behavioral characteristics, and relations with business. Mayor Chen, a charismatic mayor, relied on his personal 'brains trust' and preferred to see significant performance in a short time by pressuring the city bureaucracy. Taipei 101, a landmark for Taipei's finance-oriented world/ global-city goal, is an example of Chen's determination to show his governing capabilities.

Like his predecessor, Ma is a charismatic mayor, but in contrast to Chen, his approach to the city bureaucracy was more moderate. He tends to spend more time in communicating with the private sector and groups with interests in urban and community development. He also prefers to make decisions after considering many factors, such as laws and regulations, statistical data, suggestions of the bureaucracy and of scholars, as well as the opinions and demands of stakeholders.

In terms of their relations with business, the two mayors have shown different approaches and have used contrasting mechanisms. While a Taipei city councilor and a congress legislator, before becoming mayor, Chen had already built close connections with many business groups and enterprises, which frequently gave him donations. The Formosa Foundation was established in 1987 to organize his business supporters and to manage political donations from business for his campaign spending. While he was mayor, Chen continued these efforts through the Taipei Culture Foundation. Business either contributed to the Taipei Culture Foundation or sponsored the TMG's cultural activities, such as the Taipei Lantern Festival and Taipei Arts Festival. The two foundations constituted an important mechanism for channeling resources between business and the mayor and his team.

This type of state-business relationship tended to fall into grey areas. These mechanisms appeared to be legal, but could and did cause problems. For example, a construction firm bought a piece of land in 1997 for industrial development, but the firm was not able to obtain approval for its project from the Taipei Urban Planning Commission until it contributed 20 million NT dollars to the Taipei Culture Foundation in October 1997. In March 1998, the commission quickly approved the company's application and the industrial land was converted to commercial land, which greatly increased its market value and brought higher profits to the firm. This was not the only case [of such happenings, as] the Taipei Culture Foundation received nearly 100 million NT dollars from many businesses, most of which were related to projects involving the rezoning of land. In other words, while leading the city bureaucracy to raise Taipei's standing in its quest for world-city status through various policies and strategies, Mayor Chen and his administration also formed a politico-economic alliance with businesses, especially those having interests in real estate development.

It seems that as Mayor, Ma, a charismatic leader with an image of integrity, has not built similar politico-economic alliances. He won the mayoral election in 1998, but the Taipei Culture Foundation was in debt before his team took over the foundation; that is, the money raised for the Foundation during Chen's term had disappeared. Thereafter, Mayor Ma turned the foundation into a purely non-profit organization dedicated to promoting cultural activities and established the New Taiwanese Culture Foundation by using surplus money from campaign contributions. The foundation has held conferences, forums, and workshops to promote democratic ideas and to encourage youth participation.

Although some city councilors from the opposition party have questioned his relations with some business groups, this does not mean that Mayor Ma has not built connections with business. Rather, Ma tends to communicate with business through more formal channels, such as colloquia and other formal communication mechanisms.

Bureaucracy-Steered Public–Private Partnerships

In Taiwan and Taipei, the use of public–private partnerships has become increasingly prevalent and mainly takes the form of build/operate/transfer (BOT) projects. The Taipei Financial Centre Corporation (Taipei 101) is a representative example of a public–private partnership. However, the practice of public–private partnerships has always been steered by the bureaucracy. The shadow of the central bureaucracy can be seen in the Taipei 101 project because the Taiwan Stock Exchange Corporation (TSEC), China Telecom and the Chiaotung Bank are the investors and the government provided a significant proportion of the loans for constructing the Centre. The Taiwan High Speed Rail Project is another example in which the politicians and national bureaucracy have been deeply involved.

In the Taipei context, public–private partnerships are only part of the city bureaucracy's plans and strategies for promoting the city's socio-economic development. Under the mayor's leadership, the TMG has been promoting Taipei's industrial and economic development by reforming its organizational structure, establishing new laws and providing administrative resources.

In terms of reorganization, the Economic Development Commission was established in July 1999 and consists of representatives from the city bureaucracy, the business community and academics. The commission's functions include formulating economic development plans (e.g. the White Book of Taipei's Industrial Development) and strengthening communication between the bureaucracy and business. To promote investment, the Autonomous Statute of Promoting Private Investment in Taipei (2004–08) was passed to promote targeted industries by giving businesses various subsidies. The city bureaucracy has been encouraging the private sector to invest in public construction, the so-called BOT projects, most of which are cases of land development associated with the mass rapid-transit system and cultural projects.

The use of public–private partnerships needs to be appreciated in the context of Taiwan's deep-rooted bureaucratic system and tradition. The XPA and the World Trade Centre complex are the policy achievements of the MOEA and the TMG. The XPA and the buildings planned to provide producer services, such as financial services and convention/exhibition facilities, are a key part of the economic development plan of the national government and the urban planning vision of the TMG. This developmental approach is led by the national economic bureaucracy and bureaucrats from the TMG.

Thus, in the TMG's mode of governance, the so-called public–private partnerships barely resemble those used in European and American city-regions. There are some similarities in institutional arrangements and in the reasons for adopting strategies, such as lowering fiscal burden. However, the use of public–private partnerships in Taipei primarily has been influenced and directed by the city bureaucracy.

Citizen Participation: Limited Participation and Grassroots Movements

Citizen participation in Taipei's strategic planning and . . . governance have been limited although some social groups, such as the Organization of Urban Re-s (OURs) and TSUEI MA MA Foundation for Housing and Community Service, have been active in community affairs and have voiced their concerns about urban development policies and are devoted to community service.

The Urban Planning Law does provide opportunities for citizens to participate in the urban planning process, but these opportunities are limited to information dissemination and consultation, rather than initiation and planning. . . . [Citizens] can seek the assistance of city councilors when they want to introduce certain urban policy changes that would or might influence their interests. They can organize social movements to make demands on or protest against the government. Without a doubt, the TMG has tried to provide resources and opportunities for citizen participation. For example, the TMG promoted the Neighboring Rebuilding Program in 1996 and the Program of Community Planners in 1999, both of which allowed citizens to participate in community landscape redesigning. However, most of these programs were experimental and minor operations under the framework of the TMG's strategic planning. Some of these were steered by the bureaucracy—for instance, the 'Community Taipei 2005: International Conference Series' was delegated to OURs by the Department of Urban Development.

However, it is difficult to argue that citizens have gained a leading role in formulating strategic planning and in influencing Taipei's MOG. . . . While there have been many grassroots groups and community activities,

Taipei's strategic planning has always been directed by political leaders, the city bureaucracy, urban planning scholars, and a few business groups. The laws and processes related to local governance and urban development present an image of a pluralist system, but the actual operation of Taipei's MOG could be categorized as an elitist and bureaucracy-steered urban regime.

CONCLUSION

This paper describes Taipei's nodal status within the world-city system, delineates Taipei's strategic planning efforts and their specific features, as well as analyzing Taipei's MOG through constructing a conceptual framework. The framework not only acknowledges that a world city is embedded in—and structured by—the capitalist world system and world-city hierarchy, but also involves consideration of how . . . [national] and local contextual settings have conditioned a city's strategic planning. By following the logic of the conceptual framework it has been found that, on the surface, Taipei's strategic planning in the past decade matches an ideal type, but in reality it is a complex and evolutionary product of Taipei's politico-economic situation and conditions which have been structured by Taipei's MOG.

This conceptual framework is relevant not only to the study of Taipei, but could [also] to conduct comparative analyses elsewhere. . . . Enumerating the defining attributes and calculating the networking indexes of world cities constitute a top-down approach. However, one needs a conceptual framework, both 'top down' and 'bottom up', to compare the contextual settings that have influenced strategic planning in world cities, to formulate more localized and historical explanations, and to avoid the reductionist tendency of the globalization discourse.

This conceptual framework and the type of analysis structured by it are not original ideas. There are excellent writings attempting to explain the process and concept of globalization and world/global cities, such as the 'transnational urbanism' by Smith (2001). Through describing the experience of Taipei, a city that has received relatively little research attention, the conceptual model presented here is merely another attempt to add to our understanding on the world-city system. This framework, of course needs refinement, as it does not account for and fully explain all factors. [As a result], investigations into the dynamic relationships among the macro world-city hierarchy, meso-scale cross-border politics, and micro-governance settings warrant further study.

QUESTIONS FOR DISCUSSION

1. In two or three paragraphs, discuss the major themes and theories introduced in Wang's chapter.
2. In 1–2 pages, provide specific examples from his chapter to explain what the author means by contextual settings.
3. Now that you have read both Friedmann and Sassen's World/Global City and Hill and Fujita's Nested City Theory, in 2–3 pages discuss the major similarities and differences between Wang's framework and these theories.
4. Utilizing the 'Further Readings', the 'Helpful Web Links', and other sources, conduct some further research on Taipei and a couple of other cities in Taiwan. Then, in 2–3 pages, write up some of the most interesting facts you discovered about these cities and present your findings to your class.

FURTHER READINGS

Hu, T., C. Lin, and S. Chang. 2005. Technology-based Regional Development Strategies and the Emergence of Technological Communities: A Case Study of HSIP, Taiwan. *Technovation*, 25 (4): 367–380.

Kwok, R. 2005. *Globalising Taipei: The Political Economy of Spatial Development*. London: Routledge.

Ng, M. and P. Hills. 2003. World Cities or Great Cities? A Comparative Study of Five Asian Metropolises. *Cities*, 20 (3): 151–165.

Wang, C. 2003. Taipei as a Global City: A Theoretical and Empirical Examination. *Urban Studies*, 40 (2): 309–334.

Wang, C. 2007. Is Taipei an Innovative City? An Institutional Analysis. *East Asia*, 24 (4): 381–398.

Wang, J. 2004. World City Formation, Geopolitics and Local Political Process: Taipei's Ambiguous Development. *International Journal of Urban and Regional Research*, 28 (2): 384–400.

HELPFUL WEB LINKS

Chiayi, City of. 2012. Chiayi City Government Home Page. Online. Available at: http://www.chiayi.gov.tw/2011web/en/index.aspx, last accessed, January 8, 2012.

Hsinchu, City of. 2012. Welcome to Official Hsinchu City Government Web Site. Online. Available at: http://en.hccg.gov.tw/, last accessed, January 8, 2012.

Kaohsiung, City of. 2012. Welcome to Kaohsuing City. Online. Available at: http://www.kcg.gov.tw/EN/Index.aspx, last accessed, January 8, 2012.

Keelung, City of. 2012. Welcome to Keelung City Government. Online. Available at: http://www.klcg.gov.tw/en/index.jsp, last accessed, January 8, 2012.

New Taipei, City of. 2012. New Taipei City Government Home Page. Online. Available at: http://foreigner.ntpc.gov.tw/web/Home, last accessed, January 8, 2012.

Taichung, City of. 2012. Taichung City Government Home Page. Online. Available at: http://english.taichung.gov.tw/internet/english/index.aspx, last accessed, January 8, 2012.

Tainan, City of. 2012. Tainan City Government Home Page. Online. Available at: http://www.tncg.gov.tw/tainan/defaulte.asp, last accessed, January 8, 2012.

Taipei, City of. 2012. Taipei City Government Home Page. Online. Available at: http://english.taipei.gov.tw/MP_100002.html, last accessed, January 8, 2012.

Taiwan, Republic of China. 2012. Government Information Office, Republic of China (Taiwan) Home Page. Online. Available at: http://www.gio.gov.tw/, last accessed, January 8, 2012.

Taoyuan, City of. 2012. Taoyuan City Office Home Page. Online. Available at: http://www.taocity.gov.tw/en/, last accessed, January 8, 2012.

CHAPTER 13

Expanding Income Stratification in the Tokyo Region (2013)

A.J. Jacobs

Tokyo and the Tokyo Metropolitan Region (TMR) have been portrayed both as similar to American metropolitan areas, as well as lacking the many problems they have experienced. Whereas some scholars have suggested that its levels of residential segregation by income have converged with the West, others have refuted this claim. Yet, neither side has verified their position with statistics. Moreover, the dearth of data in these studies has resulted in a general lack of clarity regarding the Tokyo being observed by urban scholars.

So it is fair question to ask, which Tokyo were these theorists writing about? Were they describing conditions in the:

1. 23 Tokubetsu-Ku, an area which consists of 23 quasi-independent municipalities or *Ku* that until 1943 encompassed the legally defined territory of the City of Tokyo, and according to preliminary counts from the *2010 Population Census of Japan,* had a population of 8.95 million? (see Figure 13.1);[1]

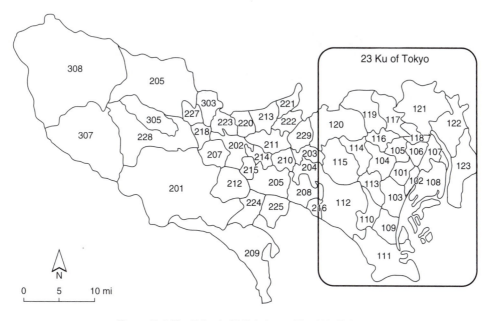

Figure 13.1 The Tokyo's 23 Tokubetsu-Ku within Tokyo-to

2. Tokyo Metropolitan Prefecture (*Tokyo-to*), an area governed by the TMG, containing 23 Ku and 39 other municipalities, and which had a preliminary 2010 population count of 13.16 million? (see Figures 13.1 and 13.2);

3. South Kanto Region, an area sometimes called the Greater Tokyo Area, and defined as the four prefectures of Tokyo, Kanagawa, Saitama, and Chiba, which in 2010 contained Tokyo's 23 Ku and 190 other municipalities, and had a population of 35.62 million? (see Figure 13.2);

4. Shuto-ken or the National Capital Region, an area which was one of eight nationally designated planning regions,

was sometimes called the Kanto Region, traverses South Kanto plus four others prefectures, Ibaraki, Tochigi, Gumma, and Yamanashi, contained the 23 Ku and 323 other municipalities, and which had a combined population of 43.47 million? (see Figure 13.2); or,

5. Kanto Major Metropolitan Area, a census-defined metropolitan region representing the commuter shed for the central cities of Tokyo, Yokohama, Chiba, and Saitama, which in 2010 included 23 Ku and 205 other municipalities situated in parts of nine prefectures, and had 36.87 million inhabitants? (see Figures 13.2 and 13.3).

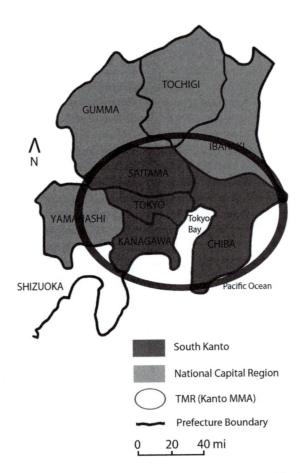

Figure 13.2 Three Tokyo regions: TMR, South Kanto, and the National Capital Region

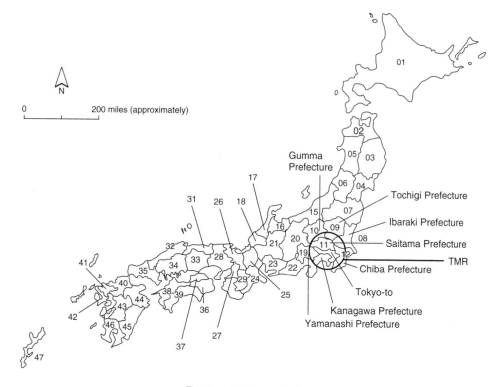

Figure 13.3 The TMR in Japan

To avoid any confusion, this chapter clearly defines its unit of analysis, its Tokyo Metropolitan Region (heretofore, TMR), as the last of these areas, the Tokyo's census-delineated Kanto Major Metropolitan Area. Its purpose is to investigate which position is correct on the TMR: convergence or continued uniqueness. It does this by examining changes in inter-municipal income indicators among municipalities within the TMR between 1980 and 2007; the latter year was the most recent available income data for municipalities in Japan at the time this chapter was completed. It finds that while income inequality among TMR municipalities has risen noticeably since 1980, the region's levels of inter-local household income (HHI) and per capita (PCI) stratification have remained relatively lower as compared with those for America's three largest census-defined Consolidated Metropolitan Statistical Areas

(CMSAs): New York, Los Angeles, and Chicago. This analysis also shows that much of TMR's increase in HHI and PCI inequality occurred after 1999.

Following its statistical analysis, the chapter chronicles some of the factors contributing to the TMR's increasing inter-municipal income stratification, namely: (1) the region's (and Japan's) declining industrial employment since 1991; (2) Japan's rising HHI inequality nation-wide; and (3) the rapid population growth of the TMR's central core, the 23 Ku, since 2000. The last of these was provoked by two concurrent forces: (a) the dramatic fall in central city land prices following the bursting of the Japanese bubble in the early 1990s; and (b) the entrepreneurial waterfront redevelopment activities of the Tokyo Metropolitan Government (TMG). The latter was greatly supported by the policies of the Japanese Developmental State. Finally, the study offers two of the many nested factors (i.e., forces driving its development that were embedded within its national and sub-national contexts), which help explain why the TMR's level of spatial inequality has remained lower than America's largest regions. More specifically, it discusses the city-region's unique racial-ethnic context and the municipal merger policies of Japan's Central Government. In the process, it reinforces the position of Nested City theorists who claimed that embedded factors have been the most decisive determinants shaping spatial outcomes in the TMR.

ASSESSING INCOME STRATIFICATION BY PLACE IN THE TMR, 1980–2007

As mentioned, in 2010, the TMR contained 23 Ku and 195 cities, towns, and villages. As of June 1, 2007, the date of the most recent income data available at the time of this study however, this total was 23 and 205,

respectively, or effectively 228 municipalities (Japan, Government of, 2010b). At that time, these localities contained 36.09 million residents. In this study, the Coefficient of Variation (COV) was utilized to assess changes in the level of income stratification by place among these localities between 1980 and 2007. The COV measures how closely bunched a data set is, and is computed by dividing the absolute value of the standard deviation of a given data group by its mean. The larger the proportion netted from this calculation, the greater the level of unevenness among points (places) in the data set. While far from perfect, this statistic provides a reasonable indicator with which to compare inter-municipal income stratification in the TMR and American largest metropolitan regions.

Based upon the COV, inter-local income stratification has clearly expanded among the 228 municipalities in the TMR since 1980. As shown in Figure 13.4, the COV for HHI

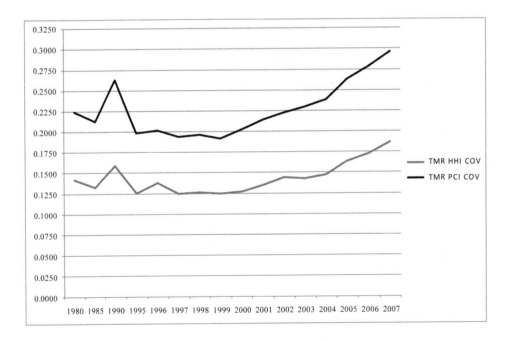

Figure 13.4 Coefficient of Variation (COV) for PCI and HHI for the TMR, 1980–2007

in the TMR rose by .0447 points between 1980 and 2007, from .1421 to .1868. Meanwhile, the region's COV for PCI expanded by .0722, from .2245 to .2967. Investigating more deeply into these numbers shows that whereas the region's COVs for HHI rose dramatically during the late between 1985 and 1990 from .1328 to .1587, it fell precipitously during the 1990s to only .1248 in 1999. Since that time COV for HHI it has risen unabated to a post-1980 high of .1868 in 2007. Meanwhile, after the COV for PCI increased from .2127 in 1985 to .2629 in 1990, it then shrank to a low of .1917 in 1999, before soaring to a new post-1980 peak of .2629 in 2007.

COMPARING INCOME STRATIFICATION BY PLACE IN THE TMR AND AMERICA'S LARGEST REGIONS

This then leads to the question, if income stratification by place has risen significantly in the TMR since 1980, how does its current level of inequality compare with that of America's three largest census-defined CMSA, New York, Los Angeles, and Chicago? For the purposes of fairly comparing the TMR with America's largest urban regions, one adjustment in the COV calculations had to be made: the 23 Ku encompassing the former city of Tokyo had to be considered as one city, similar to the central cities of New York, Los Angeles and Chicago. While this lowered the TMR COVs, it did not fundamentally change any of the findings of the statistical comparison. As a result, as shown in Table 13.1, inter-place income stratification for the TMR was measured among 206 municipalities (i.e., the Ku plus 205 other municipalities); the New York CMSA had 565 local areas, including its five boroughs as one; Los Angeles CMSA 280; and the Chicago CMSA 235. Tables 13.1 and 13.2 present the results of these comparisons.

As illustrated in Table 13.1, with the 23 Ku considered as one jurisdiction, the TMR's COV for HHI was only .1112 in 2007. This figure that was significantly lower than that for the New York (.4023), Los Angeles (.5283), and Chicago (.2977) CMSAs. Parallel outcomes were found for PCI. As illustrated in Table 13.2, with a COV of .1497 for PCI, the TMR was again much less stratified than the New York (.5109), Los Angeles (.7111), and Chicago CMSAs (.3104). In other words, while income stratification by place has expanded over time in the TMR, its inter-municipal income has remained much more evenly distributed than it was in America's three largest regions. In light of these findings, the next questions then are: (1) why has inter-municipal income inequality expanded in the TMR since 1980; and (2) why has its level of spatial income inequality remained much less severe than that in America's three largest CMSAs?

DECLINING REGIONAL INDUSTRIAL EMPLOYMENT AND EXPANDING HHI INEQUALITY IN JAPAN

According to the *Establishment and Enterprise Census*, manufacturing employment peaked in the TMR in 1991, at 3.64 million (Japan, Government of, 1992–2008). As illustrated in Table 13.3, it then declined over the next fifteen years by 1.31 million. This was the case despite the fact that total employment in the TMR expanded by 231,988 to 17.18 million between 1991 and 2006. Total employment growth, however, was contracted severely after 1996, declining by 548,085 between 1996 and 2006. Meanwhile, industrial jobs sank by 893,219, during the latter period. No area was more severely hit than the 23 Ku, which saw its manufacturing employment contract by 354,253 between 1996 and 2006, to 702,931, the Ku lost 541,026 industrial jobs between 1991 and 2006 (again see Table 13.3).

The TMR's manufacturing employment decline was essentially a microcosm of the nation as a whole, which after also hitting its

Table 13.1 HHI Stratification by Place: Tokyo MMA 2007 vs. America's Three Largest CMSAs in 2000

	Tokyo MMA 2007	*New York CMSA 2000 Census*	*Los Angeles CMSA 2000 Census*	*Chicago CMSA 2000 Census*
Population[1]	36.09 million	21.20 million	16.37 million	9.16 million
Land Area (sq. miles)	5,295	10,450	33,955	6,927
Number of Local Areas[1]	206	565	280	235
Mean HHI[2]	$37,124	$60,254	$45,903	$51,046
Coefficient of Variation[1]	**.1112**	**.4023**	**.5283**	**.2977**
Highest HHI[1]	$47,998 Urayasu city, Chiba	$182,792 Scarsdale town, NY	$200,000+ Hidden Hills city, CA Rolling Hills city, CA	$122,641 New Trier twp, IL
Lowest HHI[3]	$20,911 Katsuura city, Chiba	$14,143 Shinnecock Res. NY $22,250 Walpack twp, NY	$18,750 Bluewater CDP $25,987 Desert Hot Springs city, CA	$21,815 Pembroke twp, IL

Sources: JPS (2005–2008); TMR (2011); U.S. Census Bureau (2010a).

Notes:
1. The TMR conforms to the Kanto Major Metropolitan Area as of 2007, and includes Tokyo's Ku as one municipality. The American CMSAs were derived from the June 30, 1999 Office of Management and Budget memorandum related to the *2000 U.S. Census of Population*. They represent the: New York-Northern New Jersey-Long Island; Los Angeles-Riverside-Orange County; and the Chicago-Gary-Kenosha CMSAs. Los Angeles includes 102 CDP. The incomes for Hidden Hills and Rolling Hills were listed in the Census as 200,000+.
2. TMR municipal income was calculated at 117.5 Yen to $1 US, which was the exchange rate on the date of the income survey, March 30, 2007.
3. For comparison purposes, the lowest Native American Reservation and municipal PCI were listed for the New York CMSA, and the lowest CDP and municipal PCI for Los Angeles.

Table 13.2 PCI Stratification by Place: the TMR in 2007 versus America's Three Largest CMSAs in 2000

	TMR 2007	*New York CMSA 2000 Census*	*Los Angeles CMSA 2000 Census*	*Chicago CMSA 2000 Census*
Population[1]	36.09 million	21.20 million	16.37 million	9.16 million
Number of Local Areas[1]	206	565	280	235
Mean PCI[2]	$16,250	$26,604	$21,170	$24,581
Coefficient of Variation[1]	**.1497**	**.5109**	**.7111**	**.3104**
Highest PCI[1]	$22,237 Musashino city, Tokyo	$114,017 Mantoloking boro, NJ	$111,131 Rolling Hills city, CA	$70,331 New Trier twp, IL
Lowest PCI[3]	$8,417 Kyonan town, Chiba	$8,127 Poospatuck Reservation, NY $12,874 Passaic city, NJ	$6,389 Mecca CDP, CA $7,416 Coachella city, CA	$9,642 Pembroke twp, IL

Sources and Notes: See Table 13.1.

Table 13.3 Change in Manufacturing, Total Employment, and Population: TMR, 23 Ku, and Japan Since 1990

Period	Change TMR[1]	% Change TMR	Change Tokyo 23 Ku	% Change Tokyo 23 Ku	Change Japan	% Change Japan
Manufacturing Employment[2]						
1991–2006	−1,308,795	−3.60%	−541,026	−43.49%	−3,995,907	−28.35%
1991–1996	−415,576	−11.42%	−186,773	−15.01%	−1,165,522	−8.27%
1996–2006	−893,219	−27.70%	−354,253	−33.51%	−2,830,385	−23.33%
Total Employment						
1991–2006	231,988	1.37%	−180,491	−2.44%	−1,384,516	−2.31%
1991–1996	780,073	4.60%	82,578	1.12%	2,762,422	4.60%
1996–2006	−548,085	−3.09%	−263,069	−3.52%	−4,146,938	−6.61%
Population						
1990–2010	4,299,409	13.20%	785,874	9.63%	4,444,859	3.60%
1990–2000	2,079,700	6.39%	−28,885	−0.35%	3,314,675	2.68%
2000–2010	2,219,709	6.41%	814,759	10.02%	1,130,183	0.89%

Source: Japan, Government of (1992–2008, 1991–2011)

1 Based upon 2007 TMR boundaries
2 Not adjusted for post-2001 industrial classifications

apex in 1991 at 14.10 million, declined by roughly four million, thereafter (again, see Table 13.3). Similarly, the bulk of its contraction, 2.83 million, occurred between 1996 and 2006. On the other hand, total employment nation-wide contracted by approximately 1.38 million between 1991 and 2006, to 58.63 million. This included a fall of 4.15 million between 1996 and 2006.

A rapid rising Japanese Yen, import quotas/tariffs in foreign exports markets, and the search for cheaper labor were some of the reasons provoking the manufacturing shift out of the TMR and Japan after 1991. For example, in reaction to these pressures and rising demand, Nissan closed its auto production complex in Zama city, Kanagawa in 1995, and now builds only about one-quarter of its total vehicles in Japan. Except for Toyota, the situation was similar for Japan's other automakers.

Not surprisingly, declining total and manufacturing employment coincided with a rise in HHI inequality in Japan. As shown in Table 13.4, between 1989 and 2009, Japan's Gini Coefficients for HHI rose from .293

Table 13.4 Japan's Gini Coefficients for HHI as compared with the TMR's HHI COV: 1979 to 2009

Year	Japan's Gini Coefficient	Change From Previous Period	Year	TMR COV HHI	Change From Previous Period
1979	.271		1980	.1421	
1984	.280	+ .009	1985	.1328	− .093
1989	.293	+ .021	1990	.1587	+ .261
1994	.297	+ .004	1995	.1251	− .337
1999	.301	+ .008	1999	.1248	− .003
2009	.311	+ .010	2007	.1868	+ .620

Sources: Japan, Government of (2010a); Nihon Marketing Center (1981–2004), JPS (2005–2008)

to .311. This coincided with an in an increase in inter-municipal income stratification in the TMR, which rose from .1587 to .1868 between 1990 and 2007. In both cases, again the large majority of the increase took place after 1996. In other words, the TMR's rising income stratification by place was representative of, and greatly influenced by, a changing development (industrial) context in the nation as a whole.

FALLING LAND PRICES, KU POPULATION GROWTH, AND EXPANDING INEQUALITY NATION-WIDE

In contrast to its post-1991 industrial decline, the TMR has experienced a sizeable increase in its population over the past 20 years. As illustrated again in Table 13.3, between 1990 and 2010 the region's population swelled by 4.30 million or 13.20%, each decade adding more than two million residents. On the other hand, growth has been rather unevenly distributed region-wide. This unevenness has contributed to rising income stratification by place, particularly since 1999.

As presented in Table 13.5, the 23 Ku combined to gain 814,759 inhabitants or 10.02% between 2000 and 2010. In other words, about 10% of TMR's municipalities captured nearly 20% of its population growth. What made this even more surprising was the fact that the 23 Ku's population had contracted by nearly one million between 1965 and 1995. Also of note, the 23 Ku actually began growing in 1997, a situation which occurrence concurrent with the TMR's and the manufacturing decline (again, see Table 13.3). As a result, by 2010 the 23 Ku had not only replenished their three decades population loss, but, at 8.95 million, had also surpassed their 1965 post-war high of 8.89 million.

Population growth in the 23 Ku was induced by an assortment of factors, most prominent among them were a dramatic drop in land prices during the early 1990s, especially in the 23 Ku. The connection among the 1990s precipitous fall in land prices, rapid population expansion in the core, and rising spatial income inequality can be back to the Japan's infamous 1980s bubble economy. During this decade, the Nikkei Stock Index quadrupled to almost 39,000 and land prices, especially in the 23 Ku, rose at an even faster rate. Returning to Table 13.5, the average price of one square meter (m^2) of residential land in the 23 Ku jumped by 404.14% between 1980 and 1990, when it peaked at 1.29 million yen ($10,980). In the central core, Chiyoda, Chuo, and Minato-Ku, prices soared by more than 1,000%.

Unfortunately, the rewards from the bubble economy were not spread equally. As a result, for the first time in the post-war period, HHI inequality increased significantly nation-wide during the 1980s, with Japan's Gini Coefficient for HHI rising from .271 to .293 between 1979 and 1989 (again, see Table 13.4 and Figure 13.4). Meanwhile, inter-municipal income stratification in the TMR expanded from .1421 to .1587, between 1980 and 1990. During this period, incomes in the 23 Ku grew much more rapidly than they did in the remainder of the region, led by Minato and Chiyoda-Ku.

Predictably, soaring stock and land prices proved unsustainable and detrimental to the TMR's, and Japan's industrial economy. At the height of the bubble in 1989, it became too expensive to produce goods in many parts of the region, let alone the 23 Ku. As a result, manufacturers either moved out of these cities or went out of business. Over the next couple of years, this situation was exacerbated by the bankruptcies of several large property-related firms and brokerage houses, along with a series of regional banks and few major financial institutions. Moreover, as prices plummeted, "companies that had borrowed heavily to acquire real estate had to sell anything they could [to stay afloat], driv-

Table 13.5 Recent Changes in Population and Residential Land Value, Tokyo's 23 Ku[1,2]

Locality[3]	Population 2010	Population Change 2000–2010	% Pop. Change 2000–2010	Average Price for 1 m² Residential Land (in yen)				% Change Land Value 1990–2010	% Change Land Value 1980–1990
				2010	2005	2000	1990		
Tokyo Prefecture	13,161,751	1,097,650	9.10%	312,700	293,400	329,000	858,600	-63.58%	338.51%
23 Tokyo Ku	8,949,447	814,759	10.02%	480,200	439,700	461,100	1,290,100	-62.78%	404.14%
101-Chiyoda	47,174	11,139	30.91%	2,110,000	1,640,000	1,510,000	8,732,500	-75.84%	1,102.33%
102-Chuo	122,831	50,305	69.36%	700,000	572,500	630,000	3,935,000	-82.21%	1,410.56%
103-Minato	205,303	45,905	28.80%	1,211,300	980,400	890,000	5,462,000	-77.82%	1,284.19%
104-Shinjuku	326,332	39,606	13.81%	556,100	533,000	542,300	2,003,900	-72.25%	435.52%
105-Bunkyo	206,692	30,675	17.43%	753,600	645,700	660,600	1,741,400	-56.72%	421.53%
106-Taito	176,092	19,767	12.64%	753,600	517,500	527,000	1,295,000	-56.02%	229.94%
107-Sumida	247,645	31,666	14.66%	569,500	288,000	305,000	992,000	-70.87%	376.92%
108-Koto	460,585	83,745	22.22%	289,000	335,600	370,200	985,800	-64.03%	388.75%
109-Shinagawa	365,412	40,804	12.57%	573,600	525,600	543,100	1,469,100	-60.96%	360.24%
110-Meguro	268,719	18,579	7.43%	640,000	586,900	593,400	1,595,400	-59.88%	386.40%
111-Ota	693,426	43,095	6.63%	432,400	426,600	444,000	1,255,200	-65.55%	312.89%
112-Setagaya	878,056	63,155	7.75%	514,400	490,400	511,100	1,151,900	-55.34%	309.49%
113-Shibuya	204,753	8,071	4.10%	923,400	785,000	717,900	2,707,900	-65.90%	624.42%
114-Nakano	314,900	5,374	1.74%	465,800	467,600	482,500	1,141,300	-59.19%	296.15%
115-Suginami	549,723	27,620	5.29%	445,100	441,800	460,600	1,084,200	-58.95%	308.82%
116-Toshima	284,768	35,751	14.36%	484,900	432,500	504,500	1,343,200	-63.90%	328.73%
117-Kita	335,623	8,859	2.71%	343,000	375,500	437,400	893,200	-55.35%	270.32%
118-Arakawa	204,646	24,178	13.40%	398,000	386,000	437,500	873,000	-54.41%	265.27%
119-Itabashi	534,564	20,989	4.09%	356,000	343,000	386,200	766,200	-53.52%	253.32%
120- Nerima	714,384	58,252	8.85%	330,600	327,900	367,800	786,800	-57.98%	260.09%
121-Adachi	684,063	66,940	10.85%	270,800	235,600	268,300	535,900	-49.47%	249.80%
122-Katsushika	442,848	21,329	5.06%	292,800	275,100	310,900	616,700	-52.52%	269.06%
123-Edogawa	678,908	58,955	9.51%	300,500	286,700	330,100	751,900	-60.03%	333.62%

Sources: Japan, Government of (2001–2011), TMG (2011)

Notes:
(1) 2010 figures are preliminary Census counts.
(2) Italicized numbers estimated from data in prior years.
(3) Locality corresponds to Figure 13–1.

ing prices down further, as banks refused to lend" (Mikuni & Murphy, 2003, p. 168).

After the bubble collapsed, land prices plunged throughout the TMR, most precipitously in the 23 Ku. By the 2000, the average price of 1 m² of residential land in the Ku had fallen to 461,100 Yen (or $3,924), or essentially one-third its 1990 level. In all but region's most exclusive residential areas, prices continued to drop until 2005, when they bottomed-out. By 2010, however, even in the three most central Ku, Chiyoda, Minato, and Chuo, residential land prices still were equivalent to only about one-fourth their 1990 peaks (again, see Table 13.5). Moreover, in 19 of 20 of Tokyo's remaining Ku (excepting Shibuya), it had become less expensive to purchase a new condominium than it had been to buy a house in most of the region's first and second-ring suburbs in 1990.

In reaction to this, a 'back to Ku' movement ensued during the 2000s, resulting in the aforementioned rise in their population by a combined 814,759. Only 5% of this increase came from natural population change (i.e., births minus deaths). The largest share of new residents, approximately 70%, was migrants from other prefectures, predominantly those within the TMR. Similar trends took place in Yokohama and Kawasaki, the region's two next largest cities, which added 262,952 and 175,773 residents, respectively, between 2000 and 2010. Not coincidentally, Kawasaki was adjacent to Ota and Setagaya-Ku, while Yokohama was just south of Kawasaki. Both cities also gained the majority of their new residents from communities within the TMR, albeit from municipalities located further away from central Tokyo than they were. Meanwhile, 18 of the 26 municipalities on the region's outer fringe, in Ibaraki, Tochigi, Gumma, Yamanashi, and Shizuoka Prefectures experienced population declines, as did 59 others in the Kanagawa, Chiba, and Saitama Prefectures; almost all of the latter were in the TMR's distant subareas.

As falling land prices allowed young managers and professionals to move closer to the center of the region, HHI and PCI stratification expanded in the TMR. As mentioned, between 1999 and 2007, the TMR's COV for HHI rose from .1248 to .1868. Meanwhile, the region's COV for PCI advanced from .1917 to .2967. In the meantime, as illustrated in Table 13.6, nine of the top ten increases in municipal HHI change between 2000 and 2007 in the TMR were Tokyo Ku; overall, the 23 Ku secured 18 of the region's top 24 HHI gains. This situation was essentially repeated for PCI. In both cases, the largest advances were in the wealthiest and most central Ku, Minato, Chiyoda, Chuo, and Shibuya, the first three also experienced the fastest population growth rates among the Ku during the 2000's (again, see Table 13.5).

THE TMG'S WATERFRONT POLICIES AND EXPANDING PLACE STRATIFICATION

A final important factor contributing to the widening inter-place stratification in the TMR has been the waterfront development policies of the TMG. The most visible signs of these efforts have been the numerous high-rise condominium developments built: (1) along the Sumida River in Chuo-Ku; (2) abutting the canals in Koto-Ku; and (3) on reclaimed land on Tokyo Bay in what is known as the O'Daiba Area. Although the latter was the locus of the TMG's Waterfront City Project/Plan, the revitalization of Koto-Ku during the 2000s has been one of the most interesting cases. First, because in the early 2000s it was home to the second most public housing units among the 23 Ku. Second, because in an effort to attract young white-collar workers with families, almost all of the housing units built in the district during the period have been spacious private condominiums made affordable through public–private partnerships. While many of these new complexes were located on industrial brownfields, most

Table 13.6 Top 10 Municipalities in HHI and PCI Change, TMR: 2000 to 2007[1,2,3,4]

Municipality	Prefecture	HHI Change 2000 to 2007 (Yen)	Municipality	Prefecture	PCI Change 2000 to 2007 (Yen)
1 Minato-Ku (103)	Tokyo	3,409,705	1 Minato-Ku (103)	Tokyo	2,248,720
2 Chiyoda-Ku (101)	Tokyo	1,963,154	2 Chiyoda-Ku (101)	Tokyo	1,544,553
3 Shibuya-Ku (113)	Tokyo	1,720,083	3 Shibuya-Ku (113)	Tokyo	1,247,505
4 Chuo-Ku (102)	Tokyo	1,256,003	4 Chuo-Ku (102)	Tokyo	1,043,515
5 Meguro-Ku (110)	Tokyo	1,133,991	5 Meguro-Ku (110)	Tokyo	760,742
6 Bunkyo-Ku (105)	Tokyo	522,430	6 Shinjuku-Ku (104)	Tokyo	473,787
7 Shinjuku-Ku (104)	Tokyo	502,431	7 Bunkyo-Ku (105)	Tokyo	461,719
8 Setagaya-Ku (112)	Tokyo	471,366	8 Setagaya-Ku (112)	Tokyo	347,131
9 Koto-Ku (108)	Tokyo	309,466	9 Shinagawa-Ku (109)	Tokyo	292,621
10 Inba-mura, Inba-gun	Chiba	299,744	10 Toshima-Ku (116)	Tokyo	280,215
TMR		−154,952	**TMR**		72,979
Japan		−302,273	**Japan**		−498

Sources: Nihon Marketing Center (1981–2004), JPS (2005–2008).

Notes:

(1) Change figures are based upon the 2007 boundaries of each municipality.

(2) Source data was typically from March 31 of the given year. On March 31, 2007, approximately 117.5 yen were equal to $1 US.

(3) The numbers in parentheses are the Ku place numbers as indicated on Figure 1. Tokyo's 23 Ku are defined by Local Autonomy Law as Special Municipal Wards with similar powers to cities, towns, and villages in Tokyo Prefecture. As a result, their Ku are capitalized to not confuse them with the administrative districts or "ku" of Japan's Government Ordinance Designated Cities, such as Yokohama, Kawasaki, Saitama, and Chiba in the TMR.

(4) Shi is equivalent to city, machi is equivalent to town, and mura is equivalent to village. Since there are duplicate names for machi and mura in Japan and in the region, they are delineated within their gun, which represents the prefectural district they are in, similar to an American county.

were constructed on land controlled by the TMG, including several sites containing large public housing projects.

Energized by subsidized land prices now equivalent to most second ring suburbs, and its close proximity to Tokyo's downtown business districts—only 15 minutes via subway—Koto-Ku added 83,375 new residents between 2000 and 2010, the most of any Ku during this period (again, see Table 13.5). Approximately one-third of this new population settled in neighborhoods located within the Toyosu District (ex. Toyosu, Shiohama, and Edagawa), one of the TMG's new planned sub-centers designated to serve as new satellite growth cores outside of the Toshin (downtown) Area.

One outcome of Toyosu's growth was that HHI expanded by 309,466 yen ($2,634) in Koto-Ku between 2000 and 2007. While seemingly small, this increase occurred in a region in which, on average, suffered a drop in HHI of 154,932 yen ($1,319) or 3.43% during the period (see Table 13.6). As a result, Koto's HHI increased by an incredible 92.48% between 1980 and 2007. On the other hand, impressive as they were, Koto's income gains still paled in comparison to those achieved by Minato and Chuo-Ku, both located in Tokyo's Toshin Area and with large waterfront areas.

While the two central Ku added a smaller number of residents than Koto-Ku, 45,905 and 50,305, respectively, between 2000 and 2010, their population growth rates were higher: 28.80% and 69.36%, respectively, compared with Koto's 22.22%. More significant, however, were their amazing increases in income during the 2000s. As again presented in Table 13.6, Minato, home to numerous ultra-exclusive high-rise developments and foreign embassies, had the largest HHI and PCI gains in the TMR by far, between 2000 and 2007. In fact, at 3.41 million yen ($29,019), Minato's HHI expansion was ten times that of Koto-Ku and represented a growth rate of 31.84% from 2000. Bolstered by tens of thousands of new high-rise waterfront condominiums, Chuo-Ku's HHI expanded by 1.26 million yen ($10,689) or 19.83%, between 2000 and 2007, both ranking fourth-best in the TMR.

Unfortunately, these major waterfront developments helped to fuel a concurrent rise in HHI and PCI stratification by place in the TMR, between 1999 and 2007. Nonetheless, despite a steady rise, spatial inequality in the TMR has remained much less severe than in America's largest CMSAs. The next sections briefly offer two important embedded factors which help to explain why this has been the case: The municipal amalgamation policies of the Japanese Government and the TMR's unique racial-ethnic context.

MUNICIPAL AMALGAMATIONS HELP KEEP INEQUALITY LOWER THAN IN URBAN AMERICA

One of the major differences between the TMR and the New York, Los Angeles, and Chicago CMSA, has been that its municipalities have not evolved within a decentralized intergovernmental system. Japan has centralized unitary state. As such, whereas local governments have a great deal of functional autonomy in America, Japanese municipalities have been directed by national laws and the national government ministries. Within this context, the Japanese Government has instituted laws and policies which have severely limited municipal fragmentation, protected the territorial expansion of cities, and encouraged the consolidation of small, declining, and/or lower income localities. In

short, since the late 19th century the central government has operated under the premise that larger municipalities were more efficient than smaller ones, economically, administratively, and in the delivery of services. When growth was occurring too rapidly, or economic conditions resulted in a significant shrinkage in national and local revenues, it government has promulgated Municipal Mergers Promotion Laws, backed by incentives intended on persuading local governments to consolidate.

As a result of this perspective, at the time of its most recent Census, November 1, 2010, Japan had 128.06 million people but only 1,727 municipalities. In contrast, America had more than 36,000 cities, villages, towns, and townships. Of course, America's has a much larger land area. Nonetheless, considering that Illinois had 2,731 localities and New York 1,547, but had a combined 32.45 million people, clearly municipal fragmentation has influenced inter-local spatial inequality in the Chicago and New York CMSAs. More specifically, whereas in 2007 the TMR had 206 municipalities (228 counting the 23 Ku) serving 36.09 million people (down from 286 in 1980), Chicago had 235, governing a population one-fourth the size of the TMR, 9.16 million (again, see Table 13.1). The New York CMSA had 565 municipal governments serving 21.20 million people, or an area with 58% of the TMR's population. On the other hand, the Los Angeles CMSA, with less than half of Tokyo's population, was served by only 178 cities and towns. However, it also contained miles of unincorporated urbanized county land, including 102 Census Defined Places.

Thorough a series of local amalgamate initiatives, the Japanese Government reduced the number of municipal governments nation-wide. This began when the number of localities was cut from 71,497 in 1883 to 15,859 in 1889, and then to 11,498 by 1940. The latter included the 1932 annexation by the then City of Tokyo of 82 adjacent towns and villages, which expanded its territory almost five-fold to essentially encompass the present-day 23 Ku. Next, in 1953, in order to better accommodate explosive urban-suburban growth, the central government introduced the Town and Village Merger Promotion Law. In response, the number of localities nation-wide contracted to 3,510 in 1960 and the total in TMR's four largest prefectures—Tokyo, Kanagawa, Saitama, and Chiba—was reduced from 836 in 1950 to 278 in 1960.

Finally, in 1995, in response to a dramatic contraction in national and local revenues following the collapse of the Japanese asset-bubble economy, the government re-authorized the Municipal Merger Law, which offered sizeable financial incentives to municipalities willing to amalgamate. The government's plan was to shrink the number of municipalities nation-wide to 1,000, or at least in half, by 2010. Coupled with its Law for the Promotion of Decentralization and revisions to Local Autonomy Law, both also introduced in 1995, the central government also granted municipalities expanded powers over the administration of, and planning for, local development and services. These changes directly tied local authority to population size, meaning that the larger a municipality became, the greater its local autonomy was. In response, between

November 1, 1997 and 2010, the number of municipalities was reduced from 3,232 to 1,727. During this same time period the count in the TMR declined from 281 to 218. Such a retrenchment would be impossible in America.

In sum, whereas American intergovernmental system has encouraged municipal fragmentation and spatial income segregation, the Japan's system has discouraged such outcomes and promoted municipal mergers when it believed it was in the best interest of local government fiscal capacity and administrative efficiency. Municipal amalgamations have brought together communities with varying levels of income, with growing and declining populations, and/or with falling revenues. In the process, such consolidations have helped to limit inter-municipal income stratification in the TMR relative to America's largest CMSAs.

TMR'S RACIAL-ETHNIC EMBEDDEDNESS AND ITS UNIQUE SOCIO-ECONOMIC OUTCOMES

The TMR's quite dissimilar racial-ethnic context also helped explain its level of inter-municipal income stratification relative to America's largest metropolitan regions. As presented in Table 13.7, as of January 1, 2007, only 2.15% of the TMR's 36.09

Table 13.7 Regional vs. Central City, Minority Population and Income: TMR and America's Three Largest CMSA

	TMR 2007	New York CMSA 2000 Census	Los Angeles CMSA 2000 Census	Chicago CMSA 2000 Census
Region % Minority	2.15 %	43.61 %	60.99 %	40.65 %
Central City % Minority[1]	3.57 %	65.02 %	70.25 %	69.68 %
Region Mean HHI	$37,124	$60,254	$45,903	$51,046
Central City HHI [1]	$40,090	$38,293	$36,687	$38,625
Region Mean PCI	$16,250	$26,604	$21,170	$24,581
Central City PCI [1]	$20,275	$22,402	$20,671	$20,175

Sources and Notes: See Table 13.1.

million inhabitants, or 775,007, were non-Japanese. Roughly 40 % of these minorities, or 307,741, resided within Tokyo's 23 Ku. Despite this sizeable amount, this total still amounted to only 3.57% of the Ku's population in that year; in 2007 Japan's population was just 1.69% non-Japanese.

At 10.04%, and with 20,715 minority residents, Minato-Ku had the largest percentage of its population that was non-Japanese among the 23 Ku. The home of many foreign embassies and foreign multinational corporations, roughly one-third of Minato's non-Japanese were from the USA, UK, and Australia. The greatest numeric concentration of minorities among the Ku was in Shinjuku, which had 30,337 non-Japanese residents, equivalent to 9.87% of its population. About three-fourths of Shinjuku's minority residents were ethnic Korean and Chinese. It should be noted here, as a result of Japan's strict citizenship laws, this figure included persons who were third or fourth generation native-born, but unable to naturalize unless they renounced their heritage.

Outside of the 23 Ku, only 13 of the remaining 205 municipalities in the TMR had populations that were above 3% minority: 172 had populations that were less than 2% non-Japanese in 2007 and 135 less than 1.5% minority. Joso city (pop. 70,860) in Ibaraki Prefecture, at 6.78%, had the highest percentage of its population that was non-Japanese. It was followed by the Aikawa town in Kanagawa Prefecture, at 6.43%. In both municipalities, about two-thirds of the minorities were Brazilian and/or Peruvian brought to Japan on labor contracts to work in local factories. No other suburb had as much as 4% of its population that was non-Japanese.

The TMR's relative lack of diversity was striking when juxtaposed against America's largest urban areas. As again shown in Table 13.7, according to the U.S. Census, 43.61% of the New York CMSA's population was Minority (non-White and Hispanics persons)

in 2000. Blacks constituted 17.16% of the area's population, Asian & Pacific Islander (API) 6.82%, while 18.17% were Hispanic. The Los Angeles CMSA was 60.99% Minority in 2000, including 10.68% API, 7.60% Black, and 25.71% classified as 'Other' Race. It also was 40.30% Hispanic. Lastly, the Chicago CMSA was 40.65% Minority, including 18.65% Black, 9.95% Other Races and 16.36 % Hispanic. The region also was 4.29% API. This last relatively small figure was still a greater percentage than the combined percentage of minorities living within Tokyo's 23 Ku, the TMR's central city area.

Related to this, racial-ethnic composition, economic standing, and place were tightly intertwined in the American regions. For example, as shown in Table 13.7, whereas New York City was 65.02% Minority and had a HHI of $38,293, its CMSA was 43.61% Minority and had an HHI of $60,254. That meant that its HHI was almost $22,000 below its CMSA. Los Angeles City was 70.25% Minority and had an HHI of $36,687, the latter being more than $9,000 below its regional median. Lastly, the City of Chicago was 69.68% Minority and had an HHI that was more than $12,000 below its CMSA median. In contrast, while the 23 Ku had a slightly higher percentage of minorities than its region, 3.57% versus 2.15%, their combined HHI of $40,090 was $2,966 above its regional median; its PCI was $4,025 higher.

Two other major differences between the TMR and the American CMSAs related to the spatial location of wealth and poverty, and the connection between minority populations and low incomes. Whereas high incomes were clustered in the suburbs of all three American regions, they were concentrated in the TMR's central core. Moreover, whereas the localities with the highest concentrations of minorities in the American regions generally had among the lowest incomes, this was not the case in the TMR. For example, Minato and Shinjuku-Ku, had among the highest and fastest growing incomes in the TMR; Minato ranked first in the region and in Japan in HHI, PCI, and income growth indicators (again, see Table 13.6).

Conversely, in the New York CMSA, the highest incomes were clustered in the city's northeast suburbs, particularly in Westchester (NY) and Fairfield (CT) Counties, while area's with the largest percentage and concentrations of minorities (ex. Newark, Patterson, and East Orange, NJ, and New York city's Brooklyn borough), ranked among the bottom ten in the region in HHI and PCI in 2000. Similarly, whereas affluence was clustered in Los Angeles' western and southwestern suburbs (parts of Los Angeles and Orange Counties), and in Chicago's northern and northwest suburbs (Lake and DuPage Counties), in both regions lower incomes and poverty were over-concentrated in central city neighborhoods and in adjacent inner ring suburbs with the region's highest percent minority populations. Los Angeles city ranked 216th out of 280 in HHI and Chicago 220th among its region's 235 localities. These central cities also had among the slowest growth rates in income.

A final factor differentiating TMR's racial-ethnic context relative to America's largest metro regions has been Japan's immigration and citizenship laws. These policies have strictly regulated the number of foreigners who have entered the country and discouraged foreign nationals from becoming naturalized. As mentioned, to accomplish the latter, even native-born non-Japanese have not been considered Japanese citizens unless they renounced their ancestral nationality. As a result, most non-Japanese in the TMR were second and third generation Koreans and Chinese, born in Japan. Moreover, as compared with America's largest metro areas, which have served as the nation's gateways for immigrants into the country, the number of foreign workers relocating from periphery nations to the TMR and its central core has been purposely limited by the Japanese Gov-

ernment. It also should be mentioned here that, although it has harshly treated its historic caste (Burakumin), aboriginal peoples (Ainu), and other minorities forcibly brought to the country during its imperialist past (Koreans and Chinese), Japan and the TMR have not experienced anything comparable to America's legacy of Black slavery nor its historically racist public and private housing policies. In sum, the TMR's embedded racial-ethnic context, combined with the central government's promotion of municipal amalgamations, among other policies, has served to inhibit income stratification by place in the TMR.

SUMMARY AND CONCLUSIONS ON THE TMR

This chapter examined changes in income stratification by place within the TMR since 1980. Utilizing the statistic COV, it found that spatial income inequality has widened considerably among its 228 (206) municipalities between 1980 and 2007. It compared the TMR's situation with levels of inter-municipal income stratification in the New York, Los Angeles, and Chicago CMSAs. This analysis suggested that despite its post-1980 rise, the TMR's spatial inequality has remained much less severe than in America's three largest urban regions. In the process, the article's findings supported the idea that embedded factors unique to the TMR, rather than global capitalist flows, have remained the decisive determinants driving its development outcomes.

It demonstrated this by discussing how declining industrial employment, expanding income inequality nation-wide, falling land prices in the region's central core, and the waterfront redevelopment policies of the TMG, have contributed to the TMR's rise in income stratification by place. On the other hand, it also showed how the municipal merger policies of Japanese Government and the TMR's unique racial-ethnic context, as compared with New York, Los Angeles, and Chicago, were two of the many embedded factors that have helped to keep TMR's level of spatial inequality noticeably below that in America's largest regions. These last findings were significant as they not only reinforce the claims of Nested City theorists but also refute one of the main tenets of World/Global City theory, that is, that the TMR has been dis-embedded from its national development context.

Nevertheless, Japan's development context has evolved significantly since 1980. Among the many changes have been the greater devolution of authority to municipalities and the liberalization of the nation's retail sector. Moreover, international political and economic events have always influenced Japan's domestic development agenda; they were what prompted the sizeable shift of manufacturing jobs abroad, especially to low-wage Asian countries. If the 2009 oust-ing from national power of the long-ruling Liberal Democratic Party was any indication, however, it appears its citizens have remained unwilling to completely embrace western-style neo-liberalism and its accompanying levels of inequality and employment uncertainty. As to whether the TMR's rising spatial inequality signifies it is converging with the West, this remains a topic for another study to assess.

NOTES

1 Data sources for this and other sections of the chapter can be found on Tables 13.1 through 13.7. Also, see Jacobs, 2005, 2012). All data pre-dates the massive March 11, 2011 earthquake and tsunami that devastated the coast of Northeastern Japan. Since the epicenter of the earthquake was located 232 miles (373 kilometers) northeast of central Tokyo, the TMR suffered a relatively small number of deaths related to these events. Nevertheless, some of the affected population has been temporarily relocated to the municipalities within the region.

QUESTIONS FOR DISCUSSION

1. In 2–3 paragraphs, discuss the main themes Jacobs' chapter.
2. In 1–2 pages, use specific examples from the chapter which demonstrate how the TMR fits the concepts introduced in Hill and Fujita's Nested City Theory.
3. In 2–3 pages, provide some examples of how embedded factors, such as race-ethnic relations, national and local government policies, have affected development in your region.
4. Utilizing the 'Further Readings', 'Helpful Web Links', and other sources, conduct some further research on three or four cities located within the Tokyo Metropolitan Region. Then, in 2–3 pages, describe some of the most interesting facts you discovered about these places and present your findings to the class.

FURTHER READINGS

Cybriwsky, R. 1998. *Tokyo: The Shogun's City at the Twenty-first Century*. New York: Wiley.

Edgington, D. 1991. Economic Restructuring in Yokohama: From Gateway Port to International Core City. *Asian Geographer,* 10 (1): 62–78.

Fujita, K. and R. Hill, eds. 1993. *Japanese Cities in the World Economy*. Philadelphia: Temple University Press.

Jacobs, A. 2008. Developmental State Planning, Sub-national Nestedness, and Reflexive Public Policy-making: Keys to Employment Growth in Saitama City, Japan. *Cities*, 25 (1): 1–20.

Shapira, P., I. Masser, and D. Edgington, eds. 1994. *Planning for Cities and Regions in Japan.* Liverpool, UK: Liverpool University Press.

Waley, P. 2007. Tokyo-as-World-City: Reassessing the Role of Capital and the State in Urban Restructuring, *Urban Studies,* 44 (8): 1465–1490.

HELPFUL WEB LINKS

Chiba, City of. 2012. Chiba City English Information Page. Online. Available at: http://www.city.chiba.jp/somu/shichokoshitsu/kokusai/EnTop.html, last accessed January 7, 2012.

Hachioji, City of. 2012. Hachioji City English Language Website. Online. Available at: http://www.city.hachioji.tokyo.jp/english/index.html, last accessed January 7, 2012.

Ichikawa, City of. 2012. City of Ichikawa: Official English Website. Online. Available at: http://www.city.ichikawa.lg.jp/english/index.html, last accessed January 7, 2012.

Kanagawa Prefecture. 2012. About Kanagawa Prefecture. Online. Available at: http://www.pref.kanagawa.jp/menu/page/040103.html, last accessed January 7, 2012.

Kawasaki, City of. 2012. Welcome to Kawasaki City. Online. Available at: http://www.city.kawasaki.jp/index_e.htm, last accessed January 7, 2012.

Minato-Ku. 2012. Welcome to Minato City. Online. Available at: http://www.city.minato.tokyo.jp/e/index.html, last accessed January 7, 2012.

Saitama, City of. 2012. Welcome to the Official Website of Saitama City. Online. Available at: http://web.archive.org/web/20080520011305/http://www.city.saitama.jp/en/index.html, last accessed January 7, 2012.

Shibuya-Ku. 2012. Shibuya City Office, English Website. Online. Available at: http://www.city.shibuya.tokyo.jp/eng/index.html, last accessed January 7, 2012.

TMG. 2012. Tokyo Metropolitan Government. Online. Available at: http://www.metro.tokyo.jp/ENGLISH/, last accessed January 7, 2012.

Yokohama, City of. 2012. City of Yokohama Official Website. Online. Available at: http://www.city.yokohama.lg.jp/en/, last accessed January 7, 2012.

CHAPTER 14

Experiencing Jakarta (2008)

Christopher Silver

Few cities in history have experienced the pace of growth and change of Jakarta in the twentieth century. In 1900, the colonial capital of the Netherland Indies, then known as Batavia, was a compact city of approximately 150,000 inhabitants. Over the twentieth century, but especially after 1950, it was transformed into a sprawling metropolis, a 'megacity', of more than 9 million in an urbanized region which by 2000 was home to nearly 18 million. How this metamorphosis occurred, and what it meant for the lives of the city's residents, are key questions addressed in the following pages (see Figure 14.1).

To understand how Jakarta became a megacity requires examination of the role of both the state and private interests in planning its dramatic transformation. The planning processes of government and the private development community that figured so prominently in the emerging form and character of Southeast Asia's largest urban complex were also bound up with the larger project of consolidating and fashioning the new Indonesian nation.

FASHIONING THE COLONIAL CAPITAL CITY

Batavia, as Jakarta was called under colonial rule, was the first foothold of the Dutch in the East Indies in the seventeenth century. Nearly 300 years of colonization and occupation produced only modest changes in the landscape of the original settlement. Only after 1900 did the Dutch begin to treat Batavia with the dignity and determination befitting their colonial capital city and by far the region's most important commercial centre. The period from 1900 through the 1930s witnessed, the 'political integration of Java and the Outer Islands into a single colonial polity' with Batavia positioned administratively and economically at the head of the regime (Lindbald, 2002 p.111). Through the military force of the Royal Netherlands Indies Army, tranquillity and order (*ruste en orde*) had been achieved in the colonies by 1910 and internal vigilance ensured the continuation of Dutch rule until the archipelago was seized by the Japanese in 1942.

The glory of Batavia of the seventeenth and eighteenth centuries was not as a colonial capital, but as the nerve centre of an overseas economy directed by the privately-held Dutch East India Company (or *Vereenigde Oost-Indische Compagnie*) or, as it was commonly known, the VOC. Under the VOC during the seventeenth and eighteenth centuries, and subsequently during the nineteenth century under both Dutch and English control, Batavia was not so much a colonial capital as an international trading port. 'Batavia was outward-looking, and not keen to engage itself in territorial control of inner Java' let alone the vast network of Outer Islands. It drew its population from overseas (Europe and China), it secured its wealth from overseas trade, and only

Figure 14.1 Jakarta in Indonesia and Southeast Asia

tentatively did the city expand in the nineteenth century beyond the boundaries of the fortified commercial hub that had been erected at the mouth of the Ciliwungi River two centuries earlier. It was a place that modelled in its physical form the frugality with which the colonial administration attended to its needs. Its modest size was sufficient for the administrative and commercial functions it was expected to accommodate.

Batavia's population in 1900 was approximately 115,000, only slightly greater than its estimated size nearly a century earlier. The total population for the Batavia region, including agricultural communities located adjacent to the city, was 331,015 in 1810. Batavia's nineteenth-century population grew slowly until 1870 when the pace of European arrivals to Java picked up considerably. Between 1900 and 1930, the population of the city increased from 115,000 to 435,000 which represented an average annual growth rate of 9 per cent. Five years later, through annexation of the previously independent adjacent municipality of Meester Cornelis, Batavia's population jumped to over half a million.

Much of the city's population growth during this period resulted from immigration from rural areas and overseas and was accommodated by the conversion of agricultural estates to urban uses, together with higher densities in the native *kampung* settlements. A concurrent decline in Batavia's high mortality rate was also a contributing factor. Based on its population growth in the late 1930s, and supported by a thriving local economy, Batavia could be described as a prosperous place in the early twentieth century, and with its ascent above rival Surabaya, the largest city in the Netherland Indies.

The spatial distribution of population within Batavia underscored the traditionally deep social divisions based on race, class and ethnicity. In turn this reflected the uneven division of power in the colonial capital. In 1905 the European community represented just 9 per cent of the total population but occupied 50 per cent of the residential land, while the native population, which made up 71 per cent of Batavia's residents, crowded onto just 20 per cent of the city's land. That left the Chinese (and Arabs and Indians), who constituted 20 per cent of the population and occupied a more generous 30 per cent of the land.

[While Surabaya's economy thrived as] the leading port for the thriving sugar processing and export business, as well as the main Dutch naval base in the East Indies, Batavia benefited from the consolidation of centralized governance. Expanded government functions required new buildings and more space to accommodate them. This led to the transformation of Batavia from a compact walled fortress city of warehouses, shops and brokerage facilities into an open, more extensive urban area distinguished by large residential and government buildings on vast stretches of land. As Batavia expanded well beyond the confines of the early nineteenth-century port city it became a place differentiated by ethnicity, class, and race as well as by its multiple urban functions. However, the most important change and the foundation for the colonial capital of the twentieth

century was development of the European enclave of Weltevreden. While the old city centre, referred to as Kota (meaning 'city'), remained largely a commercial hub attached to port activities, Weltevreden emerged as the new centre of the colonial capital. Its development signalled the intention of the Dutch to elevate Batavia to a city on a par with the best in Europe.

THE CHINESE COMMUNITY OF BATAVIA

The huge economic power of the Chinese community in Batavia, in contrast to that of the so-called native population, was both a creation of the Dutch governance system and a continuing challenge to that system. Under the racially-based Dutch governance structure in the Netherland Indies, the Chinese community was not only separated, from Europeans, but also from the indigenous population. The race-based system was hierarchical and stratified, with Europeans at the top, and separate branches below for the indigenous population (*Inlandsch Bestuur*) and for the non-native, non-European communities consisting of Arabs, Moors, Bengalis and Chinese grouped under the umbrella designation, *Bestuur voor Vreemde Oosterlingen*. As the largest of the non-native, non-European community the Chinese community had its own system of local governance, the *Chineesch Bestuur*. Like all native and non-native groups, the Chinese had headsmen drawn from the community who were answerable to the colonial government for ensuring that Dutch policies were followed and taxes collected. The Chinese officials, known as *Kapitan Cina*, were especially important since they were responsible for governing both the largest and most affluent group. In the nineteenth century, the Chinese managed key segments of the agricultural system, especially the opium trade, which brought substantial revenues into the colonial coffers. The largest proportion of Batavia's revenues came from land taxes and the Chinese were the largest land holding group. Although shifting economic policies undermined the advantageous position of the Chinese, their extensive land holdings and firm base in the urban economy helped to mitigate the negative effects of losing a monopoly position.

The Chinese involvement in land in the Batavia regency was the foundation of their powerful economic position. In 1910, they controlled approximately 40 per cent of all private lands, although a policy of the Dutch government to purchase these lands reduced their holdings to only about 10 per cent by 1920. The Chinese accumulation of land in Batavia had begun in the seventeenth century, and when Governor General Daendels initiated public land sales to fill the empty government coffers between 1809 and 1811, it was the Chinese who bought up the largest share of the offerings. By 1836, 83 of the 187 private estates in the Batavia regency were owned by Chinese. Although the Agrarian Law of 1870 closed off the opportunity for non-natives to purchase property, the Chinese land owners shifted their holdings into companies that operated outside the restrictions of the law and this enabled them to retain a substantial share of the land. And on these lands they grew various crops, but largely rice, for local consumption; they employed native labourers and tenants to cultivate the land and bring them profits. The move by the Dutch government in the early 1900s to reduce the amount of private land was initially aimed at the extensive holdings of the British, and in three separate purchases in 1906, 1910 and 1918, the influence of private British land owners was virtually eliminated. However, the plan to purchase lands in Tangerang and Meester Cornelis which were owned by the Chinese was 'to facilitate city development, where space was needed for transportation networks, railways, roads, bridges and an irrigation system'. Between 1912 and 1930, the Dutch government invested over 81 million guilders to repurchase 911,140 *bouws* (210,500 hectares) of private land.

While there were Chinese communities scattered throughout the colony, the largest were in the cities of Batavia, Semarang and Surabaya. The best available estimates indicate that there were approximately 92,520 Chinese within the greater Batavia region, with more living outside the city than within it in 1905. Roughly one-third of this population, or 28,000, lived inside Batavia, mostly within the Glodok area. By 1920, the Batavia area Chinese population had grown to 116,525. When the Europeans moved the major government institutions and their primary residential functions to Weltevreden in the nineteenth century, the predominantly commercially-based Chinese population expanded into the space that was vacated, and created its own institutional base, including Chinese temples, schools, hospitals, offices for Chinese organizations, and a great variety of business establishments.

But the movements of the Chinese were closely regulated by a passport system that had been set up in 1835 which not only ensured strict residential segregation but made it possible to know who was coming and going from the community. A similar system operated within the native community. The Chinese officers working for the colonial government were responsible for enforcing the system, but technically were not employed by the Dutch since they received no remuneration. These officers were typically wealthy individuals whose income derived from their agricultural holdings or businesses in Glodok, and they served for indeterminate terms.

THE COLONIAL BACKDROP

The Dutch colonial leadership in pre-independence Batavia undertook a variety of development initiatives but none seems to have considered the tremendous changes underway in the city as a whole. Plans were

prepared but they were simply detailed map-
pings of existing uses and went out of date
almost on a daily basis. Batavia had grown
to 800,000 by 1940, with a near doubling of
the land area of the city through development
of suburban Weltevreden, and its formal
annexation (along with the adjacent residential enclave, Meester Cornelis) into the city in
the 1930s. These crucial decisions to enlarge
the city were undertaken without reference
to any scheme for the desired outcome. The
only plans were those for specific sub-areas of
the city, such as the residential development
of Menteng, the proposed revamping of the
Fatahillah civic area and the redesign of the
Konigsplein. In fact Batavia progressed using
me tradition of municipal-level regulation of
the city's development that began in 1909.
This typically involved laying out the expanding city's street pattern to accommodate new
European residential areas such as Menteng
and Gondangdia. The so-called Kubatz plan
of 1918 consisted of a single city map with
the most up-to-date inventory of the existing
infrastructure and the proposed street network for the Menteng neighbourhood.

Given that there were ample precedents for
a comprehensive approach to city planning,
how was it that such a piecemeal approach
characterized the situation in Batavia in the
early twentieth century? It was not that the
city's small but energetic band of planners and
architects failed to keep abreast of what was
going on elsewhere . . . the leading advocates
of better planning in Batavia were well connected to the international planning movement. Perhaps the best explanation is that at
that time there was no planning tradition in
The Netherlands to serve as a model for such
an approach. Planning in Holland in the early
twentieth century was principally a matter of
regulating land development to address the
immediate housing needs of the nation; its
essence was street platting and subdivision
design rather than the monumental schemes
that had come out of the nineteenth-century
tradition of city planning in Paris and were

implemented in so many United States cities
in the first three decades of the century.

Another notable factor was that Batavia
apparently lacked powerful, wealthy and
enthusiastic planning sponsors to back and
possibly even fund preparation of a plan.
Those who were the leading advocates for
better planning in Batavia were a handful of
architects, and not the business elite, and these
professionals were in many cases constrained
in their advocacy by the need to make a living. To rally support for public planning was
incidental to their primary work of designing
residences and commercial structures.

There was little chance that a movement
for civic improvement could spring from
indigenous sources in Batavia. For one thing,
its commercial-civic elite was divided along
race and ethnic lines. The existence of two
separate commercial groupings, one based in
the Chinese community and the other dominated by the Europeans, prevented the city's
business community from galvanizing into
a force for civic improvement of any kind.
Under the colonial regime, planning for the
needs of the city stuck to the bare necessities. The key challenges faced in the 1930s,
such as the increasing number and size of
substandard *kampung* housing areas and
the need to improve services to the expanding European enclaves, would have benefited
from an integrated and strategic approach,
but each was dealt with separately and incrementally. Perhaps the reluctance to invest
heavily in the reconstruction of Batavia was
related to the fact that The Netherlands government was aiming to transfer the functions
of the colonial capital from Batavia to Bandung, the cool hill city some 150 kilometres
south-east of the port. The Ministry of Public
Works and the télécommunications ministry
were moved there in the 1930s, but the outbreak of World War II diverted attention and
resources from this project. When the Japanese took control of the Netherland Indies in
1942, the capital building effort in Bandung
ceased. The new occupiers reasserted the

role of Batavia as the administrative centre of the archipelago. Later, it was the locus of the struggle to create a new nation on ashes of the former colonial capital. At that point, planning for the future began to matter.

Reconstruction of Batavia following the Japanese withdrawal from Java in 1945 and the Dutch reoccupation provided the initial impetus for an aggressive and more comprehensive approach to planning urban development. In the midst of the turmoil accompanying its attempt to reassert authority over the Indonesian islands, and despite the declaration of Indonesian independence in 1945, the Dutch government embarked on infrastructure planning for post-war recovery.

When national sovereignty was officially transferred to the Indonesians [in 1950 however], government agencies and private developers jumped into the post-war rebuilding efforts with neither a plan nor a legal framework to guide urban development.

There: was no more vexing issue for the local administrators and planners, and their consultants, than deriving accurate figures for the population of Jakarta, and its rate of growth due to natural increases and the seeming flood tide of migrants to the city in the 1950s. Since there had been no population census in Indonesia since 1931, and given the tumultuous circumstances, during the Japanese occupation and the subsequent war with the Dutch, gauging Jakarta's population size was little more than guesswork.

[In 1931, Jakarta's population was approximately 533,000 (see Table 14.1)]. By the 1961 census it had grown to 2.9 million, an increase of nearly 1.8 million since 1948. This translated into an average annual overall increase of 133,000 over this period. In fact, the rate of annual population growth would grow even more in the ensuing decade, rising to approximately 167,000 persons per year between the 1961 and 1971 censuses. No matter what was the precise figure, there was no more discussed issue among Jakarta planners, and local leaders throughout the 1950s

Table 14.1 Population of Large Indonesian Cities, 1931–1971 (000s).

City	1931	1961	1971
Jakarta	533.0	2,907.0	4,576.0
Bandung	116.8	972.8	1,201.7
Surabaya	341.7	1,007.9	1,556.3
Semarang	217.8	503.1	646.6
Medan	76.6	479.1	635.6
Palembang	108.1	474.9	582.9

Source: Wirosardjono (1974).

and 1960s than how to deal with the seemingly unstoppable flow of migrants to the city and the increasing inability of the city to accommodate them. A widely cited solution was to make improvements, to those rural areas the migrants were leaving so as to make the trek to the capital city less attractive.

[Nevertheless] despite uncertain (or nonexistent) employment opportunities, inadequate housing, higher costs of living, and the difficulty of surviving in a chaotic urban environment, there seemed to be no effective way to discourage the flow. For Jakarta's planners, the test was handling this sustained population increase both in the short run and in terms of long range improvements to the city.

EXPANSION, REVITALIZATION AND RESTRUCTURING, THE 1970S–1990S

In 1976, Indonesia's President Suharto issued an official order concerning the future development of the capital city. That executive act set in motion a process of expansion in Jakarta that would radically revamp both the form and quality of the urban environment over the next three decades. Presidential Instruction No 13/1976 (*Inpres* 13/1976) specified that the regional city of Bogor, located approximately 60 kilometres to the south of Jakarta, along with the smaller administrative cities of Tanggerang to the west, and Bekasi to the east, would be designated as the nodes of development in the capital city, area connected by the emerging modern highway system. This presidential directive formally sanctioned the new planning strategy referred to as 'bundled déconcentration', an approach prescribed for the Jakarta region in 1973 by the Dutch consultant team headed by Lambert Giebels.

Yet where the Dutch planners saw an opportunity to implement a managed system of spatial decentralization through investment in a mass transit system linking the centre city to these designated suburban development centres, the Indonesian government and the real estate development community saw a rationale for encouraging fringe area development that did not have to wait for such expensive transport infrastructure. Adding to the highway system started by Sukarno in the early 1960s seemed a much more feasible approach, especially since there was an opportunity for the toll roads to generate revenue as well as to lure in private investment. A modern highway system offered a more flexible transport network that could more easily serve the ten identified business groups that were poised to expand the urbanized area into the periphery. So with promulgation of *Inpres* 13/1976, it was the automobile, the bus and the truck that triumphed over transit in delivering a modern public transport system to Jakarta.

LAND DEVELOPMENT

While completing the toll road construction programme was a critical ingredient of Jakarta's suburbanization process, planning for alternative models of urban communities was underway long before the pavement dried. According to Leaf (1994, pp. 344, 353):

> the two important areas which have been instrumental in fostering the suburbanization of Jakarta . . . [are] . . . a massive programme of subsidized housing finance . . . and a municipal permit system for land development created specifically to feed urban lands into the corporate development sector.

And these, he said, were supported by 'government-sponsored provision of trunk infrastructure'. Dick noted that even before large-

scale suburban development occurred the artificially low fares charged on the public transit system, subsidized fuel prices for car owners, and the aggressive development of a highway network to support this transport system discouraged high density development. 'In effect', he observed, 'the government is subsidizing urban sprawl, a trend which has been most evident in Jakarta over the past decade [1970s] but which can be found in most other large Indonesian cities' (Dick 1981, p. 87).

The generosity of Indonesia's National Land Agency in issuing permits to allow development of more than 80,000 hectares of land on the fringes of Jakarta between 1985 and 1999 hastened the sprawling decentralized pattern of development. Although only 40 per cent of the permitted land was actually built on prior, to the economic crisis of 1997, the net effect of the wholesale granting of development authorizations was to encourage developers to favour peripheral locations over those more centrally located. This was a repetition of a process of land conversion that had first occurred with government encouragement during the third national development plan 1978–1983 (*Repelita III*). During that 5 year period, agricultural areas immediately adjacent to the city, including Pasar Minggu, Jati Padang, Warung Buncit, Pejaten, Pondok Labu, Klender, Ciputat, Cilenduk and Depok were drawn into the urban settlement system. All these communities were located along Jakarta's southern edge, and all were linked spatially and functionally to the only satellite city, Kebayoran Baru. Both the Jakarta to Bogor highway, as well as expanded radial roadways emanating from the inner ring highway, provided ready access to these areas.

Given the scale of new housing, commercial, and industrial development at the edges of metropolitan Jakarta from the late 1970s to the 1990s, it would be reasonable to expect that this would have been accompanied by equally dramatic population losses and commercial decline in the inner city. Even when abundant lands were made available for new development at the edges, this did not dampen demand for land in the city. According to a study of land speculation in the Jakarta region, land prices in strategic areas of central Jakarta rose rapidly during the 1980s and 1990s. In Jakarta's so-called 'Golden Triangle', a new commercial zone framed by Jalan Sudirman, Jalan Gotot Subroto, and Jalan Rasuna Said, the land price per square metre rose from Rp 2500 in 1970 to Rp 700,000 by 1988 (US$7 to 438). But this was just the start. By the early 1990s, land prices in this area averaged Rp 5 million per square metre but in some transactions were known to go as high as Rp 12 million (or US$4,800) per square metre. These inflated prices made it extremely attractive to transform the remaining residential, manufacturing and trade properties to new uses to capture the land value. No wonder that the locus of Jakarta's office boom shifted to the Golden Triangle area. According to the best available data, from 1980 to 1992, there were 600 new buildings constructed in Jakarta, with a total value of US$3 billion, the greatest proportion in or adjacent to the Golden Triangle. Escalating land prices in central Jakarta led to

> the changing function of the core area, from being a center of manufacturing activities to ... a center for finance and services ... Slum areas are being converted into a business zone, with shopping centers, hotels, offices, condominiums and the like. (Firman, 1996 p.109)

The physical transformation and consequent displacement of previous functions in so many areas of central Jakarta, especially near strategic commercial zones, was profound. Yet available population data suggest that population growth in Jakarta's inner areas remained robust in the face of such massive development outside its boundaries, at least through the early 1990s. Only one of Jakar-

ta's five administrative areas, Jakarta Pusat (Central Jakarta), experienced a population loss in the wake of explosive commercial development, but that loss was relatively modest—from 1,182,393 to 1,001,000 (15 per cent) between 1984 and 1994, (see Table 14.2). At the same time, the other four administrative areas increased in population between 37 per cent and 77 per cent. In other words, development in Jakarta's suburban periphery and the dramatic restructuring of older sections of the inner city did not produce the abandonment of the city centre that was so typical of Western cities also experiencing rapid decentralization.

In Jakarta, there was a steady outflow of inner-city residents to new developments along the periphery. A study of who was populating Jakarta's expanding fringe found that migrants moved there from central Jakarta in order to obtain affordable housing. Whether pushed out because their housing was cleared for new development, or facing the pressures of escalating rents (or the chance to make some money by letting a city centre house at an inflated rate while renting something for much less but further out), inner-city neighbourhoods fed the emerging suburbs with a steady flow of new residents. The continuous influx of new migrants from outside the Jakarta region replenished inner urban areas and more than offset the population losses due to out-migration. What is remarkable is that the residential density of Jakarta actually increased from an average of 99.7 persons per hectare in 1980 to 135.7 persons per hectare in 1994.

Table 14.2 Central City Population Increases, Jakarta, 1984 to 1994

	1984	1994	Change
South Jakarta	1,476,201	2,023,300	+37%
East Jakarta	1,395,877	2,337,200	+67%
Central Jakarta	1,182,393	1,001,000	−15%
West Jakarta	1,260,818	2,097,700	+66%
North Jakarta	869,553	1,539,400	+77%
Total	6,184,842	8,998,600	+46%

Sources: Jakarta, DKI, (1984, 1990).

The increased population density in the inner city, coupled with a continuous process of land-use conversion and rapid development of peripheral areas, constituted a unique urban dynamic that confounded the prevailing planning model devised to manage change.

The transition process in Jakarta's inner and outer cities during the 1980s and 1990s had a disruptive effect, especially in low-income neighbourhoods. Displacement of virtually all the remaining pockets of affordable residential neighbourhoods adjacent to the Jalan Sudirman, Jalan Thamrin and Jalan Rasuna Said commercial areas forced many to crowd into residential areas not directly in the path of the business boom or to join the exodus to the urban fringe. Almost all the replacement housing built in or near the Golden Triangle was geared to an upper-income market. Throughout the 1980s and early 1990s, *kampung* residents in the path of inner-city commercial development tried to resist displacement or at least hold out for improved compensation, but in most cases, residents were forced to move with little compensation. One exception was redevelopment of the abandoned Kemayoran airport in Central Jarkarta. The project displaced 5,200 families in three adjacent sub-districts (*kelurahan*). While the centrepiece of the Kemayoran project was a new international trade centre, it included new replacement low-income apartments. The project plan called for displaced families to have first priority for occupancy in these units. Not all accepted the new housing because it was more expensive than their previous shelter (costing between Rp 30,000 (US$24) and 115,000 (US$52) per month). Others did not like apartment living (it seemed like living in a 'bird cage') and chose to take the compensation for their land and moved to a cheaper area. What was most significant in the case of the Kemayoran redevelopment plan was the introduction of an explicit commitment to replacement housing for low-income families. Although the final dispensation of the project did not work exactly as planned, it is significant that Jakarta's planners recognized that the displacement factor of centre city restructuring was a matter to be addressed.

VISIONS FOR THE FUTURE

Planning has become even more important to twenty-first-century democratic Jakarta than it was in implementing the competing colonial and nationalist visions of the twentieth. This can be seen in the carefully crafted 'strategic plan' now being used to frame development of the capital city. In its discussion of the challenges currently confronting Jakarta, the strategic plan reads much like many of the earlier assessments of urbanization in the capital city, suggesting that perhaps little has changed in the realities of life for many despite the outward appearance of a much larger and more modern city. The social challenges are identified as uncontrolled urbanization which has produced a whole new collection of slum areas, and a higher incidence of crime and social conflict, especially in the aftermath of the economic crisis. Unemployment remains high despite the return of economic growth, income disparity has increased, and there is the general perception that social institutions are not able to suppress 'increasing conflict among social groups'. These inequalities are exacerbated by unequal distribution of the benefits of education and health. Of course, contributing to all of these problems has been the 'slow economic recovery' since the crisis, of 1997. Although by 2000 economic growth had increased to 3.98 per cent and then held at roughly the same level (3.64 per cent) in 2001, unemployment has remained high, causing even more to turn to the informal sector, mainly street vending.

Lingering effects of the economic crisis limited the city's financial capacity to address longstanding infrastructure needs. As expected, the strategic plan underscores the problems of limited water supply, annual flooding, inadequate garbage and sewage management, and the continuing challenge of providing enough decent and affordable housing for low income families. But what is notable about this plan is its emphasis on the environmental deficiencies of the megacity that involve more than just poor infrastructure service. A lack of open space and massive air and water pollution problems topped the list. 'Like problems in most mega cities', the plan observes, 'Jakarta faces a problem of limited open space' largely because it is being crowded out by economic activities. Air and water pollution, including industrial waste, are cited as related environmental deficiencies that helped to give Jakarta the dubious distinction of being 'the third highest polluted city in the world'.

The plan also acknowledges that the low level of trust and acceptance of the government after the reform movement has made it even more difficult to govern and plan effectively. Both the economic crisis and the collapse of the New Order government contributed to a higher level of social disorder and insufficient community participation in governance, despite the changes in the structure of local government. From the standpoint of Jakarta's leadership, decentralization gave new authority to local government officials but did not immediately supply sufficient resources to enable the new responsibilities to be handled effectively There seemed to be fewer resources to take on more responsibilities, Which contributed to the 'low spirit' among government officers now confronted with massive challenges previously taken on in partnership with a powerful central government.

Although the litany of urban ills identified in the plan was essentially the same as those which planners confronted throughout the last half of the century, this new plan is grounded in a fundamentally different notion of the purpose of planning. The vision presented is for the megacity Jakarta to become

'a humane, efficient, and competitive capital supported by a participative, prosperous, well behaved and, civilized society in a safe and sustainable environment'. This vision is framed within a series of mission statements that call for an efficient and honest government that will ensure a 'just and sound environmental and community-focused development process' supported by the necessary infrastructure. The plan calls for a phased-in process, beginning with a focus on full economy recovery, improved governance and law enforcement, and some new infrastructure between 2002 and 2004. By 2005, the emphasis would shift from recovery to sustaining the prosperity that had been restored and to ensure that the foundations for social, political and economic development in place would be sustainable.

Throughout the list of specific strategies runs the theme of good planning and management in order to support communities and to minimize social conflicts. It is not just a matter of dealing with the historically big challenges of traffic congestion, flood control, spreading slum areas, and an increasing informal sector in conflict and competition with the formal sector. The sustainable megacity is one that needs to meet the important social needs of its ever changing citizenry, from health care, to education, to supporting community organizations and elevating the moral tone in a capital city traditionally concerned more with generating wealth rather than sharing it. As Jakarta, the megacity, faces the ongoing planning challenges early in the twenty-first century, its leadership now understands more clearly than at any point in the previous century that planning is, in effect, largely a social process even with its obvious physical manifestations. Effective planning for cities are those policies and initiatives that improve the social conditions of the greatest number of its citizens. That had been true during the waning years of the colonial capital in the early twentieth century and it remains ever more true as Jakarta is poised to step onto the global stage as a world city in its own right, one in which newly created democratic planning processes might ultimately enable all its citizens to share in the greatness of Southeast Asia's grandest city.

QUESTIONS FOR DISCUSSION

1. In two or three paragraphs, discuss the main themes in Silver's chapter on Jakarta.
2. List three or four of the factors mentioned by Silver that suggest Jakarta fits Nested City Theory. Then, in 1–2 pages, use the chapter and others examples from the book to explain these factors and their impact on Jakarta.
3. List three or four of the similarities and differences between Jakarta and two other cities you have already read about in Parts One or Two. Now, based only upon what you have read in the book, in 1–2 pages explain these similarities and differences.
4. Using the 'Further Readings', 'Helpful Web Links', and other sources, conduct some further research on Jakarta and another large city in Southeast Asia. Then, in 2–3 pages, describe some of the most interesting new events and facts you discovered about these places and present your findings to the class.

FURTHER READINGS

Castles, L. 1991. Jakarta: The Growing Centre. In H. Hill, ed., *Unity and Diversity: Regional Economic Development in Indonesia since 1970.* New York: Oxford University Press.

Dick, H., V. Houben, J. Linbald, and T. Wie, eds., 2002. The *Emergence of a National Economy: An Economic History of Indonesia, 1800–2000.* Crows Nest, NSW: Allen and Unwin.

Firman, T. 1999. From Global City to City of Crisis: Jakarta Metropolitan Region under Economic Turmoil. *Habitat International,* 23 (4): 447–466.

Huabarat, L. 2010. The City as a Mirror: Transport, Land Use and Social Change in Jakarta. *Urban Studies,* 47 (3): 529–555.

Leaf, M. 1996. Building the Road for the BMW: Culture, Vision and the Extended Metropolitan Region of Jakarta. *Environment and Planning A,* 28 (9): 1617–1635.

Marcussen, L. 1990. *Third World Historical in Social and Spatial Development: The Case of Jakarta.* Aldershot, UK: Avebury.

HELPFUL WEB LINKS

Bangkok Post. 2012. Home Page of Bangkok Post Newspaper: The World's Window on Thailand. Online. Available at: http://www.bangkokpost.com/, last accessed, January 6, 2012.

Ho Chi Minh City. 2012. Welcome to Ho Chi Minh City: HCM City People's Committee. Online. Available at: http://www.eng.hochiminhcity.gov.vn/eng/news/, last accessed, January 6 2012.

Indonesia, Republic of. 2012. Portal Nasional Republik Indonesia: English Portal of the National Republic of Indonesia. Online. Available at: http://indonesia.go.id/en/, last accessed, January 6, 2012.

Jakarta, City of, 2012. Enjoy Jakarta. Official Tourism Portal. Jakarta City Government, Tourism and Culture Office. Online. Available at: http://www.jakarta-tourism.go.id/, last accessed, January 6, 2012.

Jakarta, DKL 2012. Official Website of the DKI Jakarta Governance. Jakarta Daerah Khusus Ibukota (Special Capital Region of Jakarta). Online. Available at: http://www.jakarta.go.id/english/, last accessed, January 6, 2012.

Jakarta Post, 2012. Home Page of the Jakarta Post Newspaper. Online. Available at: http://www.the-jakartapost.com/, last accessed, January 6, 2012.

Kuala Lumpur, City of. 2012. Official Portal of City of Kuala Lumpur (Malaysia) City Hall. Online. Available at: http://www.dbkl.gov.my/portalv7/index.php?lang=en, last accessed, January 6, 2012.

Manila, City of. 2012. Welcome to the Official Website of the City of Manila, Philippines. Online. Available at: http://www.manila.gov.ph/, last accessed, January 6, 2012.

Phnom Penh, City of. 2012. Phnom Penh, Cambodia: The Charming City. Online. Available at: http://www.phnompenh.gov.kh/, last accessed, January 6, 2012.

Singapore, Government of. 2011. Singapore Government Home Page. Online. Available at: http://www.gov.sg/govemment/web/content/govsg/classic/home, last accessed, December 31, 2011.

CHAPTER 15

Actor Networks and Hybrid Developmental States: Malaysia's Multimedia Super-corridor and New York's Silicon Alley (2003)

Michael Indergaard

In recent years, many nations have looked to digital industry enclaves as motors that might propel their economies through the uncertain tides of globalisation. Public officials around the world have long been entranced by Silicon Valley. During the 1990s, a new kind of digital enclave made a spectacular emergence in US cities. 'New media' districts such as the San Francisco's 'Multimedia Gulch', the 'Digital Coast' of Los Angeles and New York's 'Silicon Alley' drew billions in investment and generated large numbers of jobs. These districts were touted as evidence of a 'new economy' fuelled by a combination of neo-liberal policies and new technology. However, there are a variety of ways in which digital districts are being made. Central states in east Asian nations such as Japan, Singapore and Malaysia have devised development schemes featuring 'smart' buildings, technopoles and 'intelligent' cities. Now that the dot-com bubble has burst, it is a good time to examine state-led alternatives.

Research shows that settings with different institutional profiles may produce distinctive forms of innovation Hill and Kim (2000) offer a starting-point for examining how institutional differences matter in the making of digital districts in east Asia and the US. In what might be termed a 'nested city' thesis, they argue that cities are shaped by "the national development model and regional context" in which they are "embedded" (Hill and Kim, 2000, p. 2188). They especially stress differences between cities of the west Atlantic and east Asian regions—bastions of neo-liberalism and developmental states, respectively. While unfettered equity markets dominate under neo-liberalism, states in late-developing east Asian nations have used a mix of regulation and non-market governance mechanisms to concentrate resources in key sectors.

The question of whether developmental states are a viable alternative when it comes to nurturing digital districts is of special relevance for students of east Asia. The explosive growth of digital industries in the US during the 1990s led many observers to ask whether east Asia's developmental states are outmoded. In this light, Malaysia's efforts to build a Multimedia Super-corridor (MSC) are very important. The MSC is a striking state attempt to nurture a digital district—all the more audacious considering Malaysia's standing as a second-tier newly industrialising country (NIC). The Malaysian state has had success in supporting the growth of basic industry but it is not clear that the same strategy can work for developing advanced technology. Malaysia is also strategic because it is more representative of the world's NICs than classic east Asian cases. At the same time, it has special importance as a secular state trying to balance the demands of development and Islam. Finally, the case allows a look at contradictory trends in developmentalism. Prime Minister Mahathir has promoted the MSC as a flagship in the state's effort to develop its society and as an alternative model for developing nations. Yet, his regime has also embraced some neo-liberal policies.

In this paper, the cases of Malaysia's MSC project and New York's Silicon Alley are used to examine how the ability of a second-tier developmental state to create a digital district compares with that of a neo-liberal framework. While New York is a centre of global finance and business services, it too felt compelled to play digital catch-up in the 1990s, Silicon Alley's rise was imprinted by neo-liberal policies—and the kind of free market sensibilities concerning technology that inflect the musings of Secretary Summers. Compared with the MSC project, the direct role of government was muted and the organisation of images, relationships and space is quite different. Moreover, Silicon Alley's decline in the wake of the market crash allows a look at neo-liberalism's shortcomings.

[It argues that, Malaysia represents a hybrid which] departs from the developmental state model, mixing features of both developmentalism and neo-liberalism. In order to attain a more nuanced and dynamic analysis, it is proposed that the development of digital districts be conceptualised as cases of 'translation' rather than of embeddedness: ideas and power relations alike have to be reconstituted when they are enacted in new settings. The study shows that neo-liberal regimes had an indirect effect on districts such as Silicon Alley through informal policies that promoted the financial and technological sectors. In Silicon Alley itself, there was little public-sector involvement; entrepreneurial actors and visions proliferated, with venture capitalists and real estate interests taking the lead in bringing together diverse participants. In contrast, Malaysia's state devised a comprehensive vision of how the MSC will support national development and has created a public agency to enroll and co-ordinate participants. Some MSC elements have a neo-liberal cast (for example, recruitment of transnational corporations and a NASDAQ-like market for technology stocks) but are enmeshed in a framework where state entities and developmental goals remain central. The digital ensemble being assembled in the MSC is proving to be more resilient than that created in Silicon Alley during a flood of speculation. It is concluded that the state-led path is more desirable for developing nations that need to construct a digital industry base.

The nested city thesis provides important insights, but has some limitations. First, its reliance on the idea of 'embeddedness' limits its ability to deal with change—a liability when assessing the 1990s and the rise of digital districts. Relatedly, city traits are sometimes derived from national characteristics in a rather mechanical fashion. Secondly, the emphasis on regional types (west Atlantic neo-liberalism, east Asian developmentalism) has benefits, but comes at a cost: an underspecification of the nestedness of cities in national settings.

In sum, the nested city thesis requires further theoretical specification that deals with the dynamic and hybrid nature of contemporary institutional change.

THE MALAYSIAN QUESTION

It is tempting to view Malaysia as a developmental state that is embedded in an east Asian regional system orchestrated by Japan. The formation of the east Asian economy was spurred by Japan's extension of its production system across Singapore, Taiwan, Hong Kong and South Korea, and its subsequent fanning out into Malaysia, Thailand, China, Indonesia and Vietnam. Under the 'Look East' and 'Malaysia Inc.' policies of the 1980s, Malaysia emulated development strategies of Japan and South Korea; as Japan had done earlier, the Malaysian state devised a strategy to upgrade its industries into higher-value-added areas. Castells (1998, p. 308) even calls Malaysia "the fifth tiger". Indeed, by some indicators, Malaysia has been at the forefront of 'second-tier' NICs. It achieved an annual growth in GDP that averaged 8.9 per cent between 1988 and 1995 and a rise in per capita income from US$978 in 1970 to US$9470 in 1995; the povery rate declined from 16.5 per cent of households in 1990 to 8.9 per cent in 1995 (Tressini, 2001, pp. 336–337) (see Figure 15.1).

However, to the extent to which Malaysia is a 'tiger', it is one of a different stripe. In various respects it is more representative of second-tier NICs than the classic east Asian success stories. Its population is more heterogeneous in terms of ethnicity and religion. As of 1991, 57 per cent of Malaysia's population was Malay and indigenous peoples (together referred to as 'Bumiputeras') while 27 per cent were of Chinese ethnicity and 8

per cent were of Indian ancestry (Huff, 2001, p. 452). Its political economy is ethnically segmented. Chinese dominate the indigenous business sector, while Malays are the political élites. Of special interest is the fact that the Malay-dominated state has cultivated a secular form of Islam In the area of information technology Malaysia is far and away the leader amongst Muslim countries. These traits, along with the MSC project, leads Huff (2001) to propose that Malaysia's ability to create "the cultural and institutional conditions conducive to creativity and innovation" (p. 457) make it "a vanguard model not only for the Muslim World, but perhaps for all developing countries" (p. 447).

Figure 15.1 Malaysia's Multimedia Super-corridor in context

However, other observers question Malaysia's record as a developmental state (Henderson, 1999; Jomo, 2001). The ethnic segmentation between its economic and political élites seems a special constraint. Export-oriented industrialisation policy was initiated in response to ethnic riots in 1969. Industrialisation, along with a redistribution of wealth towards the Bumiputera majority, was said to be a pre-condition for ethnic harmony. The ensuing New Economic Policy (NEP) bypassed the country's small and medium-sized firms, which were owned by ethnic Chinese, and turned to foreign capital. Thus, in contrast to the classic east Asian cases, industrialisation in Malaysia was driven by foreign direct investment. During the 1980s, Mahathir's regime dropped the goal of uplifting the Bumiputera masses, stressing national development as a means of achieving ethnic harmony, However, the Bumiputera élite continues to receive preferential treatment. From the late 1980s to the mid-1990s, the Mahahir regime adopted a number of neo-liberal policies (for example, privatisation and financial liberalisation) that favoured his political allies among the Bumiputera élite.

Critics claim that dependence on foreign investment and favouritism towards regime allies have compromised the state—especially, its ability to channel capital to key sectors (Henderson, 1999; Jomo, 2001). Rasiah (2001, p. 59) argues that Malaysia "has failed to ensure the kind of strong institutional supports for technological change that have been achieved by first-tier Asian NIEs". While the 1990 Action Plan for Industrial Technological Development directed investment into technology-deepening projects (including the MSC), few mechanisms were created to co-ordinate and discipline enterpreneurs or to upgrade the skill-base or R&D. Thus, firms have not "developed productive capabilities to increase their participation in foreign firms value-added chains" (Rasiah, 2001, p. 63),

Based on its "asymmetical capacities", Henderson (1999) terms Malaysia's state, "semi-developmental" or, following Evans (1995), an "intermediate" case (i.e. on a continuum between developmental and predatory states). Since it is also semi-neo-liberal, there is ample reason to treat Malaysia as an institutional hybrid. Which institutional face is enacted—and how—may depend on the circumstances.

NEW YORK'S SILICON ALLEY

Hill and Kim (2000) claim that neo-liberal policies (such as privatisation, deregulation) helped to spur the globalisation of New York's financial and producer services and that US monetary policies, trade policies and geopolitical posturing continue to boost the ensemble's position in the world economy. To this account of US neo-liberalism, one must add the strong, although indirect, influence of federal technology and financial policy on the development of digital technology. The growth of the computer sector in the 1980s was fuelled by permissive regulation of the financial sector. The federal government played a lead role in setting rules that favoured entrepreneurship by facilitating "risky investments": laws on taxation, bankruptcy, stock listings, options and financing (Rowen, 2000, p. 189). The link between technology and finance was re-invigorated by Clinton policies that treated the sectors as twin engines of the economy, The Telecommunications Act of 1996 aimed to spark restructuring across the computer, media and telecommunications sectors in order to boost competition, investment and innovation, especially *vis-à-vis* the Internet Policies to increase firm access to capital added fuel to the mix. When an ensuing stock boom spread to the dot-com sector, federal officials (the Federal Reserve Chairman, the Secretary of Treasury) joined in to celebrate the rise of a 'new economy'—one where technology would allow a transcending of old limits.

These policies influenced the building of new media districts in several ways. First, telecommunications deregulation promoted the unravelling of what had been separate technological networks while an increased availability of capital—in combination with new economy 'models'—provided resources for assembling new networks. Secondly, the lack of direct state participation in the creation of new media districts opened the door for diverse kinds of entrepreneurs, although neo-liberal policy favoured particular kinds of entrepreneurs (financiers) and enrolment devices (venture capital, stock options).

Thirdly, the focus on financial actors and devices promoted a particular form of enrolment—a rapid (but short-lived) mobilisation to connect with new media financing networks and the market for technology stocks. Fourthly, neo-liberal policy helped to shape a new division of labour that emerged among digital enclaves in the US. The division of labour that followed the rise of the Internet in the 1990s featured: computer industry centres (such as Silicon Valley) that rely on engineer-ing and science workers to create technologi-cal infrastructures for the Internet (such as net-work systems, operating software); and, new media districts (such as Silicon Alley) that use creative firms and workers in areas such as graphic design, marketing and advertising to prototype commercial applications of Internet technology. Neo-liberal policy-makers could take for granted the rich technological and business assets of the US and focus on the cir-culation of capital; their promotion of devices to link technological development to finance capital helped to intensify competition among digital enclaves in the US for capital.

Silicon Alley Problematisations

Silicon Alley emerged along a stretch of Broadway running from the Flatiron District, through Greenwich Village and into SoHo—the domain of young creative types attracted to New York University and old factory lofts (Zukin, 1982) (see Figure 15.2).

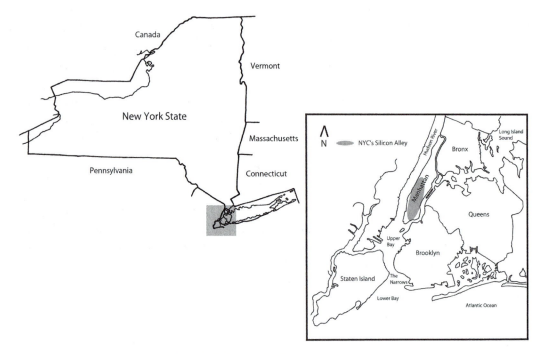

Figure 15.2 New York's Silicon Alley in context

As the ensemble grew, it spilled over into the financial district and then into other parts of the city and the metro region.

Silicon Alley is the product of myriad entrepreneurs and visions. Assorted web pioneers, venture capitalists, an industry association, real estate interests and corporations have tried to establish translations involving the district. An examination of their efforts highlights two points about the making of new media districts: network-building, not impersonal market forces, linked the new media to the financial sector; and, powerful actors, even financial firms and transnational corporations, need networks to extend their power into new domains.

The initial problematisation of New York's new media district came from Lower Manhattan creative types who had begun to experiment with CD-ROMs, electronic bulletin boards and the World Wide Web. These web pioneers argued that the advent of the World Wide Web meant that one could be an on-line publisher without having to go through corporations. As many of them started businesses to sustain their creative pursuits, the enclave's own media—newsletters like @NY, *Silicon Alley Reporter* and *AlleyCat News* —helped to articulate a commercial problematisation. They proposed that the 'out of control' nature of digital technology meant that corporations would not be able to control the new markets. Advocates of on-line magazines claimed that "You could put out a professional-looking daily publication with only . . . an editor or two, an HTML jockey, maybe a Unix geek" (Johnson, 1997, p. 2). As corporations turned to start-ups to design websites, web shops asserted that their 'nimbleness' and ability to tailor 'content' for niches would allow them to become 'strategic partners' of corporations; however, most found themselves to be mere sub-contractors without much leverage.

As the alternative media vision dimmed, venture capitalists, the Silicon Alley media and new media entrepreneurs argued that the enclave's purpose was to make creative applications for corporations. This view stressed its advantages *vis-à-vis* other districts. Silicon Alley's name signals the rise of a rival to Silicon Valley.

Deeming Internet business to be a new segment of the media placed New York at the centre of the digital era. It also resonated with perceptions of New York's dominance as a commercial and cultural centre.

More typically, Silicon Alley promoters argued that its role in making creative applications complemented Silicon Valley's role in developing technologies.

After a bull market for technology stocks spread to Internet firms, financiers began to tout Silicon Alley as a gateway to the stock market. Venture capitalists and investment banks exaggerated the potential of firms and cast aside normal criteria. The stock market vision overshadowed all others as firms with modest records received enormous stock valuations. A @NY editor remarked on the rise of a "vision of a mythical digital Oz" that led companies to make "their single-minded goal raising money and going public" (Watson, 1998, p. 1). The finance problematisation linked the possibilities of windfall profits to the new media's role in leading a revolution against the old economy.

Competing entrepreneurs sometimes offered rival problematisations. This was the case with the most noteworthy attempt to create wired space in Silicon Alley—the New York Information Technology Center (NYITC). Two very different kinds of group influenced the project. The first group—a coalition composed of media giants Time Warner, McGraw-Hill and Forbes, along with IBM, several utilities and the New York New Media Association—made the inital problematisation for a new media centre. They advanced the idea of opening up a Midtown facility that provided subsidised office space, equipment and research facilities for new media start-ups. They proposed that the new sector needed a hub that would strategically focus resources, interactions and attention. [The second group was a downtown property coalition that wanted to use the new media industry to revitalise the depressed downtown real estate market. The stock market crash of 1987 and the ensuing recession had left the financial district with mothballed buildings and a vacancy rate of 23 per cent. The lead actor was the Alliance for Downtown, a business improvement district (BID) for the Downtown area.] Also in the coalition was city government, which had made revitalisation of Downtown real estate a priority. After the city offered tax credits, a developer agreed to wire a vacant downtown office building with satellite hook-ups, fibre optics for high-speed local area networks and high-speed Internet connections. The group later introduced a 'Plug 'n go' programme that extended to the entire Downtown area: the idea was to offer flexible wired space to attract small firms that do not know what lies ahead. The head of the Alliance remarked that the programme would develop "a Levittown for cyberspace, starter homes for young companies" (Holusha, 1997). City hall later created a "Digital New York" programme that offered subsidised wired space in other boroughs to new media firms that were being displaced by high real estate prices in Manhattan.

Efforts by individual firms to use wired offices to transform their businesses were the most ubiquitous type of Silicon Alley translation. Importantly, even TNCs such as Ericsson have couched their problematisations in terms of networks. The telecommunications giant set up a Cyberlab in the NYITC as a place where start-ups could make use of its equipment and technical assistance—if their agendas complement Ericsson's.

Silicon Alley Enrollments

In order to enact their problematisations, the entrepreneurs of Silicon Alley needed to enroll some combination of firms, workers, suppliers, investors and/or customers. The devices used included a trade association, venture capital, stock options, subsidised wired space, wired labs and industry surveys. Venture capitalists and real estate interests have had the most success in using these devices to organise positions of power within district networks.

The web pioneers enrolled support for the alernative media problematisation by creating organisations and networks that provided on-line workers/users with opportunities for face-to-face interaction. For example, Echo (East Coast Hang Out)—a virtual electronic bulletin board that became a virtual community of 3500 members—organised get-togethers at local bars. A similar interest in face-to-face interaction led to the founding of organisations that ranged from the Silicon Alley Jewish Center to Webgrrls (an association for new media women). Web pioneers drew on these ties when they started up ventures to support their creative exploits; they also attempted to enroll corporations as 'partners'. However, they usually lacked devices to establish leverage with corporations, perhaps because their products were creative, rather than technical, in nature.

Other organisations were created for the explicit purpose of enrolling new media actors in commercial networks. The most important is the New York New Media Association (NYNMA), which two venture capitalists helped to form in autumn 1994 with 8 members: By 2000, there were some 8000 members, consisting of firms' owners, consultants, graphic artists, musicians and lawyers from over 3000 firms.

Their success in enrolling large numbers of diverse actors stems from a device that venture capitalists control: venture capital itself.

The NYNMA has become the main collective actor in Silicon Alley. The full spectrum of new media entrepreneurs and participants makes use of arenas that NYMNA provides—seminars, forums and special-interest groups—in order to meet each other or customer groups.

The NYNMA has also made strategic efforts to enrol the local media and government as supporters of the district. To this end, it organised several surveys of the new media industry. After the surveys indicated large gains in the number of new media firms and workers, NYNMA was able to enrol the local media into its public relations network. However, it has had little success in enrolling material support from either state or local government.

The NYITC project allows us to examine the kind of contingencies that come into play when rival entrepreneurs seek to enroll the same entities. In this case, two sets of entrepreneurs competed to enroll the centre into their respective ensembles in Midtown and Downtown. The real estate coalition prevailed, shifting the project from the heart of Silicon Alley to a location where it boosted the Downtown real estate market—even though NYNMA's president (a venture capitalist) criticised the location as not convenient for clients in the publishing and entertainment industries with Midtown offices. The real estate coalition had several advantages in a situation where the object to be enrolled, a major building, was itself a major device for gaining leverage *vis-à-vis* the project; to gain control of such a building one has to go through real estate interests. The tax credit offered by its ally—city hall—was itself a device that allowed the real estate group to enroll the building's owner. Through 'Plug 'n go' the Downtown coalition has used the device of wired facilities to enrol many more new media firms: 14 participating buildings drew 250 new media tenants and a total of 600 new media firms settled Downtown. Property developers played a gatekeeper role: the NYITC's owner, for example, claimed to screen prospective tenants to ensure that they were 'real' new media firms.

In the case of Ericsson's Cyberlab, part of the appeal of the wired facilities is the particular network that the facility connects with: Ericsson's global extranet, The Cyberlab—little more than a large wired room—is a multifaceted networking device. So that the lab could connect with the 'right' start-ups, its staff was drawn from Silicon Alley.

This is the crux of Cyberlab's mission: enrol Silicon Alley firms to apply Ericsson's technologies in order to establish them as standards. Ericsson has also cultivated ties with the NYNMA by sponsoring its events and Cyberlab's director recently became a NYNMA board member. Finally, Cyberlab took a loan from the New York City Investment Fund in order to make ties with its members, which include investment firms such as Bear Stearns, Citicorp and J. P. Morgan. Fund representatives now sit on Cyberlab's board of directors.

A financial translation dominated Silicon Alley by 1999. In 1997, 21 Silicon Alley firms received US$161 million in venture capital; 110 firms received US$4.6 billion in 1999. In the same span, the number of IPOs grew from 2 to 41, while the sum raised rose from US$115 million to US$3.5 billion (PwC, 2000, p. 25). Founders and CEOs became worth hundreds of millions of dollars and 1000 employees held stock worth at least US$1 million dollars. Firms used stock options to enroll workers, service providers and landlords (Indergaard, 2001, 2002).

Silicon Alley Unravels

Silicon Alley's most characteristic elements stabilised around its role in tying start-ups to the stock market. However, stock market glory cloaked a fundamental flaw on the part of Silicon Alley's new public firms; few had enrolled enough *paying* customers to generate profits or even a promising revenue stream. Some insiders, worried that Silicon Alley's development was being distorted, advocated more active government involvement. A venture capitalist (interview, July 1998) cited "a systemic problem from overvaluation of unsound businesses" and noted institutional gaps: "at the state and local level there is not a concentrated effort to support this business. You need a strategic vision and analysis". A *Silicon Alley Reporter* executive (interview, July 1998) called on city hall to

> provide tax incentives, support putting the technology in the schools, internship programs, adult technical education . . . They should showcase the industry.
>
> There is a battle to become the lead ecosystem for Internet companies. . . . In LA government is involved in the community, doing tangible things for the industry. They also sent planeloads of executives to Asia.

Such concerns were submerged as Silicon Alley bathed in apparent prosperity. At the start of 2000, 29 public companies were worth US$29 billion (Watson, 2000). Between 1997 and 1999, the number of new media firms and workers in the city grew from 2128 firms and 48,828 workers, to 4000 firms employing 138,000 workers (PwC, 2000). Manhattan real estate boomed.

When the market bubble finally burst in April 2000 and stock values began a free-fall, the basic credibility of Silicon Alley became an issue.

After the dot-com crash, many of Silicon Alley's trademark arrangements came unraveled. *The Silicon Alley Reporter* and *AlleyCat News* have shut down. Venture capitalists are fleeing; the enclave's flagship financier, Flatiron Partners, left the Flatiron District to move into the Midtown offices of Chase Manhattan–J.P. Morgan. The NYNMA has lost 2000 members and has been absorbed by a national association. Some public firms may survive through mergers or by being acquired by corporations A mass of small firms, the less visible backbone of the enclave, had credible prospects as service providers for corporations—until the World Trade Center attack destabilised New York's role as a centre for the organisation and conspicuous display of global capitalism. It is unclear how the resources that were assembled during the 1990s as elements of Silicon Alley will be recombined.

MALAYSIA'S MULTIMEDIA SUPER-CORRIDOR

To some observers, the Multimedia Supercorridor reflects the strivings of a *city*—Kuala Lumpur (Malaysia's capital). Yeung (2000, p. 245) comments that Kuala Lumpur is "one of the best examples of a city in Pacific Asia planning to move purposefully into the Information Age". Morshidi (2000, p. 2237) also draws attention to the city, proposing that the MSC may "put the city's drive towards 'world city' status back on track". Such accounts mesh with claims that east Asian cities are now competing to gain the 'regional HQ functions' of transnational corporations (Ho, 2000).

Others perceive the initiative of a *region*. Scott's treatise on the rise of regional centres opens with a vignette about a 1997 trip during which Prime Minister Mahathir approached firms in Silicon Valley and Hollywood about participating in the MSC (Scott, 1998b).

However, one cannot adequately account for the MSC without addressing its state patron. My study reveals that the Malaysian state has made ample use of its sovereign powers in the MSC: it has presented a comprehensive problematisation that focuses on creating and weaving together digital industry infrastructure, actors and markets. Moreover, the state has used (as well as created) devices to enroll participants. In these respects, its framework for making a digital district differs sharply from the neo-liberal one that influenced Silicon Alley,

I propose that the Malaysian state is, in fact, a *developmental hybrid:* some neo-liberal elements are evident in the MSC project but are largely subordinated to developmental agendas. With that qualification, the state's involvment in the project fits the developmental state profile outlined by Hill and Kim (2000). The MSC stresses national development and strategic interests; some neo-liberal images and themes are present, but are framed in developmental terms. State entities are the main entrepreneurial actors; transnational corporations participate but the terms of their involvment are, in large part, set by the state. A mix of developmental and neo-liberal measures is used to channel capital to strategic sectors. First, the place-based strategy directs capital to targetted sectors. Secondly, some MSC financial devices that seem similar to those found in Silicon Alley (technology stocks, venture capital) are intertwined in a very different context—one in which the state actors and goals remain central. The state has implemented some measure of developmental discipline in an enrolment process that has been slower, but which has created more enduring outcomes than was the case in Silicon Alley. The project has stressed stability and planning—qualities that have become much more appealing since the crashing of the US stock market and the destruction of the World Trade Center. Finally, a regional context does imprint the MSC: in contrast to Silicon Alley, whose rivals were located in the US, the MSC competes with enclaves that are located in other east Asian nations.

MSC Problematisations

Kuala Lumpur, with a population of 1.4 million, is the commercial, financial and administrative centre of Malaysia. Although there are aspirations that the city reach world city status, the manner in which the goal is pursued bears the state's imprint. The city's producer services sector, for example, reflects "the government's policy of nurturing indigenous rather than overseas producer services in the city" (Morshidi, 2000, p. 2237). In fact, the MSC problematisation includes grand plans for Kuala Lumpur, envisioning that it will become a mega-city that can be compared with centres like Tokyo–Yokohama.

In his "Vision 2020" speech (1991) Mahathir called for the public–private partnerships of 'Malaysia Inc.' to be extended into the digital realm, in order to bring a unified nation into the Information Age. The MSC problematisation that has resulted is something of a hybrid—containing a mix of development principles and the kind of techno-utopian imagery that would sound familiar in Silicon Alley. For example, in an address to German investors, Mahathir claimed that the MSC entailed "a new paradigm in the creation of value for the Information Age . . . a hi-tech test-bed that will allow firms to explore multimedia technologies without any limitations" (MDC, 1998b, p. 2). This was possible because the MSC was being built on a "green-field site, unencumbered by industrial practices and legacies or entrenched interests" (p. 2).

The green-field emphasis calls to mind settings for computer industry enclaves in the US, as opposed to the city centres that host new media districts. It also conveys images of unrestrained entrepreneurship associated with neo-liberalism. Yet, the developmental state is the animating spirit in MSC problematisations. Whereas an assortment of uncoordinated schemes was presented for Silicon Alley, the MSC problematisation is a totalising vision of a set of wired spaces and projects arranged in accordance with the principles of an 'ideal' economic and social order. Wired spaces of different scales are nested within each other. At the largest scale is the *corridor*—a 750 sq km area with a fibre-optic backbone providing a high-capacity global telecommunications and logistics network. Its northern end-point is the Petronas Towers in Kuala Lumpur; its southern end-point is a new international airport. Hybridity is evident in the MSC's mission: serve as a portal to Asia for TNCs while acting as a gateway for national development. Regarding the latter, the MSC is to support the modernisation of manufacturers and to nurture small and-medium-sized enterprises (SMEs) in digital sectors while new universities, 'smart' schools and e-commerce are to take the larger society into the Information Age (MDC, 1998a, 1998c, 1998d).

The second level of wired space is that of *intelligent cities*. One of these, Putrajaya, is the new administrative capital of Malaysia, designed to host eventually a population of 75,000. It is framed as an electronic government. The second city, Cyberjaya, is to host the first 200 companies invited into the MSC and is to serve as the major residential community in the MSC, housing 15,000 knowledge-workers (MDC, 1998g). It is also the site for Multimedia University. The total population is to be 240,000 ultimately. Adjacent to the intelligent cities is a pre-existing technology park housing telecommunications firms and research labs. Within Cyberjaya is a third wired level—the *Flagship Zone* —which houses centres for 'telemedicine,' 'smart' schools, marketing, training and R&D collaborations between local and transnational firms. A final special centre is an 'E-village' that will house the MSC's creative multimedia firms and support the creative firm cluster in developing content. It includes offices, a multimedia academy that is to nurture local talent in the areas of film, theatre, music and TV, business incubators and—at yet another wired level—a 'studio precinct' that features sound effects and post-production facilities for film production, animation and game development. Later phases include a theme park and holiday resort, providing creative producers with links to a key area of commercial application In sum, the MSC brings together a variety of industry segments that are found in separate ensembles and distinctive settings in the US—suburbs, edge cities and city centres.

MSC Enrollments

The state created a public entity—the Multimedia Development Corporation (MDC)—to act as the focal entrepreneur in the MSC. The MDC is the master strategist, service provider and financier for the corridor. It also takes the lead in enrolling participants. In contrast to what we saw in the US, this state entity wields the devices created to assemble technology ventures; the devices in this case include wired facilities, consultative groups, investor conferences, a firm certification system, cyber-laws, special state markets for MSC products/services, on-line exchanges and state-supported venture capital.

Of the new consultative mechanisms, the most notable is an International Advisory Panel. Although described as a mechanism for garnering advice, one could argue that its main function is to enroll the world's telecommunications and computer powerhouses. An MDC document refers to such firms as "web-shapers"—firms that "provide the technology that defines a common architecture or open platform, which often forms the basis for a new industry standard" (MDC 1998e, p. 2). The panel, which is chaired by the Prime Minister, has included notable CEOs such as James Barksdale (Netscape), Bill Gates (Microsoft), Craig Barret (Intel), Louis Gerstner (IBM) and executives from Ericsson, Motorola, NEC, Sony, Siemens, NTT, Oracle, Compaq, Lucent Technologies, Nokia, Cisco, British Telecom and Fujitsu. The panel first met in 1997. It advised the government to safeguard intellectual property rights and voiced concern about a shortage of skilled workers. A second body, the Founders Council, meets more often to give the government feedback. The MDC says it manages representation to create a balance of local and global firms, SMEs and "web-shapers" (MDC, 1998e, p. 2). Another device used to enroll firms is the "MSC investor conference", which has been staged in Germany, Canada, Australia, Great Britain and the US. Sometimes Malaysian firms come along to find partners. Such events also were held in Malaysia to draw SMEs from areas such as Johore—a region with linkages to nearby Singapore (MDC, 1998f).

The sovereign power of the state is salient in the device through which the MDC evaluates applications of firms that wish to participate in the corridor—a sharp contrast to Silicon Alley where property developers served as gatekeepers. To qualify for 'MSC status' firms must meet several conditions: be an information technology or multimedia enterprise, be willing to transfer technology and pledge that at least 15 per cent of their workforce will be 'knowledge-workers'. In return, they are exempt from some taxes for 10 years and face few restrictions in sourcing knowledge-workers and capital. A set of 'cyberlaws' were instituted in the MSC (for example, to protect intellectual property rights) and the state has pledged not to censor the Internet, a move aimed at gaining a competitve advantage over Singapore.

A final area concerns enrolling capital for infrastucture and firms. Builders of infrastructure (private and quasi-public firms) originally were to raise money on the Malaysian stock market or procure loans. The [1997] Asian crisis forestalled these options. As the value of Malaysia's currency and stock market tumbled, the state reaffirmed its commitment to the MSC and introduced new devices to enroll capital. The MDC increased its equity stake in the Cyberview development consortium from 10 per cent to 51 per cent and took control over constructing high-priority infrastructure (MDC, 1998e). The government opened the MESDAQ—a NASDAQ-like stock market oriented to technology firms. The new exchange is meant to facilitate IPOs by start-ups in order to spur investors to create venture capital funds. Firms listed on the MESDAQ were exempted from currency controls (as were MSC status firms in general).

In a complementary move, an MDC subsidiary was created in 1999—the MSC Venture Corporation (MSCVC)—to lead the new effort to draw venture capital. Its mission suggests that the MSC s financial strategy, which appears neo-liberal on the surface, is actually hybrid in nature. The MSCVC is to make investments in "potental high-growth SMES" while also helping to "expose these companies to other venture capitalists" (MDC, 2000, p. 1). It hosts forums where it introduces companies to potential investors

and, in the manner of a Silicon Alley venture capitalist, trumpets its inside positioning as a financier.

Stabilising the MSC

As MSC entrepreneurs adjusted plans and relationships, they seemed to move in the same direction as their Silicon Alley counterparts—greater reliance on financial devices. However, the significance of devices depends on their position *vis-à-vis* the respective networks. When Silicon Alley entrepreneurs shifted their focus to connect with financial markets rather than new product markets, they narrowed their base of material supports; in contrast, MSC entrepreneurs diversified the sources of material resources by adding new financial devices. The Malaysian state has continued to use its sovereignty to stabilise networks with a mix of regulation and subsidy. Consequently, MSC entrepreneurs have had more success in stabilising networks even though they encountered international financial and political crises that their Silicon Alley counterparts never faced.

In the wake of the Asian crisis, the IMF and the US government demanded that the affected nations liberalise their markets. Mahathir blamed international speculators for undermining east Asian markets and denounced the US and the IMF as Western imperialists. As tensions rose, the US Ambassador warned, "Let us remember also how important partnerships between the two countries will be in the Multimedia Super-corridor" (Jayasankaran, 1997). In 1998, Malaysia imposed capital controls. The escalating crisis widened a rift between Mahathir and his deputy, Anwar Ibrahim, who became the standard-bearer for opposition groups ranging from Islamic fundamentalists to advocates of economic liberalisation. In 1998, Anwar was purged and then convicted on suspect morals charges, inflaming the opposition and further damaging the regime's reputation in the West.

Critics proposed that Malaysia had shut itself off from the global economy and predicted that its economy would stall. They also deemed Malaysia another case of the 'crony capitalism' that had brought fiscal crisis to east Asia. The dire predictions proved faulty, but crisis and controversy took a toll on the MSC. In a 1999 cover story entitled "Mahathir's High Tech Folly", *Business. Week* claimed that Mahathir's actions and capital controls had caused foreign corporations to hesitate in committing to the MSC. The project had hoped to draw US$4 billion in investment but only US$1 billion materialised. Corporations (such as Microsoft) that had planned to locate regional headquarters in the MSC were shifting their regional operations to places such as Singapore (Einhorn and Prasso, 1999).

However, there are increasing signs that the project is becoming stabilised as elements and relationships fall into place. Multimedia University and its incubator centre are in operation; pockets of offices, research facilities and apartments wired for broadband access have come on-line. Most importantly, the MSC has turned the corner with regard to the critical goal of enrolling firms. Some 200 firms had been granted MSC status as of the end of 1998. By 10 March 2002, a total of 650 firms had been awarded MSC status. Of the[se], 194 develop software, 144 are Internet-based (mostly e-commerce and business applications) and 76 develop content (MDC, 2002, p. 1).

There seems to be a healthy amount of involvment by established Malaysian firms. A recent report notes that 359 MSC status firms were locally owned while 142 were joint ventures with foreign firms and 46 were 'world class companies' (Karim, 2001). However, the MDC and the International Advisory Panel recently agreed that the MSC has fallen short in enrolling indigenous SMEs (Sharif, 2001b). The MDC has responded by introducing a new flagship application to enroll start-ups that features venture capital, R&D grants and a broadband network that positions the MSC's Central Incubator as a hub for other incubators.

In fact, the problem in nurturing start-ups is linked to more general problems of extending MSC networks into the larger economy and society. Compared with the ambitions of the MSC problematisation, the results achieved to this point are rather modest. As of August 2001, the MDC estimated that 12,000 jobs had been created in MSC (Sharif, 2001a, p. 3).

To some extent, the slow progress stems from problems that are inherent in extending MSC networks beyond the enclave. Extensions often require realignments in power relations. For example, the Association of the Computer and Multimedia Industy of Malaysia has demanded that state-owned Telekon Malaysia allow all telecoms and IT firms equal access to broadband infrastructure at the same price: it asserts that, without affordable access to bandwidth, "the country is not moving anywhere with the Multimedia Supercorridor (MSC) campaign" (Ng, 2002, p. 1). In fact, the process of societal change that the MSC project envisions has barely begun. Various segments of Malaysian society are holding back from committing to unfamiliar ventures that possess higher levels of risk. A manager at Sun Microsystems complains, for example, that the cream of the workforce aims to work for multinational corporations, not start-ups (Matthews, 1999). Moreover, the creation of start-ups in the MSC is being stunted by a lack of investment.

Banks are uncomfortable in granting loans to these sectors because they lack "indepth knowledge on the personalities, technologies and applications being developed" (Matthews, 1999, p. 1). Finally, Malaysian élites do not realise the need for the nation to move from a reliance on manufacturing to a second economic engine that is 'knowledge-driven'.

In fact, critics (Jomo, 2001) claim that the regime's practice of favouring its political allies has retarded entrepreneurialism.

Finally, Malaysia's position *vis-à-vis* the Islamic world lends an uncertain cast to its efforts to stabilise the MSC project. There are promising dimensions, For example, a number of Muslim countries (Syria, Eygpt, Jordan, Bahrain) are interested in importing products developed in MSC flagship applications—an indication that religious ties may help the project to enroll commercial customers. In addition, the new conflict between Western capitalism and Islamic militants has led the Bush administration to embrace Mahathir's secular regime as a champion of moderate Islam Malaysia (and others who co-operate in the 'war on terrorism') may gain the kind of breathing-space that abetted the rise of development states during the Cold War.

Despite all the shortcomings of the MSC—and its state master—its credibility is on the rise. While it would be unthinkable to market images of Silicon Alley—commentators note that 'Silicon Alley is dead'—the MSC vision is still being used to enroll businesses. Full-page ads in the *New York Times* present Malaysia as a "knowledge-driven society, where expansion and stability are the order of the day", as is evidenced by the fact that "Prime Minister Mahathir has personally . . . backed the Multimedia Super-corridor" (Summit Communications, 2002).

CONCLUSIONS

For the MSC project to fulfill its goals is likely to require substantial change on the part of the Malaysian state as well as the society itself. It is not clear that this will happen. In light of the fate of Silicon Alley and other new media districts in the US, the most positive aspect of the MSC may be that the effort continues. Neo-liberal policies encouraged US districts to shift their focus from creating new product markets to connecting with financial markets; the Silicon Alley translation that became dominant was a temporary set of arrangements for circulating resources rather than an enduring foundation for digital innovation. Recent revelations about crony capitalism USA make this path of development all the more difficult to recommend for a developing country. In contrast, the Malaysian state appears to be assembling and stabilising an ensemble of digital industry infrastructures, resources and entrepreneurial groupings. Thus, we must reject the claim that US-style neo-liberalism is a desirable path for developing countries that need to create a digital industry base. Several other conclusions follow; developmental states remain viable in a digital age for second-tier NICs in east Asia, and perhaps elsewhere; the nature of east Asia's developmental states is changing in the direction of hybridisation as they weave elements of neo-liberalism into developmental frameworks; and developmental states may be able to stabilise secular forms of Islam in east Asia, and perhaps elsewhere.

The comparison with Silicon Alley helps to clarify the nature of the MSC's state patron. Although the MSC project includes some neo-liberal imagery and practices, they are enmeshed in a framework where the state—and developmental agendas—remain at the centre. This supports my claim that Malaysia is a 'developmental hybrid'—a view that departs from the categorical distinctions that Hill and Kim (2000) draw between developmental and neo-liberal states. In other respects, this study complements their thesis that regional and national contexts influence the form that urban development takes. Although we have not focused on regional contexts, basic differences are evident. Malaysia backs the MSC as part of its competition with other east Asian nations to create regional centres; the MSC s rivalry with Johore is an exception that proves the rule, since that part of Malaysia is in Singapore's zone of influence. In contrast, Silicon Alley competed with other enclaves within the US (such as Silicon Valley, San Francisco, Los Angeles).

We have found that the developmental and neo-liberal state frameworks supported different types of entrepreneurs, visions and enrolment devices in the MSC and Silicon, respectively. As expected in a setting where developmentalism dominates, state entities were focal actors in the MSC; a state agency, which was created to act as the main institutional entrepreneur, took the lead in devising a comprehensive problematisation for the district and in enrolling participants. State sovereignty was also salient in the devices that were used to enroll participants into the positions envisioned for them in the enclave: a district-wide telecommunications infrastructure, advisory panels, investor conferences, a firm certification system, cyberlaws, state markets for new products and state-supported venture capital.

The comparison has also helped to flesh out the portrait of neo-liberalism presented by Hill and Kim (2000). As they hint, neo-liberal regimes exercise sovereignty, but in different institutional locations from those in developmental states. Whereas the state in Malaysia used its sovereignty to place itself at the centre of particular entrepreneurial projects, neo-liberal regimes in the US exercise their sovereignty at the level of the national system, shaping the conditions under which specific entrepreneurs operate—for example, in Silicon Alley. Whereas Malaysia deemed the MSC a national champion during the 1990s, the Clinton administration informally targeted the technological and financial sectors as sites of innovation, using a new regulatory framework to unsettle and reframe technology systems that were previously kept separate. Its policies vis-à-vis the financial sector helped to boost the availability of financial devices for entrepreneurs (such as venture capital, options).

This study shows that Hill and Kim were right to stress the role of equity markets and the FIRE sectors in New York, but adds that active network-building, rather than impersonal markets, is what put these entities in play during the development of Silicon Alley. And, in the midst of a multitude of entrepreneurs who tried to take advantage of the vacuum produced by the absence of public-sector entrepreneurs, it was venture capitalists and real estate developers, rather than transnational investment firms and corporations that exercised the most power in weaving together Silicon Alley, circa 1999.

QUESTIONS FOR DISCUSSION

1. In two or three paragraphs, discuss the major themes and theories introduced in Indergaard's chapter.

2. In two or three paragraphs, provide specific examples from his chapter to explain what the author means by the hybrid nature of contemporary capitalist city-regions.

3. Now that you have read Part One of the book, as well as most of Part Two, in 2–3 pages discuss some of the major differences between Indergaard's framework and Hill and Fujita's Nested City Theory and Friedman–Sassen–Taylor's World/Global City Theory.

4. Utilizing the 'Further Readings', 'Helpful Web Links', and other sources, conduct some further research on Silicon Alley, New York, and cities in the Malaysian Multimedia Super-corridor, such as Cyberjava, Kuala Lumpur, and Putrajava. Then, in 2–3 pages, describe some of the most interesting new events and facts you discovered about these places and present your findings to the class.

FURTHER READINGS

Bunnell, T. 2004. *Malaysia, Modernity and the Multimedia Super Corridor: A Critical Geography of Intelligent Landscapes.* London: RoutledgeCurzon.

Currid, E. 2006. New York as a Global Creative Hub: A Competitive Analysis of Four Theories on World Cities. *Economic Development Quarterly,* 20 (4): 330–350.

Indergaard, M. 2004. *Silicon Alley: The Rise and Fall of a New Media District.* New York: Routledge.

Indergaard M. 2009. What to Make of New York's New Economy? The Politics of the Creative Field. *Urban Studies,* 46 (5–6): 1063–1094.

Jomo, K. 1997. *Industrial Technology Development in Malaysia: Industry and Firm Studies.* London: Routledge.

Rasiah, R., and J. Schmidt, eds. 2010. *The New Political Economy of Southeast Asia.* Cheltenham, UK: Edward Elgar.

HELPFUL WEB LINKS

IT Business Edge Network. 2012. *Internet News.com.* Online. Available at: http://www.intemetoews.com/, last accessed, January 5, 2012.

Kuala Lumpur, City of. 2012. Official Portal of City of Kuala Lumpur (Malaysia) City Hall. Online. Available at: http://www.dbkl.gov.my/portalv7/index.php?lang=en, last accessed, January 6, 2012.

Matthews, J and A. Devasahayam, eds. 2012. *Malaysian Technology News.* Online. Available at: http://mytechnews.tripod.com/index.htm, last accessed, January 5, 2012.

MDEC. 2012. Home Page of Malaysia's Multimedia Development Corporation (MDeC). Online. Available at: http://www.mdec.my, last accessed, January 5, 2012,

MSC Malaysia. 2012. Home Page of MSC Malaysia: National ICT (Information & Communication Technology) Initiative. Online. Available at: http://www.mscmalaysia.my/home, last accessed, January 5, 2012.

New York, City of. 2012. NYC.gov: Official Website of the City of New York. Online. Available at: http://www.nyc.gov/portaysite/nycgov/7front_door=true, last accessed, January 9, 2012.

Putrajaya Federal Territory of. 2012. The Official Portal of Perbadanan Putrajava (Federal Territory of Putrajaya). Online. Available at: http://www.ppj.gov.my/portal/page?_pageid=311,1&_dad=portal&_schema=PORTAL#1762, last accessed, January 5, 2012.

Setia Haruman Sdn. Bhd. 2012. Setia Haruman: The Master Developer of Cyberjaya, Malaysia. Online. Available at: http://www.cyberjaya-msc.com/mainpage.asp, last accessed, January 5, 2012.

Silicon Alley. 2012. Silicon Alley, NY is the Energy Capital of the World. Online. Available at: http://www.siliconalley.com/, last accessed January 5, 2012.

The star Online. 2012. Home Page of the Malaysia Star Newspaper. Online. Available at: http://thestaronline.com/ and http://thestar.com.my/, last accessed, January 5, 2012.

CHAPTER 16

Ulsan: South Korea's *Great Industrial City* (2013)

A. J. Jacobs

Ulsan, South Korea, is home to the world's largest auto production complex, its fifth largest automaker, its biggest shipyard and shipbuilder, and the globe's second largest petrochemicals combine. In addition, these firms have export linkages on six continents. Yet, since it does not qualify as a center of international finance, the city never has been or will be ranked among the world's most important cities by Global/World City theorists. Nevertheless, similar to other current and historical *Great Industrial Cities*, such as Manchester, Essen, Detroit, and Shanghai, Ulsan has become a vital cog in, and instrument of, global capitalism.

Great Industrial Cities are defined here as large, dense regional agglomerations of capital, labor, production, infrastructure, and knowledge, which provide substantial economies of scale and scope for firms in the same industrial sector (localization economies) and in all industries (urbanization economies), whose synergies incite an enlargement in the region's output, population, employment, and income. As production expands, innovation provokes exports to other nations. What distinguishes a Great Industrial City from other urban conurbations is that its manufacturing sector(s) becomes highly influential, even dominant, internationally. Ulsan's rise to prominence in three industrial sectors suggests not only that is a *Great Industrial City*, but that it merits much greater attention than it has received in the English language literature.

Ulsan's growth path, similar to that of the world's other major city-regions, both industrial and non-industrial, has been driven by international, national, and sub-national factors. Its development as a major manufacturing hub was facilitated by the policies of its national government. Its economy has relied heavily on exports to other nations. Its growth context has been influenced by its nestedness within East Asia, including South Korea's historical relations with Japan and North Korea, and the linkages of Ulsan firms with Japanese manufacturers. Finally, Ulsan has benefited from its subnational context, particularly from its substantial concentrations of motor vehicles, shipbuilding, and petrochemicals firms, as well as its proximity to other industrial cities in its region.

Overall, through its case study of Ulsan, this chapter seeks to: (1) introduce the concept of *Great Industrial City*; (2) remind scholars and practitioners about the continued importance of industrial cities for national economies, and in global capitalism; (3) demonstrate how the world's city-regions have been decisively shaped by both international and embedded/nested factors; and (4) enhance the English language reader's knowledge of South Korean urban areas. It begins with some background data on Ulsan, followed by a reviewed of the factors driving its rise to Great Industrial City status.

BACKGROUND ON ULSAN[1]

Ulsan is situated along the East Sea, within South Korea's newly defined Dongnam (Southeast) Economic Zone and the larger Gyeongsang Region (see Figure 16.1). Originally settled as a fishing port, Ulsan's rise to *Great Industrial City* status began on January 27, 1962, when in accordance with the First National Five-Year Economic Plan or NEP (1962–66), the area was designated

as a Special Industrial District (SID). A few months later, on June 1, Ulsan Township was authorized as a city (*si*).

Over the next 15 years the Ulsan-*si's* population grew steadily, reaching 252,570 in 1975, before doubling to 550,207 in 1985. Then, on 1 January 1995, after merging with Ulsan-*gun* (county) and adding its roughly 150,000 residents, the city's Census population stood at 967,429. Two years later, after surpassing one million inhabitants, Ulsan was

Figure 16.1 Ulsan among South Korea's provinces and special cities

recognized as its nation's sixth *Gwangyeok-si* or Metropolitan City, a designation placing it in South Korea's second highest municipal status category, behind only the National Capital of Seoul. This granted the city functional independence from its province, South Gyeongsang, and allowed it to divide into five administrative wards or *Gu* (see Figure 16.2). With 1,082,567 residents within an area of 1,056 sq. km (408 sq. miles) in 2010, Ulsan was its nation's seventh most populous city (see Tables 16.1 and 16.2).

In terms of employment, based upon the national enterprise census and local estimates, in 2008 Ulsan establishments employed 391,000 workers (again, see Table 16.1). Among these, 146,481 were in manufacturing employment. Overall, employment increased by 56,735 or 16.96 % from 2000, while industrial jobs were up 17,670 or 13.72 % from eight years prior. Whereas Ulsan's total employment ranked seventh most among South Korean cities, its industrial employment was second. Moreover, Ulsan's post-2000 numeric increase in both manufacturing firms and industrial employment ranked first among the nation's seven major cities. This was significant considering manufacturing jobs expanded in only two of the seven during this period (see Table 16.3).

As for specific sectors, Ulsan has the unique distinction of being home to the world's: (1) largest automotive assembly complex and fifth biggest automaker, Hyundai Motor; (2) largest dockyard and shipbuilder, Hyundai Heavy Industries (Hyundai HI); (3) fourth

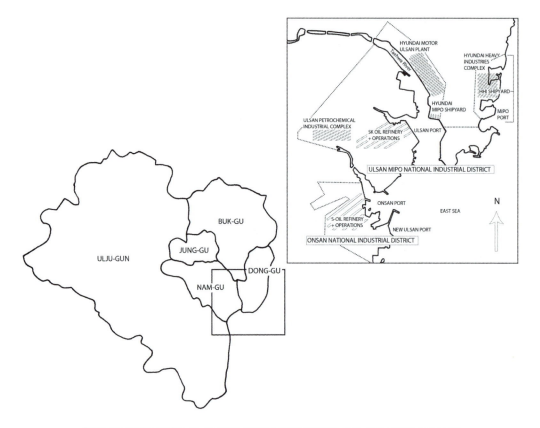

Figure 16.2 Ulsan's five *gu*, its ports and industrial districts, including HyMC and HyHI

Table 16.1 Manufacturing Employment (2008)

Population, 2010	1,126,879
Land Area, 2010	1,056 sq. km or 408 sq. miles
Total Employment, 2008[1]	391,300
Manufacturing Employment, 2008	146,481

Sources: KOSIS (2011), Ulsan (2011)

Note: (1) Estimated from source data.

Table 16.2 2010 Population of South Korean's Largest Cities

1. Seoul Special City	9,794,304
2. Busan Metropolitan City	3,414,950
3. Incheon Metropolitan City	2,662,509
4. Daegu Metropolitan City	2,446,418
5. Daejeon Metropolitan City	1,501,859
6. Gwangju Metropolitan City	1,469,293
7. Ulsan Metropolitan City	1,082,567
8. Changwon city	1,080,441
South Korea	48,580,293

Sources: KOSIS (2011); Gyeongsangnam-do (2011)

largest producer of medium-sized container vessels, Hyundai Mipo Dockyard; and (4) second largest petrochemicals complex. It also hosted two of the globe's top eight refineries,

operated by SK Energy and S-Oil, which combined to process more crude oil daily, 1.4 million barrels in 2010, than any other city on earth. As a result, Ulsan ranked first among South Korean cities in employment in four manufacturing sectors: Motor Vehicles, Motor Vehicles Parts and Trailers (MVM); 'Other' Transportation Equipment Manufacturing (OTEM), including shipbuilding; Chemicals & Chemical Products; and Coke & Refined Petroleum Products (see Table 16.4).

More specifically, in 2008 Ulsan's 410 Transportation Equipment Manufacturing (TEM) firms employed 91,819 workers, 49,378 in MVM, and 42,441 in OTEM. In all, TEM employment increased by 19,518 of 27.00% from 2000, and accounted for 62.68% of the city's total manufacturing employment in 2008. In addition, these sectors were supported by 440 firms employing 24,519 in related complementary manufacturing, for another 16.74% of the city's industrial workers. Although the Chemicals and Chemical Products sector lost 5,110 jobs or 29.94% between 2000 and 2008, the city's 169 Petrochemicals and Non-metallic Mineral firms still employed 17,889 workers in the latter year, including 11,955 in Chemicals.

Table 16.3 Manufacturing Employment Change, Metropolitan Cities & Seoul, 2000–2008[1,2]

City	Change in Manufacturing Firms 2000–2008	Change in Manufacturing Employment 2000–2008	% Change in Manufacturing Firms 2000–2008	% Change in Manufacturing Employment 2000–2008	GDP Per Capita 2008
Seoul	−1,480	−49,684	−22.21%	−27.66%	$23,375
Busan	−269	−23,826	−6.51%	−15.54%	$15,360
Incheon	−49	−22,623	−1.08%	−12.47%	$17,460
Daegu	−124	−15,150	−4.10%	−13.93%	$12,975
Gwangju	254	14,097	33.42%	33.67%	$14,790
Daejeon	60	−768	9.63%	−2.34%	$15,075
Ulsan	**325**	**17,670**	**35.79%**	**13.72%**	**$46,370**
Korea	7,311	143,358	14.29%	6.20 %	$20,210

Source: KOSIS (2011)

Notes: (1) Employment is by Place of Work (2) GDP were rounded at the source and calculated using the July 1, 2008 exchange rate of 1,048.11 KRW to USD

Table 16.4 Ulsan's Manufacturing Employment by Sector, 2008[1]

	2008 Establishments	2008 Manufacturing Employment	% of 2008 Manufacturing Employment	Employment Change 2000–2008
Total Manufacturing Employment (KIC 10~33)	**1,233**	**146,481**	**100.00%**	**17,670**
Transportation Equipment Manufacturing[2]	410	91,819	62.68%	19,518
—Motor Vehicles, Motor Vehicle Parts & Trailers[2]	220	49,378	33.71%	12,555
—Other Transportation Equipment, including Shipbuilding[2]	190	42,441	28.97%	6,963
TEM-related Complementary Manufacturing	440	24,519	16.74%	5,134
Fabricated Metals	180	7,926	5.41%	1,212
Machinery & Equipment	164	7,823	5.34%	4,278
Primary Metals	62	6,094	4.16%	513
Plastics & Rubber Products	34	2,676	1.83%	-869
Petrochemicals & Non-metallic Minerals	169	17,889	12.21%	–5,222
Chemicals & Chemical Products[2]	118	11,955	8.16%	–5,110
Coke & Refined Petroleum Products[2]	20	5,069	3.46%	179
Non-metallic Mineral Products	31	865	0.59%	–291
Other Manufacturing	214	12,254	8.37%	–1,760
Electrical Equipment & Appliances	59	2,967	2.03%	1,492
Computer & Electronics	22	2,516	1.72%	–4,722
Textiles, except Apparel	40	2,420	1.65%	103
Remaining Manufacturing Sectors (< 1% per sector)	93	4,351	2.97%	1,367

Source: KOSIS (2011)

Note:
(1) Employment is by Place of Work;
(2) Ulsan ranked first nationally in employment in this category.

Finally, all of Ulsan's manufacturing sectors were aided tremendously by the city's extensive port system, whose four harbors annually handled: (1) approximately 16% of South Korea's cargo tonnage; (2) more than 50% of the nation's crude oil imports; (3) almost 50% of the country's automobile exports; and (4) more than 40% of South Korea's shipbuilding exports. In concert with the city's industrial prowess, the port system has helped transform Ulsan into Asia's fourth largest manufacturing hub in terms of value of exports, and into a major catalyst in South Korea's economic growth over the past 35 years.

THE KOREAN DEVELOPMENTAL STATE AND ULSAN'S RISE TO 'GREAT' INDUSTRIAL CITY

Although some have questioned its effectiveness in recent years, the was no disputing that the South Korean government has been the foremost catalyst driving Ulsan's rise to

Great Industrial City status. As mentioned, this began in 1962, when under the First NEP of military leader Chung-Hee Park (1961–79), the area was designated as a SID and the base for South Korea's oil and chemicals industries. This decision was consistent with one of the primary goals of the plan: to end the nation's total reliance upon imported chemicals and fertilizers. To promote growth in its new target areas and sectors, the government offered firms locating within SIDs, sizeable tax exemptions/credits, low interest loans, utility-rate subsidies, and tariff rebates on imported goods utilized to create exports. In addition, in 1962, the national government established the Korea Petroleum Energy Corporation (KPEC) in Ulsan, which two years later would open the nation's first oil refinery.

Unfortunately, while the plan's policies led to the establishment of a major petrochemicals complex in Ulsan in 1967, and fostered rapid growth in manufacturing employment, the leading petrochemical producers in the city were primarily foreign companies involved in joint ventures with local firms. In response, under its Second NEP (1967–71) the national government targeted capital-intensive investment in chemicals, as well as in steel and machinery manufacturing.

Next, in 1970, in an effort to relieve over-crowding and congestion in Seoul and Busan, the government again provided firms tax incentives to relocate factories to Ulsan and other designated SIDs. These initiatives were accelerated under the Third NEP (1972–76), which came to be known as the Heavy Chemical Industrialization Plan (HCI Plan), which sought to turn South Korea into a world leader in petrochemicals manufacturing. In addition to subsidies and regulations affecting industrial entry, to lead this HCI drive, in 1974–75, the government designated four new growth poles: Yeocheon (now Yeosu, for petrochemicals); Changwon (machinery, especially for defense industries); Pohang (iron and steel); and Ulsan (chemicals, automobiles and ship-building). Thereafter, in 1982, Onsan (petro-

chemicals), at the time just outside of the Ulsan city limits in Ulsan-gun, was established.

As a direct result, by the 1970s, an independent Korean chemical complex had emerged in Ulsan, and the number of petrochemical plants in the city had increased from just 2 in 1963 to 51 in 1978. Finally, the HCI Plan laid the foundation for the expansion of KPEC's oil operations in Ulsan. Purchased by SK Energy in 1980, this complex would ultimately become the world's second largest single refinery and the centerpiece of a network which currently extends into 14 countries on five continents. Through SK Gas, which established its first liquefied gas plant in Ulsan in 1985, SK became South Korea's largest gas station operator; the firm currently possesses a 34% domestic market share while operating 3,670 stations, nationwide.

As for other prominent industries in Ulsan, in 1962–63, in conjunction with the First NEP, the government enacted the Automobile Industry Promotion Law and the Automobile Protection Act. These measures eventually led to Hyundai opening a factory in Ulsan in 1968, where it assembled a small lot of complete knock down (CKD) cars for Ford Motor Company. Shortly thereafter, Hyundai Motor's outlook improved dramatically, when the national government set out to build its own MVM industry.

In accordance with the HCI Plan, in 1975 the South Korean Government passed the Enterprises Affiliation Promotion Law, which encouraged and subsidized the clustering of auto parts and components makers. One of the prime foci for an auto cluster was the newly designated growth pole of Ulsan. Next, under the Fourth NEP (1977–81), the government targeted the automotive industry as a strategic industry for export promotion, and extended special subsidies to suppliers and subcontractors affiliated with domestic manufacturers. As a result, by December 1975, when the first Pony rolled off the Hyundai Motor's Ulsan assembly line, South Korea was producing its own cars (Hyundai

Motor, 2012). Within a year, the automaker was exporting the nation's first car from Ulsan. In addition, by the late-1970s, 90% of the parts in the typical Korean car were domestically manufactured.

During the 1980s, buoyed by Hyundai Motor's Excel sub-compact, export production expanded significantly in Ulsan. These efforts were greatly enhanced by the national government's passage of the Automobile Industry Rationalization Policy in 1981, which protected the domestic auto industry by limiting passenger car manufacturing to two companies: Hyundai Motor and GM-Daewoo's Saehan Motors. Over the next 15 years, this and other national policies, such as currency interventions, preferential tax and credit incentives, and periodic crackdowns on labor/the relaxation of labor laws, combined with other factors to be discussed, transformed Hyundai Motor into a major international automaker.

In 1996, annual vehicle production at the firm's Ulsan complex had exceeded one million vehicles. Then, in 1998, in the midst of the 1997 Asian fiscal crisis, which left the auto industry, among others, in financial peril, Hyundai absorbed the nation's second largest automaker, Kia Motors. By the end of the 2000s, the Hyundai-Kia brands had rebounded from the crisis and commanded a roughly 70% share of the domestic market. At that time, domestic vehicles production stood at 2.74 million, export sales had exceeded one million, and Hyundai Motor's total vehicle production had soared to 4.65 million. Meanwhile, the firm's Ulsan operations had been transformed into the world's largest assembly complex, a 5.05 square kilometers site (54.35 million square feet) containing five independent plants, with a vehicle capacity of 1.7 million vehicles and employing 34,000 people (again, see Figure 16.2). By 2010, as a direct result of its national developmental approach, the former CKD assembler based in Ulsan had become the world's fifth largest automobile producer.

National plans and policies introduced during the 1960s and 1970s also were vital to Ulsan's rise to top of the global shipbuilding industry. In order to create a private domestic shipbuilding industry, the government introduced the 1962 Shipbuilding Industry Encouragement Act, again by offering direct subsidies (up to 30% of the production costs to build local shipyards) and loans, as well as eliminating duties on imported parts and materials. Under the Second and Third NEP, two more Shipbuilding Promotion Acts were enacted (in 1967 and 1973), as well as the Machinery Promotion Act (1969). Together, supported by the Korea's Export-Import Bank, this legislation extended subsidies and favorable financing to domestic shipbuilders and parts suppliers.

Similar to Hyundai Motor, Hyundai HI's success also was greatly aided by the national political connections of its founding Jeong family, extending as high up as President Park. For example, for much of the past 50 years, a disproportionate proportion of high-ranking national officials have hailed from South Gyeongsang Province. This included Mong-Jun Jeong, then president of Hyundai HI and son of Hyundai's founder Ju-Yeong Jeong, who was elected to the national assembly in 1988 representing Ulsan. These linkages netted Hyundai HI countless government contracts to construct ships, national infrastructure, and industrial facilities projects. It was within this context that the South Korean shipbuilder broke ground on its massive operations along Ulsan's Mipo Bay in 1972, and was granted a special national policy exception allowing it to secure technical assistance from foreign companies (see Figure 16.2). As a result, by the mid-1980s, the firm had become the world's largest shipbuilder, employing as many as 30,000 workers at its Ulsan dockyard. By 2010, Hyundai HI held a 15% share of the world market and had offices and subsidiaries in 22 countries on five continents. Moreover, its Ulsan-based affiliate, HMD, had become among the top four producers of mid-sized container vessels (Hyundai HI, 2012).

In sum, while global liberalism may have loosened its grip over its economy, the South Korean Developmental State clearly led Ulsan's rise to *Great Industrial City* status. This involvement continued in 2010, when national government Korean State provided 27 billion Korean Won (KRW or $25.76 million) to construct the Ulsan Free Trade Zone, on a 1.30 square kilometers site (13.97 million square feet) in the city's Ulju-gu's Sin-Il General Industrial Complex.

INTERNATIONAL FORCES IMPACTING ULSAN'S GROWTH PATH

As a result of the export orientation of its major manufacturing firms, Ulsan's fate certainly has been tightly linked to the global economy. Recent examples of international factors which have significantly affected the city's growth path have included the: (1) 1997 Asian Fiscal Crisis; (2) friction caused by South Korean trade surpluses with the US and Canada; (3) Toyota's 2010 safety issues with its US vehicles; and (4) low KRW relative to the Japanese Yen (JPY) of the late-2000s, especially following the AIG-Lehman Shock of September 15–16, 2008.

Among the many impacts of the 1997 Asian Fiscal Crisis was the dramatic depreciation of the Korean Won (KRW), which forced the South Korean Government to turn to the IMF for aid, and left the nation's largest business conglomerates (*jaebeol*) in fiscal distress. In response, the government promulgated its *Big Deal Program*, which set out to rationalize the nation's energy, electronics, and TEM sectors by encouraging business swaps among the *jaebeol*. This was a mixed blessing for Ulsan's Hyundai Group. On the one hand, it was instructed by the government to become more focused on heavy industries and shipbuilding by divesting itself of some of its assets. On the other hand, in 1998, Hyundai Motor was allowed to take over the failing Kia Motors. This gave the firm the economies of scale and financial stability needed to invest heavily vehicle quality. This accelerated its move away from being a low-price regional producer of cars primarily for Asian markets to a company whose Ulsan exports comprised a rising share of North American and European auto sales

Finally, in pushing for a reduction in South Korea's over-reliance on exports, the IMF's Crisis-related bailout plan provoked a geographic shift in Hyundai Motor's production. As a result, while Ulsan's plants remained the core of the automaker's worldwide manufacturing activities, by 2009 it produced only about 30% of its vehicles in the city, as compared with twice that in 2000. In 2011, Hyundai-Kia vehicles were built in 22 countries on five continents. This included 16 final assembly complexes in eight nations, and 24 CKD joint-ventures in 17 countries, as compared to its manufacturing operations in six South Korean municipalities. The group had subsidiaries and sales affiliates in nearly 200 countries.

As for trade issues, during the 1980s, relations with North American were frayed due to South Korea's large trade surpluses with the US and Canada, particularly related to imported automobiles. Threatened with of import quotas from these nations, and after receiving $131 million in incentives from the Canadian and Quebec governments, Hyundai Motor constructed a $387 million plant just 45 minutes east of Montreal, in Bromont, QC. With an annual capacity of 100,000 vehicles, it began producing Sonatas there in April 1989. Despite these major investments, quality problems doomed Bromont production from the start, and the plant was shuttered in 1993.

Over the next decade, this lesson taught the automaker that any successful entry into North American required major improvements to quality. As mentioned, aided by its merger with Kia, this was accomplished during the 2000s, when North America sales from Ulsan roughly doubled to 450,000 vehicles. Meanwhile, a significantly expanding trade surplus with the US served to reignite friction between the two countries. In response, Hyundai Motor decided to once again produce cars in North America, this time constructing a manufacturing complex in Montgomery, Alabama, in 2005, with an annual capacity of 300,000 vehicles; in 2010, the plant produced 300,500 vehicles with a domestic content of 80%. Then, in November 2009, it began production at a Kia factory in West Point, Georgia, just 90 miles northeast of Montgomery, equally capable of manufacturing 300,000 vehicles annually. In contrast, the group cut back on its vehicle exports from Ulsan, where production was basically flat during the 2000s.

Hyundai Motor's new US factories also proved fortuitous in the light of a third international event in 2010: US Congressional hearings prompted by false accusations and news stories alleging safety issues with Toyota Motor's most popular vehicle models (i.e., sudden acceleration). As a direct result, US

vehicle sales of the Hyundai-Kia Group rose by 21.7% to 894,496 in 2010 as compared with 2009; sales of the Hyundai Sonata sedan rose by 63.8% from 2009 to 196,623. While very little of this increase was from exports, Ulsan-based auto suppliers benefited tremendously from a related rise in demand for parts installed in the firm's American-made models. Conversely, Hyundai Motor's decision to shift some of its Elantra subcompact model production from Ulsan to Alabama, beginning in November 2010, could prove costly to the city.

A final dramatic international factor affecting Ulsan employment was the late 2000s dramatic depreciation of the KRW relative to the currency of its major export competitors the JPY. This trend began in January 2008 and accelerated rapidly following the September 15–16, 2008 collapse of two giant US financial services firms, AIG and Lehman Brothers. Figure 16.3 illustrates how relatively 'low' against the JPY the KRW has become by comparing their annual exchange

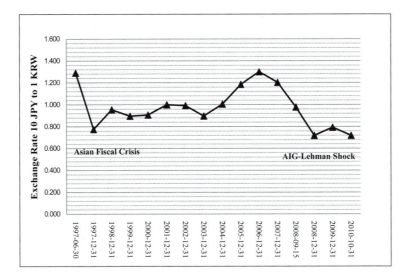

Figure 16.3 KRW to JPY normalized exchange rates, 1997–2010

Source: Oanda (2010)

Notes. Since the KRW is denominated in 1,000 to the USD as compared with 100 Yen, the figures above were adjusted or normalized by utilizing the KRW to 10 JPY rate. In other words, if the JPY to KRW was .1000, it was represented above as 1.000. Therefore, a figure of < 1.0 meant that the KRW was 'low' relative to the JPY, while > 1.0 meant the KRW was 'high'.

rates between 1997 and 2010. Since the KRW essentially has an extra digit below cents (i.e., 1000 KRW = 100 JPY), to normalize the two rates to 1.000, the KRW rate per 10 JPY was used. In the chart, a reading below 1.000 signified that the KRW's value was 'low' relative to the JPY, favoring Ulsan exporters. Conversely, a ratio of greater than above 1.000 meant that the KRW was 'high' versus the JPY, favoring Japanese exporters.

After fluctuating around par/1.000 between December 31, 2001 and December 31, 2004, the KRW appreciated against the JPY. It then returned to its 2004 level just before the AIG-Lehman shock, thereafter, international investors aggressively sold off KRW and USD and bought JPY. This led to the concurrent rapid rise in the JPY against the USD and an equally dramatic fall in the KRW. This situation resulted in the KRW being even cheaper against the JPY (.719) on October 31, 2010, than it was at the height of the 1997 Asian Fiscal crisis (see December 31, 1997, when it was at .775). This translated into a significant pricing advantage for Ulsan exporters over their Japanese competitors, which was enhanced by two factors: (1) in the late 2000s Ulsan manufacturers were much less dependent on Japanese imports as compared with 1997; (2) during the Asian Fiscal Crisis, the JPY also dramatically depreciated against the USD, resulting in equivalent KRW to JPY rates against the USD, rather than a 'low' KRW (again, see Figure 16.3). One outcome of this was, despite Hyundai Motor's new US plants, Ulsan city manufacturing employment expanded by 6,201 or 17.11% between 2007 and 2008. Approximately 94% of this was in MVM and OTEM, both of which added more than 2,200 workers.

In sum, the Asian Fiscal Crisis, trade friction with North America, the Toyota safety controversy, and the AIG-Lehman shock/'low' KRW versus the JPY, all demonstrate how Ulsan's growth cycles, similar to that of other *Great Industrial Cities*, have been forcefully shaped by international forces. Meanwhile, with firm linkages on six continents, South Korea's industrial heartland has become an important node in global capitalism.

ULSAN'S EMBEDDEDNESS IN NORTHEAST ASIA

South Korea is located in Northeast Asia, on a peninsula just 120 miles across the Korean Strait from Japan. To its north is North Korea, itself bordered by China and Russia. Historically, this geographical embeddedness has placed South Korean cities and firms in the middle of some precarious and advantageous political-economic circumstances. For example, from 1910 to 1945, Korea was a colony of Imperial Japan. This marked a period of severe repression and exploitation of its people that the two nations have yet to overcome.

In addition to its socio-political ramifications, Japanese colonization also had a lasting effect on South Korea's economic and industrial development. Initially, Japan dismantled Korea's feudal class divisions and its prohibitions on private property. Moreover, it constructed the energy, transportation, financial, and commercial infrastructure necessary to industrialize the country. Nevertheless, such endeavors were not part of a strategy to make Korea self-sufficient, but rather to support Japan's empire building. This was especially apparent following Japan's annexation of Manchuria in the 1931, when Korea became a frontline supply base for its military advances in China. It also was evident with regards to Japanese investments in Korean education, which although high, were not intended to build a thriving middle class, but rather to assimilate Koreans at the bottom of Japanese society. Finally, following a bloody uprising in 1919, the Japanese purposefully cultivated a Korean capitalist class, in order to quiet the masses. This bourgeois class would later resurface as the political-economic elite of post-colonial South Korea.

Following its defeat in World War II, Japan withdrew from Korea, and the country was partitioned into the present-day North and South Korea. Only five years later, foreign powers thrust the nation into the middle of a war of these territories. When peace was restored in 1953, the civil economy of South Korea's became concentrated in textiles and light manufacturing, led by a small number of large companies operating out of formerly Japanese plants, and run by the aforementioned Japanese-fostered Korean elite.

The influence of Japan continued after General Park seized power in 1961, via a military coup. Although fervently nationalistic, the new President was inspired most by the strategies of Japan's late 19th-century Meiji government, especially its 'rich nation, strong army' doctrine, which called for the cultivation of a loyal business class. As a result, members of the bourgeoisie were jailed and their fortunes commandeered, only to be released and their wealth returned, if they committed to invest in the best interest of economic nationalism. This set the stage for the formation of the *jaebeol*, such as Hyundai, whose size and diversification mirrored that of Japan's pre-war *zaibatsu* business conglomerates. Park's NEP and ambitious export-oriented strategy, which rapidly pushed South Korea's industrial mix toward HCI, also were inspired by Japan's pre- and post-WW II success. Park picked Ulsan to play a key role in this drive because of its deep harbor, vacant land, and most importantly, it was located in the nation's southeast, as far away as possible on the peninsula from North Korea.

Park's 'Look East' policy also re-established linkages with Japanese companies, a decision which proved particularly beneficial for Ulsan's post-1960s economic growth. For example, the Ulsan-based Hyundai HI and Hyundai Motor owe much of their success to the tutelage of the Japanese firms, particularly Kawasaki Heavy Industries and Mitsubishi Motors, respectively. As part of this technical assistance, Kawasaki invited 200 Korean engineers and technicians to Japan for training, provided Hyundai HI with proven designs for ships, and subcontracted with the firm to build its first two tankers. Since 1973, Hyundai Motor has received financial and technical support and has been involved in several joint ventures with Mitsubishi. Hyundai Motor's first Pony models were built with Mitsubishi engines and transmissions. In 1982, the Japanese automaker purchased a 10% stake in Hyundai Motor, with the latter agreeing to produce about 30,000 cars annually using the Mitsubishi Precis nameplate. Later, this partnership made it possible for Hyundai Motor to begin exports of its Excels to Canada in 1984, then to the US in 1986, and to the opening of Hyundai Motor's Bromont, Quebec plant in 1989.

Based upon a Mitsubishi design, between 1992 and 1998 the two firms jointly made the Hyundai Grandeur, the most popular luxury car in South Korea. The car essentially was a Mitsubishi Debonair produced in Ulsan with a Hyundai badge. After 1998, the Grandeur became solely a Hyundai production, but was succeeded by the Ulsan-built Hyundai Equus, briefly sold in Japan as the Mitsubishi Dignity limousine, and then, by the Hyundai Dynasty/Mitsubishi Proudia. Between 1988 and 1998, the Japanese automaker also supplied engineering and core components (imported or licensed) to the Hyundai Sonata, modeled originally on its Gallant platform, then built in Ulsan. Mitsubishi's equity holdings in the firm remained around 15% during this period, before declining through 2003, when it sold off its remaining Hyundai Motor shares. Until September 2009, when bought out by their partner Chrysler, the two firms still jointly developed engines for their Gallant and Sonata models, among others, through their Global Engine Manufacturing Alliance.

Finally, technology transfer and guidance from Japanese steel, machinery, auto and shipbuilding parts suppliers, also have greatly contributed to employment growth in Ulsan. In sum, Ulsan's historical and more recent linkages with Japan demonstrate how its post-war growth trajectory has been deeply embedded within Northeast Asia.

ULSAN'S SUB-NATIONAL AGGLOMERATIONS AND LINKAGES TO GROWTH

Finally, while Ulsan itself qualifies as an industrial agglomeration Ulsan's rise to *Great Industrial City* status also was greatly aided by its nestedness within two larger regional agglomerations: the Dongnam Economic Zone and the Gyeongsang Region. The latter encompassed Dongnam and the newly designated national economic bloc to its north, the Daegyeong Economic Zone (again, see Figure 16.1).

As previously discussed, Ulsan represented a Metropolitan City of 1.08 million people, and contained 391,000 in total employment, of which 146,481 was in manufacturing. It industrial sector included a clustering of 410 TEM firms employing 91,819, supported by another 440 firms with 24,519 workers in the complementary industries of Fabricated Metals, Machinery and Equipment, Primary Metals, and Plastics and Rubber Products manu-

facturing. In tandem, these firms, in concert with those in Petrochemicals and Non-metallic Minerals and the city's extensive port facilities, have formed a horizontally integrated industrial system in Ulsan, which has been a significant catalyst driving South Korea's economic growth over the past 35 years.

Ulsan firms also established production linkages with businesses throughout its larger economic zone and national region. As of 2010, the Dongnam Economic Zone, which encompassed the Metropolitan Cities of Ulsan and Busan, plus the localities in South Gyeongsang Province, had an estimated 7.66 million residents. In addition, in 2008, the zone had 2.54 million in total employment, and 11,346 manufacturing establishments employing 590,643 workers (see Table 16.5 and Figure 16.1). Among the latter were 1,921 firms employing 212,444 in TEM, of which, 918 establishments and 85,483 workers were in MVM, and 1,003 and 126,961, respectively, in OTEM. These firms were complemented by 5,464 Metals and Machinery manufacturers employing 209,826.

The economic zone's largest city was Busan, with 3.41 million residents in 2010 and 1.15 million in employment in 2008. It also contained 129,500 manufacturing jobs, including a Renault Samsung auto factory.

Table 16.5 Population and Employment for Ulsan and its Surrounding Area

	Population 2010	Total Employment 2008[1, 2]	Manf. Employment 2008[2]	Manf. Firms 2008[2]
Dongnam Economic Zone	7,657,671	2,541,340	590,643	11,346
–Ulsan Metropolitan City	1,082,567	391,300	146,481	1,233
–Busan Metropolitan City	3,414,950	1,150,000	129,500	3,865
–South Gyeongsang Province	3,160,154	1,000,000	314,662	6,284
—Changwon city (3)	1,080,441	NA	NA	NA
Daegyeong Economic Zone	5,046,450	1,520,000	306,285	6,874
–North Gyeongsang Province	2,600,032	800,000	212,686	3,973
–Daegu Metropolitan City	2,446,418	720,000	93,599	2,901

Sources: KOSIS (2011); Ulsan (2011); Gyeongsangbuk-do (2011); Gyeongsangnam-do (2011)

Notes
(1) Estimates from source data.
(2) Employment is by place of work.
(3) Population is for July 1, 2010, and includes the totals of the merged cities of Changwon, Masan and Jinhae.

Following Busan and Ulsan was Changwon, a city in South Gyeongsang Province which after its July 1, 2010 merger with Masan and Jinhae had 1.08 million residents. The new unified city also was a core for machinery and fabricated metals production, and home to GM-Daewoo and Ssangyong Motors engine plants.

Finally, Ulsan's industrial development also was aided by complementary manufacturing firms within the Daegyeong Economic Zone, which encompassed Daegu Metropolitan City and the municipalities in North Gyeongsang Province. In total, Daegyeong had an estimated population of 5.05 million in 2010 and approximately 1.52 million in employment in 2008, of which 306,285 were in manufacturing (again, see Table 16.5). Especially relevant for Ulsan factories were Daegyeong's: (1) automotive parts plants in Gyeongju city; (2) fabricated metals and parts suppliers in Daegu; (3) machinery makers in Gyeongnan city; and perhaps most of all, (4) POSCO steel complex in Pohang, a city of more than 500,000, located 70 km (44 miles) north of Ulsan. For nearly 40 years, a significant share of POSCO's Pohang output has been sent to Hyundai Motor and Hyundai HI's Ulsan plants. So intertwined have been these firms that in July 2010, Hyundai HI, Hyundai Mipo Dockyard, and POSCO deepened their long-held cross-shareholdings ties. Moreover, just two months later, POSCO opened a large new mill in Alabama to serve Hyundai Motor and its suppliers in the emerging US Southern Automotive Corridor.

As a result of its numerous agglomeration/production synergies, Ulsan's total value of exports, $78.8 billion in 2008, ranked first among South Korea's seven special cities; this was equivalent to 18.7% of the nation's total. In addition, as presented in Table 16.3, at 48.6 million KRW ($46,370 US), it had the highest GDP per capita among these cities, a figure that was more than twice the national average. Next, these synergies have promoted manufacturing growth in the city,

despite national economic downturns caused by international events of the 2000s. Again, between 2000 and 2008, the city added 56,735 in total employment, along with 325 industrial firms and 17,670 in manufacturing employment. Both of these increases were again tops among South Korea's seven special cities. This was noteworthy considering that industrial employment contracted in five of the seven during this period, with four suffering net losses in their manufacturing firms. Lastly, Ulsan's agglomerations have fueled population and income growth in the city. Between 2000 and 2010, the city's population increased by 70,457 or 6.96%. Additionally, its per capita income expanded to 15.3 million KRW ($14.598) in 2008. The latter ranked second highest among special cities, and trailed only the national capital, Seoul, by a mere $191.

In sum, along with the other influences previously chronicled, Ulsan's nestedness within the Dongnam Economic Zone and the Gyeongsang Region has been a decisive factor shaping its transformation into a world-connected, *Great Industrial City*, Asia's fourth largest manufacturing hub in terms of value of exports, with firm linkages on six continents.

Unfortunately, Ulsan's dense clustering of heavy and chemical industries also has resulted in it becoming its nation's most polluted city. For example, before its rehabilitation in the 1990s, the level of contaminants in its Taehwa River prompted national observers to dub it: 'the River of Death'. In addition, the growing international reputations of its firms, particularly Hyundai Motor and Hyundai HI, frequently aided by the government, have fostered highly combative management-labor relations, and have led to South Korean annual working hours ranking among the highest for OECD countries. Nonetheless, similar to its positive achievements, these negative outcomes were facilitated by its international, national, and sub-national embeddedness.

CONCLUSION: LESSONS FROM A 'GREAT' INDUSTRIAL CITY

This chapter began by claiming that Ulsan, as a result of it being the home to the world's largest shipyard and shipbuilder, its biggest auto production complex, its fifth largest auto producer, and one of its largest petrochemical complexes, qualified as a *Great Industrial City* (i.e., one of the world's major and influential industrial agglomerations). Second, it showed how Ulsan's path toward *Great Industrial City* status was decisively shaped by international, national, and sub-national factors. While the weight of each scale has fluctuated over time, all have been vitally important to Ulsan's industrial development.

Similar to other modern *Great Industrial Cities*, such as Toyota City, Stuttgart, and Sheffield, Ulsan has been significantly supported by the policies of its national government. In the case of Ulsan, the interventional Korean Developmental State, with its NEP, industrial district location decisions, and strategic targeting of specific manufacturing sectors, among other policies, was the foremost catalyst steering its growth path. However, like the others cities previously mentioned, international forces also were highly influential. For Ulsan, the Asian Fiscal Crisis of 1997, trade friction between South Korea and North American nations, the AIG-Lehman shock of 2008, and the Toyota safety recalls of 2010, were examples of such factors. Moreover, its prosperity has heavily relied upon the export of manufactured goods to other nations within an ever expanding global economy.

Next, Ulsan's growth trajectory was dramatically shaped by its location within East Asia, where South Korea's historical relations with Japan and North Korea. Related to this, connections between Ulsan industries and Japanese firms, among other factors, have been crucial. Finally, similar to all other *Great Industrial Cities*, Ulsan has benefited from its sub-national context, particularly its dense agglomeration of MVM, shipbuilders, petrochemical producers, and related supplier firms, its extensive port system, and firm linkages with complementary establishments located in other parts of the Dongnam Economic Zone and the larger Gyeongsang Region.

In sum, international, national, and sub-national contextual factors have together transformed Ulsan from a fishing port into one of the world's *Great Industrial Cities*. Ulsan's rise also demonstrates the continued importance of studying industrial cities, and hopefully encourages other English-language scholars to more closely examine South Korean city-regions. If they do, they may even learn a lot about urban areas within their own nations.

NOTE

1. Unless otherwise indicated, data sources for this and others sections of the chapter can be found in Tables 16.1 to 16.5.

QUESTIONS FOR DISCUSSION

1. In two or three paragraphs, discuss the main themes in Jacobs's chapter.
2. In 1–2 pages, citing examples from the chapter, define what Jacobs means by *Great Industrial Cities* (i.e., what are their characteristics).
3. Using specific examples from the chapter text, in 2–3 pages discuss how Jacobs's *Great Industrial Cities* match: (1) the ideas of Hill and Fujita's in their Nested City

theory; (2) the ideas put forth in Friedmann, Sassen, and/or Taylor in World/Global City Theory.

4. Utilizing the 'Further Readings', 'Helpful Web Links', and other sources, create a list of ten contemporary and past Great Industrial Cities. Then, in 2–3 pages, explain how and when they rose to (and fell from) prominence, and why these cities should be considered *Great Industrial Cities*.

FURTHER READINGS

Auty, R. 1990. The Impact of Heavy-Industry Growth Poles on South Korean Spatial Structure. *Geoforum*, 2 (1): 23–33.

Cho, L. and Y. Kim, eds. 1994. *Korea's Political Economy: An Institutional Approach*. Boulder, CO: Westview Press.

Eckert, C. 1991. *Offspring of Empire: The Koch'ang Kims & the Colonial Origins of Korean Capitalism 1876–1945*. Seattle: University of Washington.

Kirk D. 1994. *Korean Dynasty: Hyundai and Chung Ju Yung*. Armonk, NY: M.E. Sharpe.

Pirie, I. 2008. *The Korean Developmental State: From Dirigisme to Neo-liberalism*. New York: Routledge.

Stern, J., J. Kim, D. Perkins, and J. Yoo. 1995. *Industrialization and the State: The Korean Heavy and Chemical Industry Drive*. Cambridge, MA: Harvard University Press.

HELPFUL WEB LINKS

Busan Metropolitan City. 2012. Dynamic Busan: Home Page of Busan Metropolitan City. Online. Available at: http://english.busan.go.kr, last accessed, January 7, 2012.

Daegu Metropolitan City. 2012. Colorful Daegu: Daegu Metropolitan City, South Korea. Online. Available at: english.daegu.go.kr, last accessed, January 7, 2012.

Essen, City of. 2012. Welcome to Essen: Homepage of Essen, Germany. Online. Available at: http://essen.de/en/Aktuell/PortalAktuell_E.jsp, last accessed, January 3, 2012.

Gyeongsangnam-do. 2012. Welcome to Gyeongnam: Homepage of South Gyeongsong Province. Online. Available from http://english.gsnd.net/jsp/main/main.jsp, last accessed, January 4, 2012.

IPA. 2012. Invest Korea: Ulsan for you. Korean National Investment Promotion Agency. Online. Available at: http://ulsan.investkorea.org, last accessed, January 4, 2012.

Manchester City Council. 2012. Home Page of the City of Manchester, England. Online. Available at: http://www.manchester.gov.uk/, last accessed, January 3, 2012.

Pohang, City of. 2012. English Home Page of the Pohang City, South Korea. Online. Available at: http://eng.ipohang.org/site/eng/, last accessed, January 7, 2012.

Shanghai Baoshan District. 2012. Welcome to Baoshan. Online. Available at: http://english.baoshan.sh.cn/About_Baoshan/201005/t20100505_118477.html, last accessed January 7, 2012.

Sheffield City Council. Home Page of Sheffield, England. Online. Available at: https://www.sheffield.gov.uk/, last accessed, January 7, 2012.

Ulsan Metropolitan City. 2012. Home Page of Ulsan Metropolitan City. Online. Available at: http://english.ulsan.go.kr, last accessed, January 4, 2012.

PART 3

The City-Region as the Engine of Economic Activity/Growth: An Overview

The City-Region as the Engine of Economic Activity/Growth: An Overview

A.J. Jacobs

In Part Three: The City-Region as the Engine of Economic Activity/Growth eight chapters are presented offering a mixture of readings from different theoretical paradigms, which essentially contend that the city remains the locus of economic activity and regional and national economic growth. These perspectives all trace their lineage to one or more of the following seminal studies: Alfred Marshall's (1919) *Industry and Trade,* Joseph Schumpeter's (1934) *Theory of Economic Development,* Jane Jacobs' (1969) *The Economy of Cities,* Harvey Molotch's (1976) 'The City as a Growth Machine,' and David Harvey's (1989) 'From Managerialism to Entrepreneurialism.'

In *Industry and Trade,* Marshall discussed how certain local attributes, such as the existence of raw materials, population density, transportation infrastructure, and accessibility to other markets, have fostered comparative advantages for certain cities over others.[1] These advantages, he claimed, tended to facilitate growth in industrial production, foreign trade, and exports within an urban area. Expanding trade/markets for the city's industrial goods then promoted an enlargement in the number and size of the city's manufacturing firms. When these firms were concentrated in related industries, such as in textiles and apparel in Manchester, England, significant economies of scale were achieved by all firms in these sectors, creating what Marshall called a *localization economy.*

According to Marshall, Jane Jacobs (1969, 1984), and Schumpeter, this industrial synergy also provoked innovation, improved labor productivity, and led to the creation of 'new work' (new products and new ways of doing things). This combination then fostered what Schumpeter called economic development, a term he utilized to capture the ensuing virtuous cycle of revenue, employment, and population growth, which occurred not only in the urban region, but also in the nation as a whole.

Next, as Bertil Ohlin (1933, p. 219) suggested, as the region grew larger, the work force in the area came to possess "qualities entirely absent" in smaller markets. The improved quality and quantity of labor then attracted scores of firms in other manufacturing sectors, seeking to gain "access to a labor market, where any quality of worker can be found readily, whenever needed, an important element in the localization of many industries" (Ohlin, 1933, p. 219). According to Edgar Hoover (1937), as the city continued to attract new industries and expand in size, its industrial structure eventually reached a threshold at which it transformed the region from a *localization economy* to an *urbanization economy.* Based upon Hoover and Walter Isard (1956), *urbanization economies* can be defined as large, dense, diverse, agglomerations of labor, capital, production, transport and service infrastructure, social networks, information, knowledge, and experience. They also provide firms in all industries with substantial economies of scale, provoke product spin-offs, and result in extensive inter-dependence among firms in the same industry, and within all industries.

Hoover (1937, p. 108) went on to write: "Not all labor-oriented industries, of course, will be attracted to large cities. The advantage of city labor lies not in low wages, but in efficiency and flexibility of supply [and transport]." As a result, employers looking for sizeable pools of skilled labor generally will be attracted to central cities, while those requiring lower-skilled labor will locate within the region's periphery or in smaller regions. On the other hand, new firm locations in the central city will induce more skilled laborers to migrate there, and so on. In other words, economies of scale for all firms in a single industry (localization economies), and for firms in all industries in the same location (urbanization economies), produce an 'agglomerative force' ... which drives the rapid "enlargement in the total economic size (population, income, output or wealth) of that location" (Hoover, 1937, pp. 90–91). As McKenzie (1927) outlined, central city expansion then spills over into the periphery (suburbs), promoting growth in subordinate and complementary firms (e.g. regional plants and back office services), and in residents. Again, this virtuous cycle will result in regional and national economic growth and a territorial expansion in the geographic size of the local area.

Urbanization economies are exactly the kind of vibrant regional agglomerations discussed by Allen Scott and Michael Storper (2003) in their frequently cited *Regional Studies* article, 'Regions, Globalization, Development.' Chapter 17, the first reading in Part Three, presents a condensed version of this seminal article from the two most well-known scholars from the L.A. School of Urbanism. Drawing inspiration from Marshall, Schumpeter, and Piore and Sabel's (1984) seminal book, *The Second Industrial Divide*, among others, and building upon their own voluminous prior work, Scott and Storper argue that contrary to the assessments made by dominant contemporary theories of development and trade, advancing globalization has not made regional economies irrelevant.[2] Rather, they contend that global economic integration has made regional agglomerations even more indispensable to national growth. Therefore, they maintain that "to be fully general, development theories must incorporate" the active and causal roles played by cities and regions in growth processes (p. 579). Failure to do so, they claim, has led to the discounting of the positive impacts that agglomeration economies have had in initiating growth in poorer regions. This omission, they maintain, also has inhibited the formulation of policies which could slow or reverse the steady increase in inter-regional inequalities brought on by contemporary globalization.

In my Chapter 18, 'The Bratislava-Žilina Auto Corridor: Capitalist Agglomeration in the Post-Socialist CEE', I begin by chronicling the historical development of Slovakia's capital and largest city, Bratislava. I then present some background data on the present-day Bratislava Metropolitan Area (BMA). In the remainder of the chapter, I describe how foreign direct investment (FDI) has transformed the BMA from a socialist-controlled region into the core of an important tri-national, foreign capitalist-led motor vehicle manufacturing zone, the Bratislava-Žilina Auto Corridor. Due in large part to the area's growth, Slovakia has become the world's third largest auto producer per capita and was accepted into the European Union and European Monetary Union. Bratislava also represents a microcosm of emerging conditions within many other urban regions in Central and Eastern European (i.e., the CEE).

Chapter 19, 'The Development Industry and Urban Redevelopment in New York and London,' provides an edited selection from pp. 27–63 in Susan Fainstein's (2001b) book, *The City Builders: Property Development in New York and London, 1980–2000*. A long-standing observer of New York and London, Fainstein focuses upon the extraordinary boom in the 1980s and the subsequent 1990s bust cycle in the property markets in the two cities.[3] She attributes the rise and fall of New York and London property prices to expanding world capital flows and the ensuing explosion of financial and business services in these centers. She claims that the "deregulation of the financial industry coupled with the various product innovations and huge increases in capital flows to heighten the frenetic trading activity," induced a similar speculative fury in the two cities' property markets (p. 32). While generally considered a critic of *World/Global City Theory* (see Fainstein, 2001a), in this selection she concurs with Sassen's (1991) assessment that new technology has actually promoted greater agglomeration of business, financial, and real estate service firms in the world's top cities. Conversely, although she chronicles the roles played by governments in the revitalization of New York's midtown Manhattan, she rejects Moltoch's assertions and the conclusions drawn in his seminal book with John Logan (Logan and Molotch, 1987), *Urban Fortunes*, regarding the influence and machinations of a local growth machine in New York.

Chapter 20, 'Hong Kong: An Entrepreneurial City in Action,' presents an edited selection from Bob Jessop and Ngai-Ling Sum's (2000) *Urban Studies* article, 'An Entrepreneurial City in Action: Hong Kong's Emerging Strategies in and for (Inter)Urban Competition.' Drawing upon the ideas of Schumpeter and Harvey, as well as those discussed in Storper (1997a) and Jessop's (1997, 1998) earlier work, the authors offer Hong Kong as a case study of how the notion of entrepreneurship can be applied to cities which act strategically in order to facilitate economic growth. They argue that "despite its *laissez-faire* reputation, Hong Kong has a long history of urban entrepreneurship" (Jessop & Sum, 2000, p. 2287). Its strategies, however, frequently have required adapting to address its changing circumstances. More recently, they state, this has related to the city's reversion back to China, its key role as the core of an emerging cross-border region with Southern China, and its position as one of mainland China's most important gateways to the global economy.

In the chapter, they also introduce the concept of *glurbanization*, as one form of the more general phenomenon known as *glocalization*. They contend that whereas *glocalization* has become "the vogue word for all kinds of multi-scalar strategies with some global aspect" such as those pursued by global firms locally, *glurbanization* refers to strategies pursued by political units to enhance their place-based advantages in inter-urban competitions for mobile capital (pp. 2293–2294).

Chapter 21 is a condensed version of James Simmie, James Sennett, Peter Wood, and Doug Hart's (2002) *Regional Studies* article, 'Innovation in Europe: A Tale of Knowledge and Trade in Five Cities.' Here, in one of Simmie's numerous articles on innovative clusters, the authors examine why only a handful of European cities have been characterized as having especially high rates of firm innovation.[4] Utilizing the results of surveys conducted with recognized innovative firms in Amsterdam, London, Milan, Paris, and Stuttgart, they seek to explain how local assets, such as professional and technical knowledge and experience, infrastructure and educational systems, have contributed to innovation in these cities. Their analysis shows that innovative activities in Stuttgart and Milan have stayed more closely linked to their regional and national economies than those by firms in Amsterdam, Paris, and London. Therefore, they conclude that "the innovative and competitive advantages of the five cities are based upon a complex mixture of local, national and international factors" (p. 63). Nevertheless, they also suggest that the fostering of international firm links with other inventive knowledge clusters (i.e., cities with concentrations of professionally qualified technologists), in particular, were vital to the cultivation of local innovation. Such connections, they state, were important explanations for why these cities have remained "innovative trading nodes in the global economy" (p. 63).

Chapter 22 is an edited selection from John Rennie Short, Carrie Breitbach, Steven Buckman, and Jamey Essex's (2000) *City* article, 'From World Cities to Gateway Cities: Extending the Boundaries of Globalization Theory.' Building upon Short's in-depth research on some of the world's largest cities, the authors begin by claiming that the contemporary "focus on world cities has narrowed our understanding of the globalization/city relationship and ignored the processes of globalization occurring in almost all cities" (p. 317).[5] In other words, similar to the *Nested City Theorists*, Short and his colleagues reject the top-heavy focus and typology of the *World Cities Hypothesis*. Paralleling Jessup and Sum, they also attempt to improve upon the concept of *glocalization*. They seek to accomplish this through case studies of Barcelona, Beijing, Havana, Prague, Seattle, Sioux Falls, and Sydney, and by offering the concept of *Gateway Cities* to categorize these places. They then "provide a list of topics that can be explored using the gateway notion, including re-globalization, rescaling, representation, spectacle, and urban regimes" (p. 317). In summary, the *Gateway City* perspective represents a blending of Short's ideas on *Urban Boosterism* (Short, 1999), with the theories of *Entrepreneurial Cities* (Harvey, 1989; Hall & Hubbard, 1996, 1998); *Glocalization* (Swyngedouw 1997; Brenner, 1997); and *Urban Growth Machines/Regimes* (Molotch, 1976; Logan & Molotch, 1987; Elkin, 1987; Stone, 1989; Stoker & Mossberger, 1994; Lauria, 1997; Pereira, 2000; Pereira & Tong, 2005).

Chapter 23 presents a condensed version of Paul Waley's (2011) *Planning Perspectives* article, 'From Modernist to Market Urbanism: The Transformation of New Belgrade.' Here, Waley focuses upon the difficulties faced by Belgrade city leaders in their efforts to reconcile and accommodate socialist urban form, modernist architecture, and post-socialist, neoliberal development forces. He writes that the location for his inquiry "is the largest municipal district within Belgrade, known as New Belgrade, with its immense size and expanse (over 40 square kilometers/15 square miles and a population of about 250,000), grand boulevards and massive apartment buildings lined up in numbered blocks" (p. 209). He says that New Belgrade "is a mixture of modernist vision and socialist planning, far larger than any comparable urban district in CEE Cities" (p. 209).

Waley, goes on to discuss how the area, originally designed as a federal capital for Tito's Yugoslavia, eventually became a residential suburb, and is currently being redeveloped as a business hub and playground for foreign multinational corporations. He argues that the ensuing construction of large-scale office, expensive condominium, and retail and entertainment complexes has among other things: (1) led to the destruction of open space; (2) prevented the building of vital planned/needed cultural facilities; and (3) provoked a housing price bubble which was totally inappropriate for a nation as impoverished as Serbia. As a result, he states that today's New Belgrade can be characterized by its growing socio-spatial fragmentation and its associated visibly noticeable, housing differentiation. The latter consists of: new, chic, and prestigious apartments and condominiums; unique modernist architecture; and peripheral, low-income, high-rise socialist apartment blocks.

Overall, though best known for his 20 plus years of critical research on Tokyo, Japan,[6] Waley, through his case study of New Belgade, introduces the readers to one of the more interesting cases of a post-socialist urban growth regime. In the process, he also clearly shows how Belgrade's problems represent a microcosm of the same starkly contrasting forces confronting many contemporary Central, Eastern, and Southeastern European cities (i.e., socialism, modernism, and neo-liberalism).

The final reading in Part Three, Chapter 24, provides an original essay entitled 'Collaborative Regionalism and FDI Growth: The Cases of Mississippi's PUL Alliance and Alabama-

Georgia's Auto Valley Partnership.' The inclusion of an examination of small American urban regions may seem an odd match among the other major city-regions discussed in the book. However, the case studies of northeast Mississippi's PUL Alliance and the bi-state Hyundai-Kia Auto Valley Partnership represent prime examples of how communities within America's five-state Southeast Automotive Core (SEAC) have proven especially adept at attracting automotive-related FDI to their areas (also including South Carolina and Tennessee). SEAC local areas have 'won' eight of the eleven light vehicle assembly plants built in the USA since 1994. Most relevant here are the lessons I offer from my two case studies. First, I remind us how these areas demonstrate how America's development context continues to vary, not only in comparison to other countries, but among its sub-national regions. Second, and similar to the case of Bratislava, I discuss how manufacturing processes can transform multiple disconnected communities and sub-areas into one regional production belt. Finally, I reveal how these regions offer valuable examples of how economic decline can provoke even normally combative adjacent local governments to collaborate, in order to compete for FDI and job growth. The latter certainly is valuable insight for all cities to consider, regardless of their size, shape, geographical location, and assets.

Following Part Three, the volume concludes with an original essay entitled: 'The Nexus City Model: Bridging the Local, Regional, National, and International Contexts.' Here, I draw upon many of the ideas presented in the book's readings by presenting a 12-factor conceptual toolkit for use by students and scholars in their own examinations of the world's city-regions.

NOTES

1   Some might call these locational characteristics the initial conditions for urban and industrial growth.
2   For example, Scott (1998b, 1999, 2001a, 2001b, 2002); Storper (1991, 1995, 1997a, 1997b); and Scott & Storper, 1987).
3   Much of this work occurred in the late 1980s and early 1990s, and included her husband Norma Fainstein and others. See for example, Fainstein (1990, 1992, 2001a); Fainstein & Fainstein, (1987, 1988, 1989); and Fainstein et al. (1986, 1989, 1992).
4   Also see Simmie (1996, 2001, 2002, 2003, 2004); Hart & Simmie (1997); and Simmie & Sennett (1999).
5   See for example, Short (1996, 1999; Short & Kim 1998, 1999; and Short et al. (1996). This research culminated in Short's (2004) book, Global Metropolitan: Globalising Cities in a Capitalist World.
6   See for example, Waley (1991, 1992, 1997, 2002, 2003, 2007, 2010).

CHAPTER 17

Regions, Globalization, Development (2003)

Allen J. Scott and Michael Storper

The theory of economic development has had a long and tangled history extending from the classics of eighteenth- and nineteenth-century political economy, through the German historical school of the early twentieth century (above all, Schumpeter, 1934), to the many different streams of developmental ideas that were in circulation in the immediate post-war decades. . . . Notwithstanding the complexity and diversity of existing approaches to development, the vast majority of them tend to concentrate on macroeconomic variables and processes.

Macroeconomic considerations are, of course, critical in any real economic development process and we have no intention of suggesting otherwise. Nevertheless, our purpose in this paper is to point out and to deal with a silence that—with just a few exceptions—has characterized much of the development literature from the beginning. This concerns the role of selected regions as springboards of the development process in general, and as sites of the most advanced forms of economic development and innovation in particular, where by the term 'region' we mean any area of sub-national extent that is functionally organized around some internal central pole. Development does not depend on macroeconomic phenomena alone but is also strongly shaped by processes that occur on the ground, in specific regions of the type we have just defined. As

a result, development in any given country is always characterized by significant variations in the intensity and character of economic order from one place to another. Here, we are not simply calling attention to an obvious empirical state of affairs; we are also putting forward a significant clue about a complex theoretical question focused on the geographical foundations of economic growth. Any answer to this question, we argue, must consider the locational efficiency and innovation enhancing clusters of capital and labor in economic development. Cities and regions, in other words, are critical foundations of the development process as a whole. . . .

Accordingly, the theory that we shall seek to elaborate here puts considerable emphasis on the role of the *region* as a source of critical developmental assets in the form of increasing returns effects and positive externalities [i.e., firm economies of scale and scope/improved product and process efficiency, and greater firm and worker productivity, which provoke related spillovers/multipliers, expanded regional trade, and generally, regional population, employment, and economic growth]. In addition, we argue that because agglomeration is a principal source of these productivity enhancing outcomes, urbanization is less to be regarded as a problem to be reversed than as an essential condition of durable development.

REGIONS IN TODAY'S WORLD ECONOMY

These questions about the geographic foundations of development and growth are made yet more urgent by the current empirical realities of globalization. It is fundamentally mistaken to equate globalization with the notion that development today involves a simple spreading out of economy activity, or the transformation of the economic order into a liquefied space of flows. On the contrary, globalization has been accompanied by the assertion and reassertion of agglomerative tendencies in many different areas of the world, in part because of the very openness and competitiveness that it ushers in. Dense regional agglomerations of economic activity are major sources of growth in economies at virtually every stage of development today, as suggested by the worldwide expansion and spread of industrial clusters.

Thus, for example, 40% of US employment is currently located in counties constituting just 1.5% of its land area. Equally, the geographical density of employment in many sectors has been on the increase of late years. It has been suggested, as well, that 380 separate clusters of firms in the US employ 57% of the total workforce and generate 61% of the nation's output and fully 78% of its exports (Rosenfeld, 1996). . . . The OECD (1999), for its part, concludes that local industrial districts account for 30% of total employment in Italy (and 43% of that country's exports) and 30% of total employment in Holland.

The most striking forms of agglomeration in evidence today are the super-agglomerations or city-regions that have come into being all over the world in the last few decades, with their complex internal structures comprising multiple urban cores, extended suburban appendages and widely-ranging hinterland areas, themselves often sites of scattered urban settlements. These city-regions are locomotives of the national economies within which they are situated, in that they are the sites of dense masses of interrelated economic activities that also typically have high levels of productivity by reason of their jointly-generated agglomeration economies and their innovative potentials. In many advanced countries, evidence shows that major metropolitan areas are growing faster than other areas of the national territory, even in those countries where, for a time in the 1970s, there appeared to be a turn toward a dominant pattern of non-metropolitan growth. In less-developed countries, too, such as Brazil, China, India and South Korea, the effects of agglomeration on productivity are strongly apparent, and economic growth typically proceeds at an especially rapid rate in the large metropolitan regions of those countries. The same metropolitan regions are at once the most important foci of national growth and the places where export-oriented industrialization is most apt to occur.

. . . Recent accounts of the formation of an Atlantic economy in the late nineteenth and early twentieth century argue that it emerged on the basis of strong agglomeration processes in Europe and America, with the main centers of production maintaining their dominant positions through strong increasing returns to scale. Today's wave of globalization appears to be similarly anchored in (and is also partially responsible for) an expanding intercontinental patchwork of urban and regional economic systems. In sum, large-scale agglomeration—and its counterpart, regional economic specialization—is a worldwide and historically persistent phenomenon that is intensifying greatly at the present time as a consequence of the forces unleashed by globalization. This leads us to claim that national economic development today is likely not to be less but rather more tied up with processes of geographical concentration as compared with the past . . .

We now consider how the empirical realities we have alluded to can be accounted for by contemporary concepts of agglomeration, which we employ in turn as essential components of an updated development both poor and rich countries, and to shed some new light on the phenomenon of uneven spatial and economic development on a world scale.

THE FUNDAMENTALS OF AGGLOMERATION

The Analytical Decomposition of Agglomeration Processes

Cities always appear as privileged sites for economic growth because they economize on capital-intensive infrastructure (which is particularly scarce in developing areas), thus permitting significant economies of scale to be reaped at selected locations. But to this obvious basic factor underlying agglomeration, we must add three further sets of phenomena that complement and intensify its effects, namely: (1) the dynamics of backward and forward inter-linkage of firms in industrial systems; (2) the formation of dense local labor markets around multiple workplaces; and (3) the emergence of localized relational assets promoting learning and innovation effects.

Even though transport and communications costs tend to decline over time, the friction of distance in general continues to have powerful effects on locational outcomes. Improvements in transport and communications processes (e.g. the development of canal systems, railroads, the interstate highway network, the postal service, or the telegraph and the telephone) have rarely if ever slowed down the urbanizing tendencies of modern capitalism, even as they have encouraged its spatial extension. Rather, improvements of these sorts have almost always tended to reinforce the clustering of economic activity both by widening the market range of any given centre and by helping to spark off new rounds of specialization in established urban areas. This state of affairs also seems to be the case in the present period in which inter-net-based broadband communications technologies have made possible instantaneous transmission of complex messages across the globe at extremely low costs. . . .

This resistance is intensified where firms compete with one another by means of product differentiation, and where markets are characterized by much uncertainty. . . . Dense agglomerations containing large numbers of firms allow both suppliers and buyers to compensate for variability and uncertainty by providing ready access to needed resources on short notice. Considerable gains in productivity typically flow to firms from this localized concentration of many different suppliers and buyers. Among the more important of these gains is the ability to maintain low overheads while achieving high flexibility in both internal and external operations. One especially powerful phenomenon is the continuing importance of face-to-face contacts for the establishment of mutual confidence and accurate evaluation of potential partners in constantly changing business relationships.

Comparable dynamics of matching differentiated demands and supplies apply to labor markets. When firms need specialized workers, but are subject to rapid shifts in their product and process designs (as in the case of fashion-oriented or technologically-innovative industries), they usually strive as far as possible to achieve flexibility in their use of labor. At the same time, they seek to avoid the risk of costly delays in finding the various skills on which they depend. To overcome this problem, they need direct access to large and variegated pools of specialized talent. In the same way, if workers are to invest in building up their competencies, but are unable to secure long-term employment contracts, they will prefer to locate where there are many potential employers. In turn, rapid search and rehire processes will compensate them for high turnover.

In all of these circumstances, geographical concentration has major productivity-raising effects for firms, and income-raising effects for workers. Firms benefit from the possibility of adjusting their capacity levels as needed, while minimizing the risks of not finding the workers they require for expansion and change. Workers gain by having strong incentives to invest in their own talents and becoming more specialized, but are able to offset the associated risks by being in a place where the existence of multiple employment opportunities raises their chances of finding a job. . . . Geographical concentration lowers the costs of these transactions and raises the probability of successful matching for all parties.

Regional concentrations of economic activity have another advantage, which is purely dynamic in nature. The spatial proximity of large numbers of firms locked into dense networks of interaction provides the essential conditions for many-sided exchanges of information to occur, and out of which new understandings about process and product possibilities are constantly generated. Specialized regional economies are the locus of intense knowledge spillovers, thereby helping to raise the rate of innovation, and to promote long-term growth. Each of these factors underlying geographic concentration has the effect of creating positive externalities for both firms and workers. . . .

The Agglomeration Development Nexus

Cities are a necessary corollary of industrialization because they allow for complex agglomerations of specialized activities to emerge while economizing on infrastructure under conditions of national scarcity. . . . This, however, is at best a partial view of the dynamic properties of the relationship between urbanization and economic development. To begin with, the emphasis on infrastructure is only one among many reasons for agglomeration. . . . Actual agglomerations are characterized by many additional sources of productivity gain through their transac-

tional structures, local labor markets, learning effects, and so on. These phenomena can sustain the advantages of agglomeration even in the face of rapidly rising costs of urban concentration due to congestion, pollution, escalating land prices, family breakdown, etc. Such costs are especially high in developing countries, but still they fail to arrest urban growth. . . .

The particular patterns of agglomeration that make their appearance in any given instance vary widely depending upon local circumstances and the local mix of sectors, and this diversity is further augmented by the role that historical path dependencies play in the evolution of regional economies. This is an important reason why, in fact, there are many variations in the character of urban systems in both the developing and developed countries as a whole, rather than convergence toward any single type. What is common to all is the underlying functional link between agglomeration, urbanization and development. . . .

The frequency and scope of windows of locational opportunity are controlled by many factors, of which internal economies of scale (in production, R & D, transacting, and so on) are especially important. In industries where this feature results in oligopolistic supply structures (e.g. sectors producing commercial aircraft or nuclear-power generators) only a few regions will be able to attract relevant investments and to acquire production capacity. Major shifts in the core locations of these industries can generally occur only when there are important technological changes in products and processes, thereby undermining the advantages of existing producers and, by extension, the regions in which they are concentrated. By contrast, in sectors where optimal scale is achieved at low rates of output (e.g. clothing, shoes, jewelry, and many kinds of electronics industries or business services) there are numerous potential windows of locational opportunity. Sectors of this sort are able to engage in significant forms of product differentiation from one place to another, thus making it possible for latecomers to enter the market and to create distinctive niches for themselves. . . . Once agglomeration occurs (and depending on the nature of further major technological shifts), the locational pattern of these sectors becomes locked in, and local developmental effects intensify. . . .

DEVELOPMENTAL DISPARITIES IN THE CONTEMPORARY WORLD SYSTEM

Regional Divergence or Convergence?

The increasing liberalization of economic exchange as globalization has proceeded, combined with steady improvements in technologies of transportation and communication, has encouraged the world-wide spread of dense productive agglomerations. This effect is complemented by two others. First, agglomerations in different parts of the world find themselves increasingly caught up in relations of competition and complementarities with one another. Inter-agglomeration competition occurs when producers in different places operate on the same markets; complementarities are present when differentially specialized agglomerations are linked together via long-distance commodity chains. Second, agglomerations are also often deeply connected to more peripheral, less densely developed areas, especially where certain types of production units within wider commodity chains find it advantageous to locate at decentralized sites. This phenomenon is especially characteristic of branch plant operations with relatively standardized production activities and hence with low-cost procurement and distribution structures. The net result of the two tendencies . . . is the proliferation of complex trade flows, between different agglomerations and between agglomerations and peripheral areas, at national and international scales, and these flows are expanding with globalization.

Neoclassical theories of development hold that the spatial integration of economic activity in these ways tends progressively to eliminate interregional differences in living standards, by promoting some combination of structural and compositional convergence among participating economies. In fact, the actual record is quite wayward, with convergence occurring in some places at some times, and divergence occurring on other occasions. At the present moment, the play of regional and global economic forces involves many complex cross-currents in which some parts of the world (East Asia and a few metropolitan regions of Latin America) are doing relatively well, while other parts (Africa between the tropics, much of the former Soviet Union, and certain peripheral regions in more developed countries) are falling steadily behind.

The predicaments of uneven spatial development are most dramatically expressed in the observation that 50% of global Gross Domestic Product (GDP) today is produced by only 15% of the world's people [mostly concentrated in the US, Western Europe and Japan]. Conversely, the poorer half of the world's population produces just 14% of global GDP. . . . At the same time, much of the world's most important trading activities (increasingly in the form of intra-firm trade) occur between a relatively limited number of sub-national regions or agglomerations. This process accentuates the growth of selected regions, and helps to generate the contemporary phenomenon of large city-regions scattered across the continents in an integrated world-wide mosaic. Many different parts of the developing world are deeply involved in relationships like these, as exemplified by city-regions such as Mexico, Sao Paulo, Cairo, Bombay, Kuala Lumpur, Jakarta, and so on. One consequence of this trend, however, is that inter-regional income inequalities within many developing countries are increasing. Indeed, even in many developed countries, the recent period of intensive globalization combined with a turn to neo-liberal [free-market] policy measures has been accompanied by widening gaps in per capita incomes between sub-national regions. . . .

Per capita income differences among countries diverged over much of the nineteenth and twenteith centuries, but showed signs of convergence from the 1960s to the 1980s. Over the last decade or so, this [latter] tendency has been reversed, notwithstanding the dramatic improvements in technologies of spatial interaction that have been occurring.

The Dynamics of Differential Regional Development

Considerable light can be shed on these issues by further analysis of the ways that regional development processes contribute to durable structural and compositional differences between economies. In particular, why do some regions succeed in establishing high-performing economic systems while others remain stillborn, stagnate or decline even as spatial interaction costs fall?

We have already shown in our earlier discussion of windows of locational opportunity how increasing returns effects reinforce growth opportunities for regions that begin (even accidentally) to move ahead as production foci in any given sector, while progressively closing off opportunities for others. Certain endogenous features of agglomerations also have great impacts on local developmental prospects. Economic historians and geographers have shown, for example, that even industries where best practices diffuse rapidly from country (as in the case of cotton mills and railroads in the nineteenth century), factor productivity is often quite uneven over space. What is additionally puzzling is that such differences emerge not only in cases where technologies and managerial practices are similar, but also in industries uniformly to locate in large urban centers (as of the electronics industry today). All this

implies that there are significant endogenous determinants—local and national—of how well agglomerations function, and hence how much they contribute to economic development in their local and national contexts. By the same token, increasing trade, foreign investment and the international diffusion of technology do not automatically bring about convergence in productivity and development levels.

Many of the endogenous conditions underlying local economic development and facilitating entry into the world economy are cultural or institutional, in the specific sense that they entail the formation of routines of economic behavior that potentiate and shape activities such as production, entrepreneurship and innovation. These routines are, in effect, untraded forms of interdependency between economic agents, and hence, they collectively constitute the relational assets of the regional economy. Standard theories of economic development do not probe adequately into these processes. Neoclassical theories, including newer augmented versions, assume that successful behavior will emerge more or less spontaneously out of the wider economic or social context. Others, like the new growth theory, put their faith in the accumulation of stocks of knowledge leading to generalized positive externality effects throughout the economy.

The latter idea, though it may be useful as a starting point, says little about the concrete habits and relationships through which knowledge and savoir faire are created and deployed in economic action. Relational assets of this sort are not freely reproducible from one place to another, and access to them is determined at least in part through network membership. This is why untraded interdependencies tend to have a strongly place-bounded and culturally-rooted character and often cannot be transferred easily, if at all, from successful to less successful regions. Because access to these assets is spatially and organizationally on local limited, they enhance the economic advantages of their and home regions (as well as local business enterprises and in network members) and enable them to engage in monopolistic forms of competition.

These observations indicate that regional economic development involves a mixture of exogenous constraints, the reorganization and build-up of local asset systems, and political mobilization focused on institutions, socialization, and social capital. More generally, the extent to which any region succeeds in creating with much localized increasing returns effects—which depends importantly on these cultural and institutional foundations—is critical to the entire development process. A direct extension of this point is the claim that the success of national economies (as indicated above all by accession to membership in the global high-income convergence club) is, in significant ways, related to the rise of dynamic and creative agglomerations, as illustrated by the case of the high-performance Asian economies. If this claim is correct, it follows that for countries to join the high-income convergence club in today's world, they will have to sustain successful agglomerated development processes (though this remark in no way implies that balanced and sustainable rural development is not also an essential ingredient of any pathway to national development). Agglomeration is a central concern that can neither be equated to urbanization as a simple demographic phenomenon nor dissolved away into the realm of macroeconomics . . .

CONCLUSION: DEVELOPMENT THEORY THROUGH THE LENS OF ECONOMIC GEOGRAPHY

Conventional economic theories of development and trade have by and large ignored questions of economic geography. Today some of this neglect is being rectified by economists with an interest in agglomeration economies and regional dynamics (see,

for example, Fujita et al., 1999). In our view, however, this perspective can be taken further. The existence of pervasive agglomeration economies based on externalities and increasing returns effects, calls for a full recognition of the region as an organic unit of economic reality. This is because agglomeration economies represent a potent, immobile and—given their status as quasi-public goods—a highly-problematical element of the entire development process. As such, regions exist as keystones of economic organization just as firms, sectors and nations do. Development theory needs now to recognize this point and take it into account.

As we indicated at the beginning of this paper, economists have tended to privilege macroeconomic variables as the best possible line of attack on the problem of development. But this level of observation, though obviously important, is no longer (if it ever was) the uniquely privileged point of entry to an understanding of development, and all the more so today given that the barriers between national economies are in certain respects breaking down, thus enhancing tendencies to agglomeration at selected locations all over the world. Moreover, while development theories directed at poorer countries have at times recognized the fundamental two-way connection between industrialization and urbanization, they have tended to focus on the problem of hyper-urbanization and its negative social repercussions, rather than on the region as a locus of high-productivity outcomes. Our point is that one of the most fundamental issues for developing countries today is how to create and sustain the kinds of agglomerations without which they can never hope for entry into the highest ranks of the global economy, while ensuring that income disparities remain well within the limits of the socially just and politically tolerable.

This state of affairs poses many new questions for development theory and policy at the regional, national and international scales. We have sought in the present paper to move beyond elements of development theory that impede a fuller recognition of the geographical realities of the globalization process and to sketch out the beginnings of some broad responses to the questions raised by this exercise.

QUESTIONS FOR DISCUSSION

1. In two or three paragraphs, discuss the main themes of Scott and Storper's chapter.
2. In 1–2 pages, use examples from their chapter to illustrate their main themes. Also try to discuss what you think were the strongest and weakest points in their arguments.
3. Think about changes in the global economy and in technology that have taken place in the past 20 years. Discuss, in 2–3 pages, whether you think that city–regional agglomerations will continue to be in important engines of local and national economic growth. In your response, consider how transportation and communication may change over the next 20 years.
4. Utilizing the 'Further Readings', 'Helpful Web Links', and other sources, conduct some research on three industrial regions and, in 2–3 pages, describe how they fit or do not Scott and Storper's regional agglomeration thesis. Present your findings to class in a 10–15 minute speech.

FURTHER READINGS

Hurley, N. 1959. The Automotive Industry: A Study in Industrial Location. *Land Economics*, XXXV (1): 1–14.

Jacobs, J. 1984. *Cities and the Wealth of Nations*. New York: Penguin.

Sabel, C. 1989. Flexible Specialization and the Re-Emergence of Regional Economies. In P. Hirst and J. Zeitlin, eds., *Reversing Industrial Decline? Industrial Structure and Policy in Britain and Her Competitors*. New York: St. Martin's Press, pp. 17–69.

Scott, A. 1998. *Regions and the World Economy: The Coming Shape of Global Production, Competition, and Political Order*. Oxford: Oxford University Press.

Storper, M. 1997. *The Regional World: Territorial Development in a Global Economy*. New York: Guilford Press.

Storper , M. and A. Scott. 1995. The Wealth of Regions: Market Forces and Policy Imperatives in Local and Global Context. *Futures*, 27 (5): 505–526.

HELPFUL WEB LINKS

Birmingham City Council. 2012. City of Birmingham, England Home Page. Online. Available at: http://www.birmingham.gov.uk/, last accessed, January 3, 2012.

Cambridge, City of. 2012. Welcome to the City of Cambridge, MA. Online. Available at: http://www.cambridgema.gov/, last accessed, January 3, 2012.

Flemish, Department of Foreign Affairs. 2012. Welcome to Flanders: Official Portal Site of Flanders Region of Belgium. Online. Available at: http://www.flanders.be/, last accessed, January 13, 2012.

Florence, City of. 2012. Comune de Firenze: The Official Website of the City of Florence, Italy. Online. Available at: http://en.comune.fi.it/, last accessed, January 3, 2012.

Kyoto, City of. 2012. Kyoto City Web: Home Page of City of Kyoto, Japan. Online. Available at: http://www.city.kyoto.jp/koho/eng/index.html, last accessed, January 3, 2012

Lowell, City of. 2012. Welcome to the City of Lowell, MA. Online. Available at: http://www.lowellma.gov/, last accessed, January 3, 2012.

Pittsburgh, City of. 2012. City of Pittsburgh, Pennsylvania: Pghgov.com Online. Available at: http://www.city.pittsburgh.pa.us/, last accessed, January 9, 2012.

Santa Clara, City of. 2012. City of Santa Clara, California Home Page. Online. Available at: http://santaclaraca.gov/, last accessed, January 3, 2012.

Sunnyvale, City of. 2012. City of Sunnyvale, California Home Page. Online. Available at: http://sunnyvale.ca.gov/, last accessed, January 3, 2012.

Youngstown, City of. 2012. City of Youngstown, OH Home Page. Online. Available at: http://www.cityofyoungstownoh.org/, last accessed, January 3, 2012.

CHAPTER 18

The Bratislava-Žilina Auto Corridor: Capitalist Agglomeration in the Post-Socialist CEE (2013)

A. J. Jacobs

Since the fall of the Iron Curtain and state socialism, the world's largest automakers have established several auto production complexes in Central and Eastern Europe (CEE). Enticed by significant government incentive packages, the most prominent of these were Poland, the Czech Republic, Hungary, and Slovakia (i.e., the Visegrad-4).[1] This process began in earnest in early 1990–91, when Fiat took control of Poland's state-owned FSM, Magyar Suzuki was established in Hungary, and Volkswagen acquired Czechoslovakia's Škoda and BAZ.[2] These facilities quickly attracted many of the world's largest auto suppliers, and later, during the 2000s, other major carmakers. All of these manufacturers located in the CEE in order to gain access to its largely untapped consumer markets and to take advantage of its relatively inexpensive, skilled labor force. The central locations of the Visegrad-4 nations also made them prime production bases for exporting automobiles and parts to both the emerging CEE and developed Western European nations.

Initially, as a result of their greater political stability and more aggressive liberalization strategies, foreign direct investment (FDI) expanded most rapidly in Hungary and Poland, and thereafter, in the Czech Republic (or Czechia). On the other hand, "Slovakia missed much of the CEE's FDI boom of the 1990s . . . both quantitatively and qualitatively" (Fifekova & Hardy, 2010, p. 8). This dramatically changed in the 2000s and by 2007 Slovakia had the highest vehicle output per capita of any country in the world; it stood third in 2010.

Despite this, very little has been written in English about Slovakia's industrial regions, as compared with those in its larger Visegrad-4 neighbors. This chapter attempts to help rectify this situation by examining Bratislava Metropolitan Region (BMR), the heart of that Slovakia and that nation's auto industry. The chapter begins with a short history of the development of Bratislava, followed by some demographic background information on the BMR. Thereafter, the chapter reveals how the Slovak Government, Volkswagen (VW), and auto production in general have transformed the post-socialist BMR into the Bratislava-Žilina Auto Corridor, an important industrial agglomeration in global capitalism.

THE HISTORICAL DEVELOPMENT OF THE BMR

As shown in Figure 18.1, situated in southwestern Slovakia and centered on the capital city of Bratislava, the BMR can be defined as the territory encompassing the present-day Provinces Bratislava and Trnava (see OECD, 2003; Brzica, 2009).[3] While the provinces of Bratislava and Trnava generally have been considered as two separate urban areas, national development policies and the auto production processes of VW, Hyundai, and Peugeot have led to their convergence into

Figure 18.1 The Bratislava Metropolitan Region in Slovakia

one economic region. Moreover, history suggests that the combined area, located at the confluence of four CEE nations, Slovakia, the Czech Republic, Austria, and Hungary, has placed the entire BMR on the frontline of several of Europe's major political-ideological and military conflicts (see Figure 18.2).

The area was initially settled around 5,000 BC, but first began to really develop in the 2nd century BC, when the Celts established a fortress and political center in the territory. It was not until around AD 500, however, that the Slavic people began migrating to the area from the east. During this period, Bratis-

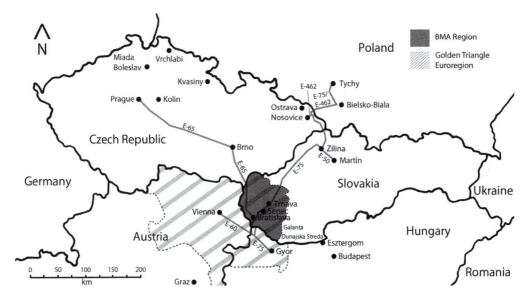

Figure 18.2 The BMA and the Golden Triangle Euroregion within the larger CEE context

lava Castle became a prominent political and economic center in what was known as the Principality of Nitra. The Nitra Area encompassed the present-day Slovak Provinces of Bratislava, Trnava, Nitra, Trenčín, and Žilina (again, see Figure 18.1). By AD 833, the peoples of Nitra and neighboring Moravia (essentially eastern and central Czech Republic) would align forces to create the first Slavic state, Great Moravia. The Slavs ruled the land until around AD 907, when they were defeated by the Magyars and annexed into the Kingdom of Hungary. Following the rise of the Magyars, Bratislava, then generally known by its German name of Pressburg (Pozsony in Hungarian or Prešpork in Slovak), became the seat of power in Hungary's Pozsony County, an area whose boundaries conformed to the present-day BMR. Unfortunately, this status also made it a frequent target for enemy military attack.

From 1536 to 1783, Pressburg served as the capital of Hungary, where it housed members of the ruling Habsburg Family. This transformed the city into the heart of politics and culture in the Kingdom, as well as its largest municipality. In 1783, the Hungarian capital and royal court were returned to their former home, Buda (now part of Budapest), prompting a major exodus from Pozsony County. From the 1830s until the end of World War I in November 1918, the area experienced economic growth as a regional center of commerce and industry, with the Danube River acting as a vital mode of transportation for international trade. During this period, Buda and Vienna would become the twin capitals of the new Austro-Hungarian Empire.

Following WWI, Austria-Hungary was dissolved and Pressburg became part of a new Slavic nation, the Czechoslovak Republic (1918–1938). In February 1919, the city was tabbed the new capital of the Republic's State of Slovakia. Then, on March 27, 1919, it was officially rechristened with a Slovak name, Bratislava. Over the next two decades, although Prague was anointed the national

capital, Bratislava acted as the political core for the Czechoslovakia's Social Democratic Party and the Slovak nationalist movement. It also became well known for its institutions of higher education (universities, technical schools, and secondary schools), its ethnic diversity, and its inter-group tolerance, with Slovak, Czechs, Germans, Hungarians, Croats, and Jews living, working, and worshiping side-by-side.

This harmonious situation was changed dramatically in 1938, when the Nazis annexed Prague and much of the nation's Czech lands. As a result, during WWII, Bratislava, despite its exposure to the Austrian and Hungarian borders, and thereby, Nazi attack, became the base for political power in the newly chartered Slovak Republic (1939–1945). After WWII, the boundaries of Czechoslovakia were essentially restored. In the interim, two-thirds of Bratislava's Jewish population were deported and/or massacred, and the great majority of its Germans and Hungarians were relocated to their ancestral homelands. In contrast, thousands of Slovaks were resettled in the area. As a consequence, Bratislava lost its unique pre-war multiculturalism.

Only a few years later, the Stalinists seized power and turned the nation into a buffer zone between the East and West, Socialism and Capitalism. In the process, Bratislava's western borders were sealed off by an Iron Curtain of barbed wire. Meanwhile, the city's factories, devastated by WWII, were rebuilt and nationalized, to best serve the interests of the USSR. Over the next 40 years, manufacturing plants in Bratislava and in neighboring regions would produce more than 40,000 tanks and heavy-duty vehicles to support the Soviets in their Cold War with the USA. Bratislava's position was forcefully reinforced in the Spring of 1968, when the Soviet-led forces invaded Prague and Bratislava, effectively dissipating any democratization movements in Czechoslovakia.

The events of November 1989 brought another dramatic change to the city, as it marked the fall of the Iron Curtain and State Socialism. This opened the city to West and ultimately its local economy to global capitalist forces. A little over three years later, on January 1, 1993, Czechoslovakia was split into two nations, the Czech Republic and Slovakia, with the latter taking Bratislava as its capital city. While this would initially lead to a period of political and economic uncertainty and tumult, by the first decades of the 21st century, the capital region had become one of CEE's most dynamic and productive metropolitan areas. In fact, as a direct result of the BMR's rapid post-Socialist economic growth, on May 1, 2004, Slovakia was welcomed into the European Union (EU), and then, on January 1, 2009, into the European Monetary Union or EMU (i.e., it was allowed to adopt the euro as its currency). It accomplished the latter an expected decade ahead of its three larger Visegrad-4 neighbors: Hungary, Poland, and the Czech Republic.

THE PRESENT-DAY BMR: SOME BACKGROUND DATA

As shown in Table 18.1, as of December 31, 2009, the BMR contained 1,184,231 residents living within an area of 2,404 square miles (6,226 square kilometers).[4] As suggested, the City of Bratislava has long stood as the central core of the BMR. In 2009, the capital had 431,061 inhabitants within its 141.95 square miles (367.65 km²) in land area. A second important fact about Bratislava city was that it was only 37 miles (60 km) east of Vienna, Austria. This meant that the two cities owned the distinction of being the two closest national capitals in distance in all of Europe. As again shown in Figure 18.2, together with Győr, Hungary, itself just 46 miles (75 km) south of Bratislava, these twin capital regions also have been referred to as the Golden Triangle Euroregion (OECD, 2003; Brzica, 2009). In 2009, this economic region, including: (1) the BMR; (2) the three Austrian States (Länder) of Vienna, Lower

Austria and Burgenland (i.e., the Vienna Metropolitan Area); and (3) Hungary's Győr-Moson-Sopron County, contained 5.22 million people within an area of 13,078 sq. miles (33,871 sq. km).

Focusing again on the BMR, in terms of ethnic composition, 82.44%, the metro area's residents where Slovaks in 2009. On the other hand, 13.33% of the BMR's population was Hungarian, 1.43% was Czech, and 2.80% was from 'Other' ethnicities (again, see Table 18.1). As for its sub-regions, Bratislava Province was even less diverse, with a population that was 90.38% Slovak, 4.36% Hungarian, and 5.26% other groups. The vast majority of these residents lived in Bratislava city, which was 90.04% Slovak. Conversely, 16.66% (10,608 of the 63,680) of the inhabitants in Bratislava Province's Senec District, situated in Bratislava city's northeast suburbs, were Hungarian. The Trnava Province was even more multicultural, with a population that was 73.64% Slovak, 23.27% Hungarian, and 3.09% Czech and Other. In fact, it was home to 130,689 of the 157,813 Hungarian persons in the entire BMR in 2009. Almost two-thirds of these (93,804) resided in Trnava Province's Dunajská Streda District, located east/southeast of Bratislava city and adjacent to the Hungarian border, which was 79.64% Hungarian (again, see Figure 18.2). Another 36,291 Hungarians lived in its Galanta District, located approximately 30 miles (50 km) due east of the capital and situated contiguous to Dunajská Streda's northern border.

In terms of employment, as presented in Table 18.2, the BMR had 702,421 in total employment in 2009. Of this total, 132,062 jobs were in manufacturing. The region's major industries included foodstuffs, chemicals, machinery, and motor vehicles production. As a result of it being the host of the national capital, the BMR also was the site of the national headquarters of numerous large multinational corporations (MNCs), such as Citibank, ING, Allianz, IBM, Samsung,

Table 18.1 Basic Population Indicators for Bratislava Metropolitan Area

	Population Dec. 31, 2009	% Slovak	% Hungarian	% Czech[1]	% Other	Land Area (sq. miles)
Bratislava Metropolitan Area	**1,184,231**	**82.44%**	**13.33%**	**1.43%**	**2.80%**	**2404.15**
Bratislava Province	622,706	90.38%	4.36%	1.83%	3.44%	792.48
Bratislava City	431,061	90.04%	3.71%	2.15%	4.10%	141.95
Remainder Bratislava Province	191,645	91.13%	5.80%	1.10%	1.97%	650.54
Senec District	63,580	80.05%	16.66%	0.97%	2.32%	138.95
Trnava Province	561,525	73.64%	23.27%	1.00%	2.09%	1,611.67
Dunajská Streda District	118,046	17.39%	79.46%	0.63%	3.14%	414.67
Galanta District	96,262	59.42%	37.70%	0.63%	2.87%	247.76
Slovakia	5,424,925	85.24%	9.47%	0.95%	4.34%	18,933.06

Source: Slovak Republic, Statistical Office (2011)

(1) Source include Czech population includes Czech, Moravian, and Silesian persons.

Table 18.2 Basic Employment and Production Indicators[1, 2]

	Employment 2009	Manufacturing Employment 2009	Unemployment Rate 2010	GDP 2008 ($US billion)	GDP Per capita 2008 ($US)	Gross HHI 2008 ($US)
Bratislava Metropolitan Area	702,421	132,062	6.27%	35.92	34,308	NA
Bratislava Province	458,589	51,747	4.63%	24.72	40,280	12,555
Bratislava City	392,954	37,164	3.94%	NA	NA	NA
Remainder Bratislava	65,635	14,583	6.45%	NA	NA	NA
Trnava Province	243,832	80,315	8.17%	11.20	20,040	9,974
Slovakia	2,209,862	524,191	12.46%	94.46	17,473	9,524

Source: Slovak Republic, Statistical Office (2011)

(1) Slovakia for Dec. 31, 2009. Place of work employment for all enterprises and private entrepreneurs. Employment based upon Revision 2 of NACE data after January 1, 2008; change data extracted from 1995–2008 Employment table based upon Revision 1 of NACE data as of May 25, 2009.
(2) All dollar figures are based upon December 31, 2008 Exchange rate of 1 $US = .7094 Euro. Euro figures provided by the source

T-Mobile, Tesco, Kraft, Siemens, VW, and Peugeot. Another positive consequence of hosting the capital was the fact that whereas the national unemployment rate was 12.46% in 2010, the BMR's jobless rate stood at just 6.27%. This rate was bolstered tremendously by the City of Bratislava where the unemployment rate was only at 3.94%; it was 4.63%, overall in 2010, in Bratislava Province.

The 2010 jobless rate in Trnava Province was 8.17%. Conversely, a significant number of the Hungarian residents that province were employed in the multiple Samsung Electronics Plants related facilities located in that province. The largest cluster of Samsung factories was situated in the Town of Galanta, and employed approximately 4,600 people. This included: a facility employing approximately 3,000 people manufacturing laser printers, DVD players and computer screens, which opened in 2003; and the company's European logistics and distribution center, which opened in 2006, and employed 300. Samsung also had an LCD-TV monitor plant in the village of Voderady, situated about 25 miles (40 km) northeast of Bratislava in the Trnava District of Trnava Province. This plant commenced production in 2008, employed about 1,000 workers, and has attracted a host of South Korean suppliers to the Voderady.

Next, as again illustrated in Table 18.2, the BMR had a GDP of $35.92 billion (25.48 billion euro) in 2008, two-thirds of which was created in Bratislava Province. This meant that the metropolitan region produced 38.02% of Slovakia's total $94.46 billion GDP (67.01 billion euro) in that year. Finally, the BMR had a GDP per capita of $34,308 (21,655 euro) in 2008, a figure that was nearly twice the national average of $17,473 (12,395 euro). The largest proportion of this output was derived from motor vehicle manufacturing, as both the Bratislava and Trnava Provinces were major hubs for these activities. As a result of its paramount importance in the region's growth, the remainder of this chapter focuses on the rise of the auto industry in the BMR, culminating in the creation of what may be called the Bratislava-Žilina Auto Corridor.

VOLKSWAGEN, THE BMR AND THE RISE OF SLOVAKIA'S AUTO INDUSTRY

At the onset of the Cold War Period (1947–1989), the Soviet bureaucracy pegged Czechoslovakia and East Germany as the primary bases for light vehicles production in the Warsaw Pact Eastern Bloc Countries.[5] In Czechoslovakia, Tatra and Škoda were the only firms authorized to manufacturer cars. The former was instructed to build a large luxury model, while the latter was licensed to mass produce a small, inexpensive "people's passenger car" (Pavlinek, 2008, p. 67).

In the early 1950s, as the government focused its investment on the defense industry, the country's light vehicles production was reorganized and its output dramatically reduced. In the process, the manufacture of Tatra's passenger car was shifted to Škoda's Mladá Boleslav plant in the present-day central portion of the Czech Republic near Prague, and Tatra's activities were directed towards building trucks and other heavy-duty vehicles for the military.

Vehicle output increased noticeably in the late 1950s, but it was not until the early 1960s when significant public investment was targeted towards the expansion and modernization of Škoda's operations. This effort led to the construction of several new factories, including the erecting of a Škoda branch plant in the Devínska Nová Ves district of Bratislava city in 1971 (which became BAZ). Meanwhile, in 1978, the production of light commercial vehicles was transferred from Vrchlabi to Trnava, within the present-day Slovak Regions of Trnava, and large agricultural tractors shifted from Brno to Martin, within today's Žilina Province (Pavlinek, 2008); Martin already was producing tractor engines since 1973. Although these state-owned endeavors would never manufacture more than a few thousand Škoda annually under socialism, the Bratislava, Trnava, and Žilina-Martin areas would later become the core production nodes of the Slovak Auto Industry.

While the 1970s was a period of growth, the Czechoslovak Auto Industry was stalled during the 1980s, by misguided and insufficient state investment. This situation combined with Škoda's monopolistic position resulted in the technology, reliability, and fit and finish quality of its automobiles lagging far behind the West. This made Škoda's small, inexpensive models, along with the components made by its suppliers, completely unprepared when, in 1989, the Iron Curtain fell and the Czechoslovak government decided to open up its economy to market competition. Sensing that its own privatization scheme was failing, the central government sought out foreign automakers to partner with its debt-ridden domestic producers. On December 9, 1990, it selected VW over 23 other companies to partner with Škoda, allowing the West German group to purchase a 31% stake in the firm for $416 million. Three months later, on March 12, 1991, VW outbid five others for an 80% share in BAZ, and in the process securing the firm's Škoda branch plant in Bratislava.

As presented in Table 18.3, VW-BAZ assembled its first two VW Passat models at its completely re-tooled Bratislava plant on December 21, 1991, with serial production beginning on February 14, 1992. In 1993, a paint shop was added. Then, in 1994, when VW would secure a 100% stake in BAZ, the Bratislava factory was expanded with the additions of the VW Golf model and a gearbox assembly line; the firm gained total control of Škoda in May 2000 (VW, 2011c).

Next, in 1996, VW widened its Slovak footprint by establishing Volkswagen Electrical Systems (VES), east of the BMR in Nitra, where it employed 800 people manufacturing gearboxes, engines, and a small batch of VW Golf (again, see

Table 18.3 Light Vehicles Production in the BMR and adjacent regions in 2012

Light Vehicles Assembly Plants in the BMR

Firm	Origin	Slovak Province	Production Launched	Employment	Vehicle Capacity
Volkswagen[1]	Germany	Bratislava	Dec 1991	7,500	400,000
Peugeot-Citroen	France	Trnava	Oct. 2006	3,200	300,000

Related Assembly Plants in Adjacent Provinces of Slovakia

Firm	Origin	Slovak Province	Production Launched	Employment	Vehicle Capacity
Kia	South Korea	Zilina	Dec. 2006	3,000	300,000

Related Assembly Plants in Adjacent Regions of Hungary and the Czech Republic

Firm	Origin	Region	Production Launched	Employment	Vehicle Capacity
Audi/VW [2]	Germany	Gyor, Hungary	Dec. 1993 engines; Apr. 1998 cars	7,900	125,000
Hyundai	South Korea	Moravian-Silesian, Czech	Nov. 2008	3,400	300,000

VW (2011a, 2011b); PSA (2007–2011), Audi (2011); Kia Motors Slovakia (2011); HMMC (2011).

(1) Includes major expansion to be completed by 2012 or 2013. Totals do not include the Martin Powertrain and components operations in the Zilina Region. Including Martin, Volkswagen was expected to employ between 8,400 and 8,500 by 2013.

(2) Includes major expansion to be completed by 2013 when the facility will become a full-fledged assembly plant. Pre-series engine production began in 1993, but the Audi/Volkswagen (VW) Gyor engine plant was not officially dedicated until October 1994.

Figure 18.1).[6] Further expansions were provoked by the Slovak Government's 'Development of the Automotive Industry' Initiative, which granted VW $44.0 million (31.2 million euro) in tax abatements in 1999. These concessions facilitated the construction of a large motor vehicles parts complex in Martin, where since May 2000 VW has manufactured gearboxes, chassis components, and other parts for its Audi, Škoda, and Porsche brands. In addition, in January of 2000, production of the VW Polo was launched in Bratislava. Government subsidies also helped to attract numerous foreign auto suppliers to the BMR, such as Johnson Controls, Magna, Faurecia, Lear, SAS Automotive, and Brose, many of which located just north of VW's Bratislava in the Lozorno

Industrial Park, situated off highway E-65 in the city's Malacky District (VW, 2011c; Jakubiak et al., 2008).

By June 2002, VW was building its Touareg SUV in Bratislava, as well as body frames for the Porsche Cayenne model. In January 2003, the plant added a small batch of the group's SEAT brand Ibiza models. Then, in November 2005, to complement its Czech and Hungarian operations, the factory began assembling some ultra-luxury Audi Q7 SUVs. Finally, in late 2007, Polo production was halted and replaced in March 2008, by the Škoda Octavia model.

In summary, since its arrival in 1991, VW has been Slovakia's largest industrial enterprise, employer, and exporter. According to its most recent 2010 Annual Report, the group employed 6,964 people nation-wide (VW, 2011b). This total was expected to climb to around 8,500 by 2013, as the Bratislava plant was retooled and expanded in preparation for the launching of VW's new 'UP' series brand of small family sedans. As again shown in Table 18.3, at that time, about 7,500 of this employment would be in Bratislava. Upon production of the UP cars, annual production capacity at the Bratislava Plant will rise to 400,000, and the complex will become one of a select few operations worldwide manufacturing five separate brands at the same site (VW, Škoda, Seat, Audi, and UP).

By 1995, almost two-thirds of all FDI into in Slovakia was spent in the BMR. This total had increased to nearly three-quarters by 2008 (Pavlinek & Smith, 1998; SARIO, 2011). Twenty years later, the VW Bratislava plant has remained Slovakia's largest single FDI project. This and the other activities chronicled here suggest that VW will continue to act as a major force driving the BMR's economy, as well as national growth, for many years to come.

THE BRATISLAVA-ŽILINA AUTO CORRIDOR

In total, VW has produced more than 2.5 million vehicles in Bratislava (VW, 2011c). However, in the early 2010s, the German automaker was far from the only major car manufacturer with facilities in the BMR or Slovakia. After receiving a government incentives package of $225 million (160 million euro), in January 2003, Peugeot of France agreed to build an auto assembly plant in Trnava (see Figures 18.2 and 18.3). As shown again in Table 18.3, Peugeot's factory, which launched production in October 2006, currently employs 3,200 people and has an annual capacity of 300,000 vehicles. Only a year after Peugeot's announcement, in March 2004, Hyundai of South Korea accepted nearly $1.3 billion (900 million euro) in state financial incentives and infrastructure upgrades to construct a plant the central Slovakia province of Žilina (Jakubiak et al., 2008). The facility, which began manufacturing Kia automobiles in December 2006, presently employs 3,000 workers and also has a capacity of 300,000 vehicles.

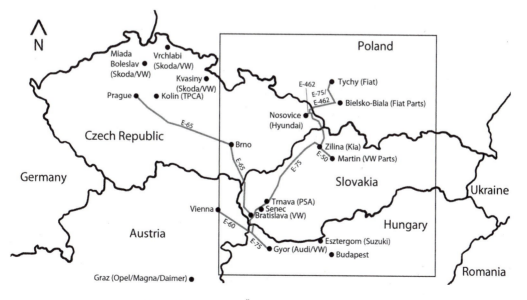

Figure 18.3 Bratislava-Žilina Auto Corridor in the CEE

Both Peugeot and Kia were attracted to Slovakia by the nation's skilled but relatively affordable and non-militant labor force. In addition, while each brought along several of their own Tier-I, Tier-II, and Tier-III suppliers to the area, both automakers selected sites in Slovakia near Central Europe's E-75 Highway Corridor, in order to tap into VW's existing multinational supplier network; Kia located just 20 miles (32 km) west of VW's Martin Plant. In 2011, there were more than 200 auto suppliers located in nearby regions of Western and Central Slovakia, the large majority of which were foreign owned, primarily based in Germany, France, America, and more recently, South Korea. Another 30, including U.S. Steel Kosice, were located in Eastern Slovakia (SARIO, 2011).

As a result of the VW, Peugeot, and Kia facilities, employment in motor vehicles and parts related manufacturing in Slovakia expanded from less than 1,000 in 1990 to 22,000 in 1993 and then to 74,000 by 2008 (ACEA, 2010; SARIO, 2011). Nearly three-quarters of this employment was in the BMR. Moreover, in 2010, Slovakia produced 556,941 motor vehicles, an increase of 375,158 or 206.38% from 2000. Although this figure was slightly lower than the nation's 2008 high of 575,776 vehicles, it still represented a 188-fold gain from the 2,958 vehicles assembled in the country in 1993 (OICA, 2002, 2011; Ward's, 1995–2010). Comparatively speaking, auto production in the former Czechoslovakia peaked in 1989 at only 239,181 cars and trucks (Pavlinek, 2008).

Overall, Slovakia was Europe's ninth largest auto producer in 2010. More impressively, in that year, the nation ranked third worldwide in vehicles manufactured per capita; it was first in this category in 2007. As shown in Table 18.4, in 2010, at 101.81 vehicles per 1,000 in population, Slovakia narrowly trailed the Czech Republic and Slovenia for this prestigious title. No other CEE nation was even remotely close to the top three per capita producers.

Table 18.4 Vehicle Production per 1,000 in Population in Selected Nations

Nation	2010 Vehicles Produced	2010 Population (millions)	Vehicles produced per 1,000 in Population
Czech Republic	1,076,385	10.20	105.51
Slovenia	205,711	2.00	102.69
Slovakia	*556,941*	*5.47*	*101.81*
South Korea	4,271,941	48.64	87.83
Japan	9,625,940	126.80	75.91
Germany	5,905,985	81.64	72.34
Canada	2,071,026	33.76	61.35
Spain	2,387,900	46.51	51.35
France	2,227,742	64.77	34.40
Belgium	338,290	10.42	32.45
USA	7,761,443	310.23	25.02
Other CEE Nations			
Hungary	167,890	9.99	16.80
Romania	350,912	21.96	15.98
Austria	104,814	8.21	12.76
Russia	1,403,244	139.39	10.07
Ukraine	83,133	45.42	1.83
Serbia	6,470	7.34	0.88

Source: OICA (2011); U.S. Census Bureau (2011)

In addition, VW's presence in Bratislava has served as a catalyst for economic growth not only in Slovakia, but also in nearby regions in Hungary and the Czech Republic. This began in earnest in December 1993, when the German automaker commenced building engines in a plant less than 50 miles (80 km) south of the VW Bratislava in Győr, a city situated in northwest Hungary's Győr-Moson-Sopron County. As shown again in Table 18.3, the facility added the Audi TT sports car to its operations in April 1998. This was followed in September 2005 by the making of components, and in November 2007, by the assembling of approximately 200 Audi A3 convertibles. More recently, VW announced another major expansion in Győr, which in 2013 will transform the complex into a full-fledged assembly plant. In the process, the firm will raise its total employment there from the present 6,138 to 7,900, and its annual vehicle production

capacity from 55,000 to 125,000; the plant built 38,541 cars and 1.65 million engines in 2010. Another long-term potential project could bring Győr's automobile output to more than 300,000 by 2018 (Audi, 2011; VW, 2011b; Reuters, 2011).

Finally, as a result of its success in Žilina, in September 2005, Hyundai Motor announced it would build a second assembly plant in the CEE, this time within the Ostrava Metropolitan Area of northeastern Czech. This came to fruition on November 3, 2008, when Hyundai i30 began rolling off the firm's Nosovice assembly line, located just 53 miles (85 km) west of Kia's Žilina Plant. In mid-2011, the plant employed 3,400 workers and had an annual vehicle capacity of 300,000 (again, see Figures 18.2 and 18.3).

The net result of these investments has been the development of what might be called the Bratislava-Žilina Auto Corridor. As shown in Figures 18.3 and 18.4, this zone

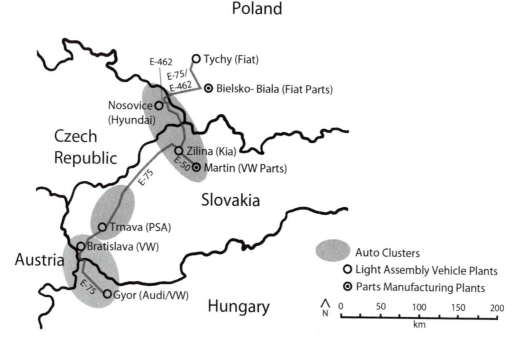

Figure 18.4 Auto clusters in the Bratislava-Žilina Auto Corridor

has a nucleus of Bratislava, forms a spine running along Highway E-75, and traversed parts of three nations: western Slovakia, eastern Czech, and northwestern Hungary. Within this automotive production region there were five foreign light vehicles assembly plants situated in three interconnected auto clusters: VW Bratislava-Audi Győr; Peugeot Trnava; and Kia Žilina-Hyundai Ostrava (again, see Figures 18.3 and 18.4); VW also had a major supply facility in Martin near Žilina.

The area could soon gain another cluster, as the Chinese manufacturer Jianghuai (JAC Motors) was in discussions with Slovak Government about establishing a plant somewhere in the country. If such developments were a sign of things to come, it would not be long before the Bratislava-Žilina Auto Corridor converged with Fiat's Polish auto plants in Tychy (assembly) and Bielsko-Biala (formerly assembly and currently powertrain components), both of which also were situated along/near the E-75 Corridor, to create an even larger capitalist automotive production agglomeration.

In summary, the BMR's development as a motor vehicles manufacturing hub has been a perfect example of how State subsidies and capitalist forces have combined to drive economic growth within certain post-socialist CEE regions. In the interim, the BMR's industrial base has transformed from a state-owned, Soviet-led military apparatus, into an export base for the world's largest private foreign automakers, targeting customers not just domestically, but throughout Europe. Although there remained concerns for the region's over-dependence on the highly cyclical auto industry, Slovakia's rise to EU and European Monetary Union Member suggest the BMR's future appears bright. Depending upon how you looked at it, this represented a major positive shift from, or a potential repetition of, its long tumultuous history as a territory occupied by non-Slovak powers.

CONCLUSION: CAPITALIST AGGLOMERATIONS IN THE POST-SOCIALIST BMR

This chapter chronicled some of the important moments in the historical development of Bratislava, from its initial settlement through its time in Great Moravia, Hungary, Austria-Hungary, Czechoslovakia, and now Slovakia. It then presents some background data on the present-day BMR. The remainder of the paper describes how foreign direct investment (FDI) has transformed the BMR into the nucleus of an emerging tri-national automotive production agglomeration, the Bratislava-Žilina Auto Corridor. As a result of these two attributes, the BMR was a major catalyst behind its nation being accepted into the EU in 2004, and ascending to the EMU in 2009. Slovakia accomplished the latter before any of the Visegrad-4 nations, despite having the smallest population among them.

Following the fall of the Iron Curtain, the former Government of Czechoslovakia laid the groundwork for Slovakia's procession to the EU and EMU with its sale of the former state-owned Škoda's Bratislava operations (BAZ) to VW in 1991. Since that time, the Slovak Government has played an extremely proactive role in the BMR's economic growth, particularly with its aggressive policies targeting FDI, most notably luring major foreign automakers and components suppliers to the area. These efforts have won it the praise from some of the globe's largest institutions and MNCs. The World Bank rated Slovakia's investment environment as the most progressive among post-Socialist nations and one of its top 20 most favorable business climates worldwide. According to the European Automobiles Manufacturers' Association (ACEA, 2008) and Ernst & Young (2010), Slovakia's liberalization reforms, its low corporate flat-rate income and value-added taxes, together with its advantageous geographical location and its educated, relatively lower-wage and productive labor force, have made the nation an ideal target for prestigious FDI, such as auto assembly projects. Price-Waterhouse wrote that Slovakia's elimination of administrative barriers for new start-up companies; flexible, non-adversarial labor market relations; streamlined tax system; low direct taxes; and other investment incentives, have aggressively promoted job growth (PwC, 2006, p. 196).

As a result of its development context, Slovakia's motor vehicles production exploded from just 2,958 in 1993 to 556,941 in 2010, and its automotive related employment more than tripled from 22,000 to 74,000. Led by VW, the BMR was the destination for approximately three-quarters of all FDI entering its nation and more than half of this new employment. Spillover projects and employment connected to these activities then have stimulated regional economies throughout western and central Slovakia, as well as in eastern Czech and northwestern Hungary. So much so that the motor vehicle production complexes in these areas have congealed to form what could be called the Bratislava-Žilina Auto Corridor, an area with a core of Bratislava, intertwined by Highway E-75, and containing three interconnected auto clusters: Bratislava-Győr (VW-Audi); Trnava (Peugeot); and Žilina-Ostrava (Kia-Hyundai).

Among the major negatives to these developments have been that the economies of the BMR and Slovakia have become overly-dependent on both motor vehicle manufacturing and FDI from MNCs based in larger core nations. As for the latter, according to the OECD (2010), in 2007, 60.5% of Slovakia's manufacturing employment worked for firms of 250 or more employees, the highest total among OECD nations. By comparison, among CEE nations this percentage was 48.3% in the Czech Republic and 45.4% in both Poland and Hungary; it was 54.3% for Germany, 32.2% for Japan, and 26.3% for Italy. Moreover, MNCs accounted for roughly one-third of Slovakia's GDP.

Combined this situation has left the BMR and national economy extremely vulnerable to the volatile nature of global corporate restructuring, especially in the auto industry, a sector well-known for its hyper-sensitivity to world and domestic economic cycles and for its tendency to downside and/or relocate production and employment to lower-wage nations.

Nonetheless, the massive commitment made by the Volkswagen, Peugeot, and Hyundai, several hundred auto suppliers, potential new producers (JAC of China), and by MNCs in other industries, suggests that the BMR has become an important capitalist core in the post-socialist CEE. This combined with Bratislava city's historical and present role as a national capital, which has attracted numerous large financial services and other non-manufacturers to the area, should continue to bolster the metropolitan region's economy for many years to come.

NOTES

1   Established during a February 15, 1991 summit convened in Visegrád, Hungary, the Visegrád Group or the Visegrad Four (or V4), is a politico-economic alliance among the four aforementioned CEE nations. Its original purpose was to promote regional cooperation in a collective effort towards all four achieving integration into the European Union (EU); all four attained EU status on May 1, 2004 (International Visegrad Fund, 2012).

2   FSM was an acronym for Fabryka Samochodow Małolitrazowych, while BAZ was short for Bratislavské Automobilové Závody (Bratislava Automobile Company) of Slovakia.

3   Slovakia has eight self-governing regions (samosprávne kraje), which are constitutionally defined as upper-tier administrative provinces (vyššie územné celky or VUC). The term 'Province' is used in this chapter.

4   Unless otherwise specified, data in this chapter were obtained from Statistical Office of the Slovak Republic (2011) and SARIO (2011).

5   Bus manufacturing was assigned to Hungary. By the 1970s, plants in Poland and Yugoslavia were also producing more than 100,000 light vehicles.

6   Originally a joint venture between Volkswagen and Siemens, VES Nitra was sold to Sumitomo Electric of Japan in April 2006 and changed its name to SE Bordnetze-Slovakia.

QUESTIONS FOR DISCUSSION

1. In two or three paragraphs, discuss the main themes from Jacobs's chapter on Bratislava.
2. In 1–2 pages, utilizing specific examples from the chapter, explain how Jacobs's discussions about the BMR resemble and contrast with the arguments put forth in World/Global City, Nested City, and Scott and Storper's agglomeration theory.
3. Does World/Global City, Nested City, or Scott and Storper's agglomeration theory best explain the transformation of the BMR into an important capitalist agglomeration? In 2–3 pages, explain your choice, citing examples from this chapter and others.
4. Using the 'Further Readings', 'Helpful Web Links', and other sources, conduct some further research on Bratislava and another city-region in the CEE. Then, in 2–3 pages, write up some of the most interesting facts you discovered about those cities and present your findings to your class.

FURTHER READINGS

Kirschbaum, S. 2005. *A History of Slovakia: The Struggle for Survival*. New York: Macmillan.

Pavlinek, P., B. Domanski, and R. Guzik. 2009. Industrial Upgrading through Foreign Direct Investment in Central European Automotive Manufacturing. *European Urban and Regional Studies,* 16 (1): 43–63.

Pavlinek, P., and J. Zenka. 2010. The 2008–2009 Automotive Industry Crisis and Regional Unemployment in Central Europe. *Cambridge Journal of Regions, Economy and Society*, 3 (3): 349–365.

Seton-Watson, R. 1943. *The History of the Czech and Slovaks*. Hamden, CT: Archon Books.

Smith, A. 1998. *Reconstructing the Regional Economy: Industrial Transformation and Regional Development in Slovakia*. Cheltenham, UK: Edward Elgar.

Smith, A. and S. Ferencíkova. 1998. Inward Investment, Regional Transformations and Uneven Development in Eastern and Central Europe: Enterprise Case-Studies from Slovakia. *European Urban and Regional Studies*, 5 (2): 155–173.

HELPFUL WEB LINKS

Bratislava, City of. 2012. Bratislava History. Online. Available at: http://www.bratislava-city.sk/bratislava-history-general, last accessed, January 2, 2012.

Bratislava, Province of. 2012. Bratislavsky Samosprávne Kraje Region [Bratislava Self-Governing Region]. Online. Available at: http://www.region-bsk.sk/EN/default.aspx, last accessed January 2, 2012.

Budapest, City of. 2011. Budapest Portal. Online. Available at: http://english.budapest.hu/Engine.aspx, last accessed, December 29, 2011.

Győr-Moson-Sopron County, Local Government of. 2012. Welcome to the Homepage of Győr-Moson-Sopron County. Online. Available at: http://www.gymsmo.hu/index_portal.php?nyid=2&hlid=2, last accessed, January 2, 2012.

Ostrava, City of. 2012. Official Website of the City Ostrava, Czech Republic. Online. Available at: http://www.ostrava.cz/en, last accessed, January 15, 2012.

Pilsen, City of . 2012. Official Information Server of the City of Pilsen, Czech Republic. Online. Available at: http://www.pilsen.eu/en/, last accessed January 7, 2012.

Prague, City of. 2011. Prague Portal. Online. Available at: http://www.praha.eu/jnp/en/home/index. html, last accessed, December 30, 2011.

SARIO. 2012. Slovak Investment and Trade Development Agency. Online. Available http://www.sario. sk/?home, last accessed January 9, 2012.

St. Petersburg, City of. 2012. Internet Guide to St. Petersburg, the Cultural Capital of Russia. Online. Available at: http://petersburgcity.com/news/, last accessed January 7, 2012.

Tychy, City of. 2012. Tychy. A Good Place. Online. Available at: http://www.umtychy.pl/artykul. php?j=2, last accessed, January 2, 2012.

CHAPTER 19

The Development Industry and Urban Redevelopment in New York and London (2001)

Susan Fainstein

The 1980s marked an extraordinary surge in property development in London and New York, followed by an equally precipitous drop at the end of the decade. A new boom gathered force in the mid-1990s and continued through 2000. The two property booms closely tracked spurts in the economies of the two cities, largely attributable to growth in finance and business service sectors throughout the twenty years, but also to expansion in media and tourism, especially in the latter part. Although in many respects the 1990s represented a continuation of previous trends, that decade, as we shall see, had some elements that differentiated it from the earlier period.

As the 1980s boom hit its peak, high-ranking public officials were celebrating an "urban renaissance," embodied in the grand new building complexes of London and New York. At the same time, writers, academics, and community-based critics were condemning the pretensions and social impacts of the recently constructed projects (see Figures 19.1 and 19.2).

The real-estate investment market, while not quartered on a few trading floors like the stock and bond exchanges, formed a very significant part of the 1980s speculative milieu. It uniquely combined the visible, physical endeavor of constructing the environment in which that activity took place. Property development belonged to the 1980s financial boom as cause, effect,

and symbol. Profits on large projects, huge tax benefits from real-estate syndication in the United States, and trading margins from mortgage securitization formed the basis for vast fortunes. As their wealth and visibility made them prominent actors in the cultural and social scene, the names of developers like Donald Trump, William Zeckendorf, Jr., and Mortimer Zuckerman in New York, or Stuart Lipton, Godfrey Bradman, and Trevor Osborne in London became widely publicized. Financial institutions that underwrote the property market likewise prospered. For example, the mortgage department of Salomon Brothers, headed by Lewis Ranieri, had made the bond-trading firm into the most profitable business on Wall Street.

The burgeoning space needs of the expanding financial institutions, the businesses that provided them with services, and their suddenly wealthy employees produced a great surge in demand that was in part refueled by the office requirements of the development industry itself, its financial backers, and its service providers. The steeply climbing curve of returns from real-estate investment prompted a stream of new development proposals, which justified their costs with prognoses of ever-increasing earnings. The shiny skyscrapers housing the boisterous trading floors of the fabulously profitable investment banks; the high-rise condominiums and converted lofts affording havens for the

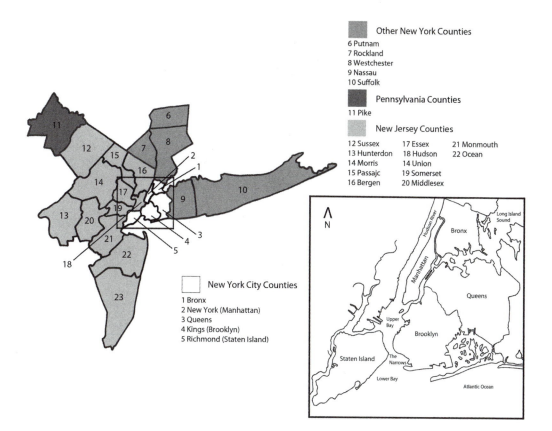

Figure 19.1 The New York City-Region and the five boroughs of New York

young urban professionals; the renovated mansions and penthouses sheltering their bosses; and the glamorous marble-clad shopping malls, festive marketplaces, deluxe hotels, and opulent restaurants catering to their consumption whims constituted the symbolic setting for the excesses of the period.

Few would dispute that speculative property investment did indeed transform the functions and appearance of New York and London during the 1980s; nor would they disagree that while the public purse helped finance physical change, private entrepreneurs using borrowed money were in charge. Since developers saw little profit in building factories or working-class housing, they confined their activities to producing offices and luxury residential units. The consequence of their development strategies was an economic and spatial restructuring of London and New York that was dramatically uneven in its components.

Simultaneous investment and disinvestment created not just the juxtaposition of rich and poor, made obvious by the ubiquitous homeless within even the most affluent neighborhoods, but also sent whole communities on opposite trajectories (Mollenkopf & Castells, 1991). The growing numbers of relatively and absolutely impoverished city residents, displaced from factory jobs as a consequence of economic restructuring, dislodged from their homes by gentrification and financial catastrophe, or deinstitutionalized and suffering from disabilities, provided the counterpoint

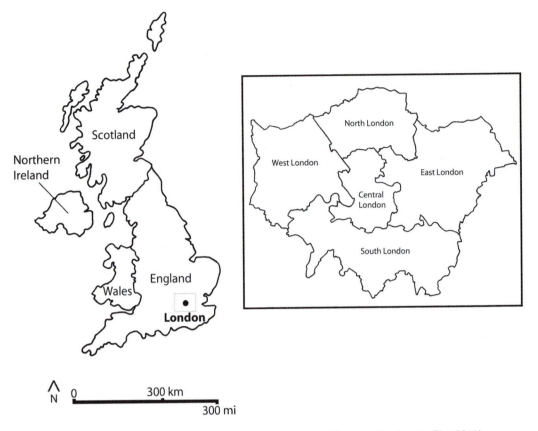

Figure 19.2 London in the UK with London's sub-regions as defined by 'The London Plan 2011'

to good fortune. The symbolism of these contrasts was interpreted by the left as revealing the injustice of privately led economic development programs and by the right as a moral lesson demonstrating the differential in rewards to the deserving and undeserving, the entrepreneurs and the wastrels.

For most of the 1980s the constant fanfare trumpeting new development projects and the army of building cranes punctuating the London and New York skylines did appear to herald progress, whatever its imperfections. The visibility and hopefulness of new construction tended to override the caveats of critics. Community representatives who railed against the overwhelming effects of large projects on their neighborhoods were

derided for standing in the way of progress. Despite soaring office vacancy rates in other American cities as the 1980s progressed, New York developers continued to propose ever-larger projects. And in London, memories of the property-market collapse of the mid-1970s faded, as banks ratcheted up their real-estate investments.

In 1980 it was by no means obvious that London and New York would witness such accelerated growth. Employment and population had been declining in both cities; existing levels of development made land acquisition difficult-and expensive; very high occupancy costs discouraged prospective commercial tenants; while planning restrictions combined with community opposition to create formidable obstacles to developers' ambitions. Then, abruptly, the economic trajectories of London and New York reversed, as increased world trade, global financial deals, and expanding national markets for their producer services complexes caused economic transactions within them to multiply exponentially during the decade.

The 1987 stock market crash, however, heralded another turn in the fortunes of the two cities. In 1989 the property market, which had lagged the decline of equity markets, also collapsed and for a five-year period manifested soaring vacancy rates, plummeting prices, and developer bankruptcies. The enormous increase in office space resulting from the speculative investments of the 1980s ran into declining demand. But again, as the national economies of the two nations recovered from the steep but short recession that started the decade, the economies of the two cities revived also. The cheap, vacant space proved an advantage, as growing firms found that they could expand without hindrance. Moreover, developers and financial institutions proved more cautious than in the past, with the result that new development did not race ahead of demand. In fact, by the beginning of the new century the slack had been absorbed, rents were rising far faster than the overall rate of inflation, and firms were having trouble acquiring sufficient space for their needs. Much of the development that did occur involved the conversion of vacant or underutilized warehouse and industrial space into offices and condominiums rather than new construction. Consequently, the face of the two cities changed relatively little; rather, the physical transformation achieved during the 1980s solidified.

This chapter examines, first, the heightened importance of global cities within the world economy during the latter part of the twentieth century. Second, it describes changes in the production of, and demand for, space. Finally, it analyzes the effect of economic change and government policy on the physical development of London and New York. The following chapter investigates the causes and consequences of cyclicity in real-estate markets and the similarities and differences in the property development cycle that occurred in London and New York between 1980 and 2000.

THE INCREASED IMPORTANCE OF GLOBAL CITIES

New York and London, along with Tokyo, are the preeminent global cities, as defined by their influence on world financial markets. Recent work emphasizes that these cities are not unique in being heavily involved in global flows of capital, that international transactions do not comprise the largest share of their economic base, and that other cities have more rapidly growing financial and business services (FBS) sectors (Logan, 2000). Nevertheless, in the sheer magnitude of their FBS sector, the number of foreign firms doing business within them, and their cultural and social connections with the rest of the world, London and New York can claim to be in a different league from other cities. An investigation of the driving forces behind real-estate investment in recent decades uncovers the dominant role played by those economic sectors most closely tied to the global economy in stimulating development. Especially during the 1980s the EBS sectors were key; in the 1990s, although the two economies became somewhat more diverse, EBS—especially the securities industry—continued to play a major role.

Initial analyses of the rising importance of global cities generally offered three reasons for the phenomenon: (1) the greater size and velocity of world capital flows; (2) the increased need for centralized command-and-control posts in a decentralized world economy; and (3) the extensive technical infrastructure needed by the FBS industries. These arguments were based on observations of growth driven by FBS in the 1980s.

Later, renewed expansion of these cities was dependent also on the surprising rapid growth of media-related, informational, and cultural enterprises. In New York particularly, the 1990s saw an eruption of Internet and telecommunications firms, which were nowhere evident when the first edition of this book was written (Sassen, 1991; Healy & Nabarro, 1990; Beauregard, 1991).

World Capital Flows

Several factors produced the explosion in the FBS sectors that fueled the economies of both London and New York in the boom years at the end of the century and spurred their physical redevelopment The internationalization of investment and the growth of international trade had greatly heightened the importance of the financial industry and financial markets. The restructuring of companies, the rapid expansion of mergers and acquisitions, and the restless search by corporations for low-cost production sites and marketing advantages accelerated the volatility of capital and thereby enlarged the role of firms that specialized in managing flows of capital. According to Sassen, transactions increasingly took place between firms located in financial centers rather than within the large American banks. In other words, while the management of manufacturing and retail industries became more and more integrated *within* large corporations, ever-greater financial flows were increasingly controlled through joint ventures, deals, and trades involving numerous actors. During the 1990s the soaring stock market, growth in venture capital and other niche investment firms, and expansion of the NASDAQ exchange in New York further enlarged the financial sector, more than compensating for contraction in the traditional banking sector resulting from downsizing and mergers.

The debt crisis that began in the 1970s had cut off third-world outlets for investment at the same time as financial institutions continued to acquire massive amounts of capital from pension and mutual funds. Moreover, this capital was increasingly either lent directly to borrowers by investors, who purchased interest-bearing bonds, or used to purchase equity in firms. Thus, instead of savings flowing into commercial banks and then being lent by these banks to firms seeking to grow, funds circumvented the traditional banking system (a process known as "disintermediation"). This shift greatly increased the activity level and profits of investment bankers, who were the underwriters and traders of these instruments, and investment banking firms accordingly added personnel and operational space.

A host of other financial "products" was invented, including "swaps"—exchanges of debt holdings among institutions; junk bonds—high-yield notes that were rated below investment grade; and index futures—agreements to purchase a group of stocks at a preestablished price at a later date. Globalization of investment and production increased the possibility of loss through currency devaluation or sudden, unforeseen market shifts, stimulating the development of new financial instruments as hedges against risk. The securitization of debt (initially mortgages and third-world debt, then consumer debt, including student loans) meant that banking institutions could "bundle"—that is, aggregate—their loans to businesses and individuals, then convert them to attain liquidity through selling their loans for an amount based on the present value of their expected returns.

The development of markets for all of these novel financial products magnified the number of instruments traded within what had become an increasingly closed and volatile system of circulation of capital among the most developed countries. In the meantime, takeovers and leveraged buyouts fueled the volume of new debt issues. Once-conservative investment institutions, ranging from university endowments to major insurance companies, sought the high rates of return offered by speculative financial instruments and became far more dynamic players in the hyperactive financial world.

Deregulation of the financial industry combined with the various product innovations and huge increases in capital flows to heighten the frenetic trading activity and deal making that characterized the financial world of the two cities. In the United States the Reagan and Bush administrations' distaste for enforcing antitrust laws allowed the mergers and acquisitions and leveraged buyouts to involve more and more companies and greater and greater sums of money, along with ever-larger phalanxes of legal and financial advisers. Despite wide publicity surrounding its prosecution of Microsoft for violating antitrust laws, the Clinton administration was no more zealous in blocking the giant buyouts and vast mergers that transpired during the 1990s, especially in banking and media. The relaxation of the barriers that had existed between different types of financial institutions, such as investment, savings, and commercial banks, further stimulated growth within the financial service industries.

Changes in the world financial system during the last quarter-century were direct causes of London's spatial restructuring, especially within the "square mile" constituting the City. Response to foreign competition led to the weakening of restrictions on London's financial firms, culminating in the "Big Bang" of 1986. At the same time as fixed commissions on all domestic securities transactions were eliminated (a move that had taken place in the United States a decade earlier), membership on the stock exchange was opened to foreign institutions for the first time. Not only did these changes directly result in greater business activity, but they attracted numerous foreign firms, which mainly sought space in the vicinity of the City of London. As described by Michael Pryke, "The City was to become the hub not of a culturally familiar, slow-paced,

empire-oriented regime of trade finance but of a new fast-moving capitalism in which the City itself was to become equally international" (Pryke, 1991, p. 210). Many of the newcomers, however, ultimately found that the increase in financial activity did not meet their anticipations.

As corporate debt shifted from bank loans to direct borrowing, the major banks lost their previous dominance of financial transactions. Nonetheless, from the early 1970s onward, branches of foreign banks increased in number within both London and New York and continued to expand throughout the rest of the century. The growing volume of international trade; the greater presence of foreign subsidiaries in all economic sectors, the increasing numbers of executives from abroad in connection with this internationalized economic activity, and the end of fixed exchange rates all contributed to the demand for retail and commercial banking services. Growth in the real-estate industry itself stimulated bank expansion, since almost all construction loans emanated from the banking sector. Moreover, as large international banks like Barclay's and Citibank increasingly took on functions similar to those of investment banks by acting as financiers for corporate merger and acquisitions, they too got caught up in the cycle of speculative growth within the corporate investment arena.

Agglomeration Effects

Transactions in the various securities took place mainly on trading floors within individual firms rather than through the exchanges. Nevertheless, the major investment banks and the headquarters of commercial banks felt it necessary to cluster close to the old markets. Because there is a very high level of interaction both among financial firms and between the financial sector and the concerns that provide it with legal, public relations, management consulting, and other services, this group of enterprises is led to settle only in those locations where agglomeration of financial and advanced-services firms already exist (Amin & Thrift, 1992). Accountants, lawyers, tax consultants, and other advisers to the deal-makers also highly valued proximity to the investment bankers, since their presence at meetings of the various parties to a deal was frequently required. Large suburban firms have continued to rely on Manhattan for most of their service needs despite some gradual decentralization (Schwartz, 1992). Thus, even firms headquartered outside the London and New York central business districts (CBDs) apparently found it more convenient to obtain business services within the supermarket of their dense advanced-services agglomerations rather than closer to home.

Proximity was crucially important for the participants in a major deal. For example, the marathon negotiations in the buyout of RJR Nabisco shows that numerous investors, as well as virtually every significant law firm and investment bank in the country, took part. Although Nabisco's headquarters was in Atlanta, Georgia, and its subsidiaries were scattered around the world, the action, which involved hundreds of corporate officers, investment bankers, lawyers, and financial advisers, took place in New York. On numerous occasions discussions lasted until dawn, and the presence of principals would suddenly be required at extremely odd hours. One cannot imagine where else but in Manhattan it would have been possible to assemble all the participants. Only the common location within a major financial center of the financial and legal involved permitted the necessary transactions.

As well as responding to the burgeoning demand for space to house the rapidly growing FBS sector and their workforce, property development activity was fueled by the ready supply of fund flowing into the real-estate industry. Property investment became interchangeable with other kinds of debt and equity commitment. Previously, because of its low liquidity and unique property investment

had been the province of a limited group of financial institutions and knowledgeable individuals. Now, however, greater opportunities real-estate investment syndication, in which limited partners did not take an active role but received an income stream and could sell their interests in a project fairly easily, eliminated any reason but rate of return to prefer one type of investment over another. The prospect of high speculative gains attracted many to the property market. Moreover the favorable tax treatment that real estate received in both the United Kingdom and the United States, although especially the latter, often tipped the balance of investment decisions toward it, there by increasing the flow of capital into the development industry.

Technological Factors

A number of contemporary theorists have stressed the importance of information, rather than natural resources or physical capital, to economic development. The impact of télécommunications and computer technology on the locational choices of firms cuts two ways. Even though new technologies foster decentralization by reducing the need for physical proximity among participants in a production process, they free those units that find advantages in city-center locations to seek out core areas, rather than staying with the routine processing sections of the enterprise. Thus, headquarters can remain in London and New York after routine operations have departed, and firms headquartered elsewhere can maintain a presence within them.

Within the "space of flows," certain places stand out because they have the labor pools and technological structures to support the computer and telecommunications systems necessary for the management of the global economy. The enormous expansion in financial and advanced business services depended on the development of a technology adequate to handle the soaring volume of transactions. And, in a circular process, only relatively few centers had sufficient activity to support the necessary infrastructure (Castells, 1985, 1990; Sassen, 1991).

Nevertheless, according to a study by Coopers & Lybrand Deloitte, London and New York did not have an absolute advantage in these technologies. At least six other office centers (New Jersey, Chicago, Los Angeles, Paris, Tokyo, and Singapore) all offered a sufficient technological base, and the number is rapidly increasing. The requirements for modern firms relying on information retrieval and processing include a heavily backed-up communications grid and a pool of technical personnel to operate and repair equipment. Modern office structures with building managers who continuously upgrade the information and telecommunications systems are also necessities. In 1980 many old buildings were not sufficiently adaptable for renovation to accommodate the demand for large trading floors and adequate space for cables and outlets. Business leaders and public officials in many cities, however, were aware of these needs and increasingly invested in their provision. The rapid installation of fiber-optics systems linking most large office centers further reduced the edge of London and New York. By the end of the century, even all second-tier cities offered linkages to broadband fiber-optic cables. In addition, within the two global cities the high level of traffic congestion and histories of insufficient investment in transport (a non-high-tech but equally significant part of the infrastructure) meant that both failed to provide easy physical access to their business districts. Thus, while the technological infrastructure of London and New York has been a necessary underpinning of their global-city status, it does not guarantee their future dominance.

In summary, then, London and New York used their preeminence as the world's leading locations for securities and money markets to capture, in absolute terms, substantial growth in the financial and advanced-services industries during the last two decades of the twentieth century. At the same time, their relative position was declining in relation to competing cities (for New York, in the rest of the United States, and for London, in Europe). They already possessed the critical mass of resources needed to direct the financial flows that energized the world economy, but they also needed to provide appropriate space for expansion. The requirement was provision of offices that met the technological demands of the computer age and construction of luxury residential and high-end consumption facilities to cater to the needs of the leaders of the expanding industries. Although other cities competed vigorously to attract office-based industries, even the appeal of much lower operating costs elsewhere did not shake loose many of the firms anchored in London and New York. Their competitive edge, however, was threatened, and one of the factors driving policy was fear that rivals could offer superior, less expensive space.

London

By the end of the 1980s London was witnessing the largest office-building boom in its history. During the mid-1970s a rise in interest rates had meant that property companies were no longer able to meet their obligations based on current earnings; their shaky financial situation, following on a decade of speculative growth, had threatened many banks and required intervention by the Bank of England. A decade afterward, however, surplus space had been absorbed, and the anticipated advent of the Big Bang and, later, of European integration provoked high expectations of exploding demand and the seeming assurance of ever-higher rates of return: The ensuing boom signaled the reentry of banks into large-scale property lending after the secondary bank crisis of the 1970s, although insurance companies and pension funds remained wary of risking their assets on the property market. A small number of development companies was behind most of the new speculative enterprises, and much of the financing came from Japanese banks.

The initiative for promoting redevelopment activity in London did not come from a local-growth coalition of business leaders and governmental officials, as had been the case in many American cities (Mollenkopf, 1983). Rather, the urgings of the national government, which incorporated Margaret Thatcher's views that private investors operating in a free market would create local economic growth, opened up London's once highly regulated property development arena for speculative ventures. According to Harding, the shift in local government priorities from an emphasis on social welfare to economic boosterism "was forced through from the national level" (Harding, 1994, p. 374).

After the Thatcher government took office 1979, it introduced a series of measures intended to spur private economic activity and. diminish local-authority activism. In 1982 the capital gains tax was indexed to the rate of inflation, greatly increasing the potential profitability of property ownership; reduction of corporation taxes further encouraged activity by property companies. The Bank of England relaxed its requirement that primary banks be located within the square mile around its building on Threadneedle Street, thereby opening up additional territory for office space to house banking operations. The government's establishment of the London Docklands Development Corporation (LDDC) and of an enterprise zone in the Isle of Dogs portion of Docklands attracted a massive influx of capital to that partially abandoned area. In addition, the central government put considerable pressure on local authorities to relax planning regulations, sell property, and enter into joint ventures with the private sector. Through a series of circulars, legislation, and decisions by the Secretary of State for the Environment, it pressed local authorities to grant planning permission more readily. It capped (i.e., put a ceiling on) local-authority expenditure,

forcing localities to look to the private sector for benefits that had previously been publicly financed. Centrally imposed limits on their revenue-raising capacity caused local authorities to regard sales of publicly owned land to property developers as a potential revenue source; central-government interdictions on land banking also stimulated localities to put land in the hands of developers.

Each of the 33 local authorities that made up Greater London set its own development policy. Until the abolition of the Greater London Council (GLC) in 1986, London's boroughs nominally conformed to the Greater London Development Plan, which the GLC approved in 1969. This plan gave high priority to construction of council housing and stimulation of manufacturing employment Lack of support for the plan by the Conservative central government, however, weakened its mandate well before its actual abrogation (Thornley, 1991). Once the GLC was abolished, its plan had no status, and the Secretary of State for the Environment had the task of providing "strategic planning guidance" to the local authorities, each of which was required to formulate a development plan that would "facilitate development while protecting the local environment." During the 1980s developers avoided building in jurisdictions whose councils made life difficult for them. Even though the British tax system stopped rewarding local authorities that attracted business enterprises when Parliament established a national business tax, few authorities could afford to ignore the benefits of new investment in terms of increased employment and services. Therefore, they became increasingly competitive with one another, and even the more recalcitrant borough councils eventually assumed a pro-development posture. By the end of the 1990s all local authorities had become willing partners in development schemes. At the same time, the renewed importance of London-wide strategic planning and the termination of special status for the Docklands meant that competition among the boroughs had lessened (in contrast to the New York metropolitan region, where the battle between New York and New Jersey for office occupants had, if anything, intensified).

Much of the new office construction went up on land that had been in the possession of public bodies, which they released initially as a consequence of the Thatcher government's promptings. Local authorities had originally acquired large holdings in anticipation of building housing or other public facilities on them. Other governmental corporations—for example, British Rail and the Port of London Authority—found themselves owning tracts on which the previous uses had become obsolete. Such vacant or derelict property became the sites for major construction projects.

The freeing up of developable sites, especially around London's numerous railroad stations, along with demands from potential tenants for more modern buildings, spurred many schemes. Developers, accustomed to the formidable barriers to planning permission that had long restricted new construction within London, responded quickly to their new opportunities. The unaccustomed compliance of local authorities loosed a flood. At the same time, changes in technology had made the low ceilings and small floor areas of most existing office buildings obsolete. Potential tenants had begun to indicate a preference for high-quality space over a central location, which until then had been the sine qua non of site selection. This shift, combined with the early successes of fringe-area projects like Broadgate, which was located on the edge of the City of London, made feasible the development of property formerly considered unsuitable for offices.

The City of London

Nowhere did governmental efforts to instigate local development activity have a greater effect than in the City, where more than 16.5 million square feet of office space was con-structed between 1985 and 1990. Until 1983, concerns with historic preservation and the obduracy of the various guilds and titled families holding ancient freehold rights had blocked much potential development within the square mile. Since the City did not harbor the antagonism to business evident in the Labour-dominated boroughs, however, once the economic benefits of restricting growth ended, attitudes toward physical change easily became more flexible, and the commitment to tradition weakened.

For a long period, financial firm that already possessed space adjacent to the Bank of England benefited from their monopoly position and had no motivation to favor expansionary policies. Financial deregulation and competition changed the stakes. Competitive office development in the nearby Docklands threatened the interests represented within the Corporation of the City of London. If the City refused to accommodate expansion when deregulation was prompting accelerated financial-sector activity, firms already located there risked losing their locational advantage as the center of gravity shifted eastward. On the other hand, landowning interests within the Corporation, as well as the Corporation itself, which owned 20 percent of the land in its jurisdiction, stood to make considerable money through more intensive development of their holdings. Moreover, when the central government introduced a uniform national business tax, to be distributed to localities on a formula basis, it gave to the City of London alone the right to keep 15 percent of the business rate collected within its boundaries. Thus, increasing local commercial property values would greatly enhance the City's revenue position.

Once the Corporation decided to reverse the previous conservationist direction, the City's administrative officers embarked on an active promotional effort. The planning director solicited advice from firms concerning their space needs and encouraged developers to seek planning permission for buildings to accommodate them. In addition, he identified new developable land, including space over highways and railroad tracks. In the process, the local development plan was modified to raise floor area ratios ("plot ratios") sufficiently to permit an average 25 percent expansion in the size of buildings. While the local authority relaxed regulations and made discreet contacts with developers and potential tenants, it did not engage in an elaborate sales effort on the LDDC model nor deal making in the frenzied New York City mode. Only in the case of the European Bank for Reconstruction and Development, which had been contemplating a site in the Docklands, was there an outright effort at enticing it to take a City location. An influential member of the governing body claimed that "it would be beneath us" to set up such an operation. Rather, he said, that "we create an atmosphere." He did note that the Lord Mayor possessed a trust fund allowing him to entertain foreign visitors, adding that "we like to meet people and mix, but we do it in a private way" (Fainstein, 2001b, p. 48).

Initially, either because of this subtle form of public relations or simply in response to availability of new, first-class space, tenants rushed to let the additions to the City's office stock. The new space that came on the market in the City between 1981 and mid-1987 boasted almost 100 percent occupancy by the time of the October stock-market crash, 57 percent of it by banking and finance enterprises. By far the largest single project adding to the stock during the latter part of the decade was the Broadgate, a joint venture between the privately owned development firms of Stanhope and Rosehaugh and the publicly owned British Rail. Costing more than £2 billion by 1991, this still ongoing enterprise transformed derelict railroad yards adjacent to Liverpool Street Station into a mixed-use retail and office complex. Its siting in the City "fringe," adjacent to the low-income East London commercial and residential borough of Tower Hamlets, represented a distinctive break with tradition.

As the development's first fourteen buildings reached completion, initial success in attracting stellar tenants, even after the 1987 jolt to financial markets, seemed to augur unlimited possibilities for those developers willing to invest in the most technologically advanced, luxuriously appointed projects.

The story changed radically by 1990, then reversed itself again later in the decade. As a result of sustained contraction in the financial industry and simultaneous continued large-scale speculative construction, the City considerably exceeded the rest of central London in the amount of commercial space left unoccupied during the recession. Like downtown Manhattan, however, it recovered rapidly by century's end. As the surplus space was absorbed, the vacancy rate plunged to 5 percent, while rents climbed to £52 per square foot on average and considerably above that for prime sites.

New York

The last quarter of the twentieth century saw New York riding an economic roller coaster. After the city suffered huge job losses and virtual governmental bankruptcy in the mid-1970s, an unexpected economic recovery began in 1977. The city's decline in the preceding years had been sharper than London's; likewise, its revival was more dramatic. By 1981 office construction skyrocketed, rivaling, although never equaling, the pace of the early 1970s. During the 1990s recession, office construction halted altogether, and during the late 1990s it revived only slowly, as lenders were reluctant to engage in the speculative financing of the earlier decade. Redevelopment in the 1990s largely took the form of rehabilitation and conversion rather than new development According to *Crain's New York Business,* upgrades of older office properties and conversions of industrial space added 15 million square feet of prime office space in two years (1998–1999), comprising an investment of $3 billion. This compared to an average annual rate of new construction of 6.9 million square feet during the peak years (1987–1989) of the 1980s boom. In particular, Manhattan's far West Side, south of 42nd Street, became a coveted location for telecommunications and Internet-related firms. It profited from numerous fiberoptic cable linkages and proximity, to the main cable, exceptionally large spaces, heavy weight-bearing floors, and huge elevators in old factory buildings. The area also became the home of scores of art galleries, driven out of SoHo by boutiques and rising prices and attracted by cheap, disused industrial space (Fainstein & Fainstein, 1987; Fainstein, Gordon & Harloe, 1992).

Downtown Manhattan prospered in the 1990s as well. Having suffered from the highest vacancy rates in the city during the downturn, it became the focus of development policy. Business interests in the area formed the Downtown Alliance, a business improvement district (BID) and effective lobbying group. Because policy-makers were pessimistic that the surplus of office space, particularly Class B space, would soon, if ever, be absorbed, the city sponsored a program of tax incentives to promote the conversion of office buildings into residences in this previously all-commercial area. As described in *New York* magazine,

> Preservationists, good-government types, techies—and the free market—are working together to do nothing less than turn this skyscraper national park into a 24-hour urban 'village' that breaks down the geographic and psychic space between commerce recreation, and daily life. The working model of Tomorrowland Wall Street is a hot-wired urban hive—dense, frenetic, whirring with synergies, a critical mass of art, industry, and communications. (Williams, 1996. p. 35)

The city also offered incentives for upgrading the technical infrastructure of buildings to attract "new economy" firms in communications, media, and the Internet to the area.

Primarily as a result of extraordinary growth in these sectors, downtown succeeded beyond anyone's imaginings in again becoming a desirable office location. In fact, the demand for offices became so great that developers shelved plans for residential conversions to pursue the more lucrative commercial office market. Thus, New York's "Silicon Alley" consists of Chelsea, once a factory district; Midtown South, formerly a secondary office area, and downtown, previously devoted wholly to the financial industry.

New York, like London, has had no powerful business-led growth coalition to formulate a citywide planning strategy. The Real Estate-Board of New York takes positions on particular issues of concern to the industry—e.g., property and rent taxes, revisions to the zoning code. The Regional Plan Association, a nonprofit good-government group, has proposed a development plan for the New York region with little effectiveness. The New York City Partnership, an alliance of chief executive officers, sponsors affordable housing and holds occasional forums but largely plays a low-key role.

During the 1975 fiscal crisis, New York's business elite strongly promoted its conservative response to the budgetary shortfall; after that, while it has lobbied extensively against taxes and has supported public-sector redevelopment initiatives and transit improvements, it has not participated actively in redevelopment planning. Rather, particular elements of business—especially developers and securities firms—influenced politicians directly through heavy contributions to political campaigns. The approach of these political influentials was not to press for comprehensive solutions to New York's problems but to seek specific benefits such as tax abatements and zoning variances.

Public Programs

Spending on major capital projects had virtually halted during the years following the fiscal crisis and private-sector recession of the mid-1970s. After 1981, however, increased local revenues arising from the city's economic revival combined with state and federal subsidies for economic development to launch a number of major development projects. Chief among these were South Street Seaport, Battery Park City, the Javits Convention Center, and the Times Square Marriott and Grand Hyatt hotels, all located in midtown or downtown Manhattan. The city paid for supporting infrastructure and granted tax subsidies; it also used federal Urban Development Action Grants (UDAGs) to subsidize the Seaport, developer Donald J. Trump's Grand Hyatt—his first major enterprise, which adjoined Grand Central Station—and the massive Marriott, located in the heart of Times Square. The Urban Development Corporation (UDC), later renamed the Empire State Development Corporation (ESDC), a semi-independent agency of the State of New York with the mission of promoting economic development, was revived from bankruptcy by the infusion of new state funds. It managed the construction of the convention center and the planning and infrastructure for Battery Park City. The corporation's legal powers, exercised through separately incorporated subsidiaries for each project (the Convention Center Development Corporation, the Battery Park City Authority, the Times Square Redevelopment Corporation), freed it from oversight requirements that affected city-sponsored efforts: It did not heed to go through the normal process of community consultation for project approval; it did not have to request a variance if it did not conform to the zoning law; and the city's governing bodies had no authority over it.

Tax Subsidies

Besides participating in those major projects where public authorities took the initiative, private developers took advantage of tax-subsidy programs for new construction. Since under New York law all local revenue measures must be enacted by the state government, these programs were products of state legislative action; nevertheless, they applied to local property levies rather than state: tax liabilities. The Industrial and Commercial Incentives Board (ICIB), which administered a tax incentive program for businesses, participated in office-building, hotel, and retail projects, initially almost all in Manhattan. Although the initial purpose of the ICIB had been to revive New York's manufacturing base, it quickly turned into a real-estate development program, and the construction of new speculative office buildings became equated with economic growth in the views of the program's sponsors. Two tax-subsidy programs for residential development—421a for new construction and J-51 for rehabilitation—were also heavily used to assist luxury housing in Manhattan. On the East Side, always New York's wealthiest district, publicly subsidized projects included Donald Trump's Grand Hyatt hotel and his famous Trump Tower luxury retail and condominium residence, as well as the AT&T (now Sony) Building, designed by Philip Johnson as a postmodern statement, and across from it, the IBM building. In 1981 and 1982 alone, twelve office buildings, comprising more than 7 million net square feet, were completed on Manhattan's already very densely developed midtown East Side. Although restrictions were eventually placed on the tax incentive programs to direct them to less affluent parts of the city, before these limits were imposed late in the 1980s, almost every building intended for wealthy business or residential occupants made use of such subsidies.

The strategy of targeting firms facing lease expirations or seeking new or additional space and offering them tax breaks continued through the administrations of Edward Koch, David Dinkins, and Rudolph Giuliani. Tax deals have gone to very wealthy firms in the most desirable parts of Manhattan, based on the argument that high rents and operating costs would otherwise drive them out of the city. Thus, for example, the investment firm Bear Stearns got a $75 million exemption from sales taxes; part of the break was tied to the creation of new jobs. The city also gave additional tax relief to firms that had already received large tax benefits either directly or as part of a package of incentives for the buildings they occupied. Within five years the Giuliani administration had granted more than $2 billion in tax breaks and other subsidies to more than four dozen of the city's biggest corporations. Unlike the planning gain deals in London, besides stipulations for job retention and creation, the enforcement of which is dubious, there were no requirements for public benefits, and one clear detrimental effect was the shifting of the tax burden to small and medium-sized companies.

Media Responses

The New York press has largely acted as a reliable booster of real-estate investment. The failure of the mainstream media to offer a general assessment of the city's redevelopment priorities has meant that conflicts over particular schemes took the form of local skirmishes rather than contributing to a citywide debate over appropriate economic strategies. Although the architecture critics of the Times frequently found fault with particular buildings for their bulk and occasionally delivered broadsides against the city's failure to formulate coherent strategies for expansion, the media largely did not question the basic equation of real-estate development with economic growth. In particular, Donald Trump, New York's best-known (although by no means biggest) developer, adeptly used the media to promote his glamorous skyscrapers and, by inference, the whole ambiance of Upper East Side luxury that surrounded them. Trump was not only man but metaphor.

Intensity of Development

New York, unlike London between 1986 and 2000, possessed a unified, centralized city government and a department of city planning; it nevertheless never produced a citywide development plan. Development proceeded project by project as developers assembled a site, raised financing, and exploited available subsidies. If they did not require zoning variances or seek zoning bonuses; they did not need planning permission at all and could build as of right. The zoning code already offered a floor area ratio (FAR) of 12:1 (i.e., twelve square feet of floor space for every square foot of the total site) on most lots that were zoned for office use. It granted bonuses to developers who provided public amenities like plazas or subway station improvements; typically such awards raised the FAR to 15:1, three times the level of London. Developers could also purchase the air rights from adjacent buildings, pyramiding these allowances on top of their bonuses, thus building even higher.

The city government has largely refrained from developing plans that would specify its priorities as to kinds of structures, preferred locations, or desired amount of space.

New residential construction, almost all for the luxury market until 1987, continued unabated wherever potential sites were not protected by historic-district status. Extremely strong demand for residential space in the heart of the city allowed developers to obtain extraordinarily high returns on their investments. Nevertheless, the city continued to provide tax benefits for luxury residential development under the 421a program until 1986. When the city government finally decided to end subsidies for buildings in central Manhattan, developers rushed to put foundations in the ground so as to take advantage of the tax benefits before they disappeared.

The high level of development activity during the boom years of the 1980s markedly changed the appearance of Manhattan. The midtown and downtown office cores expanded and became much more dense. A number of large apartment buildings replaced low-rise structures on the Upper West Side and filled in the gaps remaining in the West Side Urban Renewal Program dating from the 1960s. Battery Park City, to the west of Wall Street, and Tribeca, an old industrial area just north of the financial district, gained thousands of housing units, producing a residential community in a part of New York that had been devoted wholly to business for well over a century. Huge new residential structures lined the East Side between the East River and Third Avenue. Almost all of the new construction in Manhattan required the demolition of existing buildings. In contrast, the development spurt of the century's end, relying much more heavily on conversions and rehabilitation, had a less obvious effect on the city's appearance.

The spin-off effects of both Manhattan booms were mainly felt across the Hudson River in New Jersey, where at the beginning of the new century, millions more square feet were on the drawing boards to house back offices of, among others, Goldman Sachs, Chase Bank, Paine Webber, American Express, and Merrill Lynch. Although New York City's boroughs felt some residential pressure, their business districts remained mostly untouched by office construction. Only one major project, MetroTech in downtown Brooklyn, represented a serious attempt to decentralize office functions to New York City's boroughs. Undertaken during the Koch administration, this precedent seemingly did not impress the Giuliani administration, which launched no major projects except for baseball stadiums outside Manhattan.

ECONOMIC AND REAL-ESTATE CYCLES

The business cycles of the last quarter of the twentieth century affected London and New York very strongly. Tied as they were to global financial markets, they had little to buffer them from either the manic investment climate of the boom periods or the depressive withdrawal of capital during the declines. Thus, during the 1980s they reached an apogee of wealth creation, physically reflected in the erection of huge new structures. Then, suddenly, a few years after the cave-in of financial markets in October 1987, the construction boom foundered, and the enthusiastic portrayal of a prosperous future for London and New York as global cities faded along with it. The newspaper business pages presented a staccato of defaults and bankruptcies where formerly they had published the press releases of the deal-makers. The cranes disappeared, and in their stead empty office buildings and vacant flats eerily recalled previous optimism. As the job gains of the decade vanished, little else remained to mark the flush times besides the millions of square feet of space that had been created. Both London and New York suffered disproportionately from the recessions affecting their countries. Worst of all, the very industries that during the 1980s had been the object of their economic strategies, the source of their growth, and the symbol of their accomplishments lost the most employment. In London, jobs in the financial and business services sectors fell by 90,000 between 1990 and 1992, wiping out all of the FBS employment gains of the preceding five years. During 1989–1991, New York sustained comparable losses, as FBS employment dropped by 91,000, returning the city's job level to the lowest figure since 1983.

Revival came quickly in London, more slowly in New York, although neither regained all of the jobs it had lost until the end of the decade. During the 1990s, for the most part, economic and construction activity followed trend lines established in the 1980s. Core strengths continued to be in finance and business services; construction focused on office and luxury residential sectors. There were, however, some differences. Tourism and media contributed strongly to economic growth. Particularly in New York, the "new economy" businesses associated with information technology exploded, while motion picture production became the fastest-growing sector as measured by percentage increase. In the words of one real estate adviser: "Nobody dreamed of them [the technology companies] in 1990. We never anticipated [entertainment and media] companies like Bertelsmann, Disney, Viacom. The nature of retailing has changed. Retail and entertainment are much more closely allied." Construction had become much less speculative. The amount of new office space added was relatively small compared to the 1980s, although as noted earlier, conversion of industrial space or upgrading of existing offices meant that much more was added than would have been obvious to an observer looking at the skyline.

QUESTIONS FOR DISCUSSION

1. In two or three paragraphs, discuss the main themes of Fainstein's chapter.
2. In 1–2 pages, use specific examples from the chapter to illustrate Fainstein's main themes.
3. From what you have just read and other articles/knowledge, list what do you think were the major forces driving both New York and London's growth in the late 20th century? Now, in about 2–3 pages, discuss how these factors similarly and differentially impacted each city's growth path (for example, compare and contrast Fainstein's descriptions of property development trends in New York and London and the actors driving their respective growth patterns).
4. Utilizing the 'Further Readings', 'Helpful Web Links', and other sources, conduct some further research on the New York and London areas. Then, in 2–3 pages, discuss some of the most interesting facts you discovered about these cities and present your findings to your class. Where possible, try to relate these comments and findings to the theoretical arguments introduced in the Friedmann, Sassen, Derudder et al., Hill-Fujita, and/or other chapters.

FURTHER READINGS

Fainstein, S. 2011. *The Just City*. Ithaca, NY: Cornell University Press.

Fitch, R. 1996. *Assassination of New York*. New York: Verso.

Kantor, P., C. Lefevre, A. Saito, H. Savitch, and A. Thornley. 2012. *Struggling Giants: City-Region Governance in London, New York, Paris, and Tokyo*. Minneapolis: University of Minnesota Press.

King, A. 1990. *Global Cities: Post-Imperialism and the Internationalization of London*. New York: Routledge.

Kynaston. D. 2010. *City of London: 1815–2000*. London: Chatto & Windus.

Logan, J. and H. Molotch. 1987. *Urban Fortunes: The Political Economy of Place*. Berkeley: University of California Press.

HELPFUL WEB LINKS

British History Online. 2012. London, Survey of. Online, Available at: http://www.british-history.ac.uk/place.aspx?gid=74&region=l, last accessed, January 14, 2012.

ePodunk. 2012a. Brooklyn New York Borough Information: Profile of Brooklyn, New York, NY. Online. Available at: http://www.epodunk.com/cgi-bin/genInfo.php?locIndex=286, last accessed, January 14, 2012.

ePodunk. 2012b. Manhattan New York Borough Information: Profile of Manhattan, New York, NY. Online. Available at: http://www.epodunk.com/cgi-bin/genlnfo.php?loclndex=1101, last accessed, January 14, 2012.

Jersey City, City of. 2012. Jersey City Redevelopment Agency. Online. Available at: http://www.thejcra. org/, last accessed, January 14, 2012.

London, City of. 2012. Home Page of the City of London, United Kingdom. Online. Available at: http://www.cityoflondon.gov.uk/Corporation/homepage.htm, last accessed, January 14, 2012.

London Councils. 2012. London Councils: Home Page of the Councils for the 33 Boroughs of London. Online. Available at: http://www.londoncouncils.gov.uk/, last accessed, January 14, 2012.

New York, City of. 2012. NYC.gov: Official Website of the City of New York. Online. Available at: http://www.nyc.gov/portal/site/nycgov/?front_door=true, last accessed, January 9, 2012.

Royal Docks Trust. 2012. Royal Docks Update. Online. Available at: http://www.royaldockstrust.org. uk/rdteam.html, last accessed, January 14, 2012.

The Port Authority. 2012. Port Authority of New York and New Jersey. Online. Available at: http://www.panynj.gov/, last accessed, January 14, 2012.

Westminster City Council. 2012. City of Westminster, United Kingdom. Online. Available at: http://www.westminster.gov.uk/, last accessed, January 14, 2012.

CHAPTER 20

Hong Kong: An Entrepreneurial City in Action (2000)

Bob Jessop and Ngai-Ling Sum

There is widespread interest among policy-makers and observers alike in the entrepreneurial city. It is less obvious what exactly being an entrepreneurial city involves. To help resolve this conundrum, our paper first provides a Schumpeterian analysis of the entrepreneurial city and then illustrates it with the Hong Kong case (see Figure 20.1). We first offer a three-part definition of the entrepreneurial city in capitalist societies. This relates urban entrepreneurship to changing forms of competitiveness, changing strategies to promote inter-urban competitiveness in both the economic and in the extra-economic fields and entrepreneurial discourses, narratives and self-images. Schumpeter (1934) identified five ways in which entrepreneurs innovate in normal economic activities; our analysis identifies parallels in urban entrepreneurialism. We then critically consider how far such an analysis is valid given the differences between the types of actor involved and the objects of their innovation—answering affirmatively in both respects and suggesting the conditions in which cities can be described as strategic actors with entrepreneurial ambitions. This theoretical analysis is further refined and justified from recent developments in Hong Kong and east Asia. Conventionally regarded as a paradigm case of *laissez-faire* and officially described in the decades before 1997 as practicing 'positive non-intervention', Hong Kong actually has a long history of urban entrepreneurship based on public–private partnerships. But its strategies have been modified as the economic and political environments have changed.

Our contribution is particularly concerned with the recent period, when Hong Kong's entrepreneurial city strategies have been developed against the background of an emerging cross-border regional space (Greater China) and its favorable insertion into the global circuits of capital. In this context we introduce the concept of 'glurbanization' as one form of the more general phenomenon of 'glocalization' and show how it can be used to illuminate current entrepreneurial city strategies in east Asia.

Thus the second part of the paper describes how, between the 1970s and the early 1990s, Hong Kong responded in two ways to the growing relocation of its local manufacturing activities to the mainland. It became the key node in coordinating 'sub-contracting management' for the 'Greater China' region; and, in addition, its increasingly internationalized financial and producer services sectors expanded to fill the gaps created by the 'hollowing-out' of Hong Kong's local manufacturing base.

Hong Kong's continuing rise from the mid-1980s onwards as a regional financial center provided ample funds for further expansion by local property capital. These structural shifts strengthened the position of finance and property capital in the local power bloc. As property became an increasingly important

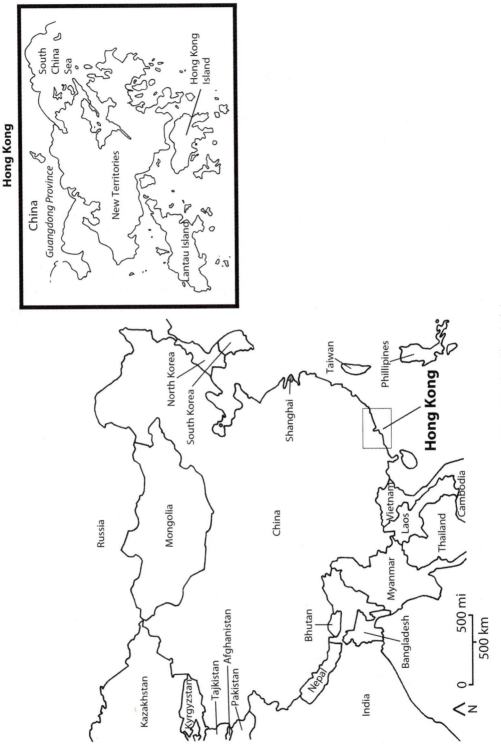

Figure 20.1 Hong Kong in Asia

sphere of capital accumulation, industrial and commercial capitals worried about the lack of high-tech investment and the rising cost of all economic activities in Hong Kong. This was reflected in the development of two major alternative urban strategic orientations organized around the competing interests of industry and producer services and concerned in their different ways with problems of . . . governance.

[Occurring] shortly after the 1997 return of Hong Kong to the mainland, the outbreak of the Asian crisis initially complicated these strategies. When the crisis stabilized in early 1999, however, the competing visions took on a new life and generated even more explicit and reflexive urban entrepreneurialism. In particular, since urban economic growth is locked into a property-related path, the government is now seeking to build a new urban bloc. This would consolidate real estate, commercial and technological interests around new entrepreneurial projects such as a science park, cyberport and Chinese-medicine port. Such projects serve to unify different interests in Hong Kong and are also mediating the emergence of a global–regional–national bloc of economic actors involved in information and communication technologies and services—in the case of the cyberport, for example, these include Microsoft, Acer from Taiwan and IT firms from Hong Kong and China. These entrepreneurial projects are by no means unique to Hong Kong and, indeed, they are facing competition from similar projects in Singapore, Kuala Lumpur and Beijing.

WHAT IS AN ENTREPRENEURIAL CITY?

It might be argued that entrepreneurial cities have existed for centuries, if not millennia and, in terms of institutional structures and strategies supporting economic innovation, this could well be true. But this argument views cities as engines of *wealth creation* regardless of the specific form in which this occurs—and so fails to capture what is novel about the role of entrepreneurial cities in *capital accumulation*. In particular, we propose three defining features of entrepreneurial cities:

- An entrepreneurial city pursues innovative strategies intended to maintain or enhance its economic competitiveness *vis-à-vis* other cities and economic spaces.
- These strategies are real and reflexive. They are not 'as if' strategies, but are more or less explicitly formulated and pursued in an active, entrepreneurial fashion.
- The promoters of entrepreneurial cities adopt an entrepreneurial discourse, narrate their cities as entrepreneurial and market them as entrepreneurial.

The first and second criteria distinguish cities that happen for whatever reason(s) to perform well economically from those that are entrepreneurial. For not all cities that perform well are entrepreneurial; and not all entrepreneurial cities perform well. Adopting the second criterion directs attention to the conditions under which cities can be said to act in a relatively unified and strategic manner and/or in which specific social forces are able to define the interests of the city and be seen to act for and on behalf of the latter. Only where explicit strategies are pursued can we talk of an entrepreneurial city. The third criterion is useful in distinguishing the entrepreneurial city from non-entrepreneurial urban regimes. Urban regimes and urban blocs pursue many different kinds of economic, political and socio-cultural strategy—for example, religious center, dream factory, imperial capital, modernist utopia, municipal socialism or tourist center. Only some adopt an explicitly entrepreneurial self-identity as well as an entrepreneurial strategy.

Our approach to the first and second criteria for identifying entrepreneurial cities is influenced by Schumpeter (1934), who defined entrepreneurship as the creation of opportunities for surplus profit through 'new combinations' or innovation; by Harvey (1989), who has presented some influential ideas on the shift from urban managerialism to urban entrepreneurialism. Their work is very useful in defining the nature of entrepreneurial strategies oriented to enhancing the competitiveness of cities and regions.

INTER-SCALAR STRATEGIES

Cities engage in different kinds of inter-scalar strategy. Even if they do not act directly as economic entrepreneurs producing commodities (for example, as sponsors of property-led development, tourist spectacles, etc.), cities may still promote an entrepreneurial environment on a range of scales that might help to sustain local growth and make the best use of any opportunities to promote entrepreneurship and/or market their places/spaces. In this regard, several strategies can be identified. These differ in at least three respects: their respective concepts and discourses of competitiveness, the spatial and scalar horizons over which they are meant to operate and their association with different local contexts and positions in prevailing urban hierarchies. What they share is an important role for urban or metropolitan authorities in their overall framing and promulgation. In this sense, for all the talk of the crisis of the state (at whatever level), public authorities still appear to have a major role in organizing entrepreneurial policies for the city (including inner cities and metropolitan regions), reflecting on them and narrating such policies in entrepreneurial terms . . .

One relatively novel form of inter-urban competition is 'glurbanization'. We have coined this term to distinguish urban from firm-level strategies within the broader concept of 'glocalization', which has lost its original precision, as it has become the vogue word for all kinds of multi-scalar strategies with at least some global aspect. As such it

clearly differs from the initial usage of glocalization to distinguish the strategy of global localization pursued by Japanese firms from the strategy of globalization favored by many US multinationals. In this context, whereas globalization is oriented to building a worldwide intra-firm division of labor with production oriented to world markets and standard tastes, glocalization is concerned with establishing a geographically concentrated interfirm division of labor in the three major trading blocs (Ruigrok and van Tulder, 1996).

Glocalization has also been used to describe de-territorialization and re-territorialization strategies by political units (see Swyngedouw, 1997, later Brenner, 1998, 1999a, 199b). But this is the other side of the contradiction of mobility-immobility in capital accumulation and has a very different dynamic. We suggest that it is more sensible to differentiate strategies on the immobile territorial side as well as on the mobile de-territorializing or even aterritorial (i.e. cyber-) side of the accumulation of capital. Failure to do so leads to the conceptual morass of a 'glocalization' concept that simply refers to any and all forms of global–local interaction . . .

To avoid these problems, we propose the term glurbanization strategies to refer to entrepreneurial strategies that are concerned to secure the most advantageous insertion of a given city into the changing inter-scalar division of labor in the world economy. For, whilst glocalization is a strategy pursued by global firms that seek to exploit local differences to enhance their global operations, glurbanisation is pursued by cities to enhance their place-based dynamic competitive advantages to capture certain types of mobile capital and/or to fix local capital in place. . . . The key analytical (and empirical) differences between glurbanization and glocalization as we propose them within the broader framework of concerns with global–local (or, better, multiscalar) articulation are summarized in Table 20.1. This table is not intended to present a complete typology of multi-scalar strategies, but aims simply to highlight some differences important for the ensuing discussion.

The concept of glurbanization is very useful for exploring the emerging strategies of contemporary entrepreneurial cities, for it . . . provides a means of exploring the articulation between firm-level, city-level and state-level strategies in the current period of globalization. It also highlights the contrasting moments of glocalization in its broadest sense—i.e. the de-territorializing mobility of flows in space versus re-territorializing attempts to fix capital in place. It is also highly relevant to the pursuit of dynamic competitive advantage in so far as entrepreneurial cities must position themselves not only in the economic sphere, but also in the many extra-economic spheres that are so important nowadays to effective structural or systemic competition. In doing so, they continue to reproduce local differences that enable transnational firms to pursue their own glocalization strategies.

AN ENTREPRENEURIAL CITY IN ACTION: THE CASE OF HONG KONG

Hong Kong has a long history of urban entrepreneurialism, with different strategies being pursued as its economic and political environments changed. Our paper focuses on the period since 1979—i.e. from the year that China first opened its doors to foreign investment through to Hong Kong's current efforts to reposition itself in the light of the Asian crisis. At stake here is a complex and still evolving dialectic between glocalization and glurbanization strategies in the broad sense in which these terms have just been defined. The opening of China provided opportunities for Hong Kong firms to adopt glocalization strategies to enhance their competitive advantage in the export market. This was partly facilitated by the corresponding glurbanization strategies of different provinces, cities and townships in southern China. This resulted in the so-called 'hollowing-out' of Hong Kong as a manufacturing center. The gap has been filled by Hong Kong's emergence as a services center for local, regional and international companies. In response to these changes, governmental and quasi-governmental as well as private economic actors proposed their own (competing) glurbanization strategies for Hong Kong—some more favorable to a reinvigorated manufacturing strategy, some more favorable to the development of a producer service role within a changing regional–global economy. These 'glurbanization' responses in Hong Kong took a new turn with the outbreak of the Asian crisis and its impact on interurban, interregional and international competition in east Asia and more widely.

The Hollowing Out/Filling In of Hong Kong

China's 1979 declaration of its open door policy was followed five years later by the

Table 20.1 Glurbanization versus Glocalization

	Glurbanization	*Glocalization*
Strategic actors	Cities (perhaps as national champions)	Firms (perhaps in strategic alliances)
Strategies	Place- and space-based strategies	Firm- or sector-based strategies
New scales of activities and temporalities	Create local differences to capture flows and embed mobile capital	Develop new forms of scalar and/ or spatial division of labor
Chronotopic (time-space) governance	Re-articulate time and space for structural or systemic competitive advantages	Re-articulate global and local for dynamic competitive advantages

signing of the Sino-British Joint Declaration in 1984. This promised that Hong Kong's capitalist way of life would not be changed for 50 years after its return to the mainland in 1997. This . . . encouraged [Hong Kong] manufacturers to look for short- to medium-term opportunities in the immediate region. . . . Taking advantage of the low land and labor costs, manufacturing firms relocated their activities to southern China. By the mid-1990s, almost 25,000 Hong Kong factories, mostly in textiles and clothing, toys and consumer electronics, moved there to exploit low labor and rent costs. They then employed directly about 3 million workers—i.e. three times the total manufacturing labor force left in Hong Kong. . . .

The combination of glocalization strategies pursued by Hong Kong firms and a glurbanisation strategy pursued by provincial, urban and township authorities in southern China contributed to Hong Kong's transformation from an industrial center to a global-gateway city. But it also prompted the so-called hollowing-out process in its status as a manufacturing center. The resulting gap has been filled by the growing importance of producer services such as retail and import/export trades, financial services, insurance, real estate and business services as well as owner-ship of premises (see Table 20.2).

The Emergence of Finance and Real Estate

On the material level, the northward march of Hong Kong's manufacturing turned it into a (sub-contracting) management hub. This new [situation] has been coupled with developments on the financial front, for, since the early 1980s, Hong Kong has become a regional financial center. Among contributory factors here are: Hong Kong's market-friendly environment; the opening of China for inward and outward investment; the growing economic importance of the Asia-Pacific Region; global financial liberalization and development of international banking and financial markets; and, developments in information technology and telecommunications. Local, regional and multinational banks/financial institutions came to specialize in on-shore and off-shore activities—for example, syndicated loans for the Southeast Asian Region and acting as a financial *entrepot* for 'Greater China'. As a regional financial center, Hong Kong became a net recipient of overseas funds, which amounted to about HK$138 billion in 1988. About half of these funds came from Chinese banks. In addition, financial deregulation in Japan and tougher competition among Japanese banks meant that Hong Kong became one of their destinations for off-shore activities. Thus, by the end of 1989, Japanese institutions came

Table 20.2 Hong Kong: Percent GDP by Selected Economic Activity

	1985	1990	1995	1997
Industry	29.8	25.3	16.6	14.7
Manufacturing	21.9	17.6	8.3	6.5
Construction	5.0	5.4	5.4	5.8
Others	2.9	2.3	2.9	2.4
Services	74.5	80.3	83.8	85.2
Wholesale/retail trade, restaurants & hotels	21.8	24.3	26.6	26.1
Transport, storage & communications	8.1	9.4	10.1	9.3
Financing, insurance, real estate and business services	16.3	20.8	24.4	26.5
Community, social and personal services	17.3	15.0	17.3	17.4
Ownership of premises	11.0	10.8	13.3	13.0

Sources: Hong Kong SAR Government (various years)

to dominate Hong Kong's foreign-currency loan market and accounted for two-thirds of Hong Kong's total foreign currency assets (Goldstein, 1990).

This ample supply of funds was not easily absorbed by Hong Kong's immature debt market . . . It was property that provided this field. . . . Between 1985 and 1997, property estate investment and speculation pushed real estate prices up eight-fold. The emergence of property as an object of capital accumulation has consolidated a close relationship between finance and property capital (ex. more than half of the Hang Seng Stock Index is made up of property and property-related shares). This property-finance relationship formed only part of a broader cross-border urban bloc that comprised not only multinational/local banks and construction companies, also legal/property professionals, government, [individual investors], and cross-border capital from China. . . . In short, we can argue that the construction of Hong Kong's structural competitiveness and glurbanization strategies are based on a place-based, [embedded] notion of urban entrepreneurialism.

THE ASIAN CRISIS AND HONG KONG'S NEW URBAN IDENTITIES

The Asian Crisis

. . . On February 5, 1997, speculators launched an attack on the Thai baht. [This was followed] by the Bank of Thailand allowing the baht to float on July 2, 1997. The [ensuing] financial contagion quickly spread to Indonesia, Malaysia, South Korea, the Philippines, and then Hong Kong . . ., [leaving] governments in short-term crisis management. The Hong Kong Government intervened in the money market initially by pushing up interest . . . and later by imposing penalty interest on borrowing of the Hong Kong (HK) dollar. The government was able to maintain the pegged exchange rate under

conditions of high interest rates [and limit] capital flight from the HK dollar. This [sent] the local stock index and residential property prices down by over 50 per cent between October 1997 and June 1998. Asset depreciation, especially in the property sector, cut at the heart of Hong Kong's internal 'growth' dynamics it had developed since the opening of China. This bursting of the 'property bubble' has given rise to fears among [some] about further asset depreciation. In order to prevent the asset from further depreciating, the government's short-term strategies were: to freeze land sales (until April 1999); to allocate HK$1390 million for home-buyer loans; and, to grant tax rebates to property owners.

The HK dollar came under further attack in August 1998 when the Japanese yen depreciated against it, with hedge funds selling the Hong Kong stock market short in the expectation that the index would fall as interest rates rose. Speculative attacks propelled significant amounts of capital outflow as some people believed that this might also force a devaluation of the Chinese yuan. This time, the government reacted with more short-term measures which included: drawing on its reserves to buy US$15 billion worth of selected Hong Kong shares (60 percent of these were property related—higher than this sector's weight in the stock market); and, introducing a package of technical measures to strengthen the transparency and operation of the linked exchange rate system (for example, a rediscount facility to reduce interest rate volatility). The pegged system was once again maintained, but at the expense of high interest rates, weak domestic demand and rising unemployment. Hong Kong's GDP fell 5 percent and the unemployment rate had reached 6 percent at the beginning of 1999. However, wages and rents are still high. In April 1999, the government resumed land sales, an action that was seen as a continuing of its support for the property sector.

A New Urban Identity for a Crisis-ridden Hong Kong

The service versus industry debate took a new turn when the crisis began to stabilize in early 1999. The Asian crisis has disarticulated the previous structured coherence of Hong Kong's political economy and has exposed it to several challenges the:

(1) decline in Hong Kong's role as agent for China's exports;
(2) over-dependence on the property sector;
(3) vulnerability of financial and other services;
(4) effects of recession (ex. negative growth rates, fall in asset values, 6 percent unemployment rate);
(5) competition from other regional cities, such as Shanghai and Singapore; and
(6) rising 'tide of the information revolution'.

Given that Hong Kong has become a global–regional–gateway city dependent on the local real estate sector as well as cross-border manufacturing, innovative attempts to recast Hong Kong's competitiveness cannot be entirely divorced from this historical growth path. Up to the time of writing, private and public actors alike are urgently seeking to construct new objects and projects of urban governance that might help to rebuild the crisis-ridden economy.

One high-profile object-project is the HK $13 billion ($US1.68 billion) 'Cyberport' that was originally the 'brain child' of 'Hong Kong's Bill Gates' (Richard Li) and his Singapore-based corporation called Pacific Century, and which is expected to create 12,000 jobs upon its completion. Li's (and Pacific Century's) vision is interesting in two aspects. First, [because] . . . it adopts the idea of a service-based cluster; but one that narrates it in terms of the metaphor 'Silicon Valley' and suggests that the Cyberport could help Hong Kong to 'catch up' with the 'information revolution'. More specifically, this project aims

to redefine Hong Kong's competitive advantages . . . by: capturing global 'information flows' and managing them within the service-space of Hong Kong and its broader region (for example, as an e-commerce hub); connecting Hong Kong's services to fast cyber-time and the knowledge-based economy; and, consolidating a social space in which to build a 'cyber culture critical mass' that links the global, regional and local. This time-space re-imagination can be seen as an innovative entrepreneurial city vision to create a new techno-urban identity.

Secondly, given that the Cyberport is an imagined *service* cluster that will be *built* to capture the information—*technology* flows, this new object can symbolically (and, perhaps, materially) bridge the traditional service-technology–property divide in the cityspace of Hong Kong. It highlights the role of (information) technology in expanding the activities of traditional service clusters—a critical mass can be (partly) nurtured by the physical form of the built environment that is modeled on the 'Silicon Valley'. The transversal potential of this construction has not gone unnoticed by the government and its advisory agency (the Commission for Innovation and Technology). In fact, the idea was selected and (partly) appropriated by the government when the Financial Secretary unveiled it in the 1999 Budget.

After the official announcement, this new object of urban governance seems to have resonated within a global–regional–local [knowledge-based] community comprising local capital (for example, Li's Pacific Century), the government (e.g., the Chief Executive, the Financial Secretary, the Commission on Innovation and Technology, the Secretary for Information and Broadcasting), quasi-governmental organizations (ex. Hong Kong Industrial Technology Center) and global–regional capitalists (for example, Microsoft's Bill Gates, Yahoo!'s Jerry Yeung, and IBM's Craig Barrett). The latter group . . . flew to Hong Kong, publicly endorsed the idea, and even highlighted their roles, therein. A techno-cultural regime of truth is beginning to emerge in this network of 'infopreneurs', which cuts across the private–public as well as global–regional–local spheres.

But this emerging regime of truth has also encountered resistance. Some market analysts criticize the Cyberport idea as comprising little more than "Cyber villas by sea" (i.e. a real estate project as opposed to a high-tech project) and claim there is no Silicon Valley (Webb, 1999). Being left out of an important strategic project, 10 real estate developers jointly denounced the government's decision-making process as being 'not open for bidding' and declared that the government is using residential land to subsidize the Cyberport project. The Democratic Party, for different reasons, challenged the government for lack of transparency, creating 'favoritism/ cronyism' and departing from its '*laissez-faire*' policy.

Despite these challenges, the emerging techno-urban discourse/identity continues to resonate and has gathered some strength in reorganizing and re-regularizing economic practices. Notable examples include new consortia of property developers proposing new innovative projects. Large developers such as Sun Hung Kai Properties (SHKP) and Hutchison Whampoa have reinvented themselves as Internet companies. SHKP created its own Internet arm (SunEvision) and, together with the Hong Kong Industrial Technology Center (HKITC), launched the Cyber-incubator project in August 1999. Under this latter scheme, developers would provide rent-free space for new 'infopreneurs' for 3 years in return for 10 per cent stakes in their businesses.

Other developers such as Cheung Kong (Holdings), Henderson Land Development, New World Development and Sino Land are planning to participate in similar rent-for-equity programs. The Chief Executive, Tung Chee-Hwa, visited Silicon Valley in July 1999 to build new linkages with the local Internet communities. The Hong Kong-Silicon Valley Association, which is mediated by a Chinese *diaspora* network, was set up to enhance possible global–local flows of knowledge, expertise and manpower. Some investors even switched from blue chips to Internet and technology and Internet-related stocks—the share price of Pacific Century CyberWorks rose 1280 per cent when it first came onto the market in May 1999. In this regard, it can be argued that the techno-cultural imagination has created a post-crisis euphoria that may be conducive towards the rebuilding of a new form of urban governance that cuts across the global–regional–local scales as well as across different fractions of commercial, financial, property and technological capital. In addition to its potential to really different capital (and their organizational and inter-organizational setups) for new strategic projects, it is also facilitating the rebuilding of cross-border private-public alliance based on the politics of (Internet) optimism.

Riding on this politics of (Internet) optimism, the Cyberport imagination was further reinforced and broadened in the Second and Final Report of the Commission of Innovation and Technology published in June 1999. Acknowledging the importance of Internet-based services linked to the Cyberport project, the Commission reintroduces some place-based manufacturing recommendations (for example, institutional/organizational changes such as institutional arrangements, building up human capital, fostering innovation and technology culture, and creating an enabling business environment). However, it is also reflexively seeking new niches. . . . More specifically, one such niche recommended by the Commission is the building of a 'Silicon Harbor'. This was planned to comprise a semi-conductor manufacturing project that would allegedly be able to 'leapfrog' existing microchip fabrication facilities. This state-of-the-art factory would cost US$1.2 billion and comprise 4 factories built in phases, along with infrastructure and supporting facilities, on over 200 hectares and would eventually accommodate 200–300 companies. Its main aim was to bypass the PC age and enter directly into the ASICs (application-specific integrated circuits) era by 2003.

More recently (February 2000), the Commission on Strategic Development, with the approval of the Chief Executive, has reinforced the importance of the financial and business services sector. This is illustrated by an official blueprint for transforming Hong Kong into Asia's 'world city' that would rival the positions of London and New York in Europe and North America, respectively. This would involve strengthening Hong Kong's links with the Pearl River Delta of China and other mainland regions (such as the Yangtze Delta and Basin and key central and western regions) as well as enhancing its ability to exploit China's imminent entry into the World Trade Organization and position itself as a 'knowledge-based economy'. This blueprint envisages a complex array of private-public partnerships and networks cooperating under Hong Kong's leadership to promote the overall competitiveness of an emerging multi-centered city-region, not only in economic terms but also in cultural and community matters. This long-term development plan is explicitly phrased in entrepreneurial terms, emphasizes the importance of marketing Hong Kong as a world-class city and is strongly committed to promoting a wide range of innovative, high-tech financial and business services to secure its position within an evolving inter-scalar division of labor (Commission on Strategic Development, 2000).

CONCLUSIONS

The analysis presented above is still preliminary for two reasons. It is based on an emerging approach to entrepreneurial cities that needs further theoretical development and refinement . . . Nonetheless we believe that four themes are worth restating as key elements in an emerging research agenda on inter-urban competition in the current period of capitalist restructuring.

First, we believe that the crisis of the national framework of the 'spatiotemporal fix' and compromise that helped to sustain post-war growth during the period of Atlantic Fordism and the emergence of national security and/or developmental states in East Asia has contributed to a 'relativization of scale'. This phenomenon refers to the fact that no new scale has emerged to replace the primacy of the national level in the organization and regularization of the global economy. This is associated with the search for new forms of chronotopic (time-space) governance, as well as new forms of material and immaterial economic, political and social organization. Indeed, we find competing spatial and scalar strategies on many different levels, pursued by a wide range of actors; but these have not yet evolved into an overall pattern of structural coherence analogous to the post-war period with its primacy of the national.

Secondly, in exploring the changing role of cities in this regard, we believe that it is useful to develop a Schumpeterian analysis of the entrepreneurial city. We believe that it is justified to treat cities as actors under certain conditions and that these are closely bound up with capacities to realize particular discursive-material accumulation strategies and hegemonic projects. Even if this is rejected, it is certainly the case that urban blocs claiming to speak for and on behalf of cities or regions as 'spaces for themselves' (Lipietz, 1985/1994) have become more explicitly entrepreneurial on all three criteria introduced above.

Thirdly, in this context we believe it is worth distinguishing between 'glocalization' and 'glurbanization' in terms of whether it is a firm-level or city-level strategy that is at stake. We concede that both terms are misleading in so far as they seem to operate with a simple global-local or a simple global–urban dichotomy, which thereby fails to grasp the real complexity and perplexity of the proliferation of increasingly tangled places, spaces and scales which can no longer be treated as if they were 'nested' like so many Russian dolls. But it is this very complexity, perplexity, proliferation and tangledness that poses uncertainties and risks demanding new entrepreneurial orientations. The concept of 'glurbanization' represents a first attempt to address some of these problems from the viewpoint of the city as actor rather than from the viewpoint of the firm. As we have also noted elsewhere, however, 'glurbanization' can also be seen as a state-level response in so far as cities are coming to replace firms as 'national champions' in international competition (Jessop, 1998).

Fourthly, we also relate these changes to shifts in the modalities of competition in an increasingly 'globally integrated' but still multi-scalar, unevenly developing and tangled economy, because these shifts have modified the nature of inter-urban, as well as international competition. Indeed, with the increasing interest in dynamic competitive advantages and the bases of structural and/or systemic competitiveness, the extra-economic dimensions of cities have gained as much significance as what used to be seen as their economic dimensions. So-called natural economic factor endowments have become far less important (despite the continuing path-dependent aspects of the positioning of places in urban hierarchies); and socially constructed, socially regularized and socially embedded factors have become more important for inter-urban competitiveness. This is why urban entrepreneurialism comes to be so significant in shaping the forms of urban hierarchies, (especially in their middle ranks), and the character of global city networks. Certainly the capacity to remain at the top of the hierarchy or to move up it depends on cities' capacities and strategies for acquiring complex strategic activities and/or promoting innovation in the areas we have sketched.

QUESTIONS FOR DISCUSSION

1. In two or three paragraphs, discuss Jessop and Sum's major themes and conclusions related to Hong Kong.
2. In 1–2 pages, provide specific examples from this chapter which help explain Jessop and Sum's main themes and conclusions.
3. In 2–3 pages compare Jessup and Sum's Entrepreneurial City theory with Global City and Nested City Theory. Use examples from their chapter and presented in Friedmann, Sassen, Hill and Fujita, Fainstein, and others to help illustrate your points.
4. Utilizing the 'Further Reading', 'Helpful Web Links' and other sources, conduct some further research on Hong Kong and other entrepreneurial cities. Make a list of ten other so-called entrepreneurial cities: five North America or Europe and five in China. Then, in 2–3 pages, describe some interesting similarities and differences between the Western cities and Chinese 'entrepreneurial cities'.

FURTHER READINGS

Brenner, N. 2004. *New State Spaces: Urban Governance and the Rescaling of Statehood.* New York: Oxford University Press.

Hall, T. and P. Hubbard, eds. 2000. *The Entrepreneurial City: Geographies of Politics, Regime, and Representation.* New York: Wiley.

Jessop, B. 1997. The Entrepreneurial City: Re-imaging Localities, Redesigning Economic Governance. In N. Jewson and S. MacGregor, eds., *Realizing Cities: New Spatial Divisions and Social Transformation*. London: Routledge, pp. 28–41.

Jessop, B. 2004. *The Future of the Capitalist State*. London: Polity Press.

Storper, M. 1997. The City: The Centre of Economic Reflexivity. *The Service Industries Journal*, 17 (1): 1–27.

Sum, N. 1995. More than a 'War of Words': Identity, Politics and the Struggle for Dominance during the Recent 'Political Reform' Period in Hong Kong. *Economy and Society*, 24 (1): 67–100.

HELPFUL WEB LINKS

Guangzhou, City of. 2011. Guangzhou International. Online. Available at: http://english.gz.gov.cn/, last accessed, December 31, 2011.

Hong Kong City Hall. 2011. Hong Kong City Hall, Leisure and Cultural Services Department. http://www.lcsd.gov.hk/CE/CulturalService/CityHall/en/index.php, last accessed, December 31, 2011.

Hong Kong Cyberport Management Company, Ltd. 2011. Hong Kong Cyberport. Online. Available at: http://www.cyberport.com.hk/en, last accessed, December 31, 2011.

Hong Kong, Government of. 2011. Hong Kong: Asia's World City. Online. Available at: http://www.gov.hk/en/nonresidents/, last accessed, December 31, 2011.

HKMA. 2011. Welcome to the Hong Kong Monetary Authority. Online. Available at: http://www.hkma.gov.hk/eng/index.shtml, last accessed, December 31, 2011.

Hong Kong Trade Development Council. Pearl River Delta (PRD): PRD Economic Profile. Online. Available at: http://www.hktdc.com/info/vp/a/prd/en/1/1/1/1X06BW84/Pearl-River-Delta--PRD-/PRD-Economic-Profile.htm, last accessed, December 31, 2011.

Macao, Special Administrative Region. 2012. Welcome to the Macao of the People's Republic of China: Macao SARG Portal, Online. Available at: http://portal.gov.mo/web/guest/citizen, last accessed, January 13, 2012.

Manhattan Institute for Policy Research. 2011. The Entrepreneurial City: A How-To Handbook for Urban Innovators. Online. Available at: http://www.manhattan-institute.org/html/ cci_the_ent_city.htm, last accessed, December 31, 2011.

Pacific Century CyberWorks. 2011. PCCW Home Page. Available at: www.pccw.com/eng/, last accessed, December 31, 2011.

Shenzhen, City of. 2011. Shenzhen Government Online. Online. Available at: http://english.sz.gov.cn/, last accessed, December 31, 2011.

CHAPTER 21

Innovation in Europe: A Tale of Networks, Knowledge and Trade in Five European Cities (2002)

James Simmie, James Sennett, Peter Wood, and Doug Hart

This paper . . . seeks to analyze why a minority of European cities are characterized by especially high rates of innovation among the firms located in them. It is particularly concerned to explain what contributions the urban assets and other arrangements in those cities make to innovation. For the purposes of this study, innovation is defined as "the commercially successful exploitation of new technologies, ideas or methods through the introduction of new products or processes, or through the improvement of existing ones. Innovation is a result of an interactive learning process that involves several actors from inside and outside the companies" (European Commission, 1996, p. 54). . . . Innovation is important because: "At the level of the economy, innovation is the single most important engine of long-term competitiveness, growth and employment" (ESN, Brussels, 2000, p. 3).

Early theorists used to view innovation as a more or less linear process. This is no longer the case. There is now general agreement with the view that "innovation is a complex interactive process involving multiple links between new science and technology, potential producers and consumers" (Rothwell, 1991). These multiple, interactive links also change over time according to industrial sector, the types of innovation involved and the timing of economic developments.

Four main groups of theory are identified that seek to explain directly or indirectly the reasons why innovation is relatively con-

centrated in some places rather than others. These groups of theory and their main [scholarly] sources of inspiration are:

1. Traditional agglomeration theory (Marshall, 1919; Schumpeter, 1934, 1939; Hoover, 1937, 1948; Perroux, 1950; Scitovsky, 1954; Vernon, 1966; Jacobs, 1969);
2. Networked and embedded production theory (Coase, 1937; Williamson, 1975; Granovetter, 1985; Becattini, 1990; Scott, 1990b; Storper, 1995);
3. Knowledge economy theory (Schumpeter, 1942; Nelson & Winter, 1982; Piore and Sabel, 1984; Lundvall, 1992; Dosi et al., 1988);
4. New competition and trade theory (Vernon, 1966, 1979; Utterback, 1988; Porter, 1990; Krugman, 1991).

Each of these theories has different starting points and has been supported by case studies in different nations and cities. . . . The hypothesis advanced in this paper is that there are genuine differences in both national and local innovation systems and the ways in which they operate in practice. These differences are reflected in these different theories . . . [and their] related case studies in various countries and cities. We therefore expect to find that different combinations of elements of these theories will offer the best explanation of the nature and working of innovation systems in different cities.

In this paper we seek to investigate [our] hypothesis empirically by selecting a sample of European city-regions that have the highest relative inputs of research and development expenditures as a basis of innovation . . . [and] produce relatively high levels of innovative outputs, at least as measured by their success in winning various awards for innovation (see Figure 21.1). Comparable locally conducted interviews with [159] innovation award winning firms were conducted in 5 out of the 10 most innovative city-regions in Europe: Amsterdam [26 firms interviewed], London [33], Milan [35], Paris [33] and Stuttgart [32].

The analysis of the results of these interviews tells a highly complex story. Its elements include differing national innovation systems; different combinations of reasons why the cities studied are home to relatively high concentrations of innovation; and some support for different explanations of the relationships between innovation and space in different types of city. . . .

ANALYSIS

The results of investigations . . . illustrate. . . . some tentative comparisons and contrasts among the five cities. The results of these analyses are structured around the latter three groups of theory outlined above.

Figure 21.1 Innovative cities in Europe: Amsterdam, London, Milan, Paris and Stuttgart

Networked and Embedded Production Theory

We [begin with an] evaluation of how far the assumptions underlying networked and embedded production theories are supported by our original empirical data, [as] . . . it has provided both a powerful critique of traditional agglomeration theory in so far as it has been applied to innovation, and an important alternative paradigm during the 1990s.

We turn first to an analysis of the evaluation by firms of the relative importance of a selection of 25 reasons why they would choose to locate the development of a new innovation in their particular city-region. Firms were asked: 'In the light of your experiences with the process of innovation how important would each of the following factors be in your decision to set up a new firm and develop an innovation in this region?' Their assessments of the importance of the 25 reasons were simplified into six groups of closely related variables by factor analysis. . . .

In terms of the overall positive importance to innovation within firms, professional and skilled labor combined with business services, transport and communications generally scored highly. Labor, premises and capital, and production and consumption linkages and networks followed these. Social networks and public knowledge, information, training and research provision were usually scored low in importance to innovation by firms. . . .

Two components indicate the importance of elements of the networked and embedded production theories: production and consumption linkages and networks; and social networks. [In our survey], the scores for the importance of the proximity of suppliers were higher for Stuttgart and Milan than they were for Amsterdam, London and Paris. This was some reflection of the differing roles played by local supply networks in the innovation systems of the two regional cities as compared with the three international cities.

Similar relationships [were] seen in the rankings of the importance of other types of collaborators. The scores were higher in Milan and Stuttgart than they were for London and Paris. In Amsterdam there was a higher score for the importance of the proximity of other collaborators than for suppliers. This may reflect the small size of the Netherlands as a whole and the sectoral dominance of the Randstadt Area (Amsterdam, Rotterdam, the Hague and Utrecht, and their surrounding areas) in innovative firms interviewed for this study.

The importance attached to the proximity of customers was more mixed. The highest score was found in Stuttgart, the lowest score was in London. The figures do not show much difference as between the three remaining cities. Therefore, some further unpacking of this analysis was required.

This is begun [by asking] firms to estimate the importance of four specified kinds of contacts for their award winning innovation. All firms attached considerable importance to business networks. These included contacts with customers, suppliers, competitors or business services. It is argued here, however, that these kinds of relationships are a general requirement of engaging in economic activity. All firms must have some business networks in order to operate at all. The key questions from the point of view of networked production theory are who are these relationships with and how geographically confined are they? [Another] key question is whether there is a significant distinction that should be drawn between the role of business networks in the everyday economic activities of firms and their roles in the specific process of innovation.

. . . Firms were asked to rate the importance of different kinds of collaborators for their innovation. [Our findings] show that the most important relationships were with clients and customers. With the exception of Milan, these were all rated more highly than relationships with suppliers. These were rated most highly in Amsterdam and moderately highly in the other four cities. The significance attached to relationships with clients and customers may be a special and general feature of demand led innovation. It tends to support demand-pull theories of the main drivers of innovation, as compared with technology push.

Turning to the locations of suppliers and customers, [our interviews] provide some contradictions to local production network theory. The mean scores by quartile for local suppliers were particularly low for Paris and London. This again confirms previous research in both cities which has shown that local suppliers do not play a significant role in their regional innovation systems. The figures were higher for Stuttgart and Milan, as expected, and even higher for Amsterdam. Even so, on average, this only places them in the 26–50% quartile for use of local suppliers.

At the other end of the locational supply scale the firms interviewed in Amsterdam, Paris and London all rated European suppliers as more important than their local counterparts. The corollary of this was that firms in Milan and Stuttgart rated them as less important than their local suppliers.

These differences in the geographic extent of supply networks, also was reflected in the locations of customers and clients. In all cases these tended to be less local than were suppliers. Thus firms in Milan and Stuttgart rated their national customers as more important than their local ones. This also was the case for the three international cities. Where the firms in these latter cities tended to differ from the two regional cities was in the significance attached to their European and American customers. Amsterdam, London and Paris scored their European customers more highly than did the firms in Milan and Stuttgart. In addition, Amsterdam and London also attached greater importance to their American customers than the firms in other cities did.

What these figures suggest is that networked local production theory has tended to over-generalize the importance of local supplier/customer production net works. This seems to be a function of the kinds of cities that have been selected as case studies to support this theory. The importance of local production networks to innovation systems may therefore be mainly limited to these particular case studies and types of city.

Much less work has been conducted on core metropolitan capital cities such as Amsterdam, London and Paris, even though they have remained major locations for innovation over many decades. The innovation systems in these types of city appear to be more open, less dependent on local suppliers and more international in their orientation than those in regional cities. These differences form the basis of a distinction that may be made between international and regional cities.

Embeddedness is argued to be an important feature of networked production systems . . . Granovetter (1985) argued that that economic activity also was a social phenomenon, [and] that one example of this . . . was the presence and importance of weak social networks in local production systems. The emergence of social networks in our analysis gives some credence to this view. . . . The firms [we] interviewed expressed some support for the view that local, informal social interaction between ex-colleagues and friends contributed to the relationships between innovation and their chosen locations. It was expected that, given their more networked local production systems, the importance of these relationships would be higher in Milan and Stuttgart than the other cities. This, however, was not the case. In practice, the importance of informal social networks to innovation was greater in the more international than the regional cities. These relationships were confirmed in [our interviews which found] that the importance of social contact networks as a source of knowledge was quite low in all cases. . . .

Taken together, these analyzes suggest that the exact nature of the embeddedness on the genesis of innovation varies in different types of city. In the regional cities, with their relatively formal and stronger institutionalized local production networks and linkages, these may supersede informal social networks in importance in their local innovation systems. In the more international cities, with their generally lower reliance on local formal production networks and linkages, less precise and more informal social networks may contribute more to the local culture of innovation and the international orientation of their regional innovation systems. Some of these weak informal social networks may have been built up over time by the more fluid labor markets in the international cities. Where there is more movement between firms, there are more opportunities to build up trails of former colleagues in other firms.

Knowledge Economy Theory

Knowledge and experience are key inputs to innovation as are national systems of innovation (Lundvall, 1992). An important characteristic of successful systems is their ability to acquire and understand new information. Knowledge and experience are required to know where to look for this information and to understand its innovative possibilities once found. Systems that achieve these tasks on a regular basis may be defined as 'learning' systems. These may have national characteristics but there is also growing evidence that there are also regional variations of these national systems.

. . . [Our] data indicate that, for the firms interviewed in this research, the crucial elements of their local learning innovation systems were highly qualified professional experts, skilled manual labor, external general and specialized business services, together with public universities, skills and training providers. The most important elements [of these] were professional and skilled

labor. The presence of both, were judged to be among the most important reasons for locating in specific city-regions in order to innovate. The availability of professional labor was regarded as important by firms in all five cities. The availability of skilled manual labor was also regarded as important in a majority of the cities. This was less the case in Paris and London. This probably reflects their greater degrees of specialization in computer, R&D and business services in the case of Paris, and medical, precision and optical instruments in the London Region. . . . These sectors presumably employ less skilled manual labor than the innovative sectors sampled in the remaining cities . . .

[From our interviews we also discovered] the importance of local recruitment of professional technologists [for innovation]. . . . One of the reasons for the presence of firms in the city-regions studied was the availability of local pools of technologists that could be recruited to work on particular innovation projects. This was the case for all cities with the exception of Stuttgart. This latter exception indicates another special characteristic of that city's learning innovation system. In that city, large companies, in particular, tend to have long-term training policies. Partly as a result of these institutional arrangements, labor tends to be trained, recruited and retained in the same firm for long periods. This long-term perspective towards highly qualified labor reduces the need to recruit new people for each innovation. It also accumulates a lot of specialized knowledge and experience within firms located in Stuttgart.

The importance of being able to retain or recruit highly qualified professional technologists is reflected in the generally high scores given to quality of life factors by firms in all the cities studied. . . . The availability of good housing, schools, leisure facilities, public services and environments were generally regarded [by the firms interviewed] as relatively important reasons for the concentration of labor and innovations in the cities studied. Good schools, the seed of innovation, received the highest overall scores. . . . [This] suggests that public policy makers are right to emphasize the importance of quality of life factors with respect to those locations where innovative activities are particularly concentrated. The reasons for their importance, however, are not so much because they are necessary to retain and attract firms, [but because they are vital to retaining and attracting the] professional and technical labor that is essential for innovation. . . . All of the city-regions studied here are widely regarded as desirable places in or around which to live. This image makes an important contribution to the presence of suitable qualified pools of labor in their regions.

Returning to the significance of knowledge and experience for innovation systems, much of these key ingredients are internal firm resources and represent technology push factors driving innovation. . . . On the other hand, [there were] major external sources of knowledge used in the particular innovation projects studied here. Overall, the highest importance was attached to customers followed by suppliers and experts from other parts of the company group. This signifies the importance of demand-pull as a driver of innovation. Customers were regarded as the most important external sources of knowledge by firms in all of the cities, except Milan. In Milan, suppliers were regarded as more important than customers as sources of knowledge. In Paris, Stuttgart, and London, suppliers were ranked second in importance to customers. In Amsterdam, suppliers were ranked third after customers and experts from other parts of the company. . . .

Generally, the importance of local commercial, professional knowledge providers, external to the firms, was rated lower than those of the customer and production supply chains. . . . With the notable exception of firms in Amsterdam, most local external business services were not rated highly as knowledge providers to innovation. . . . Tech-

nical consultants were rated most highly, particularly in Amsterdam and Milan. . . . Finally, firms attached high importance to public providers of knowledge, information, and training. Some importance [also] was attached to collaboration with universities or other higher education institutes. Academics, however, were regarded as quite important sources of knowledge, and universities as quite important sources of information in the international cities of Amsterdam, Paris, and London. They are both regarded as less important in the regional cities of Milan and Stuttgart. Conversely, firms in Milan and Stuttgart rated the contributions of their local education and training networks more highly than firms in the other three cities.

These figures suggest that the structure and balance of local innovation systems are different in the more international cities as compared with those in the more regional cities. While firms in Amsterdam, Paris and London seem to access high level public knowledge on a more ad hoc project-by-project basis, those in Milan and Stuttgart seem to [have] more systematic and regular linkages with their local education and training systems. This could also reflect the greater choice of public sources of knowledge in the larger cities as compared with the more limited and sectorally tailored systems in the smaller ones. Here size leads to greater variety and to new types of agglomeration advantages connected with the emerging knowledge economy.

New Competition and Trade Theory

Krugman (1991) emphasized the importance of specialization and absolute trading advantages in driving economic growth in successful regions. Turning first to the trading success of the firms interviewed in the five cities, overall, nearly half of the innovations produced by firms that were on the market were exported. The highest proportions of innovations exported were in the international cities of Amsterdam, Paris and London, cities [with long] histories as centers of international trade. The constant coming and going of personnel from other international trading centers makes a major contribution to the cosmopolitan and outward orientation of these cities [making them attractive to innovative creating workers]. Significantly lower proportions of innovations were exported from the more regional cities of Milan and Stuttgart. Although these cities also have international trading connections, they are not of the same level and variety as those of the three capital cities.

[Among] the sample of firms interviewed for this study, there were noticeable degrees of specialization in each of the cities. In Amsterdam, the main specialization was the chemicals, rubber, non-metallic minerals sector; in Milan, television, radio and communications; in Paris, computer, R&D and business services; for Stuttgart, computing and electrical machinery; and in London, medical, precision and optical instruments. What was noticeable, however, was that the more international cities have more minor specializations than the more regional cities. . . . These degrees of specialization were related to the number of possible sectors in which firms may be innovating to acquire absolute competitive advantages. Generally speaking, the more specialized sectors characterized by higher rates of innovation there were in any particular city, the greater the competitive international trading advantages of those cities.

[On the other hand], not only was specialization by sector important to innovation but also the quality of the labor within those sectors . . . The firms interviewed in this study [also believed] that professionally qualified technologists were key contributors to innovation. Such labor has tended to concentrate in the types of city studied here and its preference for such locations was an important reason why they continued to be innovative trading nodes in the global economy.

[According to] Porter (1990), local rivalries and project collaboration between competitors are said to be important in making some regions more competitive than others. Among the firms and cities investigated here, local clustering of competitors is the exception rather than the rule. With the notable exception of firms in Amsterdam, the main competitors for most innovative firms are not clustered in the same locality or region. Overall, more of the firms' main competitors are located either in the U.S. or other European countries than in their home regions. Once again this is more the case in the international cities than the regional centers of Milan and Stuttgart. In addition, as already discussed, the international cities acquire more external knowledge for their innovation from their competitors than the firms in the regional cities do.

This also suggests that international competition rather than local rivalries drive innovation. Therefore, firms located in the more international cities with their more numerous networks and linkages to the international economy gain some locational advantages over firms based in more regional cities. Access to international competitors thus appears to make a more significant contribution to innovation than local rivalries and competitors.

Porter's argument that competitive economic clusters require both best practice global and local supply chains is often misconstrued to refer only to local suppliers. Only the firms [we] interviewed in Amsterdam fulfill this original requirement. They used local/regional suppliers as well as national and international suppliers in the production of their innovations. In this way they were the only firms in the sample that reflect Porter's original conditions. In contrast, suppliers based in Europe and the U.S., were regarded as more important than local suppliers with respect to innovation by the firms interviewed in Paris and London. Conversely, local suppliers were rated as more important than international suppliers by firms in Milan and Stuttgart.

This suggests that few cities meet Porter's argument that regional competitiveness is partially based on the use of best practice suppliers located both within regions and internationally. To some extent the location of suppliers is a result of differences between local innovation systems. There appear to be a number of different pathways to success. The evidence provided by the surveys conducted here [implies] that there are entrepôt systems like that of Amsterdam that are open to both international and local best practice suppliers. These arrangements have the merit of transferring the latest ideas from around the world to local producers and suppliers. This probably helps to prevent lock-ins by introducing new ideas from outside the region.

Secondly, there are international systems like Paris and London. These appear to prefer using suppliers from other advanced economies. They draw in best practice from other international sources and supply a stream of new innovations that way. Such systems do not seem to rely much on the reception or transfer of new ideas from local suppliers. They are mainly oriented outwards from their local regions.

Thirdly, there are local systems in such cities as Milan and Stuttgart. Although the innovation systems in these cities do have international connections, the firms located in them tend to regard local suppliers as more important than those in the other cities studied. As such, they correspond more to local networked production theories than they to Porter's explanation for regional competitive success. This is not too surprising, as cities in Italy and Germany, are among the main case studies cited in support of the former theory.

[Another key] element in Porter's explanation of regional competitiveness is the existence of demanding national and local customers. As already [discussed], in all cities the importance of national customers was rated more highly than local customers by the firms interviewed. With the notable exception of Amsterdam, national customers were rated as more important than either European or, in the case of all cities, U.S. customers.

[This demonstrates] the importance of demand-pull in stimulating innovation. [It] also shows the significance of strong home markets as the basis for innovations that may then achieve export success. London's innovative specializations in, for example, medical instruments and pharmaceuticals, supply many of the needs of markets stimulated by the procurements of the National Health Service. This creates demands that stimulate innovation for a large home market.

Finally, Porter also stresses the importance of local factor conditions to enable innovation and therefore, competitiveness. Governments, particularly in the case of innovation systems external to firms, may create these. These include the publicly provided education and training systems; basic services such as electricity and water; and also transport and telecommunication systems. (e.g., one of the most important pieces of infrastructure for innovation is an international airport). These enabling factor conditions are present to varying degrees in all five cities studied here. The more international of them have the most important international hub airports of Schiphol, Charles de Gaulle and Heathrow. These offer unrivalled European access to other international trading centers in the global economy. This is one of the ways in which the innovative cities studied differ from some of the less innovative and often more peripheral regions in Europe.

CONCLUSIONS

The research reported in this paper started with the hypothesis that there are genuine differences in both national and local innovation systems and the ways in which they operate in space. It was expected that these differences would be reflected in both the relevance of the available theories for explaining the evidence collected, and in the characteristics of that evidence in the five different cities studied. Even allowing for various caveats concerning the nature and size of the samples of innovative firms in the individual cities, the empirical evidence presented largely substantiates these propositions.

The evidence presented suggests that, even among the crème de la crème of innovative European cities, there are significant differences in the ways in which their regional innovation systems are structured and work. A broad distinction may be made between the more international capital cities and their more regional counterparts.

Much of the post-1970s local production network explanations of the relationships between economic activity and space have been built upon the study of regional cities in places like Emilia-Romagna and Baden-Wurttemberg. The evidence presented here has shown that there is some justification in the cases of Milan and Stuttgart for the view that local factors such as suppliers, education and technology transfer institutions do play important parts in the innovation systems of those city regions. Their supplier, producer, and customer chains do seem to extend mainly over local to national geographic space. Consequently, one of the, main reasons for the concentration of innovations in these cities is the importance of the geographic proximity of the various elements of these chains.

Nevertheless, these regional cities also share with the international capital cities the need to attract, recruit and retain highly qualified professional technical labor. This is the key requirement of innovative, knowledge based learning economies. In all five cities the availability of pools of specialists is crucial to their success. The regional cities seem to achieve this mainly by remaining so attractive to their own indigenous labor that it 'sticks', often for life, to the same region. Even the more open capital cities rely heavily on local labor supplies for innovation. This labor, as with the regional cities, often remains in the region primarily for perceived quality of life advantages. At the moment, language differences within Europe also tend to reinforce the commitment of specialists to their limited numbers of national concentrations of innovation. Thus, a major reason for the geographic concentration of local, knowledge-based innovation systems is the relationship between the need for highly qualified professional technical labor on the one hand, and, on the other hand, the combination of economic opportunities and quality of life factors that are attractive to that kind of labor.

Competition and trade are further reasons why innovative firms are located in the five cities. In the case of the competitive advantages of the five cities, these are built first on some distinctive local factor conditions. These include sophisticated education and training systems made up of varying mixes of universities, research establishments, technology transfer institutions and technical training. They also include high-speed and capacity telecommunications systems that frequently have been installed earlier, to higher capacity or that radiate from the cities studied. International airports also constitute an important element in the local factor conditions enabling firms to innovate in these five cities.

These factor conditions are also important in facilitating the supply chains used by innovative firms. In cases these are locally based, but in others they are national and international. Good local factor conditions mean that innovative firms can take advantage of both geographic and time proximity to suppliers. The latter a particular advantage for the international cities as it brings a huge range and variety of possible best practice suppliers within the reach of innovative firms located in them.

Much the same arguments also apply to competitors. The evidence gathered here shows that most of the innovative firms' main competitors were not located in home city region. Nevertheless, much is learned from competitors and knowledge is required of what they are doing. This can also be achieved as a result of the time proximity afforded to competitors by the transport and communication systems, particularly of the international cities in this study.

Demanding customers and clients are among the main drivers of innovation. For most of the firms interviewed in this study, their main customers were located either nationally or in other European countries or the U.S. Local demand as such was not therefore a main reason for the firms to be located in the five cities. Strong national demand, however, for their innovative specializations was important. This influenced their clustering tendencies either because central governments were key national clients or because they could serve both national and international markets from the five cities.

It may be seen from these various reasons for locating innovations in the cities studied that international trading advantages play a major role in all of them. First, the physical ability to trade with suppliers and customers based on competitive local factor conditions is an important advantage. Second, the ability to generate world-class specializations is increasingly important as the basis of the absolute trading advantages needed by first-world economies to compete in the global economy. Third, the concentrations of highly qualified professional and technical labor in the five cities, and some the systems that produce them, form the basis of their positions as knowledge nodes in the international economy. It gives them the ability not only to innovate in ways that are not available without them, but also to scan the international economy and understand the leading edges in their particular specializations.

The innovative and competitive advantages of the five cities are therefore based upon a complex mixture of local, national and international factors. These are combined on the one hand to form their distinctive local innovation systems. No two of these systems are their exactly the same. On the other hand, all five cities are major or important nodes in the international economy. Their abilities to innovate and trade in the global economy are the key to their competitive success.

QUESTIONS FOR DISCUSSION

1. In two or three paragraphs, discuss the major themes and theories introduced in the Simmie et al. chapter.
2. In 1–2 pages, using specific examples from the chapter, explain how the innovative and competitive advantages of the five cities studied by Simmie et al. were based upon a "complex mixture of by local, national and international factors".
3. Now that you have read chapters on World/Global, Nested, and Entrepreneurial Cities, as well as explaining agglomeration theory, in 2–3 pages discuss the major similarities and differences between Simmie et al.'s framework and two of these other theories.
4. Utilizing the 'Further Readings', 'Helpful Web Links', and other sources on the internet, conduct some further research on three other Innovative Cities. Then, in 2–3 pages, write up a report of some interesting facts about those cities to present in class.

FURTHER READINGS

Lambooy, J. 2002. Knowledge and Urban Economic Development: An Evolutionary Perspective. *Urban Studies,* 39 (5–6): 1019–1035.

Simmie, J., ed. 1996. *Innovation, Networks, and Learning Regions?* London: Jessica Kingsley Publishers.

Simmie, J., ed. 2001a. *Innovative Cities.* New York: Spon Press.

Simmie, J. 2002. Trading Places: Competitive Cities in the Global Economy. *European Planning Studies,*10(2): 201–214.

Simmie, J. 2003. Innovation and Urban Regions as National and International Nodes for the Transfer and Sharing of Knowledge. *Regional Studies,* 37 (6–7): 607–620.

Strambach, S. 2002. Change in the Innovation Process: New Knowledge Production and Competitive Cities – The Case of Stuttgart. *European Planning Studies,* 10 (2): 216–231.

HELPFUL WEB LINKS

Amsterdam, City of. 2011. I amsterdam: Portal to Amsterdam. Online. Available at: http://www.iamsterdam.com/, last accessed, December 31, 2011.

Boston, City of. 2011. Welcome: City of Boston. Online. Available at: http://www.cityofboston.gov/last accessed, December 31, 2011.

Greenberg, A. 2010. America's Most Innovative Cities. *Forbes.com.* May 24. Online. Available at: http://www.forbes.com/2010/05/24/patents-funding-jobs-technology-innovative-cities.html, last accessed, December 31, 2011.

Innovation Cities Program. 2011. Innovation Cities Top 100 Index 2011: City Rankings. Online. Available at: http://www.innovation-cities.com/, last accessed, December 31, 2011.

London, City of. 2011. Welcome to the City of London Corporation. Online. Available at: http://www.cityoflondon.gov.uk/Corporation/homepage.htm, last accessed, December 31, 2011.

Milan, Municipality of. 2011. Comune di Milano: Welcome to the Municipality of Milan Website. Online. Available at: http://www.comune.milano.it/portale/wps/portal/CDMHome, last accessed, December 31, 2011. In multiple languages, select English.

Montreal, City of. 2012. Ville de Montreal: Official City Portal of Montreal, Quebec. Online. Available at: http://ville.montreal.qc.ca/, last accessed, January 15, 2012.

San Jose, City of. 2011. Welcome to the City of San Jose. Online. Available at: http://www.sanjoseca.gov/depts.asp, last accessed, December 31, 2011.

Stuttgart Region Economic Development Corporation. 2011. Region Stuttgart. Online. Available at: http://www.region-stuttgart.de/sixcms/sr_home/, last accessed, December 31, 2011.

Tsukuba, City of. 2012. Welcome to Tsukuba, Ibaraki, Japan! Tsukuba City Information, City of Science and Nature. Online. Available at: http://www.tsukubainfo.jp/, last accessed, January 6, 2012.

CHAPTER 22

From World Cities to Gateway Cities: Extending the Boundaries of Globalization Theory (2000)

John Rennie Short, Carrie Breitbach, Steven Buckman and Jamey Essex

Globalization is now the subject of a growing number of books, articles, conferences and even whole careers. . . . While the academic treatment of globalization has produced numerous insights into the workings of global capital, especially as it occurs in 'world cities' like New York, London, and Tokyo, it has tended to neglect the causes and effects of globalization farther down the urban hierarchy. What does globalization mean for people in these smaller cities and how are they involved in directing the process? The work that follows provides a series of seven theorized case studies of cities from around the world to illustrate how globalization works outside the capitals of worldwide finance and banking. The notion of 'world city' is put aside in favor of 'gateway city' to illustrate that globalization is indeed global, taking many forms in many cities. By looking at cities below the top echelon, we seek to broaden the understanding of the globalization/city connection. We want to build upon the notion of gateway city, a term developed by Grant (1999) and Grant and Nijman (2000). We use the term 'Gateway' to refer to the fact that almost any city can act as a gateway for the transmission of economic, political and cultural globalization.

The focus on gateway as opposed to world city shifts our attention away from which cities dominate to how cities are affected by globalization. We also suggest a provisional list of topics that can be considered in this new perspective.

'GLOCALIZATION'

One common model of globalization is as a wave of change sweeping away local distinctiveness. In this scenario, more often assumed than articulated, globalization is a tsunami of change wiping out the uniqueness of localities. However, a more critical view of globalization acknowledges a more complex set of relationships between the global and the local. The local is not simply a passive recipient of single, unitary global processes. Processes flow from the local to the global as much as from the global to the local (good examples are the growth in ethnic cuisines throughout the world and the blending of hybrid cuisines). The city is not simply a passive recipient of global processes. We are eager to move away from the view of globalization as an unfettered phenomenon towards a theory that grounds it in time and space. The term 'glocalization' refers to this more subtle relationship between the global and the local.

In the next sections we present case studies of 'glocalization'. By presenting a range of cities we seek to widen the canvass of globalization/city studies. These case studies help us to lay the basis for a sounder theoretical understanding of the impact of globalization on different cities in the world and for a more profound explanation of the connection between urbanization and globalization. We use a range of cities rather than focusing on world cities that are common in the literature. Their population sizes are shown in Table 22.1. . . . Our case study cities—Barcelona, Sydney, Seattle, Sioux Falls, Havana, and Prague—are not the usual suspects of world city research (see Figure 22.1). [They] are Gateway Cities in that they embody, reflect and transmit processes of globalization.

Sydney

Sydney grew as an outpost of the British Empire, developed as a primate city, and more recently blossomed into a global city. An understanding of Sydney's growth and change allows us to see two things: how pulses of globalization affect one city over time; and the competition between cities for a country's gateway city designation.

The city first became global in 1788, when it was established as a gulag for the British state's overcrowded jails. Previously, many convicts had been dumped in the North American colonies, but the US declaration of independence closed off this possibility. Sydney was a carceral city, an outpost of the British state, its connections more overseas than national. In that sense it has always been a global city.

[During] the 19th century its function broadened, [acting as] an economic node in the British imperial system, [and] the transmission point between the wider world and the interior of Australia, which was being commodified to produce wheat, timber, minerals and a range of primary commodities. These goods were sent to Britain, which in turn sent labor, capital and finished goods. Prior to 1901, Australia was in reality a collection of semi-autonomous states, including

Table 22.1 Gateway Cities Populations

City	Population	Year
Barcelona	1,454,695	1998
Havana	2,175,888	1993
Prague	1,202,552	1998
Seattle	536,978	1998
Sioux Falls	116,762	1998
Sydney	3,934,700	1997

Sources: Compiled by Editor from the United Nations (1999) and U.S Census Bureau (2000)

Figure 22.1 Gateway cities in the world context

New South Wales, South Australia, Victoria, Queensland and West Australia. Each state acted as a separate economic and political unit with its own capital city: Sydney, Adelaide, Melbourne, Brisbane, and Perth, respectively. Although Sydney dominated the state of New South Wales, it was not the only gateway city in Australia. The other cities played similar roles for their respective states. Indeed, throughout the latter half of the 19th century Melbourne could lay legitimate claim to being Australia's dominant city. After the Gold Rush of the 1850s in Victoria, Melbourne's growth was spectacular and it was referred to as Marvelous Melbourne. When the new federal state needed a temporary capital, before Canberra was built, Melbourne was selected. In the period when Australia's globalization hinged around primary commodity production, Melbourne dominated. It housed the economic elite and the headquarters of the commodity companies. Melbourne's claim to being Australia's global city was reinforced when it hosted the 1956 Olympic Games.

In the second half of the 20th century, the competition to be Australia's gateway city was fought between Sydney and Melbourne. Each city represented the hopes and aspirations of their respective state governments, New South Wales and Victoria, as well as private-sector interests. Each city had competing growth machines. But in comparison to the USA, state governments played an enormous role in the growth machine and civic boosterism. Both groups realized that Australia could only sustain one global city, [and] both wanted it to be their city.

Sydney began to pull away from Melbourne in terms of international recognition. While both were approximately the same size (including the outer suburban areas, approximately 4 million for Sydney and 3.5 million for Melbourne), Sydney began to achieve more international visibility. The completion of the Opera House in 1973 gave the city a globally recognized icon; the project

was begun in. When it opened, the Opera House joined the Harbour Bridge in giving the city international recognition with a global signifier.

An economic shift also occurred when Britain joined the European Community in 1973. As part of the entry requirements, Britain jettisoned its old trading relations with Australia and New Zealand. Australia now had to operate in a global market rather than an imperial one, initiating a new round of globalization. In this new round of reglobalization, economic orientation shifted to the Pacific Rim and 60% of Australia's exports now go to Japan. There was also a reconnection with the world financial system as the country is less connected through London. It is in this recent reglobalization that Sydney . . . has emerged as Australia's global gateway city.

The 2000 Olympic Games both embody and reinforce Sydney's position. The preparations for the Games, strongly supported by the State Government, included improvements to the international airport, transport connections between the airport to the city centre and a host of infrastructural improvements. These and other remedial projects will further enhance Sydney's global connectivity.

Barcelona

> The town had a gaunt untidy look, roads and buildings were in poor repair, the streets at night were dimly lit for fear of air-raids, the shops were mostly shabby and half-empty. (Orwell, 1980, p. 6)

George Orwell's 1938 portrait of Barcelona, torn and debilitated by the Spanish Civil War, contrasts sharply with the modern bustling image the city presented to the world at the 1992 Summer Olympics. . . . The jump from the Orwellian world of the war and the Francoist state repression that followed to that of the Olympic Games is no small feat and illustrates the reglobalization of Barcelona and the city's attempts to earn 'world city' status in the past quarter century. The themes of global spectacle and rescaling have marked Barcelona's recent trajectory.

Barcelona was the last Catalan stronghold of political resistance to fall in the Spanish Civil War (1933–1939). Before the war, Barcelona had been the head and home of Catalonia, a region sporting a long history of rivalry with Madrid and Castile. Catalan nationalism had thrived in the decades prior to the civil war, but in 1939, Franco established a fascist state that emphasized Castilian control and Madrid's eminence in Spain. Franco moved quickly afterwards to quash Catalan nationalism, with particular emphasis on repression of the Catalan language.

The globalization of Barcelona since Franco's death in 1975 has much to do with the death ushered in a transition to democratization and decentralization in Spain that allowed regional identities to strengthen and flourish, and the new national constitution gave Catalonia considerable autonomy. Barcelona again openly celebrated and dominated Catalan identity as new political actors took the stage in the region and began to push Barcelona towards its current world city position. Accompanying this assertion of Catalan identity was a further decentralization and democratization of government on the municipal level within Barcelona. The devolution of government to the *barrio* (neighborhood) in Barcelona and its metropolitan area encouraged local initiative, the greening of the city and a strong sense of civic pride and unity, resulting in economic revival, improved public services and metropolitan co-ordination on large projects (Borja, 1996, p. 85).

Perhaps most important to Barcelona's globalization was Spain's 1986 entry into the European Union. Catalonia, with six million people, 21% of Spain's GNP, over a quarter of its exports and a third of its foreign investment, has firmly established itself as a vital component of both Spain and the new integrated Europe (Thomas, 1990, p. A1). Barcelona, as the gateway to a prospering Catalonia, is reaping the rewards of integration and repositioning itself within Spain, the Mediterranean and Europe.

The 1992 [Summer] Olympics offered Barcelona the opportunity to make great changes in its physical appearance as city leaders undertook numerous large urban projects. Montjuic Stadium, the Olympic village and the Macba (Contemporary Art Museum) were accompanied by many smaller urban projects designed to 'green' the city and make it more pedestrian-friendly. . . .

Urban iconography is a powerful component of city representation, and in Barcelona's case the works of Catalan architect Antoni Gaudi epitomize the city's unique culture and distinctive built form. Working in the late 19th and early 20th centuries, Gaudi was a leader in the architectural style *modernisme*, distinctively Catalan and marked by fluid shape, bright color and a highly original feel. Gaudi's architecture is the keystone of Barcelona's urban form. The 1992 Olympics provided an ideal arena in which to celebrate, update and expand this tradition.

The Olympic spectacle and the physical changes accompanying it remain building blocks for Barcelona and the high point of its process of reglobalization. Barcelona's role at multiple scales (Catalonia, Spain and Europe) retains great importance, though Barcelona has yet to reach the world status of other European cities such as London and Paris. The world urban hierarchy can be extremely fluid and Barcelona's place in it is not completely secure.

Prague

The cities of post-Soviet Europe are now important sites of reglobalization into a capitalist global economy. One example [is] Prague and its attempts to build on its rich cultural heritage to become a global tourist centre. The city has played a key role in the European cultural scene. [In additional to its history of diverse architecture, Prague is famous for its classical music and opera houses], including the F.A. Nostitz theatre (later renamed the Stavovske theatre). It was here that Mozart premiered *Don Giovanni* (in 1787) and *La Clemenza di Tito* (in 1791). The city is also well known as the home and burial ground of Franz Kafka.

Some 215 years after *Don Giovanni* premiered in Prague the city was once again recognized by its European neighbors as a cultural Mecca, selected by the European Union Council of Ministers of Culture as a European City of Culture in 2000. This prestigious award [has been] given annually since 1985 to the city that best exemplifies European cultural heritage. The honor has great significance for the city in terms of tourist publicity [and] in shedding its socialist image. Tourism has become an important element in the city's capitalist revival and reglobalization. The increase in tourism retail has had positive and negative implications for the character of the region. Even though residents welcome tourist activity they shun the increase in tourist retail shops in the city centre; nearly half of residents feel that there are too many souvenir shops in the historic core. [In addition], tourists are beginning to feel that they are not seeing the 'real city' or mingling with the locals which is advertised as being Prague's charm (Simpson, 1999).

Prague is now at a crossroads in its reglobalization. On the one hand, the city is experiencing tremendous economic growth through its expanding tourist industry. On the other hand, the influx of tourists is threatening to destroy the type of city which it markets and sells.

Sioux Falls

Globalization is a phenomenon that impacts more than just world cities. Though small and rarely appearing in tables of world cities, Sioux Falls is also a crucible of globalization trends. Sioux Falls has long been the largest city in South Dakota. [It also] is an example of how the idea of a gateway city can be applied to a small-scale regional city.

In recent years, Sioux Falls . . . has been receiving accolades from a range of sources as widely read as *USA Today* and as specific as *Builder Magazine*. Behind these acclaims is a city with a complex range of features that have been managed by city leaders to take advantage of globalization. Understanding how globalization processes have occurred in Sioux Falls requires looking at the structures of business and government as well as at the lives of its citizens.

Urban regimes and strategies of place promotion are among the key tactics cities use to connect with global capital. In Sioux Falls, alliances between the private business community and the local and state government are specifically designed to attract new businesses and residents and to make Sioux Falls more competitive. The Sioux Falls Development Foundation, [has been] a key actor in the city's globalization.

One of the more common activities of cities engaged in the . . . global economy is to enlist the services of a location consultant. The Sioux Falls Development Foundation has retained the services of The Boyd Company . . . in order to [promote] the relative benefits of doing business in Sioux Falls as compared to other American and Canadian cities in the Midwest region. The strategies of the Foundation . . . are clearly paying off financially, since *Site Selection Magazine* named the Foundation-owned Sioux Empire Development Park one of the top 10 industrial parks in the world.

Despite the boosterism, there are segments of the population not benefiting from the growth of the city. In 1998, 432 homeless people were counted in Sioux Falls, 82 more than the previous year. In fact, the number of homeless in Sioux Falls jumped dramatically after *Money Magazine* named the city the best place to live in America in

1992. Conflicts [have occurred] over the use of the downtown, which has been altered significantly by the opening of the Washington Pavilion of Arts and Science in 1999. Making the cultural consumers who visit the Pavilion comfortable, though, means regulating the activities of youth who have a tradition of making use of downtown Sioux Falls by 'cruising the loop'. Ideas suggested by members of the Downtown Task Force, composed of government officials, downtown merchants and residents, include measures to ban cruising and the installation of surveillance cameras on downtown buildings. The changes in the streets of Sioux Falls signal tensions between the small town practices that once defined the area and the ambitions of business and community leaders who want to redefine Sioux Falls as an urban cultural centre.

Sioux Falls' leaders have sought to further define the city as a viable part of the global economy by establishing a US port of entry and a foreign trade zone. The Governor of South Dakota, Bill Janklow, lobbied for these features in Sioux Falls to encourage local business owners to become involved in international trade . . . and to have international deliveries made directly to Sioux Falls, rather through Minneapolis or other larger regional cities.

The case of Sioux Falls illustrates global processes at a small scale. By taking advantage of their location in a low-tax state and by keeping abreast of trends in the economy, the leaders of Sioux Falls have successfully established the city as a gateway to the global economy in the Great Plains region. The city is connected to the global economy through its businesses negotiations and through transactions at the new port of entry and foreign trade zone. For individuals in Sioux Falls, there are new spaces, such as the revitalized cultural downtown, and new scales, such as overcrowded homeless shelters and large corporations [such as Citibank Credit Card Services] that are becoming part of daily experiences. Globalization impacts small cities, as well as world cities.

Seattle

The World Trade Organization (WTO) meetings that took place in Seattle in November 1999 became a scene of massive protest against what critics claimed was an unfettered global capitalism. What was meant to be an economic trade meeting became a global spectacle. As the WTO protest ravaged downtown Seattle, the city itself was embracing the notions of global capitalism.

The WTO meetings were not the first time that the city has hosted a trade conference. During the 1990s city leaders actively sought trade conferences and global events to help highlight the city as a global arena of commerce and culture. Conferences have included the Quadrilateral Trade Ministerial meeting in 1996, the Asia Pacific Economic Cooperation (APEC) summit in 1993, the first US meeting of the North American Free Trade Agreement (NAFTA) in 1990 and in 2001 Seattle will host the Asian Development Bank Annual Meeting. Also in 1990 the city brought together Olympic caliber athletes from around the world to participate in the Goodwill Games.

The city also has an active trade alliance committee (Trade Development Alliance of Greater Seattle) that forms ties with other cities in the region and abroad. The 'Cascadia Region' that Seattle has formed ties with is a 400 mile long, 8 million resident corridor that runs from Vancouver, BC to Eugene, Oregon. It accounts for more than $250 billion in annual output (Harvey, 1996; TDAGS, 2000). In conjunction with regional alliances the city has been an active proponent of international alliances. Over the last 40 plus years an extensive sister city campaign includes 21 sister cities, making it the second largest such effort in the USA. The sister city program helps to establish not only economic but also cultural links between cities.

Companies such as Amazon.com, Boeing, Weyehaeuser, Microsoft, Nordstrom, and Starbucks all have their headquarters in the Greater Seattle region, which contributes to considerable job increases in the area. In turn, Seattle has become a leading centre for advanced technology software, biotechnology, electronics, medical equipment and environmental engineering; the world's software giant Microsoft is just one of 2200 software development firms in the area (TDAGS, 2000).

Starbucks, once a small coffee shop that opened its doors in 1971 in Pike Place Market, has prospered along with the city of Seattle, and is now a global empire that has approximately 2200 stores worldwide. . . . The company is not about merely selling coffee, as much as they are about selling a lifestyle.

While Seattle's exploding global economy has brought many economic and cultural benefits to the area, it has come with a downside. As more and more people have moved into the area, rising housing prices and rates of congestion have become a major concern. Affordable city living has become a thing of the past. For instance from 1988 to 1998, the median sales price of a single-family home in the Seattle Metropolitan Area increased by 86%, compared with a national increase of 46% (Caggiano, 1999).

Along with a massive increase in housing prices, the area has experienced increased traffic congestion. The area's freeways during rush hours have become a bottleneck of cars. This has meant a [long] commute for many who, due to metropolitan prices, must live outside the metropolitan region and commute into the city for work. Adding to the problems is the fact that the city has not implemented an adequate public transit system to cope with the situation (Enlow, 1999).

Yet this [growth is not spreading to] the entire Seattle Region. While Seattle city is booming, Bremerton, just a short ferry ride across the Puget Sound, is on the decline.

Bremerton is a traditional 'blue collar' machinist/navy town that has experienced the downside of Seattle's boom. The same things that have helped Seattle to foster growth such as trade liberalization and the ending of the cold war have had a negative impact on Bremerton through shop/base closings and a loss of good paying 'blue collar' jobs. As with globalization everywhere, the effects have been uneven in spatial and social terms. However, the dominant narrative is of the Seattle of Starbucks and Microsoft rather than Bremerton and expensive housing.

Havana

On 25 January 1998, Pope John Paul II delivered a lengthy open-air Mass to hundreds of thousands of Cubans in Havana's Plaza of the Revolution in which he encouraged Cuba to 'open itself up to the world' while inviting the world to do the same for Cuba (Schwab, 1999, p. 126). Havana's experience in the last decade illustrates its hazardous road toward reglobalization and the dangers of being left out of the world economy. Havana has been a global city since the Spanish founded it in 1519. By the early 17th century Havana had become the primary city in the Spanish Caribbean, serving as the commercial and military pivot of Cuba and the principal node in the trading network connecting Spain with its New World colonies. The sugar boom of the 19th century helped finance extensive urban projects in Havana, particularly during the 1830s under the direction of colonial Governor Miguel Tacón, and by the 1860s urban sprawl forced leaders to tear down the city walls (Segre *et al.*, 1997). Havana expanded rapidly after the Spanish-American War in 1898.

With the influx of American tourists and investment a definite Yankee influence emerged in the newer suburban quarters of the city. The housing stock in Havana's older sections deteriorated rapidly even as new high-rise sprang up in Habana Vieja (Old

Havana) and the city's infrastructure was reoriented for the automobile (Segre *et al.*, 1997). Firmly within the American orbit in 1898, Cuba, especially Havana, was dominated by American investment by the 1950s. Havana became a playground for American tourists and a haven for organized crime. The city remained a colonial entrepot and the principal Caribbean node for an expanding commercial empire, with the USA replacing Spain after 1898.

[With] the Cuban Revolution . . . in January 1959, Havana's global connections [were] altered suddenly and drastically. The Socialist state headed by Fidel Castro established ties to the Soviet Union and its European satellites. Official links to the USA ended as the American embargo against the island took hold. The 'Special Period' that followed the end of the Soviet connection brought to a head the urban problems that had been building in Havana for decades.

In the past decade, Havana has faced many of the same problems confronting other large cities in the Third World. Yet Havana is unique because of the persistence of the Castro Government's open hostility towards the primary channels and attributes of economic globalization. At a January 2000 conference in Havana, Castro labeled the International Monetary Fund (IMF) 'the backbone of the New World Order of Globalization' and the 'executioner' of the Third World (Anderson, 2000, p. 224). Cuba's resistance to traditional Third World links to the world economy meant alternative routes to reglobalization and reintegration had to be found. The desperate search for new global links made the period of economic restructuring in the early and mid-1990s a desperately hard time for Havana.

By the end of the decade, these links had been established in Havana through the growth of tourism and an emphasis on neighborhood improvement. Many analysts predicted that the only solution for Cuba's economic woes would be a lifting of the American embargo. There are signs that the embargo, while still in effect, has weakened. The primary goal of the embargo, the ousting of Fidel Castro, "has been singularly unsuccessful" (Ritter and Kirk, 1995, p. 7). Increased American pressure and attempts to expand the embargo failed as well in the

1990s, and only served to alienate American allies, the United Nations (UN) and other international groups (notably the WTO and OAS) from Washington's position. Furthermore, American economic penetration has not been stopped within Cuba as dollars have flowed into Havana via the tourist industry and Cuban-Americans sending money to relatives at home. In fact, US dollars have been accepted in Cuba as legal currency since 1993 (Putnam, 1999).

Castro's criticism of globalization illustrates another important trend present in Havana's current round of reglobalization. The Cuban state in recent years has identified itself with the Third World, especially Latin America, in reintegrating itself into the world. Castro has realized that Cuba's (and Havana's) place in the world order is inextricably tied to the fate of its neighbors. The economic crises experienced in Southeast Asia brought forth fears from leaders in Havana that Brazil would succumb to economic turmoil next, making Latin America and Cuba equally susceptible to the global dilemma (*The Economist*, 1999). Cuba has tried hard to establish itself as a leader in the Third World, with Havana playing host to numerous international conferences, including the Ibero-American Summit in November 1999 and the UN South Summit, organized by the Group of 77 in April 2000.

The UN has taken a further interest in historic Havana, naming Old Havana, the city's colonial core, a UNESCO World Heritage Site in 1982 (Williams, 1999, p. 38). This and the economic crisis of the 1990s created a widespread interest in the preservation and rehabilitation of Havana's historic districts, a trend that called for the devolution of urban planning and construction to the neighborhood level. These developments have also aided the tourist industry and promoted increased foreign investment in the city.

The Pope's 1998 visit to Cuba marked a watershed in the reglobalization of Havana. The Pontiff's appeal for the opening of Cuba to the world, and the world to Cuba, symbolizes the tensions Cuba's leadership has dealt with in reintegrating itself into the world system after the breakdown of the Soviet alliance.

CONCLUSIONS

This paper has argued that to understand fully the connection between globalization and the city, it is important to extend our understanding beyond the narrow focus on world cities. While the top level of the global urban hierarchy is an important object of consideration, when it becomes the sole focus of globalization, understanding is skewed and partial. Theories of globalization that only build upon the experiences of a few world cities have a precariously narrow grip on the full range of the urban experience, while the search for world cityness dooms a large number of cities to marginality or even exclusion from research on globalization and the city.

We argued that the idea of Gateway City extends the range of theorizing on how globalization takes place. Gateway city is a shorthand term for the idea that many, if not all, cities act as transmission points for globalization and are the focal point for a whole nexus of globalization/localization relationships. . . .

We selected [six] cities ranging in population size from just over 100,000 to almost [four] million, and ranging in world-city measures from relatively high to not even registering. We purposely selected cities that were not on the usual list of world cities and below the top echelon of the global urban hierarchy. Our case studies could have been different, but the general point remains that even small non-world cities can be examined for evidence of globalization. The case studies were brief. Each city could have been the focus of the entire paper. However, they were indicative of the rich possibilities of using the gateway themes and the selected topics. . . .

Globalization is a universal phenomenon that is occurring around the world in a range of cities. By moving beyond the narrow focus on world cities, our understanding of both globalization and the city can only be enriched and deepened.

QUESTIONS FOR DISCUSSION

1. In two or three paragraphs, discuss the main themes in Short et al.'s chapter. Make sure to discuss their view of Global City Theory.
2. List three or four of the factors mentioned by Short et al. as being important influences in city globalizing processes. Then, in 1–2 pages, use the case studies to explain these factors.
3. Now that you have read Abu-Lughod and Short et al., in 2–3 pages discuss some of similarities and differences between their views of the factors affecting major cities.
4. Utilizing the 'Further Readings', 'Helpful Web Links', and other sources, make a list of seven to ten other cities which might be considered Gateway Cities. Then, pick three and write a page about each explaining why you think these cities fit Short et al.'s perspective.

FURTHER READINGS

Lauria, M. 1997. *Reconstructing Urban Regime Theory: Regulating Urban Politics in a Global Economy*. London: Sage.

Short, J. 1996. *The Urban Order: An Introduction to Cities, Culture, and Power*. Oxford: Blackwell.

Short, J. 2004. *Global Metropolitan: Globalising Cities in a Capitalist World*. London: Routledge.

Short, J., Y. Kim, M, Kuus, and H. Wells. 1996. The Dirty Little Secret of World Cities Research—Data Problems in Comparative Analysis. *International Journal of Urban and Regional Research*, 20 (4): 697–719.

Stone, C. 1989. *Regime Politics: Governing Atlanta, 1946–1988*. Lawrence, KS: University of Kansas Press.

Ward, S. 1998. *Selling Places: The Marketing and Promotion of Towns and Cities, 1850–2000*. London: Spon Press.

HELPFUL WEB LINKS

Accra, City of. 2011. Welcome to the City of Accra, Ghana. Online. Available at: http://ama.gov.gh/, last accessed, December 30, 2011.

Auckland, City of. 2012. Auckland Council: Home Page of Auckland, New Zealand. Online. Available at: http://www.aucklandcouncil.govt.nz/EN/Pages/default.aspx/, last accessed, January 11, 2011.

Barcelona, City of. 2011. Felic Barcelona: The Website of Barcelona City. Online. Available at: http://www.bcn.es/english/ihome.htm, last accessed, December 30, 2011.

Den Haag (The Hague). 2012. Home Page of Den Haag, Netherlands. Online. Available at: http://www.denhaag.nl/en.htm, last accessed, January 13, 2012.

Miami-Dade County. 2011. Miami-Dade County, Florida Portal. Online. Available at: http://miami-dade.gov/, last accessed, December 30, 2011.

Prague, City of. 2011. Prague Portal. Online. Available at: http://www.praha.eu/jnp/en/home/index.html, last accessed, December 30, 2011.

Seattle, City of. 2011. The Official Website of the City of Seattle. Online. Available at: http://seattle.gov/, last accessed, December 30, 2011.

Sioux Falls, City of. 2011. The City of Sioux Falls. Online. Available at: http://www.siouxfalls.org/, last accessed, December 30, 2011.

Sydney, City of. 2011. City of Sydney Home Page. Online. Available at: http://www.cityofsydney.nsw.gov.au/, last accessed, December 30, 2011.

United Nations, 2011. *Demographic Yearbook*. New York: United Nations Statistics Division. Online. Available at: http://unstats.un.org/unsd/demographic/products/dyb/dyb2.htm, last accessed, December 30, 2011.

CHAPTER 23

From Modernist to Market Urbanism: The Transformation of New Belgrade (2011)

Paul Waley

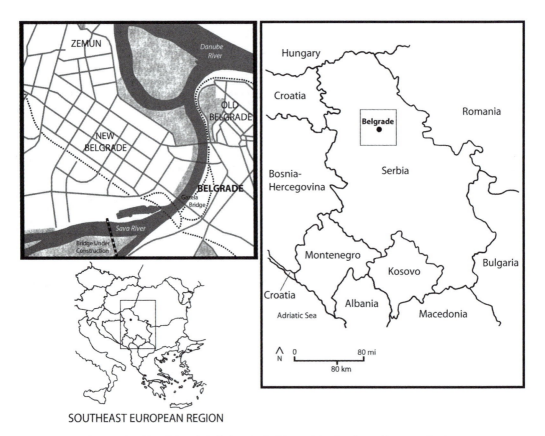

Figure 23.1 New Belgrade in Belgrade, Serbia, and the Southeast European Region

New Belgrade is one of the biggest—if not, the biggest—of the 'new cities' that sprang up on the outskirts of the major urban settlements of Central and Eastern Europe (CEE) during the Socialist period. It is however dif-ferent in a number of important respects from places such as Nova Huta, the steel city that stands next door to Krakow, or Petržalka, the Bratislava district on the south side of the Danube. It was designed with a strategic political intent: to serve as the capital of the Socialist Republic of Yugoslavia. Never really completed, it has become a fascinating landscape testimony to changing concepts and practices in urban design and urban policy over the last sixty years. Today, with its 4,100 hectares (10,000 acres), it is the easily the largest of Belgrade's sixteen districts. A city within the city, its population of about a quarter million would today make it Serbia's third largest urban settlement.

New Belgrade is, in the first place, a paradigm for the meeting of modernism and socialism in urban form and space. It is, secondly and more recently, paradigmatic of postmodern and post-socialist urbanism and of the attendant insinuations of the neoliberal market into modernist urban form and space. It is also, is a "near-anomaly in post-Socialist urban change, showing that prime location and quality of development may beat the grim predictions of some scholars issued during the 1990s that the Socialist districts would inevitably become ghettoes of decay" (Hirt, 2009, p. 30).

Paradigmatic it may be, but it bears notable differences both from Western modernism and Soviet socialist realism. While New Belgrade illustrates patterns of change in the CEE, it does so in extreme ways. And yet, strangely, it has seldom been inserted into histories of modernist and socialist urbanism. Why should this be so? Part of the answer probably lies in the distinctive nature of its genesis, and part in the destructive nature of Yugoslavia's disintegration. Unlike Petržalka, New Belgrade was not intended to be a residential district. Unlike Nova Huta, industry was not its raison-d'être. That it became (largely if not totally) a giant residential suburb is a commentary on the project's lack of economic sustainability— Yugoslavia simply could not afford to realise such an ambitious project. But it was far from ever becoming just another monotonous series of high-rise apartment blocks. The lively architectural ambience that existed in Socialist Belgrade, in frequent contact with devel-

opments in Western Europe and elsewhere, ensured that the new city within a city was changing form and appearance in response to stimuli from elsewhere.

This paper attempts to address some of the ironies and apparent contradictions . . . of New Belgrade, while telling the story of [its] growth and mutations. The paper starts with a discussion of some salient characteristics of socialist cities within which New Belgrade can be set. The main sections of the paper present an account of the development of New Belgrade that juxtaposes transformations in the built environment with a sense of daily lived experiences, setting this within the context of the momentous changes that have affected Yugoslavia and Serbia during this period. In doing so, I will argue for a reading of New Belgrade that emphasizes the nature of the urban landscape as mirror of social change. The very nature of the never-complete New Belgrade, with its large open spaces and broad avenues, has made it particularly prone to the construction of the built landscape of neo-liberal capital. These accretions have multiplied to the point where they now populate nearly all the remaining empty plots, creating thus a patchwork of different styles of urbanism and a highly distinctive record of changing approaches to urban development and urban life. They provide an unusually complete setting from which to explore the broader issues surrounding the nature of modernist and socialist and postmodernist and post-socialist urbanism. It is in this sense that New Belgrade manages to be both paradigmatic and exceptional.

MODERNIST URBANISM, SOCIALIST URBANISM

The first stone for New Belgrade was laid in 1948, the year of the break with the Soviet Union. This is an important pointer to the way the new district developed. Unusually, New Belgrade was both a modernist city and a socialist city, in its adherence to a geometric street plan and in its combination of a separation of functions and provision of services within its housing blocks. Under socialism, urban form and space were seen as ways of shaping and improving society in a direction congenial to socialist ideals, but socialist cities in practice varied enormously. Modernist urbanism was of course predicated on the belief that urban form could be used as a conditioning tool for society.

Discussion of socialist urbanism cannot be conducted in isolation from consideration of the modernist movement. Modernist urbanism has much more readily identifiable and consistent features than does socialist urbanism, while of course lacking socialism's ideological foundations. However, they share a backbone of central characteristics, from which each diverges at various times in different places. These include:

1. A fundamental faith in the centrality of the plan.
2. Functional zoning.
3. A generous use of space. This was made possible in socialist cities as a result of state ownership of land.
4. There was a specific emphasis on the importance of green space.
5. An emphasis on the city as locus for production and widespread provision of land for industry.
6. The use of industrialised and therefore standardised building techniques.
7. A parallel sense of standardised, uniform human life.
8. Large housing estates.
9. Building *ex novo* (from scratch). New cities sprang up from Siberia to Brazil.

New Belgrade incorporates or reflects many of these common features. And it encapsulates a further one: 'Projects in socialist new towns were hardly ever completed'.

In a similar vein, New Belgrade reflects may of the changes that have overtaken CEE cities in the last 20 years including the introduction of a planning regime that is subservient to the dictates of the market and the requirements of international capital and a restructuring of urban areas leading to the development of a central business district and the growth of suburbs and beyond them an urban sprawl.

Market-oriented planning . . . and entrepreneurial urban governance has clearly become the central tenet in Serbia, as it has in the rest of the CEE. Within this model, FDI plays a transformative role. The influx of capital investment from Western Europe and North America, as well as Japan and Korea, has created a new hierarchy of cities, with a rapid development of central cities but under-urbanisation in smaller cities of a newly cast periphery. . . . Corporate regional headquarters, supported by an array of advanced producer services, have already transformed the three largest cities of the CEE countries, Budapest, Prague and Warsaw, and are having similar effects on Moscow.

On the ground, a process of spatial restructuring has occurred as a result of which the cities of the CEE have developed features previously more familiar in the urban areas of western Europe. Alongside the creation of CBDs and the process of suburbanisation have come other phenomena such as the commercialisation and privatization of sites vacated by industry and a growing number of hypermarkets and shopping malls in peripheral areas of large cities. At the same time, the commodification of urban space and the diffusion of extra-legal construction have led to a growing impromptu infill urbanisation, often through the construction of commercial buildings . . . and have triggered socio-spatial segregation.

Yugoslav cities have not been immune to these changes. But many of them have occurred somewhat later or in intensified form as a result of the far more disruptive and retarded nature of transition in the former Yugoslav countries. And, as we shall see, many of these developments are visible in contemporary New Belgrade. However, perhaps because of what is perceived as the exceptional nature of the post-Yugoslav tradition, and with a few exceptions many of which are listed above, consideration of the ex-Yugoslav case has been largely absent from wider discussion.

THE PLANNING AND EARLY CONSTRUCTION OF NEW BELGRADE

New Belgrade occupies what was once a highly strategic site between two rivers, the Danube and the Sava, and between two empires, the Ottoman and the Austro-Hungarian. Plans for construction of a new settlement on the marshes between the existing settlements of Belgrade and Zemun had existed during the first incarnation of the Yugoslav state, in the 1920s and 1930s. The 1923 Master Plan for Belgrade envisaged the construction of neo-baroque avenues and boulevards, but all that materialised on the far bank of the Sava was Belgrade Fairgrounds, which was later transformed by the occupying Nazis into an extermination camp.

The destruction of about one-third of Belgrade during both German and allied air raids in the Second World War and the establishment of a socialist republic with its capital in Belgrade gave a new impetus and significance to the idea of constructing a federal capital outside the existing urban settlement. A series of plans were announced for New Belgrade in the 1950s, after a hiatus caused by the break with Moscow and the many associated disruptions. . . . The plan that was finally adopted was . . . designed around a central axis, running from the federal executive building to the station, which consisted of buildings with commercial, cultural and recreational functions, built around a central open space. Plans to include federal government ministries along this central axis were dropped during the 1950s.

While this plan was never realised, three landmark buildings were completed in New Belgrade, mitigating what was otherwise to become an exclusively residential landscape. The most significant of the three was the Federal Executive Council Building (Savezno Izvršno Veće, known to all as SIV) (see Figure 23.2). . . . The resultant building presents itself as an unusual compromise between two

Figure 23.2 New Belgrade's Federal Executive Council (SIV) Building

Source: Waley (2011, p. 215).

prevalent contemporary tendencies, the one modernist, light and clean, suggesting the lines and forms emanating from Brasilia, the other, perhaps less visible on the exterior, the vernacular references of a classicised modernism. While this building is very much one of a kind, the second of the three landmark buildings, the CK building, housing the Central Komitet (Committee) of the League of Socialists of Yugoslavia materialised in the end in the guise of a fairly standard internationalist modernist office block, showing the clear influence of Mies van der Rohe. It dominated its environs, allowing for all-round observation, fittingly, one might argue, for the headquarters of the Central Committee of the League of Socialists.

While the CK building was placed in a prominent position at the entry point to New Belgrade for those crossing the river from the old city, a third landmark, the Hotel Jugoslavije, was located more discretely on the banks of the Danube on the far (west) side of the Federal Executive building (see Figure 23.3). The Hotel Jugoslavije, built over a number of years between 1947 and 1961, as a prestigious riverside lodging for visiting foreign guests. These three buildings were the only completed expressions of New Belgrade's assumed role as federal capital. They were, however, to be joined by others, regardless of the quickly aborted plans to build government offices along the central axis. Foreign embassies were to be encouraged to move to New Belgrade, and, while several were reported to be considering a move, only the Chinese government . . . moved its embassy to this bank of the Sava. In addition, there were plans to locate a number of museums and other cultural buildings in New Belgrade, on land near

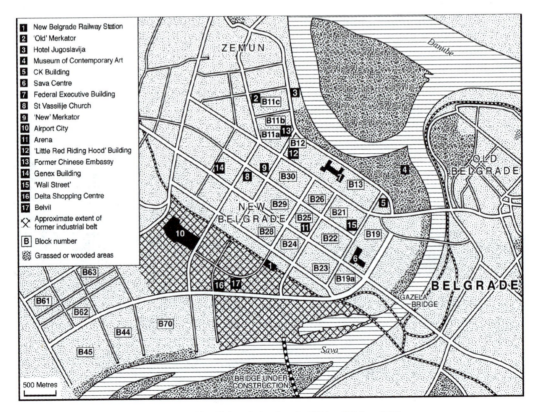

Figure 23.3 New Belgrade landmarks (Waley 2011, p. 216)

the confluence of the Sava and the Danube next to the CK building. Of these, only one was completed, the Museum of Contemporary Art. A Museum to the Revolution of the People of Yugoslavia was to have been built there too, but work was abandoned in the 1970s with only the foundations built.

BUILDING LIVES IN NEW BELGRADE

New Belgrade was built on marshlands that flooded every spring and autumn, and the initial work of preparing the terrain was very hard. Eight million cubic meters of sand from the Sava and the Danube was laid over the terrain to bed it down. The work was done without proper equipment but with much genuine enthusiasm, especially on the part of the thousands of youth brigade members from all over Yugoslavia who took part. Lacking specialist machinery, most work was done by hand. Contemporary accounts are cast very much in the idiom of the triumph of civilisation and the human will over the forces of nature, represented by the treacherous marshy terrain.

New Belgrade was laid out, in true Corbusian style, in orthogonal matrix blocks, 300 meters square. In this it adhered closely to the 1957 General Urban Plan. The vast extent of the planned new part of Belgrade led inevitably to a permanently unfinished appearance, an impression reinforced by the fact that construction of apartment blocks had started on the furthest side of the district from Belgrade, preceded by work on blocks closer to the Sava and the old city. In the middle, the three central blocks remained empty. With the Danube to the north, Zemun to the west and the Sava and beyond it central Belgrade to the east, a large swath of land to the south was earmarked for industrial purposes. A power station, shipyards and machinery factories eventually filled some of this area, but a steelworks located there early on was bankrupted in the 1970s. Perhaps the single largest departure from a 'pure' Corbusian approach was the construction in the 1970s

and 1980s of massive apartment blocks on the far side of the industrial zone, in Blocks 61, 62 and 63 (again, see Figure 23.3). This was a clear move away from a more sensitive—and expensive—modernism towards the technocratic monumentalism of socialist urbanism.

The huge scale of New Belgrade made it a very expensive enterprise, and it was not possible to rely long on the enthusiasm of youth brigades. Contributing to the expense was the lavish choice of materials, both inside and out, and the care given to the configuration of buildings in the blocks. But, as with so many Yugoslav development plans, such expenses were only made possible through centralized funding predicated on loans from abroad. But if the state controlled the whole process of construction, at a local level there was a degree of experimentation with community organizations. In the various plans of the 1950s, New Belgrade was laid out along lines similar to the Soviet *raion* and *mikro raion*, community structures for new housing estates. These were implemented as residents associations. These later developed into the *mesne zajednice* (wards or local communities below the municipal level) alongside reforms of national systems of government which introduced throughout Yugoslavia the concept of self-management). In line with Soviet planning prescriptions, each block was to have a number of community facilities, including a post office, nursery, elementary school and supermarket as well as sufficient green space and playgrounds. These were to be centrally placed, with residential buildings aligned around them.

New Belgrade had originally been planned to become the federal capital for the new Yugoslavia. It is ironic then, that with the exception of a few isolated landmark buildings, it became a giant residential suburb. It is also ironic that this residential suburb came to incorporate a fairly distinct hierarchy. The best housing was to be found in the central blocks located on either side of New Belgrade's empty axis. These were allocated to employees of various federal ministries and agencies and of the military, according to the Yugoslav system of 'socially owned property', where state institutions and companies invested in housing for their employees.

If New Belgrade can be seen as a space that was, in the end, hierarchically organised, it also enshrined an important sense of being representative of the whole of Yugoslavia. The system of balances that existed meant that top federal military and civilian officials needed to reflect the national composition of the whole country. The residents of the more central blocks were as a consequence drawn from all over the country. New Belgrade was considered to belong to the people of all Yugoslavia, while old Belgrade on the other side of the Sava River was the home of residents of the city of longer standing.

Perhaps the dominant impression that New Belgrade conveyed was one of open space and incompleteness. The very center of New Belgrade was an open space, Block 26, on the axis between the SIV and the railway station. The land between the blocks and the rivers, in which the Museum of Contemporary Art still stands, never really fulfilled its potential as park land. The station remained marginal within the country's transport network, little more than a suburban stop, and the blocks by its entrance were undeveloped. Cultural facilities were planned but not built. Schools and shops were insufficient. The sense of incompleteness was reinforced by certain responsiveness to changing architectural ideas, both within Yugoslavia and beyond, and buildings, arguably creating thereby an urban landscape that is anything but static. . . . As if to emphasise the unfinished nature of New Belgrade, what should have been one of the most prestigious spaces, along the Sava, was occupied, as a result of tenancy rights contracted with one of the big state-owned companies, by small, self-built rural-style houses, many of them inhabited by Roma (Gypsies).

THE WIDER FRAMEWORK OF CHANGE IN SERBIA

War and the deprivations that coloured the lost decade of the 1990s greatly exacerbated living conditions in Belgrade and throughout Serbia. Sanctions only served to strengthen the grip on power of Slobodan Milošević and those around him, who had monopolistic control of many strategic commodities. The opposition to Milošević and his Socialist Party was always strong, but he managed, ruthlessly, to control and suppress it. Serbia (at the time, part of residual Yugoslavia) became a highly centralized country, with all the key levers of political and economic power under the control of the Socialist Party and its lackeys. A country that had become decentralized to the point of no return now became suffocatingly centralized. Planning in Belgrade became inevitably centralized.

In some ways the transition in Serbia has followed patterns set in other CEE countries. In other ways, Serbia has very much followed its own path (or, perhaps, a specifically Western Balkan path), characterised by what is generally known as a blocked, prolonged delayed transition, caused by war and authoritarian government. Both these divergent interpretations can be seen reflected in housing policy and housing conditions in the 1990s. On the face of it, housing privatization bore much in common with other transitional CEE countries. It was conducted rapidly and ruthlessly, but this very rapidity and the political calculations that lay behind it set Serbia apart. Housing privatization was conducted so as to solidify the grip on power of the ruling elite around Milošević. As little as between 2 and 5 percent of housing, she points out, was left in public hands by 1993. Those who benefited principally, alongside the political elite, were urban dwellers, and in particular professional, managerial and other members of the middle class. "Housing privatization acted as a shock absorber that gave impoverished middle class households the impression that they were not among the 'losers' in the transformation" (Djordjevic, 2004, pp. 100–101). Flats were released to tenants at a third of their market value on highly favorable loan terms. But this extent of privatization was highly inappropriate for a country as poor as Serbia, in which, once a period of raging inflation had been overcome, salaries were low when they were paid at all and prices remained very high.

The 1990s saw a decline in legal housing construction. At the same time illegal construction of housing continued apace, as more and more people were pushed into the black market to meet their housing needs. An estimated 10% of housing stock in Belgrade is illegal, representing over 40,000 separate buildings. . . . Illegal construction was generally a problem of the old city. In the apartment blocks of New Belgrade, maintenance was the problem in the 1990s for those who had recently purchased the apartments in which they lived. The country for which New Belgrade had originally been conceived as a capital was falling apart around them, and there was little available for the upkeep of the buildings themselves and their surrounding land. In a number of blocks, permission was granted for the construction of small apartments on the roofs of buildings whose occupants would be contracted to undertake maintenance tasks. The experiments appear to have been less than successful. Elevators ceased to function, and rubbish chutes became blocked. The centralized heating systems failed. Established residential communities were disrupted and dispersed by the war, as they were in some areas by the privatization process. Refugees from Croatia and Bosnia moved into apartments, especially in the massive southwest bocks, and there was a rise in drug-related crime in a number of areas (the two developments seen by many as being linked). Then, at the end of the 1990s, the coup de grace was delivered by NATO bombs. A number of landmark buildings were damaged in the bombing campaign of 1999, notably the CK building, which had been appropriated by Milošević's Socialist Party. The top storeys of that building, an obvious target, were severely damaged, and were subsequently removed entirely when the building was renovated. Meanwhile, perhaps the most infamous casualty of the NATO bombing was the Chinese Embassy, damaged beyond repair by a bomb that had apparently been intended for a different target.

THE CONTEMPORARY PLANNING FRAMEWORK IN SERBIA AND ITS CAPITAL

Milošević's regime was finally deposed in October 2000. From then on, Serbia's trajectory followed a path more similar to that pursued by other CEE countries, albeit with a number of distinctive characteristics. For those who envision a fairly predictable 'transition' away from socialism towards western European welfare capitalism, Serbia certainly presents some difficulties and ambiguities. Not least of these involves planning regulation and the ownership of urban land, where Serbia has occupied an ambivalent place somewhere between state and market. Planning itself remains dominated by a technocratic approach, with a focus on the provision of physical infrastructure.

The principal piece of post-2000 legislation has been the Planning and Construction Act of 2003, which lays out various measures introduced over several years in a somewhat tortuous process. This crucial legislative act was designed to lead the way to the private ownership of urban land. It has, however, been widely criticised for turning its back on participatory, integrated planning and for a restricted interpretation of the role of planning. A revised version of the law, which was passed in September 2009, leaves important procedures open to interpretation. Thus, a number of questions remain concerning the establishing of monetary value for usage rights as well as the current value of urban land. And it has obfuscated rather than clarified various anomalies and grey areas: it fails, for example, to provide a definition of the public realm, leaving it unclear as to whether developers should also be made to install infrastructure. The law covers several other important issues; for example, it introduces various measures that facilitate the legalisation of illegal constructions. The law is designed above all to harmonise planning, construction and property ownership with EU norms.

A main issue tackled by the legislation is the conjoined one of ownership and restitution of urban land. Urban land in Serbia is owned by the state, but in the case of Belgrade, including New Belgrade, the national government delegates responsibilities to the Belgrade municipal government. To complicate matters, in New Belgrade, large old state-owned companies occupy important blocks and have tended to act as if they were owners of the land. In a system not at all dissimilar to that which exists in China, property users pay a 'use fee'—in effect, a lease—to the state. This lease, which had reached quite a high level in New Belgrade in 2008, covers the total potential floor space on new build and thus encourages vertical construction; what is more, floor area ratios can be raised if a case is made to the city assembly.

Compared with the rest of Belgrade, urban development is much easier in New Belgrade because interested parties know that issues of restitution do not exist. New Belgrade has, indeed, seen the lion's share of development projects in the first decade of the 21st century. Almost all the empty plots in New Belgrade have been leased, and the rest have been earmarked for development. However, New Belgrade, like the rest of the city, presents various drawbacks for property investors. These relate to the various obstacles and bureaucratic hurdles that are placed in front of developers; it has taken longer to obtain construction permits in Serbia than in most other countries in the world, and there have been more of them to be obtained. In this context, it remains to

be seen how effective the new legislative measures will be. The lack of transparency and excess of bureaucracy in this process is recognised by the government in Belgrade, and the new Law on Planning and Construction is designed in part to speed up this process, although relevant changes will also have to be implemented at the municipal level.

While the ambiguities that have clouded the regulatory environment have put off many investors, others appear to have been attracted by the possibility of making considerably greater profits than would be possible in a more tightly regulated and transparent market. A steady rise in property prices in the mid-2000s, saw the price of residential property in New Belgrade reach €2,000 per square meter ($263 per square foot). The 'purchase' price of a lease on newly built property lagged behind, so that even when the per-square-meter cost of construction was thrown in, a clear profit was accrued for developers. It is interesting to note that many investments in the property market in New Belgrade over the last decade have come, as well as from domestic and foreign-based Serbian interests, from the wider Southeast European Region (understood here as stretching from Austria to Greece), with the important addition of Israel.

Slovenian investors were the first in, as they were familiar with the system of state ownership of urban land, and they reaped the initial benefits. Greek and Israeli interests are active in a number of sites in New Belgrade, most notably in the central Block 26. Conversely, Turkish investors, responsible for a significant number of construction projects in Moscow, while reportedly keen to work in Serbia, have been put off by the regulatory environment and high prices.

The political climate through the first decade of this century was not uniformly favorable for foreign investments, as the prevailing mood lurched between a defensive nationalism and a more outward-looking liberalism. Nevertheless, the wide open spaces that remained in New Belgrade at the turn of the century were tempting targets. The unfinished nature of the terrain appeared to be inviting investments. There were plenty of positive factors for the boosters to draw upon. These included Belgrade's central position in southeastern Europe and its location at the crossroads of two European transport corridors (7 and 10) . . . The talk of the town towards the end of the decade was all about Russians buying property in Montenegro, and the nouveaux riches of Montenegro buying up property in New Belgrade. The economic downturn of the last years of the decade only really impacted on property development in Belgrade in 2009, but there is no special reason to believe that construction work will not pick up again in the following few years. . . .

THE PATTERNS AND TENOR OF LIFE IN NEW BELGRADE TODAY

Today's New Belgrade is characterised by ever greater differentiation, a catastrophic deterioration of public space, unplanned development, and growing socio-spatial fragmentation. In trying to pick one's way through these various interpretations, one should be mindful of the variety of housing types (existing already by the end of 1980s) which have led, inevitably perhaps, to differentiated neighborhoods. The almost total privatization of housing in New Belgrade (as elsewhere in the city) has contributed to the differentiation between blocks. But at the same time, it has reinforced a district-wide socio-spatial patterning. Flats in central blocks have risen in price, some of them quite steeply, while in more peripheral blocks, a much more uneven pattern of occupation has arisen, with many flats rented out on the private market. This contrast is borne out by surveys [chronicling] wide variations in perceived safety between residents of New Belgrade's central blocks and its more peripheral ones. . . . The very earliest blocks, dating from the 1960s, have begun to look rather shabby, while the architectural and design pedigree of the central blocks of the 1970s remains

strikingly visible. On the one hand [are] mega blocks of the district's southern reaches followed in short order by a much more varied constellation of housing styles, including some very well designed low-rise housing near the Sava River and a widespread and ever-growing infill of more recent housing, culminating in the huge Belvil development, constructed for the 2009 Student Games, and then sold off to the private sector.

Amidst this rather unlikely diversity, three types of residential environment can be identified: prestige, modernist and peripheral. Apartments have become extremely expensive (compared to average income levels) throughout the central blocks of New Belgrade, but the buildings that have a special cache as the residences of the rich are those of recent construction, such as in the Little Red Riding Hood and Belvil developments. However, apartments are expensive throughout much of the central blocks of New Belgrade. For example, in the early 1990s, at the time of privatisation, an apartment in Block 30, in the center of the district, cost roughly 4,500 DM (about £1,500 or $2,125 at the time. In 2008, apartments in the same block were selling for €150,000 to €200,000 ($212,500 to $283,000), with a minimum price of €70,000 ($99,000) for one of the smallest apartments. The average was €2,000 per square meter ($263 per square foot), while across the road in the block containing the Little Red Riding Hood building, the average cost of a square meter was €3,500 ($460 per square foot).

The second type is the modernist apartment building, a feature of the central blocks of New Belgrade. The finest examples, in Blocks 21–23, have generous windows with wooden shutters, recessed balconies, and richly profiled facades. In addition, these central blocks still have central spaces that contain various communal amenities—shops, post offices, playgrounds, football and basketball courts, etc. For the most part, these spaces are reasonably well maintained, certainly nothing like the bleakness and anomie that one associates with socialist new towns in the CEE. . . . The neighborhood associations still exist, although no longer as social meeting places but as administrative, locally based offices of the New Belgrade government. . . . There are however now fewer residential associations in New Belgrade—eighteen in all—meaning that each association covers several blocks and a large number of residents. Each building has its own residents' organizations, but unlike the president of the neighborhood associations who receives a salary from the local government, officials are unpaid, and therefore the organizations, are not always as effective as they might be. Given the size of the buildings and the fact that there are many elderly residents who have been there since the days of Yugoslavia, difficulties arise in organising and financing maintenance.

The third category is that of peripheral residential environments, found in particular in the southwestern extension of New Belgrade. These blocks, which vary between huge prefabricated concrete slabs and more amenable buildings closer to the river Sava, were completed after the central and northwestern blocks, and built for a different type of resident: ordinary low-income people, many of whom worked in the old city on the other side of the river. With the disintegration of Yugoslavia and the economic and political disruption that ensued, a breakdown of social norms occurred throughout Yugoslavia, especially in its capital. In New Belgrade this manifested itself predominantly in the harsher environments of the monolithic blocks and surrounding spaces of the southwestern part of the district. Drug-use became widespread, and poverty and dislocation created a sense of fragmentation.

It was against this background of an already degraded environment that an influx of Chinese occurred, the 'beneficiaries' of an open visa regime negotiated by the Chinese and Yugoslav governments. One particular area within New Belgrade, in Block 70, became the basing point and distribution center for Chinese commercial undertakings throughout the Balkans. The presence of a relatively large number of Chinese at a time of great economic hardship produced reactions that ranged between bewilderment and hostility. The Chinese, however, remained, and today, there are many signs that their presence is accepted and in some quarters welcomed. A much older community in New Belgrade is that of the Roma, a settlement lying under the Gazela Bridge which crosses the Sava River. Roma living there were making money through recycling, but were moved out and dispersed in the summer of 2009 to make way for the reconstruction of the bridge. This was just the last of numerous attempts to remove the settlement and re-house its inhabitants.

Despite its social fragmentation, New Belgrade remains a district of choice for a significant number of people. Undoubtedly one of the main reasons is its proximity to the Sava and Danube Rivers. The Sava, in particular, is lined with bars and cafés which are particularly popular with people from both banks of the river. The ability to sit on a barge on the river sipping a drink is an amenity the like of which is not to be found in many other large European cities. In addition, the residents of New Belgrade have about 25 square meters of green space per capita (269 square feet), as opposed to an estimated seven to eight square meters in the old city (86 square feet). There are of course issues and problems. The large expanse of parkland near the confluence of the Sava and the Danube, part of which was formally designated Friendship Park, is sorely in need of maintenance. The same can be said of many of other green spaces within blocks. The lack of car parking is already a significant problem and likely to worsen. The lack of bridges – a situation only being remedied now – leads to traffic congestion and overcrowded buses crawling back and forth across the Sava to old Belgrade. In the end, however, there are plentiful signs that New Belgrade remains an attractive residential choice for many of the inhabitants of Belgrade.

CONCLUDING THOUGHTS

New Belgrade might have been built according to classic modernist prescriptions, but it is testimony to the rapid change in ideas, styles and the technology of residential architecture. There are prominently located parts of New Belgrade where modernist apartment blocks give way suddenly to housing from the 1980s, 1990s and 2000s, with coloured wall panels, curved corners and sloping roofs, very different in spirit and style from the natural concrete, wooden frames, and strong lines of the modernist buildings. Away from the center of New Belgrade, the purer spirit of the plans of the 1960s and the buildings of the 1970s have been replaced by an approach that is more functional in certain areas while more eclectic in others, with little attempt to provide community structures and no investment in high-quality materials and design. Here, open spaces along the main thoroughfares have been absorbed by kiosks, small businesses and larger commercial outlets. In the former industrial belt that divided the 'old' center of New Belgrade from the massive apartment blocks built to the south, large commercial and housing projects are being completed, on the plots left vacant by departing industries.

Despite being such a large-scale and thorough example of socialist modernism, there have been no attempts to date to preserve any part of New Belgrade, although there is support for the idea in some quarters. This lack of interest stems no doubt from three factors: the failings of modernist urbanism, the shortcomings of socialist urbanism, and the collapse of Yugoslavia. Modernist urbanism calls for a sense of completeness. . . . Construction work in parts of the district had already departed from the prescriptions of modernism by the 1980s. The shortcomings of socialism were manifested both in failures of management and of equity. The scale of the project put it beyond the resources of Yugoslavia's socialist government, while on the ground the inability to secure a sufficient supply of housing led to the construction of monumental apartment blocks that lacked the architectural quality and communal facilities of earlier blocks. Although the plan to locate the federal ministry buildings there was abandoned very early, New Belgrade was seen by its residents as Yugoslavia's, as opposed to Serbia's, old Belgrade. Residents of the older blocks worked in the armed forces and national ministries and so by definition came from all over the country. When the country itself collapsed, so too did the belief in the transformative power of New Belgrade. It would be highly misleading however, to suggest that the district is decaying or moribund. On the contrary, the vigorous construction projects that have filled empty spaces in the district and built new infrastructure, including bridges, suggests that the district Belgrade is likely to become one of the leading centers for business activity in Southeast Europe. One can only regret that this is happening with little regard for the possibilities of preserving, if only in some of the more central blocks, a sense of the modernist urbanism of which New Belgrade is such an egregious example.

QUESTIONS FOR DISCUSSION

1. In two or three paragraphs, discuss Waley's major themes and conclusions related to New Belgrade.
2. In 1–2 pages, provide specific examples from his chapter explaining Waley's main themes and conclusions.
3. Now that you have read Friedman, Sassen, Hill and Fujita, and other chapters, in 2–3 pages discuss whether Global City, Nested City Theory, or some other theory

best helps understand recent developments in New Belgrade. Use examples from the chapter and other chapters to help illustrate your points.

4. Utilizing the 'Further Readings', 'Helpful Web Links', and other sources, conduct some further research on Belgrade and another post-socialist capital city-region in southeastern Europe. Examples include: Bucharest (Romania), Ljubljana (Slovenia), Sarajevo (Bosnia & Herzegovina), Sofiya (Bulgaria), or Zagreb (Croatia). Then, in 2–3 pages, write up some of the most interesting facts you discovered on the two cities and present them to class.

FURTHER READINGS

Hamilton, F., K. Dimitrovska Andrews, and N. Pichler-Milanovic, eds. 2005. *Transformation of Cities in Central and Eastern Europe: Towards Globalization*. Tokyo: United Nations University.

Hirt, S. 2000. Belgrade, Serbia. *Cities, 26* (5): 293–303.

Petrovic, M. 2001. Post-socialist Housing Policy Transformation in Yugoslavia and Belgrade. *European Journal of Housing Policy,*1 (2): 211–231.

Vujosevic, M. and Z. Nedovic-Budic. 2006. Planning and Societal Context: The Case of Belgrade, Serbia. In S. Tsenkova and Z. Nedovic-Budic, eds., *The Urban Mosaic of Post-Socialist Europe: Space, Institutions and Policy*. Heidelberg: Physica-Verlag, pp. 275–294.

Vujovic, S. and M. Petrovic. 2007. Belgrade's Post-socialist Urban Evolution: Reflections by the Actors in the Development Process. In K. Stanilov, ed., *The Post-Socialist City: Urban Form and Space Transformation in Central and Eastern Europe after Socialism*. Dordrecht: Springer, pp. 361–384.

Waley, P. 2002. Moving the Margins of Tokyo. *Urban Studies,*39 (9): 1533–1550.

HELPFUL WEB LINKS

Airport City Belgrade. 2011. Airport City Belgrade. Online. Available at: http://www.airportcitybelgrade.com, last accessed, December 29, 2011.

Athens, City of. 2012. Home Page of the Municipality of Athens, Greece. Online. Available at: http://www.cityofathens.gr/en/, last accessed. January 11, 2012.

Belgrade, City of. 2011. Beograde: Welcome to the City of the Future in Southern Europe. Online. Available at: http://www.beograd.rs/cms/view.php?id=220, last accessed, December 29, 2011.

Blagojevic, L. 2004. New Belgrade: The Capital of No-City's-Land. *Art-e-fact*. Online. Available at: http://artefact.mi2.hr/_a04/lang_en/theory_blagojevic_en.htm#_ednref16, last accessed, December 29, 2011.

Bucharest, City of. 2011. Bucharest: Local Administration. Online. Available at: http://www1.pmb.ro/pmb/index_en.htm, last accessed, December 29, 2011.

Ljubljana, City of. 2011. Welcome to Ljubljana: The Capital City of Slovenia. Online. Available at: http://www.ljubljana.si/en/, last accessed, December 29, 2011

Sarajevo, City of. 2011. Welcome to the Official Sarajevo Website. Online. Available at: http://www.sarajevo.ba/en/, last accessed, December 29, 2011.

Serbia, Government of. 2011. Welcome to the Official Web Site of the Serbian Government. Online. Available at: http://www.srbija.gov.rs/?change_lang=en, last accessed, December 29, 2011.

Sofia Municipality. 2011. Welcome to the Official Web Site of Sofia Municipality! Online. Available at: http://www.sofia.bg/en/index_en.asp, last accessed, December 29, 2011

Zagreb, City of. 2011. City of Zagreb: Official Website. Online. Available at: http://www.zagreb.hr/default.aspx?id=1979, last accessed, December 29, 2011.

CHAPTER 24

Collaborative Regionalism and FDI Growth: The Cases of Mississippi's PUL Alliance and Alabama–Georgia's Auto Valley Partnership (2013)

A.J. Jacobs

Over the past 20 years, inter-local competition has become especially fierce, as globalization has expanded the battlefield beyond regional and national borders. This particularly has been the case in battles for prestigious Foreign Direct Investment (FDI), such as motor vehicle assembly plants. Communities within the Southeast Automotive Core (SEAC), encompassing Alabama, Georgia, Mississippi, South Carolina, and Tennessee, have proven especially adept in this environment, attracting of eight of the eleven light vehicle assembly plants built by foreign motor vehicle manufacturers (i.e., the 'New Domestics') in the USA since 1994 (see Figure 24.1).[1] Such success certainly merits closer examination.

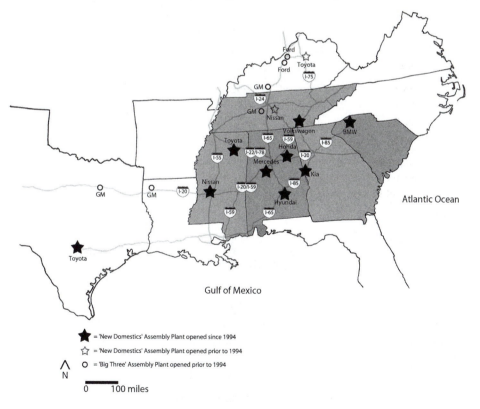

Figure 24.1 The Southeast automotive core

Although their large incentive giveaway packages and right-to-work laws have received the most coverage in the scholarly discourse, right or wrong, as Karl Polanyi (1957 [1944]) would have predicted, the primary purpose of SEAC market interventions has been to improve the economic well-being of their citizens, among the least affluent, nationally. As shown in Table 24.1, between 1969 and 1999 (i.e., the 1970 and 2000 Census), with the exception of Georgia, the five SEAC states have consistently ranked in the bottom-third nationally in Household Income (HHI) and Per Capita Income (PCI); Census estimates for 2009 suggest Georgia's HHI and poverty rate. What has been especially unique and significant since the 2000s, at least in parts of the SEAC, has been that local areas have come to realize that *collaborative regionalism* (i.e., joint/cooperative economic development policy planning and action among neighboring, even rival jurisdictions), rather than cutthroat parochialism, was the best method in which to compete for FDI.

Through case studies of the Toyota-PUL Alliance of northeast Mississippi and the Hyundai-Kia Auto Valley Partnership of east-central Alabama and west-central Georgia, this chapter examines how collaboration among certain local regions within the SEAC has created a comparative advantage for their areas in their competitions for the FDI of the 'New Domestics'. In the process, they also have improved the FDI competitiveness of the entire five-state region.

Table 24.1 Income & Poverty Rates Rankings for SEAC among the 50 States, 1969 to 1999[1]

Year	Median Household Income (highest income to lowest)	Median Per Capita Income (highest income to lowest)	Percent Poverty (lowest percentage to highest)
1969	35. Georgia	37. Georgia	41. Georgia
	41. South Carolina	41. Tennessee	42. Tennessee
	42. Tennessee	47. Alabama	46. South Carolina
	48. Alabama	48. South Carolina	47. Alabama
	50. Mississippi	50. Mississippi	50. Mississippi
1979	36. Georgia	36. Georgia	41. Tennessee
	39. South Carolina	39. Tennessee	42. Georgia
	44. Tennessee	45. Alabama	43. South Carolina
	47. Alabama	46. South Carolina	48. Alabama
	50. Mississippi	50. Mississippi	50. Mississippi
1989	23. Georgia	21. Georgia	36. Georgia
	35. South Carolina	36. Tennessee	37. South Carolina
	39. Tennessee	37. South Carolina	38. Tennessee
	41. Alabama	39. Alabama	44. Alabama
	50. Mississippi	50. Mississippi	50. Mississippi
1999	20. Georgia	21. Georgia	34. Georgia
	38. South Carolina	35. Tennessee	36. Tennessee
	39. Tennessee	37. South Carolina	38. South Carolina
	42. Alabama	38. Alabama	46. Alabama
	49. Mississippi	50. Mississippi	50. Mississippi

Sources: U.S. Census Bureau (2010a, 2010b, 2011a, 2011d)

Notes
(1) To provide symmetry in the table, the state with the lowest% poverty was ranked first and with the highest ranked 50th.

SOME BACKGROUND ON THE SEAC[2]

As illustrated in Table 24.2a, the first New Domestics automaker to locate an assembly plant in the SEAC was Nissan, which began producing cars in Smyrna, TN in June 1983. This facility, combined with Toyota's May 1988 opening of its first stand alone U.S. assembly facility in the Georgetown, KY, and General Motors (GM) of the USA's October 1990 launch of its Spring Hill, TN Saturn Plant, attracted hundreds of supplier plants to Tennessee.[3] Nonetheless, it was not until after BMW began building cars in the Upstate Region of South Carolina near Spartanburg in 1994, and Mercedes opened near Tuscaloosa, Alabama in 1997, that any real automotive-related agglomeration synergies formed in the SEAC.

The arrival of the German automakers, along with the area's growing reputation for its business friendly policymaking and diligent workers, helped the region secure six more New Domestics assembly plants between 1999 and 2008: Alabama won Honda and Hyundai plants; Mississippi landed Nissan and Toyota; Georgia gained a Kia factory; and Tennessee was selected by VW (again, see Table 24.2a). Overall, local markets in the five-state SEAC have captured eight of the eleven New Domestics light vehicle assembly complexes built in the USA between 1994 and 2011.[4]

As a result of these events, between 1993 and 2008, New Domestics' light vehicles output grew by 999,386. Alabama led the way with an increase of 672,338 vehicles during this period. These totals offset a loss of 840,000 in vehicle capacity caused by Ford and GM's shuttering of their Atlanta, GA plants, in October 2006 and September 2008, respectively, and GM's idling of its Spring Hill Plant, in November 2009 (see Table 24.2b).[5] New Domestics output was expected to surpass two million by 2013, when the new Kia, Toyota, and VW plants have reached their capacity, and expansions at Nissan and BMW were completed.

Related to this, whereas Motor Vehicle, Motor Vehicle Bodies, Trailers, and Parts Manufacturing (MVM) employment in the U.S. fell by 286,233 or 24.56% between 1998 and 2008, it rose by 7,102 or 5.77% in the SEAC. The SEAC's gains were most pronounced during the 2002 to 2008 period, when the region added 18,744 or 16.81% in MVM employment, including 11,583 or 16.07% in Motor Vehicle Parts Manufacturing (MVPM). In contrast, the U.S. suffered a decline of 109,000 or 11.03% in MVM, while MVMP contracted by 96,180 or 14.64%; MVMP was down 240,539 or 30.01% from 1998 to 2008.

While Alabama received the overwhelming majority of the SEAC's growth between 2002 and 2008, the other SEAC states, including more recently Georgia, have also added MVM jobs. As the next sections describe, one of the most important catalysts behind the region's success has been the collaborative efforts of neighboring jurisdictions in local areas which have attracted New Domestics' FDI. Two prime examples of this have been the Toyota-PUL Alliance in NE Mississippi and the Hyundai-Kia Auto Valley Partnership of east-central Alabama and west-central Georgia.

NE MISSISSIPPI'S TOYOTA-PUL ALLIANCE

PUL's Development Context

In February 2007, Toyota announced it would construct an auto assembly plant in NE Mississippi near US 78/Future I–22, a highway corridor that runs between Birmingham and Memphis (again, see Figure 24.1). Originally considered a dark horse for the factory, the area's Wellspring Project won out over sites in Chattanooga, TN and Marion-Crittenden County, AR, (near Memphis). The successful location, a relatively rural area of 127,843 residents and 69,154 in total private

Table 24.2a Foreign Light Vehicle Assembly Plants Opened in the SEAC since 2006

Automaker	Announced	State	State Region	Location	Incentive Package	Production Began	Emp.	Vehicle Capacity
Active New Domestics Light Vehicles Assembly Plants opened in the SEAC before 1994								
1. Nissan	Oct-1980	TN	Central	Smyrna town, Rutherford Co.	$19 mill	Jun-1983	3,900	550,000
New Domestics Plants opened in SEAC since 1994								
1. BMW	Jun-1992	SC	Northwest	near Greer in Spartanburg Co.	$150 mill	Sep-1994	7,000	240,000
2. Mercedes	Sep-1993	AL	West-central	Vance town, Tuscaloosa Co.	$258 mill	Feb-1997	3,000	160,000
3. Honda	May-1999	AL	Central	near Lincoln city in Talladega Co.	$158 mill	Nov-2001	4,500	300,000
4. Nissan	Nov-2000	MS	Central	Canton city, Madison Co.	$363 mill	May-2003	3,300	400,000
5. Hyundai	Apr-2002	AL	South-central	Montgomery city, Montgomery Co.	$253 mill	Mar-2005	3,200	300,000
6. Kia	Mar-2006	GA	West-central	West Point city, Troup Co.	$399 mill	Nov-2009	2,500	300,000
7. Toyota	Feb-2007	MS	Northeast	Blue Springs village, Union Co.	$294 mill	Nov-2011	2,000	150,000
8. VW	Jul-2008	TN	Southeast	near Chattanooga in Hamilton Co.	$577 mill	Apr-2011	2,000	200,000

Table 24.2b Light Vehicle Assembly Plants Closed in the SEAC since 2006

Closed	State	State Region	Location	Production Began	Emp. (1)	Vehicle Capacity
1. Ford	Oct-2006	GA	Central	Hapeville city in Fulton County, near Atlanta	Dec-1947	–1,900	300,000
2. GM	Sep-2008	GA	Central	Doraville city in DeKalb County, near Atlanta	Nov-1947	–3,200	300,000
3. GM	Nov-2009	TN	Central	Spring Hill city, Maury County	Oct-1990	–2,500	240,000

Sources: Compiled by the author from Ward's (1995–2010); McGhee (2006); Atlanta Journal-Constitution (2008); Davis (2010); BMW (2011); Ford (2011); GM (2011); HMMA (2011); Honda (2011); KMMG (2011); MBUSI (2011); Nissan (2011); SAC (2011); Toyota (2011); and VW (2011a).

Notes:
(1) Employment at the time of closing. All three plants employed more at various points during the 1990's and 2000's. GM still has 1,189 workers at its Spring Hill engine facility and has announced that it will re-open its assembly plant in the second half of 2012, and employ 685 there.

employment, has come to be known as PUL Region. The name was derived from the economic development alliance of Pontotoc, Union, and Lee Counties, created with the express purpose of recruiting Toyota to the region (see Figure 24.2).

As shown in Table 24.3, the PUL Region had 29,861 in manufacturing employment in 2000. This total was equivalent to 43.18% of the area's total private employment in 2000. Nearly half of the former in that year, or 14,626, was in Furniture manufacturing (Furn. Mfg). This meant that this sector was responsible for 21.15% of the region's private employment. Moreover, although PUL contained only 4.49% of the state's 2.84 million in population in 2000, and just 7.23% of its employment, the region was home to 44.41% of the state's Furn. Mfg employment.

Unfortunately, over the next eight years, total private employment in the PUL Region would contract by 3,789 or 5.48%, led by a manufacturing decline of 9,679 jobs or 32.41% (again, see Table 24.3). Meanwhile,

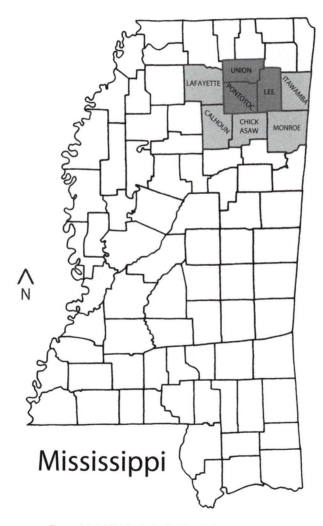

Figure 24.2 NE Mississippi's Toyota PUL Alliance Region

Table 24.3 PUL Region: Change in Furniture Manufacturing (Furn. Mfg) Employment, 2000 to 2008[1]

Area	Change Total Emp. 2000–08	% Change Total Emp. 2000–08	Mfg. Emp. 2000	Change Mfg Emp. 2000–08	% Change Mfg. Emp. 2000–08	Furn. Mfg. Emp. 2000[2]	Change Furn. Mfg Emp. 2000–08	% Change Furn. Mfg Emp. 2000–08
Pontotoc Co.	297	3.08%	6,842	−635	−9.28%	5,510	−188	−3.41%
Union Co.	−2,059	−20.37%	5,213	−2,534	−48.61%	3,121	−1,529	−48.99%
Lee County	−2,027	−4.10%	17,806	−6,510	−36.56%	5,995	−1,738	−28.99%
PUL Region	**−3,789**	**−5.48%**	**29,861**	**−9,679**	**−32.41%**	**14,626**	**−3,455**	**−23.62%**
%PUL Emp.	—	—	43.18%	—	—	21.15%	—	—
% of State	31.49%	—	13.57%	16.85%	—	44.41%	29.37%	—
TRPDD Area	−6,553	−6.19%	44,069	−14,925	−33.87%	20,293	−5,177	−25.51%
% of State	54.45%		20.03%	25.99%	—	61.61%	44.01%	—
Mississippi	**−12,034**	**−1.26%**	**220,046**	**−57,431**	**−26.10%**	**32,936**	**−11,764**	**−35.72%**
%Tot. Emp	—	—	—	—	—	3.44%	—	—

Source: U.S. Census Bureau (2011b)

Notes:
(1) Private Employment only;
(2) Furn. Mfg represents the total employment for NAICS 337.

between 2000 and 2008, Furn. Mfg shrank by 3,455 or 23.62%. Faced with rising unemployment and declining tax revenues provoked by the shifting of a large segment of Furn. Mfg production to China, local officials concluded that proactive collaborative intervention was necessary in order to protect their citizens from any related negative impacts.

Recruiting Toyota

Toyota's surprise selection of NE Mississippi revolves around the yeomen efforts of the PUL Alliance, a consortium representing a level of inter-jurisdictional collaboration unprecedented in Mississippi's history. The Alliance was formed in late-2001, and is governed by a nine-member board consisting of two supervisors from each of the three PUL counties, and the mayor's of their respective county seats, the aforementioned Pontotoc, New Albany, and Tupelo. Other important actors in the project have included the: Pontotoc County Chamber of Commerce; Union County Development Association; North Mississippi Industrial Development Association; the Three Rivers Planning & Development District (TRPDD);[6] and Community Development Foundation of Tupelo/Lee County (CDF). These local entities also were greatly aided by state and federal agencies, particularly, the Mississippi Development Authority (MDA), the Office of Governor Haley Barbour, the state legislature, the Tennessee Valley Authority (TVA), and the U.S. Department of Transportation (US DOT).

The idea to pursue a New Domestics auto assembly plant was conceived in the Fall 2000, during a retreat of TRPDD and CDF officials. At the time, the PUL Region was beginning to experience the effects of what ultimately would be a sizable decline in its furniture industry, especially upholstered furniture. Economic analyses conducted by region officials suggested that three manufacturing sectors had the best long-term growth prospects for job creation: Food (processing);

Motor Vehicles (auto assembly plants); and Motor Vehicle Parts (auto suppliers). The food industry was ruled out, due to its large demand for water and wastewater capacity. The focus then turned to the auto industry, with the top priority of attracting a light vehicle assembly plant. This decision was further supported by the belief that the work skills required in Furn. Mfg. were highly transferrable to auto manufacturing

The next phases involved creating a local structure and securing a massive site that would serve the needs of a major automaker. Accomplishing these steps, however, required several amendments to Mississippi's Constitution, allowing for the authorization of a multi-jurisdictional entity that would share in both the costs and benefits of acquiring and servicing such a site. These endeavors spawned the PUL Alliance in late-2001. These efforts were advanced by the 1995 success of TRPDD planners in creating a seven-county solid waste authority/regional landfill.

As for assembling a site, once the eventual 1,730 acres in Union County were identified, $30 million worth of purchase options were acquired on related parcels; an additional 450-acre buffer zone was requested by Toyota. Since neither Union nor the other two counties had the fiscal capacity to issue such a large bond, TRPDD secured bridge financing, until each county issued a bond for their $10 million, one-third share. In addition to the cost of purchasing the land, the site required significant clearing and grading, and its connecting infrastructure were in need of major upgrading.

Next, the development team, which included the MDA and TVA, began identifying potential tenants for the site, dubbed the Wellspring Project. This process involved visits to Europe and Asia. According to local officials, however, the area was not far enough along in the process to truly compete for the Hyundai factory awarded to Montgomery, AL in April 2002, or for the Toyota

pickup truck plant awarded to San Antonio in February 2003. At the time, PUL did not even control the Wellspring site, and highway connections to the area were considered below automaker standards.

The situation began to change in January 2004, when US 78 was re-branded as the Future I–22. This event required grueling negotiations between Mississippi and the US DOT, culminating in the latter's endorsement of a $500 million project to extend and enhance the highway. The outlook further improved in January 2005, when the TVA certified Wellspring as one of its recommended 'Megasites,' at the time, only the third such designation of its kind in the seven-state TVA Region. Together, these changes stamped the site as a prime location ready for a large-scale industrial development, and significantly raised the profile of the PUL Alliance's development team. This was especially relevant for Toyota, who played a lead role in developing the TVA's Megasite concept, and whose Japanese officials viewed their auto complexes as multi-local regional developments rather than parochial projects.

Still, although Toyota privately ranked Wellspring as its top choice, the PUL Alliance had several other significant hurdles to overcome. First among them was the pending fall 2006 expiration of their land options for the site. In response, the PUL Board unanimously voted to renew these agreements and to even raise the payouts, in order to buyout a few disgruntled land owners, effectively doubling the projected land costs. A second obstacle was cleared only after Mississippi Governor Barbour's Administration intervened by agreeing to purchase all mineral rights claims to the site held by any current and prior landowners.

As a result, in February 2007, when Toyota officially announced the location for its new U.S. vehicle factory, the alliance had all of its proverbial 'ducks in a row'. In the process, Toyota and the region relied and will rely upon several long-term multi-jurisdictional service agreements and structures created for the project. In particular, the site receives water service from the PUL Alliance, its railroad spur is maintained by the TRPDD, its natural gas is supplied by Ponotoc city, its sewer by Tupelo, and its electricity by New Albany, through a PUL built sub-station.

PUL Incentives and Outcomes

The final piece in PUL's successful landing of Toyota was a large state and local incentive package, although surprisingly, this was not a deal breaker for the automaker; Marion, AR offered a larger package. Rather, the site's environmental suitability and other related factors proved more important. For example, Toyota shied away from Marion because its region, the Memphis Metropolitan Area, was designated as in 'non-attainment' of Federal air quality standards under the Clean Air Act Amendments. Additionally, there were some concerns regarding potential flooding, as a result of the Arkansas site's proximity to the Mississippi River. Although the Chattanooga tract would become a TVA Megasite, Toyota similarly was worried about it being the former home to an ammunition facility.

Ultimately, Toyota received $293.9 million in incentives to locate in the region: $253.6 million from the State of Mississippi and $40.3 million from PUL entities. The package included: $67 million in site preparation costs; $136.6 million for infrastructure; $80 million targeted for job-training; and another $10.3 million in miscellaneous incentives. Thirty million of the site costs, and the miscellaneous subsidies were borne by local bodies. The state also allocated an additional $30 million to attract Toyota Tier-I suppliers.

While Toyota's direct incentive package represents an incredibly high figure, considering Nissan received $19 million in giveaways in 1980, its package was still $70 million less than the $363 million received by Nissan from Canton and the State of Mississippi in November 2000. Toyota's award also was

$105 million lower than what was given to Kia Motors in 2006, to lure its assembly factory to southwest Georgia, and almost one-half the $577 million garnered in 2008 by VW in Chattanooga (again, see Table 24.2).

Toyota broke ground in Blue Springs in April 2007. The plant's completion, however, was delayed for 18-months, and its launch date pushed back until November 17, 2011. Three factors stalled the start of its production: (1) the near doubling of gasoline prices between January 2007 and July 2008 to $4 per gallon; (2) the world economic crisis of 2008–09; and (3) the fallout from the spring 2010 alleged safety issues with, and recalls of, its American-sold vehicles. In exchange for the incentives it received, the automaker has brought 2,000 jobs to the PUL Region, paying an average of $61,000 annually. This was significant considering that *U.S. Census* estimates suggest that Mississippi had the lowest Median HHI and PCI in the nation in 2009: $36,650 and $19,743, respectively. A number of Japanese suppliers also have constructed factories in the region. These firms and others were expected to add 4,900 supplier jobs to the area by 2012–13, paying an average of $34,250/year.

Incorporating the other expected 1,400 indirect jobs, the MDA (2008) estimated that the Wellspring Project should generate nearly $318 million in annual taxable payroll earnings in the PUL Region by 2013. Including the $161 million in wages earned from the 2,232 two-year construction jobs generated to complete the project, the MDA projected that state and local governments would recoup their investments and its related interest within 17 years, several years prior to the maturation of the bonds they issued. Finally, of its own volition, Toyota pledged $50 million to the area public schools over a period of 10 years. Despite not opening until the Fall, the firm already made its first payment of $2.5 million in January 2011. It also created a public nature preserve adjacent to the site.

In sum, realizing that no one municipality or county alone could successfully accommodate a project the size of a Toyota factory and related supplier cluster, PUL officials went against the nation, state, and local tide of inter-local combativeness, and banded together to form a regional economic development alliance to land the project. The Alliance's ten-year odyssey, offers a prime example of the comparative advantages (and pitfalls) accrued by competing local governments willing to act together as a collaborative region in order to recruit FDI. Most importantly, by attracting Toyota, PUL officials took a giant step towards overcoming the social dislocation confronting their area, and towards improving the quality of life of their residents.

ALABAMA–GEORGIA'S HYUNDAI-KIA AUTO VALLEY PARTNERSHIP

Auto Valley Partnership's Development Context

Situated in east-central Alabama and west-central Georgia, the Hyundai-Kia Auto Valley Partnership encompasses a 110-plus mile, 10-county corridor along Interstates 65 and 85, between Hyundai Motors' Montgomery (AL) Assembly Plant and Meriwether County, GA. The latter county was just east of Troup County, GA's and Hyundai's new Kia Motors West Point Assembly Plant (see Figures 24.1 and 24.3). The Auto Valley's name was derived from the fact that the Hyundai and Kia supply clusters have now

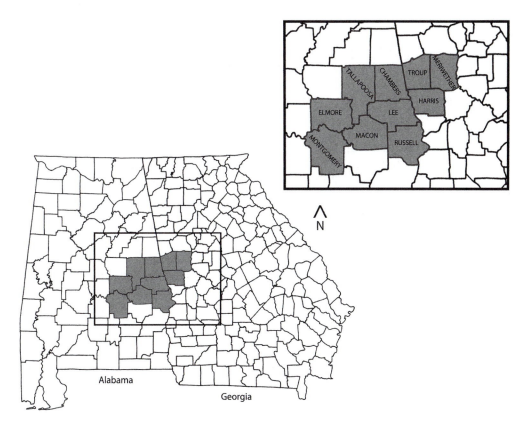

Figure 24.3 Alabama-Georgia's Hyundai-Kia Auto Valley Partnership Region

converged within the Chattahoochee River Valley bioregion, an area whose communities have regularly collaborated on projects governed by the Valley Partnership Joint Development Authority (VPJDA).[7]

The area's attractiveness to the Hyundai-Kia Auto Group was greatly advanced by the State of Alabama's prior reputation for accommodating other automakers, including: Daimler, which since February 1997 has built Mercedes Benz in the Town of Vance, Tuscaloosa County, and now employed 3,000; and Honda, which has assembled vehicles in central Alabama's Talladega County since November 2001, and employed 4,500 (again see Table 24.2). These two firms have contributed more than 30,000 new MVM jobs to the state. Alabama also recruited two engine plants to Madison County-Huntsville: Navistar, a heavy-duty truckmaker also supplying Ford (opened in 2001); and Toyota (2003). Unfortunately, while these three Alabama counties prospered, very little growth trickled down to the Montgomery or Chattahoochee Valley Regions.

As illustrated in Table 24.4, total manufacturing employment in the ten-county Hyundai-Kia Auto Valley declined by 8,585 or 18.00% between 1998 and 2008. More specifically, Textiles and Apparel Manufacturing (TAM) lost 13,064 or 70.13% jobs between 1998 and 2008. This followed a contraction of 7,277 in TAM employment between 1987 and 1997. The central portion of the Valley (particularly, Chambers and Tallapoosa), was hit hardest during all three periods. Mirroring Furn. Mfg in the PUL Region, the primary catalyst driving this decline was the global shift of TAM to Developing Asia, particularly China.

In response to the ensuing rising unemployment and declining incomes suffered by residents in the area, state and local governments aggressively pursued MVM related FDI. Due exclusively to their recruitment of Hyundai to Montgomery and Kia to West Point, MVM employment in the Auto Valley Region expanded by 6,051 between 1998 and 2008. In other words, without this FDI induced increase in MVM, the area would have suffered a contraction of 14,636 industrial jobs after 1998.

The Auto Valley Development Team and the Recruitment of Hyundai and Kia

The Hyundai-Kia Auto Valley began to take shape on April 2, 2002, when Hyundai announced it would build its first U.S. assembly complex near I–65 in Montgomery. The South Korean automaker selected the site over Glendale/Hardin County, KY, an area located 45 miles south of Ford Motor's Louisville Assembly and 60 miles north of GM's Bowling Green, KY plant. Montgomery became the preferred site when legal challenges delayed Kentucky's attempts to condemn the property it had purchased options on for the project. However, Hyundai was already leaning toward Montgomery for two reasons: (1) Alabama's track record with Daimler/Mercedes, whom the group had been involved with on several joint ventures; and (2) Montgomery's development team, a regional coalition of municipal, county, and state officials complemented by private sector representatives.

The Montgomery team consisted of representatives from the State of Alabama Development Office (ADO), the Office of then Governor Don Siegelman, the Montgomery Area Chamber of Commerce, Montgomery County, Montgomery city, and the Economic Development Partnership of Alabama (EDPA). The latter, a private, nonprofit funded by the Alabama companies, included among its membership, Bill Taylor, then President and CEO of Mercedes-Benz U.S. International. While the Montgomery Plant was the initial impetus for growth, it was the recruitment of Kia to west-central Georgia that really turned the Auto Valley into a prime example of collaborative regionalism.

Table 24.4 Change in Hyundai-Kia Auto Valley Motor Vehicles (MVM) and Textiles & Apparel (TAM) Manufacturing[1]

Area	Change Mfg Emp. 1998–2008	% Change Mfg Emp. 1998–2008	Change TAM Emp. 1998–2008[2]	% Change TAM Emp. 1998–2008	Change TAM Emp. 1987–1997[3]	Change MVM Emp. 1998–2008[4]	% Change MVM Emp. 1998–2008
Auto Valley	**-8,585**	**-18.00%**	**-13,064**	**-70.13%**	**-7,277**	**6,051**	**646.67%**
Alabama (pt)	-4,213	-12.18%	-11,623	-85.78%	-6,145	5,930	1,174.26%
Chambers Co.	-3,777	-67.75%	-3,832	-84.22%	-2,070	5	******
Elmore Co.	1,236	55.01%	-306	-50.92%	-375	78	458.82%
Lee County	23	0.35%	-1,631	-98.43%	-869	877	******
Macon Co.	291	346.43%	-35	-100.00%	-10	350	******
Montgomery Co.	2,585	24.10%	-112	-40.43%	175	3,997	972.51%
Russell County	-284	-8.22%	-1,553	-89.00%	-23	343	445.45%
Tallapoosa Co.	-4,287	-72.42%	-4,154	-88.67%	-285	280	******
Georgia (pt)	-4,372	-33.40%	-1,441	-28.38%	-1,132	121	28.07%
Harris County	-398	-34.37%	-173	-98.86%	100	0	0
Meriwether Co.	-1,445	-64.19%	-377	-100.00%	-100	24	32.00%
Troup County[5]	-2,529	-26.12%	-891	-19.69%	-1,132	97	27.25%
Alabama	**-73,814**	**-20.94%**	**-47,997**	**-72.16%**	**-20,996**	**17,929**	**105.38%**
Georgia	**-137,121**	**-25.63%**	**-67,762**	**-53.99%**	**-33,537**	**-7,788**	**-34.83%**

Source: U.S. Census Bureau (2011b)

(1) Private Employment only, in some cases, extrapolated from range values.
(2) SIC sectors 22 and 23
(3) NAICS sectors 313 through 315.
(4) NAICS sectors 3361 to 3363.
(5) Does not include new Kia plant, which opened in November 2009.
****** Division by zero.

The Kia competition came down to three finalists: West Point, GA; Marion, AR; and Meridian/Lauderdale County Area of east-central Mississippi. Ironically, the West Point and Meridian sites were proposed by Kia to the development offices of Mississippi and Georgia, as a result of their accessibility to Hyundai Montgomery. In August 2005, due to its enormous incentive package, it appeared Meridian was Kia's preferred location; at that time, PUL and Columbus/Lowndes County, MS, just south of the larger TRPDD, were eliminated from contention. On the other hand, Hyundai privately began to fear that the Meridian Area did not possess a large enough population to sufficiently accommodate its labor demands for the plant and potential suppliers. This created a new opening for the West Point development team, which it seized upon by securing purchase options on 37 parcels and 2,176 acres of land in only 45 days. These extraordinary efforts greatly impressed Hyundai-Kia management in the U.S. and South Korea.

West Point's initiative was led by representatives from the: cities and development authorities of West Point and LaGrange; Troup and Harris Counties; LaGrange-Troup County Chamber of Commerce; Greater Columbus, GA Chamber of Commerce (GCCC); and VPJDA. Area planners also benefited tremendously from the guidance of the Montgomery, AL development team which landed Hyundai, who provided advice related to cultivating the right environment to accommodate Kia, its South Korean suppliers, and their families. Finally, West Point's bid was greatly aided by the Office of Georgia Governor Sonny Perdue, the Georgia Department of Economic Development, and several other state agencies.

The actual recruitment of Kia involved numerous clandestine meetings between state and local officials and the Hyundai Group, both in the U.S. and South Korea. This process actually began back in 2000, when the State of Georgia first was informed by Hyundai that it was planning to build an American factory. The sessions became more frequent and more intense after 2003. By then, Georgia officials were highly motivated to act, in the light of Daimler's 2003 cancellation of a proposed commercial van plant it was to build in Pooler near Savannah. This turned to more desperation in January 2006, when Ford announced it would shutter its Hapeville/Atlanta Assembly by October 2006. These decisions cost the state approximately 5,200 good paying jobs; two years later, GM also would close its Doraville Assembly complex near Atlanta, putting another 3,200 out of work.

Following Kia's decision to operate in West Point, the VPJDA took on a leadership role in the project, developing sites for Kia's supply network and recruiting suppliers to the Valley Region. Founded in 1994 under the auspices of the GCCC, and modeled after the 12-county Charlotte Regional Partnership (of NC and SC), the VPJDA is a nonprofit, public-private development organization established to help promote investment and job creation in the Chattahoochee Valley Region. The VPJDA's activities have been governed by Georgia's 'Interlocal Cooperation Act' (State Code Title 36–69), which since 1981 has allowed for collaboration among counties and municipalities in the provision of services and facilities, when these jurisdictions believed it was in the best interest of their collective citizens (GGA, 2011).

The Interlocal Act has been amended several times since, most germane being a 2005 revision (Title 36–69A) permitting Georgia jurisdictions to cooperate with public agencies in other states. In other words, whereas creating the PUL Alliance required major amendments to the Mississippi Constitution, for 25 years prior to Kia's locating in West Point, Georgia Law enabled the local structures that were necessary to attract and serve a development of its size. What was perhaps most significant about the Valley Partnership's accomplishments, was that to succeed, local officials had to overcome existing racial and class divisions between the cities of West Point and LaGrange and out-county areas in Harris and Troup Counties; over the past 30 years, the former have become much less affluent and much more proportionately Black than the latter.

Auto Valley Partnership Incentives and Outcomes

Hyundai's $1.1 billion assembly plant was lured to Montgomery by $252.8 million in state and local incentives. This included: $76.7 million in tax incentives; $61.8 million for training facilities and programs; $55 million in site improvements ($17.3 million for land); $29 million for infrastructure upgrades; $18.2 million in utility and rail improvements (provided by the EDPA); and $12.1 million in other incentives. In exchange, Hyundai commenced production in Montgomery in March 2005. Since then, the automaker has expanded twice: adding Santa Fe SUVs to its Sonata sedan production in April 2006; and building a second engine plant in September 2008. In November 2010, Santa Fe assembly was shifted to Kia's West Point Plant, in order to make room for its Hyundai Elantra model. In 2011, the Montgomery complex employed 3,200 workers and had an annual payroll surpassing $200 million, with assembly line salaries typically in the mid-$40,000s to low $50,000s. Hyundai's 35 suppliers, mostly South Korean firms, have created another 6,000 jobs, primarily in Montgomery and Lee Counties, but also in adjacent counties along I–85 in east-central Alabama and west-central Georgia. All of these coming to a state which had a 2009 Census estimated Median HHI of $42,652 and a PCI of $22,842, both ranking 44th nationally. Related multipliers from the project have generated another 14,000, retail and service jobs in the region.

Awarded in March 2006, Kia received an incentive package of $399 million. The State of Georgia contributed $248 million, consisting of: $83.1 million for the acquisition and preparation of 3,300 acres near I–85 for Kia and its suppliers; $79.5 in tax incentives, including a Georgia Mega Project Tax credit and 15-year income and sales tax abatements; $65 million in transportation improvements (not including the US DOT's 20% share, which amounted to another $16 million); and $14.5 million in training grants. The Troup County, West Point, and LaGrange local package was $151 million and included: a $130 million, 15-year property tax abatement on the buildings; and $21 million earmarked for infrastructure improvements (GDEcD, 2010).[8]

Kia, which began production in November 2009, initially hired 1,200 workers; it received 43,000 applications. By October 2011, this total was approximately 2,500, the minimum amount promised by the firm in accordance with it achieving the factory's annual vehicle production capacity of 300,000. Kia was followed to the region by more than 20 of its South Korean suppliers, which employed 3,600 workers in the Valley Region.

As for the City of West Point, it contributed $25 million for infrastructure improvements to Kia and related developments. Additionally, in order to accommodate the project, its corporate limits were expanded from 4.5 to 12 square miles. In return, the municipality gained more than 3,000 new jobs, paying an average $50,000 annually and with sizeable benefits packages. These jobs helped to bolster the well-being of West Point and Troup County residents, who as of the 2000 Census had Median HHIs of $31,886 and $35,469, respectively, and PCIs of $16,735 and $17,626; these figures were far below the state medians of $42,433 for HHI and $21,154 for PCI. They also were a blessing for Troup County, which had an unemployment rate of 14% prior to Kia's arrival; this was down to 11.4% in August 2011 (GDOL, 2011). Finally, Kia employment has greatly benefitted a state economy which had a Census estimated Median HHI of $46,570 in 2009 (ranked 37th nationally), and a PCI of $24,944 (ranked 29th).

Overall, the plant was expected to create 16,000 jobs state-wide, and have an economic impact of more than $4 billion annually. Furthermore, located just 90 miles east of Montgomery, the West Point Plant also has prompted Kia related expansions among Hyundai Montgomery suppliers. As a result, the production chains of the two assembly plants have fused from two separate subregions into one ten-county region along I–65 and I–85, containing 700,437 residents, 240,364 in private employment, and 47,692 manufacturing jobs in 2008 (again, see Figures 24.1 and 24.3). Recruiting and winning both plants required collaborative regionalism, first in Montgomery and then in the bi-state Chattahoochee Valley Partnership Region. Separately and together, their success demonstrates the potential short and long-term comparative advantages gained from acting as a collaborative region in competitions for FDI.

CONCLUSIONS AND LESSONS FOR OTHER AREAS

One of the primary functions of the governments, at the national, state, and local levels, has been to implement policies which would improve the quality of life of those dislocated by rapid progress, economic decline, or other changing conditions. Among development officials in the SEAC, this calling has fueled the aggressive pursuit of manufacturing firms, first relocations from the industrial north, and more recently from FDI. In the process, the region has attracted eight of the eleven New Domestics light vehicle assembly plants opened in the USA since 1994. A common theme among those areas that have been successful in recruiting

Motor Vehicle Manufacturing related FDI has been inter-local collaboration, or what might be called *collaborative regionalism*. Through case studies of NE Mississippi's Toyota PUL Region and the Alabama–Georgia's Hyundai-Kia Auto Valley Partnership, this chapter has chronicled two prime examples of this new commitment to inter-local cooperation for FDI.

In addition to the benefits accumulated by these areas from their successes, their experiences also provide other North American regions with other valuable lessons for consideration during their own pursuits of FDI. Among them were:

1. Large incentive packages are a given part of the costs of competing for mega FDI projects;
2. Foreign firms, especially those from Asia, have a starkly different perspective regarding municipal and state boundaries from that of Americans, and view parochialism as an American problem that must be overcome prior to their recruitment efforts;
3. Municipalities, counties, labor organizations, regional planning agencies, the state development department, the Governor's office, in concert with the state and Congressional legislatures, all have to support the project;
4. All of the necessary land must be controlled, either through acquisition or via long-term purchase options and cannot have any environmental issues;
5. Prior inter-local collaboration helps build capacity for a megasite project;
6. FDI related collaborative regionalism requires a long-term commitment;
7. A fair cost and revenue sharing agreement among participant communities is required in advance of recruitment;
8. Most areas which have won New Domestics assembly plants have failed in their first attempt. It will take a few attempts to learn how to land a big project;

9. Matching FDI job recruitment with local labor force skills is important; and

10. The demands/needs of firms will vary based upon their national and world-regional origin. Becoming familiar with the different cultures and needs of foreign firms is a must for success.

As of October 2011, Alabama, with its more than 350 MVM related firms, has gained most from to-date the New Domestics FDI competitions. Over the past 20 years, the profile and legitimacy of the entire SEAC as a site for FDI has been enhanced by Alabama's initial and continuing accomplishments. Similarly, Alabama has greatly benefitted from the many other motor vehicles plants that have been located in the SEAC, before and since 1992. By the same token, the successes in the SEAC have improved the future potential of neighboring Arkansas, Louisiana, and the Florida Panhandle.

Whereas growing ever larger incentive packages have become a given, numerous other factors also have played a role in the rise of the SEAC as one of America's major motor vehicle manufacturing agglomerations. The North American Free Trade Agreement of 1994 facilitated the movement of finished vehicles, as well as parts, to and from Mexico. This turned the SEAC into a prime location for 'New Domestics' plants. As this chapter discussed, collaborative regionalism has become a third key factor and comparative advantage in separating winning and losing areas in the SEAC. Although it will take many years to assess whether the potential returns have justified the enormous financial risks taken by the regions and states examined in this chapter, one thing is for sure: the burdens and amenities accumulated from such projects will be shared by multiple, not one, jurisdictions. Hopefully, this important lesson will spread more readily throughout the U.S., and lead to more inter-local cooperation beyond recruiting FDI.

NOTES

1 As of 2011, the New Domestics' Auto Transplants with assembly plants building light vehicles in the USA and Canada included: Honda, Mitsubishi, Nissan, Subaru, and Toyota from Japan; Hyundai and Kia for South Korea; and BMW, Mercedes, and Volkswagen from Germany. Two other Japanese producers have joint ventures with American car companies: Mazda with Ford in Michigan (i.e., Auto Alliance); and Suzuki with General Motors in Ontario (i.e., CAMI). Isuzu also formerly produced vehicles in a joint venture with Subaru's at the latter's current Indiana factory.

2 Unless otherwise indicated, data sources for this and others sections of the chapter can be found in Tables 24.1–24.4. Much of the remaining data was obtained during my interview with local officials (SEAC, 2011).

3 The SEAC represents the inner ring of what has been called the Southern Automotive Corridor, an area also generally including Arkansas, Kentucky, Louisiana, North Carolina, Texas, and sometimes Virginia, West Virginia, and Missouri (Georgia Power, 2011; SAC, 2011).

4 The other three not won by the SEAC were Toyota's Princeton, IN SUV-pickup truck factory (opened in 1999), Toyota's San Antonio pickup plant (2006), and Honda's Greensburg, IN Civic plant (2008).

5 In September 2011, GM announced that it would re-open Spring Hill in the second half of 2012 and build Chevrolet Equinox at the plant, employing a drastically reduced work force of 685.

6 In addition to the PUL Counties, the TRPDD included Calhoun, Chickasaw, Itawamba, Lafayette, and Monroe Counties.

7 There are multiple Valley Partnerships. The so named 'Valley Partnership', included: Columbus-Muscogee, Cusetta-Chattahoochee, Harris, Marion, Talbot and Taylor Counties in Georgia and Russell County, AL; and two cities, West Point (in Harris and Troup Counties) and Manchester (in Talbot and Meriwether Counties). These areas have collaborated on economic development, growth management, transportation, recreation, social services, and health care planning. The seven counties above and Talbot also belonged to Georgia's 16-county, Region 8, River Valley Regional Commission Planning Area. Next, the ten-county 'Fort Benning and Chattahoochee Valley Region', involved in the expansion of Fort Benning Army Base, included the 'Valley Partnership' jurisdictions plus: Stewart County, GA and Barbour and Lee Counties in Alabama. Interestingly, the Kia plant and most of West Point were in Troup County, along with Meriwether County, was within Georgia's ten-county Region 4, Three Rivers Regional Commission Area (see Valley Partnership 2011a, 2011b).

8 Kia's rent is $1 annually for the tax abatement period, thereafter, the land will be transferred to the firm for a nominal fee.

QUESTIONS FOR DISCUSSION

1. In two or three paragraphs, discuss the main themes of Jacobs's chapter.
2. In one page, define what Jacobs's means by *collaborative regions* (i.e., what are characteristics of such places). Then, in another 2–3 pages, conduct some research of your own and make a list of other regions in the USA, or in other countries, which are well known for their inter-local collaboration efforts. Briefly describe what such activities they are particularly known for.
3. In 2–3 pages, and using examples from the chapter, explain which theory or theories presented in other chapters, best explain the developments of the PUL and Hyundai-Kia Auto Valley Regions (i.e., Global City; Nested City; innovative city; agglomeration theory, etc).
4. Utilizing the 'Further Readings', 'Helpful Web Links', and other sources, conduct some further research of one of the two auto regions described in this chapter and then compare the projects impacts to another region in the American South which also has landed a foreign assembly plant. Then, in 2–3 pages, write a summary of the project's expected/accrued costs and benefits to present in class.

FURTHER READINGS

Bartik, T. 2005, Solving the Problems of Economic Development Incentives. *Growth and Change*, 36 (2): 139–166.

Greenbaum, R., B. Russell, and T. Petras. 2010. Measuring the Distribution of Economic Development Tax Incentive Intensity. *Economic Development Quarterly*, 24 (2): 154–168.

Kenney, M., and R. Florida. 1993. *Beyond Mass Production: The Japanese System and its Transfer to the U.S.* New York: Oxford University Press.

Klier, T., and J. Rubenstein. 2010. The Changing Geography of North American Motor Vehicle Production. *Cambridge Journal of Regions, Economy and Society*, 2010: 1–13.

Markusen, A., ed. 2007. *Reining in the Competition for Capital*. Kalamazoo, MI: W.E. Upjohn Institute for Employment Research.

Molot, M. 2005. Location Incentives and Inter-state Competition for FDI: Bidding Wars in the Automotive Industry. In L. Eden and W. Dobson, eds., *Governance, Multinationals, and Growth*. Northampton, MA: Edward Elgar, pp. 297–324.

HELPFUL WEB LINKS

CDF. 2011. Community Development Foundation: Tupelo/Lee County Mississippi. Online. Available at: http://www.cdfms.org, last accessed, December 28, 2011.

GDEcD. 2011. Georgia Department of Economic Development. Online. Available at: www.georgia,org, last accessed, December 28, 2011.

GDOL. 2011. Georgia Labor Force Estimates. *Georgia Department of Labor*. Online. Available at: http://www.dol.state.ga.us/pdf/pr/laborforce.pdf, last accessed, December 28, 2011.

Georgia Power. 2011. *Automotive Manufacturing in Georgia – 2011*. Online. Available at: http://www.georgiapower.com/select/publications/Automotive_Industry_Report.pdf, last accessed, December 28, 2011.

MDA. 2011. *Mississippi Development Authority, Economic Development*. Online. Available at: http://www.mississippi.org, last accessed, December 28, 2011.

NADO. 2007. *Regional Alliance Pulls Toyota to Tupelo.* Washington, DC: National Association of Development Organizations Research Foundation. Available at: www.ruraltransportation.org/uploads/tupelo.pdf, last accessed, December 28, 2011.

SAC. 2011. Southern Auto Corridor News. *Southern Business & Development Magazine.* Online. Available at: http://www.southernautocorridor.com, last accessed, December 28, 2011.

TVA. 2011. Accelerate Your Success with a Tennessee Valley Megasite. Online. Available at: http://www.tvaed.com/megasites.htm, last accessed, December 28, 2011.

Valley Partnership. 2011. The Valley Partnership in the Columbus, GA Region. Online. Available at: http://www.thevalleypartnership.com, last accessed, December 28, 2011.

Wellspring Project. 2011. *Northeast Mississippi Welcomes Toyota to the Wellspring Project.* Online. Available at: http://www.wellspringproject.com, last accessed, December 28, 2011.

Conclusions and Lessons

CONCLUSION

The Nexus City Model: Bridging the Local, Regional, National, and International Contexts

A.J. Jacobs

Human settlements come in all shapes and sizes, from sparsely populated rural areas, to small towns and villages with only a few hundred, to individual municipalities with populations in excess of 8 million, to vast metropolitan areas with 35 million residents and encompassing hundreds of cities, towns, and villages. They evolve in a multiplicity of contexts and contain inhabitants from all parts of the globe and from all walks of life. Jersey City, New Jersey, for example, sometimes referred to as New York's sixth borough, is a municipality city of 250,000 with residents who speak more than 50 native tongues. In stark contrast, in Tokyo's 23 Ku, an area of nearly 9 million formerly known as the City of Tokyo, 96.3% of the population is native Japanese (see Chapter 16).

As discussed in the introduction to Part III, Alfred Marshall (1919) chronicled how certain attributes, such as the existence of raw materials, population density, infrastructure, and proximity to other urban areas, have created comparative advantages for certain cities over others. These advantages then tended to promote expanding foreign trade, exports, and the enlargement in the number and size of manufacturing firms in the area. When producers in related industries became concentrated within a city, such as in textiles and apparel in Manchester, England, significant economies of scale were achieved by all firms in those sectors, creating what Marshall called a *localization economy*. This industrial synergy then fostered economic and population growth not only in the urban region, but in the nation, as a whole. These were exactly the processes that provoked the rise of the automobile industry in Detroit.

THE BEGINNING OF AN AUTO REGION: DETROIT, 1701–1900

Detroit was initially settled in 1701, when Antoine de la Mothe Cadillac established

> Fort Pontchartain, at 'la place du détroit', the strait . . . located on the one high stretch of land along the Detroit River's eighteen-mile course. . . . Though the river was little more than a half-mile wide . . . it was the outlet for the waters of Lake Superior, Lake Michigan, and Lake Huron, and linked those inland seas with the lower lakes, Erie and Ontario, the St. Lawrence River [and thence, the Atlantic Ocean] . . . Within a decade, the settlement had become one of the most important inland trading posts on the continent.
>
> (Green, 1965, pp. 193–195)

By 1750, French settlers were farming adjacent lands and Detroit had approximately 1,000 inhabitants. In 1763, when New France was conquered by the British, most of the French settlers remained in the area. The British held the city until the mid-1790s, despite the U.S. Continental Congress's ratification of the Northwest Ordinance in 1787, which annexed Michigan into the Union. In 1802, the Town of Detroit was chartered. After an 1805 fire destroyed much of the town, Michigan's Territorial Governor rescinded Detroit's charter, and ordered the rebuilding of the city based upon the guidelines set out by Judge Augustus Woodward (Green, 1965).

Detroit officially became a city in 1806. As the territorial capital and eastern port, the city began to thrive, especially after the opening of the Erie Canal in 1825. The city's population surpassed 9,000 in 1840, and thereafter, began to experience rapid growth, as a Detroit became a center for steel, metal castings, flour, and other foodstuffs manufacturing (Hill, 1983).

In 1847, the capital of the new state of Michigan was transferred to Lansing, forever changing both areas. Detroit, nevertheless, remained the state's chief commercial center, with the city's chief export at that time being flour. In close proximity to its flours mills, however, were numerous small shops which specialized in repairing mill machinery and producing new parts. In addition, "along the waterfront were small shipyards where passenger ships and ships for the flour trade were built to cross the Lakes" (Jacobs, 1969, p. 123).

By 1855, with the completion of 'Soo' canal connecting Lake Superior to Lake Huron and the Lower Great Lakes, ships heading east to other manufacturing centers began to more frequently dock in Detroit's harbors. As a result:

> Detroit shipyards [became] among the first in the world to build steamships. . . . As the export work from the shipyards grew, the yards supported a growing collection of engine manufactures and parts makers, as well as suppliers of other fittings and materials for ships. By the 1860s, marine engines themselves were a major Detroit export. . . . While the engine business was growing, it was supporting a growing collection of its own suppliers: shops that made parts and tools, others that supplied copper alloys, made from local ores, to shops where brass valves and to bits of engine brightwork were manufactured. The refineries . . . became so successful that between about 1860 and 1880 copper was Detroit's largest export.
>
> (Jacobs, 1969, pp. 123–124)

As industrial commerce grew, so did the city's population. Between 1860 and 1880 the number of city residents more than doubled from 45,619 to 116,340. This nearly doubled again in 1890 to more than 205,000 (U.S. Census Bureau, 2011a). However, during this period, the city's employment mix shifted from exporting primary goods to producing secondary goods. According to Jane Jacobs (1969, p. 124):

> In about 1880, the local ores ran out . . . the refineries . . . closed down and their proprietors built new plants in the mountain states near new mines . . . The loss of the copper business was not an economic disaster for Detroit because . . . by 1880, [it] had produced so many exports—paints, varnishes, steam generators, pumps, lubricating systems, tools, store fixtures, stoves, medicines, furniture, leather for upholstery, sporting goods—that they soon more than compensated for the loss of refineries.

The iron, steel, and railroad car manufacturing "formed the city's industrial core in the 1880s" (Thomas, 1992, p. 25). Then, in 1889, Ransom Olds launched Detroit's first successful automobile assembly company. Olds looked to the city's bustling marine and metalworking industries for many of his parts. For his new car's transmission, he contracted with Henry Leland, a "precision machinist and maker of marine engines" (Green, 1965, p. 201). To make his engines, he hired the Dodge Brothers, a well-known, second-generation operated machine shop in the city.

According to Hurley (1959, p. 1), "there were sound commercial reasons why automotive manufacturing succeeded in Detroit." First, the city's industrial base specialized "in pressed steel, malleable iron, brass parts, springs, rubber tires, paints and varnishes, materials which were indispensable for the assembly of the horseless carriage" (p. 2). Second, "the importance of motor boats and commercial vessels on the Great Lakes resulted in an important marine-engine industry developing in the area; this lent impetus to the production of all types of engines, including those for autos as well" (p. 2). Third, the city's vibrant concentration of machine shops, tool and die, and engine related parts makers supplied "an unmistakable attraction" for auto manufacturers (p. 2). Fourth, the city was equidistant between the east and west coasts of the USA, and therefore, "advantageously situated for shipment of parts to regional assembly plants in any part of the nation" (p. 4). Fifth, Detroit was in close proximity, via ship or rail, to the iron ore resources, the steel producing centers, and the rubber supplies of the Great Lakes Region. Finally, Hurley explained, in Detroit, and in Michigan in general, "gas engines were preferred . . . as opposed to steam (favored in Massachusetts) and the electric motor (in Connecticut) . . . [This gave the area] a decided advantage over . . . other places when the gas engine proved to be the most efficacious way to power an auto. Otherwise, [he said], New England could easily have become the the center of the world's motor vehicles industry" (pp. 1–2).

In summary as Hurley wrote (1959, pp. 1–2):

> Every fabricating industry . . . lends itself to the combined pull of five vector forces: raw materials; fuel and power sources; market availability; the proximity of labor and capital pools; and transport arteries. The geographic patterns which characterize different industries are a compound of economic considerations, socio-historical factors, and happenstance. This [was] especially true of . . . automotive manufacturing in the United States. . . . The development of this industry in Detroit is a classic instance of how historical accident and socio-economic factors combine to determine industrial sites.

THE AUTO INDUSTRY DRIVES URBAN AND REGIONAL GROWTH IN DETROIT, 1900–1950

By 1900, with 285,876 residents, Detroit contained a deep pool of skilled workers, most who had gravitated to the city to work in its expanding factories. By 1908, twenty companies were building automobiles in the city (Green, 1965). Among the new automakers was Cadillac, established in Detroit by Henry Leland in 1902. A year later, the Packard Motor Company moved its operations from Warren, Ohio, to the city, to take advantage of its growing industrial economy. Meanwhile, in 1908, Ransom Olds merged his company with Buick, then, the nation's largest automaker, to form General Motors (GM), headquartered in Detroit. Over the next decade, GM would bring under its umbrella several other local competitors, including Cadillac, Chevrolet, and Oakland Motors, the maker of Pontiacs (Bloomfield, 1978). The firm also acquired numerous local parts producers and distributors, reconstituting GM into a vertically and horizontally integrated conglomerate (Chandler, 1977).

Nonetheless, it was Leland's former chief engineer at Cadillac, Henry Ford, who would provide the real spark driving the emergence of the auto industry in Detroit, and ultimately, the region's now 100-plus year legacy as the home of America's auto industry. Ford formed his own vehicle company in 1903, initially operating out of an old converted wagon shop on Mack Avenue in Detroit. Later, he moved to a larger building in Detroit's New Center Area, where he operated the Ford Piquette Plant. In the beginning, Ford bought all the items he needed to assemble his cars from various suppliers in the city, such as the Dodge Brothers. Later, he began to produce more and more of his own original and replacement parts and components (Jacobs, 1999, 2009a). These activities led to the opening of a new car plant in the Detroit suburb of Highland Park in 1910, and culminated in Ford's implementation of the world's first moving assembly line at the new factory in 1913. Henry Ford's innovation, which made it possible to mass produce automobiles, would then dictate how most factory goods were manufactured for the next 75 years.

Within only two years of its installation, Ford Motor had already produced its one-millionth Model T, and Detroit had become "a boomtown more raucous even than Houston in the 1970s" (Garreau, 1991, p. 104). Meanwhile, Ford Motor would come to affect "every facet of Detroit, transforming and increasing its population and revolutionizing its cultural and political character" (Thomas, 1992, p. 24).

> Automobile production, and the magic and myth of Henry Ford attracted workers from other industrial areas, both in and outside the state. Yugoslavs, Finns, and Lithuanians who had worked in the copper mines and lumber camps of Michigan's Upper Peninsula, flocked to Detroit in pursuit of higher wages in the auto industry. Ukrainians and other Slavic Russians left the . . . coal mines of New York and Pennsylvania . . . for Detroit's auto factories. Sicilians, Poles, Bulgarians and Macedonians all were drawn into Detroit's boom industry. . . . By 1915, Henry Ford's promise of five dollars a day [had also drawn] a large influx of Black laborers from the South to Detroit. . . . In 1900, Detroit was the 13th largest city in the nation. . . . By 1920 it [had] soared to fourth.
>
> (Thomas, 1992, pp. 24–26)

Within ten years, almost 121,000 industrial workers plied their trade in the City of Detroit. Another 200,000 were employed in manufacturing in other communities state-wide, most in complementary factories serving the Motor City's plants. In 1914, Michigan's 67,538 auto workers produced nearly two-thirds of America's total value of automobile related products (U.S. Census Bureau, 1918; Jacobs, 2009a).

By 1921, Ford was manufacturing "55.7% of the passenger cars produced in the United States" (Chandler, 1990, p. 205). Henry Ford spent much of the profits constructing and expanding his new 'Industrial Colossus,' the Rouge Plant, which opened in 1919 in suburban Detroit along the Rouge River in 1919. Within five years of its construction, 'The Rouge' had its own steel mill, equipped with blast furnaces and foundries, supplying most of the iron, brass, steel, and bronze castings used in Ford factories. This enabled Ford to totally integrate the production of parts, accessories, and replacement parts into his own facilities. As a result, by 1929, 'The Rouge' was an industrial city of its own, employing almost 100,000 hourly workers (Nevins and Hill, 1957). The plant operations were complemented by Ford Motor's building of hundreds of housing units in districts just west and north of the complex, in what is now the City of Dearborn; most were originally located in what was called City of Fordson, which merged with the Village of Dearborn in 1927. Only ten years after The Rouge opened in 1920, Dearborn's population had grown from less than 2,500 to more than 50,000. As for the City of Detroit, its population soared to 1.57 million in 1930. While Dearborn was no Detroit, its development represented mirrored the rapid suburbanization of population and employment that was taking in the Detroit Region, at the time, and that would proceed for the next 50 years (Jacobs, 1999).

A final important event occurring during the 1920s was Walter Chrysler's rescuing of the bankrupt Maxwell Motors. Thereafter, the once head of GM's Buick Division established Chrysler Motor Company in Detroit, and the Big Three Automakers, which would come to dominate the American industrial landscape for the next 60 years, were complete (Levin, 1995). The Big Three would not only control America's automobile production, it also would shape its physical landscape. Detroit was a microcosm of these forces. Whereas the City of Detroit served as the incubator for the initial development phase of the American auto manufacturing in the early 20th century, as the industry matured, it spilled over into nearby towns engaging in complementary work, transforming a city into a vast metropolitan region. By the late 1930s, the Big Three's production chain spread across several communities in the Detroit Region; it also produced satellite centers further west in Flint and Lansing, Michigan.

After World War II, production and growth would further intensify in the suburbs, significantly enlarging the region's geographic footprint. In 1950, the three-county Detroit Standard Metropolitan Statistical Area, encompassing the Counties of Wayne (Detroit, Highland Park, Hamtramck, and Dearborn), Oakland (Pontiac), and Macomb (Warren), was home to 3.02 million. This total was an increase of almost 839,000 from the 2.18 million in 1930. Meanwhile, the City of Detroit's population expanded from by nearly 281,000 between 1930 and 1950, to 1.85 million. Nevertheless, this meant that the city's share of its region's population had contracted from 72.04% in 1930 to 61.32% in 1950. Moreover, neither figure included the populations of neighboring Washtenaw County, then home to Ford's Willow Run Plant, nor Genesee County, home to Flint's massive Buick auto complex. Together these areas had 405,000 residents, an increase of 128,000 from 277,000 in 1930 (U.S. Census Bureau, 2011a). In the decades to follow, while the suburbs were growing in size and space, local, national, and international forces would conspire to spur a downward decline in the city. By 1980, the Region was experiencing a similar fate.

THE AUTO INDUSTRY MATURES AND DECENTRALIZES, 1950–2010

According to Mowitz and Wright (1962), the City of Detroit's population peaked in 1953 with 1.91 million inhabitants. Conversely, suburban growth continued at a torrid pace. Between 1950 and 1970 the population of the five counties of Wayne, Oakland, Macomb, Washtenaw, and Genesee County expanded by roughly 1.46 million people, from 3.42 million to 4.88 million. Meanwhile, the City of Detroit's population contracted to 1.51 million. By 1950, the city's further expansion was blocked by, among other things, a ring of home-rule suburban municipalities encircling its boundaries. As if being landlocked was not problematic enough, federal and state policies were encouraging the dispersal of population and employment in the region.

For example, the 1951 National Industrial Dispersion Program promoted the decentralization of the auto industry by offering firms accelerated tax amortization on capital machinery as part of the U.S. Defense Department's plan to de-concentrate major industries out of areas within potential Soviet nuclear target zones (Hurley, 1959; Darden et al., 1987; Thomas, 1990). Next, through subsidizing mortgage loans and building miles of limited access freeways, the Federal Housing Administration (FHA) Loan Program and the National Highway Act of 1956 made suburban housing easily accessible to many middle-class White families. This also prompted the suburbanization of retail activities. On the other hand, other policies, such as FHA and the Federal Urban Renewal Program, promoted residential racial homogeneity (segregation), discouraged inner city residential investment, and/or cleared hundreds of housing units that were never replaced. These policies combined with housing discrimination and real estate steering produced a high degree of racial and occupational place stratification within the Detroit Region (Darden et al., 1987; Hill, 1984; Thomas, 1997). This environment, which reached a boiling point in the 1960s, would dramatically impact local politics at least through the 1990s (Jacobs, 1999).

As for the Big Three Automakers, by 1970 they had established an integrated final production and parts network which extended across southeastern Michigan, as well to the Lansing and Grand Rapids Regions of the state. Contrary to Hoover's (1937) descriptions however, as the Big Three grew increasing dominant, political and economic power plays effectively blocked the establishment of other industries in the region. This prevented the much needed diversification of the Detroit Region's economy from occurring, a happenstance that would later serve to accelerate the area's demise in the post-1970 global economic age. In other words, despite exceeding four million in population, the Detroit Region never really developed a true *urbanization economy*. Combative, short-sighted management–labor relations exacerbated the situation, inhibiting labor upgrading, limiting the pool of skilled labor, and even discouraging foreign automakers from building factories in the region.

This was readily apparent following the two Arab oil embargos of the 1970s, which sent gasoline prices skyrocketing up nearly four-fold between 1973 and 1981, and effectively broke the Big Three's hold on American consumers. While the Big Three continued to focus their sales efforts on high margin, large, low fuel-economy vehicles, Japanese producers producing fuel-efficient cars, swooped in and captured an ever-increasing share of the American auto market. In addition, after going so long without any competition in the USA, the reliability of Big Three automobiles was below par. Quality issues especially haunted GM, Ford, and Chrysler sales during the 1990s and 2000s, long after gas prices stabilized. Again, Japanese automakers, now producing a growing percentage of their cars in the USA, capitalized on the Big Three's failing reputation with their low maintenance, worry-free vehicles.

The net result was the end of the Big Three as they were known for more 50 years. In 1976, the Big Three commanded an 85.52% share of U.S. motor vehicle sales. This fell to 73.43% in 1985, then to 64.71% in 2000, and to just 44.47% in 2010. GM, the world's largest car manufacturer, led the demise, its market share falling from 46.53% in 1976 to only 18.81% in 2010 (Ward's, 2011). Financial woes hit all three of the Detroit automakers, now dubbed the 'Detroit Three.' This included the near failure of GM and Chrysler, the latter being absorbed first by the German automaker Daimler (Mercedes-Benz), then by the private equity firm Cerberus Capital Management, and more recently by Fiat of Italy. These events led to plant closings and massive layoffs in the Detroit Region. In 1976, the five counties with final light vehicles assembly plants in the region, Genesee, Macomb, Oakland, Washtenaw, and Wayne, had 625,057 in manufacturing employment. By 2008, this total had fallen by more than 438,000, to just 186,374 (U.S. Census Bureau, 1978, 2011b). In contrast, expanding market share provoked employment and population growth in Toyota's home region, Nagoya, near its Northern Kentucky U.S. headquarters (i.e., the Cincinnati Metropolitan Area) and around its Georgetown, KY assembly plant (Metropolitan Lexington). Similarly, it spurred growth near Honda's Japanese plants in Sayama, Saitama Prefecture and in Central Ohio (the Columbus Metropolitan Area), as well as in proximity to Nissan's operations outside of Nashville, TN.

Finally, in the 1970s and thereafter, Detroit had become one of the most segregated and racially charged urban areas, even by American standards. Ironically, this situation actually began in the early 20th century and intensified during and after World War II, as scores of southern Blacks, displaced as a result of advances in farming mechanization, migrated to work in Detroit's bustling auto plants. In response to these multifarious forces, the population of the five auto producing counties in the Detroit Region contracted from 4.88 million in 1970 to 4.63 million in 2010. In the latter year, the City of Detroit contained only 713,777 residents, making it America's 18th largest city; it was the fourth largest from 1920 to 1940 and fifth largest 1950 to 1970 (U.S. Census Bureau, 2011a).

In sum, Detroit and its region's growth outcomes were determined by a variety of localized and non-localized forces. Similar to that of every other metropolitan area worldwide, its trajectory was shaped and re-shaped by its own particular blend of economic, spatial, institutional and social factors, and the interchange among them.

THE CITY AS THE NEXUS: A MODEL FOR STUDYING URBAN AND REGIONAL DEVELOPMENT

The Detroit case demonstrates how, a multiplicity of local, regional, national, and international forces influence a city's growth path.[1] In essence, cities are the nexus (both cores and means of), connecting or bridging the political, economic, social activities taking place on all spatial tiers (see Derudder et al.'s Chapter 3).[2] While there are countless determinants that impact urban growth, the case studies and perspectives covered in this volume suggest that the dynamic interplay among at least 12 contextual factors help explain the continued diversity of growth outcomes in the world's city-regions. These are:

1. *Natural features*—This localized factor accounts for the unique topographical features of an local area and/or region, such as the existence of a deep harbor port, mineral deposits, plains or mountainous terrain, and arable land.

    For example, many of the world's largest cities were settled along water bodies. Therefore, seaport regions, such as New York, London, Shanghai, and Durban (eThekwini), have dissimilar nested *natural features* contexts for development than inland areas in those countries, such as Dallas–Fort Worth, Birmingham–Midlands, Beijing, and Johannesburg. For that matter, seaports have different local natural contexts than river based city-regions, or a lake based regions.

2. *Time-historical*—As Abu-Lughod suggested in Chapter 10, this is a local, regional, national, and international variable, which accounts for the point in time of world and national history that a city was first settled, when it urbanized, its unique political-social history, and its nation's level of technological development, initially and presently.

    Bratislava's history of being on the frontline of numerous Central and Eastern Europe's military and ideological battles provides an illustration of how *time-historical* factors forcefully shape a city's development path. Its past then makes it unique in comparison with Chicago, Detroit, and other American which never experienced extended warfare. Next, New York, a long established metropolitan area that was first settled as a Native American territory, which then became a Dutch, British, and American colony, has a different *time-historical* development context from that of the post-railroad/dam technology Los Angeles, the 1970s oil boom town of Houston, and in the information age city-region of San Jose. By the same token, the *time-historical* growth context for a city-region in a core developed nation, such as in the USA, Germany, or Japan, will vary considerably from others within developed emerging markets/semi-periphery nations, such as the Brazil, Russia, India, and China (the BRICs), and within frontier markets/ periphery nations, such as Ecuador, Serbia, Sri Lanka, and Mongolia.[3]

3. *Scale*—This effectively is a local-regional factor, but one which is greatly impacted by national and international forces. Examples include national laws governing immigration and economic push-pull factors drawing people to or away from an area. *Scale* refers specifically to the size of a city-region's population, employment base, and territorial size, as well as its density.

   For example, as a result of their sheer size, the New York, Mexico City, Sao Paolo, Mumbai, Seoul, and Tokyo Regions, each with approximately 20 million or more inhabitants, have dissimilar contexts from city-regions of lesser size/scale within their respective nations, and worldwide.

4. *Social-demographic*—Although primarily a local and regional factor, similar to scale, this variable is greatly impacted by national and international forces. It accounts for an area's racial-ethnic and age composition, its foreign-born/immigrant population, inter-group relations, level of educational attainment, and labor skills, as well as any socio-cultural aspects that may impact its development.

   For instance, relatively less diverse city-regions, such as Mexico City, Ulsan, and Tokyo, and essentially bi-racial/bi-ethnic metro areas, such as Detroit, Cleveland, and Bratislava, have strikingly dissimilar *social-demographic* contexts as compared with the vastly multicultural regions of New York, Los Angeles, Toronto, Vancouver, and Sao Paolo. This factor was discussed in several of the chapters in Part Two: Nested City Regions, particularly, Abu-Lughod's Chapter 10 on New York, Chicago, and Los Angeles, and in my Chapters 11 and 13 on Detroit–Toronto and Tokyo, respectively.

5. *Economic-production*—This is a localized variable frequently influenced by national and international forces. It considers a city-region's industrial mix, the diversity of its economic base, and its physical infrastructure.

   For example, diverse urbanization economies, such as the New York, Toronto, or Tokyo, have different economic-production contexts than localization economies, such as Detroit (auto industry), Edmonton (oil), Kitakyushu (steel), which are overly-dependent upon one industry. Similarly, an industrial region has a different context than mercantile, government-service, or agriculturally-based region (i.e., Weber's merchant, consumer, and agricultural cities). An urban region dependent upon a sunset industry, such as textiles, has a different context than an emerging high-tech region. The *economic-production* context of an area with many transnational corporations will vary from one with only a few or none at all (e.g., see my Chapter 16 on Ulsan, and Simmie et al.'s Chapter 21).

6. *Institutional capacity/reflexiveness*—This local, regional, and national factor represents the policymaking skills/innovativeness of national and sub-national governments, and firms operating in a city-region. This element incorporates several important local influences, particularly, Amin and Thrift's (1995) concept of 'institutional thickness'; Storper's (1997a) 'city as the center of economic reflexivity'; the Urban Entrepreneurialism of Harvey (1989) and Jessop and Sum (in Chapter 20); and the Urban Boosterism of Short et al. (in Chapter 22).

   Institutional capacity/reflexiveness also represents variations in local coalition building, such as the existence of powerful pro-growth regimes or anti-growth movements in the city-region[4] or the collaborative regionalism I chronicled in my review of the PUL Alliance and Hyundai-Kia Auto Valley Partnership (Chapter 24). The influence of growth regimes were discussed in Fainstein's reading on New York and London (Chapter 19) and Waley's article on New Belgrade (Chapter 23).

Lastly, this factor considers the information transfer and related synergies emanating from the clustering of manufacturing or knowledge intensive firms. Examples of these were presented in Scott and Storper's discussion on regional economies (Chapter 17), in Simmie et al.'s review of 'Innovative Cities' (Chapter 21), and in my chapters on Ulsan, Bratislava, and the Hyundai-Kia Auto Valley (Chapters 16, 18, and 24, respectively).

7. *National urban hierarchy*—This is a national factor which has two sub-elements to it. The first draws upon the belief that every nation has its own urban hierarchy, with some having balanced and complex city systems, and others containing primate cities, or some combination, thereof. The second considers that cities at particular positions within a given *national urban hierarchy* will have their own unique development contexts.[5]

Related to the first element, the primate city of Bangkok, which is the national political, financial, and industrial capital of Thailand, will have a different *national urban hierarchy* context than a city-region within a multi-nucleated, split-functional system of cities, such as Los Angeles in the USA. Related to the second element, a national capital region will have different nested context than non-capital regions in that same country and worldwide (see Friedmann's discussion in Chapter 1). More specifically, the national capital regions of Washington DC, Ottawa, Mexico City, Paris, Berlin, Bratislava, Tokyo, Jakarta, and so on, will have a completely different *national urban hierarchy* contexts than other cities in their respective nations, including provincial/state capital cities.

8. *Intergovernmental structure*—This variable accounts for national variations in intergovernmental systems and their related impacts on city-regions, such as between centralized unitary states and non-centralized federal systems. It also considers existing diversity in vertical and horizontal intergovernmental relations among similarly structured systems (see Wang's Chapter 12 discussion on Taipei and my Chapter 13 on Detroit and Toronto).

For example, cities in federal systems, such as the USA, Canada, and Germany, all of which have expansive local autonomy to enact policies, will have dissimilar *intergovernmental structure* contexts for development than those in unitary states, such as Japan, the UK, and France. Whereas America was built upon a philosophy of strong institutions of local government which were intended to represent, first and foremost, local concerns, Japanese municipal authority has been circumscribed by national laws under the direction of the central bureaucracy. On the other hand, despite all being non-centralized federal systems, intergovernmental distributions of authority and functions have varied notably among the USA, Canada, and Germany, as well as among unitary states in Europe and Asia.[6]

9. *National development approach*—This factor accounts for diversity among liberal-regulatory, developmental, hybrid, and other states, and how national development policies impact urban trajectories (see Hill and Fujita, Chapter 9).

As a late industrializing nation, the Japanese Government determined that it was in the best interest of building a strong national economy for it, and not multinational corporations or market forces, to maintain primacy over development decisions and outcomes within its borders. Later, South Korea's President Park 'Looked East' to Japan for his country's model for economic development. Both nations, therefore, advocated developmentalism, a strategic approach to growth that believes that the national government should pro-actively cultivate ('develop') its national and local economies. As chronicled in my reading on Ulsan (Chapter 13), through its five-year National Economic Plans and related incentives to firms locating within its designated industrial districts, the South Korean Government played an important role in facilitating that city's transformation into major manufacturing hub. National Governments in Taiwan, and Malaysia acted similarly in their efforts to foster growth in Taipei, and in Malaysia's Multimedia Super Corridor (see Wang's Chapter 12 and Indergaard's Chapter 15).

In contrast, cities such as New York, Chicago, Detroit, and Los Angeles have evolved within a context governed by a quite dissimilar *national development approach*, America's Liberal-Regulatory State. Within this setting, the prevailing attitude has been that market mechanism (i.e., private supply and demand), firms, and local governments should be the most decisive shapers of urban growth outcomes, and that national governments should only react with rules and regulations (i.e., intervene) when there was a need to relieve undesirable consequences.[7] As a result, the American Government has eschewed any systematic, national long-term development planning, and instead relied upon "a patchwork of policies or a mixed bag of unrelated programs . . . intended to fix specific problems" (Noll, 1991, pp. 230–231).

10. *Regional Market*—This local, national, and international element refers to the region of the world in which a city-region is situated within, as well as its proximity to other urban markets within its nation-state and within nearby nations.

For instance, as a result of historical international relations, a city-region in East Asia would have a dissimilar *regional-market* context than one in the eastern USA or Western Europe. Similarly, differences exist between city-regions in the American north, south, east and west, between those in the Canadian Prairies and eastern and coastal provinces, and between those in Northern Italy and Southern Italy, etc. As discussed in my reading on Ulsan (Chapter 16), South Korea's spatial embeddedness and historical connections in Northeast Asia, relative to Japan, North Korea, China, and Russia have influenced that city's economic and industrial development. Variations in urban growth paths provoked by differences in *regional-market* context also were chronicled in Abu-Lughod's reading on New York, Chicago, and Los Angeles (Chapter 10), and in the Simmie et al. and Short et al. readings (Chapters 21 and 22, respectively);

11. *Degree of global economic integration*—This local, national, and international factor refers to the extent to which a local area's economy is linked to the global economy/international division of labor of production. This was a central theme of the readings in Part One: City-Regions in a World System, and in several readings in Part Three: The City-Region as the Engine of Economic Activity/Growth.

For example, Simmie et al. (Chapter 21), claimed that one of the reasons why innovative firms in London and Paris have been more internationally successful than those in Stuttgart and Milan, was because the former cities have long been globally connected, while the latter have been more closely tied to supplier and customer networks in Europe.

On the other hand, the *degree of global economic integration* among city-regions varies depending upon how globally-oriented the industrial sectors are in which their local firms are involved in. This idea represented a core argument in the readings by Friedmann, Sassen, and Derudder et al. in their classifications of *World/Global Cities and the World City Network* (Chapters 1–3). As these scholars claimed, the economies of New

York and London are fully integrated into the global economy as a result of their being to the home of major international stock markets. Somewhat similarly, the city-regions of Nagoya (Toyota-Lexus-Mitsubishi), Ulsan (Hyundai), Detroit (GM, Ford, Chrysler), and the Hannover-Braunschweig-Göttingen-Wolfsburg Metropolitan Region (Volkswagen) are globally well-integrated because their economies are highly dependent upon the export of finished automobiles and motor vehicle parts. This situation was discussed for multiple industries in my Ulsan chapter.[8] The same holds true for the oil and gas producing centers of Edmonton and Houston, as well as urban areas in northern Venezuela's Orinoco Belt, Indonesia, and in the Persian Gulf (e.g., Dubai), all of which are completely reliant upon global consumers of petroleum products. In turn, as discussed earlier in this chapter, fluctuations in worldwide gasoline prices also have dramatically impacted the economies and employment of Detroit and other car producing regions. Conversely, places without major industries and college towns, particularly those without many international or out-of-state students, have economies that are much less integrated into the global economy.

Lastly, it also could be argued that the *degree of global economic integration* accounts for variations between import dependent and export-oriented areas. Japanese and South Korean cities, for example, regardless of their economic mix, historically have been overly dependent upon foreign imports of natural resources from other areas. Therefore, they have had quite dissimilar development contexts, as compared with those in the aforementioned oil economies, and in agricultural and mining potash producing areas, such as those in West Virginia, USA, Saskatchewan, Canada, the South Wales Valley, and Queensland, Australia;

12. *Contemporary international events/forces*—This takes into account how major global events, such as economic crises, wars, natural disasters, currency fluctuations, and bilateral or multilateral trade disputes, uniquely affect certain city-regions, but may also affect all city-regions within a specific country or supranational region, regardless of their level of global integration.

The Asian Fiscal crisis provides an illustration of a *contemporary international event/ force* that affected not only human settlements within multiple Southeast Asian nations, irrespective of their industrial mix and level of global integration, but other regions worldwide. The same was true of: the 1989 events which culminated in the dissolution of the USSR, the fall of the Berlin Wall, and the end of socialism in Central and Eastern Europe (CEE), the terrorist attacks of September 11, 2001, and the AIG-Lehman shock of September 15–16, 2008, among others. In other words, development outcomes in certain cities, because of their geographic proximity or intimate connections to these *contemporary international events/forces*, were affected by these events more than others. Bratislava was an example of a city dramatically changed by the fall of socialism in the CEE discussed in this volume. Certainly, the New York Metropolitan Area was more directly affected than most by the events of September 11 (because it was a direct target) and the AIM-Lehman shock (because of its links to the global financial services sector). Nevertheless, the growth contexts for almost all American cities, and those in Canada for that matter, especially along the border, were greatly affected by these events.

Finally, the massive March 11, 2011, 'Great East Japan' earthquake and tsunami (tidal wave) that devastated the coast of eastern Japan, and the 500-year flood levels in Thailand, are two cases of how natural disasters can have dramatic ramifications beyond their immediate city-regions. Both catastrophes dramatically disrupted the lives and activities of firms, workers, and citizens not only in the local areas (Sendai/Tohoku Region and the Bangkok Metropolitan Area, respectively), but in countless other regions nationally (Japan and Thailand) and globally. This included abruptly halting the production chains of several manufacturing sectors, and the economies of countless cities networked to these places and industries.

In Japan, the 9.0 magnitude earthquake and ensuing 133-foot (40.5-meter) high tsunami is believed to have taken the lives of approximately 30,000 people. It also destroyed three reactors at a nuclear power plant in Fukushima Prefecture. The aftermath displaced hundreds of thousands of people living within 20 miles of the site. These events continue to wreak havoc on eastern Japan, even as far south as Urayasu, Chiba Prefecture, home to Tokyo Disneyland, and 250 miles from earthquake's epicenter and where the tidal wave struck landfall. On the other hand, the earthquake essentially wiped out the inventory of Renesas Electronics, the largest auto-related micro chip-maker in the world. This exacted a heavy toll not only on its home city, Hitachi Naka in Ibaraki Prefecture, but also on other cities prefectural-wide, such as Hitachi and Mito, and on countless auto producing regions in Japan and worldwide, from Nagoya to Shanghai, from Bratislava to Durban, from Sao Paulo to Tupelo, Mississippi, Japanese and non-Japanese producers alike.

Honda Motor and its manufacturing supply bases were hit especially hard by the Thai floods, which disrupted its production facilities not only in Ayutthaya, Thailand near Bangkok, but throughout its supply chain from Santa Rosa, in the Philippines near Manila, to Campana, Argentina near Buenos Aires, to Marysville, Ohio near Columbus, and so on.

In should be stated here that all 12 of these factors will have varying influences on human settlements, with the weights of each fluctuating depending upon that specific place and time. Moreover, some cities will essentially remain local, whereas some will be more regionally, nationally, and/or internationally integrated. Nonetheless, all cities are two-pronged nexus of development. First, they serve as loci of political, economic, and social activities. Second, since the local, regional, national, and international tiers are interdependent, cities act as the intersection points or bridges connecting two or more spatial levels.

Without any doubt, the above list requires further exploration, refinement, and elaboration by others. For instance, the lists of spatial tiers could be expanded by splitting regional into metropolitan and national sub-region levels, and the international tier into supranational-regional, international, and global, etc. Nevertheless, the City as the Nexus Model should provide students and scholars with a basic, yet multi-faceted framework for understanding how local, regional, national, and international factors influence urban development outcomes. It also supplies them with a toolkit to utilize in their comparisons of city-regions within the same, or different, nations.

In closing, it is hoped that the model offered here will not only provoke others to add their input to it, but also to think out of the box and develop their own new integrative theories of urban development. This is especially critical, as cities continue to confront an uncertain and challenging development context still suffering from the effects of the 2008 world economic crisis. If new ways of thinking about cities evolve from this process, then this volume certainly will have been worth significantly more than the effort put forth to complete it.

NOTES

1   This point in central to Nested City Theory, see particularly Hill & Fujita's Chapter 9, Abu-Lughod's Chapter 10, and Jacobs's Chapter 16. For perhaps the most well known perspective of what has been called multiscalar theory, however, see Kevin Cox's (1997) *Spaces of Globalization: Reasserting the Power of the Local*, and his articles: Cox (1995, 2004) and Cox & Mair (1989).

2   On this point, in addition to Derudder et al.'s Chapter 3, also see Storper (1995), Brenner (1997, 2004), and Therborn (2011). Although using the term in a slightly different way, Allen J. Scott (1980), in his book, *The Urban Land Nexus and the State*, was one of the first to call the city a nexus of development.

3   For one recent list of Frontier Markets, see Standard & Poor's (2011).

4   Also see, Logan & Molotch (1987); Stone (1989); and Orr & Stoker, (1994), to name a few.

5   The concept of system of cities draws heavily upon Bourne & Simmons (1978). Gottmann & Harper (1990) present an interesting discussion of the special development contexts of national capital cities.

6   For further details on this see Wright (1988), Pickvance & Preteceille (1991), Norton (1994), and Muramatsu (1997).

7   For detailed discussion of this point, see Johnson (1982) and Gurr & King (1987).

8   For interesting discussion on this point, also see Hill (1987) and Dicken (2011).

Rights and Permissions

Chapter	Credit Line
Part 1, Chapter 1	Edited selection from "Where We Stand: A Decade of World City Research," by John Friedmann, pp. 21–47. In P.L. Knox and P.J. Taylor (eds.) *World Cities in a World System*. Cambridge University Press, 1995. Reprinted by permission.
Part 1, Chapter 2	From *Cities in a World Economy*. 3rd ed. By Saskia Sassen, pp. 32–33, 130–148. Copyright © 2006. Used by permission of Sage Publications.
Part 1, Chapter 3	Edited selection from "Hierarchical Tendencies and Regional Patterns in the World City," by Ben Derudder, Peter Taylor, Frank Witlox and Gilda Catalano, from "Network: A Global Urban Analysis of 234 Cities," pp. 875–886 in *Regional Studies*, 37 (9). Copyright © 2003. Used by permission of Routledge.
Part 1, Chapter 4	Edited selection from "Mexico City: The Making of a Global City?" by Christof Parnreiter from *Global Networks, Linked Cities*, pp. 145–182, edited by Saskia Sassen. Copyright © 2002. Used by permission of Routledge.
Part 1, Chapter 5	Edited selection from "Location Theory in Reverse? Location for Global Production in the IT Industry of Bangalore," by Rolee Aranya, pp. 446–463 in *Environment and Planning A*, 40(2), 2008. London: Pion Ltd. Used by permission.
Part 1, Chapter 6	Edited selection from "Building Shanghai: Historical lessons from China's Gateway," by Edward Denison from *City*, 12(2). Copyright © 2008. Used by permission of Routledge.
Part 1, Chapter 7	Edited selection from "Race, Space and the Post-Fordist Spatial Order of Johannesburg," by Owen Crankshaw, from pp. 1692–1711 in *Urban Studies*, 45 (8). Copyright © 2008. Used by permission of Routledge.
Part 1, Chapter 8	Edited selection "Global Dubai or Dubaization" by Yasser Elsheshtawy, pp. 249–279 in *Dubai: Behind an Urban Spectacle*, Copyright © 2009. Used by permission of Routledge.
Part 2, Chapter 9	Edited selection from "The Nested City: Introduction," by Richard Child Hill and Kuniko Fujita, pp. 207–217, *Urban Studies*, 40(2). Copyright © 2003. Used by permission of Routledge. (*Urban Studies* is now published by Wiley-Blackwell)

Part 2, Chapter 10	Edited selection from Janet L. Abu-Lughod, p*p, 1–4, 399–426 in* New York, Chicago, Los Angeles: America's Global Cities. Copyright © 1999. Reprinted by permission of University of Minnesota Press.
Part 2, Chapter 11	Edited and revised selection from "Embedded Contrasts in Race, Municipal Fragmentation & Planning: Divergent Outcomes in the Detroit and Greater Toronto-Hamilton Regions 1990–2000," by A.J. Jacobs, pp. 147–173 in *Journal of Urban Affairs,* 31 (2). Copyright © 2009. Used by permission of John Wiley & Sons.
Part 2, Chapter 12	Edited selection from "Planning Taipei: Nodal Status, Strategic Planning and Mode of Governance," by Chia-Huang Wang, pp. 283–309 in *Town Planning Review,* 77(3), 2006. Used by permission of Liverpool University Press.
Part 2, Chapter 13	New Reading with Modified Maps. Maps used by permission of John Wiley & Sons. Copyright © 2005 and previously published in "Expanding Income Stratification in the Tokyo Region," by A.J. Jacobs, *Journal of Urban Affairs,* 27 (5): 521–555.
Part 2, Chapter 14	Edited selection from Chapters 2–3, 5, 7 in *Planning the Megacity: Jakarta in the Twentieth Century* by Chris Silver. Copyright © 2008. Used by permission of Routledge.
Part 2, Chapter 15	Edited selection from "The Webs they Weave: Malaysia's Multimedia Super-corridor and New York City's Silicon Alley," by Michael Indergaard, pp. 379–401 in *Urban Studies,* 40 (2). Copyright © 2003. Used by permission of Routledge.
Part 2, Chapter 16	New Reading. Part of this chapter was previously published in "Ulsan, South Korea's Global Nested 'Great' Industrial City," pp. 8–20 in *The Open Studies Journal* 4(1) by A.J. Jacobs.
Part 3, Chapter 17	Edited selection from "Regions, Globalization, Development," by Allen J. Scott and Michael Storper, pp. 579–593 in *Regional Studies,* 37 (6–7). Copyright © 2003. Used by permission of Routledge.
Part 3, Chapter 18	New reading. Maps used by permission of Elsevier, copyright © 2012. Maps previously published in "The Bratislava-Žilina Auto Corridor: Capitalist Agglomeration in the Post-Socialist CEE," by A.J. Jacobs, in press article in *Cities,* 29, published online November 2011.
Part 1, Chapter 19	Edited selection from "The Development Industry & Urban Redevelopment in New York & London," by Susan Feinstein from *The City Builders: Property Development in New York & London, 1980–2000,* pp. 27–63. Copyright © 2001. Used by permission of the University Press of Kansas.
Part 3, Chapter 20	Edited selection from "An Entrepreneurial City in Action: Hong Kong's Emerging Strategies in and for (Inter)Urban Competition," by Bob Jessop and Ngai-Ling Sum, pp. 2287–2313 in *Urban Studies,* 37 (12). Copyright © 2000. Used by permission of Routledge. (*Urban Studies* is now published by Wiley-Blackwell)
Part 4, Chapter 21	Edited selection from "Innovation in Europe: A Tale of Knowledge and Trade in Five Cities," by James Simmie et al., pp. 47–64 in *Regional Studies,* 36(1). Copyright © 2002. Used by permission of Routledge.

| Part 4, Chapter 22 | Edited selection from," From World Cities to Gateway Cities: Extending the Boundaries of Globalization Theory," by John R. Short et al., pp. 317–340 in *City*, 4 (3). Copyright © 2000. Used by permission of Routledge. |

| Part 3, Chapter 23 | Edited selection from "From Modernist to Market Urbanism: The Transformation of New Belgrade," by Paul Waley, pp. 209–235 in *Planning Perspectives*, 26 (2). Copyright © 2011. Used by permission of Routledge. |

| Part 3, Chapter 24 | New Reading. Maps used by permission of Sage, copyright © 2012. Maps previously published in "Collaborative Regionalism and Growth: Mississippi's PUL Alliance and Alabama-Georgia's Auto Valley Partnership," by A.J. Jacobs. From in press article in *Economic Development Quarterly*, 26, published online, July 2012. |

SOURCES OF FIGURES

i.1, 3.1, 4.1,5.1, 6.1, 7.1, 8.1, 10.1, 11.1, 11.3, 12.1, 13.2, 14.1, 15.1, 15.2, 16.1, 16.2, 18.1, 18.2, 18.3, 18.4, 19.1, 19.2, 20.1, 21.1, 22.1, 23.1, 24.1, 24.2, and 24.3, Rendered by Sarah Searcy and A. J. Jacobs

16.3 and 18.4, Rendered by A.J. Jacobs

3.1, Derudder et al. (2003, p. 881). Reprinted with permission.

5.2, Aranya (2008, p. 451). Reprinted with permission.

5.3, Aranya (2008, p. 453). Reprinted with permission.

5.4, Aranya (2008, p. 454). Reprinted with permission.

5.5, Aranya (2008, p. 455). Reprinted with permission.

6.2, Denison (2008, p. 213). Reprinted with permission.

7.2, Crankshaw (2008, p. 1693). Reprinted with permission.

7.3, Crankshaw (2008, p. 1702). Reprinted with permission.

7.4, Crankshaw (2008, p. 1705). Reprinted with permission.

11.2, Modified version originally made by author and Mark Finn and published in Jacobs (2009b, p. 151). Reprinted with permission.

13.1, Modified version of map originally published in Jacobs (2005, p. 524). Also published in Jacobs (2012, p. 123). Reprinted with permission.

13.2, Also published in Jacobs (2012, p. 124). Reprinted with permission.

13.3, Modified version of map originally published in Jacobs (2005, p. 524). Also published in Jacobs (2012, p. 125). Reprinted with permission.

13.4, Data obtained from Nihon Marketing Center (1981–2004) and JPS (2005–2008). Also published in Jacobs (2012, p. 127). Reprinted with permission.

16.1, Previously published in Jacobs (2011b, p. 10). Reprinted with permission.

16.3, Data obtained from Oanda (2010); Previously published in Jacobs (2011b, p. 15).

Reprinted with permission.

18.1, Previously published in Jacobs (2012 [2011], p. 1). Reprinted with permission.

18.2, Previously published in Jacobs (2012 [2011], p. 3). Reprinted with permission.

18.3, Previously published in Jacobs (2012 [2011], p. 6). Reprinted with permission.

23.2, Waley (2011, p. 215), Reprinted with permission.

23.3, Waley (2011, p. 216). Reprinted with permission.

References Cited in the Readings

Abdullah, A. 2006a. Dubai: Rihlat Madina Arabiya min Al Mahaliya ila Al Alamia [Dubai: An Arab City Journey from Localism to Globalism]. *Al-Mustaqbal Al-Arabi* [*The Arab Future*], January, 323: 57–84.

Abdullah, A. 2006b. Dubai: Rihlat Madina Arabiya min Al Mahaliya ila Al Alamia—Munaqashit Ta'alig Samir Amin [Dubai: An Arab City Journey from Localism to Globalism—Discussing Samir Amin's Commentary]. *Al-Mustaqbal Al-Arabi* [*The Arab Future*], August, 330: 100–106.

Abrahamson. M . 2004. *Global Cities*. New York: Oxford University Press.

Abu-Lughod, J. 1995. Comparing Chicago, New York, and Los Angeles: Testing Some World City Hypotheses. In P. Knox and P. Taylor, eds. *World Cities in a World System*. New York: Cambridge University Press, pp. 171–191.

Abu-Lughod, J. 1999. *New York, Chicago, Los Angeles: America's Global Cities*. Minneapolis, MN: University of Minnesota Press.

ACEA. 2008. Automotive Industry in the New EU Member States: Slovak Republic—Largest Per Capita Car Producer. Brussels: European Automobile Manufacturers' Association.

ACEA. 2010. *European Union—Economic Report*. Brussels: European Automobile Manufacturers' Association.

Alderson, A. and J. Beckfield. 2004. Power and Position in the World-city System. *American Journal of Sociology*, 109 (4): 811–851.

Alderson, A., J. Beckfield, and J. Sprague-Jones. 2010. Intercity Relations and Globalisation: The Evolution of the Global Urban Hierarchy. *Urban Studies*, 47 (9): 1899–1923.

Amin, A. and N. Thrift. 1992. Neo-Marshallian Nodes in Global Networks. *International Journal of Urban and Regional Research*, 16 (4): 571–587.

Amin, A. and N. Thrift. 1994. Living in the Global. In A. Amin and N. Thrift, eds., *Globalization, Institutions, and Regional Development in Europe*. Oxford: Oxford University Press, pp. 1–22.

Amin, A. and N. Thrift. 1995. Globalisation, Institutional 'Thickness" and the Local Economy. In P. Healey, S. Cameron, S. Davoudi, S. Graham, and A. Madani-Pour, eds., *Managing Cities: The New Urban Context*. New York: Wiley, pp. 91–108.

Amin, S. 2006. Munaqashit maqalit Abdulkhaleg Abdullah: Dubai: Rihlat Madina Arabiya min Al Mahaliya ila Al Alamia [Discussion of Abdul Khaleg Abdullah's Article—Dubai: An Arab City Journey from Localism to Globalism]. *Al-Mustaqbal Al-Arabi* [*The Arab Future*], January, 323: 157–160.

Amsden, A. 1989. *Asia's Next Giant: South Korea and Late Industrialization*. New York: Oxford University Press.

Anderson, L. 2000. Letter from Havana: The Old Man and the Boy. *The New Yorker*, 21 and 28 February, pp. 224–237.

Aoki, H. 2003. Homelessness in Osaka: Globalisation, Yoseba and Disemployment. *Urban Studies*, 40 (2): 361–378.

Aranya, R. 2008. Location Theory in Reverse? Location for Global Production in the IT Industry of Bangalore. *Environment and Planning A*, 40(2): 446–463.

Aris. G. 2007. Provinces Should Look to Dubai for Inspiration: Economic Miracle Can Be Mirrored in Iraq. *Gulf News*, January 11, p. 43.

Atlanta Journal-Constitution. 2008. General Motors Doraville Timeline, September 21, p. A8.

Audi. 2011. Győr Production Plant Overview. Online. Available at: http://www.audi.com/com/ brand/ en/company/production_plants/gyoer.html, last accessed June 30, 2011.

Bank for International Settlements. 2005. *Quarterly Review—December, 2005*. Basel, Switzerland: BIS.

Barnet, R. and R, Muller. 1974. *Global Reach: The Power of Multinational Corporations*. New York: Simon and Schuster.

Beall, J., O. Crankshaw, and S. Parnell. (2002) *Uniting a Divided City: Governance and Social Exclusion in Johannesburg*. London: Earthscan.

Beauregard, R. 1991. Capital Restructuring and the New Built Environment of Global Cities: New York and Los Angeles. *International Journal of Urban and Regional Research*, 15 (1): 90–105.

Beaverstock, J., R. Smith, and P. Taylor. 2000. World City Network: A New Metageography?

Beaverstock, J, P. Taylor, and R. Smith. 1999. A Roster of World Cities. *Cities*, 16 (6): 445–458.

Beavon, K. 2004. *Johannesburg: The Making and Shaping of the City*. Pretoria: UNISA Press.

Becattini, G. 1990. The Marshallian Industrial District as a Socio-Economic Notion. In F. Pyke, G. Becattini, and W. Sengenberger, eds. *Industrial Districts and inter-firm Co-operation in Italy*. Geneva: International Institute for Labor Statistics, pp. 37–51.

Berger, S., and R. Dore, eds. 1996. *National Diversity and Global Capitalism*. Ithaca, NY: Cornell University Press.

Bibby, R. 1990. *Mosaic Madness: Pluralism without a Cause*. Toronto: Stoddart.

Bloomfield, G. 1978. *The World Automotive Industry*. North Pomfret, VT: David & Charles.

BMW. 2011. BMW Premium Production Worldwide. Online. Available from: http://www.bmwgroup. com, last accessed July 16.

Borja, J. 1996. The City, Democracy and Governability: The Case of Barcelona. *International Social Science Journal*, 48 (1): 85–93.

Bourne, L. and J. Simmons, eds. 1978. *Systems of Cities: Readings on Structure, Growth, and Policy*. New York: Oxford University Press.

Boyd, M. 2000. Ethnicity and Immigrant Offspring. In M. Kalbach and W. Kalbach, eds., *Perspectives on Ethnicity in Canada*. Toronto: Harcourt, pp. 137–154.

Brenner, N. 1997. Global Cities, Glocal States: Global City Formation and State Territorial Restructuring in Contemporary Europe. *Review of International Political Economy*, 5 (1): 1–37.

Brenner, N. 1998. Global Cities, Glocal States: Global City Formation and State Territorial Restructuring in Contemporary Europe. *Review of International Political Economy*, 5 (1): 1–37.

Brenner, N. 1999a. Globalization as Reterritorialization: The Re-scaling of Urban Governance in the European Union. *Urban Studies*, 36 (3): 431–451.

Brenner, N. 1999b. Beyond State-centrism? Space, Territoriality and Geographical Scale in Globalization Studies. *Theory and Society*, 28 (1): 39–78.

Brenner, N. 2004. *New State Spaces: Urban Governance and the Rescaling of Statehood*. New York: Oxford University Press.

Brenner, N. and R. Keil, eds. 2006. *The Global Cities Reader*. New York: Routledge.

Brown, E., G. Catalano, and P. Taylor. 2002. Beyond World cities: Central America in a Space of Flows. *Area*, 34 (2): 139–148.

Brunn, S., M. Hays-Mitchell, and D. Zeigler. 2012. *Cities of the World: World Regional Urban Development*. Fifth Edition. Lanham, MD: Rowman & Littlefield.

Brzica, D. 2009. Urban Dynamism within the Vienna-Bratislava Metropolitan Area: Improving Regional Competitiveness and the Constructed Regional Advantage Concept. *Managing Global Transitions*, 7 (3): 241–258.

Bureau of Statistics. 1968. *Population Census of South Africa, 6th September, 1960, Vol. 7, No.2*.

Characteristics of the Population in Each Magisterial District and Economic Region: Occupation, Industry and Type of Abode. Pretoria: Republic of South Africa Bureau of Statistics.

Burgess, E. 1925. The Growth of the City: An Introduction to a Research Project. In R. Park, E.

Burgess, E. and R. McKenzie, eds. 1984. *The City*. Chicago, IL: University of Chicago Press, pp. 47–62.

Burgess, E., ed. 1926. *The Urban Community*. Chicago, IL: University of Chicago Press.

Burns, P. 2002. The Intergovernmental Regime and Public Policy in Hartford, Connecticut. *Journal of Urban Affairs*, 24 (1): 55–73.

Caggiano, C. 1999. Microsoft—Maybe You've Heard of It? *Inc.*, May 18, p. n/a.

Castells, M. 1977. *The Urban Question: A Marxist Approach*. Cambridge, MA: MIT Press.

Castells, M. 1983. *The City and the Grassroots: A Cross-Cultural Theory of Urban Social Movements*. Berkeley, CA: University of California Press.

Castells, M., ed. 1985. *High Technology, Space, and Society*. Beverly Hills, CA: Sage.

Castells, M. 1989. *The Informational City: Economic Restructuring and Urban Development*. Malden, MA: Blackwell.

Castells. M. 1998. *End of Millennium*. Oxford: Blackwell.

Central Statistical Service. various years. *Population Census of South Africa*. Pretoria: Central Statistical Service.

Champion, 2004. Does the Gateway to the Middle East Lie in Ruins? Golden Days Seem Far Away. *The Daily Star Online*. February 10. Online. Available at: http:/www.dailystar.com.lb, last accessed September 21, 2005.

Chan. S. 2008. Dispute Fester over Village Playhouse's Fate. *The New York Times*, October 20. Online. Available at: http//cityroom.blogs.nytimes.com/2008/20/20/dispute-festers-over-village-playhouse-fate/, last accessed, January 11, 2012.

Chandler, A. 1977. *The Visible Hand: The Managerial Revolution in American Business*. Cambridge, MA: Harvard University Press.

Chandler, A. 1990. *Scale and Scope: The Dynamics of Industrial Capitalism*. Cambridge, MA: Harvard University Press.

Chase-Dunn, C. 1984. Urbanization in the World-System. In M. Smith, ed., *Cities in Transformation*. Beverly Hills, CA: Sage, pp. 111–122

Chase-Dunn, C. 1985. The System of World Cities, AD 800–1975. In M. Timberlake, ed., *Urbanization in the World Economy*. Orlando, FL: Academic Press, Inc., pp. 269–291.

Child, C. 1924. *Physiological Foundations of Behavior*. New York: Henry Holt & Co.

Christopher, A. 2001. Urban Segregation in Post-apartheid South Africa. *Urban Studies*, 38 (3): 449–466.

Christopher, A. 2005. Does South Africa have Ghettos? *Journal of Economic and Social Geography*, 96 (3): 241–252.

Clammer, J. 2003. Globalisation, Class, Consumption and Civel Society in South-east Asian Cities. *Urban Studies*, 40 (2), 403–419.

Coase, R. 1937. The Nature of the Firm. *Economica*, 4 (16): 386–405.

Cody, J. 2001. *Building in China—Henry K Murphy's 'Adaptive Architecture' 1914–1935*. Hong Kong: The Chinese University Press.

Cohen, R. 1981. The New International Division of Labor: Multinational Corporations and Urban Hierarchy. In M. Dear and A. Scott, eds., *Urbanization and Urban Planning in Capitalist Society*, London: Methuen, pp. 287–315.

Commission on Strategic Development. 2000. *Bringing the Vision to Life: Hong Kong's Long-term Development Needs and Goals*. Hong Kong: Central Policy Unit, Hong Kong Special Administrative Region.

Cowley, P. and J. Aronson. 1993. *Managing the World Economy*. New York: Council of Foreign Relations Press.

Cox, K. 1995. Globalization, Competition, and the Politics of Local Economic Development. *Urban Studies*, 32 (2): 213–224.

Cox, K., ed. 1997. *Spaces of Globalization: Reasserting the Power of the Local*. New York: Guilford.

Cox, K. 2004. Globalization and the Politics of Local and Regional Development. *Transactions of the Institute of British Geographers (New Series)*, 29 (2): 179–194.

Cox, K. and A. Mair. 1989. From Localised Social Structures to Localities as Agents. *Environment and Planning A*, 23 (2): 197–213.

Crankshaw, O. 1996. Changes in the Racial Division of Labour during the Apartheid Era. *Journal of Southern African Studies*, 22 (4): 633–656.

Crankshaw, O. 1997. *Race, Class and the Changing Division of Labour under Apartheid*. London: Routledge.

Crankshaw, O. 2005. Class, Race and Residence in Black Johannesburg, 1923–1970, *Journal of Historical Sociology*, 18 (4): 353–392.

Crankshaw, O. 2008. Race, Space and the Post-Fordist Spatial Order of Johannesburg. *Urban Studies*, 45 (8): 1692–1711.

Crankshaw, O. and C. White. 1995. Racial Desegregation and Inner City Decay in Johannesburg. *International Journal of Urban and Regional Research*, 19 (4): 622–638.

Daher, R. 2008. Amman: Disguised Genealogy and Recent Urban Restructuring and Neoliberal Threats. In Y. Elsheshtawy, ed. *The Evolving Area City*. New York: Routledge, pp. 37–68.

Daniels, P. 1985. *Service Industries: A Geographical Appraisal*. New York: Methuen.

Daniels, P. 1995. The EU Internal Market Programme and the Spatial Development of Producer Services in Great Britain, *European Urban and Regional Studies*, 2 (4): 299–316.

Darden, J., R. Hill, J. Thomas, and R. Thomas. 1987. *Detroit: Race and Uneven Development*. Philadelphia, PA: Temple University Press.

Darden, J. 2004. *The Significance of White Supremacy in the Canadian Metropolis*. Lewiston, NY: Edwin Mellen Press.

Darden, J. 2007. Changes in Black Residential Segregation in Metropolitan Areas of Michigan. In J. Darden, C. Stokes, and R. Thomas, eds., *The State of Black Michigan, 1967–2007*. East Lansing, MI: Michigan State University Press, pp. 147–160.

Davis, M. 1990. *City of Quartz: Excavating the Future in Los Angeles*. New York: Vintage Books.

Davis, R. 2010. Alabama Auto Industry Update. Paper presented during the *2010 Southern Automotive Conference*, October 6–8, 2010, in Tunica, MS.

Dear, M. ed. 2001. *From Chicago to L.A.: Making Sense of Urban Theory*. Thousand Oaks, CA: Sage.

Dear, M. and A. Scott, eds. 1981. *Urbanization and Urban Planning in Capitalist Society*. London: Methuen.

Denison, E. 2008. Building Shanghai: Historical Lessons from China's Gateway. *City*, 12 (2): 207–216.

Department of Statistics. 1976. *Population Census 1970, Occupation and Industry by District and Economic Region*. Pretoria: Republic of South Africa Department of Statistics.

Derudder, B. et al. 2010. Pathways of Change: Shifting Connectivities in the World City Network, 2000–08. *Urban Studies*, 47 (9): 1861–1877.

Derudder, B., P. Taylor, F. Witlox, and G. Catalano. 2003. Hierarchical Tendencies and Regional Patterns in the World City Network: A Global Urban Analysis of 234 Cities. *Regional Studies*, 37 (9): 875–886.

Derudder B. and F. Witlox. 2002. Classification Techniques in Complex Spatial Databases: Assessment of Vagueness and Sparsity in a Network of World Cities. *Solstice*, 13 (1): 1–32.

Derudder, B. and F. Witlox, eds. 2010. *Commodity Chains and World Cities*. New York: Wiley.

Dick, H. 1981. Urban Public Transport, Part II. *Bulletin of Indonesian Economic Studies*, 17 (2): 72–88.

Dicken, P. 2011. *Global Shift: Mapping the Changing Contours of the World Economy*. Sixth Edition. New York: Guilford Press.

Dlamini, N. 2005. Cosmo City on Track for First Residents, *Johannesburg News Agency*. May 24 May. Online. Available at: www.joburg.org.za, last accessed, January 12, 2012.

Dlamini, N. 2007. Rich and Poor to be Neighbours, *Johannesburg News Agency*. February 22. Online. Available at: www.joburg.org.za, last accessed, January 12, 2012.

Djordjevic, M. 2004. Reducing Housing Poverty in Serbian Urban Centers: Analysis and Policy Recommendations, in J. Fearn, ed., *Too Poor To Move, Too Poor To Stay: A Report on Housing in the Czech Republic, Hungary and Serbia*. Budapest: Local Government and Public Service Reform Initiative, Open Society Institute, pp. 97–121.

Dore, R., W. Lazonick, M. and O'Sullivan. 1999. Varieties of Capitalism in the Twentieth Century, *Oxford Review of Economic Policy*, 15 (4): 102–120.

Doremus, P., W. Keller, L. Pauly, and S. Reich. 1998. *The Myth of the Global Corporation*. Princeton, NJ: Princeton University Press.

Dosi, G., C. Freeman, R. Nelson, G. Silverberg, and L. Soete. 1988. *Technical Change and Economic Theory*. London: Pinter.

Du, Y. 1935. The Consciousness that Architects Should Have. *The Builder*, 3 (6): 26.

Dubois. W. 1899. *The Philadelphia Negro*. Philadelphia, PA: The University of Philadelphia.

Dyce, C. 1906. *Personal Reminiscences of Thirty Years' Residence in the Model Settlement, Shanghai, 1870–1900*. London: Chapman & Hall.

Einhorn, D. and S. Prasso. 1999. Mahatir's High-Tech Folly. *Business Week*, March 29, pp. 83–86.

El-Fasher, J. 2006. Glittering Towers in a War Zone. *The Economist*, December 7. Online. Available at: http://www.economist.com/node/8380843, last accessed, January 11, 2012.

Elkin, S. 1987. *City and Regime in the American Republic*. Chicago, IL: University of Chicago Press.

Elsheshtawy, Y. 2004. Redrawing Boundaries: Dubai an Emerging Global City. In Y. Elsheshtawy, ed. *Planning Middle East Cities*. New York: Routledge, pp. 169–199.

Elsheshtawy, Y. 2006. From Dubai to Cairo: Competing Global Cities, Models, and Shifting Centers of Influence. In D. Singerman and P. Amar, eds., *Cairo Cosmopolitan: Politics, Culture and Urban Space in the New Middle East*. Cairo: AUC Press.

Elsheshtawy, Y. 2009. *Dubai: Behind an Urban Spectacle*. New York: Routledge.

Enlow, C. 1999. Seattle: Small is Still Beautiful. *Planning*, 65 (3): 4–12.

Ernest & Young. 2010. The Central and Eastern European Automotive Market: Industry Overview. Stuttgart & Detroit: Ernest & Young, March.

ESN, Brussels, 2000. Innovation and Creativity: Transforming Europe. Special Edition of *Innovation & Technology Transfer*. Luxembourg: European Commission, Enterprise DG. Programme. June. Online. Available at: ftp://ftp.cordis.europa.eu/pub/itt/docs/itt00–4_en.pdf, last accessed, December 31, 2011.

European Commission. 1996. *DGs XIII and XVI RITTS and RIS Guidebook, Regional Actions for Innovation*. Brussels: EC.

Evans, P. 1995. *Embedded Autonomy*. Princeton, NJ: Princeton University Press.

Fainstein, N. and S. Fainstein. 1988. Governing Regimes and the Political Economy of Development in New York City. In J. Mollenkopf, ed., *Power, Culture, and Place: Essays on the History of New York City*. New York: Russell Sage Foundation, pp. 161–199.

Fainstein, N. and S. Fainstein. 1989. New York City: The Manhattan Business District, 1945–1988. In G. Squires, ed., *Unequal Partnerships*. New Brunswick, NJ: Rutgers University Press, pp. 59–79.

Fainstein, S. 1990. Economics, Politics, and Development Policy: New York and London. *International Journal of Urban and Regional Research*, 14 (4): 553–575.

Fainstein, S. 1992. The Second New York Fiscal Crisis. *International Journal of Urban and Regional Research*, 16 (1): 129–137.

Fainstein, S. 2001a. Inequality in Global City-Regions. In A. Scott, ed., *Global City-Regions: Trends, Theory, Policy*. New York: Oxford University Press, pp. 285–298.

Fainstein, S. 2001b. *The City Builders: Property Development in New York & London, 1980–2000*. Lawrence, KS: University of Kansas Press.

Fainstein, S. and N. Fainstein. 1987. Economic Restructuring and the Politics of Land Use Planning in New York City. *Journal of the American Planning Association*, 53 (2): 237–248.

Fainstein, S., N. Fainstein, R. Hill, D. Judd, and M. Smith, eds. 1986. *Restructuring the City: The Political Economy of Urban Redevelopment.* Revised Edition. New York: Longman.

Fainstein, S., N. Fainstein, and A. Schwartz. 1989. Economic Shifts and Land Use in the Global City. In R. Beauregard, ed., *Atop the Urban Hierarchy.* Totowa, NJ: Rowan and Littlefield, pp. 45–86.

Fainstein, S., I. Gordon, and M. Harloe, eds. 1992. *Divided Cities: New York & London in the Contemporary World.* Oxford: Blackwell.

Far Eastern Review. 1927. Shanghai's New Billion-dollar Skyline, 24 (1 June), p. 254.

Feagin, J. and M. Smith. 1987. Cities and the New International Division of Labor: An Overview. In M. Smith and J. Feagin, eds., *The Capitalist City: Global Restructuring & Community Politics.* Cambridge, MA: Basil Blackwell, pp. 3–34.

Fifekova, M. and J. Hardy. 2010. Business Service Foreign Direct Investment in Central and Eastern Europe: Trends, Motives and Impacts. Project Report. Hertfordshire, UK: Economy and Society Trust and the Business School of University of Hertfordshire, February.

Firman, T. 1996. Patterns and Trends in Urbanization: A Reflection of Regional Disparity. In G. Jones and T. Hull, eds., *Indonesia Assessment: Population and Human Resources.* Canberra: Research School of Pacific and Asian Studies, Australian National University, pp. 101–117.

Fong, E., ed. 2006. *Inside the Mosaic.* Toronto: University of Toronto Press.

Ford. 2011. Ford Motor Company: Global Operations. Online. Available from: http://corporate.ford.com/about-ford/global-operations, last accessed January 15.

Foreign Policy. 2008. The Global Cities Index. Online Available at: http://www.foreignpolicy.com/, last accessed, February 24, 2009.

Frank, A. 1966. The Development of Underdevelopment. *Monthly Review,* 18 (4): 17–31.

Frank, A. 1967. *Capitalism and Underdevelopment in Latin America: Historical Studies of Chile and Brazil.* New York: Monthly Review Press.

Friedman, T. 2006. Dubai and Dunces. *The New York Times,* March 15. Online. Available at: http://www.nytimes.com/, last accessed, January 12, 2012.

Friedmann, J. 1986. The World City Hypothesis. *Development and Change,* 17 (1): 69–83.

Friedmann, J. 2001. World Cities Revisited: A Comment. *Urban Studies,* 38 (13): 2535–2536.

Friedmann, J. 1995. Where We Stand: A Decade of World City Research. In P. Knox and P. Taylor, eds., *World Cities in a World System.* New York: Cambridge University Press, pp. 21–47.

Friedmann, J. and G. Wolff. 1982. World City Formation: An Agenda for Research and Action. *International Journal of Urban and Regional Research,* 6 (3): 309–344.

Fujita K. 1991. A World City and Flexible Specialization: Restructuring of the Tokyo Metropolis. *International Journal of Urban and Regional Research,* 15 (2): 269–284.

Fujita, K. 2000. Asian Crisis, Financial Systems and Urban Development, *Urban Studies,* 37 (12): 2197–2216.

Fujita, K. 2003. Neo-industrial Tokyo: Urban Development and Globalisation in Japan's State-centred Developmental Capitalism. *Urban Studies,* 40 (2): 249–281.

Fujita, K. 2011. Financial Crises, Japan's State Regime Shift, and Tokyo's Urban Policy. *Environment and Planning A,* 43 (2): 307–327.

Fujita, K. and R. Hill, eds. 1993. *Japanese Cities in the World Economy.* Philadelphia, PA: Temple University Press.

Fujita, K. and R. Hill. 1997. Together and Equal: Place Stratification in Osaka. In P. Karan and K. Stapleton, eds., *The Japanese City.* Lexington, KT: University Press of Kentucky, pp. 106–133.

Fujita, K. and R. Hill. 1998. Industrial Districts and Urban Economic Development in Japan: Tokyo and Osaka. *Economic Development Quarterly,* 12 (2): 181–198.

Fujita M., P. Krugman, and A. Venables. 1999. *The Spatial Economy: Cities, Regions and International Trade.* Cambridge, MA: MIT Press.

Gamewell, M. 1916. *The Gateway to China.* New York: F. H. Revell Co.

Garreau, J. 1991. *Edge City: Life on the New Frontier.* New York: Anchor Books.

GaWC. 2011. Globalization and World Cities Research Network Website. Online. Available at: http://www.lboro.ac.uk/gawc/, last accessed January 15, 2012.

GDEcD. 2010. *Kia Motors Manufacturing Georgia Fact Sheet*. Atlanta: Georgia Department of Economic Development.

GDOL. 2011. Georgia Labor Force Estimates. *Georgia Department of Labor*. Online. Available at: http://www.dol.state.ga.us/pdf/pr/laborforce.pdf, last accessed October 14.

Georgia Power. 2011. *Automotive Manufacturing in Georgia—2011,* Online. Available at: http://www.georgiapower.com/select/publications/Automotive_Industry_Report.pdf, last accessed, December 28, 2011.

Geddes, P. 1915. *Cities in Evolution*. London: Benn.

Gelb, S. 1991. South Africa's Economic Crisis: An Overview. In S. Gelb, ed., *South Africa's Economic Crisis*. Cape Town: David Philip, pp. 1–32.

GGA. 2011. The Official Code of Georgia. Atlanta: *Georgia General Assembly*.

Giovanni, J. 1983. I Love New York and L.A., Too. *New York Times Magazine*, September 11, p. 147.

GJMC. 1948–2001. Population Census of Greater Johannesburg Metropolitan Council. Johannesburg: GJMC.

GM. 2011. General Motors. *GM News*. Online. Available from: http://media.gm.com/media/us/ en/ company_info.html, last accessed March 16.

Goldstein , C. 1990. High Stakes: Japanese Share of Overseas Investment Surges. *Far Eastern Economic Review*, 28 (June): 71–72.

Gottdiener, M. 1985. *The Social Production of Urban Space*. Austin, TX: University of Texas Press.

Gottdiener, M. and L. Budd. 2005. *Key Concepts in Urban Studies*. Thousand Oaks, CA: Sage.

Gottdiener, M. and J. Feagin. 1988. The Paradigm Shift in Urban Sociology. *Urban Affairs Review*, 24 (2): 163–187.

Gottdiener, M. and R. Hutchison. 2011. *The New Urban Sociology*. Fourth Edition. Boulder, CO: Westview Press.

Gottmann, J. and R. Harper, eds. 1990. *Since Megalopolis: The Urban Writings of Jean Gottmann*. Baltimore, MD: The Johns Hopkins University Press.

Granovetter, M. 1985. Economic Action and Social Structure: The Problem of Embeddedness. *American Journal of Sociology*, 91 (3): 481–510.

Grant, R. 1999. The Gateway City: Foreign Companies and Accra, Ghana. Paper presented at the *Third World Studies Association Meeting*, San Jose, Costa Rica, November 21.

Grant, R. and J. Nijman. 2000. Comparative Urbanism in the Lesser Developed World: A Model for the Global Era. Paper presented at the *Sixth Asian Urbanization Conference*. University of Madras, Cheney, India, January 5–9.

Green, C. 1965. *American Cities in the Growth of the Nation*. New York: Harper & Row.

GTMA. 2006. Investing in the GTA: Automotive & Advanced Manufacturing. Toronto: Greater Toronto Marketing Alliance.

Gulf News. 2007. Emaar Studies Proposals for Massive Libyan Project. *Gulf News*, June 18, p. 42.

Gurr, T. and D. King. 1987. *The State and the City*. London: Macmillan.

Gyeongsangbuk-do. 2011. Homepage of North Gyeongsang Province. Online. Available from: http://www.gb.go.kr/eng/main/main.jsp, last accessed October 2, 2011.

Gyeongsangnam-do. 2011. Homepage of South Gyeongsong Province. Online. Available from http://english.gsnd.net/, last accessed October 2, 2011.

Hall, P. 1966/1979. *The World Cities*. New York: McGraw-Hill.

Hall. P. 1996. The Global City. *International Social Science Journal*, 48 (1): 15–23.

Hall, T. and P. Hubbard. 1996. The Entrepreneurial City: New Urban Politics, New Urban Geographies? *Progress in Human Geography*, 20 (2): 153–174.

Hall, T. and P. Hubbard, eds. 1998. *The Entrepreneurial City: Geographies of Politics, Regime, and Representation*. New York: Wiley.

Harding, A. 1994. Urban Regimes and Urban Growth Machines: Toward a Cross National Research Agenda. *Urban Affairs Quarterly*, 29 (3): 356–382.

Harrison, P. and A. Mabin. 2006. Security and Space: Managing the Contradictions of Access Restriction in Johannesburg. *Environment and Planning B*, 33 (1): 3–20.

Hart, D. and J. Simmie. 1997. Innovation, Competition and the Structure of Local Production Networks: Initial Findings from the Hertfordshire Project. *Local Economy*, 12 (3): 235–246.

Hart, T. 1976a. The Evolving Pattern of Elite White Residential Areas in Johannesburg, 1911–1970. *The South African Geographical Journal*, 58 (1): 68–75.

Hart, T. 1976b. Patterns of Black Residence in the White Residential Areas of Johannesburg. *The South African Geographical Journal*, 58 (2): 141–150.

Harvey, D. 1973. *Social Justice and the City*. London: Edward Arnold.

Harvey, D. 1982. *The Limits to Capital*. Chicago, IL: University of Chicago Press.

Harvey, D. 1989. From Managerialism to Entrepreneurialism: The Transformation of Urban Governance in Late Capitalism. *Geografiska Annaler, Series B Human Geography*, 71 (1): 3–17.

Harvey, T. 1996. Portland, Oregon: regional city in a global economy, *Urban Geography*, 17 (1): 95–114.

Hatch, W. and K. Yamamura. 1996. Asia in Japan's Embrace: Building a Regional Production Alliance. New York: Cambridge University Press.

Hawley, A. 1950. *Human Ecology: A Theory of Community Structure*. New York: Ronald Press.

Hawley, A. 1968. *Roderick D. McKenzie on Human Ecology*. Chicago, IL: University of Chicago.

Hawley, A. 1971. *Urban Society: An Ecological Approach*. New York: Ronald Press.

Hawley, A. 1986. *Human Ecology: A Theoretical Essay*. Chicago, IL: University of Chicago Press.

Hay, C. and D. Marsh. 2000. *Demystifying Globalization*. London: Palgrave Macmillan.

Healey, P. and R. Nabarro, eds. 1990. *Land and Property Development in a Changing Context*. Aldershot, Hants, UK: Gower.

Henderson. J. 1999. Uneven Crises: Institutional Foundations of East Asian Economic Turmoil. *Economy and Society*, 28 (3): 327–368.

Henderson, J. and M. Castells, eds. 1987. *Global Restructuring and Territorial Development*. Newbury Park, CA: Sage.

Heskin, A. 1991. *The Struggle for Community*. Boulder, CO: Westview Press.

Hill, R. 1982. Transnational Capitalism and the Crisis of Industrial Cities. *Journal of Intergroup Relations*, 10 (5): 30–41.

Hill, R. 1983. Crisis in the Motor City: The Politics of Economic Development in Detroit. In S. Fainstein, N. Fainstein, R. Hill, D. Judd, and M. Smith, eds., *Restructuring the City*. New York: Longman, pp. 80–125.

Hill, R. 1984. Economic Crisis and Political Response in the Motor City. In L. Sawers and W. K. Tabb, *Sunbelt/Snowbelt: Urban Development and Regional Restructuring*. New York: Oxford University Press, pp. 313–338.

Hill, R. 1987. Global Factory and Company Town: The Changing Division of Labor in the International Automobile Industry. In J. Henderson and M. Castells, eds., *Global Restructuring and Territorial Development*. Newbury Park, CA: Sage, pp. 18–37.

Hill, R. 1989. Comparing Transnational Production Systems: The Automobile Industry in the USA and Japan. *International Journal of Urban and Regional Research*, 13 (3): 462–480.

Hill, R. 1990a. Federalism and Urban Policy: The Intergovernmental Dialectic. In T. Swartz and J. Peck, eds., *The Changing Face of Fiscal Federalism*. New York: M.E. Sharpe, pp. 35–55.

Hill, R. 1990b. Industrial Restructuring, State Intervention, and Uneven Development in the U.S. and Japan. In J. Logan and T. Swanstrom, eds., *Beyond the City Limits: Urban Policy and Economic Restructuring in Comparative Perspective*. Philadelphia, PA: Temple University Press, pp. 60–85.

Hill, R. 1996. Detroit and Osaka: Urban Life in the USA and Japan. *Michigan Sociological Review*, 10 (Fall): 1–17.

Hill, R. 2004. Cities and Nested Hierarchies. *International Social Science Journal* 56 (181): 373–384.

Hill, R. and K. Fujita. 1995. Osaka's Tokyo Problem. *International Journal of Urban and Regional Research,* 19 (2): 181–193.

Hill, R. and K. Fujita. 2000. State Restructuring and Local Power in Japan. *Urban Studies,* 37 (4): 673–690.

Hill, R. and K. Fujita. 2003. The Nested City: Introduction. *Urban Studies,* 40 (2): 207–217.

Hill, R. and J. Kim. 2000. Global Cities and Developmental States: New York, Tokyo, and Seoul. *Urban Studies,* 37 (12): 2167–2195.

Hill, R. and J. Kim. 2001. Reply to Friedmann and Sassen, *Urban Studies,* 38 (13): 2541–2542.

Hirt, S. 2009. Landscapes of Post-modernity: Changes in the Built Fabric of Belgrade and Sofia since the End of Socialism. *Urban Geography,* 29 (8): 785–810.

HMMA. 2011. Hyundai Motor Manufacturing Alabama, LLC. Online. Available from: http://www.hmmausa.com, last accessed October 12.

HMMC. 2011. Hyundai Motor Manufacturing Czech. General Information. Nosovice, CZ. Available at: http://www.hyundai-motor.cz/hyundai/english.php, last accessed July 5, 2011.

Ho, K. 2000. Competing to be Regional Centers. *Urban Studies,* 37 (12): 2337–2356.

Ho, K. 2003. Attracting and Retaining Investments in Uncertain Times: Singapore in South-East Asia. *Urban Studies,* 40 (2): 421–438.

Hollingsworth, J. and R. Boyer. 1997. *Contemporary Capitalism: The Embeddedness of Institutions.* New York: Cambridge University Press.

Holusha. J. 1997. Oversupply of Office Space is Starting to Dwindle. *The New York Times,* May 4, p. 9.

Honda. 2011. Honda in America, Operations Overview. Online. Available from: http://corporate.honda.com, last accessed January 31.

Hong Kong SAR Government (various years). *Hong Kong Annual Report.* Hong Kong: Hong Kong Special Administrative Region.

Hoover, E. 1937. *Location Theory and the Shoe and Leather Industries,* Cambridge, MA: Harvard University Press.

Hoover, E. 1948. *The Location of Economic Activity.* New York: McGraw-Hill.

Hoppner F., F. Klawon, R. Kruse, and T. Runkler. 1999. *Fuzzy Cluster Analysis.* Chichester: John Wiley.

Howe, C. 1981. *Revolution and Development in an Asian Metropolis.* Cambridge: Cambridge University Press.

Hoyt, H. 1933. *One Hundred Years of Land Values in Chicago.* Chicago, IL: University of Chicago Press.

Hou, F. 2006. Spatial Assimilation of Racial Minorities in Canada's Immigrant Gateway Cities. *Urban Studies,* 43 (7): 1191–1213.

Hsu, J. 2005. A Site of Transnationalism in the 'Ungrounded Empire': Taipei as an Interface City in the Cross-border Business Networks. *Geoforum,* 36 (5): 654–666.

Huber, T. 1994. *Strategic Economy in Japan.* Boulder, CO: Westview Press.

Huff. T. 2001. Globalization and the Internet: Comparing the Middle Eastern and Malaysian Experiences. *Middle East Journal,* 3 (3): 439–458.

Hurley, N. 1959. The Automotive Industry: A Study in Industrial Location. *Land Economics,* 35 (1): 1–14.

Hymer, S. 1972. The Multinational Corporation and the Law of Uneven Development. In J. Bhagwati, ed., *Economics and World Order: From the 1970's to the 1990's.* London: The Macmillan Company, pp. 113–140.

Hymer, S. 1979. *The Multinational Corporation: A Radical Approach.* New York: Cambridge University Press.

Hyundai HI. 2012. Hyundai Heavy Industries: Shipbuilding. Online. Available at: http://english.hhi.co.kr/Business/Shipbuilding.asp, last accessed, January 4, 2012.

Hyundai Motor. 2012. Hyundai Worldwide. Seoul: Hyundai Motor Company. Online. Available from: http://worldwide.hyundai.com/hyundai-worldwide.html, last accessed, January 4, 2012.

Ignatieff, M. 1993. *Blood and Belonging: Journeys into the New Nationalism*. New York: The Noonday Press.

Indergaard, M. 2001. Innovation, Speculation, and Urban Development. *Critical Perspectives on Urban Development*, 6: 107–146.

Indergaard, M. 2002. The Bullriders of Silicon Alley. In J. Eade and C. Mele, eds., *Understanding the City*. Cambridge, MA: Blackwell, pp. 339–362.

Indergaard, M. 2003. The Webs They Weave: Malaysia's Multimedia Super-corridor and New York City's Silicon Alley, *Urban Studies*, 40 (2): 379–401.

Indergaard, M. 2004. *Silicon Alley: The Rise and Fall of a New Media District*. New York: Routledge.

Indergaard, M. 2009. What to Make of New York's New Economy? The Politics of the Creative Field. *Urban Studies*, 46 (5): 1063–1094.

Indergaard, M. 2011. Another Washington—New York Consensus? Progressives Back in Contention. *Environment and Planning A*, 43 (2): 286–306.

INEGI. various years. Banco de Infomación Económica. Aquascalientes: Instituto Nacional de Estadisticas, Geografia y Informatica (INEGI). Online. Available at: www.inegi.gob.mx, last accessed, January 13, 2012.

International Visegrad Fund. 2012. Visegrad Group: The Czech Republic, Hungary, Poland. Slovakia. Online. Available at: http://www.visegradgroup.eu/, last accessed, January 9, 2012.

Isard, W. 1956. *Location and Space-Economy*, New York: John Wiley & Sons.

Jacobs, A. J. 1997–2008. Author Interviews with 120 State, Provincial, and Local Government Officials in the Detroit and Greater Toronto and Hamilton Regions, December 1997 to August 2008.

Jacobs, A.J. 1999. Intergovernmental Relations and Uneven Development in the Detroit (U.S.) and Nagoya (Japan) Auto Regions. Unpublished Dissertation. East Lansing, MI: Michigan State University.

Jacobs, A. J. 2002. Integrated Development Planning, Supportive Public policies, and Corporate Commitment: A Recipe for Thriving Major Cities in Aichi, Japan. *Journal of Urban Affairs*, 24 (2): 175–196.

Jacobs, A. J. 2003a. Devolving Authority and Expanding Autonomy in Japanese Prefectures and Municipalities. *Governance*, 16 (4): 601–623.

Jacobs, A. J. 2003b. Embedded Autonomy and Uneven Metropolitan Development: A Comparison of the Detroit and Nagoya Auto Regions, 1969–2000. *Urban Studies*, 40 (2): 335–360.

Jacobs, A. J. 2004. Inter-local Relations and Divergent Growth: The Detroit and Tokai Auto Regions, 1969 to 1996, *Journal of Urban Affairs*, 26 (4) 479–504.

Jacobs, A. J. 2005. Has Central Tokyo Experienced Uneven Development? An Examination of Tokyo's 23 Ku Relative to America's Largest Urban Centers. *Journal of Urban Affairs*, 27 (5): 521–555.

Jacobs, A. J. 2006. Embedded Localities: Employment Decline, Inner City Population Growth, and Declining Place Stratification among Japan's Mid-size and Large Cities. *City & Community*, 5 (3): 269–282.

Jacobs, A. J. 2008. Developmental State Planning, Sub-national Nestedness, and Reflexive Public Policymaking: Keys to Employment Growth in Saitama City, Japan. *Cities*, 25 (1): 1–20.

Jacobs, A. J. 2009a. Auto Industry & Manufacturing in Michigan. In: R. Schaetzl, J. Darden, and D. Brandt, eds., *Michigan Geography and Geology*. Boston, MA: Pearson, pp. 474–486.

Jacobs, A. J. 2009b. Embedded Contrasts in Race, Municipal Fragmentation, and Planning: Divergent Outcomes in the Detroit and Greater Toronto-Hamilton Regions 1990–2000. *Journal of Urban Affairs*, 31 (2): 147–173.

Jacobs, A. J. 2009c. The Impacts of Variations in Development Context on Employment Growth: A Comparison of Central Cities in Michigan and Ontario, 1980–2006. *Economic Development Quarterly*, 23 (4): 351–371.

Jacobs A. J. 2011a. Japan's Evolving Nested Municipal Hierarchy: The Race for Local Power in the 2000s. *Urban Studies Research*, 2011 (1): 1–14.

Jacobs A. J. 2011b. Ulsan, South Korea: A Global and Nested 'Great' Industrial City. *Open Urban Studies Journal*, 4 (1): 8–20.

Jacobs A. J. 2012. The Nested Global City-Region: Intermunicipal Income Stratification in the Tokyo Metropolitan Region, 1980–2007. *Urban Geography,* 33 (1): 120–146.

Jacobs, A. J. 2012 [2011]. The Bratislava Metropolitan Region. Cities, in press. Online. Available at: http://dx.doi.org/10.1016/j.bbr.2011.03.031.

Jacobs, J. 1969. *The Economy of Cities.* New York: Random House.

Jacobs, J. 1984. *Cities and the Wealth of Nations.* New York: Random House.

Jakarta, DKI. 1984. Statistik Wilayah Tahun (Annual Statistics by District). Jakarta: Daerah Khusus Ibukota Jakarta.

Jakarta, DKI. 1990. Proyeksi Penduduk DKI Jakarta (Population Projections for the Special Capital Region of Jakarta). Jakarta: Daerah Khusus Ibukota Jakarta.

Jakubiak, M., P. Kolesar, I. Izvorski, and L. Kurekova. 2008. The Automotive Industry in the Slovak Republic. Washington, DC: International Bank for Reconstruction and Development/World Bank, Commission on Growth and Development, Working Paper No. 29.

Japan, Government of. 1991–2011. *Population Census of Japan, 1990–2010.* Tokyo: Japan Statistical Association.

Japan, Government of. 1992–2008. *Establishment and Enterprise Census of Japan, 1991–2006.* Tokyo: Japan Statistical Association.

Japan, Government of. 2010a. *2009 National Survey of Family Income and Expenditure.* Tokyo: Statistics Bureau. Online. Available at: http://www.stat.go.jp/, last accessed May 9, 2011.

Japan, Government of. 2010b. *To-do-fu-ken betsu Shi-cho-son su no Hensen: Heisei 11–nen, 03–31 [Change in number of municipalities by prefecture: Since March 31, 1999].* Tokyo: Ministry of Internal Affairs and Communications. Online. Available at: http://www.soumu.go.jp/kouiki/ kouiki.html, last accessed September 1, 2010.

Jayasankaran. S. 1997. Two-Edged Sword: Anti-American Mood Angers U.S. but helps Mahathir. *Far Eastern Economic Review*, 27, November: 15.

Jessop, B. 1997. The Entrepreneurial City: Re-imaging Localities, Redesigning Economic Governance. In N. Jewson and S. MacGregor, eds. *Realizing Cities: New Spatial Divisions and Social Transformation.* London: Routledge, pp. 28–41.

Jessop, B. 1998. The Enterprise of Narrative and the Narrative of Enterprise: Place-Marketing and the Entrepreneurial City. In T. Hall and P. Hubbard, eds., *The Entrepreneurial City: Geographies of Politics, Regime, and Representation.* New York: Wiley, pp. 77–106.

Jessop, B. and N. Sum. 2000. An Entrepreneurial City in Action: Hong Kong's Emerging Strategies in and for (Inter)Urban Competition. *Urban Studies*, 37 (12): 2287–2313.

Johnson, C. 1982. *MITI and the Japanese Miracle: The Growth of Industrial Policy, 1925–1975.* Stanford, CA: Stanford University Press.

Johnson, S. 1997, Web Editor Argues: Believe the Hype. @ NY. Online. Available at: http://www.news-ny.com/view221.htm, last accessed, June 1, 2002.

Jomo. K., ed. 2001. *Malaysian Eclipse.* London: Zed Books.

Jou, S. and D. Chen. 2001. Keeping the High-Tech Region Open and Dynamic: The Organizational Networks of Taiwan's Integrated-Circuit Industry. *GeoJournal*, 53 (1): 81–87.

JPS, 2005–2008, *Kojin Shotoku Shihyo [Individual Income Indicators].* Tokyo: JPS.

Jun, T. 1938. Foreign Influence in Chinese Architecture. *T'ien Hsia*, 6(5): 410.

Jurgens, U. and M. Gnad. 2002. Gated Communities in South Africa: Experiences from Johannesburg. *Environment and Planning B*, 29 (3): 337–353.

Karim, Z. 2001. New MSC Flagship Application. *The Star Online*. August 28. Available at: http://thestar.com.my/, last accessed, January 5, 2012.

Keil, R. 1998. Globalization Makes States: Perspectives of Local Governance in the Age of the World Cities. *Review of International Political Economy*, 5(4): 616–646.

Keil, R. and P. Lieser. 1992. Frankfurt: Global City—Local Politics. In M. Smith, ed., *After Modernism: Global Restructuring and the Changing Boundaries of City Life.* New Brunswick, NJ: Transaction Publishers, pp. 36–69.

Kia Motors Slovakia. 2011. Kia Motors Slovakia Annual Report. Teplicka nad Vahom, Žilina, Slovakia. Online. Available at: http://eng.kia.sk/index.php?context=346, last accessed July 5, 2011.

King, A. 1989. *Urbanism and Colonialism and the World-Economy*. New York: Routledge.

King, A. 1990. *Global Cities: Post-Imperialism and the Internationalization of London*. New York: Routledge.

King, G. 1919. The Utilisation of Chinese Architecture Design in Modern Building—The Rockefeller Foundation's Hospital Plant at Peking, *Far Eastern Review*, 15 (3 August): 562.

Kingsmill, T. 1911. Early Architecture in Shanghai. *Social Shanghai*, 12 (July–December): 76–77.

KMMG. 2011. *Kia Motor Manufacturing Georgia*. Online. Available from: http://www.kmmgusa.com, last accessed January 17.

Knox, P. 1995. World Cities in a World-System. In P. Knox and P. Taylor, eds., *World Cities in a World System*. New York: Cambridge University Press, pp. 3–20.

Knox, P. and P. Taylor, eds. 1995. *World Cities in a World System*. New York: Cambridge University Press.

Kojima, K. 2000. The Flying Geese Model of Economic Development: Origins, Theoretical Extensions and Regional Policy Implications. *Journal of Asian Economics*, 11 (4): 375–401.

KOSIS. 2011. Korean Statistical Information Service Database. Daejeon: Statistics Korea. Online. Available at: http://www.kosis.kr, last accessed October 11, 2011.

Krugman, P. 1991. *Geography and Trade*. Cambridge, MA: MIT Press.

Kuo, N. 2000. The Taipei Region. In R. Simmonds and G. Hack, eds., *Global City Regions: Their Emerging Forms*. London: Spon Press, pp. 135–148.

Kwok, R. 2005. *Globalising Taipei: The Political Economy of Spatial Development*. London: Routledge.

Lamb, D. 2002. *The Arabs: Journeys beyond the Mirage*. New York: Vintage.

Lauria, M., ed. 1997. *Reconstructing Urban Regime Theory: Regulating Urban Politics in a Global Economy*. Thousand Oaks, CA: Sage Publications.

Laurie, P. 1866. *The Model Settlement*. Shanghai: Laurie Private Collection.

Leaf, M. 1994. The Suburbanization of Jakarta: A Concurrence of Economics and Ideology *Third World Planning Review*, 16 (4): 341–356.

Levin, D. 1995. *Behind the Wheel at Chrysler: The Iacocca Legacy*. New York: Harcourt Brace.

Leyshon, A. and N. Thrift. 1997. *Money/Space: Geographies of Monetary Transformation*. New York: Routledge.

Linbald, J. 2002. The Late Colonial State and Economic Expansion, 1900–1930s. In H. Dick, V. Houben, J. Linbald, and T. Wie, eds., *The Emergence of a National Economy: An Economic History of Indonesia, 1800–2000*. Crows Nest, NSW: Allen and Unwin, pp. 111–152.

Lipietz, A. 1985/1994. The National and the Regional: Their Autonomy *Vis-A-Vis* the Capitalist World Crisis. In R. Palen and B. Gills, eds., *Transcending the State-Global Divide: A Neo-statist Agenda in International Relations*. Boulder, CO: Lynne Rienner, pp. 23–43.

Lipietz, A. 1989. *Mirages and Miracles: The Crises of Global Fordism*. London: Verso.

List, F. 1966 [1885]. *The National System of Political Economy*. New York: Augustus M. Kelly.

Lo, F. and Y. Yeung, eds. 1998. *Globalization and the World of Large Cities*. Tokyo: UNU Press.

Logan, J. 2000. Still a Global City: The Racial and Ethnic Segmentation of New York. In P. Marcuse and R. Van Kempen, eds., *Globalizing Cities: A New Spatial Order?* Malden, MA: Blackwell, pp. 158–185.

Logan, J. and H. Molotch. 1987. *Urban Fortunes: The Political Economy of Place*. Berkeley, CA: University of California Press.

Lopez-Claros, A. and K. Schwab. 2005. *The Arab World Competitiveness Report 2005* (World Economic Forum). Basingstoke, UK: Palgrave Macmillan.

Lu, Y. 1929. Sun Yat-sen Memorial in Nanking and Canton. *The Far Eastern Review*, 25 (9–March), p. 98.

Lundvall, B., ed. 1992. *National Systems of Innovation: Towards a Theory of Innovation and Interactive Learning*. London: Pinter.

Machimura, T. 1992. The Urban Restructuring Process in Tokyo in the 1980s: Transforming Tokyo into a World City. *International Journal of Urban and Regional Research,* 16 (1): 114–128.

Machimura, T. 1998. The Symbolic Use of Globalization in Urban Politics in Tokyo. *International Journal of Urban and Regional Research,* 22 (2): 183–194.

Machimura, T. 2003. Narrating a 'Global City' for 'New Tokyoites.' In H. Dobson and G. Hook, eds., *Japan and Britain in the Contemporary World.* New York: Routledge, pp. 196–212.

Maitland, F. 1898. *Township and Borough.* Cambridge: Cambridge University Press.

Marcotullio, P. 2003. Globalisation, Urban Form and Environmental Conditions in Asia-Pacific Cities. *Urban Studies,* 40 (2): 219–247.

Marcuse, P. and R. Van Kempen, eds. 2000. *Globalizing Cities: A New Spatial Order.* Malden, MA: Blackwell.

Markusen, A. and S. Park. 1993. The State as Industrial Locator and District Builder: The Case of Changwon, South Korea. *Economic Geography,* 69 (2): 157–181.

Markusen, A. and V. Gwiasda. 1994. Multipolarity and the Layering of Functions in World Cities: New York City's Struggle to Stay on Top. *International Journal of Urban and Regional Research,* 18 (2): 167–193.

Marques, J. 2007. Prosperity Awaits. *Gulf News,* Weekend Supplement, May 11, p. 9.

Marshall, A. 1919. *Industry and Trade.* New York: Macmillan & Co.

Martindale, D. 1958. Prefatory Remarks: The Theory of City. In Max Weber, *The City.* Trans. and eds., D. Martindale and G. Neuwirth. New York: The Free Press, pp. 9–62.

Matthews, J. 1999. Should the Multimedia Super Corridor be reviewed? *Malaysian Technology News.* November 26. Online. Available at: http://mytechnews.tripod.com/features/19991126mscreview.htm, last accessed, January 5, 2012.

MBUSI. 2011. *Mercedes Benz U.S. International.* Online. Available from: http://mbusi.com, last accessed, January 17, 2011.

McGhee, B. 2006. Last Ford Taurus Rolls off Atlanta Assembly Line. *USA Today.* October 27. Online. Available from: http://www.usatoday.com/money/autos/2006–10–27–taurus-farewell_x. htm, last accessed, March 8, 2011.

McKenzie, R. 1924. The Ecological Approach to the Study of the Human Community. *The American Journal of Sociology,* 30 (3): 287–301.

McKenzie, R. 1927. The Concept of Dominance and World Organization. *American Journal of Sociology,* 33 (1): 18–42.

McKenzie, R. 1933. *The Metropolitan Community.* New York: McGraw-Hill.

MDC. 1998a. World IT Chiefs Meet in Cyberjaya. Online. Available at: http://www.mscmalaysia.my/, last accessed, January 5, 2012.

MDC. 1998b. Speech by the Prime Minister of Malaysia at the MSC Investors' Conference. Hanover, Germany, March 20. Online. Available at: http://www.mscmalaysia.my/, last accessed, January 5, 2012.

MDC. 1998c. Malaysia's Multimedia Super Corridor to Benefit German IT/Multimedia Companies. Online. Available at: http://www.mscmalaysia.my/, last accessed, January 5, 2012.

MDC. 1998d. New Web-Site to Facilitate Smart Partnerships. Online. Available at: http://www.mscmalaysia.my/, last accessed, January 5, 2012.

MDC. 1998e. MSC to Take up Controlling Stake in Cyberview. Online. Available at: http://www.mscmalaysia.my/, last accessed, January 5, 2012.

MDC. 1998f. MSC Promotion Continues Down Under. Online. Available at: http://www.mscmalaysia.my/, last accessed, January 5, 2012.

MDC. 1998g. Knowledge Workers Exchange Launched. Malaysia's Multimedia Development Corporation. Online. Available at: http://www.mscmalaysia.my/, last accessed, January 5, 2012.

MDC. 2000. *MSC Today.* Malaysia's Multimedia Development Corporation. July 27. Online. Available at: http://www.mscmalaysia.my/, last accessed, January 5, 2012.

MDC. 2002. Approved 650 Companies by Sectors as of March 10. Online. Available at: http://www.mscmalaysia.my, last accessed, January 5, 2012.

Mikuni, A. and R. T. Murphy. 2003. *Japan's Policy Trap: Dollars, Deflation, and the Crisis, of Japanese Finance*. Washington, DC: Brookings Institute Press.

Miller, D. 2000. The New Urban Studies: Los Angeles Scholars use their Region and their ideas to end the dominance of the 'Chicago School'. *The Chronicle of Higher Education*, August 19. Online. Available at: http://chronicle.com/article/The-New-Urban-Studies/3868, last accessed, January 11, 2012.

Millennium IT Policy. 2001. Millennium IT Policy: IT for the Common Man. Government of Karnataka, Department of Information Technology.

MMAH. 1996. *1996 Provincial Policy Statement*. Toronto: Ontario Ministry of Municipal Affairs and Housing.

MMAH. 2003. Municipal Act 2001 E-Guide. Ontario Ministry of Municipal Affairs and Housing. Online. Available at http://www.mah.gov.on.ca/, last accessed January 8, 2006.

MMAH. 2005a. *Greenbelt Plan, 2005*. Toronto: Ontario Ministry of Municipal Affairs and Housing. Online. Available at: http://www.mah.gov.on.ca/Page189.aspx, last accessed January 9, 2012.

MMAH. 2005b. *2005 Provincial Policy Statement*. Toronto: Ontario Ministry of Municipal Affairs and Housing.

Molavi, A. 2007. The New Silk Road. *Washington Post*, April 9. Online. Available at: http://www.susris.com/articles/2007/ioi/070410–silk-road.html, last accessed, January 12, 2012.

Mollenkopf, J. 1983. *Contested City*. Princeton, NJ: Princeton University Press.

Mollenkopf, J. and M. Castells, eds. 1991. *Dual City: Restructuring New York*. New York: Russell Sage Foundation.

Molotch, H. 1976. The City as a Growth Machine. *American Journal of Sociology*, 82 (2): 309–332.

Montalto de Jesus, C. 1909. *Historic Shanghai*. Shanghai: Shanghai Mercury.

Morshidi, S. 2000. Globalising Kuala Lumpur and the Strategic Role of the Producer Services Sector. *Urban Studies*, 37 (12): 2217–2240.

Mowitz, R. and D. Wright. 1962. *Profile of a Metropolis: A Case Book*. Detroit, MI: Wayne State University Press.

MPIR. 2006. *Places to Grow, Better Choices, Brighter Future: Growth Plan for the Greater Golden Horseshoe*. Toronto: Ontario Ministry of Public Infrastructure Renewal. Online. Available at: https://www.placestogrow.ca/index.php?lang=eng, last accessed, January 9, 2012.

MRG. 2003. *The Dubai Economy*. Dubai: Madar Research Group.

Muramatsu, M. 1997. *Local Power in the Japanese State*. Berkeley, CA: University of California Press.

Nelson, R. and S. Winter. 1982. *An Evolutionary Theory of Economic Change*. Cambridge, MA: Harvard University Press.

Nevins, E. and F. Hill. 1957. *Ford: Expansion and Challenge, 1915–1933*. New York: Charles Scribner's Sons.

Newman, P. and G. Verpraet. 1999. The Impacts of Partnership on Urban Governance: Conclusions from Recent European Research. *Regional Studies*, 33 (5): 487–491.

Ng, P. 2002. Pikom: Equal Access Needed to Boost ICT. *The Star Online*. April 10. Online. Available at: http://thestar.com.my/, last accessed, January 5, 2012.

Nihon Marketing Kyoiku Center. 1981–2004, *Kojin Shotoku Shihyo [Individual Income Indicators]*. Tokyo: Nihon Marketing Kyoiku Center.

Nijman, J. 1996. Breaking the Rules. Miami in the Urban Hierarchy. *Urban Geography*, 17 (1): 5–22.

Nissan. 2011. Nissan Corporate Information: Facilities Overseas, North America. Online. Available from: http://www.nissan-global.com, last accessed last accessed, October 13.

Noll, R. 1991. Structural Policies in the United States. In S. Kernel, ed., *Parallel Politics: Economic Policymaking in the United States and Japan*. Washington, DC: Brookings Institution, pp. 230–280.

Norton, A. 1994. *International Handbook of Local and Regional Government: A Comparative Analysis of Advanced Democracies*. Brookfield, VT: Edward Elgar.

Oanda. 2010. Historical Currency Data. Online. Available at: www.oanda.com, last accessed, January 4, 2012.

O'Brien, R. 1992. *Global Financial Integration: The End of Geography*. London: Pinter.

O'Connor, K. and R. Stimson. 1995. *The Economic Role of Cities: Economic Change and City Development, Australia 1971–1991*. Canberra: AGPS.

OECD. 1999. *Boosting Innovation: The Cluster Approach*. Paris: Organization for Economic Cooperation and Development.

OECD. 2003. *OECD Territorial Reviews: Vienna-Bratislava Austria/Slovak Republic*. Paris: Organization for Economic Co-operation and Development.

OECD. 2010. *OECD Economic Outlook*, Volume 2010/2, No. 86, December. Paris: Organization for Economic Co-operation and Development.

Ohlin, B. 1933. *Interregional and International Trade*. Cambridge, MA: Harvard University Press.

OICA. 2002. World Motor Vehicle Production by Country and Type: 2000–2001. Paris: International Organization of Motor Vehicle Manufacturers. Online. Available at: http://oica.net/category/production-statistics/, last accessed, January 2, 2012.

OICA. 2011. World Motor Vehicle Production by Country and Type: 2009–2010. Paris: International Organization of Motor Vehicle Manufacturers. Online. Available at: http://oica.net/category/production-statistics/, last accessed, January 2, 2012.

Olds, K. and H. Yeung. 2004. Pathways to Global City Formation: A View from the Developmental City-state of Singapore. *Review of International Political Economy*, 11 (3): 489–521.

OMB. 2004. *Ontario Municipal Board and Board of Negotiation Annual Report 2002–2003*. Toronto: Ontario Municipal Board.

Ontario, Province of. 1998. *Greater Toronto Services Board Act, 1998. Statutes of Ontario, 1998, Chapter 23*. Toronto: Office of the Legislative Assembly of Ontario.

Ontario, Province of. 2005. *Planning Act. Statutes of Ontario, 1990, Chapter 13*. Toronto: Office of the Legislative Assembly of Ontario.

Ontario, Province of. 2006. *Municipal Statute Law Amendment Act, 2006. S. O. 2006, Chapter 32*. Toronto: Office of the Legislative Assembly of Ontario. December 26. Online. Available at: http://www.e-laws.gov.on.ca/html/source/statutes/english/2006/ elaws_src_s06032_e.htm, last accessed, January 9, 2012.

Orr, M. and G. Stoker. 1994. Urban Regimes and Leadership in Detroit. *Urban Affairs Quarterly*, 30 (1): 48–73.

Orwell, G. 1980 [1938]. *Homage to Catalonia*. San Diego, CA: Harvest/HBJ.

Oweis, K. 2007. Syria's Opening Up for Investment. *Gulf News*, April 28, p. 48.

Pahl, R. 1970. *Whose City? And Further Essays on Urban Society*. London: Longman.

Park, R. 1915. The City: Suggestions for the Investigation of Human Behavior in an Urban Environment. *American Journal of Sociology*, 20 (5): 577–612.

Park, R., E. Burgess, and R. McKenzie, eds. 1925. *The City*. Chicago, IL: University of Chicago Press.

Parnreiter, C. 2002. Mexico City: The Making of a Global City? In S. Sassen ed., *Global Networks, Linked Cities*. New York: Routledge, pp. 145–182.

Pauly, L. 1997. *Who Elected the Bankers?* Ithaca, NY: Cornell University Press.

Pavlinek, P. 2008. *A Successful Transformation? Restructuring of the Czech Automobile Industry*. New York: Physica-Verlag.

Pavlinek, P. and A. Smith. 1998. Internationalization and Embeddedness in East-Central European Transition: The Contrasting Geographies of Inward Investment in the Czech and Slovak Republics. *Regional Studies*, 32 (7): 619–638.

Pereira, A. 2000. State Collaboration with Transnational Corporations: The Case of Singapore's Industrial Programmes (1965–2000). *Competition and Change*, 4 (4): 423–451.

Pereira, A. and C. Tong. 2005. Power and Developmental Regimes in Singapore, China and Malaysia. *Global Economic Review*, 34 (1): 128–143.

Perroux, F. 1950. Economic Space: Theory and Applications. *Quarterly Journal of Economics*. 64 (1): 89–104.

Pickvance, C. and E. Preteceille, eds. 1991. *State Restructuring and Local Power: A Comparative Perspective*. London: Pinter Publishers.

Pieterse, E. 2003. Unravelling the Different Meanings of Integration: The Urban Development Framework of the South African Government. In P. Harrison, M. Huchzermeyer, and M. Mayekiso, eds., *Confronting Fragmentation: Housing and Urban Development in a Democratising Society*. Cape Town: University of Cape Town Press, pp. 122–139.

Piore M. and C. Sabel. 1984. *The Second Industrial Divide*. New York: Basic Books.

Polanyi, K. 1957 [1944]. *The Great Transformation: The Political and Economic Origins of Our Time*. Boston, MA: Beacon Press

Porter, M. 1990. *The Competitive Advantage of Nations*. New York: Free Press.

Preston, R. 1978. The Structure of Central Place Systems. In L. Bourne and J. Simmons, eds., *Systems of Cities: Readings on Structure, Growth, and Policy*. New York: Oxford University Press, pp. 185–206.

Prinsloo, D. and C. Cloete. 2002. Post-Apartheid Residential Mobility Patterns in Two South African Cities. *Property Management*, 20 (4): 264–277.

Pryke, M. 1991. An International City Going 'Global': Spatial Change in the City of London. *Environment and Planning D: Society and Space*, 9 (2): 197–222.

PSA. 2007–2011. PSA Peugeot Citroen Annual Reports, 2006 through 2010. Paris. Online. Available at: http://www.psa-peugeot-citroen.com/, last accessed April 12, 2011.

Putnam, J. 1999. Cuba: Evolution in the Revolution, *National Geographic*, 195 (6): 2–35.

PwC. 2000. *Third Annual New York Media Survey*. New York: Price-Waterhouse Coopers.

PwC. 2006. From Beijing to Budapest—Winning Brands, Winning Formats. New York: Price-Waterhouse Coopers. Online. Available at: http://www.pwc.com/en_GX/gx/retail-consumer/pdf/ slovak_republic.pdf, last accessed 4 April 2011.

Rasiah, R. 2001. Pre-crisis Economic Weakness and Vulnerabilities. In K. Jomo, ed. *Malaysian Eclipse*. London: Zed Books, pp. 47–66.

Reitz, J. and R. Breton. 1994. *The Illusion of Difference: Realities of Ethnicity in Canada and the United States*. Toronto, ON: C.D. Howe Institute.

Reuters. 2011. Audi May Expand Hungary Plant Further from 2018. 26 January 2011. Online. Available at: http://autonews.gasgoo.com/global-news/audi-may-expand-hungary-plant-further-from-2018–110126.shtml, last accessed June 30, 2011.

Rimmer, P. 1986. Japan's World Cities: Tokyo, Osaka, Nagoya or Tokaido Megalopolis? *Development and Change*, 17 (1): 121–157.

Ritter, A. and J. Kirk, eds. 1995. *Cuba in the International System: Normalization and Integration*. New York: St. Martin's Press.

Rogerson, C. and J. Rogerson. 1997. The Changing Post-Apartheid City: Emergent Black-Owned Small Enterprises in Johannesburg. *Urban Studies*, 34 (1): 85–103.

Rodriguez, N. and J. Feagin. 1987. Urban Specialization in the World-System. *Urban Affairs Quarterly*, 22 (2): 187–220.

Rosenfeld S. 1996. United States: Business Clusters. In OECD, *Networks of Enterprises and Local Development*. Paris: Organization for Economic Cooperation and Development.

Rothwell, R. 1991. External Networking and Innovation in Small and Medium Sized Manufacturing Firms in Europe. *Technovation*, 11(2): 93–112.

Rowen, H. 2000. Serendipity or Strategy: How Technology and Markets came to Favor Silicon Valley. In C. Lee, W. Miller, M. Hancock, and J. Rowen, eds., *Silicon Valley Edge*. Stanford. CA: Stanford University Press, pp. 184–199.

Ruigrok, W. and R. Van Tulder. 1996. *The Logic of International Restructuring*. New York: Routledge.

SAC. 2011. Southern Auto Corridor News. *Southern Business & Development Magazine*. Online. Available from: http://www.southernautocorridor.com, last accessed, October 13.

SACN. 2007. Housing in Joburg 'for Rich and Poor'. *South African Cities Network Newsletter*. 41. Online. Available at: http://sacities.net/, last accessed, September 2007.

Sancton, A. 1998. Policymaking for Urban Development in American and Canadian Metropolitan

Regions. In D. Rothblatt and A. Sancton, eds., *Metropolitan Governance Revisited: American/Canadian Intergovernmental Perspectives*. Berkeley, CA: University of California, pp. 1–12.

Saito, A. 2003. Global City Formation in a Capitalist Developmental State: Tokyo and the Waterfront Sub-centre Project. *Urban Studies*, 40 (2): 283–308.

SARIO. 2011. Slovak Investment and Trade Development Agency, various documents. Online. Available http://www.sario.sk/?home, last accessed July 4, 2011.

Sassen, S. 1991. *The Global City: New York, London, Tokyo*. Princeton: Princeton University Press.

Sassen, S. 1995. On Concentration and Centrality in the Global City. In P. Knox and P. Taylor, eds., *World Cities in a World-System*. New York: Cambridge University Press, pp. 63–78.

Sassen, S. 1998. *Globalization and Its Discontents: Selected Essays*. New York: New Press.

Sassen, S. 1999. Global Financial Centers. *Foreign Affairs*, 78 (1): 75–87.

Sassen, S. 2001. Global Cities and Developmentalist States: How to Derail What Could Be an Interesting Debate. A Response to Hill and Kim. *Urban Studies*, 38 (13): 2357–2540.

Sassen, S. 2002. *Global Networks, Linked Cities*. New York: Routledge.

Sassen, S. 2006. *Cities in a World Economy*. Third Edition. Thousand Oaks, CA: Pine Forge.

Sassen-Koob. 1982. Recomposition and Peripheralization at the Core. *Contemporary Marxism*, 5 (Summer): 88–100.

Sato M., Y. Sato, and L. Jain. 1997. *Fuzzy Clustering Models and Applications*. Heidelberg: Physica-Verlag.

Saxenian, A. and J. Hsu. 2001. The Silicon Valley–Hsinchu Connection: Technical Communities and Industrial Upgrading. *Industrial and Corporate Change*, 10 (4): 893–920.

Schiller, R. 2001. *The Dynamics of Property Location: Value and the Factors which Drive the Location of Shops, Offices and Other Land Uses*. London: Spon.

Schumpeter, J. 1934. *Theory of Economic Development: An Inquiry into Profits, Capital, Credit, Interest, and the Business Cycle*. Cambridge, MA: Harvard University Press.

Schumpeter, J. 1939. *Business Cycles: A Theoretical, Historical and Statistical Analysis of the Capitalist Process*. New York: McGraw-Hill.

Schumpeter, J. 1942. *Capitalism, Socialism and Democracy*. New York: McGraw-Hill.

Schwab, P. 1999. *Cuba: Confronting the U.S. Embargo*. New York: St. Martin's Press.

Schwartz, A. 1992. The Geography of Corporate Services: A Case Study of the New York Urban Region. *Urban Geography*, 13 (1): 1–24.

Scitovsky, T. 1954. Two Concepts of External Economies. *The Journal of Political Economy*, 62 (4): 143–151.

Scott, A. 1980. *The Urban Land Nexus and the State*. London: Pion.

Scott, A. 1990a. *Metropolis: From the Division of Labor to Urban Form*. Berkeley, CA: University of California Press.

Scott, A. 1990b. *New Industrial Spaces*. London: Pion.

Scott, A. 1998a. From Silicon Valley to Hollywood: Growth and Development of the Multimedia Industry in California. In. H. Braczyk, P. Cooke, and M. Heidenreich, eds. *Regional Innovation Systems*. London: UCL Press, pp. 136–162.

Scott, A. 1998b. *Regions and the World Economy: The Coming Shape of Global Production, Competition, and Political Order*. Oxford: Oxford University Press.

Scott, A. 1999. The Cultural Economy: Geography and the Creative Field, *Media, Culture & Society*, 21 (6): 807–817.

Scott, A., ed. 2001a. *Global City-Regions: Trends, Theory, Policy*. New York: Oxford University Press.

Scott, A. 2001b. Industrial Revitalization in the ABC Municipalities, Sao Paulo: Diagnostic Analysis and Strategic Recommendations for a New Economy and a New Regionalism. *Regional Development Studies*, 7 (1): 1–32.

Scott, A. 2002. Regional Push: Towards a Geography of Development and Growth in Low- and Middle-Income Countries. *Third World Quarterly*, 23 (1): 137–161.

Scott, A. and E. Soja. 1998. *The City: Los Angeles and Urban Theory at the End of the Twentieth Century*. Berkeley, CA: University of California Press.

Scott, A. and M. Storper, eds. 1986. *Production, Work, Territory: The Geographical Anatomy of Industrial Capitalism*. Boston, MA: Allen and Unwin.

Scott, A. and M. Storper. 1987. High Technology Industry and Regional Development: A Theoretical Critique and Reconstruction. *International Social Science Journal*, 112 (2): 215–232.

Scott, A. and M. Storper. 2003. Regions, Globalization, Development. *Regional Studies*, 37 (6–7): 579–593

SEAC. 2011. Author interviews with state and local development officials in Alabama, Georgia, Mississippi, South Carolina, and Tennessee.

Searcy, S. and A. J. Jacobs. 2011. Maps Rendered and Revised for *The World's Cities: Contrasting Regional, National, and Global Perspectives*, A. J. Jacobs, ed., New York: Routledge.

Segre, R., M. Coyula, and J. Scarpaci. 1997. *Havana: Two Faces of the Antillean Metropolis*. Chichester: John Wiley & Sons.

Shanghai Mercury Office. 1893. *Shanghai 1843–1893, The Model Settlement: Its Birth, Its Youth, Its Jubilee*. Shanghai: Shanghai Mercury Office.

Sharif, R. 2001a. MDC: We've Streamline the Process. *The Star Online*, August 7. Available at: http://thestar.com.my/, last accessed, January 5, 2012.

Sharif, R. 2001b. More Effort Needed: IAP. *The Star Online*, September 11. Available at: http://thestar.com.my/, last accessed, January 5, 2012.

Shin, K. and M. Timberlake. 2000. World Cities in Asia: Cliques, Centrality and Connectedness, *Urban Studies*, 37 (12): 2257–2285.

Short, J. 1996. *The Urban Order: An Introduction to Cities, Culture, and Power*. Oxford: Blackwell.

Short, J. 1999. Urban Imaginers: Boosterism and the Representation of Cities. In A. Jonas and D. Wilson, eds., *The Urban Growth Machine*. Albany, NY: SUNY Press, pp. 37–54.

Short, J. 2004. *Global Metropolitan: Globalising Cities in a Capitalist World*. New York: Routledge.

Short, J., C. Breitbach, S. Buckman, and J. Essex. 2000. From World Cities to Gateway Cities: Extending the Boundaries of Globalization Theory. *City*, 4 (3): 317–340.

Short, J. and Y. Kim. 1998. Urban Crises/Urban Representations: Selling the City in Difficult Times. In T. Hall and P. Hubbard, eds., *The Entrepreneurial City*. New York: Wiley, pp. 55–76.

Short, J. and Y. Kim. 1999. *Globalization and the City*. New York: Addison Wesley Longman.

Short, J., Y. Kim, M, Kuus, and H. Wells. 1996. The Dirty Little Secret of World Cities Research-Data Problems in Comparative Analysis. *International Journal of Urban and Regional Research*, 20(4): 697–719.

Short, J., Y. Kim, M, Kuus, and H. Wells. 1996. The Dirty Little Secret of World Cities Research-Data Problems in Comparative Analysis. *International Journal of Urban and Regional Research* 20 (4): 697–719.

Silver, C. 2008. *Planning the Megacity: Jakarta in the Twentieth Century*. New York: Routledge.

Simmie, J., ed. 1996. *Innovation, Networks, and Learning Regions?* London: Jessica Kingsley Publishers.

Simmie, J. ed. 2001. *Innovative Cities*. New York: Spon.

Simmie, J. 2002. Knowledge Spillovers and the Reasons for the Concentration of Innovative SMEs. *Urban Studies*, 39 (5/6): 885–902.

Simmie, J. 2003. Innovation and Urban Regions as National and International Nodes for the Transfer and Sharing of Knowledge. *Regional Studies*, 37 (6–7): 607–620.

Simmie, J. 2004. Innovation and Clustering in the Globalised International Economy. *Urban Studies*, 41 (5/6): 1095–1112.

Simmie, J. and J. Sennett. 1999. Innovative Clusters: Global or Local linkages? *National Institute Economic Review*, 170 (1): 87–98.

Simmie, J. J. Sennett, P. Wood, and D. Hart. 2002. Innovation in Europe: A Tale of Knowledge and Trade in Five Cities. *Regional Studies*, 36 (1): 47–64.

Simmel, G. 1950. Metropolis and Mental Life. In K. Wolff, ed. and trans. *The Sociology of Georg Simmel*. New York: The Free Press, pp. 409–424.

Simpson, F. 1999. Tourist Impact in the Historic Centre of Prague: Resident and Visitor Perceptions of the Historic Built Environment. *The Geographical Journal*, 165 (2): 173–185.

Sklair, L. 1991. *Sociology of the Global System: Social Change in Global Perspective*. Baltimore, MD: Johns Hopkins University Press.

Slovak Republic, Statistical Office. 2011. Slovak Population and Employment Data. Online. Available at: http://portal.statistics.sk/, last accessed July 4, 2011.

Smith, D. and M. Timberlake. 1995a. Cities in Global Matrices: Toward Mapping the World-system's City System. In P. Knox and P. Taylor, eds., *World Cities in a World System*. New York: Cambridge University Press, pp. 79–97.

Smith, D. 2004. Global Cities in East Asia: Empirical and Conceptual Analysis. *International Social Science Journal*, 56 (181): 399–412.

Smith, D. and M. Timberlake. 1995b. Conceptualising and Mapping the Structure of the World System's City System. *Urban Studies*, 32 (2), 287–302.

Smith, D. and M. Timberlake. 2001. World City Networks and Hierarchies, 1977–1997: An Empirical Analysis of Global Air Travel Links. *American Behavioral Scientist*, 44 (10): 1656–1678.

Smith, L. 2006. The Road to Tech Mecca. *Wired Magazine*. Online. Available at: http:/www.wired.com.wired.12.07/dubai_pr.html, last accessed September 6, 2006.

Smith M., ed. 1984. *Cities in Transformation*. Beverly Hills, CA: Sage.

Smith, M., ed. 1992. *After Modernism: Global Restructuring and the Changing Boundaries of City Life*. New Brunswick, NJ: Transaction Publishers.

Smith, M. 2001. *Transnational Urbanism: Locating Globalization*. Malden, MA: Blackwell.

Smith, M. and J. Feagin, eds. 1987. *The Capitalist City: Global Restructuring & Community Politics*. Cambridge, MA: Basil Blackwell.

Soja, M., R. Morales, and G. Wolff. 1983. Urban Restructuring: An Analysis of Social and Spatial Change in Los Angeles. *Economic Geography*, 59 (2): 195–230.

Soja, E. 1989. *Postmodern Geographies: The Reassertion of Space in Critical Social Theory*. New York: Verso.

Soja, E. 1992. The Stimulus of a Little Confusion: A Contemporary Comparison of Amsterdam and Los Angeles. In M. Smith, ed., *After Modernism: Global Restructuring and the Changing Boundaries of City Life*. New Brunswick, NJ: Transaction Publishers, pp. 17–38.

Stallings, B., ed. 1995. *Global Change, Regional Response*. New York: Cambridge University Press.

Standard & Poor's. 2011. S&P Frontier Indices Methodology. New York: Standard & Poor's, September. Online. Available at: http://www.standardandpoors.com/, last accessed January 20, 2012.

Statistics Canada. 2007. *Census of Canada: Census of Population, 1986–2006*. Online. Available at: http://www.statcan.gc.ca/start-debut-eng.html, last accessed, January 9, 2012.

Stoker, G. and K. Mossberger. 1994. Urban Regime Theory in Comparative Perspective. *Environment and Planning C: Government and Policy*, 12 (2): 195–212.

Stone, C. 1989. *Regime Politics: Governing Atlanta, 1946–1988*. Lawrence, KS: University of Kansas Press.

Storper, M. 1991. *Industrialization, Economic Development, and the Regional Question in the Third World*. London: Pion.

Storper, M. 1995. The Resurgence of Regional Economies, Ten Years Later: The Region as a Nexus of Untraded Interdependencies. *European Urban and Regional Studies*, 2(3): 191–221.

Storper, M. 1997a. The City: The Centre of Economic Reflexivity. *The Service Industries Journal*, 17 (1): 1–27.

Storper, M. 1997b. *The Regional World: Territorial Development in a Global Economy*. New York: Guilford Press.

Storper, M. and R. Walker. 1989. *The Capitalist Imperative: Territory, Technology and Industrial Growth*. Oxford: Basil Blackwell.

STPI. 2004. Software Technology Parks of India. Government of Karnataka, Department of IT, BT, and S&T. Online. Available at: http://www.bangaloreitbt.in/, last accessed, January 13, 2012.

Strong, J. 1898. *The Twentieth Century City*. New York: Baker and Taylor.

Sudjic, D. 1992. *The 100 Mile City*. London: Andre Deutsch.

Summit Communications. 2002. The 21st Century Vision of a Hi-Tech Economy. *The New York Times,* March 21, p. A27.

Swyngedouw, E. 1997. Neither Global nor Local: 'Glocalization' and the Politics of Scale. In K. Cox, ed., *Spaces of Globalization: Reasserting the Power of the Local*. New York: Guilford Press, pp. 137–166.

Taipei Metropolitan Government. 2004. TMG Website. Online. Available at: http://www.taipei.gov. tw/MP_100001.html, last accessed, January 8, 2012 (in Chinese).

Taylor, P. 1995. World Cities and Territorial States: The Rise and Fall of Their Mutuality. In P. Knox and P. Taylor, eds. *World Cities in a World System*. New York: Cambridge University Press, pp. 48–63.

Taylor, P. 1997. Hierarchical Tendencies amongst World Cities: A Global Research Proposal. *Cities,* 14 (6): 323–332.

Taylor, P. 2000. World Cities and Territorial States under Conditions of Contemporary Globalization. *Political Geography,* 19 (1): 5–32.

Taylor, P. 2001. Specification of the World City Network. *Geographical Analysis,* 33 (2): 181–194.

Taylor, P. 2004a. Regionality in the World City Network. *International Social Science Journal,* 56 (181): 361–372.

Taylor, P. 2004b. *World City Network: A Global Urban Analysis*. New York: Routledge.

Taylor, P. and R. Aranya. 2008. A Global 'Urban Roller Coaster'? Connectivity Changes in the World City Network, 2000–04. *Regional Studies,* 42(1): 1–16.

Taylor P., G. Catalano, and D. Walker. 2002a. Measurement of the World City Network. *Urban Studies,* 39 (13): 2367–2376.

Taylor P., G. Catalano, and D. Walker. 2002b. Exploratory Analysis of the World City Network. *Urban Studies,* 39 (13): 2377–2394.

Taylor, P., B. Derudder, P. Saey, and F. Witlox, eds. 2006. *Cities in Globalization: Practices, Policies and Theories*. London: Routledge.

Taylor P. and M. Hoyler. 2000. The Spatial order of European Cities under Conditions of Contemporary Globalization. *Tijdschrift voor Economische en Sociale Geografie (Journal of Economic & Social Geography),* 91 (2): 176–189.

Taylor, P., P. Ni, B. Derudder, M. Hoyler, J. Huang, and F. Witlox, eds. 2010. *Global Urban Analysis: A Survey of Cities in Globalization*. London: Earthscan.

Taylor P. and D. Walker. 2001. World Cities: A First Multivariate Analysis of Their Service Complexes. *Urban Studies,* 38 (1): 23–47.

Taylor P., D. Walker, G. Catalano, and M. Hoyler. 2002. Diversity and Power in the World City Network. *Cities,* 19 (4): 231–241.

TDAGS. 2000. About Greater Seattle. Seattle: Trade Development Alliance of Greater Seattle. Online. Available at: http://www.seattletradealliance.com. 25 January.

Therborn, G. 2011. End of a Paradigm: The Current Crisis and the Idea of Stateless Cities. *Environment and Planning A,* 43 (2): 272–285.

The Economist.1999. Fidel's Dismal Science, 350 (8103), June 23: 67.

The Economist. 2006. Fake Parks: Dubai in America. *The Economist*, July 13. Online. Available at: www.economist.com, last accesed December 2, 2008.

The Economist. 2007. A Road That Is Not Straight. *The Economist*, August 4, p. 35.

Thomas, B. 1990. Catalonia: The Factory of Spain (Special Advertising Supplement), *Forbes* 145 (12), pp. A1–A3.

Thomas, J. 1990. Planning and Industrial Decline: Lessons from Postwar Detroit. *Journal of American Planning Association,* 56 (3): 297–310.

Thomas, J. 1997. *Redevelopment and Race: Planning a Finer City in Postwar Detroit*. Baltimore, MD: The Johns Hopkins University Press.

Thomas, R. 1992. *Life for Us Is What We Make It: Building Black Community in Detroit, 1915–1945*. Bloomington, IN: Indiana University Press.

Thornley, A. 1991. *Urban Planning under Thatcherism*. London: Routledge.

Tillman, R. and M. Indergaard. 2008. *Pump and Dump: The Rancid Rules of the New Economy*. New Brunswick, NJ: Rutgers University Press.

Timberlake, M., ed. 1985. *Urbanization in the World Economy*. Orlando, FL: Academic Press, Inc.

Timberlake, M. 1987. World System Theory and the Study of Comparative Urbanization. In M. Smith and J. Feagin, eds., *The Capitalist City*. Cambridge, MA: Basil Blackwell, pp. 37–65.

TMG, 2006–2010, Overview: Tokyo's History, Geography, and Population. Tokyo: Tokyo Metropolitan Government. Online. Available at: http://www.metro.tokyo.jp/ENGLISH/ PROFILE/overview02.htm, last accessed, May 21, 2011.

TMG. 2011. Tokyo Metropolitan Standard Land Price Survey. Tokyo: Tokyo Metropolitan Government. Bureau of Finance.

TMR, 2011, Population and Registered Foreign Residents by Country of Origin: Ibaraki, Tochigi, Gumma, Chiba, Saitama, Tokyo, Kanagawa, Yamanashi, and Shizuoka Prefectures. Unpublished data, available on prefectural websites in Japanese. See, for example, from Saitama, Available at: http://www.pref.saitama.lg.jp/site/kensaku, last accessed January 7, 2012.

Toyota. 2011. *Toyota, About us: Engineering & Manufacturing*. Online. Available from: http://www.toyota.com/about/our_news/corporate.html, last accessed, October 10.

Tressini, B. 2001. Embedded State Autonomy and Legitimacy: Piecing Together the Malaysian Development Puzzle. *Economy and Society*, 30 (3): 325–353.

ULI. 2008. ULI Launches Global City Index Report: London, New York Still Rank as World Leaders but Face Competition from Other Global Cities. Washington, DC: Urban Land Institute. Online. Available at: http:\ww.uli.org, last accessed, December 2, 2008.

Ulsan. 2011. Ulsan Metropolitan City. Online. Available at: http://english.ulsan.go.kr, last accessed on October 1, 2011.

United Nations. 1999. *Demographic Yearbook*. New York: United Nations Statistics Division.

U.S. Census Bureau. 1918. *Census of Manufactures, 1914*. Washington, DC: Government Printing Office.

U.S. Census Bureau. 1978. *County Business Patterns, 1976*. Washington, DC: Government Printing Office.

U.S. Census Bureau. 2000. Population Estimates for Places (Sorted Alphabetically within State), SU-99–7: Annual Time Series, July 1, 1990 to July 1, 1999 (includes April 1, 1990 Population Estimates Base). U.S. Census Bureau, Population Division, Population Estimates Program, Washington, DC. Online. Available at: http://www.census.gov/popest/data/cities/totals/ 1990s/SU-99–07.html, Internet release, October 20, 2000, last accessed, December 30, 2011.

U.S. Census Bureau. 2010a. *1890–2000 Census of Population*. Online. Available from http://www.census.gov, last accessed, January 9, 2012.

U.S. Census Bureau. 2010b. *State and County Estimates for 2009*. Online. Available from http://www.census.gov/did/www/saipe/data/statecounty/data/2009.html, last accessed, March 1.

U.S. Census Bureau. 2011a. *2007–2009 American Community Survey 3–Year Estimates*. Online. Available from: http://factfinder.census.gov, last accessed, March 1.

U.S. Census Bureau. 2011b. *County Business Patterns*. Online. Available from: http://censtats.census.gov, last accessed January 19, 2012.

U.S. Census Bureau. 2011c. Country Rankings. Online. Available at: http://www.census.gov/ ipc/www/idb/rank.php, last accessed, July 4, 2011.

U.S. Census Bureau. 2011d. *Current Population Survey, 2008–2010 Annual Social and Economic Supplements*. Online. Available from: http://www.census.gov/hhes/www/income/data/, last accessed, February 14.

Utterback, J. 1988. Innovation and Industrial Evolution in Manufacturing Industries. In B. Guile, and H. Brooks, eds. *Technology and Global Industry: Companies and Nations in the World Economy.* Washington, DC: National Academy Press.

Valley Partnership. 2011a. Fort Benning and the Valley Region: Welcome to the Chattahoochee

Valley Partnership. 2011b. The Valley Partnership in the Columbus, GA Region. Online. Available from: http://www.thevalleypartnership.com, last accessed, October 14.

Valley. Online. Available from: http://www.fortbenningandthevalley.com, last accessed, March 8.

Vernon, R. 1966. International Investment and International Trade in the Product Cycle. *Quarterly Journal of Economics*, 80 (2): 190–207.

Vernon, R. 1979. The Product Cycle Hypothesis in a New International Environment. *Oxford Bulletin of Economics and Statistics*, 41 (4), 255–267.

VW. 2011a. Volkswagen Group of America: Chattanooga Plant. Online. Available at: http://www.volkswagengroupamerica.com, last accessed, August 11.

VW. 2011b. Volkswagen Production Plants. Online. Available at: http://www.volkswagenag.com/vwag/vwcorp/content/en/the_group/production_plants.html, last accessed July 4, 2011.

VW. 2011c. Volkswagen Slovakia. Online. Available at: https://www.volkswagen-media-services.com/, last accessed July 4, 2011.

Waley, P. 1991. *Tokyo: City of Stories*. New York: Weatherhill.

Waley, P. 1992. *Fragments of a City: A Tokyo Anthology*. Tokyo: Japan Times.

Waley, P. 1997. Tokyo: Patterns of Familiarity and Partitions of Difference. *American Behavioral Scientist,* 41 (3): 396–429.

Waley, P. 2002. Moving the Margins of Tokyo. *Urban Studies,* 39 (9): 1533–1550.

Waley, P. 2003. By Ferry to Factory: Crossing Tokyo's Great River into a New World. In N. Fieve and P. Waley, eds. *Japanese Capitals in Historical Perspective: Power, Memory and Place in Kyoto, Edo and Tokyo,* London: RoutledgeCurzon, pp. 208–232.

Waley, P. 2007. Tokyo-as-World-City: Reassessing the Role of Capital and the State in Urban Restructuring, *Urban Studies,* 44 (8): 1465–1490.

Waley, P. 2010. From Flowers to Factories: A Peregrination through Changing Landscapes on the Edge of Tokyo. *Japan Forum,* 22 (3): 281–306.

Waley, P. 2011. From Modernist to Market Urbanism: The Transformation of New Belgrade. *Planning Perspectives,* 26 (2): 209–235.

Walks, R.A. and L. Bourne. 2006. Ghettos in Canada's Cities? Racial Segregation, Ethnic Enclaves and Poverty Concentration in Canadian Urban Areas. *Canadian Geographer,* 50 (3): 273–297.

Wallerstein, I. 1974a. *The Modern World System I: Capitalist Agriculture and the Origins of the European World-Economy in the Sixteenth Century.* New York: Academic Press, Inc.

Wallerstein, I. 1974b. The Rise and Future Demise of the World Capitalist System: Concepts for Comparative Analysis. *Comparative Studies in Society and History,* 16 (4): 387–415.

Wallerstein, I. 1979. *The Capitalist World-Economy.* New York: Cambridge University Press.

Walton, J. 1976. Political Economy of World Urbna Systems: Directions for Comparative Research. In J. Walton and L. Masotti, eds., *The City in Comparative Perspective: Cross-National Research and New Directions in Theory.* London: Sage, pp. 301–313.

WAM [Emirates News Agency]. 2007. Sama Dubai set for $14bn Tunisia Deal. *Arabian Business*, July 18. Online, http://www.arabianbusiness.com/companies/sama-dubai-uae-70012.html?page=2, last accessed January 11, 2012.

Wang, C. 2003. Taipei as a Global City: A Theoretical and Empirical Examination. *Urban Studies*, 40 (2): 309–334.

Wang, C. 2006. Planning Taipei: Nodal Status, Strategic Planning and Mode of Governance. *Town Planning Review,* 77(3): 283–309.

Wang, C. 2007. Is Taipei an Innovative City? An Institutional Analysis. *East Asia,* 24 (4): 381–398.

Wang, J. 2004. World City Formation, Geopolitics and Local Political Process: Taipei's Ambiguous Development. *International Journal of Urban and Regional Research*, 28 (2): 384–400.

Ward's. 1995–2010. *Ward's Automotive Yearbooks, 1995–2010*. Detroit: Ward's Communications, Inc.

Ward's. 2011. *U.S. Total Vehicle Sales Market Share by Company, 1961–2010*. Online. Available at: http:// http://wardsauto.com/keydata/, last accessed October 28, 2011.

Watson, T. 1998. Will Stock Dive Finally Kill Net Hype Once and for All? @NY. Online. Available at: http://www.news-ny.com/view401.htm, last accessed, June 1, 2002.

Watson, T. 2000. Billions Flowed into Silicon Valley, as Internet Industry grew up in 1999. @NY. January 6. Online. Available at: http://www.news-ny.com, last accessed, June 1, 2002.

Weber, A. 1899. *The Growth of Cities in the Nineteenth Century*. New York: Macmillan.

Weber, M. 1958. *The City*. D. Martindale and G. Neuwirth, trans. and eds. New York: The Free Press. Originally published in 1925.

Weber, M. 1978. The City (Non-Legitimate Domination). In M. Weber, *Economy and Society: An Outline Interpretive Sociology*, G. Roth and C. Wittich, trans. and eds. Berkeley, CA; University of California Press, pp. 1212–1372. Originally published in 1925.

Webb, D. 1999. Pacific Century CyberWork, 5 May. Online. Available at: http://webb-site.com/articles/pccyber- wok.htm.

Williams, A. 1996. Wall Street Wonderland. *New York Magazine*, November 4, pp. 33–39.

Williams, A. 1999. The Rebirth of Old Havana. *National Geographic,* 195(6): 36–45.

Williamson, O. 1975. *Markets and Hierarchies*. New York: Free Press.

Wilson, G. 1930. Architecture, Interior Decoration and Building in Shanghai Twenty Years Ago and Today. *China Journal of Science & Arts*, 12 (5), May: 249.

Wirosardjono, S. 1974. Conditions Leading to Rapid Urbanization in Jakarta and Its Policy Implications. Paper presented at the United Nations Conference, Nagoya, Japan, October 28 to November 8.

Wirth, L. 1928. *The Ghetto*. Chicago, IL: University of Chicago Press.

Wirth, L. 1938. Urbanism as a Way of Life. *American Journal of Sociology*, 44 (1): 3–24.

World Bank. 1993. *The East Asian Miracle: Economic Growth and Public Policy*. New York: Oxford University Press.

Wright, A. 1908. *Twentieth Century Impressions of Hong Kong, Shanghai and Other Treaty Ports of China*. London: Lloyds Greater Britain Publishing Company.

Wright, D. 1988. *Understanding Intergovernmental Relations: Public Policy and Participants Perspectives in Local, State, and National Governments,* Third Edition. Pacific Grove, CA: Brooks/Cole Publishing.

Wu, F. 2000a. Place Promotion in Shanghai, PRC. *Cities*, 17 (5): 349–361.

Wu, F. 2000b. The Global and Local Dimensions of Place Making: Remaking Shanghai as a World City. *Urban Studies*, 37 (8): 1359–1377.

Yawar, A. 2006. Viva Las Dubai? Does the UAE Metropolis Show the Path to Economic Development? Online. Available at: http://english.ohmynews.com/article/article_view.asp? no=336337&rel_no.1, last accessed, March 29, 2009.

Yeung, Y. 2000. *Globalization and Networked Societies*. Honolulu, HI: University of Hawaii Press.

You, D. 1936. Architecture Chronicle. *T'ien Hsia*, 3(4): 358.

Zukin, S. 1982. *Loft Living*. New Brunswick, NJ: Rutgers University Press.

Zukin, S. 1992. The Bubbling Cauldron: Global and Local Interactions in New York City Restaurants. In M. Smith, ed., *After Modernism: Global Restructuring and the Changing Boundaries of City Life*. New Brunswick, NJ: Transaction Publishers, pp. 105–132.

Index

Managing Hospitality Organizations
Second Edition

SAGE PUBLISHING: OUR STORY

We believe in creating fresh, cutting-edge content that helps you prepare your students to make an impact in today's ever-changing business world. Founded in 1965 by 24-year-old entrepreneur Sara Miller McCune, SAGE continues its legacy of equipping instructors with the tools and resources necessary to develop the next generation of business leaders.

- We invest in the right **authors** who distill the best available research into practical applications.

- We offer intuitive **digital solutions** at student-friendly prices.

- We remain permanently independent and fiercely committed to **quality, innovation, and learning.**

Sara Miller McCune founded SAGE Publishing in 1965 to support the dissemination of usable knowledge and educate a global community. SAGE publishes more than 1000 journals and over 800 new books each year, spanning a wide range of subject areas. Our growing selection of library products includes archives, data, case studies and video. SAGE remains majority owned by our founder and after her lifetime will become owned by a charitable trust that secures the company's continued independence.

Los Angeles | London | New Delhi | Singapore | Washington DC | Melbourne